CULTURAL ANTHROPOLOGY

CULTURAL ANTHROPOLOGY

Twelfth Edition

Conrad Phillip Kottak
University of Michigan

Boston   Burr Ridge, IL   Dubuque, IA   New York   San Francisco   St. Louis
Bangkok   Bogotá   Caracas   Kuala Lumpur   Lisbon   London   Madrid   Mexico City
Milan   Montreal   New Delhi   Santiago   Seoul   Singapore   Sydney   Taipei   Toronto

To the memory of my mother,
Mariana Kottak Roberts

Higher Education

CULTURAL ANTHROPOLOGY

Published by McGraw-Hill, a business unit of The McGraw-Hill Companies, Inc., 1221 Avenue of the Americas, New York, NY, 10020. Copyright © 2008, 2006, 2004, 2002, 2000, 1997, 1994, 1991, 1987, 1982, 1978, 1974 by The McGraw-Hill Companies, Inc. All rights reserved. No part of this publication may be reproduced or distributed in any form or by any means, or stored in a database or retrieval system, without the prior written consent of The McGraw-Hill Companies, Inc., including, but not limited to, in any network or other electronic storage or transmission, or broadcast for distance learning.

Some ancillaries, including electronic and print components, may not be available to customers outside the United States.

This book is printed on acid-free paper.

2 3 4 5 6 7 8 9 0 DOW/DOW 0 9 8 7

ISBN-13: 978-0-07-353095-6
ISBN-10: 0-07-353095-6

Vice President and Editor-in-Chief: *Emily Barrosse*
Publisher: *Phillip A. Butcher*
Sponsoring Editor: *Monica N. Eckman*
Senior Developmental Editor: *Thomas B. Holmes*
Editorial Assistant: *Teresa C. Treacy*
Senior Marketing Manager: *Daniel M. Loch*
Managing Editor: *Jean Dal Porto*
Project Manager: *Jean R. Starr*
Art Director: *Jeanne Schreiber*
Senior Art Editor: *Katherine McNab*
Map Preparation: *Mapping Specialists*
Design Manager: *Robin Mouat*
Senior Designer: *Preston Thomas*
Interior Design: *Linda Robertson*
Cover Image: © *Frans Lanting/Corbis*
Senior Photo Research Coordinator: *Alexandra Ambrose*
Photo Researcher: *Barbara Salz*
Media Project Manager: *Ron Nelms*
Media Producer: *Michele Borrelli*
Production Supervisor: *Jason I. Huls*
Copyeditor: *Sharon O'Donnell*
Proofreader: *David M. Shapiro*
Permissions: *Wesley Hall*
Composition: *9.5/11 Palatino, by Precision Graphics*
Printing: **45# Pub Matte, R. R. Donnelley & Sons**

Credits: The credits section for this book begins on page C1 and is considered an extension of the copyright page.

Library of Congress Cataloging-in-Publication Data
Kottak, Conrad Phillip.
  Cultural anthropology / Conrad Phillip Kottak. -- 12th ed.
    p. cm.
  Includes bibliographical references and index.
  ISBN-13: 978-0-07-353095-6 (pbk. alk. paper)
  ISBN-10: 0-07-353095-6 (pbk. : alk. paper)
    1. Ethnology. I. Title.
GN316.K64 2008
306--dc22
                                                    2006046621
The Internet addresses listed in the text were accurate at the time of publication. The inclusion of a Web site does not indicate an endorsement by the authors or McGraw-Hill, and McGraw-Hill does not guarantee the accuracy of the information presented at these sites.

www.mhhe.com

Brief Contents

Contents

10 Marriage 227

11 Gender 251

About the Author

Conrad Phillip Kottak (A.B. Columbia College, 1963; Ph.D. Columbia University, 1966) is a professor of Anthropology at the University of Michigan, where he has taught since 1968. He served as Anthropology Department chair from 1996 to 2006. In 1991 he was honored for his teaching by the university and the state of Michigan. In 1992 he received an excellence in teaching award from the College of Literature, Sciences, and the Arts of the University of Michigan. In 1999 the American Anthropological Association (AAA) awarded Professor Kottak the AAA/Mayfield Award for Excellence in the Undergraduate Teaching of Anthropology. In 2005 he was elected to the American Academy of Arts and Sciences.

Professor Kottak has done ethnographic fieldwork in Brazil (since 1962), Madagascar (since 1966), and the United States. His general interests are in the processes by which local cultures are incorporated—and resist incorporation—into larger systems. This interest links his earlier work on ecology and state formation in Africa and Madagascar to his more recent research on global change, national and international culture, and the mass media.

The fourth edition of Kottak's popular case study *Assault on Paradise,* based on his continuing field work in Arembepe, Bahia, Brazil, was published in 2006 by McGraw-Hill. In a research project during the 1980s, Kottak blended ethnography and survey research in studying "Television's Behavioral Effects in Brazil." That research is the basis of Kottak's book *Prime-Time Society: An Anthropological Analysis of Television and Culture* (Wadsworth 1990)—a comparative study of the nature and impact of television in Brazil and the United States.

Kottak's other books include *The Past in the Present: History, Ecology and Cultural Variation in Highland Madagascar* (1980), *Researching American Culture: A Guide for Student Anthropologists* (1982) (both University of Michigan Press), and *Madagascar: Society and History* (1986) (Carolina Academic Press). The most recent editions (twelfth) of his texts *Anthropology: The Exploration of Human Diversity* (this book) and *Cultural Anthropology* are being published by McGraw-Hill in 2007. He is also the author of *Mirror for Humanity: A Concise Introduction to Cultural Anthropology* (5th ed., McGraw-Hill, 2007) and *Window on Humanity: A Concise Introduction to Anthropology* (2nd ed., McGraw-Hill, 2007). With Kathryn A. Kozaitis, he wrote *On Being Different: Diversity and Multiculturalism in the North American Mainstream* (2nd ed., McGraw-Hill, 2003).

Conrad Kottak's articles have appeared in academic journals, including *American Anthropologist, Journal of Anthropological Research, American Ethnologist, Ethnology, Human Organization,* and *Luso-Brazilian Review.* He also has written for more popular journals, including *Transaction/SOCIETY, Natural History, Psychology Today,* and *General Anthropology.*

In recent research projects, Kottak and his colleagues have investigated the emergence of ecological awareness in Brazil, the social context of deforestation and biodiversity conservation in Madagascar, and popular participation in economic development planning in northeastern Brazil. Since 1999 Professor Kottak has been active in the University of Michigan's Center for the Ethnography of Everyday Life, supported by the Alfred P. Sloan Foundation. In that capacity, for a research project titled "Media, Family, and Work in a Middle-Class Midwestern Town," Kottak has investigated how middle-class families draw on various media in planning, managing, and evaluating their choices and solutions with respect to the competing demands of work and family.

Conrad Kottak appreciates comments about his books from professors and students. He can be readily reached by e-mail at the following Internet address:

ckottak@bellsouth.net

Preface

Since 1968, I've regularly taught Anthropology 101 ("Introduction to Anthropology") to a class of 375 to 550 students. Constant feedback from students, teaching assistants, and my fellow instructors keeps me up to date on the interests, needs, and views of the people for whom this text is written. I continue to believe that effective textbooks are rooted in enthusiasm and enjoyment of one's own teaching experience.

As a college student, I was drawn to anthropology by its breadth and because of what it could tell me about the human condition. I believe that cultural anthropology has compiled an impressive body of knowledge about human similarities and differences, and I'm eager to introduce that knowledge in the pages that follow. I believe strongly in anthropology's capacity to enlighten and inform. Anthropology's subject matter is intrinsically fascinating, and its focus on diversity helps students understand and interact with their fellow human beings in an increasingly interconnected world and an increasingly diverse North America.

I decided to write this book back in 1972, when there were far fewer introductory anthropology texts than there are today. The texts back then tended to be overly encyclopedic. I found them too long and too unfocused for my course and my image of contemporary anthropology. The field of anthropology was changing rapidly. Anthropologists were writing about a "new archaeology" and a "new ethnography." Studies of language as actually used in society were revolutionizing overly formal and static linguistic models. Symbolic and interpretive approaches were joining ecological and materialist ones within cultural anthropology.

Cultural anthropology hasn't lost its excitement. Since 1972, profound changes have affected the people and societies ethnographers traditionally have studied. In cultural anthropology it's increasingly difficult to know when to write in the present and when to write in the past tense. Yet many texts ignore change—except maybe with a chapter tacked on at the end—and write as though cultural anthropology and the people it studies were the same as they were a generation ago. While any competent text must present cultural anthropology's core, it also should demonstrate anthropology's relevance to today's world. *Cultural Anthropology,* 12th edition, has a unique set of goals and themes.

GOALS

This book has three main goals. My first goal is to offer a thorough and up-to-date introduction to cultural anthropology. Anthropology is a *science*— a "systematic field of study or body of knowledge that aims, through experiment, observation, and deduction, to produce reliable explanations of phenomena, with reference to the material and physical world" (*Webster's New World Encyclopedia* 1993, p. 937). Cultural anthropology is a humanistic science devoted to discovering, describing, and explaining social and cultural similarities and differences in time and space. In *Mirror for Man*, one of the first books I ever read in anthropology, I was impressed by Clyde Kluckhohn's (1944) description of anthropology as "the science of human similarities and differences" (p. 9). Kluckhohn's statement of the need for such a field still stands: "Anthropology provides a scientific basis for dealing with the crucial dilemma of the world today: how can peoples of different appearance, mutually unintelligible languages, and dissimilar ways of life get along peaceably together?" (p. 9).

Cultural anthropology is a science with clear links to the humanities, as it brings a comparative and cross-cultural perspective to forms of creative expression. One might say that cultural anthropology is among the most humanistic academic fields because of its fundamental respect for human diversity. Cultural anthropologists routinely listen to, record, and attempt to represent voices and perspectives from a multitude of times, places, nations, and cultures. Through its four subfields, the larger discipline known as general anthropology—or simply anthropology—brings together biological, social, cultural, linguistic, and historical approaches. Multiple and diverse perspectives offer a fuller understanding of what it means to be human than is provided by academic fields that lack anthropology's broad vision.

My second goal was to write a book that would be good for students. This book would be user-friendly in approach and pedagogy. It would stress to students why cultural anthropology should matter to them and how it can be used to understand themselves. By discussing current events in relation to anthropology's core, it would show how anthropology affects their lives. Through the unique "Beyond the Classroom" boxes (see below), the book also would highlight the work that students just like them are doing in anthropology.

It's been my aim throughout my 12 editions to write the most current, timely, and up-to-date textbook available. I try to be fair and objective in covering various and sometimes diverging approaches, but I make my own views known and write in the first person when it seems appropriate. I've heard colleagues who have used other textbooks complain that some authors seem so intent on presenting every conceivable theory about an issue—the role of the arts in society, for example—that students are bewildered by the array of possibilities. Anthropology should not be made so complicated that it is impossible for beginning students to appreciate and understand. Thus, the textbook author, like the instructor, must be able to guide the student.

My third goal was to write a book that professors, as well as students, would appreciate. The organization of this text is intended to cover core concepts and basics while also discussing prominent current issues and interests. I sought to create a text that is readable, attractive, amply illustrated, and up to date and that features an extraordinary support package, including supplements that benefit both student and professor.

THEMES

This 12th edition of *Cultural Anthropology* has two themes that mirror the three goals just discussed. These themes are "Bringing It All Together" and "Understanding Ourselves."

Bringing It All Together   Most texts give lip service to the fact that anthropology is an integrated, comparative, holistic approach to human similarities and differences. This book, however, takes a truly holistic approach through the "Bringing It All Together" essays that come after Chapters 6, 11, and 16. These essays show how anthropological approaches combine to interpret and explain a common topic. The topics that are "brought together" are (1) issues involving unity and diversity, in terms of ethnicity, "race," culture, and language in Canada; (2) archaeological, physical, linguistic, and cultural features of the Basques, including their place in Europe and Basque migration to the United States; and (3) the use of cultural and linguistic symbols in the proliferation of fast food, and the public health implications of this spread, in terms of increasing obesity. Marginal icons in each chapter direct the reader to a "Bringing It All Together" essay that complements the topic at hand.

Understanding Ourselves   It's common and proper for texts to present facts and theories prominent in the field of study, but often such material seems irrelevant to the student. In anthropology particularly, facts and theories should be presented not just to be read and remembered, but because they help us understand ourselves. "Understanding Ourselves" paragraphs, found in each chapter, answer the question "So what?" For example, we see how both men and women are constrained by their cultural training, stereotypes, and expectations (Chapter 11), and how people manage the transition from their family of orientation to their family of procreation (Chapter 9).

ORGANIZATION

The 12th edition of *Cultural Anthropology*, guided by very thoughtful reviewers, covers core and basics, as well as prominent current issues and approaches.

Part I ("The Dimensions of Anthropology") introduces anthropology as a four-field, integrated discipline, with academic and applied dimensions, that examines human biological and cultural diversity in time and space. Anthropology is discussed as a comparative and holistic science, featuring biological, social, cultural, linguistic, and historical approaches. Part I explores links between anthropology and other fields—other natural sciences as well as social sciences and the humanities. Examples of applied anthropology from the various subfields are provided. This part was designed with one of my goals (as mentioned previously) for the text in mind—introducing a holistic field consisting of four subfields and two dimensions.

Part II ("Cultural Diversity") begins with a discussion of the concept of culture and its roots in human biological evolution. A new Chapter 4 examines "The Evolutionary Origins of Human Culture." When in human evolution did culture emerge, how did it develop, and what is its significance for human nature and adaptability? Next comes an examination of ethnicity, in relation to race and its social construction. We see in Part II that culture and language are linked through learning, sharing, and reliance on symbolic thought. Throughout Part II, discussions of relevant concepts, theory, and explanations are combined with rich ethnographic examples and case studies. Part II examines how sociocultural diversity is manifest and expressed in such domains as language, economic and political systems, family and kinship, marriage, gender, religion, and the arts.

Having explored diversity in the major domains of cultural life in Part II, we examine their transformations and expressions in the modern world in Part III ("The Changing World"). Part III is one of the key differences between this anthropology text and others. Several important questions are addressed in Part III: How and why did the modern world system emerge? How has world capitalism affected patterns of stratification and inequality within and among nations? What were colonialism and imperialism and their legacies? What was Communism, and what has happened since its fall? How do economic development and globalization affect the peoples, societies, and communities among which anthropologists have traditionally worked? How do people actively interpret and confront the world system and the products of globalization? What factors threaten continued human diversity? How can anthropologists work to ensure the preservation of that diversity?

SPECIAL FEATURES

Working closely together, the author, editors, designer, and photo researcher have developed a format for this text that supports the goal of a readable, practical, up-to-date, and attractive book. I tried to follow through with my goal of making the book student-friendly.

The text, its accompanying student CD-ROM, and the Online Learning Center website work together as an integrated learning system to bring the theories, research findings, and basic concepts of anthropology to life for students. Offering a combination of print, multimedia, and web-based materials, this comprehensive system meets the needs of instructors and students with a variety of teaching and learning styles. The material that follows describes the many features of the text,

student CD-ROM, and Online Learning Center, as well as the supplementary materials that support those resources.

Chapter Opener and Overview

The opening of each chapter is designed to engage the reader immediately in the chapter content. Each chapter begins with an outline of key points. The Overview is located in a box on the second page. Both of these elements help students organize their reading and concentrate on the chapter's critical concepts and main points.

News Briefs

A news story begins on the fourth page of each chapter. These stories serve as a bridge between the world we live in and the chapter content. They convey the excitement and relevance of anthropological inquiry and demonstrate that topics raised in every chapter can be found in today's headlines.

Living Anthropology Videos

This feature, indicated on the page margin in each chapter, directs students to video clips on the student CD-ROM that accompanies each copy of this book. These clips bring anthropological practices to life, showing practitioners at work and providing an intimate view of their research and subjects. The CD-ROM has 25 clips, each corresponding to particular chapters in the textbook. Ranging in length from about 1.5 to 5 minutes, the clips can be used for assignments, discussion groups, or in-class activities. These clips were chosen because they are especially informative and contain visual content that can be difficult to present in a lecture format. Examples range from glimpses at the lives of different cultures to animated sequences depicting hominid ancestors in motion. Other clips were chosen because they provide a provocative look at a topic and can be useful for sparking students' interest and for starting a lecture or a discussion. A videotape version of the clips is also offered for instructor use as an in-class lecture launcher.

Every clip has been selected from a video published by *Films for the Humanities and Sciences*. The video programs from which these clips were excerpted are detailed on the student CD-ROM for those who would like to obtain a complete version on videotape.

Anthropology Atlas

The *Anthropology Atlas*, designed as an insert in the text, includes 17 maps covering topics important to all four fields in anthropology. This feature allows students to explore the geographic and visual dimensions of anthropology through a series of annotated maps and exercises associated with each one. Cross-references to individual maps are found in the margins of most chapters. Maps also include interpretive questions to test a student's skill with map usage.

Bringing It All Together Cross-References

Callouts appear in the text to direct students to one of the three essays that complement the topic being discussed in the chapter (see "Themes" above). These provide ready access to the "Bringing It All Together" essays at related points within the chapters.

Beyond the Classroom Boxes

These thematic boxes, which are found in most chapters, report on student-based research. They enable students to read about the work of their peers, further highlighting the relevance of anthropology in the real world and suggesting possible research and academic options as well.

Interesting Issues Boxes

Coverage of current issues in anthropology, often with maps and photos, raises students' awareness of some of the more provocative aspects of anthropology today. These boxes are located in each chapter.

Chapter Summaries

Each chapter includes a clearly written, concise numbered summary to aid the student in reviewing key themes and concepts.

Key Terms

Care has been taken to present understandable and accurate definitions of each key term found in a chapter. These terms are highlighted in bold type when they are introduced. A list of key terms and definitions in each chapter is found at the end of the chapter. In addition, the glossary at the end of the book includes a complete list of key terms and definitions for the entire text.

Critical Thinking Exercises

After the summary and key terms, each chapter includes exercises that challenge students to use their critical thinking skills to apply what they have read about in that chapter.

Suggested Additional Readings

An up-to-date list of additional reading materials, briefly annotated, comes at the end of each chapter to help guide student research.

Linkages

At the end of each chapter are comments and questions that link a text chapter to information in three other McGraw-Hill books: *Assault on Paradise*, 4th ed., by Conrad Phillip Kottak; *Culture Sketches*, 4th ed., by Holly Peters-Golden; and *The Gebusi*, a new case study by Bruce Knauft. Instructors may want to use one or more of these books to supplement the main text.

Internet Exercises

Included here are suggested exercises for the student to explore on the World Wide Web. Internet Exercises take students online to analyze anthropological issues relevant to chapter topics.

Appendixes

Appendix 1: A History of Theories in Anthropology This essay provides an overview of anthropological theories and their development and relevance to contemporary thought.

Appendix 2: Ethics and Anthropology This essay provides an overview of ethical issues faced by practitioners in the field of anthropology.

Appendix 3: American Popular Culture This essay explores the nature of popular culture from an anthropological point of view.

Appendix 4: Methods in Cultural Anthropology This essay surveys ethnographic and field methods, which it compares and contrasts with those of the other social sciences, especially with survey methodology. This chapter is related to, and should be read in conjunction with, Appendix 2, "Ethics and Anthropology."

Inside Covers

This edition includes two informative visual guides. The first, located on the inside front cover, highlights the coverage and chapter locations of anthropological theories in the text. The inside back cover features a similar guide to the coverage and chapter locations of race, ethnicity, class, and gender topics.

IMPORTANT FEATURES OF THE TWELFTH EDITION

Design

The large page size and contemporary design enhance the readability of the text and the clarity of its pedagogical features.

Content

- Besides the thorough updating I do with all editions, I've added new content to most chapters. To avoid increasing the length of the book, I've made cuts as well.

- An **all new** Chapter 4, titled "The Evolutionary Origins of Human Culture," examines the fact and the theory of biological evolution, along with primate and human evolution, including similarities and differences between humans and other primates. It identifies distinctive attributes that make us human and that make human culture unique. We see that, over millions of years, biological and cultural changes eventually led to anatomically modern humans, whose fossils date back more than 150,000 years, and to human behavioral modernity, which emerged somewhat later than that.

- I believe that systematic consideration of race, ethnicity, and gender is vital in an introductory cultural anthropology text. Two chapters present here are not found consistently in other anthropology texts: "Ethnicity and Race" (Chapter 5) and "Gender" (Chapter 11). Race and gender studies are fields in which anthropology has always taken the lead. I'm convinced that anthropology's special contributions to understanding the biological, social, cultural, and linguistic dimensions of race, ethnicity, and gender should be highlighted in any introductory text. They certainly are highlighted in this one—not just in their special chapters, but throughout the text, starting in Chapter 1. So important are these topics in this textbook that there is an *Inside Back Cover Guide to Race and Ethnicity, Gender, and Social Class/Stratification.* That table locates by chapter discussions of specific topics involving race and ethnicity, gender, and social class/stratification.

- The history of anthropological theory is a field I teach regularly and enjoy reading and writing about, but reviewers have been mixed about the need for a formal chapter on this topic in the book. Some say they would never have time to assign it; others think it's needed in an introductory text. I believe that Appendix 1, "A History of Theories in Anthropology," is substantial enough for instructors who want a chapter on theory. For those who don't see the need for such a chapter, its placement as an appendix doesn't interfere with the flow of the book. An *Inside Front Cover Theory Guide* highlights by chapter the major theoretical approaches discussed in the book.

- The color *Anthropology Atlas* insert includes 17 maps covering topics important to all four fields in anthropology.

- *Linkages* sections at the end of each chapter integrate the text through comments and questions to three ethnographic studies also published by McGraw-Hill: *Assault on Paradise,* 4th ed., by Conrad Phillip Kottak; *Culture Sketches,* 4th ed., by Holly Peters-Golden; and *The Gebusi,* a recent case study by Bruce Knauft.

- *News Briefs,* including several from 2005 and 2006, introduce each chapter and show how anthropology attracts public attention and how it relates to contemporary events, issues, and world affairs.

- *Interesting Issues* boxes have been updated and revised. These features, which offer unique coverage of current issues in anthropology, many with maps and photos, raise students' awareness of some of the more provocative aspects of anthropology today.

- *Critical Thinking Questions* and *Suggested Additional Readings,* found at the end of each chapter, have been updated. There are five critical thinking questions per chapter. These questions allow the student to extend and apply information in that chapter beyond the context in which it was presented originally. The readings direct students to additional work related to the theme of the chapter. This is useful when papers have been assigned on particular topics.

Pedagogy

- *Chapter Overviews* are presented in a concise box on the second page of each chapter.

- *Living Anthropology entries* are textual callouts directing the student to relate video content and exercises on the new student CD-ROM.

- *Internet Connection icons* appear throughout the text signaling where more information on a particular topic is available for the student to explore online. These links connect with websites chosen for their quality and relevance to the topic of a given chapter.

- *Understanding Ourselves* paragraphs, providing valuable context for anthropology concepts (see "Themes" above), are designed as callouts within the text for easier reading.

- *Atlas icons* appear in the text margins to direct students to related map activities in the atlas. *Interpret the world questions* are critical thinking questions about the maps and geography, and appear on the map pages of the *Anthropology Atlas.*

SUPPORT FOR STUDENTS AND INSTRUCTORS

For the Student

Kottak Living Anthropology Student CD-ROM This supplement features a powerful marriage of anthropological video clips and pedagogy to reinforce concepts from the text. Video clips link to particular chapters in the textbook. Selected from full-length anthropology-related films distributed by *Films for the Humanities and Sciences*, these clips can be used for assignments, discussion groups, or in-class activities. Each clip is accompanied by a text overview and probing questions to exercise the student's critical thinking skills. These clips also correspond to the clips provided on the Lecture Launcher VHS tape provided to instructors.

Student's Online Learning Center, www.mhhe. com/kottak (originated by Chris Glew and Patrick Livingood and revised by Jennifer Winslow) This free web-based student supplement features a large number of helpful tools, interactive exercises and activities, links, and useful information. Students will need a new copy of the textbook to access the areas of the site that are password-protected. Designed specifically to complement the individual chapters of the text, the Kottak Online Learning Center gives students access to material such as the following:

- *Internet Exercises:* Offer chapter-related links to the World Wide Web and activities for students to complete based on the sites.

- *Student Self-Quizzes:* Offer students the chance to reinforce their learning through multiple choice, true and false, and essay questions.

- *Virtual Explorations:* These activities are based on anthropology-related film clips, animations, and simulations. They are excellent tools for improving one's understanding of complex processes and phenomena related to anthropology.

- *Interactive Exercises:* Available for many chapters of the text, they allow students to work interactively with visuals, maps, and line drawings to review chapter content.

- *Chapter Objectives, Outlines, and Overviews:* Provide guidance for understanding key chapter content.

- *PowerPoint Lecture Notes:* Offer point-by-point synopses of critical ideas for each chapter.

- *Glossary* of key terms, including audible pronunciation guide to select terms.

- *Vocabulary Flash Cards:* Allow students to test their mastery of key terms.

- *FAQs:* These give students answers to common chapter-related questions.

- *Career Opportunities:* Offer students links to information about careers in anthropology.

- Helpful *web links* are provided to the following:

  General anthropology web links for each chapter of the text.

  Bringing It All Together links that offer students the opportunity to further explore background related to the Bringing It All Together sections in the text.

PowerWeb PowerWeb is a resource for the introductory course that is fully integrated with the Online Learning Center website. PowerWeb content is password-protected and includes referenced course-specific web links, articles, and news briefs about anthropology. It also provides study tools and other resources for the student.

Linkages Case Studies Chapters end with a section titled "Linkages," in which the content of that chapter is linked to three other McGraw-Hill titles: *Assault on Paradise*, 4th ed., by Conrad Phillip Kottak; *Culture Sketches*, 4th ed., by Holly Peters-Golden; and *The Gebusi* by Bruce Knauft. Instructors may wish to use one or more of these short books as a supplement to the main text. Based on more than 40 years of longitudinal field work, *Assault on Paradise* tells the story of how globalization has affected a small but rapidly growing community in northeastern Brazil. *Culture Sketches* provides short and very up-to-date case studies of 13 different societies, several of which are classic ethnographic examples. *The Gebusi* is a new and highly readable book by the eminent anthropologist Bruce Knauft, based on his field work among the people of that name in Papua New Guinea.

For the Instructor

The Instructor Online Learning Center (originated by Chris Glew and Patrick Livingood and revised by Jennifer Winslow, with revisions to the Instructor's Manual by Britt Halvorson and an updated Test Bank by Maria Perez) This password-protected site offers access to all the student online materials plus important instructor support materials and downloadable supplements such as:

- *Instructor's Manual:* The definitive guide for teaching with Kottak *Cultural Anthropology.*

- *PowerPoint Lecture Slides:* Provide instructors with a ready-made resource to organize their lectures.

- *Computerized Test Bank:* Offers numerous multiple choice, true and false, and essay questions in an easy-to-use program that is compatible with Windows and Macintosh computers. A printed version of the test bank is also provided in a Word-compatible format. McGraw-Hill's EZ Test is a flexible and easy-to-use electronic testing program. The program allows instructors to create tests from book specific items. It accomodates a wide range of question types and instructors may add their own questions. Multiple versions of the test can be created and any test can be exported for use with course management systems such as WebCT, BlackBoard or PageOut. EZ Test Online is a new service and gives you a place to easily administer your EZ Test created exams and quizzes online. The program is available for Windows and Macintosh environments.

- *A Question Bank for the Classroom Performance System (CPS):* CPS is a revolutionary wireless response system that gives instructors immediate feedback from every student in the class. CPS units include easy-to-use software and hardware for creating and delivering questions and assessments to your class. Every student simply responds with his or her individual wireless response pad, providing instant results. CPS questions for classroom use are included on the Instructor's OLC for instructors who choose to adopt this technology, which is available from your school's McGraw-Hill service representative.

- Information previously included in the printed Instructor's Resource Binder is now provided electronically on the Instructor OLC. These useful guides include:

  Chapter outlines

  Suggested lecture topics

  Suggested films for classroom use

  Guide to the Lecture Launcher video supplement

  Correlation guide to popular anthologies and supplements, offering chapter-by-chapter suggestions for integrating other materials into the course.

- *An Image Bank:* Offers professors the opportunity to create custom-made, professional-looking presentations and handouts by providing electronic versions of many of the maps, charts, line art, and photos in the text along with additional relevant images not included in the text. All the images are ready to be used in any applicable teaching tools, including PowerPoint slides.

- *Links to Professional Resources:* Provide useful links to professional anthropological websites and organizations on the Internet.

Lecture Launcher VHS Tape   This supplement offers professors a dynamic way to kick off lectures or illustrate key concepts by providing short (two- to four-minute) film clips pulled from the collection of *Films for the Humanities and Sciences.* Clips are tied to particular chapters in the text. A complete guide to correlating and using these clips with the text is provided on the Instructor OLC. Most of these clips are also available on the student OLC and have been incorporated into the Living Anthropology feature highlighted in the chapters. This allows the videos to be used in a variety of ways—from in-class viewing to homework assignments or independent study. The Living Anthropology feature in the text effectively links the videos to specific topics discussed by the author.

Faces of Culture Video Correlation Guide   For instructors using the *Faces of Culture* video series, this guide correlates each video to the appropriate chapter in the text and recommends chapter-by-chapter uses of the video series.

WHAT'S NEW IN EACH CHAPTER?

Chapter 1: What Is Anthropology?

Chapter 1 introduces anthropology as a four-field, integrated, biocultural discipline that focuses on human biological and cultural diversity in time and space. Anthropology is discussed as a comparative and holistic science, with links to the natural and social sciences and the humanities. Chapter 1 concludes with a section titled "Science, Explanation, and Hypothesis Testing." A new "News Brief" on anthropological field work in northern Kenya begins the chapter. The section "Cultural Forces Shape Human Biology" has been revised. A redundant section on applied anthropology has been incorporated into Chapter 2. There is new information on early American anthropology, garbology, and the Trobriand Islands.

Chapter 2: Applying Anthropology

In Chapter 2, applied anthropology is presented as a second dimension, rather than a fifth subfield, of anthropology. Examples of applied anthropology from the various subfields are provided. A new "News Brief" on an anthropologist's role in New Orleans after Hurricane Katrina begins the chapter. The chapter introduction has been totally rewritten. There is an expanded discussion of ethical dilemmas in applied anthropology.

Chapter 3: Culture

Chapter 3, which examines the anthropological concept of culture including its symbolic and adaptive features, has been updated based on recent writing and statistics. A new "News Brief" updates efforts by the Makah Indians to return to their whaling past. A new discussion distinguishes between the moral and methodological meanings of cultural relativism.

Chapter 4: The Evolutionary Origins of Human Culture

This **all new** chapter examines the fact and the theory of biological evolution, along with primate and human evolution, including similarities and differences between humans and other primates. It identifies distinctive attributes that make us human and that make human culture unique. We see that, over millions of years, biological and cultural changes eventually led to anatomically modern humans, whose fossils date back more than 150,000 years, and to human behavioral modernity, which emerged somewhat later than that.

Chapter 5: Ethnicity and Race

Chapter 5, which discusses the social construction of race and ethnicity, offers cross-cultural examples of variation in racial classification and ethnic relations. This chapter has been thoroughly updated, with the most recent sources and census data for the United States and Canada available in several key tables. A new "News Brief" describes dilemmas in racial classification that African Americans face when they visit Ghana.

Chapter 6: Language and Communication

Chapter 6 introduces methods and topics in linguistic anthropology, including descriptive and historical linguistics, sociolinguistics, and language and culture. A new "News Brief" begins the chapter with a discussion of sociolinguistic discrimination in the American Midwest.

Chapter 7: Making a Living

Chapter 7 surveys economic anthropology, including adaptive strategies (systems of food production) and exchange systems. The idea of industrial alienation is now illustrated here by Ong's study of Malaysian factory women, formerly in Chapter 14. The discussion of potlatching has been revised. The "Interesting Issues" box on scarcity has been updated based on a revisit to Madagascar.

Chapter 8: Political Systems

Using case material from various societies, Chapter 8 discusses political systems in terms of scale and types of conflict resolution. The section on "Foraging Bands" has been revised. Sections titled "Hegemony" and "Weapons of the Weak," formerly in Chapter 16, have been moved here, where they are discussed as forms of social control, along with "Politics, Shame, and Sorcery."

Chapter 9: Families, Kinship, and Descent

Chapter 9 discusses families, households, and descent groups cross-culturally, and also with reference to updated U.S. and Canadian census data. There is new material, including a new table, on changes in the divorce rate in the United States.

Chapter 10: Marriage

Chapter 10 examines exogamy, endogamy, the incest taboo, caste, postmarital residence rules, marital prestations, replacement marriage, and plural marriage cross-culturally. Also covered are divorce and same-sex marriage, updated to reflect recent events and legal decisions in the United States and Canada. There is a new section titled "Although Tabooed, Incest Does Happen." The section on royal endogamy has been revised.

Chapter 11: Gender

A thoroughly updated Chapter 11 examines cross-cultural similarities and differences in male and female roles, rights, and responsibilities. Systems of gender stratification and multiple genders are examined. There is information on contemporary gender roles and issues, including the feminization of poverty. The latest relevant census data is included.

Chapter 12: Religion

Chapter 12 surveys time-honored anthropological approaches to religion, while also discussing contemporary world religions and religious movements. This chapter features a "News Brief" on Islam's expansion, along with revisions of the sections titled "Antimodernism and Fundamentalism" and "A New Age." The section on contemporary world religions has been revised and updated, with a new table and figure illustrating number of adherents.

Chapter 13: The Arts

Chapter 13 explores major themes across various arts and cultures, from the definition and nature of art to links between art and religion, art as work, and art in its social context and transmission across the generations. New Sections are titled "Ethnomusicology," "Representations of Art and Culture," "Art and Communication," and "Art and Politics." A new "News Brief," "Narratives of Social Class and the Social Gap," focusing on film and print narratives, begins the chapter. The discussion of music has been expanded.

Chapter 14: The Modern World System

Chapter 14 examines the emergence and nature of the modern world system, including industrial and postindustrial systems of socioeconomic stratification and their impact on nonindustrial societies. The chapter has been revised and updated, particularly with discussions of outsourcing and global energy consumption.

Chapter 15: Colonialism and Development

Chapter 15 discusses the colonial systems and development policies that have impinged on the people and societies anthropology traditionally has studied. Major sections examine neoliberalism, Communism and its fall, and postsocialist transitions.

Chapter 16: Cultural Exchange and Survival

Chapter 16 continues the examination of how development and globalization affect the peoples, societies, and communities in which anthropologists traditionally have worked. Using recent examples, it shows how local people actively confront the world system and the products of globalization. There is a major new section titled "Indigenous Peoples," including a new "Beyond the Classroom" box. The chapter concludes with a final consideration of the role of the anthropologist in ensuring the continuance and preservation of cultural diversity.

Appendix 1: A History of Theories in Anthropology

Appendix 1 surveys theories in anthropology from 19th-century evolutionism, through Boasian anthropology, functionalism, structural functionalism, neoevolutionism, cultural materialism, structuralism, symbolic and interpretive anthropology, practice theory, world-system theory and political economy, to anthropology today.

Appendix 2: Ethics and Anthropology

Appendix 2 is a general treatment of ethics in anthropology, including the AAA Code of Ethics.

Appendix 3: American Popular Culture

Appendix 3 illustrates how culture is shared in contemporary society through case studies of American popular culture.

Appendix 4: Methods in Cultural Anthropology

Appendix 4 (formerly Chapter 3) focuses on methods in cultural anthropology, beginning with a section titled "Ethical Considerations: Networking and Reciprocation." Ethnography and survey research are among the methods considered. This appendix should be read in conjunction with Appendix 2, "Ethics and Anthropology."

ACKNOWLEDGMENTS

As always, I'm grateful to many colleagues at McGraw-Hill. Thom Holmes once again has done an outstanding job as developmental editor. His ideas about design have been implemented to give this book a clean, modern look. I also appreciate Thom's suggestions for content revision and his guidance and substantial help as we've worked on this edition. Thanks, too, to Dan Loch, a knowledgeable, creative, and enthusiastic marketing manager. I'm also pleased to continue my association with my friend Phil Butcher, McGraw-Hill's editorial director for social sciences and humanities. Phil has provided support and encouragement for well over a decade.

I thank Jean Starr once again for her work as project manager, guiding the manuscript through production and keeping everything moving on schedule. Jason Huls, production supervisor, worked with the printer to make sure everything came out right. It's always a pleasure to plan and choose photos with Barbara Salz, freelance photo researcher, with whom I've worked for almost 20 years. Thanks, too, to Susan Mansfield, Barbara's assistant, who also worked on the photo program for this edition. I thank Britt Halvorson and Maria Perez for their work on the Instructor Manual and Test Bank for this book. Jennifer Winslow did an outstanding job updating the online components for the student and instructor websites for the book. Gerry Williams updated the instructor PowerPoint files, and Mark Stephens provided editing help on all the Internet links and bibliographic references found in the book. Sincere thanks to Sharon O'Donnell for another excellent job of copyediting; and David Shapiro for proofreading. Preston Thomas worked with Thom Holmes to conceive and execute the design.

Robin Mouat, design manager, and Alex Ambrose, photo research coordinator, also deserve thanks along with Jeanne Schreiber, art director, and Katherine McNab, art editor. Teresa Treacy, McGraw-Hill's editorial assistant for anthropology, helped tremendously with reviews and all phases of manuscript preparation. Tara Maldonado worked with Thom and Teresa to assemble the visual arts manuscript, relieving me of that time-consuming responsibility. For the creation of the attractive maps, I would like to acknowledge the work of Mapping Specialists.

Thanks, too, to Michele Borrelli, media producer, for creating the OLC and student CD-ROM with video clips, and all the other supplements. Once again I thank Wesley Hall, who has handled the literary permissions.

I'm especially indebted to the professors who reviewed the 11th edition of this book and of my *Anthropology: The Exploration of Human Diversity*. They suggested many of the changes I have implemented here. Their names and schools are as follows.

Reviewers of Eleventh Edition

E. F. Aranyosi
University of Washington

Lisa Kaye Brandt
North Dakota State University

Margaret S. Bruchez
Blinn College

Andrew Buckser
Purdue University

Darryl de Ruiter
Texas A&M University

William W. Donner
Kutztown University

Todd Jeffrey French
University of New Hampshire, Durham

Vance Geiger
University of Central Florida

Dr. Stevan R. Jackson
Radford University

Brian Malley
University of Michigan

De Ann Pendry
University of Tennessee–Knoxville

Mary S. Willis
University of Nebraska–Lincoln

I'm also grateful to the reviewers of the seventh, eighth, ninth, and tenth editions of this book and my *Anthropology: The Exploration of Human Diversity* text. Their comments also helped me plan this 12th edition. Their names are as follows:

Other Reviewers

Julianna Acheson
Green Mountain College

Mohamad Al-Madani
Seattle Central Community College

Robert Bee
University of Connecticut

Kathleen T. Blue
Minnesota State University

Daniel Boxberger
Western Washington University

Vicki Bradley
University of Houston

Ethan M. Braunstein
Northern Arizona University

Ned Breschel
Morehead State University

Peter J. Brown
Emory University

Margaret Bruchez
Blinn College

Andrew Buckser
Purdue University

Karen Burns
University of Georgia

Richard Burns
Arkansas State University

Mary Cameron
Auburn University

Joseph L. Chartkoff
Michigan State University

Dianne Chidester
University of South Dakota

Inne Choi
*California Polytechnic State University–
San Luis Obispo*

Jeffrey Cohen
Penn State University

Fred Conquest
Community College of Southern Nevada

Barbara Cook
*California Polytechnic State University–
San Luis Obispo*

Norbert Dannhaeuser
Texas A&M University

Michael Davis
Truman State University

Robert Dirks
Illinois State University

Bill Donner
Kutztown University of Pennsylvania

Paul Durrenberger
Pennsylvania State University

George Esber
Miami University of Ohio

Grace Fraser
Plymouth State College

Laurie Godfrey
University of Massachusetts–Amherst

Bob Goodby
Franklin Pierce College

Tom Greaves
Bucknell University

Mark Grey
University of Northern Iowa

Homes Hogue
Mississippi State University

Kara C. Hoover
Georgia State University

Alice James
Shippensburg University of Pennsylvania

Richard King
Drake University

Eric Lassiter
Ball State University

Jill Leonard
University of Illinois–Urbana–Champaign

Kenneth Lewis
Michigan State University

David Lipset
University of Minnesota

Jonathan Marks
University of North Carolina–Charlotte

H. Lyn Miles
University of Tennessee at Chattanooga

Barbara Miller
George Washington University

Richard G. Milo
Chicago State University

John Nass, Jr.
California University of Pennsylvania

Frank Ng
California State University–Fresno

Martin Ottenheimer
Kansas State University

Leonard Plotnicov
University of Pittsburgh

Janet Pollak
William Patterson College

Howard Prince
CUNY–Borough of Manhattan Community College

Frances E. Purifoy
University of Louisville

Steven Rubenstein
Ohio University

Mary Scott
San Francisco State University

Brian Siegel
Furman University

Megan Sinnott
University of Colorado–Boulder

Esther Skirboll
Slippery Rock University of Pennsylvania

Gregory Starrett
University of North Carolina–Charlotte

Karl Steinen
State University of West Georgia

Noelle Stout
Foothill and Skyline Colleges

Susan Trencher
George Mason University

Mark Tromans
Broward Community College

Christina Turner
Virginia Commonwealth University

Donald Tyler
University of Idaho

Daniel Varisco
Hofstra University

Albert Wahrhaftig
Sonoma State University

David Webb
Kutztown University of Pennsylvania

George Westermark
Santa Clara University

Donald A. Whatley
Blinn College

Nancy White
University of South Florida

I was delighted by the enthusiasm expressed in their comments.

Students, too, regularly share their insights about this and my other texts via e-mail and so have contributed to this book. Anyone—student or instructor—with access to e-mail can reach me at the following Internet address: **ckottak@bellsouth.net.**

As usual, my family has offered me understanding, support, and inspiration during the preparation of this book. Dr. Nicholas Kottak, who received his doctorate in anthropology in 2002, regularly shares his insights with me, as does Isabel (Betty) Wagley Kottak, my companion in the field and in life for four decades. I renew my dedication of this book to my mother, Mariana Kottak Roberts, for kindling my interest in the human condition, for reading and commenting on what I write, and for the insights about people and society she provided. For the first time, sadly, this edition must be dedicated to her memory, as she died in the fall of 2005.

After almost four decades of teaching, I've benefited from the knowledge, help, and advice of so many friends, colleagues, teaching assistants, and students that I can no longer fit their names into a short preface. I hope they know who they are and accept my thanks.

I'm especially grateful to my many colleagues at Michigan who regularly share their insights and suggest ways of making my books better. Thanks especially to my fellow 101ers: Kelly Askew, Tom Fricke, Stuart Kirsch, Holly Peters-Golden, Elisha Renne, and Andrew Shryock.

Their questions and suggestions help me keep this book current. Special thanks to Joyce Marcus and Kent Flannery for providing me with the domestication dates included in the map on the spread of agriculture. I renew my thanks to Joyce for her guidance on Chapter 11 of previous editions. Throughout my career at Michigan, I've been privileged to work with scholars such as Kent, Joyce, Jeff Parsons, and Henry Wright, who share my interest in state formation. I also thank Roberto Frisancho, John Mitani, and Milford Wolpoff, who are always willing to answer my questions about biological anthropology.

Since 1968 I've taught Anthropology 101 ("Introduction to Anthropology"), with the help of several teaching assistants (graduate student instructors) each time. Feedback from students and graduate student instructors keeps me up to date on the interests, needs, and views of the people for whom this book is written. I continue to believe that effective textbooks are based in enthusiasm and in practice—in the enjoyment of teaching. I hope this product of my experience will be helpful to others.

Conrad Phillip Kottak
Ann Arbor, Michigan
ckottak@bellsouth.net

Walkthrough

Chapter Openers

Each chapter begins with an outline of key points.

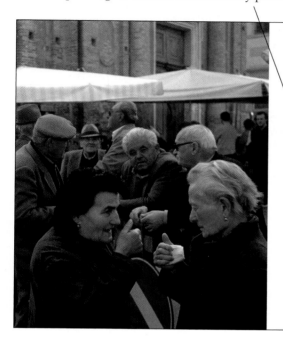

15

Language and Communication

CHAPTER OUTLINE

What Is Language?

Nonhuman Primate Communication
 Call Systems
 Sign Language
 The Origin of Language

Nonverbal Communication

The Structure of Language
 Speech Sounds

Language, Thought, and Culture
 The Sapir-Whorf Hypothesis
 Focal Vocabulary
 Meaning

Sociolinguistics
 Linguistic Diversity
 Gender Speech Contrasts
 Language and Status Position
 Stratification
 Black English Vernacular (BEV)

Historical Linguistics

WHAT IS LANGUAGE?

Language, which may be spoken (*speech*) or written (*writing*), is primary means of communication. Writing has existed for ab 6,000 years. Language originated thousands of years before that, no one can say exactly when. Like culture in general, of which l guage is a part, language is transmitted through learning, as par enculturation. Language is based on arbitrary, learned associati between words and the things for which they stand. The complex

A concise **Overview** helps students organize their reading and focus on critical concepts.

Ethnographers (field workers in cultural anthropology) typically have done field work outside their nations of origin. In the host country, the ethnographer seeks permission, cooperation, and knowledge from government officials, scholars, and many others, most importantly the people of the community being studied. Cultural sensitivity is paramount when the research subjects are living people into whose lives the anthropologist intrudes. Anthropologists need to establish and maintain appropriate, collaborative, and nonexploitative relationships with colleagues and communities in the host country.

To work in a host country and community, researchers must inform officials and colleagues there about the purpose and funding, and the anticipated results and impacts, of the research. Researchers have to gain the informed consent of all affected parties—from the authorities who control access to the field site to the members of the community to be studied. Before the research begins, people should be informed about the purpose, nature, and procedures of the research and its potential costs and benefits to them. *Informed consent* (agreement to take part in the research) should be obtained from anyone who provides information or who might be affected by the research.

A process of culturally appropriate networking, which will vary from country to country, is necessary before field work can begin. As one illustration, consider how I prepared for my first field work in Madagascar, which began in 1966. Before arriving in Madagascar I obtained a visa to

do research there from Madagascar's embassy in France, where I spent six months on language preparation. I needed to learn Malagasy, the language of Madagascar, a former colony of France. Once I reached Antananarivo, Madagascar's capital, I visited university anthropologists there to draw on their expertise and get their advice about my plans. Later, when I arrived in the territory of the ethnic group (Betsileo—Figure 12.1) I planned to study, I met with the head of the province chief. Eventually I met with the heads of all the lower-level administrative units where I would be working. Next, I became friendly with knowledgeable people in the small town where I first settled. Townsfolk have social networks that extend to rural areas—where I would be doing the bulk of my ethnographic field work. Through personal contacts, I created a network that eventually enabled me to work in several rural villages, one of which was my primary field site. Throughout my stay in Madagascar, I tried to stay in touch with the scholars and officials who had helped me at the outset. When I later applied for grants to return to Madagascar, I included two of those scholars as funded participants in the research. Such networking is an important part of any field research project in cultural or linguistic anthropology.

See the Internet Exercises at your CLS for examples of ethical dilemmas in anthropology

mhhe.com/kottak

OVERVIEW

The anthropologist's deepest ethical commitment is to the people he or she studies. Ethnography refers to the firsthand study of local cultural settings—field sites. Observing and working closely with local people, ethnographers learn the details of their lives. Life histories reveal personal experiences with culture. Genealogical information is important in societies in which kinship, descent, and marriage organize social life. Longitudinal research is the systematic study of an area or field site over time. Multisited ethnography, involving more than one field site, by a team or individual, is increasingly common.

Traditionally, cultural anthropologists worked in small-scale societies; sociologists, in modern nations. How does survey research, which typifies sociology, differ from ethnography? With more literate populations, survey researchers use questionnaires, which research subjects fill out. Sociologists study samples to make inferences about a larger population. Given the diversity that exists in modern nations, even anthropologists may adopt some survey procedures. However, anthropologists also retain the firsthand investigation characteristic of ethnography.

FIGURE 12.1 Location of the Betsileo in Madagascar.

News Briefs

A news story, beginning on the fourth page of each chapter, conveys the excitement and relevance of anthropological inquiry, even to today's headlines.

◆ N E W S B R I E F ◆

Restoring Lost Languages: A Form of Cultural Heritage Management

NEW YORK TIMES NEWS BRIEF
by John Noble Wilford
March 7, 2006

Language is a key ingredient in being human. Language and culture go together. Cultural transmission depends on language, and language is a vital part of culture. Contemporary Native Americans display a revived pride in cultural heritage, accompanied by an interest in the languages spoken by their ancestors. As we'll see in Chapter 15, "Language and Communication," any language helps organize and express modes of thought, systems of meaning, worldviews, and cultural understandings. When languages die, so do meaning systems; cultural diversity is reduced. This story describes one form of cultural heritage management—the science of reconstructing lost languages, known as language revitalization.

In the new movie about Jamestown, the first permanent English settlement in North America, founded in 1607, the paramount Indian chief Powhatan asks Capt. John Smith where his people came from. The sky?

Responding to the question, translated by an Indian whose smattering of English probably came indirectly from the earlier failed Roanoke colony in North Carolina, Smith replies: "The sky? No. We come from England, an island on the other side of the sea."

The dialogue continues as the interpreter puts Smith's reply in Powhatan's own words, Virginia Algonquian, a language not spoken for more than two centuries. Like most of the 800 or more indigenous languages of North America when Europeans first arrived, Powhatan's became extinct as Indians declined in number, dispersed and lost their cultural identity.

But a small yet growing number of linguists and anthropologists has been busy in recent years recreating such dead or dying Indian speech.

Their field is language revitalization, the science of reconstructing lost languages. One byproduct of the scholarship is the dialogue in Virginia Algonquian for the movie "The New World."

More than moviemaking is behind the research. A revival of ethnic pride and cultural studies among Indians has stimulated Indians' interest in their languages, some long dead. Of the more than 15 original Algonquian languages in eastern North America, the two still spoken are Passamaquoddy-Malecite in Maine and Mikmaq in New Brunswick . . .

The passing of a language diminishes cultural diversity, anthropologists say, and the restoration of at least some part of a language is an act of reclaiming a people's heritage. Blair A. Rudes, a linguist at the University of North Carolina, Charlotte, who specializes in reconstructing Indian languages, said several Algonquian communities in the East had efforts under way to recover their lost languages and return them to daily use . . .

When the director of "The New World," Terrence Malick, decided that for authenticity Powhatan should speak in his own language, he called in Dr. Rudes, who has worked with Dr. Goddard in reconstructing the defunct Algonquian language of the Pequot of Connecticut. He is also engaged in language restoration for the Catawba of North Carolina and is collaborating with Helen Rountree, emeritus professor of anthropology at Old Dominion University, on a dictionary of Virginia Algonquian.

Dr. Rudes was asked what Powhatan and his daughter Pocahontas would say and how they would say it. It was a daunting assignment.

The related Algonquian languages were among the first in America to die out, and no one is known to have spoken Virginia Algonquian since 1785 . . . Just two contemporary accounts—one by Captain Smith and the other by the Jamestown colony secretary, William Strachey—preserved some Virginia Algonquian words, including ones

In recent years linguists and anthropologists have worked to recreate dead and dying Native American speech. This field is known as language revitalization. One byproduct of the scholarship is the dialogue in Virginia Algonquian for the movie The New World. Shown here, from that 2005 film, are Colin Farrell and Q'orianka Kilcher, who play Captain Smith and Pocahontas.

xxix

Interesting Issues Boxes

These boxes feature discussions of provocative aspects of anthropology today and promote critical thinking.

Ethnic Nationalism Runs Wild

The Socialist Federal Republic of Yugoslavia was a nonaligned country outside the former Soviet Union (U.S.S.R.). Like the U.S.S.R., Yugoslavia fell apart, mainly along ethnic and religious lines, in the early 1990s. Among Yugoslavia's ethnic groups were Roman Catholic Croats, Eastern Orthodox Serbs, Muslim Slavs, and ethnic Albanians. Citing ethnic and religious differences, several republics broke away from Yugoslavia in 1991–1992. These republics included

For more on Bosnia see the Virtual Exploration and the Internet Exercises at your OLC

mhhe.com/kottak

Slovenia, Croatia, and Bosnia-Herzegovina (see Figure 14.3). Serbia and Montenegro are the two remaining republics within Yugoslavia. In Kosovo, which is a province in Serbia, but one whose population is 90 percent ethnic Albanian, there has been a strong movement for independence, led by the Kosovo Liberation Army.

Much of the ethnic differentiation in Yugoslavia has been based on religion, culture, political and military history, and some differences involving

language. Serbo-Croatian is a Slavic language spoken, with dialect variation, by Serbs, Croats, and Muslim Slavs alike. (Albanian is a separate language.) Croats and Serbs use different alphabets. The Croats have adopted the Roman alphabet, but the Serbs use the Cyrillic alphabet, which they share with Russia and Bulgaria. The two alphabets help promote ethnic differentiation and nationalism. Serbs and Croats, who share speech, are divided by writing—by literature, newsprint, and political manifestos.

The Yugoslav Serbs reacted violently—with military intervention—after a 1992 vote for the independence of Muslim-led Bosnia-Herzegovina, whose population is one-third Serbian. In Bosnia, the Serbs initiated a policy of forced expulsion—"ethnic purification"—against Croats, but mainly against Muslim Slavs. Serbs in Yugoslavia, who controlled the national army, lent their support to the Bosnian Serbs in their "ethnic-cleansing" campaign.

Backed by the Yugoslav army, Bosnian Serb militias rounded up Bosnian Muslims, killed groups of them, and burned and looted their homes. Thousands of Slavs fled. Hundreds of thousands of Muslims became involuntary refugees in tent camps, school gyms, and parks.

The Serbs had no use for the ethnic coexistence that the previous Yugoslav socialist government had encouraged. The Serbs also wished to avenge historic affronts by Muslims and Croats. In the 15th century, Muslim Turks had overthrown a Serbian ruler, persecuted the Serbs, and—eventually—converted

FIGURE 14.3 Former Yugoslavia, with Province and Republics.
The former Yugoslavia, although a socialist nation, was a nonaligned country outside the former Soviet Union. Like the U.S.S.R., Yugoslavia disintegrated in the early 1990s. The breakaway portions included Slovenia, Croatia, and Bosnia-Herzegovina.

In creating multiethnic states, former colonial powers such as France and England often erected boundaries that corresponded poorly with preexisting cultural divisions. But colonial institutions also helped create new "imagined communities" beyond nations. One example is the idea of *négritude* ("black association and

identity"). This concept was developed by dark-skinned intellectuals from the Francophone (French-speaking) colonies of West Africa and the Caribbean. (Günther Schlee, ed. [2002] provides cases illustrating the role of "imagined differences" in ethnic conflict—the dark side of imagining communities.)

Unique Beyond the Classroom Boxes

These boxes highlight undergraduate student research in anthropology and enable students to read about the work that students just like them are doing in anthropology.

BEYOND THE CLASSROOM

Stories from Women Domestics of the Yucatán

BACKGROUND INFORMATION

STUDENT:
Angela C. Stuesse

SUPERVISING PROFESSOR:
Allan F. Burns

SCHOOL:
University of Florida

YEAR IN SCHOOL/MAJOR:
Senior/Anthropology

FUTURE PLANS:
Master's in Latin American Studies

PROJECT TITLE:
The *Patrona-Empleada** Relationship Revealed: Stories from Women Domestics of the Yucatán

What research techniques are illustrated in this account of undergraduate research? Think about this student's approach in terms of the issues raised in the section on the evolution of ethnography.

My fascination with anthropology sprang to life in early 1996, during a semester of study abroad in the Yucatán of Mexico. It was also there that I first came into contact with domestic workers of Latin America. Witness to the daily interactions between my host-family and their servant, I became intrigued by the complex nature of their relationship and decided to return the following year to do research for my honors thesis.

The testimonial of a domestic worker is often the story of both her

personal and professional life. This is because she works not in an office, but rather in her *patrona's* home. Over time, the distinction between employee and family member blurs. The indefinite relationship that results gives rise to many questions: To what extent is the servant influenced by the values and attitudes of her *patrona*? How does the way she perceives her own life compare with the way her *patrona* sees her? Under what conditions does their bond become less work-related and more analogous to family? What causes their association to be hierarchical in nature, and in what ways is this verticality expressed and/or mediated? These themes were the driving force of my investigations.

Through personal contacts, I met four domestic workers who agreed to participate in my research. They ranged in age from 17 to 70 years old, and had between 5 and 50 years of experience. Research methods included auto-photography, unstructured and semi-structured interviews, and participant observation. Our conversations were sometimes lighthearted, sometimes very serious, and always key to a deeper understanding of each individual. Apart from listening and discussing, I also learned from these women by watching and doing. I helped them hang the laundry, set the table, sweep the patio, and fill the swimming pool. I visited their pueblas and met their families. We spent hours exchanging thoughts and discussing life. I laughed along with many and I held a hand as one woman cried. It was by participating in simple events like these that I began to understand

the profundity and strength of these unique women. By interviewing and getting to know their patronas as well, I was able to analyze the nature of their relationships and place them within the context of existing ethnographic literature and theory.

The resulting thesis gives identity to the faceless numbers common in survey and demographic research. Through my writing I have attempted to let these women speak, to give them decision, control, and value. I also have explored the genre known as "narrative ethnography," which, by including first-person experiences, rejects the idea that a valid, professional study must be "objective" and "scientific." My research adds to the growing body of narrative ethnographic, testimonial, and introspective literature about women domestics and change in the Yucatán and Latin America. With each new study we are a few steps closer to a greater cultural understanding.

*Patrona literally means patron or boss, referring to the female head of the household who oversees the domestic servants.

Empleada literally means employee, here referring to the female domestic servant.

cal analysis can support and round out an ethnographic account of local social life.

However, in the best studies, the hallmark of ethnography remains: Anthropologists enter the community and get to know the people. They participate in local activities, networks, and associations, in the city or in the countryside. They

observe and experience social conditions and problems. They watch the effects of national policies and programs on local life. I believe that the ethnographic method and the emphasis on personal relationships in social research are valuable gifts that cultural anthropology brings to the study of a complex society.

End-of-Chapter Features For Easy Review

Clear, numbered
chapter **Summaries**

Critical Thinking Questions
challenge one's understanding
of key chapter concepts.

**Suggested
Additional
Readings**
guide
student
research

Key Terms
for quick
review

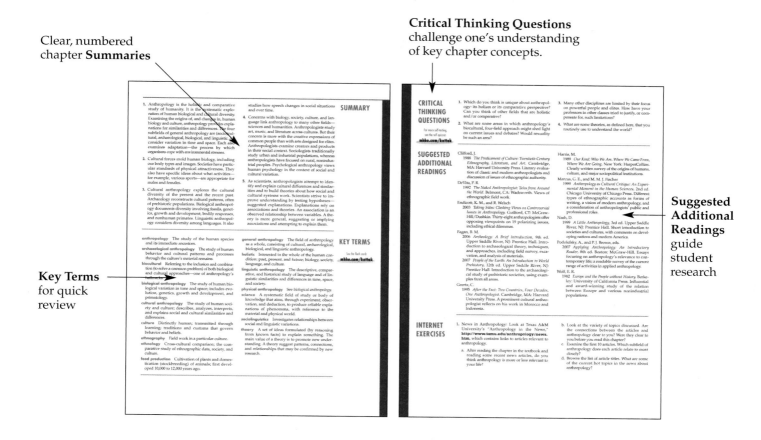

Internet Exercises take
students online to analyze
issues relevant to the chapter.

The **Linkages** feature
encourages additional
exploration of key chapter
topics by linking the student
to information in three other
McGraw-Hill books: *Assault
on Paradise*, 4th ed., by Conrad
Phillip Kottak; *Culture Sketches:
Case Studies in Anthropology*,
4th ed., by Holly Peters-Golden;
and *The Gebusi*, a new case
study by Bruce Knauft.

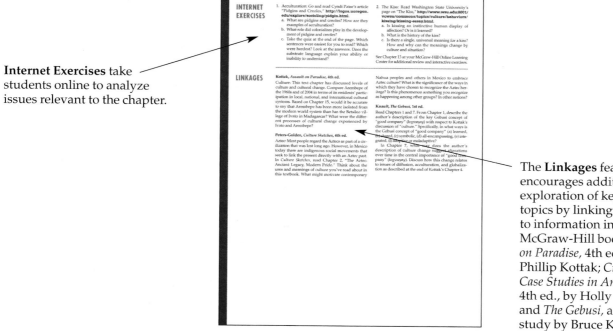

Bringing It All Together Essays

Unique thematic essays—appearing after groups of related chapters—show how anthropology's subfields combine to interpret and to explain a common topic. The essays offer a truly integrated, comparative, and holistic approach to anthropology. Through multiple and diverse perspectives, they offer students a fuller understanding of what it means to be human.

BRINGING IT ALL TOGETHER

Canada: Unity and Diversity in Culture and Language

See your OLC Bringing It All Together tests:
mhhe.com/kottak

There are levels of culture, as was pointed out in Chapter 13 titled "Culture." National culture consists of the beliefs, values, behavior patterns, and institutions that people share through growing up in a given nation. Cultures also can be smaller than nations. Such "subcultures" may originate in region, ethnicity, language, class, or religion. Thus, the religious backgrounds of American Jews, Baptists, Roman Catholics, and Muslims create subcultural differences among them. French-speaking Canadians contrast with English-speaking people in the same country.

Studying a modern nation, anthropologists may focus on either unity or diversity—on what is common or what is different. A focus on unity would examine themes, values, behavior, institutions, and experiences that transcend regions and social divisions. A focus on diversity would look at the cultures within the national culture.

The two approaches shouldn't be mutually exclusive. Despite diversity, we can still detect a series of nationally relevant institutions, norms, and expectations. As we saw in Chapter 14 on "Ethnicity and Race," the pressure on members of an ethnic group to observe a set of common national values comes not only from the national culture, but also from other ethnic groups. For example, African Americans in Los Angeles, after that city's 1992 riots, complained about their Korean neighbors. In doing so they referred to such general American values as openness, mutual respect, community participation, and "fair play." They saw their Korean neighbors as deficient in these traits. The Koreans countered by stressing another set of American national values, involving education, family unity, discipline, hard work, and achievement.

We focus now on unity and diversity in Canada. (American national culture is examined in Appendix 3.) One key feature of Canadian national consciousness is the contrast with the United States. Canadians, when traveling internationally, often are taken for Americans, which emphatically they are not. To be sure, Canada and the United States share many cultural traits. Some reflect the shared English-language heritage of most Canadians and Americans. Some reflect common experiences in the colonization of North America. Still others reflect participation in a global system, or diffusion of products and information across porous borders.

The media, especially television, have helped bring nationalism and its symbols, including cultural contrasts with the United States, to prominence in Canada. In spring 2000, a TV commercial produced in Toronto for Molson Canadian beer gained instantaneous national prominence. The ad featured the character Joe Canadian, delivering what came to be known as The Rant, soon to become a nationalist mantra for 30 million Canadians:

"I'm not a lumberjack or a fur trader; I don't live in an igloo, eat blubber or own a dogsled."

"I have a prime minister, not a president. I speak English and French, not American."

"I can proudly sew my country's flag on my backpack." (This refers to Canada's gender-neutral school curriculum, in which sewing is taught to both boys and girls.)

"I believe in peacekeeping, not policing; diversity, not assimilation."

Images of maple leaves and beavers flashed on the screen as Joe reached his climax:

"Canada is the second-largest land mass, the first nation of hockey and the best part of North America. My name is Joe and I am Canadian" (quoted in Brooke 2000).

The Rant spurred the government of Ontario, Canada's most populous province, to announce that starting in September 2000, each student would start the day by singing "O Canada," and pledging allegiance to the queen (since Canada is a member of the British Commonwealth). Although The Rant was recited by ordinary Canadians from Vancouver to Halifax, one province did not join in this affirmation of national identity. In French-

■ Jeff Douglas, who plays Joe Canadian, delivers "The Rant" in Ottawa, Ontario, on Canada Day—July 1, 2000.

Understanding Ourselves paragraphs point out the relevance of anthropology to the student's life.

Internet Connection Icons denote where more information on a particular topic is available for the student to explore online.

UNDERSTANDING OURSELVES

How does the emic–etic distinction help us understand ourselves? To exemplify an emic versus an etic perspective, consider that laypeople (including many Americans) may believe that chills and drafts cause colds, which scientists know are caused by germs. In cultures that lack the germ theory of disease, illnesses are emically explained by various causes, ranging from spirits, to ancestors, to witches. *Illness* refers to a culture's (emic) perception of bad health, whereas *disease* refers to the scientific—etic—explanation of poor health, involving known pathogens. Like people raised in any culture, we suffer both from illness (what we think we have) and from disease (what we really have), which may not be the same. Bad health has both emic and etic roots.

Another example is the emics and etics of color terminology, to which we return in the chapter on language. In different cultures, people label colors differently. Some cultures have only 2 basic color terms—for light and dark—whereas others have all 11 primary color terms, plus a series of additional ones that recognize finer discriminations of shade and hue. Etically, the color spectrum exists everywhere, but emically, people interpret and classify it differently in different societies.

classic *Argonauts of the Western Pacific* (1922/1961), were similar to earlier traveler and explorer accounts in describing the writer's discovery of unknown people and places. However, the *scientific* aims of ethnographies set them apart from books by explorers and amateurs.

More recently, the style that dominated "classic" ethnographies has been characterized as *ethnographic realism*. The writer's goal was to present an accurate, objective, scientific account of a different way of life, written by someone who knew it firsthand. This knowledge came from immersion in an alien language and culture. Ethnographers derived their authority—both as scientists and as voices of "the native" or "the other"—from this personal research experience.

Malinowski's ethnographies were guided by the assumption that aspects of culture are linked and intertwined. Beginning by describing a Trobriand sailing expedition, the ethnographer then follows the links between that entry point and other areas of the culture, such as magic, religion, myths, kinship, and trade. Compared with Malinowski, today's ethnographies tend to be less inclusive and holistic, focusing on particular topics, such as kinship or religion.

■ Bronislaw Malinowski (1884–1942), seated with villagers in the Trobriand Islands. A Polish anthropologist who spent most of his professional life in England, Malinowski is generally considered the father of ethnography. Does this photo suggest anything about Malinowski's relationship with the villagers?

According to Malinowski, a primary task of the ethnographer is "to grasp the native's point of view, his relation to life, to realize *his* vision of *his* world" (1922/1961, p. 25—Malinowski's italics). This is a good statement of the need for the emic perspective, as was discussed earlier. Since the 1970s, *interpretive anthropology* has considered the task of describing and interpreting that which is meaningful to natives. Interpretivists such as Clifford Geertz (1973) view cultures as meaningful texts that natives constantly "read" and ethnographers must decipher. According to Geertz, anthropologists may choose anything in a culture that interests them, fill in details, and elaborate to inform their readers about meanings in that culture. Meanings are carried by public symbolic forms, including words, rituals, and customs. (For more on Malinowski and Geertz, see Appendix 1.)

One trend in ethnographic writing since the 1980s has been to question traditional goals, methods, and styles, including ethnographic realism and salvage ethnography (Clifford 1982, 1988; Marcus and Cushman 1982). Marcus and Fischer argue that experimentation in ethnographic writing is necessary because all peoples and cultures have already been "discovered" and must now be "rediscovered . . . in changing historical circumstances" (1986, p. 24).

In general, experimental anthropologists see ethnographies as works of art as well as works of science. Ethnographic texts may be viewed as literary creations in which the ethnographer, as mediator, communicates information from the "natives" to readers. Some experimental ethnographies are "dialogic," presenting ethnography as a dialogue between the anthropologist and one or more native informants (e.g., Behar 1993;

been followed for five decades. Periodic village censuses provide basic data on population, economy, kinship, and religious behavior. Censused people who have moved are later interviewed to see how their lives compare with those of people who have stayed in the villages.

A series of different research questions have emerged, while basic data on communities and individuals continue to be collected. The first focus of study was the impact of a large hydroelectric dam, which subjected the Gwembe people to forced resettlement. The dam also spurred road building and other activities that brought the people of Gwembe more closely in touch with the rest of Zambia (Colson 1971; Scudder 1982; Scudder and Habarad 1991).

Later on, education became the research focus. Scudder and Colson (1980) examined how education provided access to new opportunities as it also widened a social gap between people with different educational levels. A third major study then examined a change in brewing and drinking patterns, including a rise in alcoholism, in relation to changing markets, transportation, and exposure to town values (Colson and Scudder 1988).

Team Research

As mentioned, longitudinal research is often team research. My own field site of Arembepe, Brazil, for example, first entered the world of anthropology as a field-team village in the 1960s. It was one of four sites for the now-defunct Columbia-Cornell-Harvard-Illinois Summer Field Studies Program in Anthropology. For at least three years, that program sent a total of about 20 undergraduates annually, the author included, to do brief summer research abroad. We were stationed in rural communities in four countries: Brazil, Ecuador, Mexico, and Peru. Since my wife, Isabel Wagley Kottak, and I began studying it in 1962, Arembepe has become a longitudinal field site. Three generations of researchers have monitored various aspects of change and development. The community has changed from a village into a town. Its economy, religion, and social life have been transformed.

Brazilian and American researchers worked with us on team research projects during the 1980s (on television's impact) and the 1990s (on ecological awareness and environmental risk perception). Graduate students from the University of Michigan have drawn on our baseline information from the 1960s as they have studied various topics in Arembepe. In 1990, Doug Jones, a Michigan student doing biocultural research, used Arembepe as a field site to investigate standards of physical attractiveness. In 1996–1997, Janet Dunn studied family planning and changing female reproductive strategies (Dunn 2000). Chris O'Leary, who first visited Arembepe in summer 1997, has investigated a

See the Virtual Exploration for a discussion of anthropologists' responsibilities to the communities they study.
mhhe.com/kottak

FIGURE 12.2 Location of Gwembe in Zambia.

striking aspect of religious change in Arembepe— the arrival of Protestantism. Later he did a study of changing food preferences (O'Leary 2002).

Arembepe is thus a site where various field workers have worked as members of a longitudinal team. The more recent researchers have built on prior contacts and findings to increase knowledge about how local people meet and manage new circumstances. I think that scholarship should be a community enterprise. The information we gathered in the past is there for new generations to use. To monitor changing attitudes and to understand the relation between television and family planning, Janet Dunn reinterviewed many of the women we had interviewed in the 1980s. Similarly, Chris O'Leary, who compared food habits and nutritional status in Arembepe and another Brazilian town, had access to dietary information from our 1964 interviews.

Contemporary forces of change are too pervasive and complex to be understood fully by a "lone ethnographer"—a researcher who starts

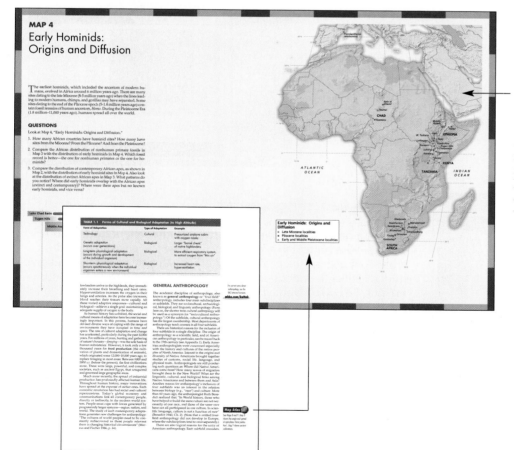

Living Anthropology Videos

Notes within each chapter direct students to video clips on the **Living Anthropology student CD-ROM.** These clips provide an intimate inside look at anthropological practices.

Anthropology Atlas

The in-text Atlas includes 17 maps covering topics important to all four fields of anthropology. Cross-references to individual maps are found in the chapter margins. Maps also include interpretive questions to test a student's skill with map usage.

Appendix 4
Methods in Cultural Anthropology

This appendix begins with a brief discussion of some of the ethical considerations that anthropologists face as they plan and conduct their fieldwork. See also Appendix 2, which summarizes the Code of Ethics of the American Anthropological Association (AAA). That code offers guidelines for anthropologists as they plan and conduct research, and as they deal with colleagues at home and abroad. The discussion of methods here focuses on cultural anthropology, especially on ethnography.

ETHICAL CONSIDERATIONS: NETWORKING AND RECIPROCATION

Ethnographers (fieldworkers in cultural anthropology) typically have done fieldwork outside their nations of origin. In the host country, the ethnographer seeks permissions, cooperation, and knowledge from government officials, scholars, and many others, most importantly the people of the community being studied. Cultural sensitivity is paramount when the research subjects are living people into whose lives the anthropologist intrudes. Anthropologists need to establish and maintain appropriate, collaborative, and nonexploitative relationships with colleagues and communities in the host country.

To work in a host country and community, researchers must inform officials and colleagues there about the purpose and funding, and the anticipated results and impacts, of the research. Researchers have to gain the informed consent of all affected parties—from the authorities who control access to the field site to the members of the community to be studied. Before the research begins, people should be informed about the purpose, nature, and procedures of the research and its potential costs and benefits to them. *Informed consent* (agreement to take part in the research) should be obtained from anyone who provides information or who might be affected by the research.

A process of culturally appropriate networking, which will vary from country to country, is necessary before fieldwork can begin. As one illustration, consider how I prepared for my first fieldwork in Madagascar, which began in 1966. Before arriving in Madagascar I obtained a visa to do research there from Madagascar's embassy in France, where I spent six months on language preparation. I needed to learn Malagasy, the language of Madagascar, a former colony of France. Once I reached Antananarivo, Madagascar's capital, I visited university anthropologists there to draw on their expertise and get their advice about my plans. Later, when I arrived in the territory of the ethnic group (Betsileo) I planned to study, I met with the province chief. Eventually I met with the heads of all the lower-level administrative units where I would be working. Next, I became friendly with knowledgeable people in the small town where I first settled. Townfolk have social networks that extend to rural areas—where I would be doing the bulk of my ethnographic fieldwork. Through personal contacts, I created a network that eventually enabled me to work in several rural villages, one of which was my primary field site. Throughout my stay in Madagascar, I tried to stay in touch with the scholars and officials who had helped me at the outset. When I later applied for grants to return to Madagascar, I included two of those scholars as funded participants in the research. Such networking is an important part of any field research project in cultural or linguistic anthropology.

Anthropologists have a debt to the people they work with in the field, and they should reciprocate in appropriate ways. For example, it is highly appropriate for North American anthropologists

A19

Appendix: "Methods in Cultural Anthropology"

This foundational essay examines ethical considerations in cultural anthropology as well as widely used ethnographic practices and research methods.

Kottak Living Anthropology Student CD-ROM

This CD-ROM combines selected anthropological video clips and review questions to reinforce concepts from each chapter of the text. Each of the clips is accompanied by a text overview and probing questions to exercise the student's critical thinking skills.

Online Learning Center

A fully updated Kottak Online Learning Center offers a rich assortment of media and content to accompany the text. The website provides professors with an Image Bank and other valuable resources, and gives students all of their book-specific, technology-based resources and activities in one convenient place.

Lecture Launcher VHS Videotape

This supplement offers professors a dynamic way to begin lectures or illustrate key concepts, by providing short (two- to four-minute) video segments taken from full-length, anthropology-related films from *Films from the Humanities and Sciences*. Video segments are tied to specific text chapters.

MAURITANIA

SENEGAL

GAMBIA

GUINEA-BISSAU

GUINEA

SIERRA LEONE

LIBERIA

IVORY COAST

MALI

BURKINA FASO

GHANA

TOGO

NIGER

BENIN

NIGERIA

ATLANTIC OCEAN

| 0 | 150 | 300 Miles |
| 0 | 150 | 300 Kilometers |

GREENLAND (DENMARK)

Arctic C

ICEL

UNITED KINGDO

IRELAND

ANDOR

PORTUGAL

MOROCCO

MAURITANIA

CAPE VERDE

CA

CENTRAL AFRICAN

SÃO TOMÉ AND P

EQUATORIAL

CONGO R

U.S.

CANADA

UNITED STATES

MEXICO

U.S.

NORTH PACIFIC OCEAN

NORTH ATLANTIC OCEAN

Tropic of Cancer

Equator

GUYANA

SURINAME

FRENCH GUIANA (FR)

COLOMBIA

VENEZUELA

ECUADOR

PERU

BRAZIL

BOLIVIA

PARAGUAY

CHILE

ARGENTINA

URUGUAY

WESTERN SAMOA

TONGA

Tropic of Capricorn

SOUTH PACIFIC OCEAN

SOUTH ATLANTIC OCEAN

Antarctic Circle

U.S.

THE BAHAMAS

| 0 | 300 Miles |
| 0 | 300 Kilometers |

CUBA

MEXICO

JAMAICA

HAITI

DOMINICAN REPUBLIC

PUERTO RICO

BELIZE

GUATEMALA

HONDURAS

EL SALVADOR

NICARAGUA

COSTA RICA

PANAMA

COLOMBIA

CARIBBEAN SEA

ST. KITTS AND NEVIS

ANTIGUA AND BARBUDA

DOMINICA

MARTINIQUE

ST. LUCIA

ST. VINCENT AND THE GRENADINES

BARBADOS

GRENADA

TRINIDAD AND TOBAGO

VENEZUELA

Scale: 1 to 125,000,000

| 0 | 1000 | 2000 Miles |
| 0 | 1000 | 2000 | 3000 Kilometers |

Note: All world maps are Robinson projection.

0   100 Miles

0   100 Kilometers

NORTH SEA
NORWAY
SWEDEN
ESTONIA
DENMARK
LATVIA
RUSSIA
LITHUANIA
RUSSIA
NETHERLANDS
BELARUS
GERMANY
POLAND
BELGIUM
LUXEMBOURG
CZECH REPUBLIC
UKRAINE
FRANCE
LIECHTENSTEIN
SLOVAKIA
SWITZERLAND
AUSTRIA
HUNGARY
MOLDOVA
SLOVENIA
ROMANIA
SAN MARINO
CROATIA
YUGOSLAVIA (SERBIA-MONTENEGRO)
BLACK SEA
MONACO
BOSNIA-HERZEGOVINA
ITALY
BULGARIA
MACEDONIA
ALBANIA
GREECE
TURKEY
MEDITERRANEAN SEA
MALTA

OCEAN
NORWAY
SWEDEN
FINLAND
RUSSIA
KAZAKSTAN
MONGOLIA
NORTH PACIFIC OCEAN
TURKEY
UZBEKISTAN
KYRGYZSTAN
TUNISIA
CYPRUS
SYRIA
TURKMENISTAN
TAJIKISTAN
NORTH KOREA
LEBANON
IRAQ
IRAN
AFGHANISTAN
CHINA
SOUTH KOREA
JAPAN
ISRAEL
JORDAN
KUWAIT
NEPAL
LIBYA
EGYPT
BAHRAIN
QATAR
PAKISTAN
BHUTAN
Tropic of Cancer
NIGER
SAUDI ARABIA
UNITED ARAB EMIRATES
INDIA
MYANMAR (BURMA)
TAIWAN
CHAD
BANGLADESH
LAOS
MARSHALL ISLANDS
NIGERIA
YEMEN
OMAN
THAILAND
VIETNAM
PHILIPPINES
ERITREA
SUDAN
DJIBOUTI
SRI LANKA
CAMBODIA (KAMPUCHEA)
PALAU
MICRONESIA
UGANDA
ETHIOPIA
MALDIVES
BRUNEI
SOMALIA
Equator
MALAYSIA
KIRIBATI
RWANDA
DEM. REP. OF THE CONGO
KENYA
SINGAPORE
I N D O N E S I A
NAURU
BURUNDI
SEYCHELLES
PAPUA NEW GUINEA
SOLOMON ISLANDS
TANZANIA
MALAWI
TUVALU
ANGOLA
COMOROS
MOZAMBIQUE
INDIAN OCEAN
EAST TIMOR
ZAMBIA
VANUATU
FIJI
MADAGASCAR
NAMIBIA
BOTSWANA
MAURITIUS
Tropic of Capricorn
AUSTRALIA
ZIMBABWE
SWAZILAND
SOUTH AFRICA
LESOTHO
NEW ZEALAND

0   100 Miles

0   100 Kilometers

RUSSIA
CASPIAN SEA
BLACK SEA
GEORGIA
AZERBAIJAN
TURKEY
ARMENIA
AZERBAIJAN
IRAN

CULTURAL ANTHROPOLOGY

What Is Anthropology?

HUMAN ADAPTABILITY

Anthropologists study human beings wherever and whenever they find them—in northern Kenya (see the "News Brief"), a Turkish café, a Mesopotamian tomb, or a North American shopping mall. Anthropology is the exploration of human diversity in time and space. Anthropology studies the whole of the human condition: past, present, and future; biology, society, language, and culture. Of particular interest is the diversity that comes through human adaptability.

Humans are among the world's most adaptable animals. In the Andes of South America, people wake up in villages 16,000 feet above sea level and then trek 1,500 feet higher to work in tin mines. Tribes in the Australian desert worship animals and discuss philosophy. People survive malaria in the tropics. Men have walked on the moon. The model of the *Starship Enterprise* in Washington's Smithsonian Institution symbolizes the desire to "seek out new life and civilizations, to boldly go where no one has gone before." Wishes to know the unknown, control the uncontrollable, and create order out of chaos find expression among all peoples. Creativity, adaptability, and flexibility are basic human attributes, and human diversity is the subject matter of anthropology.

Students are often surprised by the breadth of **anthropology,** which is the study of the human species and its immediate ancestors. Anthropology is a uniquely comparative and **holistic** science. Holism refers to the study of the whole of the human condition: past, present, and future; biology, society, language, and culture. (See the "News Brief" for an account of the varied techniques that anthropologists have used to study the Ariaal people of northern Kenya since the 1970s.) Most people think that anthropologists study fossils and nonindustrial, non-Western cultures, such as the Ariaal, and many of them do. But anthropology is much more than the study of nonindustrial peoples: It is a comparative field that examines all societies, ancient and modern, simple and complex. The other social sciences tend to focus on a single society, usually an industrial nation like the United States or Canada. Anthropology, however, offers a unique cross-cultural perspective by constantly comparing the customs of one society with those of others.

People share society—organized life in groups—with other animals, including baboons, wolves, and even ants. Culture, however, is distinctly human. **Cultures are traditions and customs, transmitted through learning, that form and guide the beliefs and behavior of the people exposed to them.** Children learn such a tradition by growing up in a particular society, through a process called enculturation. Cultural traditions include customs and opinions, developed over the generations, about proper and improper behavior. These traditions answer such questions as: How should we do things? How do we make sense of the world? How do we tell right from wrong? What is right, and what is wrong? A culture produces a degree of consistency in behavior and thought among the people who live in a particular society.

The most critical element of cultural traditions is their transmission through learning rather than through biological inheritance. Culture is not itself biological, but it rests on certain features of human biology. For more than a million years, humans have had at least some of the biological capacities on which culture depends. These abilities are to learn, to think symbolically, to use language, and to employ tools and other products in organizing their lives and adapting to their environments.

Anthropology confronts and ponders major questions of human existence as it explores human biological and cultural diversity in time and space. By examining ancient bones and tools, we unravel the mysteries of human origins. When did our ancestors separate from those remote great-aunts and great-uncles whose descendants are the apes? Where and when did *Homo sapiens* originate? How has our species changed? What are we now, and where are we going? How have changes in culture and society influenced biological change? Our genus, *Homo,* has been changing for more than one million years. Humans continue to adapt and change both biologically and culturally.

ADAPTATION, VARIATION, AND CHANGE

Adaptation refers to the processes by which organisms cope with environmental forces and stresses, such as those posed by climate and *topography* or terrains, also called landforms. How do organisms change to fit their environments, such as dry climates or high mountain altitudes? Like other animals, humans use biological means of adaptation. But humans are unique in also having cultural means of adaptation. Table 1.1 summarizes the cultural and biological means that humans use to adapt to high altitudes.

Mountainous terrains pose particular challenges, those associated with high altitude and oxygen deprivation. Consider four ways (one cultural and three biological) in which humans may cope with low oxygen pressure at high altitudes. Illustrating cultural (technological) adaptation would be a pressurized airplane cabin equipped with oxygen masks. There are three ways of adapting biologically to high altitudes: genetic

OVERVIEW

Exploring human biological and cultural diversity in time and space, anthropology confronts basic questions of human existence and survival: how we originated, how we have changed, and how we are still changing. Anthropology is holistic, studying the whole of the human condition: past, present, and future; biology, society, language, and culture. Anthropology's four subfields are cultural, archaeological, biological, and linguistic anthropology.

Culture is a key aspect of human adaptability and success. Cultures are traditions and customs, transmitted through learning, that guide the beliefs and behavior of the people exposed to them. Cultural forces constantly mold and shape human biology and behavior. Cultural anthropology examines cultural diversity of the present and recent past. Archaeology reconstructs behavior by studying material remains. Biological anthropologists study human fossils, genetics, and bodily growth. They also study nonhuman primates (monkeys and apes). Linguistic anthropology considers how speech varies with social factors and over time. Anthropology is related to many other fields: both natural sciences (e.g., biology) and social sciences (e.g., sociology).

Remote and Poked, Anthropology's Dream Tribe

NEW YORK TIMES NEWS BRIEF

by Marc Lacey
December 18, 2005

"Been on any digs lately?" Anthropologists are accustomed to that question, after announcing their profession. Often people confuse anthropology with archaeology, which is one—but just one—of anthropology's four subfields. Many anthropologists do dig in the ground, but others dig into the intricacies of human biology and living cultural expression. Anthropologists are known for their close observation of human behavior in natural settings and their focus on diversity. It is typical of the anthropological approach to go right to—and live with—the local people, whether in northern Kenya, as described here, or in middle-class America.

Anthropologists study human biology and culture in varied times and places and in a rapidly changing world. This news story focuses on a remote population, the Ariaal of northern Kenya, whom anthropologists have been studying since the 1970s. This account previews the multifaceted research interests that anthropologists have. Among the Ariaal, anthropologists have studied a range of topics, including kinship and marriage customs, conflict, and even biomedical issues such as illness and body type and function. As you read this account, consider, too, what anthropologists get from the people being studied and vice versa.

Anthropologists and other researchers have long searched the globe for people isolated from the modern world. The Ariaal, a nomadic community of about 10,000 people in northern Kenya, have been seized on by researchers since the 1970's, after one anthropologist, Elliot Fratkin—stumbled upon them and began publishing his accounts of their lives . . . .

Other researchers have done studies on everything from their cultural practices to their testosterone levels. *National Geographic* focused on the Ariaal in 1999, in an article on vanishing cultures.

But over the years, more and more Ariaal—like the Masai and the Turkana in Kenya and the Tuaregs and Bedouins elsewhere in Africa—are settling down. Many have emigrated closer to Marsabit, the nearest town, which has cellphone reception and even sporadic Internet access.

The scientists continue to arrive in Ariaal country, with their notebooks, tents and bizarre queries, but now they document a semi-isolated people straddling modern life and more traditional ways.

"The era of finding isolated tribal groups is probably over," said Dr. Fratkin, a professor at Smith College who has lived with the Ariaal for long stretches and is regarded by some of them as a member of the tribe.

For Benjamin C. Campbell, a biological anthropologist at Boston University who was introduced to the Ariaal by Dr. Fratkin, their way of life, diet and cultural practices make them worthy of study.

Other academics agree. Local residents say they have been asked over the years how many livestock they own (many), how many times they have had diarrhea in the last month (often) and what they ate the day before yesterday (usually meat, milk or blood).

Ariaal women have been asked about the work they do, which seems to exceed that of the men, and about local marriage customs, which compel their prospective husbands to hand over livestock to their parents before the ceremony can take place . . .

The researchers may not know this, but the Ariaal have been studying them all these years as well.

The Ariaal note that foreigners slather white liquid on their very white skin to protect them from the sun, and that many favor short pants that show off their legs and the clunky boots on their feet. Foreigners often partake of the local food but drink water out of bottles and munch on strange food in wrappers between meals, the Ariaal observe.

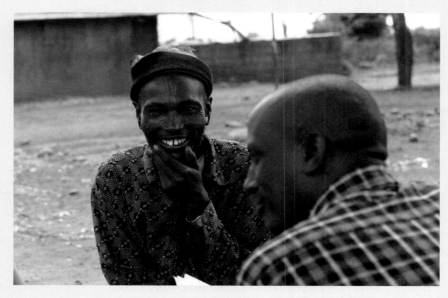

■ *Koitaton Garawale (left) is amused by questions posed by researcher Daniel Lemoille in Songa, Kenya, on December 1, 2005. The Ariaal, a nomadic community of about 10,000 people in northern Kenya, have been studied since the 1970s by Eliot Fratkin and other anthropologists, representing various subfields.*

The scientists leave tracks as well as memories behind. For instance, it is not uncommon to see nomads in T-shirts bearing university logos, gifts from departing academics.

In Lewogoso Lukumai, a circle of makeshift huts near the Ndoto Mountains, nomads rushed up to a visitor and asked excitedly in the Samburu language, "Where's Elliot?"

They meant Dr. Fratkin, who describes in his book "Ariaal Pastoralists of Kenya" how in 1974 he stumbled upon the Ariaal, who had been little known until then. With money from the University of London and the Smithsonian Institution, he was traveling north from Nairobi in search of isolated agro-pastoralist groups in Ethiopia. But a coup toppled Haile Selassie, then the emperor, and the border between the countries was closed. So as he sat in a bar in Marsabit, a boy approached and, mistaking him for a tourist, asked if he wanted to see the elephants in a nearby forest. When the aspiring anthropologist declined, the boy asked if he wanted to see a traditional ceremony at a local village instead. That was Dr. Fratkin's introduction to the Ariaal, who share cultural traits with the Samburu and Rendille tribes of Kenya.

Soon after, he was living with the Ariaal, learning their language and customs while fighting off mosquitoes and fleas in his hut of sticks covered with grass.

The Ariaal wear sandals made from old tires and many still rely on their cows, camels and goats to survive. Drought is a regular feature of their world, coming in regular intervals and testing their durability.

"I was young when Elliot first arrived," recalled an Ariaal elder known as Lenampere in Lewogoso

Lukumai, a settlement that moves from time to time to a new patch of sand. "He came here and lived with us. He drank milk and blood with us. After him, so many others came." . . .

Not all African tribes are as welcoming to researchers, even those with the necessary permits from government bureaucrats. But the Ariaal have a reputation for cooperating—in exchange, that is, for pocket money. "They think I'm stupid for asking dumb questions," said Daniel Lemoille, headmaster of the school in Songa, a village outside of Marsabit for Ariaal nomads who have settled down, and a frequent research assistant for visiting professors. "You have to try to explain that these same questions are asked to people all over the world and that their answers will help advance science." . . .

The Ariaal have no major gripes about the studies, although the local chief in Songa, Stephen Lesseren, who wore a Boston University T-shirt the other day, said he wished their work would lead to more tangible benefits for his people.

"We don't mind helping people get their Ph.D.'s," he said. "But once they get their Ph.D.'s, many of them go away. They don't send us their reports . . . We want feedback. We want development."

Even when conflicts break out in the area, as happened this year as members of rival tribes slaughtered each other, victimizing the Ariaal, the research does not cease. With tensions still high, John G. Galaty, an anthropologist at McGill University in Montreal who studies ethnic conflicts, arrived in northern Kenya to question them.

In a study in *The International Journal of Impotence Research*, Dr.

Campbell found that Ariaal men with many wives showed less erectile dysfunction than did men of the same age with fewer spouses.

Dr. Campbell's body image study, published in the *Journal of Cross-Cultural Psychology* this year, also found that Ariaal men are much more consistent than men in other parts of the world in their views of the average man's body [one like their own] and what they think women want [one like their own].

Dr. Campbell came across no billboards or international magazines in Ariaal country and only one television in a local restaurant that played CNN, leading him to contend that Ariaal men's views of their bodies were less affected by media images of burly male models with six-pack stomachs and rippling chests.

To test his theories, a nonresearcher without a Ph.D. showed a group of Ariaal men a copy of *Men's Health* magazine full of pictures of impossibly well-sculpted men and women. The men looked on with rapt attention and admired the chiseled forms.

"That one, I like," said one nomad who was up in his years, pointing at a photo of a curvy woman who was clearly a regular at the gym. Another old-timer gazed at the bulging pectoral muscles of a male bodybuilder in the magazine and posed a question that got everybody talking. Was it a man, he asked, or a very, very strong woman?

SOURCE: Marc Lacey, "Remote and Poked, Anthropology's Dream Tribe," *New York Times*, December 18, 2005, Late Edition—Final, Section 1, p. 1.

adaptation, long-term physiological adaptation, and short-term physiological adaptation. First, native populations of high-altitude areas, such as the Andes of Peru and the Himalayas of Tibet and Nepal, seem to have acquired certain genetic advantages for life at very high altitudes. The Andean tendency to develop a voluminous chest and lungs probably has a genetic basis. Second, regardless of their genes, people who grow up at a high altitude become physiologically more efficient there than genetically similar people who have grown up at sea level would be. This illustrates long-term physiological adaptation during the body's growth and development. Third, humans also have the capacity for short-term or immediate physiological adaptation. Thus, when

TABLE 1.1   Forms of Cultural and Biological Adaptation (to High Altitude)

Form of Adaptation	Type of Adaptation	Example
Technology	Cultural	Pressurized airplane cabin with oxygen masks
Genetic adaptation (occurs over generations)	Biological	Larger "barrel chests" of native highlanders
Long-term physiological adaptation (occurs during growth and development of the individual organism)	Biological	More efficient respiratory system, to extract oxygen from "thin air"
Short-term physiological adaptation (occurs spontaneously when the individual organism enters a new environment)	Biological	Increased heart rate, hyperventilation

lowlanders arrive in the highlands, they immediately increase their breathing and heart rates. Hyperventilation increases the oxygen in their lungs and arteries. As the pulse also increases, blood reaches their tissues more rapidly. All these varied adaptive responses—cultural and biological—achieve a single goal: maintaining an adequate supply of oxygen to the body.

As human history has unfolded, the social and cultural means of adaptation have become increasingly important. In this process, humans have devised diverse ways of coping with the range of environments they have occupied in time and space. The rate of cultural adaptation and change has accelerated, particularly during the past 10,000 years. For millions of years, hunting and gathering of nature's bounty—*foraging*—was the sole basis of human subsistence. However, it took only a few thousand years for **food production** (the cultivation of plants and domestication of animals), which originated some 12,000–10,000 years ago, to replace foraging in most areas. Between 6000 and 5000 B.P. (before the present), the first civilizations arose. These were large, powerful, and complex societies, such as ancient Egypt, that conquered and governed large geographic areas.

Much more recently, the spread of industrial production has profoundly affected human life. Throughout human history, major innovations have spread at the expense of earlier ones. Each economic revolution has had social and cultural repercussions. Today's global economy and communications link all contemporary people, directly or indirectly, in the modern world system. People must cope with forces generated by progressively larger systems—region, nation, and world. The study of such contemporary adaptations generates new challenges for anthropology: "The cultures of world peoples need to be constantly rediscovered as these people reinvent them in changing historical circumstances" (Marcus and Fischer 1986, p. 24).

GENERAL ANTHROPOLOGY

The academic discipline of anthropology, also known as **general anthropology** or "four-field" anthropology, includes four main subdisciplines or subfields. They are sociocultural, archaeological, biological, and linguistic anthropology. (From here on, the shorter term *cultural anthropology* will be used as a synonym for "sociocultural anthropology.") Of the subfields, cultural anthropology has the largest membership. Most departments of anthropology teach courses in all four subfields.

There are historical reasons for the inclusion of four subfields in a single discipline. The origin of anthropology as a scientific field, and of American anthropology in particular, can be traced back to the 19th century (see Appendix 1). Early American anthropologists were concerned especially with the history and cultures of the native peoples of North America. Interest in the origins and diversity of Native Americans brought together studies of customs, social life, language, and physical traits. Anthropologists are still pondering such questions as: Where did Native Americans come from? How many waves of migration brought them to the New World? What are the linguistic, cultural, and biological links among Native Americans and between them and Asia? Another reason for anthropology's inclusion of four subfields was an interest in the relation between biology (e.g., "race") and culture. More than 60 years ago, the anthropologist Ruth Benedict realized that "In World history, those who have helped to build the same culture are not necessarily of one race, and those of the same race have not all participated in one culture. In scientific language, culture is not a function of race" (Benedict 1940, Ch. 2). (Note that a unified four-field anthropology did not develop in Europe, where the subdisciplines tend to exist separately.)

There are also logical reasons for the unity of American anthropology. Each subfield considers

For current news about anthropology, see the OLC Internet Exercises **mhhe.com/kottak**

Map Atlas

See Maps 8 and 9. Map 8 shows the origin and spread of agriculture (food production). Map 9 shows ancient civilizations.

Chapter 1   What Is Anthropology?   **7**

For a quiz on the subdisciplines of anthropology, see the Interactive Exercise

mhhe.com/kottak

variation in time and space (that is, in different geographic areas). Cultural and archaeological anthropologists study (among many other topics) changes in social life and customs. Archaeologists have used studies of living societies and behavior patterns to imagine what life might have been like in the past. Biological anthropologists examine evolutionary changes in physical form, for example, anatomical changes that might have been associated with the origin of tool use or language. Linguistic anthropologists may reconstruct the basics of ancient languages by studying modern ones.

The subdisciplines influence each other as anthropologists talk to each other, read books and journals, and associate in professional organizations. General anthropology explores the basics of human biology, society, and culture and considers their interrelations. Anthropologists share certain key assumptions. Perhaps the most fundamental is the idea that sound conclusions about "human nature" cannot be derived from studying a single nation, society, or cultural tradition. A comparative, cross-cultural approach is essential.

Cultural Forces Shape Human Biology

For example, anthropology's comparative, biocultural perspective recognizes that cultural forces constantly mold human biology. (**Biocultural** refers to the inclusion and combination of both biological and cultural perspectives and approaches to comment on or solve a particular issue or problem.) Culture is a key environmental force in determining how human bodies grow and develop. Cultural traditions promote certain activities and abilities, discourage others, and set standards of physical well-being and attractiveness. Physical activities, including sports, which are influenced by culture, help build the body. For example, North American girls are encour-

aged to pursue, and therefore do well in competition involving figure skating, gymnastics, track and field, swimming, diving, and many other sports. Brazilian girls, although excelling in the team sports of basketball and volleyball, haven't fared nearly as well in individual sports as have their American and Canadian counterparts. Why are people encouraged to excel as athletes in some nations but not others? Why do people in some countries invest so much time and effort in competitive sports that their bodies change significantly as a result?

Cultural standards of attractiveness and propriety influence participation and achievement in sports. Americans run or swim not just to compete but to keep trim and fit. Brazil's beauty standards accept more fat, especially in female buttocks and hips. Brazilian men have had some international success in swimming and running, but Brazil rarely sends female swimmers or runners to the Olympics. One reason Brazilian women avoid competitive swimming in particular may be that sport's effects on the body. Years of swimming sculpt a distinctive physique: an enlarged upper torso, a massive neck, and powerful shoulders and back. Successful female swimmers tend to be big, strong, and bulky. The countries that produce them most consistently are the United States, Canada, Australia, Germany, the Scandinavian nations, the Netherlands, and the former Soviet Union, where this body type isn't as stigmatized as it is in Latin countries. Swimmers develop hard bodies, but Brazilian culture says that women

UNDERSTANDING OURSELVES

Our parents may tell us that drinking milk and eating vegetables promote healthy growth, but they don't as readily recognize the role that culture plays in shaping our bodies. Our genetic attributes provide a foundation for our growth and development, but human biology is fairly plastic. That is, it is malleable; the environment influences how we grow. Identical twins raised from birth in radically different environments (e.g., one in the high Andes and one at sea level) will not, as adults, be physically identical. Nutrition matters in growth; so do cultural guidelines about what is proper for boys and girls to do. Culture is an environmental force that affects our development as much as do nutrition, heat, cold, and altitude. One aspect of culture is how it provides opportunities for various activities. We get to be good at sports by practicing them. When you grew up, which was it easiest for you to engage in—baseball, golf, mountain climbing, fencing, or some other sport? Think about why.

Years of swimming sculpt a distinctive physique: an enlarged upper torso, a massive neck, and powerful shoulders and back. Shown here are members of the Stanford University swim team.

should be soft, with big hips and buttocks, not big shoulders. Many young female swimmers in Brazil choose to abandon the sport rather than the "feminine" body ideal.

THE SUBDISCIPLINES OF ANTHROPOLOGY

Cultural Anthropology

Cultural anthropology is the study of human society and culture, the subfield that describes, analyzes, interprets, and explains social and cultural similarities and differences. To study and interpret cultural diversity, cultural anthropologists engage in two kinds of activity: ethnography (based on field work) and ethnology (based on cross-cultural comparison). Ethnography provides an account of a particular community, society, or culture. During ethnographic field work, the ethnographer gathers data that he or she organizes, describes, analyzes, and interprets to build and present that account, which may be in the form of a book, article, or film. Traditionally, ethnographers have lived in small communities (such as Arembepe, Brazil—see "Interesting Issues" on pages 12–13) and studied local behavior, beliefs, customs, social life, economic activities, politics, and religion. What

kind of experience is ethnography for the ethnographer? The box offers some clues.

The anthropological perspective derived from ethnographic field work often differs radically from that of economics or political science. Those fields focus on national and official organizations and policies and often on elites. However, the groups that anthropologists have traditionally studied usually have been relatively poor and powerless, as are most people in the world today. Ethnographers often observe discriminatory practices directed toward such people, who experience food shortages, dietary deficiencies, and other aspects of poverty. Political scientists tend to study programs that national planners develop, while anthropologists discover how these programs work on the local level.

Cultures are not isolated. As noted by Franz Boas (1940/1966) many years ago, contact between neighboring tribes has always existed and has extended over enormous areas. "Human populations construct their cultures in interaction with one another, and not in isolation" (Wolf 1982, p. ix). Villagers increasingly participate in regional, national, and world events. Exposure to external forces comes through the mass media, migration, and modern transportation. City and nation increasingly invade local communities with the arrival of tourists, development agents, government and religious officials, and political candidates. Such linkages are prominent components of regional, national, and international systems of politics, economics, and information. These larger systems increasingly affect the people and places anthropology traditionally has studied. The study of such linkages and systems is part of the subject matter of modern anthropology.

Ethnology examines, interprets, analyzes, and compares the results of ethnography—the data gathered in different societies. It uses such data to compare and contrast and to make generalizations about society and culture. Looking beyond the particular to the more general, ethnologists attempt to identify and explain cultural differences and similarities, to test hypotheses, and to build theory to enhance our understanding of how social and cultural systems work. (See the section "Science, Explanation, and Hypothesis Testing" at the end of this chapter.) Ethnology gets its data for comparison not just from ethnography but also from the other subfields, particularly from archaeological anthropology, which reconstructs social systems of the past. (Table 1.2 summarizes the main contrasts between ethnography and ethnology.)

Archaeological Anthropology

Archaeological anthropology (more simply, "archaeology") reconstructs, describes, and interprets human behavior and cultural patterns through material remains. At sites where people live or have lived, archaeologists find artifacts, material items that humans have made, used, or modified, such as tools, weapons, camp sites, buildings, and garbage. Plant and animal remains and ancient garbage tell stories about consumption and activities. Wild and domesticated grains have different characteristics, which allow archaeologists to distinguish between gathering and cultivation. Examination of animal bones reveals the ages of slaughtered animals and provides other information useful in determining whether species were wild or domesticated.

Analyzing such data, archaeologists answer several questions about ancient economies. Did the group get its meat from hunting, or did it domesticate and breed animals, killing only those of a certain age and sex? Did plant food come from wild plants or from sowing, tending, and harvest-

ing crops? Did the residents make, trade for, or buy particular items? Were raw materials available locally? If not, where did they come from? From such information, archaeologists reconstruct patterns of production, trade, and consumption.

Archaeologists have spent much time studying potsherds, fragments of earthenware. Potsherds are more durable than many other artifacts, such as textiles and wood. The quantity of pottery fragments allows estimates of population size and density. The discovery that potters used materials that were not locally available suggests systems of trade. Similarities in manufacture and decoration at different sites may be proof of cultural connections. Groups with similar pots may be historically related. Perhaps they shared common cultural ancestors, traded with each other, or belonged to the same political system.

Many archaeologists examine paleoecology. *Ecology* is the study of interrelations among living things in an environment. The organisms and environment together constitute an ecosystem, a patterned arrangement of energy flows and exchanges. Human ecology studies ecosystems that include people, focusing on the ways in which human use "of nature influences and is influenced by social organization and cultural values" (Bennett 1969, pp. 10–11). *Paleoecology* looks at the ecosystems of the past.

In addition to reconstructing ecological patterns, archaeologists may infer cultural transformations, for example, by observing changes in the size and type of sites and the distance between them. A city develops in a region where only towns, villages, and hamlets existed a few

TABLE 1.2	Ethnography and Ethnology—Two Dimensions of Cultural Anthropology
Ethnography	**Ethnology**
Requires fieldwork to collect data	Uses data collected by a series of researchers
Often descriptive	Usually synthetic
Group/community specific	Comparative/cross-cultural

An archaeological team works at Harappa, one site from an ancient Indus River civilization dating back some 4,800 years.

centuries earlier. The number of settlement levels (city, town, village, hamlet) in a society is a measure of social complexity. Buildings offer clues about political and religious features. Temples and pyramids suggest that an ancient society had an authority structure capable of marshaling the labor needed to build such monuments. The presence or absence of certain structures, like the pyramids of ancient Egypt and Mexico, reveals differences in function between settlements. For example, some towns were places where people came to attend ceremonies. Others were burial sites; still others were farming communities.

Archaeologists also reconstruct behavior patterns and lifestyles of the past by excavating. This involves digging through a succession of levels at a particular site. In a given area, through time, settlements may change in form and purpose, as may the connections between settlements. Excavation can document changes in economic, social, and political activities.

Although archaeologists are best known for studying prehistory, that is, the period before the invention of writing, they also study the cultures of historical and even living peoples. Studying sunken ships off the Florida coast, underwater archaeologists have been able to verify the living conditions on the vessels that brought ancestral African Americans to the New World as enslaved people. In a research project begun in 1973 in Tucson, Arizona, archaeologist William Rathje has learned about contemporary life by studying modern garbage. The value of "garbology," as

Rathje calls it, is that it provides "evidence of what people did, not what they think they did, what they think they should have done, or what the interviewer thinks they should have done" (Harrison, Rathje, and Hughes 1994, p. 108). What people report may contrast strongly with their real behavior as revealed by garbology. For example, the garbologists discovered that the three Tucson neighborhoods that reported the lowest beer consumption actually had the highest number of discarded beer cans per household (Podolefsky and Brown 1992, p. 100)! Rathje's garbology also has exposed misconceptions about how much of different kinds of trash are in landfills: While most people thought that fast-food containers and disposable diapers were major waste problems, in fact they were relatively insignificant compared with paper, including environmentally friendly, recyclable paper (Rathje and Murphy 2001).

Biological, or Physical, Anthropology

The subject matter of **biological, or physical, anthropology** is human biological diversity in time and space. The focus on biological variation unites five special interests within biological anthropology:

1. Human evolution as revealed by the fossil record (paleoanthropology).

2. Human genetics.

Even Anthropologists Get Culture Shock

I first lived in Arembepe (Brazil) during the (North American) summer of 1962. That was between my junior and senior years at New York City's Columbia College, where I was majoring in anthropology. I went to Arembepe as a participant in a now defunct program designed to provide undergraduates with experience doing ethnography—firsthand study of an alien society's culture and social life.

Brought up in one culture, intensely curious about others, anthropologists nevertheless experience culture shock, particularly on their first field trip. Culture shock refers to the whole set of feelings about being in an alien setting, and the ensuing reactions. It is a chilly, creepy feeling of alienation, of being without some of the most ordinary, trivial (and therefore basic) cues of one's culture of origin.

As I planned my departure for Brazil in 1962, I could not know just how naked I would feel without the cloak of my own language and culture. My sojourn in Arembepe would be my first trip outside the United States. I was an urban boy who had grown up in Atlanta, Georgia, and New York City. I had little experience with rural life in my own country, none with Latin America, and I had received only minimal training in the Portuguese language.

New York City direct to Salvador, Bahia, Brazil. Just a brief stopover in Rio de Janeiro; a longer visit would be a reward at the end of field work. As our prop jet approached tropical Salvador, I couldn't believe the whiteness of the sand. "That's not snow, is it?" I remarked to a fellow field team member . . .

My first impressions of Bahia were of smells—alien odors of ripe and decaying mangoes, bananas, and passion fruit—and of swatting the ubiquitous fruit flies I had never seen before, although I had read extensively about their reproductive behavior in genetics classes. There were strange concoctions of rice, black beans, and

FIGURE 1.1 Location of Arembepe, Bahia, Brazil.

3. Human growth and development.

4. Human biological plasticity (the body's ability to change as it copes with stresses, such as heat, cold, and altitude).

5. The biology, evolution, behavior, and social life of monkeys, apes, and other nonhuman primates.

These interests link physical anthropology to other fields: biology, zoology, geology, anatomy, physiology, medicine, and public health. Osteology—the study of bones—helps paleoanthropologists, who examine skulls, teeth, and bones, to identify human ancestors and to chart changes in anatomy over time. A paleontologist is a scientist who studies fossils. A paleoanthro-

pologist is one sort of paleontologist, one who studies the fossil record of human evolution. Paleoanthropologists often collaborate with archaeologists, who study artifacts, in reconstructing biological and cultural aspects of human evolution. Fossils and tools are often found together. Different types of tools provide information about the habits, customs, and lifestyles of the ancestral humans who used them.

More than a century ago, Charles Darwin noticed that the variety that exists within any population permits some individuals (those with the favored characteristics) to do better than others at surviving and reproducing. Genetics, which developed later, enlightens us about the causes and transmission of this variety. However, it isn't just genes that cause variety. During any

Conrad Kottak, with his Brazilian nephew Guilherme Roxo, on a revisit to Arembepe in 2004.

our car through the village streets until we parked in front of our house, near the central square. Our first few days in Arembepe were spent with children following us everywhere. For weeks we had few moments of privacy. Children watched our every move through our living room window. Occasionally one made an incomprehensible remark. Usually they just stood there . . .

The sounds, sensations, sights, smells, and tastes of life in northeastern Brazil, and in Arembepe, slowly grew familiar . . . I grew accustomed to this world without Kleenex, in which globs of mucus habitually drooped from the noses of village children whenever a cold passed through Arembepe. A world where, seemingly without effort, women . . . carried 18-liter kerosene cans of water on their heads, where boys sailed kites and sported at catching houseflies in their bare hands, where old women smoked pipes, storekeepers offered cachaça (common rum) at nine in the morning, and men played dominoes on lazy afternoons when there was no fishing. I was visiting a world where human life was oriented toward water—the sea, where men fished, and the lagoon, where women communally washed clothing, dishes, and their own bodies.

This description is adapted from my ethnographic study *Assault on Paradise: The Globalization of a Little Community in Brazil*, 4th ed. (New York: McGraw-Hill, 2006).

gelatinous gobs of unidentifiable meats and floating pieces of skin. Coffee was strong and sugar crude, and every tabletop had containers for toothpicks and for manioc (cassava) flour to sprinkle, like Parmesan cheese, on anything one might eat. I remember oatmeal soup and a slimy stew of beef tongue in tomatoes. At one meal a disintegrating fish head, eyes still attached, but barely, stared up at me as the rest of its body floated in a bowl of bright orange palm oil . . .

I only vaguely remember my first day in Arembepe (Figure 1.1). Unlike ethnographers who have studied remote tribes in the tropical forests of interior South America or the highlands of Papua New Guinea, I did not have to hike or ride a canoe for days to arrive at my field site. Arembepe was not isolated relative to such places, only relative to every other place I had ever been . . .

I do recall what happened when we arrived. There was no formal road into the village. Entering through southern Arembepe, vehicles simply threaded their way around coconut trees, following tracks left by automobiles that had passed previously. A crowd of children had heard us coming, and they pursued

individual's lifetime, the environment works along with heredity to determine biological features. For example, people with a genetic tendency to be tall will be shorter if they are poorly nourished during childhood. Thus, biological anthropology also investigates the influence of environment on the body as it grows and matures. Among the environmental factors that influence the body as it develops are nutrition, altitude, temperature, and disease, as well as cultural factors, such as the standards of attractiveness we considered previously.

Biological anthropology (along with zoology) also includes primatology. The primates include our closest relatives—apes and monkeys. Primatologists study their biology, evolution, behavior, and social life, often in their natural environ-

ments. Primatology assists paleoanthropology, because primate behavior may shed light on early human behavior and human nature.

Linguistic Anthropology

We don't know (and probably never will) when our ancestors acquired the ability to speak, although biological anthropologists have looked to the anatomy of the face and the skull to speculate about the origin of language. And primatologists have described the communication systems of monkeys and apes. We do know that well-developed, grammatically complex languages have existed for thousands of years. Linguistic anthropology offers further illustration of anthropology's interest in comparison, variation, and

The Utility of Hand and Foot Bones for Problems in Biological Anthropology

BACKGROUND INFORMATION

STUDENT:
Alicia Wilbur

SUPERVISING PROFESSOR:
Della Collins Cook

SCHOOL:
Indiana University

YEAR IN SCHOOL/MAJOR:
Junior and Senior/Anthropology

FUTURE PLANS:
Ph.D. in Biological Anthropology

PROJECT TITLE:
The Utility of Hand and Foot Bones for Problems in Bioanthropology

How does this account suggest common problems of interest to more than one subfield of anthropology? Does the research have implications for cultural as well as for biological and archaeological anthropology?

The large, well-preserved skeletal series from west-central Illinois, housed in the Department of Anthropology at Indiana University, has been the focus of many archaeological and bioanthropological research projects over the years. I became interested in the use of hand and foot bones to determine the stature and sex of the individuals buried in those mounds. This information is important for both archaeological and biological studies of past peoples and their cultures, but is also relevant to modern forensic and mass disaster situations. In both archaeological and modern situations, the human remains recovered may be extremely fragmentary. A single hand or foot can play an important role in identifying modern victims of crime or mass disasters.

Most equations used for estimating adult stature or determining sex from skeletal material are constructed from data on modern Europeans or modern Americans of European or African extraction. Because body proportions differ between populations, applying these equations to skeletal remains of other groups may give inaccurate results. A benefit of my study was that it was constructed on Native American remains and thus could be used for modern Native Americans' remains in forensic cases or mass disasters.

I measured femurs (the thigh bone) and hand and foot bones for 410 adult skeletons and used statistical methods to predict the sex of the individuals, with accuracies exceeding 87 percent. Stature estimation also was found to be possible with hand and foot bones, although the range given was too large to be useful in a court of law. Still, estimates resulting from these equations may be useful for delimiting a range of possible heights for preliminary identification purposes.

The project was published in the *International Journal of Osteoarchaeology* in 1998. While running statistical analyses on the hand and foot data, I noticed a discrepancy in the body proportions of one female adult. Upon carefully examining the rest of her skeleton, I discovered a suite of skeletal anomalies that suggest a rare genetic syndrome called Rubinstein-Taybi Syndrome that affects many organs. Symptoms include delayed growth, mental retardation, and abnormalities of the head and face, including widely spaced eyes and an abnormally large nose. Affected individuals also may have abnormally large big toes and thumbs. There also may be breathing and swallowing difficulties.

It may yet prove possible to analyze DNA from this sample to determine if my diagnosis is correct. If so, it would be the earliest known case of this syndrome. Knowing that this individual lived to mid- to late adulthood with several physical and mental disabilities tells us something about her culture.

These types of studies on skeletal material are important for the information they give us about the past and also for their relevance to modern problems. Future research will focus on genetic and infectious diseases that beset ancient peoples as well as application of this work to modern problems.

change. **Linguistic anthropology** studies language in its social and cultural context, across space and over time. Some linguistic anthropologists make inferences about universal features of language, linked perhaps to uniformities in the human brain. Others reconstruct ancient languages by comparing their contemporary descendants and in so doing make discoveries about history. Still others study linguistic differences to discover varied perceptions and patterns of thought in different cultures.

Historical linguistics considers variation in time, such as the changes in sounds, grammar, and vocabulary between Middle English (spoken from approximately A.D. 1050 to 1550) and modern English. **Sociolinguistics** investigates relationships between social and linguistic variation. No language is a homogeneous system in which everyone speaks just like everyone else. How do different speakers use a given language? How do linguistic features correlate with social factors, including class and gender differences (Tannen 1990)? One reason for variation is geography, as in regional dialects and accents. Linguistic variation also is expressed in the bilingualism of ethnic groups. Linguistic and cultural anthropologists collaborate in studying links between language and many other aspects of culture, such as how people reckon kinship and how they perceive and classify colors.

ANTHROPOLOGY AND OTHER ACADEMIC FIELDS

As mentioned previously, one of the main differences between anthropology and the other fields that study people is **holism**, anthropology's unique blend of biological, social, cultural, linguistic, historical, and contemporary perspectives. Paradoxically, while distinguishing anthropology, this breadth is what also links it to many other disciplines. Techniques used to date fossils and artifacts have come to anthropology from physics, chemistry, and geology. Because plant and animal remains often are found with human bones and artifacts, anthropologists collaborate with botanists, zoologists, and paleontologists.

As a discipline that is both scientific and humanistic, anthropology has links with many other academic fields. Anthropology is a **science**—a "systematic field of study or body of knowledge that aims, through experiment, observation, and deduction, to produce reliable explanations of phenomena, with reference to the material and physical world" (*Webster's New World Encyclopedia* 1993, p. 937). The following chapters present anthropology as a humanistic science devoted to discovering, describing, understanding, and explaining similarities and differences in time and space among humans and our ancestors. Clyde Kluckhohn (1944) described anthropology as "the science of human similarities and differences" (p. 9). His statement of the need for such a field still stands: "Anthropology provides a scientific basis for dealing with the crucial dilemma of the world today: how can peoples of different appearance, mutually unintelligible languages, and dissimilar ways of life get along peaceably together?" (p. 9). Anthropology has compiled an impressive body of knowledge that this textbook attempts to encapsulate.

Besides its links to the natural sciences (e.g., geology, zoology), and social sciences (e.g., sociology, psychology), Anthropology also has strong links to the humanities. The humanities include English, comparative literature, classics, folklore, philosophy, and the arts. These fields study languages, texts, philosophies, arts, music, performances, and other forms of creative expression. Ethnomusicology, which studies forms of musical expression on a worldwide basis, is especially closely related to anthropology. Also linked is folklore, the systematic study of tales, myths, and legends from a variety of cultures. One might well argue that anthropology is among the most humanistic of all academic fields because of its fundamental respect for human diversity. Anthropologists listen to, record, and represent voices from a multitude of nations and cultures. Anthropology values local knowledge, diverse worldviews, and alternative philosophies. Cultural anthropology and linguistic anthropology in particular bring a comparative and nonelitist perspective to forms of creative expression, including language, art, narratives, music, and dance, viewed in their social and cultural context.

Cultural Anthropology and Sociology

Cultural anthropology and sociology share an interest in social relations, organization, and behavior. However, important differences between these disciplines arose from the kinds of societies each traditionally studied. Initially sociologists focused on the industrial West; anthropologists, on nonindustrial societies. Different methods of data collection and analysis emerged to deal with those different kinds of societies. To study large-scale, complex nations, sociologists came to rely on questionnaires and other means of gathering masses of quantifiable data. For many years, sampling and statistical techniques have been basic to sociology, whereas statistical training has been less common in anthropology (although this is changing as anthropologists increasingly work in modern nations).

Traditional ethnographers studied small and nonliterate (without writing) populations and relied on methods appropriate to that context. "Ethnography is a research process in which the anthropologist closely observes, records, and engages in the daily life of another culture—an experience labeled as the fieldwork method—and then writes accounts of this culture, emphasizing descriptive detail" (Marcus and Fischer 1986, p. 18). One key method described in this quote is participant observation—taking part in the events one is observing, describing, and analyzing.

In many areas and topics, anthropology and sociology now are converging. As the modern world system grows, sociologists now do research in developing countries and in other places that were once mainly within the anthropological orbit. As industrialization spreads, many anthropologists now work in industrial nations, where they study diverse topics, including rural decline, inner-city life, and the role of the mass media in creating national cultural patterns.

Anthropology and Psychology

Like sociologists, most psychologists do research in their own society. But statements about "human" psychology cannot be based solely on observations made in one society or in a single type of society. The area of cultural anthropology known as psychological anthropology studies cross-cultural variation in psychological traits. Societies instill different values by training children differently. Adult personalities reflect a culture's child-rearing practices.

Bronislaw Malinowski, an early contributor to the cross-cultural study of human psychology, is famous for his field work among the Trobriand Islanders of the South Pacific (Figure 1.2). The Trobrianders reckon kinship matrilineally. They consider themselves related to the mother and her relatives, but not to the father. The relative who disciplines the child is not the father but the mother's brother, the maternal uncle. Trobrianders show a marked respect for the uncle, with whom a boy usually has a cool and distant relationship. In contrast, the Trobriand father–son relationship is friendly and affectionate.

Malinowski's work among the Trobrianders suggested modifications in Sigmund Freud's famous theory of the universality of the Oedipus complex (Malinowski 1927). According to Freud (1918/1950), boys around the age of five become sexually attracted to their mothers. The Oedipus complex is resolved, in Freud's view, when the boy overcomes his sexual jealousy of, and identifies with, his father. Freud lived in patriarchal Austria during the late 19th and early 20th centuries—a social milieu in which the father was a strong authoritarian figure. The Austrian father was the child's primary authority figure and the mother's sexual partner. In the Trobriands, the father had only the sexual role.

If, as Freud contended, the Oedipus complex always creates social distance based on jealousy toward the mother's sexual partner, this would have shown up in Trobriand society. It did not. Malinowski concluded that the authority structure did more to influence the father–son relationship than did sexual jealousy. Although Melford Spiro (1993) has critiqued Malinowski's conclusions (see also Weiner 1988), no contemporary anthropologist would dispute Malinowski's contention that individual psychology is molded in a specific cultural context. Anthropologists continue to provide cross-cultural perspectives on psychoanalytic propositions (Paul 1989) as well as on issues of developmental and cognitive psychology (Shore 1996).

SCIENCE, EXPLANATION, AND HYPOTHESIS TESTING

A key feature of anthropology is its comparative, cross-cultural dimension. As was stated previously (see p. 10), *ethnology* draws on ethnographic, as well as archaeological, data to compare and contrast, and to make generalizations about, societies and cultures. As a scientific pursuit, ethnology attempts to identify and explain cultural

FIGURE 1.2 Location of Trobriand Islands.

How much would we know about human behavior, thought, and feeling if we studied only our own kind? What if our entire understanding of human behavior were based on analysis of questionnaires filled out by college students in Oregon? A radical question but one that should make you think about the basis for statements about what humans are like. A primary reason why anthropology helps us understand ourselves is the cross-cultural perspective. One culture can't tell us everything we need to know about what it means to be human. Earlier we saw how cultural forces influence our physical growth. Culture also guides our emotional and cognitive growth and helps determine the kinds of personalities we have as adults. Among scholarly disciplines, anthropology stands out as the field that provides the cross-cultural test. How does television affect us? To answer that question, study not just North America in 2006 but some other place—and perhaps also some other time (such as Brazil in the 1980s; see Kottak 1990b). Anthropology specializes in the study of human variation in space and time.

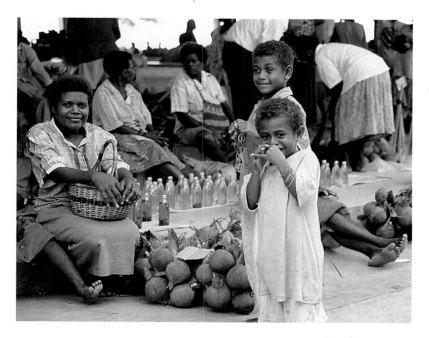

■ Bronislaw Malinowski is famous for his fieldwork among the matrilineal Trobriand Islanders of the South Pacific. Does this Trobriand market scene suggest anything about the status of Trobriand women?

differences and similarities, test hypotheses, and build theory to enhance our understanding of how social and cultural systems work.

In their 1997 article "Science in Anthropology," Melvin Ember and Carol R. Ember stress a key feature of science as a way of viewing the world: Science recognizes the tentativeness and uncertainty of our knowledge and understanding. Scientists strive to improve understanding by testing *hypotheses*—suggested explanations of things and events. In science, understanding means *explaining*—showing how and why the thing to be understood (the *explicandum*) is related to other things in some known way. Explanations rely on associations and theories. An association is an observed relationship between two or more variables. A theory is more general, suggesting or implying associations and attempting to explain them (Ember and Ember 1997).

A thing or event, for example, the freezing of water, is explained if it illustrates a general principle or association. "Water solidifies at 32 degrees" states an association between two variables: the state of the water and the air temperature. The truth of the statement is confirmed by repeated observations. In the physical sciences, such relationships are called "laws." Explanations based on such laws allow us to understand the past and predict the future.

In the social sciences, associations usually are stated probabilistically: Two or more variables *tend to be* related in a predictable way, but there are exceptions (Ember and Ember 1997). For example, in a worldwide sample of societies, the anthropologist John Whiting (1964) found a strong (but not 100 percent) association or correlation between a low-protein diet and a long postpartum sex taboo—a prohibition against sexual intercourse between husband and wife for a year or more after the birth of a child.

Laws and statistical associations explain by relating the explicandum (e.g., the postpartum sex taboo) to one or more other variables (e.g., a low-protein diet). We also want to know why such associations exist. Why do societies with low-protein diets have long postpartum sex taboos? Scientists formulate theories to explain the correlations they observe.

A **theory** is a set of ideas formulated (by reasoning from known facts) to explain something. A theory provides a framework that helps us understand *why* (something exists). Returning to the postpartum sex taboo, why might societies with low-protein diets develop this taboo? Whiting's theory is that the taboo is adaptive; it helps people survive and reproduce in certain environments. With too little protein in their diets, babies may develop a protein-deficiency disease called kwashiorkor. But if the mother delays her next pregnancy, her current baby, by breast-feeding longer, has a better chance to survive. Whiting suggests that parents may be unconsciously or consciously aware that having another baby too soon might jeopardize the survival of the first one. Thus, they avoid sex for more than a year after the birth of the first baby.

■ *This child's bloated body is due to protein malnutrition. This condition, known as kwashiorkor, comes from a West African word meaning "one-two." This refers to the practice in some societies of abruptly weaning one infant when a second one is born. With no mother's milk, the first baby may get no protein at all. What are some cultural ways of fending off kwashiorkor?*

When such abstinence becomes institutionalized, everyone is expected to respect the taboo.

A theory is an explanatory framework containing a series of statements. An association simply states an observed relationship between two or more known variables. Parts of a theory, by contrast, may be difficult or impossible to observe or to know directly. With Whiting's theory, for example, it would be hard to determine whether people developed the sex taboo because they recognized that it would give babies a better chance to survive. Typically, some elements of a theory are unobservable (at least at present). In contrast, statistical associations are based entirely on observations (Ember and Ember 1997).

If an association is tested and found to recur again and again, we may consider it proved. Theories, by contrast, are unprovable. Although much evidence may support them, their truth isn't established with certainty. Many of the concepts and ideas in theories aren't directly observable or verifiable. Thus, scientists may try to explain how light behaves by postulating that it consists of "photons," which can't be observed even with the most powerful microscope. The photon is a "theoretical construct," something that can't be seen or verified directly (Ember and Ember 1997).

Why should we bother with theories if we can't prove them? According to the Embers, the main value of a theory is to promote new understanding. A theory can suggest patterns, connections, or relationships that may be confirmed by new research. Whiting's theory, for example, suggests hypotheses for future researchers to test. Because the theory proposes that the postpartum taboo is adaptive under certain conditions, one might hypothesize that certain changes would lead the taboo to disappear. By adopting birth control, for instance, families could space births without avoiding intercourse. So, too, might the

taboo disappear if babies started receiving protein supplements, which would reduce the threat of kwashiorkor.

Although theories can't be proved, they can be rejected. The method of *falsification* (showing a theory to be wrong) is our main way of evaluating theories. If a theory is true, certain predictions should stand up to tests designed to disprove them. Theories that haven't been disproved are accepted (for the time being at least) because the available evidence seems to support them.

What is acceptable evidence that an explanation is probably right? Cases that have been personally selected by a researcher don't provide an acceptable test of a hypothesis or theory. (Imagine that Whiting had combed the ethnographic literature and chosen to cite only those societies that supported his theory.) Ideally, hypothesis testing should be done using a sample of cases that have been selected randomly from some statistical universe. (Whiting did this in choosing his cross-cultural sample.) The relevant variables should be measured reliably, and the strength and significance of the results should be evaluated by using legitimate statistical methods (Bernard 1994).

UNDERSTANDING OURSELVES

Science is a powerful tool for understanding ourselves. Properly, science isn't rigid or dogmatic; scientists recognize the tentativeness and uncertainty of knowledge and understanding, which they try to improve and enhance. Working to confirm laws, refine theories, and provide accurate explanations, scientists strive to be objective. Science relies on unbiased methods, such as random sampling, impartial analytic techniques, and standard statistical tests. But complete objectivity is impossible. There is always observer bias—that is, the presence of the scientist and his or her tools and methods always affects the outcome of an experiment, observation, or analysis. Through their very presence, anthropologists influence the living people and social conditions they study, as do survey researchers when they phrase questions in certain ways. Statisticians have designed techniques to measure and control for observer bias, but observer bias can't be eliminated totally. As scientists, we can only strive for objectivity and impartiality. Science, which has many limitations, certainly is not the only way we have to understand ourselves. Nevertheless, its goals of objectivity and impartiality help distinguish science from ways of knowing that are more biased, more rigid, and more dogmatic.

1. Anthropology is the holistic and comparative study of humanity. It is the systematic exploration of human biological and cultural diversity. Examining the origins of, and changes in, human biology and culture, anthropology provides explanations for similarities and differences. The four subfields of general anthropology are (socio)cultural, archaeological, biological, and linguistic. All consider variation in time and space. Each also examines adaptation—the process by which organisms cope with environmental stresses.

2. Cultural forces mold human biology, including our body types and images. Societies have particular standards of physical attractiveness. They also have specific ideas about what activities—for example, various sports—are appropriate for males and females.

3. Cultural anthropology explores the cultural diversity of the present and the recent past. Archaeology reconstructs cultural patterns, often of prehistoric populations. Biological anthropology documents diversity involving fossils, genetics, growth and development, bodily responses, and nonhuman primates. Linguistic anthropology considers diversity among languages. It also studies how speech changes in social situations and over time.

4. Concerns with biology, society, culture, and language link anthropology to many other fields—sciences and humanities. Anthropologists study art, music, and literature across cultures. But their concern is more with the creative expressions of common people than with arts designed for elites. Anthropologists examine creators and products in their social context. Sociologists traditionally study urban and industrial populations, whereas anthropologists have focused on rural, nonindustrial peoples. Psychological anthropology views human psychology in the context of social and cultural variation.

5. As scientists, anthropologists attempt to identify and explain cultural differences and similarities and to build theories about how social and cultural systems work. Scientists strive to improve understanding by testing hypotheses—suggested explanations. Explanations rely on associations and theories. An association is an observed relationship between variables. A theory is more general, suggesting or implying associations and attempting to explain them.

SUMMARY

KEY TERMS

See the flash cards
mhhe.com/kottak

anthropology The study of the human species and its immediate ancestors.

archaeological anthropology The study of human behavior and cultural patterns and processes through the culture's material remains.

biocultural Referring to the inclusion and combination (to solve a common problem) of both biological and cultural approaches—one of anthropology's hallmarks.

biological anthropology The study of human biological variation in time and space; includes evolution, genetics, growth and development, and primatology.

cultural anthropology The study of human society and culture; describes, analyzes, interprets, and explains social and cultural similarities and differences.

culture Distinctly human; transmitted through learning; traditions and customs that govern behavior and beliefs.

ethnography Fieldwork in a particular culture.

ethnology Cross-cultural comparison; the comparative study of ethnographic data, society, and culture.

food production Cultivation of plants and domestication (stockbreeding) of animals; first developed 10,000 to 12,000 years ago.

general anthropology The field of anthropology as a whole, consisting of cultural, archaeological, biological, and linguistic anthropology.

holistic Interested in the whole of the human condition: past, present, and future; biology, society, language, and culture.

linguistic anthropology The descriptive, comparative, and historical study of language and of linguistic similarities and differences in time, space, and society.

physical anthropology See *biological anthropology.*

science A systematic field of study or body of knowledge that aims, through experiment, observation, and deduction, to produce reliable explanations of phenomena, with reference to the material and physical world.

sociolinguistics Investigates relationships between social and linguistic variations.

theory A set of ideas formulated (by reasoning from known facts) to explain something. The main value of a theory is to promote new understanding. A theory suggest patterns, connections, and relationships that may be confirmed by new research.

CRITICAL THINKING QUESTIONS

For more self-testing, see the self-quizzes
mhhe.com/kottak

1. Which do you think is unique about anthropology: its holism or its comparative perspective? Can you think of other fields that are holistic and/or comparative?

2. What are some areas in which anthropology's biocultural, four-field approach might shed light on current issues and debates? Would sexuality be such an area?

3. Many other disciplines are limited by their focus on powerful people and elites. How have your professors in other classes tried to justify, or compensate for, such limitations?

4. What are some theories, as defined here, that you routinely use to understand the world?

SUGGESTED ADDITIONAL READINGS

Clifford, J.
  1988 *The Predicament of Culture: Twentieth-Century Ethnography, Literature, and Art.* Cambridge, MA: Harvard University Press. Literary evaluation of classic and modern anthropologists and discussion of issues of ethnographic authority.

DeVita, P. R.
  1992 *The Naked Anthropologist: Tales from Around the World.* Belmont, CA: Wadsworth. Views of ethnographic field work.

Endicott, K. M., and R. Welsch
  2003 *Taking Sides: Clashing Views on Controversial Issues in Anthropology.* Guilford, CT: McGraw-Hill/Dushkin. Thirty-eight anthropologists offer opposing viewpoints on 19 polarizing issues, including ethical dilemmas.

Fagan, B. M.
  2006 *Archeology: A Brief Introduction,* 9th ed. Upper Saddle River, NJ: Prentice Hall. Introduction to archaeological theory, techniques, and approaches, including field survey, excavation, and analysis of materials.
  2007 *People of the Earth: An Introduction to World Prehistory,* 12th ed. Upper Saddle River, NJ: Prentice Hall. Introduction to the archaeological study of prehistoric societies, using examples from all areas.

Geertz, C.
  1995 *After the Fact: Two Countries, Four Decades, One Anthropologist.* Cambridge, MA: Harvard University Press. A prominent cultural anthropologist reflects on his work in Morocco and Indonesia.

Harris, M.
  1989 *Our Kind: Who We Are, Where We Came From, Where We Are Going.* New York: HarperCollins. Clearly written survey of the origins of humans, culture, and major sociopolitical institutions.

Marcus, G. E., and M. M. J. Fischer
  1999 *Anthropology as Cultural Critique: An Experimental Moment in the Human Sciences,* 2nd ed. Chicago: University of Chicago Press. Different types of ethnographic accounts as forms of writing, a vision of modern anthropology, and a consideration of anthropologists' public and professional roles.

Nash, D.
  1999 *A Little Anthropology,* 3rd ed. Upper Saddle River, NJ: Prentice Hall. Short introduction to societies and cultures, with comments on developing nations and modern America.

Podolefsky, A., and P. J. Brown, eds.
  2007 *Applying Anthropology: An Introductory Reader,* 8th ed. Boston: McGraw-Hill. Essays focusing on anthropology's relevance to contemporary life; a readable survey of the current range of activities in applied anthropology.

Wolf, E. R.
  1982 *Europe and the People without History.* Berkeley: University of California Press. Influential and award-winning study of the relation between Europe and various nonindustrial populations.

INTERNET EXERCISES

1. News in Anthropology: Look at Texas A&M University's "Anthropology in the News," **http://www.tamu.edu/anthropology/news.htm**, which contains links to articles relevant to anthropology.

   a. After reading the chapter in the textbook and reading some recent news articles, do you think anthropology is more or less relevant to your life?

   b. Look at the variety of topics discussed. Are the connections between the articles and anthropology clear to you? Were they clear to you before you read this chapter?

   c. Examine the first 10 articles. Which subfield of anthropology does each article relate to most closely?

   d. Browse the list of article titles. What are some of the current hot topics in the news about anthropology?

2. Careers in Anthropology: Go to the American Anthropological Association's Jobs Page (**http://aaanet.jobcontrolcenter.com/search/results/**) and Northern Kentucky University's list of organizations in their area hiring anthropologists (**http://www.nku.edu/~anthro/careers.html**).

   a. What kinds of organizations are hiring anthropologists?
   b. What kinds of qualifications are these employers looking for? Do they require a graduate degree, or are they seeking people with an undergraduate degree in anthropology?
   c. What subfields are being sought by employers?

Note that these are just two job listing pages on the Web, and there are many others. If you have an interest in a field of anthropology that is not listed on these pages, use a Web search engine to research what kinds of jobs are available. A good place to start is **http://www.aaanet.org/careers.htm** for more information on careers in anthropology.

See Chapter 1 at your McGraw-Hill Online Learning Center for additional review and interactive exercises.

LINKAGES

Assault on Paradise

Read Chapter 1 of *Assault on Paradise,* 4th edition, by Conrad Phillip Kottak. How does the anthropological research experience described in this chapter differ from sociological research? Based on this account, does ethnography appeal to you? Do you know of, or have you ever visited, places comparable to Arembepe in the 1960s?

Culture Sketches

In *Culture Sketches,* 4th edition, by Peters-Golden, read Chapter 12, "The Samoans: Matai and Migration." Using what you've learned about the four subfields of anthropology and about holistic and comparative perspectives of anthropology, how would you address the Mead–Freeman debate? What might be the consequences, positive or negative, of such a controversy to the field of anthropology? How might the potential for such disagreement influence future field work?

2

Applying Anthropology

WHAT IS APPLIED ANTHROPOLOGY?

Anthropology is not a science of the exotic carried on by quaint scholars in ivory towers. Rather, it is a holistic, comparative, biocultural field with a lot to tell the public. Anthropology's foremost professional organization, the American Anthropological Association (AAA), has formally acknowledged a public service role by recognizing that anthropology has two dimensions: (1) academic anthropology and (2) practicing or **applied anthropology.** The latter refers to the application of anthropological data, perspectives, theory, and methods to identify, assess, and solve contemporary social problems. As Erve Chambers (1987, p. 309) states it, applied anthropology is the "field of inquiry concerned with the relationships between anthropological knowledge and the uses of that knowledge in the world beyond anthropology." More and more anthropologists from the four subfields now work in such "applied" areas as public health, family planning, business, economic development, and cultural resource management (see the "News Brief").

Applied anthropology encompasses any use of the knowledge and/or techniques of the four subfields to identify, assess, and solve practical problems. Because of anthropology's breadth, it has many

See the OLC Internet Exercises
mhhe.com/kottak

applications. For example, applied medical anthropologists consider both the sociocultural and the biological contexts and implications of disease and illness. Perceptions of good and bad health, along with actual health threats and problems, differ among cultures. Various societies and ethnic groups recognize different illnesses, symptoms, and causes and have developed different health-care systems and treatment strategies. Medical anthropologists are both biological and cultural, and both academic and applied. Applied medical anthropologists, for example, have served as cultural interpreters in public health programs, which must fit into local culture and be accepted by local people.

Other applied anthropologists work for international development agencies, such as the World Bank and the United States Agency for International Development (USAID). The job of such development anthropologists is to assess the social and cultural dimensions of economic development. Anthropologists are experts on local cultures. Working with and drawing on the knowledge of local people, anthropologists can identify specific social conditions and needs that must be addressed and that influence the failure or success of development schemes. Planners in Washington or Paris often know little about, say, the labor necessary for crop cultivation in rural Africa. Development funds are often wasted if an

STUDENT CD-ROM LIVING ANTHROPOLOGY

Unearthing Evil: Archaeology in the Cause of Justice
Track 2

This clip features archaeologist Richard Wright and his team of 15 forensic archaeologists and anthropologists working "in the cause of justice" in Bosnia-Herzegovina in 1998. The focus of the clip is the excavation of a site of mass burial or reburial of the bodies of some 660 civilians who were murdered during the conflict that followed the dissolution of Yugoslavia. Wright and his colleagues worked with the international community to provide evidence of war crimes. This evidence has led to the convictions of war criminals. Why was Wright nervous about this work? Compare the forensic work shown here with the discussion of forensic anthropology in this chapter.

anthropologist is not asked to work with the local people to identify local needs, demands, priorities, and constraints.

Projects routinely fail when planners ignore the cultural dimension of development. Problems arise from lack of attention to, and consequent lack of fit with, existing sociocultural conditions. One example is a very naive and culturally incompatible project in East Africa. The major fallacy was to attempt to convert nomadic herders into farmers. The planners had absolutely no evidence that the herders, on whose land the project was to be implemented, wanted to change their economy. The herders' territory was to be used for new commercial farms, and the herders were to be converted into small farmers and sharecroppers. The project, whose planners included no anthropologists, totally neglected social issues. The obstacles would have been evident to any anthropologist. The herders were expected to give up a generations-old way of life in order to work three times harder growing rice and picking cotton. What possibly could motivate them to give up their freedom and mobility to work as sharecroppers for commercial farmers? Certainly not the meager financial return the project planners estimated for the herders—an average of $300 annually versus more than $10,000 for their new bosses, the commercial farmers.

To avoid such unrealistic projects, and to make development schemes more socially sensitive and culturally appropriate, development organizations now regularly include anthropologists on planning teams. Their team colleagues may include agronomists, economists, veterinarians, geologists, engineers, and health specialists. Applied anthropologists also apply their skills in studying the human dimension of environmental degradation (e.g., deforestation, pollution). Anthropologists examine how the environment influences humans and how human activities affect the biosphere and the earth itself.

OVERVIEW

Anthropology has two dimensions: academic and applied. In varied settings anthropology regularly is "applied"—used to identify and solve problems involving human behavior, social conditions, and public health. Applied, aka "practicing," anthropologists work for various groups and organizations, including governments, agencies, and businesses. Many applied anthropologists work with local people to identify and realize their perceived needs and to plan and implement culturally appropriate change, while also attempting to protect those people from harmful policies.

Anthropology is applied in educational, urban, rural, medical, and business settings. Such domains may have theoretical as well as applied, and biological as well as sociocultural, dimensions. Educational anthropologists work in classrooms, homes, neighborhoods, and other settings relevant to education. Urban anthropologists study problems and policies involving migration, city life, and urbanization. Medical anthropologists examine disease and health-care systems cross-culturally. For business, key aspects of anthropology include ethnography and observation as ways of gathering data, cross-cultural expertise, and a focus on diversity. Anthropology's comparative outlook provides a valuable background for overseas work. A focus on culture and diversity is also highly relevant to work in contemporary North America.

Archaeologist in New Orleans Finds a Way to Help the Living

NEW YORK TIMES NEWS BRIEF

by John Schwartz
January 3, 2006

Anthropology is applied in identifying and solving various kinds of problems involving social conditions and human behavior, such as helping a community preserve its culture in the face of threat or disaster. Among the clients of applied anthropologists are governments, agencies, local communities, and businesses. This news story describes the work of an anthropologist doing public archaeology in New Orleans in the wake of Hurricane Katrina. Cultural resource management, as discussed here, is one form of applied anthropology: the application of anthropological perspectives, theory, methods, and data to identify, assess, and solve social problems.

"That's a finger bone."

Shannon Lee Dawdy kneeled in the forlorn Holt graveyard to touch a thimble-size bone poking up out of the cracked dirt. She examined it without revulsion, with the fascination of a scientist and with the sadness of someone who loves New Orleans.

Dr. Dawdy, a 38-year-old assistant professor of anthropology at the University of Chicago, is one of the more unusual relief workers among the thousands who have come to the devastated expanses of Louisiana, Mississippi and Texas in the aftermath of Hurricanes Katrina and Rita. She is officially embedded with the Federal Emergency Management Agency [FEMA] as a liaison to the state's historic preservation office.

Her mission is to try to keep the rebuilding of New Orleans from destroying what is left of its past treasures and current culture.

While much of the restoration of the battered Gulf Coast is the effort of engineers and machines, the work of Dr. Dawdy, trained as an archaeologist, an anthropologist and a historian, shows that the social sciences have a role to play as well. "It's a way that archaeology can contribute back to the living," she said, "which it doesn't often get to do."

Holt cemetery, a final resting place for the city's poor, is just one example of what she wants to preserve and protect.

Other New Orleans graveyards have gleaming mausoleums that keep the coffins above the marshy soil. But the coffins of Holt are buried, and the ground covering many of them is bordered with wooden frames marked with makeshift headstones.

Mourners decorate the graves with votive objects: teddy bears for children and an agglomeration of objects, including ice chests, plastic jack-o'-lanterns and chairs, on the graves of adults. There is the occasional liquor bottle . . .

Many of the objects on the graves were washed away by the storm, or shifted from one part of the graveyard to another. Dr. Dawdy has proposed treating the site as archaeologists would an ancient site in which objects have been exposed on the surface by erosion.

Before the hurricanes, the cemetery was often busy, a hub of activity on All Soul's Day, when people came to freshen the grave decorations.

"The saddest thing to me now was how few people we see," she said, looking at the empty expanse and the scarred live oaks. "I realize we're having enough trouble taking care of the living," she added, but the lack of activity in a city normally so close to the spirits of the past "drove home how far out of whack things are." . . .

Treating Holt as an archaeological site means the government should not treat the votive artifacts as debris, she said, but as the religious artifacts that they are, with some effort to restore the damaged site, to find the objects and at least record where they came from.

FEMA simply tries to clean up damaged areas, and its Disaster Mortuary Operational Response Teams—called Dmort—deal with the bodies of the dead and address problems in cemeteries that might lead to disease.

■ *Archaeologist Shannon Dawdy of the University of Chicago at work in New Orleans, post-Katrina.*

If such places are destroyed, Dr. Dawdy said, "then people don't feel as connected here." She added that they might be more willing to come back to a damaged city if they felt they were returning to a recognizable home.

Though she has deep emotional ties to New Orleans, Dr. Dawdy was born in Northern California. She came here in 1994 to write her master's thesis for the College of William & Mary, and, "I wrote it all day," she said. "If I had written a minimum of five pages, I could come out for a parade at night." Over the eight weeks it took to finish the project, she said: "I fell in love with New Orleans. I really consider it the home of my heart."

She started a pilot program at the University of New Orleans, working with city planners and grants for research projects that involved excavation, oral history and hands-on work with the city to safeguard its buried treasures.

She left that job to earn a double doctorate at the University of Michigan in anthropology and history that focused on French colonial times in New Orleans, then landed a coveted faculty position at the University of Chicago . . .

Even before Hurricane Katrina, Dr. Dawdy had found ways to return to New Orleans. In 2004, she made an intriguing discovery while researching a possible archaeological site under an old French Quarter parking garage slated for demolition. Property records and advertisements from the 1820's said that the site had been the location of a hotel with an enticing name: the Rising Sun Hotel.

Dr. Dawdy found a January 1821 newspaper advertisement for the hotel in which its owners promised to "maintain the character of giving the best entertainment, which this house has enjoyed for twenty years past."

It went on: "Gentlemen may here rely upon finding attentive Servants. The bar will be supplied with genuine good Liquors; and at the Table, the fare will be of the best the market or the season will afford." . . .

New Orleans, she noted, has always been known for its libertine lifestyle. The French all but abandoned the city as its colony around 1735 as being unworthy of the nation's support as a colony. Novels like "Manon Lescaut" portrayed the city as a den of iniquity and corruption, and across Europe, "they thought the locals were basically a bunch of rogues, immoral and corrupt," Dr. Dawdy said.

She added that she saw parallels to today, as some skepticism emerges about rebuilding the city. Dr. Dawdy characterized that posture as, "Those people in New Orleans aren't worth saving, because they're all criminals anyway." But even if the devastation makes it hard to envision the road back, the city, she said, is worth fighting for.

"The thing about New Orleans that gives me hope is they are so tied to family, place, history," Dr. Dawdy said. "If anyone is going to stick it out, out of a sense of history, out of a sense of tradition, it is New Orleans."

SOURCE: John Schwartz, "Archaeologist in New Orleans Finds a Way to Help the Living," *New York Times*, January 3, 2006, pp. F1, F4.

Applied anthropologists also work in North America. Garbologists help the Environmental Protection Agency, the paper industry, and packaging and trade associations. Applied archaeology, usually called *public archaeology,* includes such activities as cultural resource management, contract archaeology, public educational programs, and historic preservation. (This chapter's "News Brief" illustrates a form of public archaeology, involving cultural preservation in the wake of Hurricane Katrina.) An important role for public archaeology has been created by legislation requiring evaluation of sites threatened by dams, highways, and other construction activities. To decide what needs saving, and to preserve significant information about the past when sites cannot be saved, is the work of **cultural resource management (CRM).** CRM involves not only preserving sites but allowing their destruction if they are not significant. The "management" part of the term refers to the evaluation and decision-making process. If additional information is needed to make decisions, then survey or excavation may be done. CRM funding comes from federal, state, and local governments and from developers who must comply with preservation regulations. Cultural resource managers work for federal, state, and county agencies and other clients. Applied cultural anthropologists sometimes work with the public archaeologists, assessing the human problems generated by the proposed change and determining how they can be reduced.

Remember that applied anthropologists come from all four subfields. Biological anthropologists work in public health, nutrition, genetic counseling, substance abuse, epidemiology, aging, and mental illness. They apply their knowledge of human anatomy and physiology to the improvement of automobile safety standards and to the design of airplanes and spacecraft. Forensic (physical) anthropologists work with the police, medical examiners, the courts, and international organizations to identify victims of crimes, accidents, wars, and terrorism. From skeletal remains they may determine age, sex, size, ethnic origin, and number of victims. Applied physical anthropologists link injury patterns to design flaws in aircraft and vehicles.

Cultural anthropologists have influenced social policy by showing that strong kin ties exist in city neighborhoods whose social organization previously was considered "fragmented" or "pathological." Suggestions for improving education emerge from ethnographic studies of classrooms and surrounding communities. Linguistic anthropologists show the influence of dialect differences on classroom learning. In general, applied anthropology aims to find humane and effective ways of helping the people whom anthropologists have traditionally studied. Table 2.1 shows the four subfields and two dimensions of anthropology.

There are two important professional groups of applied anthropologists (also called **practicing anthropologists**). The older is the independent Society for Applied Anthropology (SfAA), founded in 1941. The second, the National Association for the Practice of Anthropology (NAPA), was established as a unit of the American Anthropological Association in 1983. (Many people belong to both groups.) Practicing anthropologists work (regularly or occasionally, full or part time) for nonacademic clients. These clients include governments, development agencies, nongovernmental organizations (NGOs), tribal and ethnic associations, interest groups, businesses, and social-service and educational agencies. Applied anthropologists work for groups that promote, manage, and assess programs and policies aimed at influencing human behavior and social conditions. The scope of applied anthropology includes change and development abroad as well as in North America (see Ervin 2005.)

THE ROLE OF THE APPLIED ANTHROPOLOGIST

By instilling an appreciation for human diversity, anthropology combats *ethnocentrism*—the tendency to view one's own culture as superior and to apply one's own cultural values in judging the

Supervised by archaeologists from India, with funding from the United Nations, these workers are cleaning and restoring the front facade of Cambodia's historic Angkor Wat temple. To decide what needs saving, and to preserve significant information about the past even when sites cannot be saved, is the work of cultural resource management (CRM).

behavior and beliefs of people raised in other cultures. This broadening, educational role affects the knowledge, values, and attitudes of people exposed to anthropology. Now we focus on the question: What specific contributions can anthropology make in identifying and solving problems stirred up by contemporary currents of economic, social, and cultural change?

Because anthropologists are experts on human problems and social change and because they study, understand, and respect cultural values, they are highly qualified to suggest, plan, and implement policy affecting people. Proper roles for applied anthropologists include (1) identifying needs for change that local people perceive, (2) working with those people to design culturally appropriate and socially sensitive change, and (3) protecting local people from harmful policies and projects that threaten them.

There was a time—the 1940s in particular—when most anthropologists focused on the application of their knowledge. During World War II, American anthropologists studied Japanese and German "culture at a distance" in an attempt to

TABLE 2.1 The Four Subfields and Two Dimensions of Anthropology	
Anthropology's Subfields (General Anthropology)	**Examples of Application (Applied Anthropology)**
Cultural anthropology	Development anthropology
Archaeological anthropology	Cultural resource management (CRM)
Biological or physical anthropology	Forensic anthropology
Linguistic anthropology	Study of linguistic diversity in classrooms

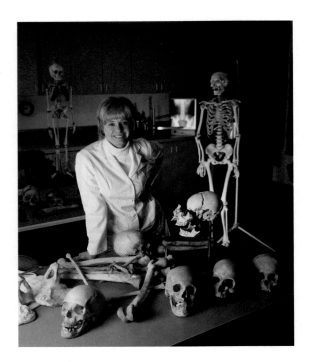

■ Like other forensic anthropologists, Dr. Kathy Reichs (shown here) and her alter ego, Temperance Brennan, work with the police, medical examiners, the courts, and international organizations to identify victims of crimes, accidents, wars, and terrorism. Brennan is the heroine of several novels by Reichs, as well as of the TV series Bones, which debuted on Fox in 2005.

predict the behavior of the enemies of the United States. After the war, Americans did applied anthropology in the Pacific, working to gain native cooperation with American policies in various trust territories.

Modern applied anthropology differs from an earlier version that mainly served the goals of colonial regimes. Application was a central concern of early anthropology in Great Britain (in the context of colonialism) and the United States (in the context of Native American policy). Before turning to the new, we should consider some dangers of the old.

In the context of the British empire, specifically its African colonies, Malinowski (1929a) proposed that "practical anthropology" (his term for colonial applied anthropology) should focus on Westernization, the diffusion of European culture into tribal societies. Malinowski questioned neither the legitimacy of colonialism nor the anthropologist's role in making it work. He saw nothing wrong with aiding colonial regimes by studying land tenure and land use, to decide how much of their land natives should keep and how much Europeans should get. Malinowski's views exemplify a historical association between anthropology, particularly in Europe, and colonialism (Maquet 1964).

Today, many applied anthropologists see their work as a helping profession, devoted to assisting local people, as anthropologists speak up for the disenfranchised in the international political arena. But applied anthropologists also solve problems for clients who are neither poor nor

powerless. Applied anthropologists working for businesses try to solve the problem of expanding profits for their employer or client. In market research, ethical issues may arise as anthropologists attempt to help companies operate more efficiently and profitably. Ethical ambiguities are present as well in cultural resource management. A CRM firm typically is hired by someone seeking to build a road or a factory. In such cases, the client may have a strong interest in an outcome in which no sites are found that need protecting. To whom does the researcher owe loyalty, and what problems might be involved in holding firm to the truth?

Like the colonial anthropologists, applied anthropologists still face ethical dilemmas because they do not set the policies they have to implement, and because it is difficult to criticize programs in which they have participated (see Escobar 1991, 1994). Anthropology's professional organizations have addressed these problems by establishing codes of ethics and ethics committees. See Appendix 2 and http://www.aaanet.org for the code of ethics of the AAA. As Tice (1997) notes, attention to ethical issues is paramount in the teaching of applied anthropology today.

ACADEMIC AND APPLIED ANTHROPOLOGY

Applied anthropology did not disappear during the 1950s and 1960s, but academic anthropology did most of the growing after World War II. The baby boom, which began in 1946 and peaked in 1957, fueled expansion of the American educational system and thus of academic jobs. New junior, community, and four-year colleges opened, and anthropology became a standard part of the college curriculum. During the 1950s and 1960s, most American anthropologists were college professors, although some still worked in agencies and museums.

This era of academic anthropology continued through the early 1970s. Especially during the Vietnam War, undergraduates flocked to anthropology classes to learn about other cultures. Students were especially interested in Southeast Asia, whose indigenous societies were being disrupted by war. Many anthropologists protested the superpowers' apparent disregard for non-Western lives, values, customs, and social systems.

During the 1970s, and increasingly thereafter, although most anthropologists still worked in academia, others found jobs with international organizations, government, businesses, hospitals, and schools. About half of students graduating with Ph.D.s in anthropology today will have careers outside academia. This shift toward application has benefited the profession. It has forced anthropologists to consider the wider social value and implications of their research.

Theory and Practice

One of the most valuable tools in applying anthropology is the ethnographic method. Ethnographers study societies firsthand, living with and learning from ordinary people. Ethnographers are participant-observers, taking part in the events they study in order to understand local thought and behavior. Applied anthropologists use ethnographic techniques in both foreign and domestic settings. Other "expert" participants in social-change programs may be content to converse with officials, read reports, and copy statistics. However, the applied anthropologist's likely early request is some variant of "take me to the local people." We know that people must play an active role in the changes that affect them and that "the people" have information that "the experts" lack.

Anthropological theory—the body of findings and generalizations of the subdisciplines—also guides applied anthropology (see Appendix 1). Anthropology's holistic and biocultural perspectives—its interest in biology, society, culture, and language—permit the evaluation of many issues that affect people. Theory aids practice, and application fuels theory. As we compare social-change policy and programs, our understanding of cause and effect increases. We add new generalizations about culture change to those discovered in traditional and ancient cultures.

Anthropology's systemic perspective recognizes that changes don't occur in a vacuum. A program or project always has multiple effects, some of which are unforeseen. For example, dozens of economic development projects intended to increase productivity through irrigation have worsened public health by creating waterways where diseases thrive. In an American example of unintended consequences, a program aimed at enhancing teachers' appreciation of cultural differences led to ethnic stereotyping (Kleinfeld 1975). Specifically, Native American students did not welcome teachers' frequent comments about their Indian heritage. The students felt set apart from their classmates and saw this attention to their ethnicity as patronizing and demeaning.

ANTHROPOLOGY AND EDUCATION

Anthropology and education refers to anthropological research in classrooms, homes, and neighborhoods (see Spindler 2000, 2005). Some of the most interesting research has been done in class-

Is change good? American culture seems to think so. "New and improved" is a slogan we hear all the time—a lot more often than "old reliable." But new isn't always improved. People often resist change, as the Coca Cola Company (TCCC) discovered in 1985 when it changed the formula of its premium soft drink and introduced "New Coke." When hordes of customers protested, TCCC brought back old, familiar, reliable Coke under the name "Coca Cola Classic," which thrives today. New Coke is history.

TCCC tried a *top-down change* (a change decided and initiated at the top of a hierarchy rather than by the communities affected by the change). The people, that is, customers, didn't ask TCCC to change its product; executives made the decision to change Coke's taste. Executives are to business decisions as policy makers are to social change programs; both stand at the top of organizations that provide goods and services to people. Smart executives and policy makers listen to people to try to determine *locally based demand*—what the people want. What's working well (assuming it's not discriminatory or illegal) should be maintained, encouraged, and strengthened. What's wrong, and how can it be fixed? What changes do the people—and which people—want? How can conflicting wishes and needs be accommodated? Applied anthropologists help answer these questions, which are crucial in understanding whether change is needed, and how it will work.

rooms, where anthropologists observe interactions among teachers, students, parents, and visitors. Jules Henry's classic account of the American elementary school classroom (1955) shows how students learn to conform to and compete with their peers. Anthropologists also follow students from classrooms into their homes and neighborhoods, viewing children as total cultural creatures whose enculturation and attitudes toward education belong to a context that includes family and peers (Zou and Trueba 2002).

Sociolinguists and cultural anthropologists work side by side in education research, for example, in a study of Puerto Rican seventh-graders in the urban Midwest (Hill-Burnett 1978). In classrooms, neighborhoods, and homes, anthropologists uncovered some misconceptions by teachers. For example, the teachers had mistakenly assumed that Puerto Rican parents valued education less

In this bilingual class, kids point as their teacher holds up cards that say "point" in English and Spanish. In such classrooms, and extending out into the community, anthropologists of education study the backgrounds, behavior, beliefs, and attitudes of teachers, students, parents, and families in their (multi)cultural context.

than did non-Hispanics. However, in-depth interviews revealed that the Puerto Rican parents valued it more.

Researchers also found that certain practices were preventing Hispanics from being adequately educated. For example, the teachers' union and the board of education had agreed to teach "English as a foreign language." However, they had not provided bilingual teachers to work with Spanish-speaking students. The school started assigning all students (including non-Hispanics) with low reading scores and behavior problems to the English-as-a-foreign-language classroom.

This educational disaster brought together a teacher who spoke no Spanish, children who barely spoke English, and a group of English-speaking students with reading and behavior problems. The Spanish speakers were falling behind not just in reading but in all subjects. They could at least have kept up in the other subjects if a Spanish speaker had been teaching them science, social studies, and math until they were ready for English-language instruction in those areas.

A dramatic illustration of the relevance of applied sociolinguistics to education comes from Ann Arbor, Michigan. In 1979, the parents of several black students at the predominantly white Dr. Martin Luther King Jr. Elementary School sued the board of education. They claimed that their children faced linguistic discrimination in the classroom.

The children, who lived in a neighborhood housing project, spoke Black English Vernacular (BEV) at home. At school, most had encountered problems with their classwork. Some had been labeled "learning-impaired" and placed in remedial reading courses. (Consider the embarrassment that children suffer and the effect on self-image of such labeling.)

The African American parents and their attorney contended that the children had no intrinsic learning disabilities but simply did not understand everything their teachers said. Nor did their teachers always understand them. The lawyer argued that because BEV and Standard English (SE) are so similar, teachers often misinterpreted a child's correct pronunciation (in BEV) of an SE word as a reading error.

The children's attorney recruited several sociolinguists to testify on their behalf. The school board, by contrast, could not find a single qualified linguist to support its argument that there was no linguistic discrimination.

The judge ruled in favor of the children and ordered the following solution: Teachers at the King School had to attend a full-year course designed to improve their knowledge of nonstandard dialects, particularly BEV. The judge did not advocate that the teachers learn to speak BEV or that the children do their assignments in BEV. The school's goal remained to teach the children to use SE, the standard dialect, correctly. Before this could be accomplished, however, teachers and students alike had to learn how to recognize the differences between these similar dialects. At the end of the year, most of the teachers interviewed in the local newspaper said the course had helped them.

In a diverse, multicultural populace, teachers should be sensitive to and knowledgeable about linguistic and cultural differences. Children need to be protected so that their ethnic or linguistic background is not used against them. That is what happens when a social variation is regarded as a learning disability.

URBAN ANTHROPOLOGY

By 2025, the developing nations will account for 85 percent of the world's population, compared with 77 percent in 1992 (Stevens 1992). Solutions to future problems will depend increasingly on understanding non-Western cultural backgrounds. The fastest population growth rates are in the less developed countries, especially in urban areas. The world had only 16 cities with more than a million people in 1900, but there are more than 300 such cities today. By 2025, 60 percent of the global population will be urban, compared with 37 percent in 1990 (Stevens 1992). Rural migrants often move to slums, where they live in hovels without utilities and public sanitation facilities.

In 2003 the United Nations (UN) estimated that some 940 million people, about a sixth of earth's population, were living in urban slums, mostly without water, sanitation, public services, and legal security (Vidal 2003). The UN estimates that in three decades the urban population of the developing world will double—to 4 billion people. Rural populations will barely increase and will start declining after 2020 (Vidal 2003). The concentration of people in slums will be accompanied by rising rates of crime and water, air, and noise pollution. These problems will be most severe in the less-developed countries. Almost all (97 percent) of the projected world population increase will occur in developing countries, 34 percent in Africa alone (Lewis 1992). Although the rate of population increase is low in northern countries, such as the United States, Canada, and most European nations, global population growth will continue to affect the Northern Hemisphere, especially through international migration. There has been substantial recent migration to the United States and Canada from developing countries with high growth rates, such as India and Mexico.

As industrialization and urbanization spread globally, anthropologists increasingly study these processes and the social and health problems they create. Urban anthropology, which has theoretical (basic research) and applied dimensions, is the cross-cultural, ethnographic, and biocultural

During the Vietnam War, many anthropologists protested the superpowers' disregard for the values, customs, social systems, and lives of Third World peoples. Several anthropologists (including the author) attended this all-night Columbia University "teach-in" against the war in 1965.

study of global urbanization and life in cities (see Aoyagi, Nas, and Traphagan, eds. 1998; Gmelch and Zenner 2002; Stevenson 2003). The United States and Canada also have become popular arenas for urban anthropological research on topics such as ethnicity, poverty, class, and subcultural variations (Mullings 1987).

Urban versus Rural

Recognizing that a city is a social context that is very different from a rural community, an early student of Third World urbanization, the anthropologist Robert Redfield, focused on contrasts between rural and urban life. He contrasted rural communities, whose social relations are on a face-to-face basis, with cities, where impersonality characterizes many aspects of life. Redfield (1941) proposed that urbanization be studied along a rural–urban continuum. He described differences in values and social relations in four sites that spanned such a continuum. In Mexico's Yucatán peninsula, Redfield compared an isolated Maya-speaking Indian community, a rural peasant village, a small provincial city, and a large capital. Several studies in Africa (Little 1971) and Asia were influenced by Redfield's view that cities are centers through which cultural innovations spread to rural and tribal areas.

In any nation, urban and rural represent different social systems. However, migrants bring rural social forms, practices, and beliefs to town. They also take back urban and national patterns when they visit, or move back permanently to, their villages of origin. Inevitably, the experiences and social units of rural areas affect adaptation to city life. City folk also develop new institutions to meet specific urban needs (Mitchell 1966).

See the OLC Internet Exercises
mhhe.com/kottak

In Peshawar, Pakistan, young boys receive instruction. What do you see here that differs from classrooms in your country?

Applying anthropology to urban planning starts by identifying the key social groups in the urban context. After identifying those groups, the anthropologist elicits their wishes for change and helps translate those needs to funding agencies. The next step is to work with the agencies and the people to ensure that changes are implemented correctly and that they correspond to what the people said they wanted at the outset. African urban groups that an applied anthropologist would consult include ethnic associations, occupational groups, social clubs, religious groups, and burial societies. Through membership in these groups, urban Africans have wide networks of personal contacts and support. Ethnic or "tribal" associations are common in both West and East Africa (Banton 1957; Little 1965). These groups maintain links with, and provide cash support and urban lodging for, their rural relatives.

The ideology of such associations is that of a gigantic kin group. The members call one another "brother" and "sister." As in an extended family, rich members help their poor relatives. When members fight among themselves, the group acts as judge. A member's improper behavior can lead to expulsion—an unhappy fate for a migrant in a large ethnically heterogeneous city.

Modern North American cities also have kin-based ethnic associations. One example comes from Los Angeles, which has the largest Samoan immigrant community (over 12,000 people) in the United States. Samoans in Los Angeles draw on their traditional system of *matai* (*matai* means chief; the *matai* system now refers to respect for elders) to deal with modern urban problems. One example: In 1992, a white police officer shot and killed two unarmed Samoan brothers. When a

judge dismissed charges against the officer, local leaders used the *matai* system to calm angry youths (who have formed gangs, like other ethnic groups in the Los Angeles area). Clan leaders and elders organized a well-attended community meeting, in which they urged young members to be patient.

Los Angeles Samoans also used the American judicial system. They brought a civil case against the officer in question and pressed the U.S. Justice Department to initiate a civil-rights case in the matter (Mydans 1992b). One role for the urban applied anthropologist is to help relevant social groups deal with larger urban institutions, such as legal and social-service agencies with which recent migrants, in particular, may be unfamiliar (see Holtzman 2000).

MEDICAL ANTHROPOLOGY

Medical anthropology is both academic/theoretical and applied/practical. It is a field that includes both biological and sociocultural anthropologists (see Anderson 1996; Brown 1998; Joralemon 1999). Medical anthropology is discussed in this chapter because of its many applications. Medical anthropologists examine such questions as: Which diseases affect different populations? How is illness socially constructed? How does one treat illness in effective and culturally appropriate ways?

This growing field considers the biocultural context and implications of disease and illness (Helman 2001; Strathern and Stewart 1999). **Disease** refers to a scientifically identified health threat caused by a bacterium, virus, fungus, para-

See the Virtual Exploration
mhhe.com/kottak

site, or other pathogen. **Illness** is a condition of poor health perceived or felt by an individual (Inhorn and Brown 1990). Cross-cultural research shows that perceptions of good and bad health, along with health threats and problems, are culturally constructed. Different ethnic groups and cultures recognize different illnesses, symptoms, and causes and have developed different health-care systems and treatment strategies.

. Disease also varies among cultures (Baer, Singer, and Susser 2003). Traditional and ancient hunter-gatherers, because of their small numbers, mobility, and relative isolation from other groups, were not subject to most of the epidemic infectious diseases that affect agrarian and urban societies (Cohen and Armelagos 1984; Inhorn and Brown 1990). Epidemic diseases such as cholera, typhoid, and bubonic plague thrive in dense populations, and thus among farmers and city dwellers. The spread of malaria has been linked to population growth and deforestation associated with food production.

Certain diseases have spread with economic development. *Schistosomiasis* or bilharzia (liver flukes) is probably the fastest-spreading and most dangerous parasitic infection now known (Heyneman 1984). It is propagated by snails that live in ponds, lakes, and waterways, usually ones created by irrigation projects. A study done in a Nile Delta village in Egypt (Farooq 1966) illustrated the role of culture (religion) in the spread of schistosomiasis. The disease was more common among Muslims than among Christians because of an Islamic practice called *wudu,* ritual ablution (bathing) before prayer. The applied anthropology approach to reducing such diseases is to see if natives perceive a connection between the vector (e.g., snails in the water) and the disease, which can take years to develop. If they do not, such information may be spread by enlisting active local groups and schools. With the worldwide diffusion of the electronic mass media, culturally appropriate public information campaigns have increased awareness and modified behavior that has public health consequences.

In eastern Africa, AIDS and other sexually transmitted diseases (STDs) have spread along highways, via encounters between male truckers and female prostitutes. STDs also are spread through prostitution, as young men from rural

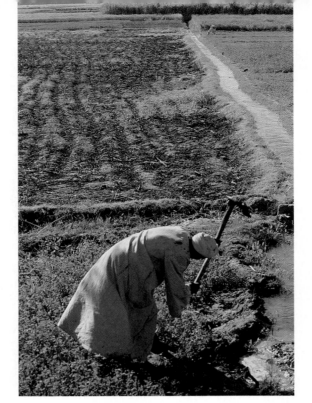

Schistosomiasis is among the fastest spreading and most dangerous parasitic infections now known. It is propagated by snails that live in ponds, lakes, and waterways (often ones created by irrigation projects) such as this one in Luxor, Egypt. As an applied anthropologist, what would you do to cut the rate of infection?

areas seek wage work in cities, labor camps, and mines. When the men return to their natal villages, they infect their wives (Larson 1989; Miller and Rockwell 1988). Cities are also prime sites of STD transmission in Europe, Asia, and North and South America (Baer, Singer, and Susser 2003; French 2002).

The kind and incidence of disease vary among societies, and cultures interpret and treat illness differently. Standards for sick and healthy bodies are cultural constructions that vary in time and space (Martin 1992). Still, all societies have what George Foster and Barbara Anderson (1978) call "disease-theory systems" to identify, classify, and explain illness. According to Foster and Anderson (1978), there are three basic theories about the causes of illness: personalistic, naturalistic, and emotionalistic. _Personalistic disease theories_ blame illness on agents (often malicious), such as sorcerers, witches, ghosts, or ancestral spirits. _Naturalistic disease theories_ explain illness in impersonal terms. One example is Western medicine or _biomedicine_, which aims to link illness to scientifically demonstrated agents that bear no personal malice toward their victims. Thus, Western medicine attributes illness to organisms (e.g., bacteria, viruses, fungi, or parasites), accidents, or toxic materials. Other naturalistic ethnomedical systems blame poor health on unbalanced body fluids. Many Latin cultures classify food, drink, and environmental conditions as "hot" or "cold." People believe their health suffers when they eat or drink hot or cold substances together or under

inappropriate conditions. For example, one shouldn't drink something cold after a hot bath or eat a pineapple (a "cold" fruit) when one is menstruating (a "hot" condition).

Emotionalistic disease theories assume that emotional experiences cause illness. For example, Latin Americans may develop _susto, or soul loss,_ an illness caused by anxiety or fright (Bolton 1981; Finkler 1985). Its symptoms include lethargy, vagueness, and distraction. Of course, modern psychoanalysis also focuses on the role of the emotions in physical and psychological well-being.

All societies have **health-care systems.** These consist of beliefs, customs, specialists, and techniques aimed at ensuring health and preventing, diagnosing, and curing illness. A society's illness-causation theory is important for treatment. When illness has a personalistic cause, shamans and other magico-religious specialists may be good curers. They draw on varied techniques (occult and practical) that comprise their special expertise. A shaman (magico-religious specialist) may cure soul loss by enticing the spirit back into the body. Shamans may ease difficult childbirths by asking spirits to travel up the birth canal to guide the baby out (Lévi-Strauss 1967). A shaman may cure a cough by counteracting a curse or removing a substance introduced by a sorcerer.

All cultures have health-care specialists. If there is a "world's oldest profession" besides hunter and gatherer, it is **curer,** often a shaman. The curer's role has some universal features (Foster and Anderson 1978). Thus, curers emerge through a culturally defined process of selection (parental prodding, inheritance, visions, dream instructions) and training (apprentice shamanship, medical school). Eventually, the curer is certified by older practitioners and acquires a professional image. Patients believe in the skills of the curer, whom they consult and compensate.

We should not lose sight, ethnocentrically, of the difference between **scientific medicine** and Western medicine per se (Lieban 1977). Despite advances in pathology, microbiology, biochemistry, surgery, diagnostic technology, and applications, many Western medical procedures have little justification in logic or fact. Overprescription of tranquilizers and drugs, unnecessary surgery, and the impersonality and inequality of the physician–patient relationship are questionable features of Western medical systems. Also, overuse of antibiotics, not just for people, but also in animal feed and antibacterial soaps, seems to be triggering an explosion of resistant microorganisms, which may pose a long-term global public health hazard.

Still, Western medicine surpasses tribal treatment in many ways. Although medicines like quinine, coca, opium, ephedrine, and rauwolfia were discovered in nonindustrial societies, thousands of effective drugs are available today to treat myriad diseases. Preventive health care improved during the 20th century. Today's surgical procedures are safer and more effective than those of traditional societies.

But industrialization has spawned its own health problems. Modern stressors include noise, air, and water pollution; poor nutrition; dangerous machinery; impersonal work; isolation; poverty; homelessness; and substance abuse. Health problems in industrial nations are due as much to economic, social, political, and cultural factors as to pathogens. In modern North America, for example, poverty contributes to many illnesses. These include arthritis, heart conditions, back problems, and hearing and vision impairment (see Bailey 2000). Poverty is also a factor in the differential spread of infectious diseases.

Medical anthropologists have served as cultural interpreters in public health programs, which must pay attention to native theories about the nature, causes, and treatment of illness. Successful health interventions cannot simply be forced on communities. They must fit into local cultures and be accepted by local people. When Western medicine is introduced, people usually retain many of their old methods while also accepting new ones (see Green 1987/1992). Native curers may go on treating certain conditions (like spirit possession), whereas M.D.s may deal with others. If both modern and traditional specialists are consulted and the patient is cured, the native curer may get as much credit as or more credit than the physician.

A more personal treatment of illness that emulates the non-Western curer-patient-community

A traditional healer at work in Malaysia. Shown here, mugwort, a small, spongy herb, is burned to facilitate healing. The healer lights one end of a moxa stick, roughly the shape and size of a cigar, and attaches it, or holds it close, to the area being treated for several minutes until the area turns red. The purpose of moxibustion is to strengthen the blood, stimulate spiritual energy, and maintain general health.

relationship could probably benefit Western systems. Western medicine has tended to draw a rigid line between biological and psychological causation. Non-Western theories usually lack this sharp distinction, recognizing that poor health has intertwined physical, emotional, and social causes. The mind-body opposition is part of Western folk taxonomy, not of science.

ANTHROPOLOGY AND BUSINESS

Carol Taylor (1987) discusses the value of an "anthropologist-in-residence" in a large, complex organization such as a hospital or a business. A free-ranging ethnographer can be a perceptive oddball when information and decisions usually move through a rigid hierarchy. If allowed to observe and converse freely with all types and levels of personnel, the anthropologist may acquire a unique perspective on organizational conditions and problems. For many years, anthropologists have used ethnography to study business settings (Arensberg 1987; Jordan 2003). For example, ethnographic research in an auto factory may view workers, managers, and executives as different social categories participating in a common social system. Each group has characteristic attitudes, values, and behavior patterns. These are transmitted through *microenculturation*, the process by which people learn particular roles in a limited social system. The free-ranging nature of ethnography takes the anthropologist from worker to executive. Each of these people is both an individual with a personal viewpoint and a cultural creature whose perspective is, to some extent, shared with other members of a group. Applied anthropologists have acted as "cultural

New Life, Good Health

BACKGROUND INFORMATION

STUDENT:
Ann L. Bretnall

SUPERVISING PROFESSOR:
David Himmelgreen

SCHOOL:
University of South Florida

YEAR IN SCHOOL/MAJOR:
Senior/Anthropology

FUTURE PLANS:
After completion of master's in applied anthropology, work with the local social-service agencies in community outreach projects

PROJECT TITLE:
Establishing a Farmers Market for the Local Hispanic Community

Note how this essay links the worlds of commerce, nutrition, health, and social interaction. The comfortable and convivial atmosphere of the local farmers' market is an appropriate setting for applying anthropology—aimed at culturally appropriate education and innovation. As immigration has increased, work demands and ready access to fast foods have changed the nature of meals and diet among Latinos and Latinas in the Tampa area. Ann Bretnall discusses her work organizing educational events and the participation of local community members in the farmer's market.

The Applied Anthropology program at the University of South Florida, in Tampa, gives students practical experience with community projects. The Project New Life-Good Health (Nueva Vida-Buena Salud) is one of many projects the Anthropology Department is currently working on. This project is designed to develop and implement a community-engaged nutrition and health education program targeting recently arrived Latino immigrant families. My project is to develop a church-based farmer's market for the local Hispanic community.

In recent years the Hispanic population of Hillsborough County, which includes Tampa, has significantly increased. Immigrants have arrived from Central and South America and from the Caribbean. According to U.S. Census Bureau data, the 1990 Hispanic population of Hillsborough County was 106,908, rising to 179,692 in 2000.

Project New Life-Good Health rests on two previous projects focusing on the local Hispanic community. Those projects were called "Acculturation and Nutritional Needs Assessment of Tampa" (ANNA-T) and "Promoting Adequate Nutrition" (PAN). The ANNA-T project investigated food consumption and physical activity patterns of recently arrived Latino immigrants. The research of ANNA-T helped to develop project PAN. PAN was a series of culturally tailored nutrition-education and disease-prevention seminars targeting low-income Latino families. Projects ANNA-T and PAN found there had been a significant change in diet, with a new emphasis on fast food and sodas and a reduced consumption of fresh fruits and vegetables. ANNA-T also discovered that lack of time and of social support were barriers to traditional family meals.

The goals of project New Life-Good Health are to: 1) develop a culturally appropriate nutrition-education and disease-prevention curriculum, 2) conduct a series of healthy-eating and disease-prevention seminars, and 3) develop a church-based farmers' market that includes nutrition-education and health-promotion activities for the larger community. Local farmers' markets have an open and informal setting, which provides a unique ambiance to the shopping experience. This social setting allows customers to converse easily with vendors, unlike the sometimes uncomfortable interactions with employees in a grocery store.

My work with the Project New Life-Good Health farmers' market involves organizing the resources necessary to implement farmers' market events. In interviews and observations, I have found genuine interest among community members and vendors. The literature I reviewed also confirms advantages to individuals involved in local farmers' markets. Efforts by community members to organize and establish the farmers' market as their own will be crucial to the success of the market as a permanent institution in their community.

To summarize, the goal of the farmers' market is to provide a venue to understand community needs, to educate, and to improve the nutrition and health of the local Hispanic community. This can be accomplished by ensuring the availability of some culturally specific foods and by introducing other healthful foods into the Hispanic diet. Our ongoing research will provide the local community with the resources to continue and manage the farmers' market as a positive and sustainable alternative within their local economy.

brokers," translating managers' goals or workers' concerns to the other group.

Closely observing how people actually use products, anthropologists work with engineers to design products that are more user-friendly. Increasingly, anthropologists are working with high-tech companies, where they use their observational skills to study how people work, live, and use technology. Such studies can be traced to 1979, when the Xerox Palo Alto (California) Research Center (PARC) hired the anthropologist Lucy Suchman. She worked in a laboratory where researchers were trying to build artificial intelligence to help people use complicated copiers. Suchman observed and filmed people having trouble with a copying job. From her research came the realization that simplicity is more important than fancy features. That's why all Xerox copiers, no matter how complex, now include a single green copy button for when someone wants an uncomplicated copy.

"[Our] graduate students keep getting snatched up by companies," says Marietta Baba (dean of social science at Michigan State University), former chair of the anthropology department at Wayne State University (WSU) in Detroit (quoted in Weise 1999). WSU trains anthropology students to observe social interactions to understand the underlying structures of a culture, and to apply those methods to industry. Baba estimates that about 9,000 American anthropologists work in academia and that about 2,200 hold applied anthropology positions in industry. "But the proportions are shifting, so you're getting more and more applied ones," she says (quoted in Weise 1999). Companies hire anthropologists to gain a better understanding of their customers and to find new products and markets that engineers and marketers might never imagine (see "Interesting Issues" on p. 38). Andrea Saveri, a director at the Institute for the Future in Menlo Park, California, contends that traditional market research is limited by its question-and-answer format. "In the case of surveys, you're telling the respondent how to answer and you're not giving them any room for anything else" (quoted in Weise 1999). Saveri, who thinks ethnography is more precise and powerful than surveys, employs anthropologists to investigate the consequences of technology (Weise 1999).

For business, key features of anthropology include (1) ethnography and observation as ways of gathering data, (2) cross-cultural expertise, and (3) a focus on cultural diversity. The cross-cultural perspective enters the picture when businesses seek to know why other nations have higher (or lower) productivity than we do (Ferraro 2006). Reasons for differential productivity are cultural, social, and economic. To find them, anthropologists must focus on key features in the organization of production. Subtle but potentially important differences can emerge from workplace ethnography—close observation of workers and managers in their natural (workplace) setting.

CAREERS AND ANTHROPOLOGY

Many college students find anthropology interesting and consider majoring in it. However, their parents or friends may discourage them by asking, "What kind of job are you going to get with an anthropology major?" The first step in answering this question is to consider the more general question "What do you do with any college major?" The answer is "Not much, without a good bit of effort, thought, and planning." A survey of graduates of the literary college of the University of Michigan showed that few had jobs that were clearly linked to their majors. Medicine, law, and many other professions require advanced degrees. Although many colleges offer bachelor's degrees in engineering, business, accounting, and social work, master's degrees are often needed to get the best jobs in those fields. Anthropologists, too, need an advanced degree, most typically a Ph.D., to find gainful employment in academic, museum, or applied anthropology.

A broad college education, and even a major in anthropology, can be an excellent foundation for success in many fields. Many University of Michigan undergraduates who are planning careers in medicine, public health, or dentistry

At a major information technology company, Marietta Baba examines one of the world's fastest supercomputers. She is studying that firm's adaptation to the rise of the service economy. Professor Baba, a prominent applied anthropologist and Dean of the College of Social Science at Michigan State University, also has studied Michigan's automobile industry.

Hot Asset in Corporate: Anthropology Degrees

More and more businesses are hiring anthropologists because they like anthropology's characteristic observation of behavior in natural settings and its focus on cultural diversity. Thus, as we see in this article, Hallmark Cards has hired anthropologists to observe parties, holidays, and celebrations of ethnic groups to improve its ability to design cards for targeted audiences. Anthropologists go into people's homes to see how they actually use products. This permits better product design and more effective advertising.

Don't throw away the MBA degree yet.

But as companies go global and crave leaders for a diverse workforce, a new hot degree is emerging for aspiring executives: anthropology.

The study of man is no longer a degree for museum directors. Citicorp created a vice presidency for anthropologist Steve Barnett, who discovered early warning signs to identify people who don't pay credit card bills.

Not satisfied with consumer surveys, Hallmark is sending anthropologists into the homes of immigrants, attending holidays and birthday parties to design cards they'll want.

No survey can tell engineers what women really want in a razor, so marketing consultant Hauser Design sends anthropologists into bathrooms to watch them shave their legs.

Unlike MBAs, anthropology degrees are rare: one undergraduate degree for every 26 in business and one anthropology Ph.D. for every 235 MBAs.

Textbooks now have chapters on business applications. The University of South Florida has created a course of study for anthropologists headed for commerce.

Motorola corporate lawyer Robert Faulkner got his anthropology degree before going to law school. He says it becomes increasingly valuable.

"When you go into business, the only problems you'll have are people problems," was the advice given to teenager Michael Koss by his father in the early 1970s.

Koss, now 44, heeded the advice, earned an anthropology degree from Beloit College in 1976, and is today CEO of the Koss headphone manufacturer.

Katherine Burr, CEO of The Hanseatic Group, has masters in both anthropology and business from the University of New Mexico. Hanseatic was among the first money management programs to predict the Asian crisis and last year produced a total return of 315% for investors.

"My competitive edge came completely out of anthropology," she says. "The world is so unknown, changes so rapidly. Preconceptions can kill you."

Companies are starving to know how people use the Internet or why some pickups, even though they are more powerful, are perceived by consumers as less powerful, says Ken Erickson, of the Center for Ethnographic Research.

It takes trained observation, Erickson says. Observation is what anthropologists are trained to do.

SOURCE: Del Jones, "Hot Asset in Corporate: Anthropology Degrees," *USA Today*, February 18, 1999, p. B1.

choose a joint major in anthropology and zoology. A recent survey of women executives showed that most had not majored in business but in the social sciences or humanities. Only after graduating did they study business, obtaining a master's degree in business administration. These executives felt that the breadth of their college educations had contributed to their business careers. Anthropology majors go on to medical, law, and business schools and find success in many professions that often have little explicit connection to anthropology.

Anthropology's breadth provides knowledge and an outlook on the world that are useful in many kinds of work. For example, an anthropology major combined with a master's degree in business is excellent preparation for work in international business. However, job seekers must always convince employers that they have a special and valuable "skillset."

Breadth is anthropology's hallmark. Anthropologists study people biologically, culturally, socially, and linguistically, in time and space, in developed and underdeveloped nations, in simple and complex settings. Physical anthropologists teach about human biology in time and space, including our origins and evolution. Most colleges have cultural anthropology courses that compare cultures and others that focus on particular world areas, such as Latin America, Asia, and Native North America. The knowledge of geographic areas acquired in such courses can be useful in many jobs. Anthropology's comparative outlook, its long-standing Third World focus, and its appreciation of diverse lifestyles combine to provide an excellent foundation for overseas employment (see Omohundro 2001).

Even for work in North America, the focus on culture is valuable. Every day we hear about cultural differences and about social problems whose solutions require a multicultural viewpoint—an ability to recognize and reconcile ethnic differences. Government, schools, and private firms constantly deal with people from different social classes, ethnic groups, and tribal backgrounds. Physicians, attorneys, social workers, police officers, judges, teachers, and students can all do a better job if they understand social differences in a part of the world that is one of the most ethnically diverse in history.

Knowledge about the traditions and beliefs of the many social groups within a modern nation is important in planning and carrying out programs that affect those groups. Attention to social background and cultural categories helps ensure the welfare of affected ethnic groups, communities, and neighborhoods. Experience in planned social change—whether community organization in North America or economic development overseas—shows that a proper social study should be done before a project or policy is implemented. When local people want the change and it fits their lifestyle and traditions, it will be more successful, beneficial, and cost effective. There will be not only a more humane but a more economical solution to a real social problem.

People with anthropology backgrounds are doing well in many fields. Furthermore, even if the job has little or nothing to do with anthropology in a formal or obvious sense, anthropology is always useful when we work with fellow human beings. For most of us, this means every day of our lives.

1. Anthropology has two dimensions: academic and applied. Applied anthropology uses anthropological perspectives, theory, methods, and data to identify, assess, and solve problems. Applied anthropologists have a range of employers. Examples: government agencies; development organizations; NGOs; tribal, ethnic, and interest groups; businesses; social services and educational agencies. Applied anthropologists come from all four subfields. Ethnography is one of applied anthropology's most valuable research tools. Another is the comparative, cross-cultural, biocultural perspective. A systemic perspective recognizes that changes have multiple consequences, some unintended.

2. Anthropology and education researchers work in classrooms, homes, and other settings relevant to education. Such studies may lead to policy recommendations. Both academic and applied anthropologists study migration from rural areas to cities and across national boundaries. North America has become a popular arena for urban anthropological research on migration, ethnicity, poverty, and related topics. Although rural and urban are different social systems, there is cultural diffusion from one to the other. Rural and tribal social forms affect adjustment to the city.

3. Medical anthropology is the cross-cultural, biocultural study of health problems and conditions, disease, illness, disease theories, and health-care systems. Medical anthropology includes biological and cultural anthropologists and has theoretical (academic) and applied dimensions. In a given setting, the characteristic diseases reflect diet, population density, economy, and social complexity. Native theories of illness may be personalistic, naturalistic, or emotionalistic. In applying anthropology to business, the key features are (1) ethnography and observation as ways of gathering data, (2) cross-cultural expertise, and (3) a focus on cultural diversity.

4. A broad college education, including anthropology and foreign-area courses, offers excellent background for many fields. Anthropology's comparative outlook and cultural relativism provide an excellent basis for overseas employment. Even for work in North America, a focus on culture and cultural diversity is valuable. Anthropology majors attend medical, law, and business schools and succeed in many fields, some of which have little explicit connection with anthropology.

anthropology and education Anthropological research in classrooms, homes, and neighborhoods, viewing students as total cultural creatures whose enculturation and attitudes toward education belong to a larger context that includes family, peers, and society.

applied anthropology The application of anthropological data, perspectives, theory, and methods to identify, assess, and solve contemporary social problems.

cultural resource management (CRM) The branch of applied archaeology aimed at preserving sites threatened by dams, highways, and other projects.

curer Specialized role acquired through a culturally appropriate process of selection, training, certification, and acquisition of a professional image; the curer is consulted by patients, who believe in his or her special powers, and receives some form of special consideration; a cultural universal.

disease A scientifically identified health threat caused by a bacterium, virus, fungus, parasite, or other pathogen.

health-care systems Beliefs, customs, and specialists concerned with ensuring health and preventing and curing illness; a cultural universal.

illness   A condition of poor health perceived or felt by an individual.

medical anthropology   Unites biological and cultural anthropologists in the study of disease, health problems, health-care systems, and theories about illness in different cultures and ethnic groups.

practicing anthropologists   Used as a synonym for applied anthropology; anthropologists who practice their profession outside academia.

scientific medicine   As distinguished from Western medicine, a health-care system based on scientific knowledge and procedures, encompassing such fields as pathology, microbiology, biochemistry, surgery, diagnostic technology, and applications.

CRITICAL THINKING QUESTIONS

For more self-testing, see the self-quizzes

mhhe.com/kottak

1. What else are you studying this semester? Do those fields have an applied dimension, too? Are they more or less useful than anthropology is?

2. Describe a setting in which you might use ethnography and observation to do applied anthropology. What other research methods might you also use in that setting?

3. Think back to your grade school or high school classroom. Were there any social issues that might have interested an anthropologist? Were there any problems that an applied anthropologist might have been able to solve? How so?

4. What do you see as the costs and benefits of Western medicine compared with tribal medicine? Are there any conditions for which you'd prefer treatment by a tribal curer than a Western curer?

5. Think of a business context you know well. How might applied anthropology help that business function better? How would the applied anthropologist gather the information to suggest improvements?

6. Besides the examples given in this chapter, think of some other problems or issues in the modern world to which applied anthropology might contribute.

SUGGESTED ADDITIONAL READINGS

Anderson, R.
   1996   *Magic, Science, and Health: The Aims and Achievements of Medical Anthropology.* Fort Worth: Harcourt Brace. Up-to-date text, focusing on variation associated with race, gender, ethnicity, age, and ableness.

Bailey, E. J.
   2000   *Medical Anthropology and African American Health.* Westport, CT: Bergin and Garvey. Medical issues affecting, and anthropological research involving, African Americans.

Brown, P. J.
   1998   *Understanding and Applying Medical Anthropology.* Boston: McGraw-Hill. Medical anthropology, basic and applied.

Chambers, E.
   1985   *Applied Anthropology: A Practical Guide.* Upper Saddle River, NJ: Prentice Hall. How to do applied anthropology, by a leader in the field.
   2000   *Native Tours: The Anthropology of Travel and Tourism.* Prospect Heights, IL: Waveland. How anthropologists study the world's number one business—travel and tourism.

Eddy, E. M., and W. L. Partridge, eds.
   1987   *Applied Anthropology in America,* 2nd ed. New York: Columbia University Press. Historical review of applications of anthropological knowledge in the United States.

Ervin, A. M.
   2005   *Applied Anthropology: Tools and Perspectives for Contemporary Practice,* 2nd ed. Boston: Pearson/Allyn & Bacon. Up-to-date treatment of applied anthropology.

Ferraro, G. P.
   2006   *The Cultural Dimension of International Business,* 5th ed. Upper Saddle River, NJ: Prentice Hall. How the theory and insights of cultural anthropology can influence the conduct of international business.

Gmelch, G., and W. Zenner
   2002   *Urban Life: Readings in the Anthropology of the City.* Prospect Heights, IL: Waveland. Up-to-date anthology.

Gwynne, M. A.
   2003   *Applied Anthropology: A Career-Oriented Approach.* Boston: Allyn & Bacon. Various applied opportunities in anthropological careers.

Holtzman, J.
   2000   *Nuer Journeys, Nuer Lives.* Boston: Allyn & Bacon. How immigrants from Sudan adapt to Minnesota's Twin Cities and to the American social-service system.

Human Organization
   The quarterly journal of the Society for Applied Anthropology. An excellent source for articles on applied anthropology and development.

Joralemon, D.

1999 *Exploring Medical Anthropology.* Boston: Allyn & Bacon. Recent introduction to a growing field.

McDonald, J. H., ed.

2002 *The Applied Anthropology Reader.* Boston: Allyn & Bacon. Recent descriptions of case experiences and approaches.

Omohundro, J. T.

2001 *Careers in Anthropology,* 2nd ed. Boston: McGraw-Hill. Offers some vocational guidance.

Sargent, C. F., and C. B. Brettell

1996 *Gender and Health: An International Perspective.* Upper Saddle River, NJ: Prentice Hall. How culture affects the relation among gender, health-care organization, and health policy.

Spindler, G. D., ed.

2000 *Fifty Years of Anthropology and Education, 1950–2000: A Spindler Anthology.* Mahwah, NJ: Erlbaum. Survey of the field of educational anthropology by two prominent contributors, George and Louise Spindler.

Stephens, W. R.

2002 *Careers in Anthropology: What an Anthropology Degree Can Do for You.* Boston: Allyn & Bacon. Making the most of an anthropology degree.

Stevenson, D.

2003 *Cities and Urban Cultures.* Philadelphia: Open University Press. A cross-cultural consideration.

Strathern, A., and P. J. Stewart

1999 *Curing and Healing: Medical Anthropology in Global Perspective.* Durham, NC: Carolina Academic Press. Cross-cultural examples of medical anthropology.

Van Willigen, J.

2002 *Applied Anthropology: An Introduction,* 3rd ed. Westport, CT: Bergin and Garvey. Excellent review of the growth of applied anthropology and its links to general anthropology.

INTERNET EXERCISES

1. Go to the website for the Central Identification Laboratory, Hawaii (CILHI), **http://www.qmmuseum. lee.army.mil/mortuary/worldwide_cilhi_ mission.htm** and read about what this organization does.
   a. What does the CILHI do?
   b. The CILHI is one of the largest employers of forensic anthropologists in the world. How are forensic anthropologists important for its mission?
   c. What kind of educational background do many of the staff members have? Where are some of the institutions they attended?

2. Go to the publication from the United States Agency for International Development (USAID) titled "Population and the Environment: A Delicate Balance" (**http://pdf.dec.org/pdf_docs/ PNACP195.pdf**).
   a. What are some of the major environmental threats due to population growth the world faces?
   b. What can groups like USAID do in the face of these threats?
   c. What contributions does anthropology have to offer? Should organizations like USAID employ anthropologists?
   d. What is the role of applied anthropology for environmental issues?

See Chapter 2 at your McGraw-Hill Online Learning Center for additional review and interactive exercises.

LINKAGES

Assault on Paradise

In Kottak's *Assault on Paradise,* 4th edition, read the sections of Chapter 9 titled "Welfare and Education" and "Public Health," which describe improvements in public health, education, and welfare between the 1960s and the 1980s. For background information on health and education during the 1960s, see Chapter 2. In the 1960s what problems might an applied anthropologist have identified as ones with which Arembepeiros most needed help? Had those problems been solved, or at least addressed, by the 1980s? Pay particular attention to health and education.

Culture Sketches

In *Culture Sketches,* 4th edition, by Peters-Golden, read Chapter 11 on "The Ojibwa: The People Endure." Urban anthropology is one applied field presented in this text chapter, which discusses differences between rural and urban life, and the process of change through urbanization. What sorts of changes have occurred in Ojibwa life through urbanization? Might the move from reservation to city, for Native Americans, be different from urbanization experienced by other social groups? Why or why not?

3

Culture

WHAT IS CULTURE?

The concept of culture has long been basic to anthropology. Well over a century ago, in his book *Primitive Culture*, the British anthropologist Sir Edward Tylor proposed that cultures—systems of human behavior and thought—obey natural laws and therefore can be studied scientifically. Tylor's definition of culture still offers an overview of the subject matter of anthropology and is widely quoted: "Culture . . . is that complex whole which includes knowledge, belief, arts, morals, law, custom, and any other capabilities and habits acquired by man as a member of society" (Tylor 1871/1958, p. 1). The crucial phrase here is "acquired by man as a member of society." Tylor's definition focuses on attributes that people acquire not through biological inheritance but by growing up in a particular society where they are exposed to a specific cultural tradition. **Enculturation** is the process by which a child learns his or her culture.

See the Virtual Exploration for an example of how cultural values are learned

mhhe.com/kottak

Culture Is Learned

The ease with which children absorb any cultural tradition rests on the uniquely elaborated human capacity to learn. Other animals may learn from experience; for example, they avoid fire after discovering that it hurts. Social animals also learn from other members of their group. Wolves, for instance, learn hunting strategies from other pack members. Such social learning is particularly important among monkeys and apes, our closest biological relatives. But our own *cultural learning* depends on the uniquely developed human capacity to use **symbols,** signs that have no necessary or natural connection to the things they signify or for which they stand.

On the basis of cultural learning, people create, remember, and deal with ideas. They grasp and apply specific systems of symbolic meaning. Anthropologist Clifford Geertz defines culture as ideas based on cultural learning and symbols. Cultures have been characterized as sets of "control mechanisms—plans, recipes, rules, instructions, what computer engineers call programs for the governing of behavior" (Geertz 1973, p. 44). These programs are absorbed by people through enculturation in particular traditions. People gradually internalize a previously established system of meanings and symbols. They use this cultural system to define their world, express their feelings, and make their judgments. This system helps guide their behavior and perceptions throughout their lives.

Bringing It All Together

For a more detailed look at the cultural, ethnic, and linguistic aspects of unity and diversity in a contemporary nation-state, see the "Bringing It All Together" essay that immediately follows Chapter 6.

See the Internet Exercises at your OLC

mhhe.com/kottak

OVERVIEW

Culture, which is learned, passes from one generation to the next through the process of enculturation. Culture relies on symbols, which have a particular meaning and value for the people who share a culture. Cultural traditions take natural phenomena, including biological urges, and channel them in particular directions. Everyone is cultured, not just people with elite educations. Societies are integrated and patterned through dominant economic forces, social patterns, key symbols, and core values. Cultural means of adaptation have been crucial in human evolution. Cultures constrain individuals, but the actions of individuals can change cultures.

There are different levels of cultural systems. Diffusion and migration carry cultural traits and patterns across social and national boundaries. Also, nations have internal cultural diversity associated with ethnicity, region, and social class. Some aspects of culture are universal. Others are merely widespread or generalized. Still others are unique and distinctive to particular societies. Mechanisms of cultural change include diffusion, acculturation, and independent invention. Globalization describes processes that promote change in a world whose nations and people are increasingly linked.

Every person begins immediately, through a process of conscious and unconscious learning and interaction with others, to internalize, or incorporate, a cultural tradition through the process of enculturation. Sometimes culture is taught directly, as when parents tell their children to say "thank you" when someone gives them something or does them a favor.

Culture also is transmitted through observation. Children pay attention to the things that go on around them. They modify their behavior not just because other people tell them to but as a result of their own observations and growing awareness of what their culture considers right and wrong. Culture also is absorbed unconsciously. North Americans acquire their culture's notions about how far apart people should stand when they talk (see "Interesting Issues" on p. 285) not by being told directly to maintain a certain distance but through a gradual process of observation, experience, and conscious and unconscious behavior modification. No one tells Latins to stand closer together than North Americans do, but they learn to do so anyway as part of their cultural tradition.

Anthropologists agree that cultural learning is uniquely elaborated among humans and that all humans have culture. Anthropologists also accept a doctrine named in the 19th century as "the psychic unity of man." This means that although *individuals* differ in their emotional and intellectual tendencies and capacities, all human *populations* have equivalent capacities for culture. Regardless of their genes or their physical appearance, people can learn *any* cultural tradition.

To understand this point, consider that contemporary Americans and Canadians are the genetically mixed descendants of people from all over the world. Our ancestors were biologically varied, lived in different countries and continents, and participated in hundreds of cultural traditions. However, early colonists, later immigrants, and their descendants have all become active participants in American and Canadian life. All now share a national culture.

Culture Is Shared

Culture is an attribute not of individuals per se but of individuals as members of *groups.* Culture is transmitted in society. Don't we learn our culture by observing, listening, talking, and interacting with many other people? Shared beliefs, values, memories, and expectations link people who grow up in the same culture. Enculturation unifies people by providing us with common experiences.

Today's parents were yesterday's children. If they grew up in North America, they absorbed certain values and beliefs transmitted over the generations. People become agents in the enculturation

Culture Clash: Makah Seek Return to Whaling Past

NEW YORK TIMES NEWS BRIEF

by Sarah Kershaw
September 19, 2005

People do not now, nor have they ever, lived in isolation from other human beings. Links between groups have been provided by cultural practices such as marriage, kinship, religion, trade, travel, exploration, and conquest. For centuries, indigenous peoples have been exposed to a world system. Contemporary forces and events make even the illusion of autonomy hard to maintain. Nowadays, as is described in this news story, members of local cultures and communities must heed not only their own customs but also agencies, laws, and lawsuits operating at the national and international levels. As you read this account and this chapter on culture, pay attention to the various kinds of rights being asserted—animal rights, cultural rights, economic rights, legal rights, and human rights—and how those rights might clash. Also consider the levels of culture and of political regulation (local, regional, national, and global) that determine how contemporary people such as the Makah live their lives and maintain their traditions. Finally, consider the minimal impact on whale populations of the Makah hunt compared with commercial whaling.

The whaling canoes are stored in a wooden shed, idle for the past six years. They were last used when the Makah Indians were allowed to take their harpoons and a .50-caliber rifle and set out on their first whale hunt since the late 1920's.

There were eight young men in a canoe with a red hummingbird, a symbol of speed, painted on the tip. There were motorboats ferrying other hunters, news helicopters, and animal rights activists in speedboats and even a submarine.

On May 17, 1999, a week into the hunt, the Makah killed a 30-ton gray whale, striking it with harpoons and then killing it with a gunshot to the back of the head.

That rainy spring day remains etched in the minds of many Makah as a defining moment in their efforts to reach back to their cultural and historical roots. It was their first kill in seven decades, and it was their last since they were stopped by court rulings. They have asked the federal government for permission to resume hunting, and public meetings on the request are scheduled for October.

The Makah, a tribe of about 1,500 near the mouth of the Strait of Juan de Fuca on the Olympic Peninsula, see themselves as whalers and continue to identify themselves spiritually with whales.

"Everybody felt like it was a part of making history," Micah L. McCarty, a tribal council member, said of the 1999 hunt. "It's inspired a cultural renaissance, so to speak. It inspired a lot of people to learn artwork and become more active in building canoes; the younger generation took a more keen interest in singing and dancing."

The Makah, a tribe of mostly fishermen that faces serious poverty and high unemployment, were guaranteed the right to hunt whales in an 1855 treaty with the United States, the only tribe with such a treaty provision. Whaling had been the tribe's mainstay for thousands of years.

But the tribe decided to stop hunting whales early in the 20th century, when commercial harvesting had depleted the species. Whale hunting was later strictly regulated nationally and internationally, and the United States listed the Northern Pacific gray whale, the one most available to the Makah, as endangered.

The protections helped the whales rebound, and they were taken off the endangered list in 1994. Several years later, the Makah won permission to hunt again, along with a $100,000 federal grant to set up a whaling commission.

By the time they were ready, none of the Makah had witnessed a whale hunt or even tasted the meat, hearing only stories passed down through the generations. They learned that the whale was a touchstone of Makah culture—the tribe's logo today pictures an eagle perched on a whale—and that the tribe's economy was built around the lucrative trade with Europeans in whale oil, used for heating and lighting, during the 18th and early 19th centuries.

For a year before the 1999 hunt, the new Makah whale hunters prepared for their sacramental pursuit, training in canoes on the cold and choppy waters of the Pacific Ocean, praying on the beach in the mornings and at the dock in the evenings.

Animal rights groups were preparing, too. When the hunt began, the small reservation and its surrounding waters were teeming with news helicopters and protest groups. On that May afternoon, when the protesters were somewhere off the reservation,

■ *Makah Indians kill a gray whale in May 1999. More than 500 Makah Indians attended the traditional ceremony of the whale hunt, which was declared illegal in 2002.*

the Makah killed their whale. They held a huge celebration on the beach, where 15 men were waiting to butcher the animal, its meat later kippered and stewed.

But the protests and the television cameras "took a lot of the spirituality out of it," said Dave Sones, vice chairman of the tribal council.

Mr. McCarty said, "I equate it with interrupting High Mass."

The Makah went whale hunting, largely unnoticed, again in 2000, paddling out on a 32-foot cedar whaling canoe, but they did not catch anything. Soon after, animal rights groups, including the Humane Society of the United States, sued to stop the hunting. In 2002, an appeals court declared the hunting illegal, saying the National Oceanic and Atmospheric Administration had not adequately studied the impact of Makah hunting on the survival of the whale species.

Despite the strict national and international regulations on whale hunting, several tribes of Alaska Natives, subsistence whale hunters

for centuries, are exempt from provisions of the 1972 Marine Mammal Protection Act, allowing them to hunt the bowhead whale. That species, unlike the gray whale, is listed as endangered, said Brian Gorman, a spokesman for the oceanic agency.

Despite their treaty rights, the Makah were not granted an exemption under the 1972 act. Last February, the tribe asked the agency for a waiver that would grant them permanent rights to kill up to 20 gray whales in any five-year period, which they insist they already have under their 1855 treaty.

The Makah's request is "setting a dangerous precedent," said Naomi Rose, a marine mammal scientist for the Humane Society.

The Alaska hunting, Ms. Rose said, "is a true subsistence hunt," whereas the Makah, who view whale hunting mostly as ceremonial, are pursuing "cultural whaling" that is not essential to their diet.

"There are too many other bad actors out there" who might try to

apply for waivers too, she said. The Makah "have a treaty right, but we're asking them not to exercise it," she said. But other environmental groups, including Greenpeace, which is adamantly opposed to the commercial harvesting of whales, have remained neutral on the Makah's quest.

"No indigenous hunt has ever destroyed whale populations," said John Hocevar, an oceans specialist with Greenpeace. "And looking at the enormous other threats to whales and putting the Makah whaling in context, it's pretty different."

Mr. Gorman, of the federal fisheries agency, said: "They have a treaty right that the U.S. government signed. It doesn't take an international lawyer to figure out that they do have this treaty."

———
SOURCE: Sarah Kershaw, "In Petition to Government, Tribe Hopes for Return to Whaling Past," *New York Times*, September 19, 2005, p. A16.

of their children, just as their parents were for them. Although a culture constantly changes, certain fundamental beliefs, values, worldviews, and child-rearing practices endure. Consider a simple American example of enduring shared enculturation. As children, when we didn't finish a meal, our parents may have reminded us of starving children in some foreign country, just as our grandparents might have done a generation earlier. The specific country changes (China, India, Bangladesh, Ethiopia, Somalia, Rwanda—what was it in your home?). Still, American culture goes on transmitting the idea that by eating all our brussels sprouts or broccoli, we can justify our own good fortune, compared to a hungry child in an impoverished or war-ravaged country.

Despite characteristic American notions that people should "make up their own minds" and "have a right to their opinion," little of what we think is original or unique. We share our opinions and beliefs with many other people. Illustrating the power of shared cultural background, we are most likely to agree with and feel comfortable with people who are socially, economically, and culturally similar to ourselves. This is

one reason why Americans abroad tend to socialize with each other, just as French and British colonials did in their overseas empires. Birds of a feather flock together, but for people, the familiar plumage is culture.

Culture Is Symbolic

Symbolic thought is unique and crucial to humans and to cultural learning. Anthropologist Leslie White defined culture as

dependent upon symbolling . . . Culture consists of tools, implements, utensils, clothing, ornaments, customs, institutions, beliefs, rituals, games, works of art, language, etc. (White 1959, p. 3)

For White, culture originated when our ancestors acquired the ability to use symbols, that is, to originate and bestow meaning on a thing or event, and, correspondingly, to grasp and appreciate such meanings (White 1959, p. 3).

A symbol is something verbal or nonverbal, within a particular language or culture, that comes to stand for something else. There is no obvious, natural, or necessary connection between the symbol and what it symbolizes. A pet that barks is no more naturally a *dog* than a *chien, Hund,* or *mbwa,* to use the words for the animal we call "dog" in French, German, and Swahili. Language is one of the distinctive possessions of *Homo sapiens.* No other animal has developed anything approaching the complexity of language.

Symbols are usually linguistic. But there are also nonverbal symbols, such as flags, that stand for countries, as arches do for a hamburger chain. Holy water is a potent symbol in Roman Catholicism. As is true of all symbols, the association between a symbol (water) and what is symbolized (holiness) is arbitrary and conventional. Water is not intrinsically holier than milk, blood, or other natural liquids. Nor is holy water chemically different from ordinary water. Holy water is a symbol within Roman Catholicism, which is part of an international cultural system. A natural thing has been arbitrarily associated with a particular meaning for Catholics, who share common beliefs and experiences that are based on learning and that are transmitted across the generations.

For hundreds of thousands of years, humans have shared the abilities on which culture rests. These abilities are to learn, to think symbolically, to manipulate language, and to use tools and other cultural products in organizing their lives and coping with their environments. Every contemporary human population has the ability to use symbols and thus to create and maintain culture. Our nearest relatives—chimpanzees and gorillas—have rudimentary cultural abilities. However, no other animal has elaborated cultural abilities—to learn, to communicate, and to store, process, and use information—to the extent that *Homo* has.

Culture and Nature

Culture takes the natural biological urges we share with other animals and teaches us how to express them in particular ways. People have to eat, but culture teaches us what, when, and how. In many cultures people have their main meal at noon, but most North Americans prefer a large dinner. English people may eat fish for breakfast, while North Americans may prefer hot cakes and cold cereals. Brazilians put hot milk into strong coffee, whereas North Americans pour cold milk into a weaker brew. Midwesterners dine at 5 or 6 P.M., Spaniards at 10 P.M.

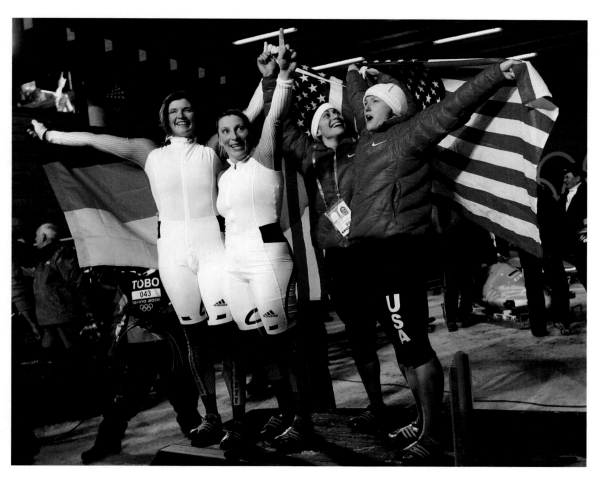

Olympic medalists and their symbols. In Cesana Pariol, Italy, on February 21, 2006, Gold Medal bobsled winners Sandra Kiriasis and Anja Schneiderheinze of Germany (left) celebrate with Silver Medal winners Valerie Fleming and Shauna Rohbock of the United States (right) on Day 11 of the 2006 Turin Winter Olympics. What are the symbols in this photo and caption?

People in the United States sometimes have trouble understanding the power of culture because of the value American culture places on the idea of the *individual.* Americans are fond of saying that everyone is unique and special in some way. In American culture, individualism itself is a distinctive *shared* value, a feature of culture. Individualism is transmitted through hundreds of statements and settings in our daily lives. Watch a morning TV show, such as *Today,* for an hour. Count how many stories focus on individuals, especially their achievements. Contrast that with the number of stories that focus on the achievements of communities. From the late Mr. Rogers from daytime TV to "real-life" parents, grandparents, and teachers, our enculturative agents insist we are all "someone special." That is, we are individuals first and members of groups second. This is the opposite of the lesson being taught in this chapter about culture. Without doubt we have distinctive features because we are individuals, but we have other distinct attributes because we are members of groups.

Cultural habits, perceptions, and inventions mold "human nature" in many directions. People have to eliminate wastes from their bodies. But some cultures teach people to defecate squatting, while others tell them to do it sitting down. A generation ago, in Paris and other French cities, it was customary for men to urinate almost publicly, and seemingly without embarrassment, in barely shielded *pissoirs* located on city streets. Our "bathroom" habits, including waste elimination, bathing, and dental care, are parts of cultural traditions that have converted natural acts into cultural customs.

Our culture—and cultural changes—affects the ways in which we perceive nature, human nature, and "the natural." Through science, invention, and discovery, cultural advances have overcome many "natural" limitations. We prevent and cure diseases such as polio and smallpox that felled our ancestors. We use Viagra to restore and enhance sexual potency. Through cloning, scientists have altered the way we think about biological identity and the meaning of life itself. Culture, of course, has not freed us from natural threats. Hurricanes, floods, earthquakes, and other natural forces regularly challenge our wishes to modify the environment through building, development, and expansion. Can you think of other ways in which nature strikes back at people and their products?

 STUDENT CD-ROM LIVING ANTHROPOLOGY

Being Raised Canela
Track 3

This clip focuses on Brazil's Canela Indians. One of the key figures in the clip is the boy Carampei, who was four years old in 1975. Another is the "formal friend" of a small boy whose finger has been burned and who has been disciplined by his mother. The clip depicts enculturation among the Canela—various ways in which children learn their culture. How does the footage of Carampei show his learning of the rhythms of Canela life? The clip shows that children start doing useful work at an early age, but that the playfulness and affection of childhood are prolonged into adulthood. How does the behavior of the formal friend illustrate this playfulness? Notice how Canela culture is integrated in that songs, dances, and tales are interwoven with subsistence activity. From an emic perspective, what is the function of the hunters' dance? Think about how the clip shows the formal and informal, the conscious and unconscious aspects of enculturation.

Culture Is All-Encompassing

For anthropologists, culture includes much more than refinement, taste, sophistication, education, and appreciation of the fine arts. Not only college graduates but all people are "cultured." The most interesting and significant cultural forces are those that affect people every day of their lives, particularly those that influence children during enculturation. *Culture,* as defined anthropologically, encompasses features that are sometimes regarded as trivial or unworthy of serious study, such as "popular" culture (see Appendix 3). To understand contemporary North American culture, we must consider television, fast-food restaurants, sports, and games. As a cultural manifestation, a rock star may be as interesting as a symphony conductor, a comic book as significant as a book-award winner.

Culture Is Integrated

Cultures are not haphazard collections of customs and beliefs. Cultures are integrated, patterned systems. If one part of the system (e.g., the economy) changes, other parts change as well. For example, during the 1950s, most American women planned domestic careers as homemakers and mothers. Most of today's college women, by contrast, expect to get paid jobs when they graduate.

What are some of the social repercussions of the economic change? Attitudes and behavior regarding marriage, family, and children have changed. Late marriage, "living together," and divorce have become more common. The average age at first marriage for American women rose

Bringing It All Together

For a more detailed look at Canadian national and popular culture, see the "Bringing It All Together" essay that immediately follows Chapter 6.

Touching, Affection, Love, and Sex

Comparing the United States to Brazil—or virtually any Latin nation—we can see a striking cultural contrast between a national culture that tends to discourage physical contact and demonstrations of affection and one in which the contrary is true.

"Don't touch me." "Take your hands off me." Such statements are not uncommon in North America, but they are virtually never heard in Brazil, the Western Hemisphere's second most populous country. Brazilians like to be touched (and kissed) more than North Americans do. The world's cultures have strikingly different notions about displays of affection and about matters of personal space. When North Americans talk, walk, and dance, they maintain a certain distance from others—their personal space. Brazilians, who maintain less physical distance, interpret this as a sign of coldness. When conversing with a North American, the Brazilian characteristically moves in as the North American "instinctively" retreats. In these body movements, neither Brazilian nor North American is trying consciously to be especially friendly or unfriendly. Each is merely executing a program written on the self by years of exposure to a particular cultural tradition. Because of different ideas about proper social space, cocktail parties in international meeting places such as the United Nations can resemble an elaborate insect mating ritual as diplomats from different cultures advance, withdraw, and sidestep.

One easily evident difference between Brazil and the United States involves kissing, hugging, and touching. Middle-class Brazilians teach their kids—both boys and girls—to kiss (on the cheek, two or three times, coming and going) every adult relative they ever see. Given the size of Brazilian extended families, this can mean hundreds of people. Females continue kissing throughout their lives. They kiss male and female kin, friends, relatives of friends, friends of relatives, friends of friends, and, when it seems appropriate, more casual acquaintances. Males go on kissing their female relatives and friends. Until they are ado-

lescents, boys also kiss adult male relatives. Brazilian men typically greet each other with hearty handshakes and a traditional male hug (*abraço*). The closer the relationship, the tighter and longer-lasting the embrace. These comments apply to brothers, cousins, uncles, and friends. Many Brazilian men keep on kissing their fathers and uncles throughout their lives. Could it be that homophobia (fear of homosexuality) prevents American men from engaging in such displays of affection with other men? Are American women more likely to show affection with each other than American men are?

Like other North Americans who spend time in a Latin culture, I miss the numerous kisses and handshakes when I get back to the United States. After several months in Brazil, I find North Americans rather cold and impersonal. Many Brazilians share this opinion. I have heard similar feelings expressed by Italian-Americans as they describe North Americans with different ethnic backgrounds.

Question: *Ethnocentrism* is the tendency to view one's own culture as superior and to apply one's own cultural values in judging the behavior and beliefs of people from other cultures (see pp. 52–54). Do you have an ethnocentric position on the matter of displays of affection?

According to clinical psychologist David E. Klimek, who has written about intimacy and marriage in the United States, "in American society, if we go much beyond simple touching, our behavior takes on a minor sexual twist" (Slade 1984). North Americans define demonstrations of affection between males and females with reference to marriage. Love and affection are supposed to unite the married pair, and they blend into sex. When a wife asks her husband for "a little affection," she may mean, or he may think she means, sex.

A certain lack of clarity in North American definitions of love, affection, and sex is evident on Valentine's Day, which used to be just for lovers. Valentines used to be sent to wives, husbands, girlfriends, and boyfriends. Now, after years of promotion by the greeting card industry, they also go to mothers, fathers, sons, daughters, aunts, and uncles. There is a blurring of sexual and nonsexual affection. In Brazil, Lovers' Day retains its autonomy. Mother, father, and children have their own separate days of recognition.

It's true, of course, that in a good marriage love and affection exist alongside sex. Nevertheless, affection does not necessarily imply sex. The Brazilian culture shows that there can be rampant kissing, hugging, and touching without sex—or fears of improper sexuality. In Brazilian culture, physical demonstrations help cement many kinds of close personal relationships that have no sexual component.

Cultures have strikingly different standards of personal space, such as how far apart people should stand in normal encounters and interactions. Contrast the distance between the American businessmen and the closeness (including touching) of the two rabbis discussing the Talmud near the Western Wall in Jerusalem. Have you noticed such differences in your own interactions with others?

■ *Cultures are integrated systems. When one behavior pattern changes, others also change. During the 1950s, most American women expected to have careers as wives, mothers, and domestic managers. As more and more women have entered the work force, attitudes toward work and family have changed. On the left, Mom and kids do the dishes in 1952. On the right (taken in January 2005), nuclear expert and Deputy Director of ISIS (Institute for Science & International Security) Corey Hinderstein uses her office in Washington, D.C. to monitor nuclear activities all over the globe.*

from 20 in 1955 to 25 in 2003. The comparable figures for men were 23 and 27 (U.S. Census Bureau 2003). The number of currently divorced Americans more than quadrupled from 4 million in 1970 to about 22 million in 2004 (Statistical Abstract of the United States 2006). Work competes with marriage and family responsibilities and reduces the time available to invest in child care.

Cultures are integrated not simply by their dominant economic activities and related social patterns but also by sets of values, ideas, symbols, and judgments. Cultures train their individual members to share certain personality traits. A set of characteristic central or **core values** (key, basic, or central values) integrates each culture and helps distinguish it from others. For instance, the work ethic and individualism are core values that have integrated American culture for generations. Different sets of dominant values influence the patterns of other cultures.

Culture Can Be Adaptive and Maladaptive

As we saw in Chapter 1, humans have both biological and cultural ways of coping with environmental stresses. Besides our biological means of adaptation, we also use "cultural adaptive kits," which contain customary activities and tools. Although humans continue to adapt biologically, reliance on social and cultural means of adaptation has increased during human evolution.

In this discussion of the adaptive features of our cultural behavior, let's recognize that what's good for the individual isn't necessarily good for the group. Sometimes adaptive behavior that offers short-term benefits to particular individuals may harm the environment and threaten the group's long-term survival. Economic growth may benefit some people while it also depletes resources needed for society at large or for future genera-

tions (Bennett 1969, p. 19). Despite the crucial role of cultural adaptation in human evolution, cultural traits, patterns, and inventions also can be *maladaptive,* threatening the group's continued existence (survival and reproduction). Air conditioners help us deal with heat, as fires and furnaces protect us against the cold. Automobiles permit us to make a living by getting us from home to workplace. But the by-products of such "beneficial" technology often create new problems. Chemical emissions increase air pollution, deplete the ozone layer, and contribute to global warming. Many cultural patterns, such as overconsumption and pollution, appear to be maladaptive in the long run.

CULTURE AND THE INDIVIDUAL: AGENCY AND PRACTICE

Generations of anthropologists have theorized about the relationship between the "system," on the one hand, and the "person" or "individual," on the other. The "system" can refer to various concepts, including culture, society, social relations, and social structure. Individual human beings always make up, or constitute, the system. But, living within that system, humans also are constrained (to some extent, at least) by its rules, and by the actions of other individuals. Cultural rules provide guidance about what to do and how to do it, but people don't always do what the rules say should be done. People use their culture actively and creatively, rather than blindly following its dictates. Humans aren't passive beings who are doomed to follow their cultural traditions like programmed robots. Instead, people learn, interpret, and manipulate the same rules in different ways—or they emphasize different rules that better suit their interests. Culture is *contested:* Different groups in society struggle with one another over whose ideas, values, goals, and beliefs will prevail. Even common symbols may have radically different *meanings* to different individuals and groups in the same culture. Golden arches may cause one person to salivate, while another person plots a vegetarian protest. The same flag may be waved to support or oppose a given war.

Even when they agree about what should and shouldn't be done, people don't always do as their culture directs or as other people expect. Many rules are violated, some very often (e.g., automobile speed limits). Some anthropologists find it useful to distinguish between ideal culture and real culture. The *ideal culture* consists of what people say they should do and what they say they do. *Real culture* refers to their actual behavior as observed by the anthropologist. This contrast is like the emic–etic distinction discussed in Appendix 4.

Culture is both public and individual, both in the world and in people's minds. Anthropologists are interested not only in public and collective behavior but also in how *individuals* think, feel, and act. The individual and culture are linked because human social life is a process in which individuals internalize the meanings of *public* (i.e., cultural) messages. Then, alone and in groups, people influence culture by converting their private (and often divergent) understandings into public expressions (D'Andrade 1984).

Conventionally, culture has been seen as social glue transmitted across the generations, binding people through their common past, rather than as something being continually created and reworked in the present. The tendency to view culture as an entity rather than a process is changing. Contemporary anthropologists now emphasize how day-to-day action, practice, or resistance can make and remake culture (Gupta and Ferguson, eds. 1997b). *Agency* refers to the actions that individuals take, both alone and in groups, in forming and transforming cultural identities.

The approach to culture known as *practice theory* (Ortner 1984) recognizes that individuals within a society or culture have diverse motives and intentions and different degrees of power and influence (see also Appendix 1). Such contrasts may be associated with gender, age, ethnicity, class, and other social variables. Practice theory focuses on how such varied individuals—through their ordinary and extraordinary actions and practices—manage to influence, create, and transform the world they live in. Practice theory appropriately recognizes a reciprocal relation between culture (the system— see above) and the individual. The system shapes the way individuals experience and respond to external events, but individuals also play an active role in the way society functions and changes. Practice theory recognizes both constraints on individuals and the flexibility and changeability of cultures and social systems.

Illustrating the international level of culture, Roman Catholics in different nations share knowledge, symbols, beliefs, and values transmitted by their church. Shown here is a Catholic seminary in Xian, China. Besides religious conversion, what other forces work to spread international culture?

Levels of Culture

Of increasing importance in today's world are the distinctions between different levels of culture: national, international, and subcultural. **National culture** refers to those beliefs, learned behavior patterns, values, and institutions that are shared by citizens of the same nation. **International culture** is the term for cultural traditions that extend beyond and across national boundaries. Because culture is transmitted through learning rather than genetically, cultural traits can spread through borrowing or *diffusion* from one group to another.

Because of borrowing, colonialism, migration, and multinational organizations, many cultural traits and patterns have international scope. For example, Roman Catholics in many different countries share beliefs, symbols, experiences, and values transmitted by their church. The contemporary United States, Canada, Great Britain, and Australia share cultural traits they have inherited from their common linguistic and cultural ancestors in Great Britain. The World Cup has become an international cultural event, as people in many countries know the rules of, play, and follow soccer.

Cultures also can be smaller than nations (see Jenks 2004). Although people who live in the same country share a national cultural tradition, all cultures also contain diversity. Individuals, families, communities, regions, classes, and other groups within a culture have different learning experiences as well as shared ones. **Subcultures** are different symbol-based patterns and traditions associated with particular groups in the same complex society. In a large nation like the United States or Canada, subcultures originate in

Bringing It All Together

For a more detailed look at the cultural, ethnic, and linguistic aspects of unity and diversity in a contemporary nation-state, see the "Bringing It All Together" essay that immediately follows Chapter 6.

region, ethnicity, language, class, and religion. The religious backgrounds of Jews, Baptists, and Roman Catholics create subcultural differences between them. While sharing a common national culture, U.S. northerners and southerners also differ in aspects of their beliefs, values, and customary behavior as a result of regional variation. French-speaking Canadians contrast with English-speaking people in the same country. Italian Americans have ethnic traditions different from those of Irish, Polish, and African Americans. Using sports and foods, Table 3.1 gives some examples of international, national, and subculture. Soccer and basketball are played internationally. Monster-truck rallies are held throughout the United States. Bocci is a bowling-like sport from Italy still played in some Italian-American neighborhoods.

Nowadays, many anthropologists are reluctant to use the term *subculture.* They feel that the prefix "sub-" is offensive because it means "below." "Subcultures" may thus be perceived as "less than" or somehow inferior to a dominant, elite, or national culture. In this discussion of levels of culture, I intend no such implication. My point is simply that nations may contain many different culturally defined groups. As mentioned earlier, culture is contested. Various groups may strive to promote the correctness and value of their own practices, values, and beliefs in comparison with those of other groups, or the nation as a whole.

Ethnocentrism, Cultural Relativism, and Human Rights

Ethnocentrism is the tendency to view one's own culture as superior and to apply one's own cultural values in judging the behavior and beliefs of people raised in other cultures. We hear ethnocentric statements all the time. Ethnocentrism is a cultural universal. It contributes to social solidarity, a sense of value and community, among people who share a cultural tradition. People everywhere think that their familiar explanations, opinions, and customs are true, right, proper, and moral. They regard different behavior as strange, immoral, or savage. The tribal names that appear in anthropology books often come from the native word for *people.* "What are you called?" asks the anthropologist. "Mugmug," reply informants. *Mugmug* may turn out to be synonymous with *people*, but it also may be the only word the natives have for themselves. Other tribes are not considered fully human. The not-quite-people in neighboring groups are not classified as *Mugmug*. They are given different names that symbolize their inferior humanity. Neighboring tribes may be ridiculed and insulted because of their customs and preferences. They may be castigated as cannibals, thieves, or people who do not bury their dead.

Opposing ethnocentrism is **cultural relativism,** the argument that behavior in one culture

TABLE 3.1 Levels of Culture, with Examples from Sports and Foods

Level of Culture	Sports Examples	Food Examples
International	Soccer, basketball	Pizza
National	Monster-truck rallies	Apple pie
Subculture	Bocci	Big Joe Pork Barbeque (South Carolina)

should not be judged by the standards of another culture. This position also can present problems. At its most extreme, cultural relativism argues that there is no superior, international, or universal morality, that the moral and ethical rules of all cultures deserve equal respect. In the extreme relativist view, Nazi Germany would be evaluated as nonjudgmentally as Athenian Greece.

In today's world, human rights advocates challenge many of the tenets of cultural relativism. For example, several cultures in Africa and the Middle East have traditions of female genital modification. *Clitoridectomy* is the removal of a girl's clitoris. *Infibulation* involves sewing the lips (labia) of the vagina to constrict the vaginal opening. Both procedures reduce female sexual pleasure and, it is believed in some cultures, the likelihood of adultery. One or both of the procedures have been traditional in several societies, but such practices, characterized as female genital mutilation (FGM), have been opposed by human rights advocates, especially women's rights groups. The idea is that the tradition infringes on a basic human right: disposition over one's body and one's sexuality. Although such practices continue in certain areas, they are fading as a result of worldwide attention to the problem and changing sex-gender roles. Some African countries have banned or otherwise discouraged the procedures, as have Western nations that receive immigration from such cultures. Similar issues arise with circumcision and other male genital operations. Is it right for a baby boy to be circumcised without his permission, as has been routinely done in the United States? Is it proper to require adolescent boys to undergo collective circumcision to fulfill cultural tradition, as is done traditionally in parts of Africa and Australia?

Some would argue that the problems with relativism can be solved by distinguishing between methodological and moral relativism. In anthropology, cultural relativism is not a moral position, but a methodological one. It states: to understand

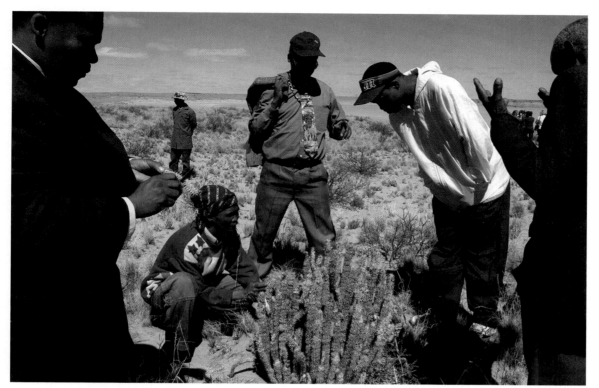

The notion of indigenous intellectual property rights (IPR) has arisen in an attempt to conserve each society's cultural base, including its medicinal plants, which may have commercial value. Shown here is the hoodia plant, a cactus that grows in the Kalahari Desert of southern Africa. Hoodia, which traditionally is used by the San people to stave off hunger, is used now in diet pills marketed on the Internet.

another culture fully, you must try to see how the people in that culture see things. What motivates them—what are they thinking—when they do those things? Such an approach does not preclude making moral judgments or taking action. When faced with Nazi atrocities, a methodological relativist would have a moral obligation to stop doing anthropology and take action to intervene. In the FGM example, one only can understand the *motivations* for the practice by looking at things from the point of view of those who engage in it. Having done this, one then faces the moral question of whether to intervene to stop it. We should recognize as well that different people and groups living in the same society—for example, women and men, old and young, the more and less powerful—can have widely different views about what is proper, necessary, and moral.

The idea of **human rights** invokes a realm of justice and morality beyond and superior to particular countries, cultures, and religions. Human rights, usually seen as vested in individuals, include the right to speak freely, to hold religious beliefs without persecution, and not to be murdered, injured, enslaved, or imprisoned without charge. These rights are not ordinary laws that particular governments make and enforce. Human rights are seen as *inalienable* (nations cannot abridge or terminate them) and international (larger than and superior to individual nations and cultures). Four United Nations documents describe nearly all the human rights that have been internationally recognized. Those documents are the UN Charter; the Universal Declaration of Human Rights; the Covenant on Economic, Social and Cultural Rights; and the Covenant on Civil and Political Rights.

Alongside the human rights movement has arisen an awareness of the need to preserve cultural rights. Unlike human rights, **cultural rights** are vested not in individuals but in *groups*, such as religious and ethnic minorities and indigenous societies. Cultural rights include a group's ability to preserve its culture, to raise its children in the ways of its forebears, to continue its language, and not to be deprived of its economic base by the nation in which it is located (Greaves 1995). Many countries have signed pacts endorsing, for cultural minorities within nations, such rights as self-determination; some degree of home rule; and the right to practice the group's religion, culture, and language. The related notion of indigenous intellectual property rights (**IPR**) has arisen in an attempt to conserve each society's cultural base—its core beliefs and principles. IPR are claimed as a cultural right, allowing indigenous groups to control who may know and use their collective knowledge and its applications. Much traditional cultural knowledge has commercial value. Examples include ethnomedicine (traditional medical knowledge and techniques), cosmetics, cultivated plants, foods, folklore, arts, crafts, songs, dances, costumes, and rituals. According to the IPR concept, a particular group may determine how indigenous knowledge

Map 10 locates classic ethnographic field sites— "cultures" or societies already studied by 1950.

and its products may be used and distributed, and the level of compensation required.

The notion of cultural rights is related to the idea of cultural relativism, and the problem discussed previously arises again. What does one do about cultural rights that interfere with human rights? I believe that anthropology's main job is to present accurate accounts and explanations of cultural phenomena. The anthropologist doesn't have to approve customs such as infanticide, cannibalism, and torture to record their existence and determine their causes and the motivations behind them. However, each anthropologist has a choice about where he or she will do field work. Some anthropologists choose not to study a particular culture because they discover in advance or early in field work that behavior they consider morally repugnant is practiced there. Anthropologists respect human diversity. Most ethnographers try to be objective, accurate, and sensitive in their accounts of other cultures. However, objectivity, sensitivity, and a cross-cultural perspective don't mean that anthropologists have to ignore international standards of justice and morality. What do you think?

UNIVERSALITY, GENERALITY, AND PARTICULARITY

In studying human diversity in time and space, anthropologists distinguish among the universal, the generalized, and the particular. Certain biological, psychological, social, and cultural features are **universal,** found in every culture. Others are merely **generalities,** common to several but not all human groups. Still other traits are **particularities,** unique to certain cultural traditions.

Universality

Universal traits are the ones that more or less distinguish *Homo sapiens* from other species (see Brown 1991). Biologically based universals include a long period of infant dependency, year-round (rather than seasonal) sexuality, and a complex brain that enables us to use symbols, languages, and tools. Psychological universals involve common ways in which humans think, feel, and process information. Most such universals probably reflect human biological universals, such as the structure of the human brain or certain physical differences between men and women, or children and adults.

Among the social universals is life in groups and in some kind of family. In all human societies, culture organizes social life and depends on social interactions for its expression and continuation. Family living and food sharing are universals. Among the most significant cultural universals are exogamy and the *incest taboo* (pro-

See the Internet Exercises at your OLC on cultural insults

mhhe.com/kottak

hibition against marrying or mating with a close relative). All cultures consider some people (various cultures differ about *which* people) too closely related to mate or marry. The violation of this taboo is *incest,* which is discouraged and punished in a variety of ways in different cultures. If incest is prohibited, *exogamy*—marriage outside one's group—is inevitable. Because it links human groups together into larger networks, exogamy has been crucial in human evolution. Exogamy elaborates on tendencies observed among other primates. Recent studies of monkeys and apes show that these animals also avoid mating with close kin and often mate outside their native groups.

Generality

Between universals and uniqueness (see the next section) is a middle ground that consists of cultural generalities. These are regularities that occur in different times and places but not in all cultures. One reason for generalities is diffusion. Societies can share the same beliefs and customs because of borrowing or through (cultural) inheritance from a common cultural ancestor. Speaking English is a generality shared by North Americans and Australians because both countries had English settlers. Another reason for generalities is domination, as in colonial rule, when customs and procedures are imposed on one culture by another one that is more powerful. In many countries, use of the English language reflects colonial history. More recently, English has spread through diffusion to many other countries, as it has become the world's foremost language for business and travel.

Cultural generalities also can arise through independent invention of the same cultural trait or pattern in two or more different cultures. For example, farming arose through independent invention in the Eastern (e.g., the Middle East) and Western (e.g., Mexico) Hemispheres. Similar needs and circumstances have led people in different lands to innovate in parallel ways. They have independently come up with the same cultural solution to a common problem.

One cultural generality that is present in many but not all societies is the *nuclear family,* a kinship group consisting of parents and children. Although many middle-class Americans ethnocentrically view the nuclear family as a proper and "natural" group, it is not universal. It is absent, for example, among the Nayars, who live on the Malabar Coast of India. The Nayars live in female-headed households, and husbands and wives do not live together. In many other societies, the nuclear family is submerged in larger kin groups, such as extended families, lineages, and clans. However, the nuclear family is prominent in many of the technologically simple societies that live by hunting and gathering. It is also a significant kin group among contemporary middle-class North Americans and Western Europeans. Later, an explanation of the nuclear family as a basic kinship unit in specific types of society will be given.

Particularity: Patterns of Culture

A cultural particularity is a trait or feature of culture that is not generalized or widespread; rather, it is confined to a single place, culture, or society. Yet because of cultural diffusion, which has accelerated through modern transportation and communication systems, traits that once were limited in their distribution have become more widespread. Traits that are useful, that have the capacity to please large audiences, and that don't clash with the cultural values of potential adopters are more likely to diffuse than others are. Still, certain cultural particularities persist. One example would be a particular food dish (e.g., pork barbecue with a mustard-based sauce available only in South Carolina, or the pastie—beef stew baked in pie dough—characteristic of Michigan's upper peninsula). Besides diffusion, which, for example, has spread McDonald's food outlets, once confined to San Bernadino, California, across the globe, there are other reasons why cultural particularities are increasingly rare. Many cultural traits are shared as cultural universals and as a result of independent invention. Facing similar problems, people in different places have come up with similar solutions. Again and again, similar cultural causes have produced similar cultural results.

At the level of the individual cultural trait or element (e.g., bow and arrow, hot dog, MTV), particularities may be getting rarer. But at a higher level, particularity is more obvious. Different cultures emphasize different things. *Cultures are integrated and patterned differently and display tremendous variation and diversity.* When cultural traits are borrowed, they are modified to fit the culture that adopts them. They are reintegrated—patterned anew—to fit their new setting. MTV in Germany or Brazil isn't at all the same thing as MTV in the United States. As was stated in the earlier section "Culture Is Integrated," patterned beliefs, customs, and practices lend distinctiveness to particular cultural traditions.

Consider universal life-cycle events, such as birth, puberty, marriage, parenthood, and death, which many cultures observe and celebrate. The occasions (e.g., marriage, death) may be the same and universal, but the patterns of ceremonial observance may be dramatically different. Cultures vary in just which events merit special celebration. Americans, for example, regard expensive weddings as more socially appropriate than lavish funerals. However, the Betsileo of Madagascar take the opposite view. The marriage ceremony is a minor event that brings together just the couple and a few close relatives. However, a funeral is a

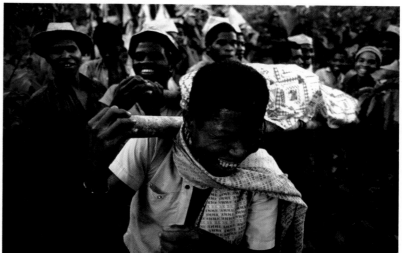

measure of the deceased person's social position and lifetime achievement, and it may attract a thousand people. Why use money on a house, the Betsileo say, when one can use it on the tomb where one will spend eternity in the company of dead relatives? How unlike contemporary Americans' dreams of home ownership and preference for quick and inexpensive funerals. Cremation, an increasingly common option in the United States, would horrify the Betsileo, for whom ancestral bones and relics are important ritual objects.

Cultures vary tremendously in their beliefs, practices, integration, and patterning. By focusing on and trying to explain alternative customs, anthropology forces us to reappraise our familiar ways of thinking. In a world full of cultural diversity, contemporary American culture is just one cultural variant, more powerful perhaps, but no more natural, than the others.

■ Cultures use rituals to mark such universal life-cycle events as birth, puberty, marriage, parenthood, and death. But particular cultures differ as to which event merits special celebration and in the emotions expressed during their rituals. Compare the wedding party (top) in Bali, Indonesia, with the funeral (bottom) among the Tanala of eastern Madagascar. How would you describe the emotions suggested by the photos?

MECHANISMS OF CULTURAL CHANGE

Why and how do cultures change? One way is **diffusion,** or borrowing of traits between cultures. Such exchange of information and products has gone on throughout human history because cultures have never been truly isolated. Contact between neighboring groups has always existed and has extended over vast areas (Boas 1940/1966). Diffusion is *direct* when two cultures trade, intermarry, or wage war on one another. Diffusion is *forced* when one culture subjugates another and imposes its customs on the domi-nated group. Diffusion is *indirect* when items move from group A to group C via group B with-out any firsthand contact between A and C. In this case, group B might consist of traders or mer-chants who take products from a variety of places to new markets. Or group B might be geographi-cally situated between A and C, so that what it gets from A eventually winds up in C, and vice versa. In today's world, much transnational dif-fusion is due to the spread of the mass media and advanced information technology.

Acculturation, a second mechanism of cul-tural change, is the exchange of cultural features that results when groups have continuous first-hand contact. The cultures of either group or both groups may be changed by this contact (Redfield, Linton, and Herskovits 1936). With acculturation, parts of the cultures change, but each group remains distinct. In situations of continuous con-tact, cultures may exchange and blend foods, recipes, music, dances, clothing, tools, technolo-gies, and languages.

One example of acculturation is a *pidgin,* a mixed language that develops to ease communi-cation between members of different societies in contact. This usually happens in situations of trade or colonialism. Pidgin English, for example, is a simplified form of English. It blends English grammar with the grammar of a native language. Pidgin English was first used for commerce in Chinese ports. Similar pidgins developed later in Papua New Guinea and West Africa.

Independent invention—the process by which humans innovate, creatively finding solu-tions to problems—is a third mechanism of cul-tural change. Faced with comparable problems and challenges, people in different societies have innovated and changed in similar ways, which is one reason cultural generalities exist. One exam-ple is the independent invention of agriculture in the Middle East and Mexico. Over the course of human history, major innovations have spread at the expense of earlier ones. Often a major inven-tion, such as agriculture, triggers a series of sub-sequent interrelated changes. These economic revolutions have social and cultural repercus-sions. Thus, in both Mexico and the Middle East, agriculture led to many social, political, and legal changes, including notions of property and dis-tinctions in wealth, class, and power. (For various theories of culture change see Appendix 1.)

GLOBALIZATION

The term **globalization** encompasses a series of processes, including diffusion and acculturation, working to promote change in a world in which nations and people are increasingly interlinked and mutually dependent. Promoting such link-ages are economic and political forces, along with modern systems of transportation and com-munication. The forces of globalization include international commerce, travel and tourism, transnational migration, the media, and various high-tech information flows (see Appadurai, ed. 2001). During the Cold War, which ended with the fall of the Soviet Union, the basis of interna-tional alliance was political, ideological, and mil-itary. Thereafter, the focus of international pacts shifted to trade and economic issues. New eco-nomic unions have been created through NAFTA (the North American Free Trade Agreement), GATT (the General Agreement on Trade and Tar-iffs), and the EU (the European Union).

Long-distance communication is easier, faster, and cheaper than ever and extends to remote areas. The mass media help propel a globally spreading culture of consumption, stimulating participation in the world cash economy. Within nations and across their borders, the media spread information about threats, products, services, rights, institu-

BEYOND THE CLASSROOM

Folklore Reveals Ethos of Heating Plant Workers

BACKGROUND INFORMATION

STUDENT:
Mark Dennis

SUPERVISING PROFESSOR:
Usher Fleising

SCHOOL:
University of Calgary

YEAR IN SCHOOL/MAJOR:
Fifth-Year Senior/
Social Anthropology

FUTURE PLANS:
Graduate school, traveling

PROJECT TITLE:
Folklore Reveals Ethos
of Heating Plant Workers

What role does folklore play among the workers described in this account? What functions do common tales serve in enabling workers to adapt to their work setting? What attributes of culture are represented here?

At the periphery of the University of Calgary campus exists a place, ironically called the central heating and cooling plant. Housed within its four walls and three levels are the industrial machinery and a tangle of pipes that snake through an eight-mile tunnel system in the bowels of the earth, bringing heat and cooling to a campus of 21,000.

Folklore is an oral form of knowledge shared by a cultural group. The objective of my research was to reveal the social and cultural manifestations of folklore among the University Central Heating and Cooling Plant (CHCP) employees. In an isolated control room, a fieldworker finds plant employees engaged in a social atmosphere filled with storytelling and humor. Accustomed to the mental and physical distance from the rest of the university, the men of the CHCP were glad to share their knowledge and folklore with me.

In addition to simple observations and document analysis, my research method consisted primarily of unstructured interviews. Using this technique I was able to control the direction of the conversation while still giving the informants (cultural consultants, community members) freedom to express themselves.

Folklore at the CHCP was passed on between employees during their shifts or during shift changes. Most stories were known by all employees. The themes included slapstick humor, disaster stories, tales about eccentric characters, practical jokes, and stories about complaints. The folklore was based entirely on oral history, with no written documentation ever produced.

During the course of fieldwork, I found that folklore functioned as an organic mechanism adapting to the needs of the employees by providing stress relief. Folklore helped them to deal constructively with job frustrations, and it created social cohesion among employees.

The last six years at the CHCP have been turbulent because of a management change. Conflicting working methods and rapid changes in technology made it hard for many employees to adapt. In this context the humor that folklore provided not only lightened the mood, but it also brought back fond memories of the easy-going past.

The CHCP has a unique working environment. At its worst, days can be filled with isolation and mundane activity, leaving the employees feeling that no one cares about the important work they do. Folklore is a healthy way of dealing with the isolation and ignorance of others. Workers share stories of the prestigious visitors, like university presidents, who have visited the plant over the years. By telling these stories the plant workers can see that there is hope for educating people about what they do. Such stories affirm that their jobs are very important.

Finally, folklore is a cohesive force whereby plant workers both old and new can celebrate the shared knowledge and unique work environment that surrounds them, leading to a happier and more productive work environment. Folklore is an interesting starting point from which to analyze subcultures and their social relations. The study of the Central Heating and Cooling Plant at the University of Calgary was one application of folklore as a theoretical basis for social analysis.

tions, and lifestyles. Emigrants transmit information and resources transnationally as they maintain their ties with home (phoning, faxing, e-mailing, making visits, sending money). In a sense, such people live multilocally—in different places and cultures at once. They learn to play various social roles and to change behavior and identity depending on the situation (see Cresswell 2006).

Local people must increasingly cope with forces generated by progressively larger systems—region, nation, and world. An army of alien actors and agents now intrudes on people everywhere. Terrorism is a global threat. Tourism has become the world's number one industry (see Holden 2005). Economic development agents and the media promote the idea that work should be for cash rather than mainly for subsistence. Indigenous peoples and traditional cultures have devised various strategies to deal with threats to their autonomy, identity, and livelihood. New forms of political mobilization and cultural expression are emerging from the interplay of local, regional, national, and international cultural forces (see Ong and Collier, eds. 2005).

SUMMARY

1. Culture, which is distinctive to humanity, refers to customary behavior and beliefs that are passed on through enculturation. Culture rests on the human capacity for cultural learning. Culture encompasses rules for conduct internalized in human beings, which lead them to think and act in characteristic ways.

2. Although other animals learn, only humans have cultural learning, dependent on symbols. Humans think symbolically—arbitrarily bestowing meaning on things and events. By convention, a symbol stands for something with which it has no necessary or natural relation. Symbols have special meaning for people who share memories, values, and beliefs because of common enculturation. People absorb cultural lessons consciously and unconsciously.

3. Cultural traditions mold biologically based desires and needs in particular directions. Everyone is cultured, not just people with elite educations. Cultures may be integrated and patterned through economic and social forces, key symbols, and core values. Cultural rules don't rigidly dictate our behavior. There is room for creativity, flexibility, diversity, and disagreement within societies. Cultural means of adaptation have been crucial in human evolution. Aspects of culture also can be maladaptive.

4. There are levels of culture, which can be larger or smaller than a nation. Diffusion, migration, and colonialism have carried cultural traits and patterns to different areas. Such traits are shared across national boundaries. Nations also include cultural differences associated with ethnicity, region, and social class.

5. Using a comparative perspective, anthropology examines biological, psychological, social, and cultural universals and generalities. There are also unique and distinctive aspects of the human condition. North American cultural traditions are no more natural than any others. Mechanisms of cultural change include diffusion, acculturation, and independent invention. Globalization describes a series of processes that promote change in a world in which nations and people are interlinked and mutually dependent.

KEY TERMS

See the flash cards

mhhe.com/kottak

acculturation   The exchange of cultural features that results when groups come into continuous first-hand contact; the cultural patterns of either or both groups may be changed, but the groups remain distinct.

core values   Key, basic, or central values that integrate a culture and help distinguish it from others.

cultural relativism   The position that the values and standards of cultures differ and deserve respect. Anthropology is characterized by methodological rather than moral relativism: In order to understand another culture fully, anthropologists try to understand its members' beliefs and motivations. Methodological relativism does not preclude making moral judgments or taking action.

cultural rights   Doctrine that certain rights are vested in identifiable groups, such as religious and ethnic minorities and indigenous societies. Cultural rights include a group's ability to preserve its culture, to raise its children in the ways of its forebears, to continue its language, and not to be deprived of its economic base by the nation-state in which it is located.

diffusion   Borrowing of cultural traits between societies, either directly or through intermediaries.

enculturation   The social process by which culture is learned and transmitted across the generations.

ethnocentrism   The tendency to view one's own culture as best and to judge the behavior and beliefs of culturally different people by one's own standards.

generality   Culture pattern or trait that exists in some but not all societies.

globalization   The accelerating interdependence of nations in a world system linked economically and through mass media and modern transportation systems.

human rights   Doctrine that invokes a realm of justice and morality beyond and superior to particular countries, cultures, and religions. Human rights, usually seen as vested in individuals, would include the right to speak freely, to hold religious beliefs without persecution, and not to be murdered, injured, enslaved, or imprisoned without charge.

independent invention   Development of the same cultural trait or pattern in separate cultures as a result of comparable needs, circumstances, and solutions.

international culture Cultural traditions that extend beyond national boundaries.

IPR Intellectual property rights, consisting of each society's cultural base—its core beliefs and principles. IPR are claimed as a group right—a cultural right—allowing indigenous groups to control who may know and use their collective knowledge and its applications.

national culture Cultural experiences, beliefs, learned behavior patterns, and values shared by citizens of the same nation.

particularity Distinctive or unique culture trait, pattern, or integration.

subcultures Different cultural traditions associated with subgroups in the same complex society.

symbol Something, verbal or nonverbal, that arbitrarily and by convention stands for something else, with which it has no necessary or natural connection.

universal Something that exists in every culture.

CRITICAL THINKING QUESTIONS

1. What cultural symbols have the most meaning for you? For your family? For your nation?

2. What are the key symbols and values that work to unite your religious group or another organization to which you belong?

3. Give some examples of cultural practices that are adaptive in the short run but probably maladaptive in the long run.

4. Do you feel you have multiple cultural identities? If so, how do you handle them?

5. What are some issues about which you find it hard to be culturally relativistic?

For more self-testing, see the self-quizzes

mhhe.com/kottak

SUGGESTED ADDITIONAL READINGS

Appadurai, A., ed.
    2001 *Globalization.* Durham, NC: Duke University Press. An anthropological approach to globalization and international relations.

Archer, M. S.
    1996 *Culture and Agency: The Place of Culture in Social Theory,* rev. ed. Cambridge, England: Cambridge University Press. Examines interrelations among individual action, social structure, culture, and social integration.

Bohannan, P.
    1995 *How Culture Works.* New York: Free Press. A consideration of the nature of culture.

Brown, D.
    1991 *Human Universals.* New York: McGraw-Hill. Surveys the evidence for "human nature" and explores the roles of culture and biology in human variation.

Geertz, C.
    1973 *The Interpretation of Cultures.* New York: Basic Books. Essays about culture viewed as a system of symbols and meaning.

Gupta, A., and J. Ferguson, eds.
    1997b *Culture, Power, Place: Explorations in Critical Anthropology.* Durham, NC: Duke University Press. New ways of conceiving and studying culture.

Hall, E. T.
    1990 *Understanding Cultural Differences.* Yarmouth, ME: Intercultural Press. Focusing on business and industrial management, this book examines the role of national cultural contrasts among France, Germany, and the United States.

Kroeber, A. L., and C. Kluckhohn
    1963 *Culture: A Critical Review of Concepts and Definitions.* New York: Vintage. Discusses and categorizes more than a hundred definitions of culture.

Lindholm, C.
    2001 *Culture and Identity: The History, Theory, and Practice of Psychological Anthropology.* New York: McGraw-Hill. An introduction to psychological anthropology, with special attention to the roles of culture and the individual.

Naylor, L. L.
    1996 *Culture and Change: An Introduction.* Westport, CT: Bergin and Garvey. Anthropology, culture, and change.

Ong, A., and S. J. Collier, eds.
    2005 *Global Assemblages: Technology, Politics, and Ethics as Anthropological Problems.* Malden, MA: Blackwell. This collection examines new ways of doing anthropology in a globalizing world.

Van der Elst, D., and P. Bohannan
    2003 *Culture as Given, Culture as Choice,* 2nd ed. Prospect Heights, IL: Waveland. Culture and individual choices.

Wagner, R.
    1981 *Invention of Culture,* rev. ed. Chicago: University of Chicago Press. Culture, creativity, society, and the self.

Wilson, R., ed.
    1996 *Human Rights: Culture and Context: Anthropological Perspectives.* Chicago: Pluto. Issues of cultural relativism and cross-cultural studies of human rights issues.

INTERNET EXERCISES

1. Acculturation: Go and read Cyndi Patee's article "Pidgins and Creoles," **http://logos.uoregon.edu/explore/socioling/pidgin.html**.
   a. What are pidgins and creoles? How are they examples of acculturation?
   b. What role did colonialism play in the development of pidgins and creoles?
   c. Take the quiz at the end of the page. Which sentences were easiest for you to read? Which were hardest? Look at the answers. Does the substrate language explain your ability or inability to understand?

2. The Kiss: Read Washington State University's page on "The Kiss," **http://www.wsu.edu:8001/vcwsu/commons/topics/culture/behaviors/kissing/kissing-essay.html**.
   a. Is kissing an instinctive human display of affection? Or is it learned?
   b. What is the history of the kiss?
   c. Is there a single, universal meaning for a kiss? How and why can the meanings change by culture and situation?

See Chapter 3 at your McGraw-Hill Online Learning Center for additional review and interactive exercises.

LINKAGES

Kottak, *Assault on Paradise*, 4th ed.

Culture: This text chapter has discussed levels of culture and cultural change. Compare Arembepe of the 1960s and of 2004 in terms of its residents' participation in local, national, and international cultural systems. Based on Chapter 15, would it be accurate to say that Arembepe has been more isolated from the modern world system than has the Betsileo village of Ivato in Madagascar? What were the different processes of cultural change experienced by Ivato and Arembepe?

Peters-Golden, *Culture Sketches*, 4th ed.

Aztec: Most people regard the Aztecs as part of a civilization that was lost long ago. However, in Mexico today there are indigenous social movements that seek to link the present directly with an Aztec past. In *Culture Sketches*, read Chapter 2, "The Aztec: Ancient Legacy, Modern Pride." Think about the uses and meanings of culture you've read about in this textbook. What might motivate contemporary

Nahua peoples and others in Mexico to embrace Aztec culture? What is the significance of the ways in which they have chosen to recognize the Aztec heritage? Is this phenomenon something you recognize as happening among other groups? In other nations?

Knauft, *The Gebusi*, 1st ed.

Read Chapters 1 and 7. From Chapter 1, describe the author's description of the key Gebusi concept of "good company" (*kogwayay*) with respect to Kottak's discussion of "culture." Specifically, in what ways is the Gebusi concept of "good company" (a) learned, (b) shared, (c) symbolic, (d) all-encompassing, (e) integrated, (f) adaptive or maladaptive?

In Chapter 7, in what way does the author's description of culture change suggest alterations over time in the central importance of "good company" (*kogwayay*). Discuss how this change relates to issues of diffusion, acculturation, and globalization as described at the end of Kottak's Chapter 4.

4

The Evolutionary Origins of Human Culture

EVOLUTION

The human capacity for culture has an evolutionary basis that extends back at least 2.5 million years—to early tool makers whose products survive in the archeological record (and perhaps even further back—based on the ape examples discussed in the "News Brief"). Contemporary humans have uniquely varied ways—cultural and biological—of evolving, of adapting to environmental stresses. Exemplifying cultural adaptation, we manipulate our artifacts and behavior in response to environmental conditions. We turn up thermostats or travel to Florida in the winter. We turn on fire hydrants, swim, or ride in air-conditioned cars to escape the summer's heat. Although such reliance on culture has increased in the course of human evolution, people haven't stopped adapting biologically. As in other species, human populations adapt genetically in response to environmental forces, and individuals react physiologically to stresses. Thus, when we work in the midday sun, sweating occurs spontaneously, cooling the skin and reducing the temperature of subsurface blood vessels.

OVERVIEW

The *theory* of evolution, through natural selection (*how* evolution occurred), was Charles Darwin's major contribution. When the environment changes, selection works with traits (variety) already present in the population. Humans, apes, and monkeys belong to the zoological order Primates. The African apes are our closest relatives. Monkeys, apes, and humans live in social groups and rely extensively on learning.

Early hominin remains come mainly from eastern and southern Africa. Upright bipedalism is a fundamental hominin trait that goes back more than 5 million years. By about 1.75 million years ago, the earliest member of our genus, *Homo habilis*, had evolved into *Homo erectus*, which extended the hominin range out of Africa. *H. erectus* had evolved into archaic *H. sapiens* by 300,000 years ago. Most scientists tend to exclude the Neandertals as ancestors of modern humans. Biological and cultural changes eventually led to anatomically modern humans, whose fossils in Africa date back more than 150,000 years.

This chapter begins by considering principles that determine human adaptation, variation, and change—and biological evolution in general. Next, human anatomy and behavior are compared with those of our closest relatives, other members of the zoological order Primates (see the "News Brief," for example, for behavioral abilities of orangutans). Then we turn to human evolution, the origin and spread of our remote ancestors— from our earliest and very apelike African forebears to the anatomically modern humans who were living in Africa by 150,000 years ago. The chapter concludes by considering the relation between anatomical and behavioral modernity: When, where, and how did the human capacity for modern cultural behavior emerge?

Let's begin with the basics of biological evolution. During the 18th century, scholars grew increasingly interested in biological diversity and human origins. At that time, the commonly accepted explanation for the origin of species came from Genesis, the first book of the Bible: God had created all life during six days of Creation. According to *creationism*, biological similarities and differences originated at the Creation. Characteristics of life forms were seen as immutable; they could not change. Through calculations based on genealogies in the Bible, the biblical scholars James Ussher and John Lightfoot even claimed to trace the Creation to a very specific time: October 23, 4004 B.C., at 9 A.M.

Fossil discoveries during the 18th and 19th centuries raised doubts about creationism. If all life had originated at the same time, why weren't ancient species still around? Why weren't contemporary plants and animals found in the fossil record? A modified explanation combining creationism with *catastrophism* arose to replace the original doctrine. In this view, fires, floods, and other catastrophes, including the biblical flood involving Noah's ark, had destroyed ancient species. After each destructive event, God had created again, leading to contemporary species. How did the catastrophists explain certain clear similarities between fossils and modern animals? They argued that some ancient species had managed to survive in isolated areas. For example, after the biblical flood, the progeny of the animals saved on Noah's ark spread throughout the world.

The alternative to creationism and catastrophism was *transformism*, also called **evolution.** Evolutionists believe that species arise from others through a long and gradual process of transformation, or descent with modification. Charles Darwin became the best known of the evolutionists. However, he was influenced by earlier scholars, including his own grandfather. In a book called *Zoonomia* published in 1794, Erasmus Darwin had proclaimed the common ancestry of all animal species.

A Revealing Behavior in "Orangutan Heaven and Human Hell"

NEW YORK TIMES NEWS BRIEF

by Connie Rogers
November 15, 2005

Primatologists study nonhuman primates, such as apes, monkeys, and lemurs. The study of monkeys, and particularly that of apes, is of particular interest to anthropology because their attributes and behavior can suggest things about human nature and origins. Of particular relevance to humans are two kinds of primates: (1) those that spend much of their time on the ground, including baboons, gorillas, chimpanzees, and, to some extent the orangutans described here, and (2) those that are most closely related to us: the great apes, which include the orangs (although chimps and gorillas are much closer relatives). Heralded in this "News Brief," based on a conversation with the Dutch primatologist Carel von Schaik, is his book Among Orangutans: Red Apes and the Rise of Human Culture *(Schaik 2004).*

Humans share many features of anatomy, temperament, and behavior, including the sociability described here, with our primate relatives. This news story reports on a learned ability—reliance on tools—that the great apes share with humans. The use and even the manufacture of crude tools by chimpanzees has been known for many years. Observation of tool use by gorillas and orangs is more recent. Schaik's book reports more fully on the studies described here. Knowing now that all the great apes can learn how to use tools, we can speculate that the common ancestor of apes and humans also had at least a rudimentary capacity for cultural learning.

People keep asking Carel van Schaik if there is anything left to discover in fieldwork.

"I tell them, 'A lot,'" said Dr. van Schaik, the Dutch primatologist. "Look at gorillas. We've been studying them for decades, and we just now have discovered that they use tools. The same is true for orangutans."

In 1992, when Dr. van Schaik began his research in Suaq, a swamp forest in northern Sumatra, orangutans were believed to be the only great ape that lived a largely solitary life foraging for hard-to-find fruit thinly distributed over a large area.

Researchers thought they were slow-moving creatures—some even called them boring—that didn't have time to do much but eat.

But the orangutans Dr. van Schaik found in Suaq turned all that on its head. More than 100 were gathered together doing things the researchers had never seen in the wild.

Dr. van Schaik worked there for seven years and came to the radical conclusion that orangutans were "every bit as sociable, as technically adept and as culturally capable" as chimpanzees.

His new conclusions about how apes—and humans—got to be so smart are detailed in his latest book, *Among Orangutans: Red Apes and the Rise of Human Culture.*

Now a professor of anthropology at the University of Zurich and the director of its Anthropological Institute and Museum, Dr. van Schaik discussed his findings in a recent telephone interview from his office there.

Q. What were you looking for in the Suaq swamp?

A. We'd been working in a mountainous area in northern Sumatra, and it felt as if we were missing the full picture of orangutan social organization. All higher primates—all of them—live in distinct social units except for the orangutan. That's a strong anomaly, and I wanted to solve it.

Q. How was Suaq different from other orangutan habitats?

A. It was an extraordinarily productive swamp forest with by far the highest density of orangutans—over twice the record number. The animals were the most sociable we'd ever seen: they hang out together,

they're nice to each other, they even share food.

Q. But you almost left this orangutan habitat after a year?

A. We'd never worked in a place like this, and it was exhausting. To get into the swamp where they were we would wade through water—sometimes chest deep, two hours in, two hours out every day. There were countless species of mosquitoes.

It was what I call orangutan heaven and human hell. But then someone noticed that they were poking sticks into tree holes. It sounded like tool use, so we decided to build boardwalks in the swamp, and things got a lot easier.

Q. Were orangutans using tools?

A. It turned out Suaq had an amazing repertoire of tool use. They shape sticks to get at honey and insects. Then they pick another kind of stick to go after the scrumptious fat-packed seeds of the neesia fruit. One of them figured out that you could unleash the seeds with a stick and that was a big improvement in their diet.

Lean times are rare at Suaq, not only because the forest is productive, but because the orangutans can get to

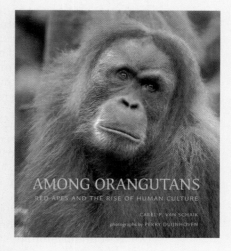

■ *The cover of Carel van Schaik's 2004 book,* Among Orangutans: Red Apes and the Rise of Human Culture, *which is described in this account.*

so much more food by using tools. So they can afford to be more sociable.

Q. How did you discover that the tool use is socially transmitted?

A. Well, one way to prove it is to see if the orangutans use tools everywhere the neesia tree exists. This was in the late 90's. Swamps were being clear-cut and drained everywhere, and the civil war in Aceh was spreading.

I felt like an anthropologist trying to document a vanishing tribe. It turned out that in the big swamps on one side of a river, the orangutans do use tools, and in the small swamp on the other side, they don't. Neesia trees and orangutans exist in both places. But the animals can't cross the river, so the knowledge hadn't spread. At that point, the penny dropped and I realized their tool use was cultural.

Q. So your discovery that the orangutans learned tool use from one another explains "the rise of human culture" part of your book's subtitle?

A. Well, yes. Orangutans split off from the African lineage some 14 million years ago. If both chimps and orangutans make tools, our common great ape ancestor probably had the capacity for culture.

Q. I always thought we got smart after we came down from the trees.

A. Actually orangutans are the largest arboreal mammal and have no predators up in the trees so they live a very long time—up to 60 years in the wild—and have the slowest life history of any nonhuman mammal including elephants and whales.

A slow life history is key to growing a large brain. The other key to intelligence is sociability.

Q. Were orangutans more social in the past?

A. I guess the rich forest areas that allowed them to live in groups were much more common in the past— they're the ones that are best for rice growing and farming—but there's no way of knowing for sure . . .

Q. You end your book with a bleak picture of the future of orangutans because of habitat conversion and illegal logging. Since then there's been a devastating tsunami and people need to cut down even more trees to put roofs over their heads. What does the future look like now?

A. One way to help people in Sumatra would be to donate wood on a large scale. But things may be better in Borneo.

There's a new Indonesian president, and in the last few months it looks as if the government is serious about cracking down on illegal logging. That leaves me more hopeful.

SOURCE: Connie Rogers, "Revealing Behavior in 'Orangutan Heaven and Human Hell': A Conversation with Carel van Schaik," *New York Times*, November 15, 2005, p. F2.

Charles Darwin also was influenced by Sir Charles Lyell, the father of geology. During Darwin's famous voyage to South America aboard the *Beagle,* he read Lyell's influential book *Principles of Geology* (1837/1969), which exposed him to Lyell's principle of **uniformitarianism,** which states that the present is the key to the past. Explanations for past events should be sought in the long-term action of ordinary forces that still operate today. Thus, natural forces (rainfall, soil deposition, earthquakes, and volcanic action) gradually have built and modified geological features such as mountain ranges. The earth's structure has been transformed gradually through natural forces operating for millions of years (see Weiner 1994).

Uniformitarianism was a necessary building block for evolutionary theory. It cast serious doubt on the belief that the world was only 6,000 years old. It would take much longer for such ordinary forces as rain and wind to produce major geological changes. The longer time span also allowed enough time for the biological changes that fossil discoveries were revealing. Darwin applied the ideas of uniformitarianism and long-term transformation to living things. He argued that all life forms are ultimately related and that the number of species has increased over time. (For more on science, evolution, and creationism, see Futuyma 1995; Gould 1999; Wilson 2002.)

Theory and Fact

Charles Darwin provided a theoretical framework for understanding evolution. He offered natural selection as a powerful evolutionary mechanism that could explain the origin of species, biological diversity, and similarities among related life forms. Darwin proposed a *theory of evolution* in the strict sense. A **theory** is a set of ideas formulated (by reasoning from known facts) to explain something. The main value of a theory is to promote new understanding. A theory suggests patterns, connections, and relationships that may be confirmed by new research. The *fact* of evolution (that evolution has occurred) was known earlier, for example by Erasmus Darwin. The *theory* of evolution, through natural selection (*how* evolution occurred), was Darwin's major contribution. But even natural selection wasn't a unique discovery of Darwin alone. Working independently, the naturalist Alfred Russel Wallace had reached a similar conclusion (Shermer 2002). In a joint paper read to London's Linnaean Society in 1858, Darwin and Wallace made their discovery public. Darwin's book *On the Origin of Species* (1859/1958) offered much fuller documentation.

Natural selection is the process by which the forms most fit to survive and reproduce in a given environment do so in greater numbers than others in the same population. Natural selection represents differential reproductive success. Natural selection operates when there is competition for strategic resources (those necessary for life) such as food and space between members of the population. There is also the matter of finding mates. You can win the competition for food and space and have no mate, and thus have no impact on the future of the species. For natural selection to work on a particular population, there must be variety within that population, as there always is.

The giraffe's neck can illustrate how natural selection works on variety within a population. In any group of giraffes, there is always variation in neck length. When food is adequate, the animals have no problem feeding themselves. But when there is pressure on strategic resources, so that dietary foliage is not as abundant as usual, giraffes with longer necks have an advantage. They can feed off the higher branches. If this feeding advantage permits longer-necked giraffes to survive and reproduce even slightly more effectively than shorter-necked ones, giraffes with longer necks will transmit more of their genetic material to future generations than will giraffes with shorter necks.

Natural selection requires variety in the population undergoing selection. Documenting and explaining such variety among humans—human biological diversity—is one of anthropology's major concerns. Scientists have learned much about **mutations**—changes in the DNA molecules of which genetic units, genes and chromosomes, are built. Evolution depends on mutations as a major source of genetically transmitted variety, raw material on which natural selection can work. Alterations in genes and chromosomes may result in entirely new types of organisms, which may demonstrate some new selective advantage. Variants produced through mutation can be especially significant if there is a change in the environment. They may prove to have an adaptive advantage they lacked in the old environment.

One classic recent example is the peppered moth, which can be light or dark (in either case with black speckles, thus the name "peppered"). A change in this species illustrates recent natural selection (in our own industrial age) through what has been called *industrial melanism*. Great Britain's industrialization changed the environment to favor darker moths (those with more melanin) rather than the lighter-colored ones that were favored previously. During the 1800s industrial pollution increased; soot coated buildings and trees, turning them a darker color. The previously typical peppered moth, which had a light color, now stood out against the dark backgrounds of sooty buildings and trees. Such light-colored moths were easily visible to their predators. Through mutations, a new strain of peppered moth, with a darker phenotype, was

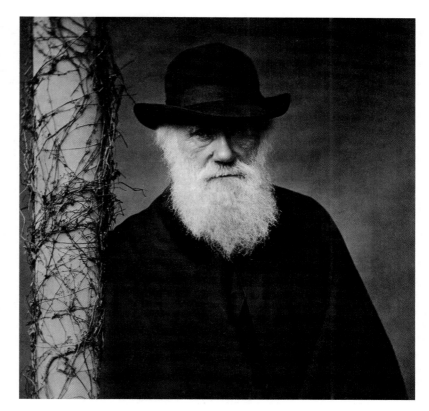

■ *Charles Darwin at his home at Down House, Kent, England, around 1880.*

favored. Because these darker moths were fitter—that is, harder to detect—in polluted environments, they survived and reproduced in greater numbers than lighter moths did. We see how natural selection may favor darker moths in polluted environments and lighter-colored moths in nonindustrial or less polluted environments because of their variant abilities to merge in with their environmental colors and thus avoid predators.

Evolutionary theory is useful because it provides explanations. Remember from Chapter 1 that the goal of science is to increase understanding through explanation: showing how and why the thing (or class of things) to be understood (e.g., the variation within species, the geographic distribution of species, the fossil record) depends on other things. Explanations rely on associations and theories. An association is an observed relationship between two or more variables, such as the length of a giraffe's neck and the number of its offspring, or an increase in the frequency of dark moths as industrial pollution spreads. A theory is more general, suggesting or implying associations and attempting to explain them. A thing or event, for example, the giraffe's long neck, is explained if it illustrates a general principle or association, such as the concept of adaptive advantage. The truth of a scientific statement (e.g., evolution occurs because of differential reproductive success due to variation within the population) is confirmed by repeated observations.

For information on common misconceptions about evolution, see the Internet Exercises at your OLC

mhhe.com/kottak

OUR PLACE AMONG PRIMATES

Our nearest relatives (animals with which we share common ancestry) are other members of the zoological order known as Primates, which includes humans, apes, monkeys, and lemurs. Apes are our closest relatives. Similarities between apes and humans are evident in anatomy, brain structure, genetics, and biochemistry. These similarities are recognized in zoological **taxonomy**—the assignment of organisms to categories (*taxa;* singular, *taxon*) according to their relationship and resemblance. Many similarities between organisms reflect their common *phylogeny*—their genetic relatedness based on common ancestry. In other words, organisms share features they have inherited from the same ancestor. Apes and humans belong to the same taxonomic superfamily, *Hominoidea* (hominoids). Monkeys are placed in two others. Apes and humans are more closely related to each other than either is to monkeys. Most closely related to humans are the African great apes: chimpanzees and gorillas. A more distant relative is Asia's great ape, the orangutan, which survives on two Indonesian islands. Gibbons and siamangs are smaller and more widespread Asian apes.

Figure 4.1 summarizes the various levels of classification used in zoological taxonomy. Each lower-level unit belongs to the higher-level unit above it. Thus, looking toward the bottom of Figure 4.1, similar species belong to the same genus (plural, *genera*). Similar genera make up the same tribe, and so on through the top of Figure 4.1. The lowest-level taxa are species and subspecies. A *species* is a group of organisms that can mate and give birth to *viable* (capable of living) and *fertile* (capable of reproducing) offspring whose own offspring are viable and fertile. *Speciation* (the formation of a new species) occurs when groups that once belonged to the same species can no longer interbreed. After a sufficiently long period of reproductive isolation, two closely related species assigned to the same genus will have evolved out of one.

The similarities used to assign organisms to the same taxon are called *homologies*, similarities they have jointly inherited from a common ancestor. We see in Table 4.1 that humans are mammals that, at a lower taxonomic level, belong to the *order* Primates. The primates share structural and biochemical homologies that distinguish them from other mammals. These resemblances were inherited from their common early primate ancestors after those early primates became reproductively isolated from the ancestors of the other mammals.

Hominidae is the zoological family that includes fossil and living humans. Also included as **hominids** are chimps and gorillas, which share a more recent ancestor with humans than they do with the orangutan. The African apes used to be assigned to the family *Pongidae* (pongids), along with Asia's orangutan. But the DNA evidence is overwhelming that chimps and gorillas are much closer to humans than to orangs, so they belong in *Hominidae*. This leaves the orangutan (genus *Pongo*) as the only member of the pongid family. What do we call the group that leads to humans but not to chimps and gorillas? A taxonomic level called *tribe* lies between family and genus. The tribe *hominini* (**hominins**) describes all the human species that ever have existed (including the extinct ones) and excludes chimps and gorillas. When scientists use the word *hominin* today, they mean pretty much the same thing as when they used the word *hominid* 20 years ago—before chimps and gorillas were included in the hominid family.

Primate Tendencies

Many trends in primate evolution are best exemplified by the **anthropoid primates:** monkeys, apes, and humans. (Anthropoids are distinguished from prosimians, such as lemurs.)

Grasping

Primates have five-digited hands that are suited for grasping. Flexible hands and feet that could encircle branches were important features in the early primates' arboreal life. Manual dexterity makes it easier to catch insects attracted to abundant arboreal flowers and fruits. Humans and many other primates have *opposable thumbs:* The thumb can touch the other fingers. Some primates

See the Virtual Exploration
mhhe.com/kottak

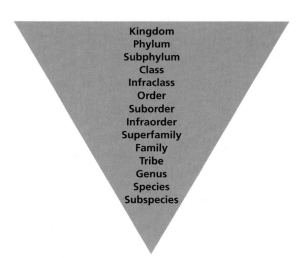

FIGURE 4.1 The Principal Classificatory Units of Zoological Taxonomy.

Moving down the figure, the classificatory units become more exclusive, so that "Kingdom" at the top is the most inclusive unit and "Subspecies" at the bottom is the most exclusive.

Kingdom
Phylum
Subphylum
Class
Infraclass
Order
Suborder
Infraorder
Superfamily
Family
Tribe
Genus
Species
Subspecies

TABLE 4.1 The Place of Humans (*Homo sapiens*) in Zoological Taxonomy

Homo sapiens is an Animal, Chordate, Vertebrate, Mammal, Primate, Anthropoid, Catarrhine, Hominoid, Hominid, and Hominin.

Taxon	Scientific (Latin) Name	Common (English) Name
Kingdom	Animalia	Animals
Phylum	Chordata	Chordates
Subphylum	Vertebrata	Vertebrates
Class	Mammalia	Mammals
Infraclass	Eutheria	Eutherians
Order	Primates	Primates
Suborder	Anthropoidea	Anthropoids
Infraorder	Catarrhini	Catarrhines
Superfamily	Hominoidea	Hominoids
Family	Hominidae	Hominids
Tribe	Hominini	Hominins
Genus	*Homo*	Humans
Species	*Homo sapiens*	Recent humans
Subspecies	*Homo sapiens sapiens*	Anatomically modern humans

also have grasping feet. However, in adapting to bipedal (two-footed) locomotion, the human line eliminated most of the foot's grasping ability.

Smell to Sight

For primates, sight is a key means of obtaining information. Monkeys, apes, and humans have excellent *stereoscopic* (able to see in depth) and color vision. The portion of the brain devoted to vision expanded, and the area concerned with smell shrank, in primate evolution. With reduction of the snout, anthropoid eyes are placed forward in the skull and look directly ahead. The fields of vision of the eyes overlap. Depth perception, impossible without overlapping visual fields, proved adaptive in the trees. Tree-dwelling primates that could judge distance better survived and reproduced in greater numbers than did those that could not. The abilities to see in depth and in color may have developed together. Both helped early anthropoids interpret their arboreal world. Superior vision made it easier to distinguish edible insects, fruits, berries, and leaves. Furthermore, having color and depth vision makes it easier to groom—to remove burrs, insects, and other small objects from other primates' hair. Grooming is one way of forming and maintaining social bonds.

Primates have five-digited feet and hands, well suited for grasping. Flexible hands and feet that could encircle branches were important features in the early primates' arboreal life. In adapting to bipedal (two-footed) locomotion, hominids eliminated most of the foot's grasping ability—illustrated here by the chimpanzee.

Think about our senses—vision, hearing, touch, smell, and taste. Where have we suffered sensory loss during our evolutionary history? Like almost all the anthropoids, humans are diurnal, active during the day. If we were night animals, we'd sense things differently. Maybe our eyes would be bigger, like those of an owl or a tarsier. Maybe we'd have biological radar systems, as bats do. Perhaps we'd develop a more acute sense of hearing or smell to penetrate the shield of the dark. As animals, humans are programmed to rise at dawn and to sleep when the sun disappears. As cultural creatures, we venture into the night with torches, lanterns, and flashlights, and we shut the dark out of our dwellings by using artificial light.

Which is most debilitating—loss of vision, hearing, or smell? Among our senses, we seem to value hearing, and above all vision, most. The anthropoids as a group are preeminently visual animals. Whole industries exist to improve our sight and hearing. But how often do you hear of a product designed to improve your ability to smell, taste, or touch things? Other animals can detect all kinds of scents and odors that help them interpret the world. Humans, by contrast, use an array of products designed *not* to improve our sense of smell, but to eliminate even the faint odors our limited olfactory apparatus permits us to smell. *Blindness* and *deafness* are common words that indicate the senses whose loss we deem most significant. The rarity of the word *anosmia,* the inability to smell, tells us something about our senses and our values. The sensory shifts that occurred in primate evolution, especially the one from smell to sight, explain something fundamental about ourselves.

Nose to Hand

Sensations of touch, conveyed by *tactile organs,* also provide information. The tactile skin on a dog's or cat's nose transmits information. Cats' tactile hairs, or whiskers, also serve this function. In primates, however, the main touch organ is the hand, specifically the sensitive pads of the "fingerprint" region. Visual and tactile changes have been interrelated. Forward placement of the eyes and depth vision allow anthropoids to pick up small objects, hold them in front of their eyes, and appraise them. Our ability to thread a needle reflects an intricate interplay of hands and eyes that took millions of years to achieve. Manual dexterity, including the opposable thumb, confers a tremendous advantage in examining and manipulating objects and is essential to a major human adaptive capacity: tool making.

Brain Complexity

The primate ratio of brain size to body size exceeds that of most mammals. Even more important, the brain's outer layer—concerned with memory, association, and integration—is relatively larger. Monkeys, apes, and humans store an array of images in their memories, which permits them to learn more. The ability to learn from experience and from other group members is a major reason for the success of the anthropoids compared to most other mammals.

Parental Investment

Most primates give birth to a single offspring rather than a litter. Because of this, growing primates receive more attention and have more learning opportunities than do other mammals. Learned behavior is an important part of primate adaptation.

Sociality

Primates tend to be social animals that live with others of their species. The need for longer and more attentive care of offspring places a selective value on support by a social group.

Humans and Apes

The so-called great apes are orangutans (large Asiatic apes), gorillas, and chimpanzees. Humans are sometimes called "the third African ape" (along with chimps and gorillas). Although apes live in forests and woodlands, gorillas, chimpanzees, and adult male orangutans spend considerable time on the ground. Nevertheless, ape behavior and anatomy reveal past and present adaptation to arboreal life. For example, apes still build nests to sleep in trees. The structure of the shoulder and clavicle (collarbone) of the apes and humans suggests that we had a brachiating ancestor. *Brachiation* refers to under-the-branch swinging. While most monkeys run and jump from branch to branch, gibbons (small Asiatic apes) and some New World monkeys swing through the trees, using their hands as hooks. Hand over hand, they move from branch to branch, propelled onward by the thrust of their bodies. Young apes still do brachiate. Adult apes tend to be too heavy to brachiate safely. Gorillas and chimps now use the long arms they have inherited from their more arboreal ancestors for life on the ground. The terrestrial locomotion of chimps and gorillas is called *knuckle-walking.* In it, long arms and callused knuckles support the trunk as the apes amble around, leaning forward.

The terrestrial locomotion of chimps and gorillas is called knuckle-walking. In it, long arms and callused knuckles support the trunk as the apes amble around, leaning forward, like this western lowland gorilla male at Washington's National Zoo.

WHAT WE SHARE WITH OTHER PRIMATES

There is a substantial gap between primate society and fully developed human culture. However, studies of primates have revealed many similarities. Scholars used to contend that learned (versus instinctive) behavior separates humans from other animals. We know now that monkeys and apes also rely on learning. Many of the differences between humans and other primates are differences in degree rather than in kind. For example, monkeys learn from experiences, but humans learn much more. Another example: Chimpanzees and orangutans make tools for specific tasks (see Mayell 2003), but human reliance on tools is much greater.

Learning

Common to monkeys, apes, and humans is the fact that behavior and social life are not rigidly programmed by the genes. All these animals learn throughout their lives. In several cases, an entire monkey troop has learned from the experiences of some of its members. In one group of Japanese macaques, a three-year-old female monkey started washing dirt off sweet potatoes before she ate them. First her mother, then her age peers, and finally the entire troop began washing sweet pota-

toes, too. The direction of learning was reversed when members of another macaque troop learned to eat wheat. After the dominant males had tried the new food, within four hours the practice had spread throughout the troop. Changes in learned behavior seem to spread more quickly from the top down than from the bottom up.

For monkeys as for people, the ability to learn, to profit from experience, confers a tremendous adaptive advantage, permitting them to avoid fatal mistakes. Faced with environmental change, primates don't have to wait for a genetic or physiological response. Learned behavior and social patterns can be modified instead.

Tools

Anthropologists once distinguished humans from other animals as tool users. Without doubt, *Homo* does employ tools much more than any other animal does. However, tool use also turns up among several nonhuman species. For example, in the Galápagos Islands off western South America, there is a "woodpecker finch" that selects twigs to dig out insects and grubs from tree bark. Sea otters use rocks to break open mollusks. Beavers are famous for dam construction.

When it became obvious that people weren't the only tool users, anthropologists started contending that only humans make tools with foresight, that is,

Compare the human and the gorilla. What similarities do you notice? What differences? Humans, gorillas, and chimps have more than 98 percent of their DNA in common.

with a specific purpose in mind. Chimpanzees show that this, too, is debatable. Chimps living in the Tai forest of Ivory Coast make and use stone tools to break open hard, golfball-sized nuts (Mercader, Panger, and Boesch 2002). At specific sites, the chimps gather nuts, place them on stumps or flat rocks, which are used as anvils, and pound the nuts with heavy stones. Breaking open the nuts requires considerable force, which must be managed carefully. When too much force is applied, the nuts shatter into inedible pieces. The chimps also must select hammer stones suited to smashing the nuts and carry them to where the nut trees grow—sophisticated behavior for an animal. Nut cracking is a learned skill, with mothers showing their young how to do it.

In 1960, Jane Goodall (1996) began observing wild chimps—including their tool use and hunting behavior—at Gombe Stream National Park in Tanzania, East Africa. From the work of Goodall and many other researchers we know that wild chimps regularly make tools. To get water from places their mouths can't reach, thirsty chimps pick leaves, chew and crumple them, and then dip them into the water. Thus, with a specific purpose in mind, they devise primitive "sponges."

The most studied form of ape tool making involves "termiting." Chimps make tools to probe termite hills. They choose twigs, which they modify by removing leaves and peeling off bark to expose the sticky surface beneath. They carry the twigs to termite hills, dig holes with their fingers, and insert the twigs. Finally, they pull out the twigs and dine on termites that were attracted to the sticky surface.

Termiting isn't as easy as it might seem. Learning to termite takes time, and many Gombe chimps never master it. Twigs with certain characteristics must be chosen. Furthermore, once the twig is in the hill and the chimp judges that termites are crawling on its surface, the chimp must quickly flip the twig as it pulls it out so that the termites are on top. Otherwise they fall off as the twig comes out of the hole. This is an elaborate skill that neither all chimps nor all human observers have been able to master.

Chimps have other abilities essential to culture. When they are trained by humans, their skills flower, as anyone who has ever seen a movie, circus, or zoo chimp knows. Wild chimps and orangs aim and throw objects. The gorilla, our other nearest relative, lacks the chimp's proclivity for tool making. However, gorillas do build nests, and they throw branches, grass, vines, and other objects. Hominids have considerably elaborated the capacity to aim and throw, which is a homology passed down from the common ancestor of humans and apes. Without it we never would have developed projectile technology and weaponry—or baseball.

Predation and Hunting

Like tool making and language, hunting has been cited as a distinctive human activity that is not shared with the apes. Again, however, primate research shows that what previously was thought to be a difference of kind is a difference of degree. The diets of other terrestrial primates are not exclusively vegetarian, as once was thought. Baboons kill and eat young antelopes, and researchers have repeatedly observed hunting by chimpanzees.

For several years John Mitani, David Watts, and other researchers have been observing chimpanzees at Ngogo in Uganda's Kibale National Park. This is the largest chimp community ever described in the wild. In 1998 it consisted of 26 adult males, 40 adult females, 16 adolescent males, 5 adolescent females, and 30 infants and juveniles (Mitani and Watts 1999). (Chimp communities have a more stable male than female core membership—adolescent males tend to stay on while adolescent females tend to leave to join other troops.)

The large community size permits the formation of large hunting parties, including an average of 26 individuals (almost always adult and adolescent males). Most hunts (78 percent) resulted in at least one prey item being caught—a much higher success rate than that among lions (26 percent), hyenas (34 percent), or cheetahs (30 percent). In most hunts (81 percent) the Ngogo chimps managed to catch multiple prey animals (three on average). The favored prey, at Ngogo as in other chimp communities, was the red colobus monkey.

As described by Mitani and Watts (1999), hunting by chimps is both opportunistic and planned.

Opportunistic hunting took place when chimps encountered potential prey as they moved about during the day. Other hunts were organized patrols, in which the chimps became silent and moved together in a single file. They would stop, look up into the trees, scan, and change direction several times. Attentive to any arboreal movement, they would stop and search whenever they detected motion. After they spotted a monkey, the chase would begin. Encountering no prey, the chimps would go on patrolling, sometimes for several hours. The Ngogo chimps also collaborate by encircling red colobus groups, blocking potential escape routes, and driving their prey down hill slopes from taller to shorter trees.

Chimps can consume a quarter pound of meat a day when they hit their hunting stride. This meat intake is comparable to that of some human hunter-gatherers (see Kopytoff 1995; Stanford 1999; Stanford and Bunn, eds. 2001). In 1992 the Japanese zoologist Toshisada Nichida described how, in Tanzania's Mahale Mountains, a high-ranking chimp male gave out pieces of meat to allies, while denying them to his enemies (Kopytoff 1995). Craig Stanford observed a similar use of meat to cement alliances at Gombe. Archeological evidence indicates that humans hunted by at least 2.5 million years ago, based on stone meat-cutting tools found at Olduvai Gorge in Tanzania. Given our current understanding of chimp hunting and tool making, we can infer that hominids may have been hunting much earlier than the first archaeological evidence attests. Since chimps seem to devour the monkeys they kill, leaving few remains after their meal, we may never find archaeological evidence for the first hominid hunt, especially if it was done without stone tools.

HOW WE DIFFER FROM OTHER PRIMATES

The preceding sections emphasize similarities between humans and other primates. *Homo* has elaborated substantially on certain tendencies shared with the apes. A unique concentration and combination of characteristics make humans distinct. However, the savanna, or open grassland, niche in which early humans evolved also selected certain traits that are not foreshadowed so clearly by the apes.

Sharing and Cooperation

Early humans lived in small social groups called bands, with economies based on hunting and gathering (foraging). Until fairly recently (12,000 to 10,000 years ago), all humans based their subsistence on foraging and lived in bands. Some such societies even managed to survive into the

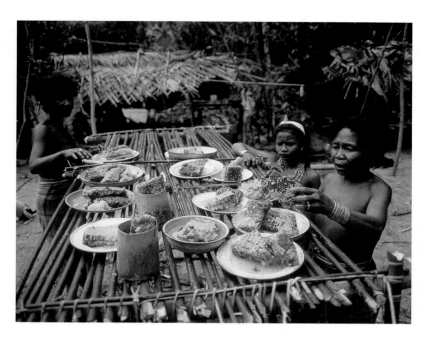

■ *Through millions of years of adaptation to an omnivorous diet, humans and their ancestors have relied on gathering, hunting, and food sharing. These three Batak women from Palawan Island, the Philippines, share wild honeycombs.*

modern world, and ethnographers have studied them. From those studies we can conclude that in such societies, the strongest and most aggressive members do not dominate, as they do in a troop of terrestrial monkeys.

Humans appear to be the most cooperative of the primates—in the food quest and other social activities. Except for meat sharing by chimps, the ape tendency is to forage individually. Monkeys also fend for themselves in getting food. Among human foragers, men and women bring resources back to the camp and share them. Older people who did not engage in the food quest get food from younger adults. Everyone shares the meat from a large animal. Nourished and protected by younger band members, elders live past reproductive age and are respected for their knowledge and experience. The amount of information stored in a human band is far greater than that in any other primate group. Through millions of years of adaptation to an omnivorous diet, hominids have come to rely, more than any other primate, on hunting, food sharing, and cooperative behavior. These are universal features in human adaptive strategies.

Mating and Kinship

Another difference between humans and other primates involves mating. Among baboons and chimps, most mating occurs when females enter estrus, during which they ovulate. Receptive females form temporary bonds with, and mate with, males. Human females, by contrast, lack a visible estrus cycle, and their ovulation is concealed. Neither a woman's sexual receptivity nor her readiness to conceive is physically evident, as it is in chimps. Not knowing when ovulation is occurring, humans maximize their reproductive success by mating throughout the year. Human pair bonds for mating tend to be more exclusive and more durable than are those of chimps. Related to our more constant sexuality, all human societies have some form of marriage. Marriage gives mating a reliable basis and grants to each spouse special, though not always exclusive, sexual rights in the other.

Marriage creates another major contrast between humans and nonhumans: exogamy and kinship systems. Most cultures have rules of exogamy requiring marriage outside one's kin or local group. Coupled with the recognition of kinship, exogamy confers adaptive advantages. It creates ties between the spouses' groups of origin. Their children have relatives, and therefore allies, in two kin groups rather than just one. The key point here is that ties of affection and mutual support between members of different local groups tend to be absent among primates other than *Homo*. There is a tendency among primates to disperse at adolescence. Among chimps and gorillas, females tend to migrate, seeking mates in other groups.

Among terrestrial monkeys, males leave the troop at puberty, eventually finding places elsewhere. The troop's core members are females. This dispersal of males reduces the incidence of incestuous matings. Females mate with males born elsewhere, which join the troop at adolescence. Although kin ties are maintained between female monkeys, no close lifelong links are preserved through males.

Humans choose mates from outside the natal group, and usually at least one spouse moves. However, *humans maintain lifelong ties with sons and daughters.* The systems of kinship and marriage that preserve these links provide a major contrast between humans and other primates.

 STUDENT CD-ROM LIVING ANTHROPOLOGY

Lucy
Track 4

This clip describes the discovery and characteristics of Lucy, the first member of *Australopithecus afarensis* to enter the fossil record. On her discovery in 1974, Lucy became the most ancient hominin and hominid in the fossil record at that time. Today that record includes several older probable or possible hominin ancestors, identified as such— like Lucy—by their upright bipedalism. The clip supplies answers to the following questions: Which of Lucy's anatomical traits were similar to those of chimpanzees? Which were similar to those of modern humans? How did Lucy's pelvis differ from an ape's pelvis? What is the explanation for this difference?

FOSSIL EVIDENCE FOR HUMANITY

DNA and fossil evidence suggests that the diversification into ancestral gorillas, chimps, and hominins began no more than 8 million years ago. Significant recent hominid or hominin discoveries have been made in Africa—Kenya, Tanzania, Ethiopia, and Chad. A skull found in 2001 in northern Chad, dated at 6–7 **m.y.a.** (million years ago), officially named *Sahelanthropus tchadensis,* more commonly called "Toumai," may or may not be the earliest hominin yet known, as may the somewhat less ancient *Orrorin tugenensis,* found in Kenya in 2001. Early hominins assigned to *Ardipithecus kadabba* lived in Africa (Ethiopia) between 5.8 and 5.5 million years ago. *Ardipithecus* was apelike in size, anatomy, and habitat. It lived in a wooded area rather than the open grassland or savanna habitat where later hominins proliferated. As of this writing, because of its probable bipedalism, *Ardipithecus kadabba* is recognized as the earliest known hominin.

In trying to determine whether a fossil is a human ancestor, should we look for traits that make us human today? Sometimes yes; sometimes no. We would look for similarities in DNA, including mutations shared by certain lineages but not others. But what about such key human attributes as bipedal locomotion, a long period of childhood dependency, big brains, and the use of tools and language? Some of these markers of humanity are fairly recent—or have origins that are impossible to date. And ironically, some of the physical markers that have led scientists to identify certain fossils as early hominins rather than apes are features that have been lost during subsequent human evolution.

Bipedalism

Fossils of *Ardipithecus,* as mentioned previously, suggest a capacity for upright bipedal locomotion by 5.8 m.y.a. (million years ago). Indeed, it was the shift toward this form of moving around that led to the distinctive hominin way of life. **Bipedalism**—upright two-legged locomotion—is the key feature differentiating early hominins from the apes. Hominin bipedalism is more than 5 million years old.

Bipedalism is considered to be an adaptation to an open grassland or savanna habitat. Scientists have suggested several advantages of bipedalism in such an environment: the ability to see over long grass, to carry items back to a home base, and to reduce the body's exposure to solar radiation. The fossil and archaeological records confirm that upright bipedal locomotion preceded stone tool manufacture and the expansion of the hominin brain. However, although the earliest hominins could move bipedally through open country during the day, they also preserved enough of an apelike anatomy to make them good climbers. They could take to the trees to sleep at night and to escape terrestrial predators.

One explanation for bipedalism centers on environmental changes that swept Africa between 8 and 5 m.y.a. As the global climate became cooler and drier, grasslands expanded in sub-Saharan Africa. The rain forests contracted, shrinking the habitat available to arboreal primates (Wilford 1995). Also, at about the same time, a geological shift deepened the Rift Valley, which runs through Ethiopia, Kenya, and Tanzania. The sinking of the valley thrust up mountains. This left the land west of the valley more humid and forested, while the east became more arid and dominated by savanna. The common ancestors of chimpanzees and hominins were divided as a result. Those adapting to the humid west became the chimpanzee family. Those in the east had to forge a new life in an open environment (Coppens 1994).

Ancestral hominins ventured more and more into open country seeking food, but retreating to the trees to escape predators and to sleep at night. Those primates increasingly stood and walked on two legs, perhaps as they kept a lookout above the grasses for food or predators. Presumably, this adaptation enhanced their chances of surviving and passing on genes that favored this stance and gait, leading eventually to bipedal hominins (Wilford 1995).

Yet another factor may have contributed to bipedalism. Early hominins might have found the intense tropical heat of the savanna very stressful. Most savanna-dwelling animals have built-in ways of protecting their brains from overheating as their body temperatures rise during the day. This isn't true of humans, nor is it likely to have been true of early hominins. The only way we can protect our brains is by keeping our bodies cool. Could it be that early hominins stood up to cool off? Studies with scale models of primates suggest that quadrupedalism exposes the body to 60 percent more solar radiation than does bipedalism. And the upright body also could catch the cooler breeze above the ground (Wilford 1995).

Brains, Skulls, and Childhood Dependency

Compared with contemporary humans, early hominins had very small brains. *Australopithecus afarensis,* a bipedal hominin that lived more than three million years ago, had a cranial capacity (430 cm^3—cubic centimeters) that barely surpassed the chimp average (390 cm^3). The form of the *afarensis* skull also is like that of the chim-

panzee, although the brain-to-body size ratio may have been larger. Brain size has increased during hominin evolution, especially with the advent of the genus *Homo.* But this increase had to overcome some obstacles.

Compared with the young of other primates, humans have a long period of childhood dependency, during which their brains and skulls grow dramatically. Larger skulls demand larger birth canals, but the requirements of upright bipedalism impose limits on the expansion of the human pelvic opening. If the opening is too large, the pelvis doesn't provide sufficient support for the trunk. Locomotion suffers, and posture problems develop. If, by contrast, the birth canal is too narrow, mother and child (without the modern option of Caesarean section) may die in childbirth. Natural selection has struck a balance between the structural demands of upright posture and the tendency toward increased brain size—the birth of immature and dependent children whose brains and skulls grow dramatically after birth.

Tool Making

Given what is known about ape tool use and manufacture, it is almost certain that early hominins shared this ability, although the first evidence for hominin stone tool making dates back only 2.5 million years. Upright bipedalism would have permitted the use of tools and weapons against predators and competitors in an open grassland habitat. Bipedal locomotion also allowed early hominins to carry things, perhaps including scavenged parts of carnivore kills. We know that primates have generalized abilities to adapt through learning. It would be amazing if early hominins, who are much more closely related to us than the apes are, didn't have even greater cultural abilities than contemporary apes have.

Teeth

One example of an early hominin trait that has been lost during subsequent human evolution is big back teeth. (Indeed a pattern of overall dental reduction has characterized human evolution.) As they adapted to the savanna, with its gritty, tough, and fibrous vegetation, it was adaptively advantageous for early hominins to have large back teeth and thick tooth enamel. This permitted thorough chewing of tough fibrous vegetation and mixture with salivary enzymes to permit digestion of foods that otherwise would not have been digestible. The churning, rotary motion associated with such chewing also favored reduction of the canines and first premolars (bicuspids). These front teeth are sharper and longer in

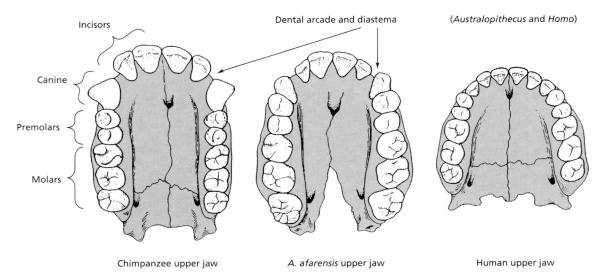

APE   A. afarensis   HOMININ
                                    (*Australopithecus* and *Homo*)

Incisors
                        Dental arcade and diastema
Canine

Premolars

Molars

Chimpanzee upper jaw   *A. afarensis* upper jaw   Human upper jaw

FIGURE 4.2   Comparison of Dentition in Ape, Human, and *A. afarensis* Palates.   SOURCE: © 1981 Luba Dmytryk Gudz/Brill Atlanta.

the apes than in early hominins (Figure 4.2). The apes use their sharp self-honing teeth to pierce fruits. Males also flash their canines to intimidate and impress others, including potential mates. Although bipedalism seems to have characterized the human lineage since it split from the line leading to the African apes, many other "human" features came later. Yet other early hominin features, such as large back teeth and thick enamel—which we don't have now—offer clues about who was a human ancestor back then.

THE EARLIEST HOMININS

Map Atlas

Map 4 shows the sites where the earliest hominid fossils have been found, along with a timeline for hominid evolution.

Early hominin evolution eventually produced a varied group known as the *australopithecines*—for which we have an abundant fossil record. This term reflects their one-time classification as members of a distinct taxonomic subfamily, the "Australopithecinae." We know now that the several species of *Australopithecus* don't form a distinct subfamily within the order Primates, but the name "australopithecine" has stuck to describe them anyway. Today the distinction between the **australopithecines** and later hominins is made on the genus level. The australopithecines are assigned to the genus *Australopithecus (A.)*; later humans, to *Homo (H.)*.

See the Internet Exercises at your OLC

mhhe.com/kottak

THE VARIED AUSTRALOPITHECINES

In the scheme followed here, *Australopithecus* had at least six species:

1. *A. anamensis* (4.2 to 3.9 m.y.a.)
2. *A. afarensis* (3.8? to 3.0 m.y.a.)
3. *A. africanus* (3.0? to 2.0? m.y.a.)
4. *A. garhi* (2.5 m.y.a.)
5. *A. robustus* (2.0? to 1.0? m.y.a.)
6. *A. boisei* (2.6? to 1.0 m.y.a.)

Remains of *A. anamensis*, a bipedal hominin, have been found at two sites in northern Kenya: Kanapoi and Allia Bay. The Kanapoi fossils date to 4.2 m.y.a., and those at Allia Bay to 3.9 m.y.a. The molars have thick enamel, and the apelike canines are large. Weighing about 110 pounds (50 kg) *A. anamensis* would have been larger than either the earlier *Ardipithecus* or the later *A. afarensis*. Because of its date and its location in the East African Rift valley, *A. anamensis* may be ancestral to *A. afarensis* (3.8–3.0 m.y.a.), which usually is considered ancestral to all the later australopithecines (*garhi, africanus, robustus,* and *boisei*) as well as to *Homo* (Figure 4.3).

Australopithecus afarensis

A. afarensis includes fossils found at two sites, Laetoli in northern Tanzania and Hadar in the Afar region of Ethiopia. Laetoli is earlier (3.8 to 3.6 m.y.a.). The Hadar fossils date to between 3.3 and 3.0 m.y.a. The Laetoli remains are mainly teeth and jaw fragments, along with some very informative fossilized footprints. The Hadar sample includes, most notably, 40 percent of the complete skeleton of a tiny female, dubbed "Lucy," who lived around 3 m.y.a. The many apelike features of *A. afarensis* are surprising in definite hominins that lived as recently as 3 m.y.a.

An ancient trail of hominin footprints fossilized in volcanic ash. Mary Leakey found this 230-feet (70-meter) trail at Laetoli, Tanzania, in 1979. It dates from 3.6 m.y.a. and confirms that A. afarensis was a striding biped.

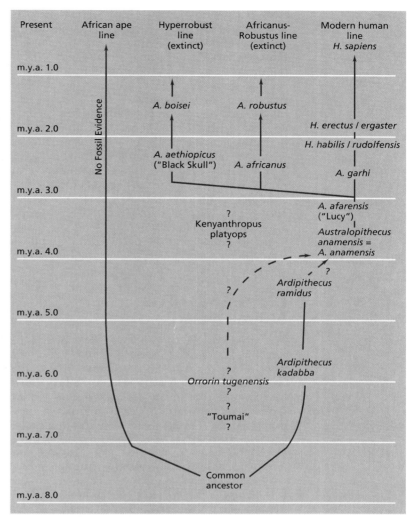

FIGURE 4.3 Phylogenetic Tree for African Apes, Hominids, and Hominins.

The presumed divergence date for ancestral chimps and hominins was between 8 and 6 m.y.a. Branching in later hominin evolution is also shown. For more exact dates, see the text and Table 4.1.

Discussion of hominin fossils requires a brief review of dentition. Moving from front to back, on either side of the upper or lower jaw, humans (and apes) have two incisors, one canine, two pre-molars, and three molars. Our dental formula is 2.1.2.3, for a total of 8 teeth on each side, upper and lower—32 teeth in all—if we have all our "wisdom teeth" (our third molars). Now back to the australopithecines. Like apes, and unlike modern humans, *A. afarensis* had sharp canine teeth that projected beyond the other teeth. Also like apes, their lower premolar was pointed and projecting to sharpen the upper canine. It had one long cusp and one tiny bump that hints at the bicuspid premolar that eventually developed in hominin evolution.

There is, however, evidence that powerful chewing associated with savanna vegetation was entering the *A. afarensis* feeding pattern. When the coarse, gritty, fibrous vegetation of grasslands and semidesert enters the diet, the back teeth change to accommodate heavy chewing stresses. Massive back teeth, jaws, and facial and cranial structures suggest a diet demanding extensive grinding and powerful crushing. The *A. afarensis* skull contrasts with those of later hominins.

The brain case is very small (430 cm^3—cubic centimeters) barely surpassing the chimp average (390 cm^3).

Below the neck, however, *A. afarensis* was unquestionably human. Early evidence of striding bipedalism comes from Laetoli, where volcanic ash covered a trail of footprints of two or three hominins walking to a water hole. These prints leave no doubt that a small striding biped lived in Tanzania by 3.6 m.y.a. The structure of the pelvic, hip, leg, and foot bones also confirms that upright bipedalism was *A. afarensis*'s mode of locomotion.

Lucy and her kind were far from dainty. Lucy's muscle-engraved bones are much more robust than ours are. With only rudimentary tools and weapons, early hominins needed powerful and resistant bones and muscles. Lucy's arms are longer relative to her legs than are those of later hominins. Here again her proportions are more apelike than ours are. Although Lucy neither brachiated nor knuckle-walked, she was probably a much better climber than modern people are, and she spent some of her day in the trees.

The *A. afarensis* fossils show that as recently as 3.0 m.y.a., our ancestors had a mixture of apelike and hominin features. Canines, premolars, and skulls were much more apelike than most scholars had imagined would exist in such a recent ancestor. On the other hand, the molars, chewing apparatus, and cheekbones foreshadowed later hominin trends, and the pelvic and limb bones were indisputably hominin. The hominin pattern was being built from the ground up.

Gracile and Robust Australopithecines

The fossils of *A. africanus* (gracile australopithecines) and *A. robustus* (robust australopithecines) come from South Africa. In 1924, the anatomist Raymond Dart coined the term *Australopithecus africanus* to describe the first fossil representative of this species, the skull of a juvenile that was found accidentally in a quarry at Taung, South Africa. Based on stratigraphy, these fossil hominins, found at five main sites in South Africa, date to the period between 3 and 2 m.y.a.

The two groups of South African australopithecines were **gracile** (*A. africanus*) and **robust** (*A. robustus*). "Gracile" indicates that members of *A. africanus* were smaller and slighter, less robust, than were members of *A. robustus*. In addition, there also were very robust—hyperrobust—australopithecines living in East Africa at this time. In the classification scheme used here, these hyperrobust specimens are assigned to *A. boisei*. However, some scholars consider *A. robustus* and *A. boisei* to be regional variants of just one species, usually called *A. robustus* (sometimes given its own genus, *Paranthropus*).

Graciles and robusts probably descend from *A. afarensis* or from a South African version of *A. afarensis*. Some scholars have argued that the graciles lived before (3.0 to 2.5? m.y.a.) and were ancestral to the robusts (2.6? to 2.0? m.y.a.). Others contend that the graciles and the robusts were separate species that may have overlapped in time. Other paleoanthropologists view the gracile and robust australopithecines as different ends of a continuum of variation in a single *polytypic species*—one with considerable phenotypic variation.

The trend toward enlarged back teeth, chewing muscles, and facial buttressing continued in the South African australopithecines. However, the canines are reduced, and the premolars are fully bicuspid. The mainstay of the australopithecine diet was the vegetation of the savanna, although these early hominins also might have hunted small and slow-moving game. As well,

TABLE 4.2 Facts about the Australopithecines Compared with Chimps and *Homo*

Species	Dates (m.y.a.)	Known Distribution	Important Sites	Body Weight (Mid-Sex)	Brain Size (Mid-Sex) (cm³)
Anatomically modern humans (AMHs)	150,000 to present			132 lb/60 kg	1,350
Pan troglodytes (chimpanzee)	Modern			93 lb/42 kg	390
A. boisei	2.6? to 1.2	E. Africa	Olduvai, East Turkana	86 lb/39 kg/	490
A. robustus	2.0? to 1.0?	S. Africa	Kromdraai, Swartkrans	81 lb/37 kg	540
A. africanus	3 to 2.0	S. Africa	Taung, Sterkfontein, Makapansgat	79 lb/36 kg	490
A. afarensis	3.8 to 3.0	E. Africa	Hadar, Laetoli	77 lb/35 kg	430
A. anamensis	4.2 to 3.9	Kenya	Kanapoi Allia Bay	Insufficient data	No published skulls
Ardipithecus	5.8 to 4.4	Ethiopia	Aramis	Insufficient data	No published skulls

they may have scavenged, bringing home parts of kills made by large cats and other carnivores. The ability to hunt large animals was probably an achievement of *Homo* and is discussed later.

Overall robustness, especially in the chewing apparatus, increased through time among the australopithecines. This trend was most striking in *A. boisei*, which survived until 1.2 m.y.a in East Africa. Compared with their predecessors, the later australopithecines tended to have larger overall size, skulls, and back teeth. They also had thicker faces and more rugged muscle markings on the skeleton.

Brain size increased only slightly between *A. afarensis* (430 cm³), *A. africanus* (490 cm³), and *A. robustus* (540 cm³) (Wolpoff 1999). These figures can be compared with an average cranial capacity of 1,350 cm³ in *Homo sapiens*. The modern range goes from less than 1,000 cm³ to more than 2,000 cm³ in normal adults (see Table 4.2).

THE AUSTRALOPITHECINES AND EARLY *HOMO*

Between 3 and 2 m.y.a., the ancestors of *Homo* split off and became isolated reproductively from the later australopithecines, such as *A. boisei*, which coexisted with *Homo* until around 1.2 m.y.a. The first evidence for speciation is dental. The fossil sample of hominin teeth dated to 2 m.y.a. has two clearly different sizes of teeth. One set is huge, the largest molars and premolars in hominin evolution; these teeth belonged to *A. boisei*. The other group of (smaller) teeth belonged to our probable ancestor, *H. habilis*, the first exemplar of the genus *Homo*.

By 1.7 m.y.a., the difference was even more evident. Two hominin groups occupied different environmental niches. One of them, *Homo*—by then *Homo erectus*—had a larger brain and a reproportioned skull; it had increased the areas of the brain that regulate higher mental functions. These were our ancestors, hominins with greater capacities for culture than the australopithecines

had. *H. erectus* hunted and gathered, made sophisticated tools, and eventually displaced its sole surviving cousin species, *A. boisei*.

The earliest members of our genus are assigned to **Homo habilis,** a name coined by L. S. B. and Mary Leakey for a fossil they found at Olduvai Gorge in Tanzania. *H. habilis* lived between 2 m.y.a. and about 1.7 m.y.a., by which time it had evolved into *H. erectus*. Another important *habilis* find is OH62 (Olduvai Hominin 62), the partial skeleton of a female *H. habilis* from Olduvai Bed I, dated to 1.8 m.y.a. This fossil was surprising because of its small size and its apelike limb bones. Not only was OH62 just as tiny as Lucy, its arms were longer and more apelike than expected. The limb proportions suggested greater tree-climbing ability than in later hominins. *H. habilis* still may have sought occasional refuge in the trees.

The small size and primitive proportions of *H. habilis* were unexpected given what was known about early *H. erectus* in East Africa. Consider the amazingly complete young male *H. erectus* fossil (WT15,000) found at West Turkana in 1984. WT15,000, also known as the Nariokotome boy, was a 12-year-old male who already had reached 5 feet 5 inches (1.7 meters). He might have grown to 6 feet had he lived.

The sharp contrast between the OH62 *H. habilis* (1.8 m.y.a.) and early *H. erectus* (1.7–1.6 m.y.a.) suggests an acceleration in hominin evolution during that 100,000–200,000-year period. Apparently hominins changed very little below the neck between Lucy (*A. afarensis*) and *H. habilis*. Then, between 1.8 and 1.6 m.y.a., a profound change—an evolutionary leap—took place. *H. erectus* looks much more human than *H. habilis* does.

Early Tools

The oldest (at that time) obviously manufactured tools were discovered in 1931 by L. S. B. and Mary Leakey at Olduvai Gorge, Tanzania. This site gave the tools their name—Oldowan pebble tools. The oldest tools from Olduvai are about 1.8 million years old. Still older (2.5 to 2.0 m.y.a.) stone tools have been found in Ethiopia, Congo,

■ *Oldowan core tools or choppers are the most common stone tools found at early African tool sites. Some may have been used for food processing, by pounding, breaking, or bashing. Other "choppers" may only have been cores from which flakes, used for cutting or scraping, were removed. Above, a chopper core tool; below, a flake tool.*

and Malawi (Asfaw, White, and Lovejoy 1999; Lemonick and Dorfman 1999).

Stone tools consist of cores and flakes. The *core* is the piece of rock from which flakes are removed; the core can be worked to become a tool itself. A *chopper* is a tool made by flaking the edge of such a core on one side. **Oldowan** pebble tools represent the world's oldest formally recognized stone tools. With the use of cores about the size of a tennis ball, flakes were struck off one or both sides to form a chopping or cutting edge. The flakes also could be fashioned into tools and were the basis of several later stone tool industries.

Significant changes in technology occurred during the 200,000-year evolutionary spurt between Bed I (1.8 m.y.a.) and Lower Bed II (1.6 m.y.a.) at Olduvai. Tool making got more sophisticated soon after the advent of *H. erectus* in Africa. Out of the crude tools in Bed I evolved better-made and more varied tools. Edges were straighter, for example, and differences in form suggest functional differentiation—that is, the tools were being made and used for different jobs, such as smashing bones or digging for tubers.

H. ERECTUS

H. erectus pushed the hominin range beyond Africa—to Asia and Europe. Small groups broke

off from larger ones and moved a few miles away. They foraged new tracts of vegetation and carved out new hunting territories. Through population growth and dispersal, *H. erectus* gradually spread and changed. Hominins were following an essentially human lifestyle based on hunting and gathering. This basic pattern survived until recently in marginal areas of the world.

The stone-tool-making techniques that evolved out of the Oldowan tradition and that lasted until about 15,000 years ago are described by the term **Paleolithic** (from Greek roots meaning "old" and "stone"). The Paleolithic, or Old Stone Age, has three divisions: Lower (early), Middle, and Upper (late). Each part is roughly associated with a particular stage in human evolution. The Lower Paleolithic is roughly associated with *H. erectus*; the Middle Paleolithic with archaic *H. sapiens,* including the Neandertals of Western Europe and the Middle East; and the Upper Paleolithic with anatomically modern humans (AMHs).

Interrelated changes in biology and culture have increased human adaptability—our capacity to live in and modify an ever-wider range of environments. Improved tools helped *H. erectus* increase its range. Biological changes also increased hunting efficiency. *H. erectus* had a rugged but essentially modern skeleton that permitted long-distance stalking and endurance during the hunt. The *H. erectus* body was much larger and longer-legged than those of previous hominins. There is archaeological evidence of *H. erectus*'s success in hunting elephants, horses, rhinos, and giant baboons.

The average *H. erectus* brain (about 1,000 cm^3) doubled the australopithecine average. *H. erectus* had an essentially modern, though very robust, skeleton with a brain and body closer in size to *H. sapiens* than to *Australopithecus*. Still, several anatomical contrasts, particularly in the cranium, distinguish *H. erectus* from modern humans. Compared with moderns, *H. erectus* had a lower and more sloping forehead accentuated by a large brow ridge above the eyes. Skull bones were thicker, and, as noted, average cranial capacity was smaller. The brain case was lower and flatter than in *H. sapiens*.

One fairly complete skull, one large mandible (jaw bone), and two partial skulls have been found recently at Dmanisi in the former Soviet Republic of Georgia. They have been assigned a date of 1.75–1.70 m.y.a. There are notable similarities between the two partial skulls and that of the Nariokotome boy from Kenya (1.6 m.y.a.). Chopping tools associated with the Kenyan and Georgian fossils also are similar. The Dmanisi finds suggest a rapid spread, by 1.7 m.y.a., of early *Homo* out of Africa and into Eurasia.

As hominins became more carnivorous, they expanded their home ranges in accordance with those of the animals they hunted. The bigger bodies and brains of early *Homo* (compared with the australopithecines) required more energy to run. Meat-rich diets provided higher quality protein as fuel. Because the australopithecines had smaller bodies and brains, they could live mainly on plants and probably used a limited range at the edge of forests, not too deep in or too exposed far out on the savanna. Once hominins developed stronger bodies and high-protein meat diets, they could (indeed had to) spread out. They ranged farther to find meat. This expansion eventually led them out of Africa, into Eurasia (Georgia) and eventually Asia (see Wilford 2000).

In 1891, the Indonesian island of Java had yielded the first *H. erectus* fossil find, popularly known as "Java man." Eugene Dubois, a Dutch army surgeon, had gone to Java to discover a transitional form between apes and humans. Of course, we now know that the transition to hominin took place much earlier than the *H. erectus* period and occurred in Africa. However, Dubois's good luck did lead him to the most ancient human fossils discovered at that time. Indonesian *H. erectus* fossils date back at least 700,000, and perhaps as many as 1.6 million, years. Fragments of a skull and a lower jaw found in northern China at Lantian may be as old as the oldest Indonesian fossils. Other *H. erectus* remains, of uncertain date, have been found in Algeria and Morocco in North Africa. The largest group of *H. erectus* fossils was found in the Zhoukoudian cave in China. The Zhoukoudian ("Peking—now Beijing—man") site, excavated from the late 1920s to the late 1930s, yielded remains of tools, hearths, animal bones, and more than 40 hominins, including five skulls. The Zhoukoudian individuals lived more recently than did the Javanese *H. erectus*, between 670,000 and 410,000 years ago, when the climate in China was colder and moister than it is today. The people at Zhoukoudian ate venison, and seed and plant remains suggest they were both gatherers and hunters. African *H. erectus* fossils have been found in Kenya, Tanzania, Ethiopia, Eritrea, and South Africa. What about Europe? A cranial fragment found at Ceprano, Italy, in 1994, has been assigned a date of 800,000 B.P. All other possible *H. erectus* remains from Europe are later and are classified as late *H. erectus*, or as transitional between *H. erectus* and early *H. sapiens*.

ARCHAIC *H. SAPIENS*

Africa, which was center stage during the australopithecine period, is joined by Asia and Europe during the *H. erectus* and *H. sapiens* periods of hominin evolution. Recent discoveries, along with reinterpretation of the dating and the

This photo shows the early (1.6 m.y.a.) Homo erectus WT15,000, or Nariokotome boy, found in 1984 near Lake Turkana, Kenya. This is the most complete Homo erectus ever found.

anatomical relevance of some earlier finds, are filling in the gap between *H. erectus* and archaic *H. sapiens*. **Archaic *H. sapiens*** (300,000? to 28,000 B.P.) encompasses the earliest members of our species, along with the **Neandertals** (130,000 to 28,000 B.P.) of Europe and the Middle East and their Neandertal-like contemporaries in Africa and Asia. Brain size in archaic *H. sapiens* was within the modern human range. (The modern average is about 1,350 cm^3.) A rounding out of the brain case was associated with the increased brain size. As Jolly and White (1995) put it, evolution was pumping more brain into the *H. sapiens* cranium—like filling a football with air.

Ice Ages of the Pleistocene

Traditionally, the geological epoch known as the *Pleistocene* has been considered the epoch of human life. Its subdivisions are the Lower Pleistocene (2 to 1 m.y.a.), the Middle Pleistocene (1 m.y.a. to 130,000 B.P.), and the Upper Pleistocene (130,000 to 10,000 B.P.). These subdivisions refer to the placement of geological strata containing, respectively, older, intermediate, and younger fossils. The Lower Pleistocene extends from the start of the Pleistocene to the advent of the ice ages in the Northern Hemisphere around one million years ago.

Each subdivision of the Pleistocene is associated with a particular group of hominins. Late *Australopithecus* and early *Homo* lived during the

Map Atlas

Map 5 locates these and other sites where fossil representatives of the genus have been found.

Lower Pleistocene. *H. erectus* spanned most of the Middle Pleistocene. *H. sapiens* appeared late in the Middle Pleistocene and dominated the Upper Pleistocene.

During the second million years of the Pleistocene, there were several ice ages, or *glacials*, major advances of continental ice sheets in Europe and North America. These periods were separated by *interglacials*, long warm periods between the major glacials. With each advance, the world climate cooled and continental ice sheets—massive glaciers—covered the northern parts of Europe and North America. Climates that are temperate today were arctic during the glacials.

During the interglacials, the climate warmed up and the *tundra*—the cold, treeless plain—retreated north with the ice sheets. Forests returned to areas, such as southwestern France, that had had tundra vegetation. The ice sheets advanced and receded several times during the last glacial, the *Würm* (75,000 to 12,000 B.P.). Brief periods of relative warmth during the Würm (and other glacials) are called *interstadials,* in contrast to the longer interglacials. Hominin fossils found in association with animals known to occur in cold or warm climates, respectively, permit us to date them to glacial or interglacial (or interstadial) periods.

H. antecessor and H. heidelbergensis

In northern Spain's Atapuerca Mountains, the site of Gran Dolina has yielded the remains of 780,000-year-old hominins that Spanish researchers call *H. antecessor* and see as a possible common ancestor of the Neandertals and anatomically modern humans. A massive hominin jaw was discovered in 1907 in a gravel pit at Mauer near Heidelberg, Germany. Originally called "Heidelberg man" or *H. heidelbergensis,* the jaw appears to be around 500,000 years old. Recently, some anthropologists have revived the species name *H. heidelbergensis* to refer to a group of fossil hominins that in this text are described as either late *H. erectus* or archaic *H. sapiens.* This group would include hominins dated (very roughly) between 700,000 and 200,000 years ago and found in different parts of the world including Europe, Africa, and Asia. These fossils, here assigned to either *H. erectus* or archaic *H. sapiens,* would be transitional between *H. erectus* and later hominin forms, such as the Neandertals and anatomically modern humans.

Besides the hominin *fossils* found in Europe, there is archaeological evidence for the presence and behavior of late *H. erectus* and then archaic *H. sapiens* in Europe. At the site of Terra Amata, which overlooks Nice in southern France, archaeologists have documented human activity dating back some 300,000 years. Small bands of hunters and gatherers consisting of 15 to 25 people made regular visits during the late spring and early summer to Terra Amata, a sandy cove on the coast of the Mediterranean. Archaeologists determined the season of occupation by examining fossilized human excrement, which contained pollen from flowers known to bloom in late spring. There is evidence for 21 such visits. Four groups camped on a sand bar, 6 on the beach, and 11 on a sand dune. Archaeologists surmise that the 11 dune sites represent that number of annual visits by the same band (deLumley 1969/1976).

From a camp atop the dune, these people looked down on a river valley where animals were abundant. Bones found at Terra Amata show that their diet included red deer, young elephants, wild boars, wild mountain goats, an extinct variety of rhinoceros, and wild oxen. The Terra Amata people also hunted turtles and birds and collected oysters and mussels. Fish bones also were found at the site. The arrangement of postholes shows that these people used saplings to support temporary huts. There were hearths—sunken pits and piled stone fireplaces—within the shelters. Stone chips inside the borders of the huts show that tools were made from locally available rocks and beach pebbles. Thus, at Terra Amata, hundreds of thousands of years ago people were already pursuing an essentially human lifestyle, one that survived in certain coastal regions into the 20th century.

THE NEANDERTALS

The first Neandertal was found in 1856 in a German valley called Neander Valley—*tal* is the German word for valley. Scientists had trouble interpreting the discovery. It was clearly human, yet different enough from modern people to be considered strange and abnormal. This was 35 years before the first *H. erectus* fossils were discovered in Java and almost 70 years before the first australopithecine was found in South Africa. Darwin's *On the Origin of Species,* published in 1859, had not yet appeared to offer a theory of evolution through natural selection. Over time, the fossil record has filled in, along with evolutionary theory. There have been numerous subsequent discoveries of Neandertals in Europe and the Middle East and of archaic human fossils with similar features in Africa and Asia.

Fossils that are not Neandertals but that have similarly large faces and brow ridges have been found in Africa and Asia. The Kabwe skull from Zambia (130,000 B.P.) is an archaic *H. sapiens* with a Neandertal-like brow ridge. There are archaic Chinese fossils with Neandertal-like features. Neandertals have been found in Central Europe and the Middle East. For example, Neandertal fossils found at the Shanidar cave in northern Iraq date to around 60,000 B.P., as does a Neander-

See the Internet Exercises at your OLC

mhhe.com/kottak

Compare these drawings of H. erectus, archaic H. sapiens, Neandertal, and AMH. What are the main differences you notice? Is the Neandertal more like H. erectus or AMH?

H. erectus

Archaic H. sapiens

Neandertal

AMH

For a quiz on human skulls, see the Interactive Exercises
mhhe.com/kottak

tal skeleton found at Israel's Kebara cave (Shreeve 1992). At the Israeli site of Tabun on Mount Carmel, a Neandertal female skeleton was excavated in 1932. She was a contemporary of the Shanidar Neandertals, and her brow ridges, face, and teeth show typical Neandertal robustness.

Cold-Adapted Neandertals

By 75,000 B.P., after an interglacial interlude, Western Europe's hominins (Neandertals, by then) again faced extreme cold as the Würm glacial began. To deal with that environment, they wore clothes, made elaborate tools, and hunted reindeer, mammoths, and woolly rhinos. The Neandertals were stocky, with large trunks relative to limb length—a phenotype that minimizes surface area and thus conserves heat. Another adaptation to extreme cold was the Neandertal face, which has been likened to a H. erectus face that has been pulled forward by the nose. This extension increased the distance between outside air and the arteries that carry blood to the brain and was adaptive in a cold climate. The brain is sensitive to temperature changes and must be kept warm. The massive nasal cavities of Neandertal fossils suggest long, broad noses. This would expand the area for warming and moistening air.

Neandertal characteristics also include huge front teeth, broad faces, and a rugged skeleton and musculature. Neandertal teeth probably did many jobs later done by tools (Brace 1995; Rak 1986). The front teeth show heavy wear, suggesting they were used for varied purposes, including chewing animal hides to make soft winter clothing out of them. The massive Neandertal face showed the stresses of constantly using the front teeth for holding and pulling.

The Neandertals and Modern People

Generations of scientists have debated whether the Neandertals were ancestral to modern Europeans. The current prevailing view, denying this ancestry, proposes that H. erectus split into separate groups, one ancestral to the Neandertals, the other ancestral to **anatomically modern humans (AMHs),** who first reached Europe around 50,000 B.P. (Early AMHs in Western Europe often are referred to as *Cro-Magnon,* after the earliest fossil find of an anatomically modern human, in France's Les Eyzies region, Dordogne Valley, in 1868.) The current predominant view is that modern humans evolved in Africa and eventually colonized Europe, displacing the Neandertals there.

Those scientists who still believe that Neandertals could have contributed to the ancestry of modern Europeans cite certain fossils to support their view. For example, the Central European site of Mladeč (33,000 to 31,000 B.P.) has yielded remains of several hominins that combine Neandertal robustness with modern features. The fossil remains of a four-year-old boy discovered at Largo Velho in Portugal in 1999 and dated to 24,000 B.P. also shows mixed Neandertal and modern features.

The Skhūl (100,000 B.P.) and Qafzeh (92,000 B.P.) skulls found at two Israeli sites cast serious doubt on the Neandertal ancestry of AMHs. Their brain cases are higher, shorter, and rounder than Neandertal skulls. There is a more filled-out forehead region and a marked chin, another modern feature. Based on these early dates from Israel, AMHs may have inhabited the Middle East before the Neandertals did. Ofer Bar-Yosef (1987) has suggested that during the last (Würm) glacial period, which began around 75,000 B.P., Western European Neandertals spread east and south (and into the Middle East) as part of a general southward movement of cold-adapted fauna. AMHs, in turn, followed warmer-climate fauna south into Africa, returning to the Middle East once the Würm ended.

ANATOMICALLY MODERN HUMANS (AMHs)

AMHs probably evolved from an archaic *H. sapiens* African ancestor. Eventually, AMHs spread to other areas, including Europe, where they replaced, or interbred with, the Neandertals. In 1987 a group of molecular geneticists at the University of California at Berkeley analyzed genetic markers in placentas donated by 147 women whose ancestors came from Africa, Europe, the Middle East, Asia, New Guinea, and Australia. The researchers focused on mitochondrial DNA (mtDNA). This genetic material is located in the cytoplasm (the outer part of a cell—not the nucleus). Ordinary DNA, which makes up the genes that determine most physical traits, is found in the nucleus and comes from both parents. But only the mother contributes mitochondrial DNA to the fertilized egg. The father plays no part in mtDNA transmission, just as the mother has nothing to do with the transmission of the Y chromosome, which comes from the father and determines the sex of the child.

To establish a "genetic clock," the Berkeley researchers measured the variation in mtDNA in their 147 tissue samples. They cut each sample into segments to compare with the others. By estimating the number of mutations that had taken place in each sample since its common origin with the 146 others, the researchers drew an evolutionary tree with the help of a computer.

That tree started in Africa and then branched in two. One group remained in Africa, while the other one split off, carrying its mtDNA to the rest of the world. The variation in mtDNA was greatest among Africans. This suggests they have been evolving the longest. The Berkeley researchers concluded that everyone alive today has mtDNA inherited from a woman (dubbed "Eve") who lived in sub-Saharan Africa around 200,000 years ago. Eve was not the only woman alive then; she was just the only one whose descendants have included a daughter in each generation up to the present. Because mtDNA passes exclusively through females, mtDNA lines disappear whenever a woman has no children or has only sons. The details of the Eve theory suggest that her descendants left Africa no more than 135,000 years ago. They eventually displaced the Neandertals in Europe and went on to colonize the rest of the world.

Besides the DNA dating, fossil and archaeological evidence has been accumulating to support the African origin, perhaps by 150,000 years ago, of AMHs. A major find was announced in 2003: the 1997 discovery in an Ethiopian valley of three anatomically modern skulls—two adults and a child. When found, the fossils had been fragmented so badly that their reconstruction took several years. Tim White and Berhane Asfaw were coleaders of the international team that made the find near the village of Herto. The skulls showed evidence of cutting and handling, suggesting they had been detached from their bodies and used—perhaps ritually—after death. Layers of volcanic ash allowed geologists to date them to 160,000–154,000 B.P. The people represented by the skulls had lived on the shore of an ancient lake, where they hunted and fished. The skulls were found along with hippopotamus and antelope bones and some 600 tools, including blades and hand axes.

Except for a few archaic characteristics, the Herto skulls are anatomically modern—long with broad midfaces, featuring tall, narrow nasal bones. The cranial vaults are high, falling within modern dimensions. These finds provide additional support for the view that modern humans originated in Africa and then spread into Europe and Asia (Wilford 2003).

Advances in Technology

Early AMHs in Africa made varied tools. For example, the people who lived at the Klasies River cave sites in South Africa made Middle Paleolithic tools, as did Neandertals in Europe and the Middle East. However, some early

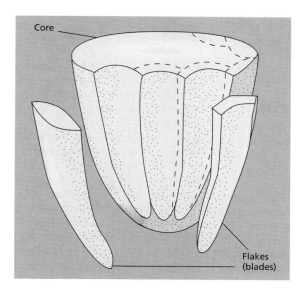

FIGURE 4.4 Upper Paleolithic Blade-Tool Making.
Blades are flakes that are detached from a specially prepared core. A punch (usually a piece of bone or antler) and a hammerstone (not shown here) were used to knock the blade off the core.

African tool finds at Blombos cave (South Africa) and in Katanda (Congo) are more reminiscent of the European Upper Paleolithic. AMHs in Europe made tools in a variety of traditions, collectively known as **Upper Paleolithic** because of the tools' location in the upper, or more recent, layers of sedimentary deposits.

Upper Paleolithic traditions emphasized *blade tools*. Blades were chipped off prepared cores 4 to 6 inches (10–15 centimeters) high, by hitting a punch made of bone or antler with a hammerstone (Figure 4.4). Blades then were modified to produce a variety of special-purpose implements. Some were composite tools that were made by joining reworked blades to other materials. Europe's Upper Paleolithic economy depended on cooperative hunting of mammoths, woolly rhinoceroses, bison, wild horses, bears, wild cattle, wild boars, and—principally—reindeer. It has been estimated that approximately 90 percent of the meat eaten by Western Europeans between 25,000 and 15,000 B.P. came from reindeer.

Illustrating increasing sophistication and diversity in tool-making techniques are the varied special-purpose tools made by Upper Paleolithic populations. Scrapers were used to hollow out wood and bone, scrape animal hides, and remove bark from trees. Burins, the first chisels, were used to make slots in bone and wood and to engrave designs on bone. Awls, which were drills with sharp points, were used to make holes in wood, bone, shell, and skin.

Upper Paleolithic bone tools have survived: knives, pins, needles with eyes, and fishhooks. The needles suggest that clothes sewn with thread—made from the sinews of animals—were being worn. Fishhooks and harpoons confirm an increased emphasis on fishing.

THE ADVENT OF BEHAVIORAL MODERNITY

Anthropologists use evidence from artifacts, art, language, and other aspects of culture, as well as genetics, anatomy, and animal remains, to reconstruct our past. Scientists agree that (1) around 6 million years ago, our hominin ancestors originated in Africa, as apelike creatures became habitual bipeds; (2) by 2.5 million years ago, still in Africa, hominins were making crude stone tools; and (3) by 1.7 million years ago, hominins had spread from Africa into Eurasia, Asia, and eventually Europe.

Most scientists agree on those three points. A smaller majority—but still a majority—of scientists think that anatomically modern humans (AMHs) had evolved by at least 130,000 years ago from ancestors who had remained in Africa. Like earlier hominins (*H. erectus*), they too spread out from Africa. Eventually they replaced—perhaps in some cases interbreeding with—nonmodern human types, such as the Neandertals in Europe and the successors of *H. erectus* in the Far East.

Disagreement remains about when, where, and how early AMHs achieved *behavioral modernity*—relying on symbolic thought, elaborating cultural creativity, and, as a result, becoming fully human in behavior as well as in anatomy. Was it 90,000 or 40,000 years ago? Was it in Africa, the Middle East, or Europe? Was it population increase, competition with nonmodern humans, or a genetic mutation that triggered the change?

The traditional view has been that modern behavior originated fairly recently, around 40,000 years ago, and only after *H. sapiens* had pushed into Europe. This theory of a "creative explosion" is based on evidence such as the impressive cave paintings at Lascaux and Chauvet (Wilford 2002b) (see "Interesting Issues"). Some researchers think this theory reflects Eurocentrism, in that anthropologists were more likely to believe evidence for early creativity in Western Europe. But when they found signs of early behavioral complexity in Africa or the Middle East, they discounted it. In fact, recent discoveries outside Europe do suggest an older, more gradual evolution of modern behavior, rather than its sudden appearance in Europe.

British archaeologist Clive Gamble observes, "Europe is a little peninsula that happens to have a large amount of spectacular archaeology. But the European grip of having all the evidence is

BEYOND THE CLASSROOM

Paleolithic Butchering at Verberie

BACKGROUND INFORMATION

STUDENT:
Kelsey Foster

SUPERVISING PROFESSOR:
Dr. James G. Enloe

SCHOOL:
University of Iowa

YEAR IN SCHOOL/MAJOR:
Senior/Anthropology

FUTURE PLANS:
Marine Archaeology Internship/
Graduate School

PROJECT TITLE:
Meat and Marrow:
Paleolithic Butchering at Verberie

How can the analysis of animal bones provide evidence for specific kinds of human activity? What kinds of animals were hunted at this Paleolithic site? What kind of eating behavior went on at the site?

The Paleolithic archaeological site of Verberie le Buisson Campin is located along the banks of the Oise River in Northern France. It was the site of repeated occupation by a small band of Paleolithic hunters to mass-kill reindeer, which make up over 98% of the faunal assemblage. Examinations of the faunal material indicate that the reindeer were killed during the fall of the year, which corresponds with the yearly migration of the reindeer herds.

Dental analysis and postcranial measurements served to determine that the majority of the reindeer remains were from sub-adult males. This shows great selectivity on the part of the Paleolithic hunters for large, healthy prey.

My research focuses on furthering the existing knowledge of Verberie by attempting to determine the butchering pattern used by the Paleolithic hunters at the site. I examined the faunal remains from the entire upper occupation level (Level II1) for any indication of human modification of bone, which is indicated by the presence of stone tool cut marks and/or impact cones. Stone tool cut marks are produced during the filleting of meat from the bones and during the dismemberment of the carcass. The impact cones are the result of the cracking of bones in order to remove the marrow.

During my research I examined 1,133 specimens of reindeer bone fragments to investigate butchering practices at Verberie. Using Lewis Binford's Meat Utility Index and Marrow Utility Index numbers for the nutritive value of reindeer limb elements, I found that the elements with high marrow index values composed a greater percentage of the assemblage, while the elements with high meat index values were much less represented.

I then compared the numbers and degree of human modification between each element and found that the higher marrow utility elements showed a higher degree of exploitation for marrow cracking than did the lower marrow utility elements. This identified the systematic processing of marrow at Ver-

berie. Conversely, the stone tool cut marks present on the assemblage were predominately the result of dismemberment and not the result of meat removal.

I finally compared the percentages of the elements with a similar ethnoarchaeologic study performed on the remains from a known marrow processing event at a Nunamuit (Alaskan Eskimos, or Inuit) residential site. The extreme similarity between these two assemblages solidified the claim of extensive marrow processing at Verberie.

When all this information is taken together, the butchering sequence at Verberie becomes clear. The butchering practice of Verberie consisted of primary dismemberment of the carcass into smaller units, with intentional snacking on the high marrow utility elements. The lack of filleting marks indicates that minimal, if any, meat exploitation occurred at the hunting camp. Therefore, if the high meat utility elements were not eaten at Verberie, they were transported to a larger residential camp for later consumption.

beginning to slip. We're finding wonderful new evidence in Africa and other places. And in the last few years, this has changed and widened the debate over modern human behavior" (quoted in Wilford 2002b).

Uncertainty about the origin of modern behavior reflects the long lag between the time when the species first looked modern (150,000–100,000 B.P.) and the time when it started acting modern

(90,000–40,000 B.P.) (Wilford 2002b). Did the capacity for behavioral modernity lie latent in early *H. sapiens* until it was needed for survival? According to archaeologist Sally McBrearty, "the earliest *Homo sapiens* probably had the cognitive capability to invent Sputnik, but they didn't yet have the history of invention or a need for those things" (quoted in Wilford 2002b). Did the need for behavioral modernity arise gradually, in the

Prehistoric Art Treasure Is Found in French Cave

In the mountains of southern France, where human beings have habitually hunted, loved and produced art, explorers have discovered an underground cave full of Stone Age paintings, so beautifully made and well preserved that experts are calling it one of the archeological finds of the century.

The enormous underground cavern [see Figure 4.5], which was found on Dec. 18, 1994, in a gorge near the town of Vallon-Pont-d'Arc in the Ardèche region, is studded with more than 300 vivid images of animals and human hands that experts believe were made more than 30,000 years ago.

In this great parade of beasts appear woolly-haired rhinos, bears, mammoths, oxen and other images from the end of the Paleolithic era, creatures large and small and variously drawn in yellow ochre, charcoal and hematite. The murals have surprised specialists because they also include a rare image of a red, slouching hyena and the era's first-ever recorded paintings of a panther and several owls. Specialists say this ancient art gallery surpasses in size that of the famous caves of Lascaux and Altamira, which are widely held to be Western Europe's finest collection of Stone Age art.

Archeologists said they were thrilled not only by the number and the quality of the images but also by the discovery that the great underground site, sealed by fallen debris, appears to have been left undisturbed for thousands of years. They see this as tantamount to finding a time capsule full of hidden treasures.

One remarkable find, they said, was the skull of a bear, placed on a large rock set in the middle of one gallery against a backdrop of bear paintings.

"Is this some kind of altar? Someone placed the skull there for a reason," said Jean Clottes, France's leading rock art specialist. Many other skulls and bones of cavebears were found in the underground warren, along with bones, flint knives, footprints and remains of fireplaces, all of which archeologists hope will provide important clues to the questions: What was the purpose of these paintings? What did their makers have in mind? . . .

The known part of the cavern consists of four great halls, up to 70 yards long and 40 yards wide, which are connected by smaller galleries roughly five by four yards, according [to] a report issued by the Ministry of Culture. The more than 300 paintings and engravings vary in size between 2 feet and 12 feet long. Some stand alone, while others are clustered in panels or painted with some cohesion, such as two rhinos head-to-head as if in a fight. As Mr. Clottes showed a videotape revealing a panel with four horses' heads close together, drawn in charcoal, he said: "These are one of the great marvels of prehistoric art." The artist or artists, he continued, made use of the natural colors of the rock and of natural stone relief to give form and bulges to the animals.

Archeologists have long believed that the deep prehistoric caves were used not as habitats, because they were too dark, but for religious ser-

FIGURE 4.5   Location of Chauvet Cave.

vices or cults about which next to nothing is known. Some specialists believe that initiation rites were held in the caves and that the drawings of the humans' hands from the Paleolithic found here and elsewhere were a token of membership in a cult or community . . .

SOURCE: Marlise Simons, "Prehistoric Art Treasure Is Found in French Cave," *New York Times*, January 19, 1995, pp. A1, A5.

context of new social conditions, environmental change, or competition with other early human types? Or did the capacity for modern behavior develop late, reflecting some kind of genetic transformation? Mary Stiner of the University of Arizona reduces the matter to one key question: "Was there some fundamental shift in brain wiring or some change in conditions of life?" (quoted in Wilford 2002*b*).

Richard G. Klein, a Stanford archaeologist, is a leading advocate for the idea that human creativity dawned suddenly, in Europe around 40,000 years ago. Before this "dawn of human culture" (Klein with Edgar 2002), *Homo* had changed very slowly—and more or less simultaneously in anatomy and behavior. After this "dawn of culture," human anatomy changed little, but behavior started changing dramatically. The pace of

■ *Cave murals dating back more than 30,000 years in Chauvet Cave at Vallon-Pont-d'Arc in southern France. How would you explain the subject matter and placement of cave paintings?*

Wilford 2002b). Reaching Europe, the rewired modern humans, the AMH Cro-Magnons, met and eventually replaced the resident Neandertals.

Klein recognizes that his genetic hypothesis "fails one important measure of a proper scientific hypothesis—it cannot be tested or falsified by experiment or by examination of relevant human fossils" (quoted in Wilford 2002b). AMH skulls from the time period in question show no change in brain size or function. According to Wilford (2002b), Klein's critics object that his concepts of "the dawn of creativity" and of an abrupt "human revolution" are too simplistic, as well as unprovable.

Other archaeologists think it inappropriate and outdated to link the origin of human behavioral modernity so closely to the European evidence. Such thinking was more understandable when few relevant sites were known elsewhere. But in the last 30 years, archaeologists working in Africa and the Middle East have found considerable evidence for early modern behavior, in the form of finely made stone and bone tools, long-distance trade, dietary changes, self-ornamentation, and abstract carvings.

In a survey of African archeological sites dating to between 300,000 and 30,000 years ago, Sally McBrearty and Alison Brooks (2000) conclude that artifacts thought to indicate the "human revolution" of the Upper Paleolithic in Europe—where they appear abruptly about 40,000 years ago—are found in Africa much earlier. In other words, what might appear to be a sudden event outside Africa was a slow process of accumulation within Africa. Given the genetic evidence that AMHs came from Africa, this makes good sense. Culture developed gradually in Africa; such cultural advances would have facilitated the spread of AMHs beyond that continent. The implication is that humans were fully "human" long before the Upper Paleolithic and that we do not need to postulate a genetic change 50,000 years ago (e.g., a mutation "for language") to account for the "human revolution."

At South Africa's Blombos Cave, an archaeological team led by Christopher Henshilwood found evidence that AMHs were making bone awls and weapon points more than 70,000 years ago. Three weapon points had been shaped with a stone blade and then finely polished. Henshilwood thinks these artifacts indicate symbolic behavior and artistic creativity—people trying to make beautiful objects. In January 2002, Henshilwood reported additional evidence from Blombos Cave for early symbolic thought: two small pieces of ocher (a soft red iron oxide stone) with inscribed triangles and horizontal lines, dating back 77,000 years (Wilford 2002b).

Earlier excavations in Congo's Katanda region had uncovered barbed bone harpoon points dating back 90,000 to 80,000 years (Yellen, Brooks,

cultural change has been accelerating ever since 40,000 B.P.

In this view, it was in Europe that modern *H. sapiens* made the first tools that confirm a pattern of abstract and symbolic thought. There, humans who were behaviorally, as well as anatomically, modern also buried their dead with ceremonies, adorned their bodies with pigments and jewelry, and fashioned figurines of fertile females. Their cave paintings expressed images from their minds, as they remembered the hunt, and events and symbols associated with it.

To explain such a flowering of creativity, Klein proposes a neurological hypothesis. About 50,000 years ago, he thinks, a genetic mutation acted to rewire the human brain, possibly allowing for an advance in language. Improved communication, in Klein's view, could have given people "the fully modern ability to invent and manipulate culture" (quoted in Wilford 2002b). Klein thinks this genetic change probably happened in Africa and then allowed "human populations to colonize new and challenging environments" (quoted in and Cornelissen 1995). Archaeologists Alison Brooks and John Yellen contend that these ancient people "not only possessed considerable technological capabilities at this time, but also incorporated symbolic or stylistic content into their projectile forms" (quoted in Wilford 2002b).

In Turkey and Lebanon, Steven Kuhn, Mary Stiner, and David Reese (2001) found evidence that, around 43,000 years ago, coastal people made and wore beads and shell ornaments with repetitive designs (see also Mayell 2004b). Some of the shells were rare varieties, white or brightly colored. The bone of a large bird was incised for use as a pendant. The Mediterranean coastal sites of Ucagizli Cave in Turkey and Ksar Akil in Lebanon are located in a corridor of ancient migrations from Africa into Europe and Asia. There the archaeologists also found remains of animal bones that offered evidence for a dietary change. Over time, the people ate fewer deer, wild cattle, and other large animals. They also hunted fewer of the slower-reproducing, easier-to-catch animals, such as shellfish and tortoises, and more of the more agile animals, such as birds and hares (Kuhn, Stiner, and Reese 2001).

Kuhn, Stiner, and Reese (2001) suggest that population increase could have caused changes in the living conditions of these AMHs—putting pressure on their resources and forcing experimentation with diet and subsistence strategies. Even a modest increase in the population growth rate could double or triple the numbers and populations of small AMH bands, forcing people to vary their subsistence strategies. People would be living nearer to one another, with more opportunities to interact. Body ornaments could have been part of a system of communication, signaling group identity and social status. Such reliance on communication through ornamentation probably implies "the existence of certain cognitive capacities and that these evolved relatively late in prehistory" (Stiner and Kuhn, quoted in Wilford 2002b; Kuhn, Stiner, and Reese 2001).

Such capacities probably were not the result of a sudden genetic mutation. "The fact that traditions of ornament making emerged almost simultaneously in the earliest Upper Paleolithic/Late Stone Age on three continents argues strongly against their corresponding to a specific event in the cognitive evolution of a single population," according to Stiner and Kuhn (quoted in Wilford 2002b).

Clive Gamble attributes the rise of behavioral modernity more to increasing social competition than to population increase. Competing with neighboring populations, including, in Europe, the Neandertals, could have produced new subsistence strategies, along with new ways of sharing ideas and organizing society. Such innovations would have advantaged AMH bands as they occupied new lands and faced new circumstances, including contact with nonmodern humans.

At South Africa's Blombos Cave, anatomically modern humans were making bone awls and weapon points more than 70,000 years ago. Shown here—some of the more than 100,000 artifacts that have been found in the cave.

According to archaeologist Randall White, an expert on Cro-Magnon creativity, early personal adornment in Africa and the Middle East shows that the human creative capacity was latent in AMHs long before they reached Europe (Wilford 2002b). Facing new circumstances, including competition, AMHs honed their cultural abilities, which enabled them to maintain a common identity, communicate ideas, and organize their societies into "stable, enduring regional groups" (quoted in Wilford 2002b). Symbolic thought and cultural advances, expressed most enduringly in artifacts, ornamentation, and art, gave them the edge over the Neandertals, with whom they may have interbred, but whom they eventually replaced in Europe.

The origin of behavioral modernity continues to be debated. We see, however, that archaeological work in many world areas suggests strongly that neither anatomical modernity nor behavioral modernity was a European invention. Africa's role in the origin and development of humanity is prominent yet again.

SETTLING THE AMERICAS

With increasing technological specialization and efficiency, humans have become increasingly adaptable. Through heavy reliance on tools and other cultural means of adaptation, Homo has become (in numbers and range) the most successful primate by far. The hominid range expanded significantly in Upper Paleolithic times with the colonization of two new continents—North America and South America. (Australia was colonized by 60,000 B.P.)

One effect of continental glaciation was to expose—during several periods of glacial advance—*Beringia,* the Bering land bridge that once connected North America and Siberia. Submerged today under the Bering Sea, Beringia was once a vast area of a dry land, several hundred miles wide. The original settlers of the Americas came from Northeast Asia. Living in Beringia thousands of years ago, these ancestors of Native Americans didn't realize they were embarking on the colonization of a new continent. They were merely big-game hunters who, over the generations, moved gradually eastward as they spread their camps and followed their prey—woolly mammoths and other tundra-adapted herbivores. Other ancient hunters entered North America along the Pacific shore by boat, fishing and hunting sea animals.

This was truly a "new world" to its earliest colonists, as it would be to the European voyagers who rediscovered it thousands of years later. Its natural resources, particularly its big game, never before had been exploited by humans. Early bands followed the game south. Although ice sheets covered most of what is now Canada, colonization gradually penetrated the heartland of what is now the United States. Successive generations of hunters followed game through unglaciated corridors, breaks in the continental ice sheets. Other colonists spread by boat down the Pacific coast.

In North America's rolling grasslands, early American Indians, *Paleoindians,* hunted horses, camels, bison, elephants, mammoths, and giant sloths. The **Clovis tradition**—a sophisticated stone technology based on a point that was fastened to the end of a hunting spear (Figure 4.6)—flourished between 12,000 and 11,000 B.P. in the Central Plains, on their western margins, and over a large area of what is now the eastern United States. The Monte Verde archaeological

FIGURE 4.6 A Clovis Spear Point.
Such points were attached to spears used by Paleoindians of the North American plains between 12,000 and 11,000 B.P. Are there sites with comparable ages in South America?

site in south central Chile has been dated firmly to 12,500 B.P. (Smith 1995). This evidence for the early occupation of southern South America suggests that the first migration of humans into the Americas may date back 18,000 years.

As hunters benefiting from the abundance of big game, bands of foragers gradually spread through the Americas. As they moved, these early Americans learned to cope with a great diversity of environments. Thousands of years later, their descendants independently invented food production, paving the way for the emergence of ethnically diverse states based on agriculture and trade in Mexico and Peru.

SUMMARY

1. The *fact* of evolution was known before Darwin and Wallace. The *theory* of evolution, through natural selection (*how* evolution occurred), was their major contribution. Natural selection requires variety in the population undergoing selection.

2. Humans, apes, monkeys, and prosimians are primates. Anthropoids include humans, apes, and monkeys. All share several primate trends, including depth vision and color vision. The great apes are orangutans, gorillas, and chimpanzees. The African apes—chimps and gorillas—are our nearest relatives.

3. Many differences between humans and other primates are of degree rather than of kind. The ability to learn—the basis of human culture—is an adaptive advantage available to all the anthro-

poids. Chimpanzees make tools and hunt and share meat. Sharing and cooperation are basic features of human bands.

4. The earliest identifiable hominin remains date to between 7.0 m.y.a. and 5.8 m.y.a. The "Toumai" find from Chad is a possible early hominin, as is *Orrorin tugenensis* from Kenya. More generally accepted hominin remains from Ethiopia are classified as *Ardipithecus* (5.8–4.4 m.y.a.). The australopithecines date back to 4.2 m.y.a. There were six species of *Australopithecus.*

5. The earliest hominins had slashing canines, elongated premolars, and a small apelike skull. Still, *A. afarensis* and its predecessors were definite hominins. *A. afarensis* was an upright biped. Remains of two later groups, *A. africanus* (graciles) and *A. robustus* (robusts), have been

found in South Africa. Both groups show the australopithecine trend toward a powerful chewing apparatus, which is more pronounced in the robusts than in the graciles.

6. By 2.0 m.y.a. there were two distinct hominin groups: early *Homo* and *A. boisei,* the hyperrobust australopithecines, which went extinct around 1.2 m.y.a. Pebble tools dating to between 2.5 and 2.0 m.y.a. have been found in Ethiopia, Congo, and Malawi. Cultural abilities developed exponentially with *Homo*'s appearance and evolution. Early *Homo, H. habilis* (2.0? to 1.7 m.y.a.) evolved into *H. erectus* (1.7 m.y.a. to 300,000 B.P.).

7. Dental, facial, and cranial robustness was reduced in *H. erectus,* which extended the hominin food quest to the hunting of large animals. *H. erectus,* with a much larger body, had smaller back teeth but larger front teeth and supporting structures, including a massive eyebrow ridge. *H. erectus*'s average cranial capacity doubled the australopithecine average. Tool complexity and evidence for cooperative hunting suggest a long period of enculturation and learning. *H. erectus* extended the hominin range beyond Africa to Asia and Europe. *H. erectus* persisted for more than a million years, evolving into archaic *H. sapiens* by the Middle Pleistocene epoch.

8. The Neandertals lived in Western Europe during the early part of the Würm glacial. Most contemporary anthropologists exclude them from the ancestry of modern Western Europeans. The ancestors of AMHs (anatomically modern humans) were other archaic *H. sapiens* groups, most probably those in Africa. AMH finds such as Skhūl (100,000 B.P.), Qafzeh (92,000 B.P.), and especially Herto (160,000–154,000 B.P.) support the view that the Neandertals (130,000 to 28,000 B.P.) and AMHs were contemporaries, rather than ancestor and descendant.

9. The Neandertals adapted physically and culturally to bitter cold, with complex tool kits. AMHs made Upper Paleolithic blade tools. The changeover from Neandertal to modern appears to have occurred in Western Europe by 28,000 B.P. It took tens of thousands of years for AMHs to achieve behavioral modernity–to express cultural abilities equivalent to those of contemporary human societies. Evidence for symbolic thought, including art and body adornment, dates back perhaps 90,000 years in Africa, and more than 40,000 years in Europe and the Middle East.

10. Humans entered the Americas perhaps as long as 18,000 years ago. Pursuing big game or moving by boat along the North Pacific Coast, they gradually moved into North America. Adapting to different environments, Native Americans developed a variety of cultures. Some continued to rely on big game. Others became generalized gatherers, hunters, and fishers.

A. afarensis Early form of *Australopithecus,* known from Hadar in Ethiopia ("Lucy") and Laetoli in Tanzania; the Hadar remains date to 3.3–3.0 m.y.a.; the Laetoli remains are older, dating to 3.8–3.6 m.y.a.; despite its many apelike features, *A. afarensis* was an upright biped.

anatomically modern humans (AMHs) Including the Cro-Magnons of Europe (31,000 B.P.) and the older fossils from Skhūl (100,000 B.P.), Qafzeh (92,000 B.P.), Herto, and other sites; continue through the present.

archaic *Homo sapiens* Early *H. sapiens,* consisting of the Neandertals of Europe and the Middle East, the Neandertal-like hominins of Africa and Asia, and the immediate ancestors of all these hominins; lived from about 300,000 to 28,000 B.P.

australopithecines Varied group of early hominins. The term is derived from their former classification as members of a distinct subfamily, the Australopithecinae; now they are distinguished from *Homo* only at the genus level, as *Australopithecus (A.).*

bipedalism Upright two-legged locomotion, the key feature differentiating early hominins from the apes.

evolution Belief that species arose from others through a long and gradual process of transformation, or descent with modification.

gracile Opposite of "robust;" indicates that members of *A. africanus* were a bit smaller and slighter, less robust, than were members of *A. robustus.*

hominid A member of the taxonomic family that includes humans and the African apes and their immediate ancestors.

hominin A member of the human lineage after its split from ancestral chimps; the term *hominin* is used to describe all the human species that ever have existed, including the extinct ones, and excluding chimps and gorillas.

Homo habilis Term coined by L. S. B. and Mary Leakey; immediate ancestor of *H. erectus;* lived from about 2.0 to 1.7 m.y.a.

mutation Change in the DNA molecules of which genes and chromosomes are built.

m.y.a. Million years ago.

natural selection The process by which the forms most fit to survive and reproduce in a given environment do so in greater numbers than others in the same population; more than survival of the fittest, natural selection is differential reproductive success.

KEY TERMS

See the flash cards

mhhe.com/kottak

Neandertals   Members of an archaic *H. sapiens* group that lived in Europe and the Middle East between 130,000 and 28,000 B.P.

Oldowan   Earliest (2.5 to 2.0 m.y.a.) stone tools; first discovered in 1931 by L. S. B. and Mary Leakey at Olduvai Gorge.

Paleolithic   Old Stone Age (from Greek roots meaning "old" and "stone"); divided into Lower (early), Middle, and Upper (late).

robust   Large, strong, sturdy; said of skull, skeleton, muscle, and teeth; opposite of *gracile*.

taxonomy   Classification scheme; assignment to categories (*taxa*; singular, *taxon*).

theory   A set of ideas formulated (by reasoning from known facts) to explain something. The main value of a theory is to promote new understanding. A theory suggests patterns, connections, and relationships that may be confirmed by new research.

uniformitarianism   Belief that explanations for past events should be sought in ordinary forces that continue to work today.

Upper Paleolithic   Blade-tool-making traditions associated with early *H. sapiens sapiens;* named from their location in upper, or more recent, layers of sedimentary deposits.

CRITICAL THINKING QUESTIONS

1. Is *Homo sapiens* more or less adaptable than other species? What makes us so adaptable? Can you think of some species that are more adaptable than we are?

2. What are the main trends in primate evolution? Compare a cat or dog with a monkey, ape, or human. What are the main differences in the sensory organs—those that have to do with vision, smell, and touch, for example?

3. If you found a new hominoid fossil in East Africa, dated to five million years ago, would it most likely be an ape ancestor or a human ancestor? How would you tell the difference?

4. What were the main differences between *Homo habilis* and *Homo erectus?* Was *Homo habilis* more like *Homo erectus,* or more like the australopithecines?

5. How does the geographic distribution of *H. erectus* differ from that of the australopithecines? What did culture have to do with this difference?

SUGGESTED ADDITIONAL READINGS

Campbell, B. G., and J. D. Loy
    2002   *Humankind Emerging,* Concise ed. New York: Longman. Well-illustrated survey of physical anthropology, particularly the fossil record.

De Waal, F. B. M.
    2001   *The Ape and the Sushi Master: Cultural Reflections by a Primatologist.* New York: Basic Books. Behavior of humans and apes.

Goodall, J.
    1996   *My Life with the Chimpanzees.* New York: Pocket Books. Popular account of the author's life among the chimps.

Gould, S. J.
    2002   *The Structure of Evolutionary Theory.* Cambridge, MA: Belknap Press of Harvard University Press. Explores the punctuated equilibrium model and other aspects of evolutionary theory.

Johanson, D. C., and B. Edgar
    1996   *From Lucy to Language.* New York: Simon & Schuster. Popular account of human evolution by a prominent contributor to understanding the fossil record.

Klein, R. G.
    1999   *The Human Career: Human Biological and Cultural Origins,* 2nd ed. Chicago: University of Chicago Press. Hominin fossils, origins, and evolution.

Klein, R. G., with B. Edgar
    2002   *The Dawn of Human Culture.* New York: Wiley. Becoming modern, physically and culturally.

Lieberman, P.
    1998   *Eve Spoke: Human Language and Human Evolution.* New York: W. W. Norton. Language and behavior in human evolution.

Mayr, E.
    2001   *What Evolution Is.* New York: Basic Books. A master scholar sums it all up.

Schick, K. D., and N. Toth
    1993   *Making Silent Stones Speak: Human Evolution and the Dawn of Technology.* New York: Simon & Schuster. Flint knapping and prehistoric tools.

Tattersall, I.
    1999   *The Last Neandertal: The Rise, Success, and Mysterious Extinction of Our Closest Human Relatives,* rev. ed. Boulder, CO: Westview. One view of what happened to the Neandertals.

Weiner, J.
    1994   *The Beak of the Finch: A Story of Evolution in Our Time.* New York: Alfred A. Knopf. An excellent introduction to Darwin and to evolutionary theory.

Wenke, R. J.
    1996   *Patterns in Prehistory: Mankind's First Three Million Years,* 4th ed. New York: Oxford University Press. Very thorough survey of fossil and archaeological reconstruction of human evolution.

1. Primate Conflict: Go to the Living Link's video collection at Emory University's Center for the Advanced Study of Ape and Human Evolution website, **http://www.emory.edu/LIVING_ LINKS/AV/conflict_28k.ram**, and watch the Chimpanzee Conflict movie.

   a. What different kinds of aggression are presented in the movie?

   b. What are the different responses to aggression? Did these responses tend to escalate or terminate the aggressive behavior?

   c. Is aggressive behavior restricted to adults? Does it take on different forms in juveniles?

   d. Which of these aggressive behaviors and responses do humans share with the chimpanzees? For example, do humans use bluff display?

2. Early Hominin Skulls: Visit Philip L. Walker and Edward H. Hagen's "Human Evolution: The fossil evidence in 3D" (**http://www.anth.ucsb. edu/projects/human/**). Then click the link to enter the gallery.

   a. Click on the human figure labeled "Human origins" and then click on the skull labeled "Australopithecine radiation." You now have a three-dimensional view of an *Australopithecus afarensis* skull, and you can use the mouse to rotate the skull. Compare it with a modern human skull. What are some of the differences you notice? What do these differences mean about diet, environment, and brain size?

   b. Go back and view the *Paranthropus boisei* (equivalent to *Australopithecus boisei* in this text) and *Australopithecus africanus* skulls. What are the major differences between the two, and what do these differences say about diet, environment, and brain size?

3. Visit the home page of the Chauvet-Pont-d'Arc cave (**http://www.culture.gouv.fr/culture/ arcnat/chauvet/en/index.html**). Read about the discovery and authentication of the cave (under "The Cave Today") and about the archaeological context, dating, and significance of the cave (under "Time and Space").

   a. How was the cave found? How do they know the paintings are as old as they claim?

   b. When was the cave occupied? What kind of hominin was using the cave?

   c. What makes the Chauvet-Pont-d'Arc cave different from other caves used during a similar time period? What do archaeologists know about the people who occupied the cave and made the paintings?

5

Ethnicity and Race

ETHNIC GROUPS AND ETHNICITY

We know from the chapter on "Culture" that culture is learned, shared, symbolic, integrated, and all-encompassing. Now we consider the relation between culture and ethnicity. Ethnicity is based on cultural similarities and differences in a society or nation. The similarities are with members of the same ethnic group; the differences are between that group and others. Ethnic groups must deal with other such groups in the nation or region they inhabit, so that interethnic relations are important in the study of that nation or region. (Table 5.1 lists American ethnic groups, based on 2004 figures.)

TABLE 5.1	Racial/Ethnic Identification in the United States, 2004 (as Claimed in Census)	
Claimed Identity	**Millions of People**	**Percentage**
Hispanic	41.3	14.1%
Asian	12.1	4.1
Two or more races	3.9	1.3
Pacific Islander	0.4	0.1
American Indian	2.2	0.8
Black	36.0	12.2
White	197.8	67.4
Total population	293.7	100.0%

SOURCE: U.S. Census Files, 2005.

As with any culture, members of an **ethnic group** *share* certain beliefs, values, habits, customs, and norms because of their common background. They define themselves as different and special because of cultural features. This distinction may arise from language, religion, historical experience, geographic isolation, kinship, or "race" (see Spickard 2004). Markers of an ethnic group may include a collective name, belief in common descent, a sense of solidarity, and an association with a specific territory, which the group may or may not hold (Ryan 1990, pp. xiii, xiv).

OVERVIEW

Ethnicity is based on cultural similarities (among members of the same ethnic group) and differences (between that group and others). Ethnicity is revealed when people claim a certain ethnic identity for themselves and are defined by others as having that identity. A race is an ethnic group that is assumed to have a biological basis.

"Races" are socially constructed, defined in terms of contrasts perceived in particular societies. In the United States children of mixed unions, no matter what they look like, tend to be classified with the minority-group parent. Other cultures have different systems of racial classification.

Environmental variables involving educational, economic, and social backgrounds provide better explanations for performance on intelligence tests by races, classes, and ethnic groups than do genetic differences in learning ability.

Most nation-states are not ethnically homogeneous. Multiculturalism contrasts with assimilation, in which minorities abandon their cultural traditions. Ethnicity can be expressed in peaceful coexistence, or in discrimination or violent confrontation. A dominant group may try to destroy ethnic practices (ethnocide) or force ethnic-group members to adopt the dominant culture (forced assimilation).

According to Fredrik Barth (1969), ethnicity can be said to exist when people claim a certain ethnic identity for themselves and are defined by others as having that identity. **Ethnicity** means identification with, and feeling part of, an ethnic group and exclusion from certain other groups because of this affiliation. But issues of ethnicity can be complex. The "News Brief" describes how African Americans who travel to Ghana to strengthen or reclaim an ethnic heritage are excluded from that heritage by many Ghanaians. Ethnic feelings and associated behavior vary in intensity within ethnic groups and countries and over time. A change in the degree of importance attached to an ethnic identity may reflect political changes (Soviet rule ends—ethnic feeling rises) or individual life-cycle changes (young people relinquish, or old people reclaim, an ethnic background).

We saw in the chapter "Culture" that people participate in levels of culture. Groups within a culture (including ethnic groups in a nation) have different learning experiences as well as shared ones. Cultural differences may be associated with ethnicity, class, region, or religion. Individuals often have more than one group identity. People may be loyal (depending on circumstances) to their neighborhood, school, town, state or province, region, nation, continent, religion, ethnic group, or interest group (Ryan 1990, p. xxii). In a complex society such as the United States or Canada, people constantly negotiate their social identities. All of us "wear different hats," presenting ourselves sometimes as one thing, sometimes as another.

In daily conversation, we hear the term *status* used as a synonym for *prestige*. In this context, "She's got a lot of status" means she's got a lot of prestige; people look up to her. Among social scientists, that's not the primary meaning of "status." Social scientists use *status* more neutrally—for any position, no matter what the prestige, that someone

Ghana's Uneasy Embrace of Slavery's Diaspora

NEW YORK TIMES NEWS BRIEF

by Lydia Polgreen
December 27, 2005

Consider racial, ethnic, and national identities. This article describes current efforts by Ghana to attract African Americans to that country as tourists, retirees, and permanent residents. It describes how millions of enslaved Africans were exported from Ghana to the Western Hemisphere and how, centuries later, Africans and African Americans shared a common struggle for independence and advancement. Also discussed are identity issues that African Americans face in Ghana, where often they are equated with white foreign tourists. Ghanaians apparently focus more on nationality and class than on skin color in classifying African Americans.

We hear the words ethnicity *and* race *frequently, but American culture doesn't draw a very clear line between them. This chapter argues that, given the lack of a precise distinction between race and ethnicity, it's probably better to use the term* ethnic group *instead of* race *to describe any such social group—for example, African Americans, Asian Americans, Irish Americans, Anglo Americans, or Hispanics.*

CAPE COAST, Ghana—For centuries, Africans walked through the infamous "door of no return" at Cape Coast Castle directly into slave ships, never to set foot in their homelands again. These days, the portal of this massive fort so central to one of history's greatest crimes has a new name, hung on a sign leading back in from the roaring Atlantic Ocean: "The door of return." . . .

Taking Israel as its model, Ghana hopes to persuade the descendants of enslaved Africans to think of Africa as their homeland—to visit, invest, send their children to be educated and even retire here . . .

In many ways it is a quixotic goal. Ghana is doing well by West African standards—with steady economic growth, a stable, democratic govern-

ment and broad support from the West, making it a favored place for wealthy countries to give aid.

But it remains a very poor, struggling country where a third of the population lives on less than a dollar a day, life expectancy tops out at 59 and basic services like electricity and water are sometimes scarce. Nevertheless, thousands of African-Americans already live here at least part of the year, said Valerie Papaya Mann, president of the African American Association of Ghana.

To encourage still more to come, or at least visit, Ghana plans to offer a special lifetime visa for members of the diaspora and will relax citizenship requirements so that descendants of slaves can receive Ghanaian passports. The government is also starting an advertising campaign to persuade Ghanaians to treat African-Americans more like long-lost relatives than as rich tourists.

That is harder than it sounds.

Many African-Americans who visit Africa are unsettled to find that Africans treat them—even refer to them—the same way as white tourists. The term "obruni," or "white foreigner," is applied regardless of skin color.

To African-Americans who come here seeking their roots, the term is a sign of the chasm between Africans and African-Americans. Though they share a legacy, they experience it entirely differently.

"It is a shock for any black person to be called white," said Ms. Mann, who moved here two years ago. "But it is really tough to hear it when you come with your heart to seek your roots in Africa."

The advertising campaign urges Ghanaians to drop "obruni" in favor of "akwaaba anyemi," a slightly awkward phrase fashioned from two tribal languages meaning "welcome, sister or brother." . . .

The government plans to hold a huge event in 2007 to commemorate

the 200th anniversary of the end of the trans-Atlantic trade by Britain and the 50th anniversary of Ghana's independence. The ceremonies will include traditional African burial rituals for the millions who died as a result of slavery. Estimates of the trade vary widely. . . .

Some perished on the long march from the inland villages where they were captured to seaports. Others died in the dungeons of slave castles and forts, where they were sometimes kept for months, until enough were gathered to pack the hold of a ship. Still others died in the middle passage, the longest leg of the triangular journey between Europe, Africa and the Americas. Of the estimated 11 million who crossed the sea, most went to South America and the Caribbean. About 500,000 are believed to have ended up in the United States.

The mass deportations and the divisions the slave trade wrought are wounds from which Africa still struggles to recover.

Ghana was the first sub-Saharan African nation to shake off its colonial rulers, winning its independence from Britain in 1957. Its founding father, Kwame Nkrumah, attended Lincoln University, a historically black college in Pennsylvania, and saw in African-Americans a key to developing the new nation. "Nkrumah saw the American Negro as the vanguard of the African people," said Henry Louis Gates Jr., chairman of the African and African-American studies department at Harvard. . . .

To Nkrumah, the struggle for civil rights in the diaspora and the struggles for independence from colonial rule in Africa were inextricably linked, both being expressions of the desire of black people everywhere to regain their freedom.

But Nkrumah was ousted in a coup in 1966, and by then Pan-Africanism had already given way

■ *Ghana's Cape Coast Castle (Fort Carolusborg). For centuries, Africans walked through this castle's infamous "door of no return" directly into slave ships. Today, that door has been renamed "the door of return." Ghana hopes to persuade the descendants of enslaved Africans to visit, invest, send their children to be educated and even retire here.*

to nationalism and cold war politics, sending much of the continent down a trail of autocracy, civil war and heartbreak. Still, African-Americans are drawn to Ghana's rich culture, and the history of slavery.

Ghana still has dozens of slave forts, each a chilling reminder of the brutality of the trade. At Elmina Castle, built by the Portuguese in 1482 and taken over by the Dutch 150 years later, visitors are guided through a Christian chapel built adjacent to the hall where slaves were auctioned, and the balcony over the women's dungeons from which the fort's governor would choose a concubine from the chattel below.

The room through which slaves passed into waiting ships is the emotional climax of the tour, a suffocating dungeon dimly lit by sunlight pouring through a narrow portal leading to the churning sea. . . .

For African-Americans and others in the African diaspora, there is lingering hostility and confusion about the role Africans played in the slave trade.

"The myth was our African ancestors were out on a walk one day and some bad white dude threw a net over them," Mr. Gates said. "But that wasn't the way it happened. It wouldn't have been possible without the help of Africans." Many Africans, meanwhile, often fail to see any connection at all between them and African-Americans, or feel African-Americans are better off for having been taken to the United States. Many Africans strive to emigrate; for the past 15 years, the number of Africans moving to the United States has surpassed estimates of the number forced there during any of the peak years of the slave trade. The number of immigrants from Ghana in the United States is larger than that of any other African country except Nigeria, according to the 2000 census.

"So many Africans want to go to America, so they can't understand why Americans would want to come here," said Philip Amoa-Mensah, a guide at Elmina Castle. . . .

The relationship is clearly a work in progress. Ghanaians are still learning of their ancestors' pivotal

roles in the slave trade, and slave forts on the coast, long used to thousands of foreign visitors, have in recent years become sites for school field trips. . . .

A recent African-American visitor to Cape Coast castle took the emotionally charged step through the door of no return, only to be greeted by a pair of toddlers playing in a fishing boat on the other side, pointing and shouting, "obruni, obruni!"

William Kwaku Moses, 71, a retired security guard who sells shells to tourists on the other side of the door of no return, shushed the children.

"We are trying," he said, with a shrug.

_____
SOURCE: Lydia Polgreen, "Ghana's Uneasy Embrace of Slavery's Diaspora." *New York Times*, December 27, 2005. Retrieved from http://travel2.nytimes.com/2005/12/27/international/africa/27ghana.html?ex=1142312400&en=9830f16f2ed71593&ei=5070.

occupies in society. In this sense, **status** encompasses the various positions that people occupy in society. Parent is a social status. So are professor, student, factory worker, Democrat, shoe salesperson, homeless person, labor leader, ethnic-group member, and thousands of others. People always occupy multiple statuses (e.g., Hispanic, Catholic, infant, brother). Among the statuses we occupy, particular ones dominate in particular settings, such as son or daughter at home and student in the classroom.

Some statuses are **ascribed:** People have little or no choice about occupying them. Age is an ascribed status; we can't choose not to age. Race and gender usually are ascribed; people are born members of a certain group and remain so all their lives. **Achieved statuses,** by contrast, aren't automatic; they come through choices, actions, efforts, talents, or accomplishments, and may be positive or negative (Figure 5.1). Examples of achieved statuses include physician, senator, convicted felon, salesperson, union member, father, and college student.

Status Shifting

Sometimes statuses, particularly ascribed ones, are mutually exclusive. It's hard to bridge the gap between black and white, or male and female. Sometimes, taking a status or joining a group requires a conversion experience, acquiring a new and overwhelming primary identity, such as becoming a "born again" Christian.

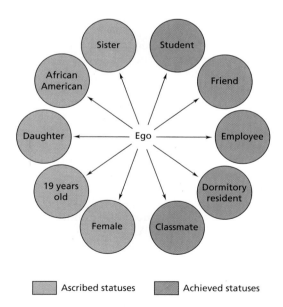

Ascribed statuses   Achieved statuses

FIGURE 5.1   Social Statuses.

The person in this figure—"ego," or "I"—occupies many social statuses. The green circles indicate ascribed statuses; the purple circles represent achieved statuses.

How do we determine who (what kind of a person) we are, and who others are? What kinds of identity cues and clues do people use to figure out who they are dealing with, and how to act in social situations? Part of human adaptive flexibility is our ability to shift statuses, varying our claimed identities in response to context. Many of the social statuses we occupy, the "hats" we wear, depend on the situation. People can be both black and Hispanic, or both a father and a ballplayer. One identity is claimed or perceived in certain settings, another in different ones. Among African Americans a "Hispanic" baseball player might be black; among Hispanics, Hispanic. When claimed or perceived identity varies depending on the audience, this is called the *situational negotiation of social identity.* As an illustration, the same man might declare any of the following, depending on the situation: "I'm Jimmy's father." "I'm your boss." "I'm African American." "I'm your professor."

We'll see in the next chapter that we vary the way we talk, as well as act, depending on our audience. In face-to-face encounters, other people can see who we are. They may expect us to think and act in certain ways based on their visual judgment of our identity, and their stereotypes about how people with that identity act. Although we can't know which aspect of identity they'll focus on (e.g., race, age, or gender), face to face it's hard to be anonymous or to be someone else. That's what masks and costumes are for.

But we don't just interact face to face. We phone, write, and—more than ever—use the Internet. Cyberspace communication is changing notions of identity and the self. Virtual worlds, such as computer role-playing games, are ways of extending ourselves into various forms of cybersocial interaction (Escobar 1994). People choose and vary their identities by using different "handles," multiple names in cyberspace. People may manipulate ("lie about") their ages and genders and create their own cyberfantasies. Of course there are subtle clues, revealed in writing. A greeting of "Dude" suggests a male. Linguistic (e.g., foreign language) background and class (educational) status may be evident in written expression. In psychology, multiple personalities are abnormal, but in anthropology, multiple identities are more and more the norm.

TABLE 5.2 American Hispanics, Latinos, 2002	
National Origin	Percentage
Mexican American	66.9%
Puerto Rican	8.6
Cuban	3.7
Central & South American	14.3
Other Hispanic/Latino origin	6.5
Total	100.0%

SOURCE: R. R. Ramirez and G. P. de la Cruz, "The Hispanic Population in the United States," *Current Population Reports,* 2003, P20-545. U.S. Census Bureau.

■ "Hispanic" and "Latino" are ethnic categories that cross-cut "racial" contrasts such as that between "black" and "white." Note the physical diversity exemplified by these Latina teenagers.

Some statuses aren't mutually exclusive, but contextual. People can be both black and Hispanic, or both a mother and a senator. One identity is used in certain settings, another in different ones. We call this the *situational negotiation of social identity.* When ethnic identity is flexible and situational, it can become an achieved status (Leman 2001).

Hispanics, for example, may move through levels of culture (shifting ethnic affiliations) as they negotiate their identities. "Hispanic" is an ethnic category based mainly on language. It includes whites, blacks, and "racially" mixed Spanish speakers and their ethnically conscious descendants. (There are also "Native American," and even "Asian," Hispanics.) "Hispanic," representing the fastest growing ethnic group in the United States, lumps together millions of people of diverse geographic origin—Puerto Rico, Mexico, Cuba, El Salvador, Guatemala, the Dominican Republic, and other Spanish-speaking countries of Central and South America and the Caribbean.

"Latino" is a broader category, which can also include Brazilians (who speak Portuguese). The national origins of American Hispanics/Latinos in 2002 were as shown in Table 5.2.

Mexican Americans (Chicanos), Cuban Americans, and Puerto Ricans may mobilize to promote general Hispanic issues (e.g., opposition to "English-only" laws) but act as three separate interest groups in other contexts. Cuban Americans are richer on average than Chicanos and Puerto Ricans are, and their class interests and voting patterns differ. Cubans often vote Republican, but Puerto Ricans and Chicanos are more likely to favor Democrats. Some Mexican Americans whose families have lived in the United States for generations have little in common with new Hispanic immigrants, such as those from Central America. Many Americans (especially those fluent in English) claim Hispanic ethnicity in some contexts but shift to a general "American" identity in others.

In many societies an ascribed status is associated with a position in the social-political hierarchy. Certain groups, called *minority groups,* are subordinate. They have inferior power and less secure access to resources than do *majority groups* (which are superordinate, dominant, or controlling). Often ethnic groups are minorities. When an ethnic group is assumed to have a biological basis (distinctively shared "blood" or genes), it is called a **race.** Discrimination against such a group is called **racism** (Cohen 1998; Kuper 2005; Montagu 1997; Scupin 2003; Shanklin 1995).

RACE

Race, like ethnicity in general, is a cultural category rather than a biological reality. That is, ethnic groups, including "races," derive from contrasts perceived and perpetuated in particular societies, such as Ghana, as described in the "News Brief," rather than from scientific classifications based on common genes (see Wade 2002).

It is not possible to define human races biologically. Only cultural constructions of race are possible—even though the average person conceptualizes "race" in biological terms. The belief that human races exist and are important is much more common among the public than it is among scientists. Most Americans, for example, believe that their population includes biologically based "races" to which various labels have been applied. These labels include "white," "black," "yellow," "red," "Caucasoid," "Negroid," "Mongoloid," "Amerindian," "Euro-American," "African American," "Asian American," and "Native American."

We hear the words *ethnicity* and *race* frequently, but American culture doesn't draw a very clear line between them. As an illustration, consider two articles in the *New York Times* of May 29, 1992. One, discussing the changing ethnic composition of the United States, states (correctly) that Hispanics "can be of any race" (Barringer 1992, p. A12). In other words, "Hispanic" is an ethnic category that cross-cuts "racial" contrasts such as that between "black" and "white." The other article reports that during the Los Angeles riots of spring 1992, "hundreds of Hispanic residents were interrogated about their immigration status on the basis of their *race* alone [emphasis added]" (Mydans 1992a, p. A8). Use of "race" here seems inappropriate because "Hispanic" is usually perceived as referring to a linguistically based (Spanish-speaking) ethnic group, rather than a biologically based race. Since these Los Angeles residents were being interrogated because they were Hispanic, the article is actually reporting on ethnic, not racial, discrimination. However, given the lack of a precise distinction between race and ethnicity, it is probably better to use the term *ethnic group* instead of *race* to describe *any* such social group, for example, African Americans, Asian Americans, Irish Americans, Anglo Americans, or Hispanics.

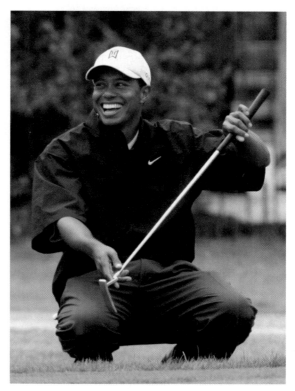

■ *Tiger Woods in Texas for the EDS Byron Nelson Championship on May 14, 2004. The number of interracial marriages and children is increasing, which has implications for the traditional American system of racial classification. What is Tiger's race?*

THE SOCIAL CONSTRUCTION OF RACE

Races are ethnic groups assumed (by members of a particular culture) to have a biological basis, but actually race is socially constructed. The "races" we hear about every day are cultural, or social, rather than biological categories. In Charles Wagley's terms (Wagley 1959/1968), they are **social races** (groups assumed to have a biological basis but actually defined in a culturally arbitrary, rather than a scientific, manner). Many Americans mistakenly assume that "whites" and "blacks," for example, are biologically distinct and that these terms stand for discrete races. But these labels, like racial terms used in other societies, really designate culturally perceived rather than biologically based groups.

Hypodescent: Race in the United States

How is race culturally constructed in the United States? In American culture, one acquires his or her racial identity at birth, but race isn't based on biology or on simple ancestry. Take the case of the child of a "racially mixed" marriage involving one black and one white parent. We know that 50 percent of the child's genes come from one parent and 50 percent from the other. Still, American culture overlooks heredity and classifies this child as black. This rule is arbitrary. From *genotype* (genetic composition), it would be just as logical to classify the child as white.

American rules for assigning racial status can be even more arbitrary. In some states, anyone known to have any black ancestor, no matter how remote, is classified as a member of the black race. This is a rule of **descent** (it assigns social identity on the basis of ancestry), but of a sort that is rare outside the contemporary United States. It is called **hypodescent** (Harris and Kottak 1963) (*hypo* means "lower") because it automatically places the children of a union or mating between members of different groups in the minority group. Hypodescent helps divide American society into groups that have been unequal in their access to wealth, power, and prestige.

The following case from Louisiana is an excellent illustration of the arbitrariness of the hypodescent rule. It also illustrates the role that governments (federal, or state in this case) play in legalizing, inventing, or eradicating race and ethnicity (Williams 1989). Susie Guillory Phipps, a light-skinned woman with "Caucasian" features and straight black hair, discovered as an adult that she was "black." When Phipps ordered a copy of her birth certificate, she found her race listed as "colored." Since she had been "brought up white and married white twice," Phipps challenged a 1970 Louisiana law declaring anyone with at least one-thirty-second "Negro blood" to be legally black. In other words, having 1 "Negro" great-great-great-grandparent out of 32 is sufficient to make one black. Although the state's lawyer

Map 7 plots the distribution of human skin color in relation to ultraviolet radiation from the sun.

admitted that Phipps "looks like a white person," the state of Louisiana insisted that her racial classification was proper (Yetman 1991, pp. 3–4).

Cases like Phipps's are rare, because "racial" and ethnic identities are usually ascribed at birth and usually don't change. The rule of hypodescent affects blacks, Asians, Native Americans, and Hispanics differently (see Hunter 2005). It's easier to negotiate Indian or Hispanic identity than black identity. The ascription rule isn't as definite, and the assumption of a biological basis isn't as strong.

To be considered "Native American," one ancestor out of eight (great-grandparents) or four (grandparents) may suffice. This depends on whether the assignment is by federal or state law or by an Indian tribal council. The child of a Hispanic may (or may not, depending on context) claim Hispanic identity. Many Americans with an Indian or Latino grandparent consider themselves "white" and lay no claim to minority-group status.

For more about race and the census, see the Virtual Exploration

mhhe.com/kottak

Race in the Census

The U.S. Census Bureau has gathered data by race since 1790. Initially this was done because the Constitution specified that a slave counted as three-fifths of a white person and because Indians were not taxed. The racial categories specified in the U.S. census include White, Black or Negro, Indian (Native American), Eskimo, Aleut or Pacific Islander, and Other. A separate question asks about Spanish-Hispanic heritage. Check out Figure 5.2 for the racial categories in the 2000 census.

An attempt by social scientists and interested citizens to add a "multiracial" census category has been opposed by the National Association for the Advancement of Colored People (NAACP) and the National Council of La Raza (a Hispanic advocacy group). Racial classification is a political issue. It involves access to resources, including jobs, voting districts, and federal funding of programs aimed at minorities. The hypodescent rule results in all the population growth being attributed to the minority category. Minorities fear their political clout will decline if their numbers go down.

But things are changing. Choice of "Some other race" in the U.S. Census more than doubled from 1980 (6.8 million) to 2000 (over 15 million)—suggesting imprecision in and dissatisfaction with the existing categories (Mar 1997). In the year 2000, 274.6 million Americans (out of 281.4 million censused) reported they belonged to just one race, as shown in Table 5.3.

Nearly 48 percent of Hispanics identified as White alone, and about 42 percent as "Some other race" alone. In the 2000 census, 2.4 percent of Americans, or 6.8 million people, chose a first-ever option of identifying themselves as belonging to more than one race. About 6 percent of Hispanics reported two or more races, compared with less than 2 percent of non-Hispanics (http://www.census.gov/Press-Release/www/2001/cb01cn61.html).

The number of interracial marriages and children is increasing, with implications for the traditional system of American racial classification. "Interracial," "biracial," or "multiracial" children who grow up with both parents undoubtedly

→ NOTE: Please answer BOTH Questions 5 and 6.

5. **Is this person Spanish/Hispanic/Latino?** *Mark* [X] *the* **"No"** *box if not Spanish/Hispanic/Latino.*

☐ **No,** not Spanish/Hispanic/Latino ☐ Yes, Puerto Rican
☐ Yes, Mexican, Mexican Am., Chicano ☐ Yes, Cuban
☐ Yes, other Spanish/Hispanic/Latino — *Print group.*

5. **What is this person's race?** *Mark* [X] *one or more races to indicate what this person considers himself/herself to be.*

☐ White
☐ Black, African Am., or Negro
☐ American Indian or Alaska Native — *Print name of enrolled or principal tribe.*

☐ Asian Indian ☐ Japanese ☐ Native Hawaiian
☐ Chinese ☐ Korean ☐ Guamanian or Chamorro
☐ Filipino ☐ Vietnamese ☐ Samoan
☐ Other Asian — *Print race.* ☐ Other Pacific Islander — *Print race.*

☐ Some other race — *Print race.*

FIGURE 5.2 Reproduction of Questions on Race and Hispanic Origin from Census 2000.

SOURCE: U.S. Census Bureau, Census 2000 questionnaire.

TABLE 5.3 Americans Reporting They Belonged to Just One Race	
White	75.1%
Black or African-American	12.3%
American Indian and Alaska Native	0.9%
Asian	3.6%
Native Hawaiian and Other Pacific Islander	0.1%
Some other race	5.5%

SOURCE: http://www.census.gov/Press-Release/www/2001/cb01cn61.html.

Perceptions of Race and Skin Color on an American College Campus

BACKGROUND INFORMATION

STUDENT:
Gretchen M. Haupt

SUPERVISING PROFESSOR:
Donna Hart

SCHOOL:
University of Missouri–St. Louis

YEAR IN SCHOOL/MAJOR:
Junior/Anthropology

FUTURE PLANS:
Complete a master's in library science and pursue research as a librarian in an academic setting.

PROJECT TITLE:
Perceptions of Race and Skin Color on an American College Campus

For her senior honors thesis, Gretchen Haupt plans to build on the research project described here. To demonstrate that Americans' perceptions of race, in relation to skin color, are arbitrary and socially constructed, Haupt asked a sample of 30 students, Euro-Americans and African Americans, to complete a task: place 30 pigment chips in order from darkest to lightest. Having done so, they were then asked to identify the dividing line between "black" and "white." How much uniformity do you expect she found in their responses? Read the essay to find out.

There is no such biological reality as separate human races. Extensive research conducted on the subject of variation within our species has only served to confirm that the biological definition of race is not applicable to humans. Despite this, people continue to put the global population in neat, concise little groups (or at least they attempt to). Inevitably, the dividing lines between geographic and/or ethnic groups cannot be genetically supported since there are no specific sets of alleles correlated with the common divisions of white, black, red, brown, or however many racial categories are postulated. While *Homo sapiens* manifests variation in physical characteristics related to a population's original geographic environment, the most commonly used method for categorization and race assignment in the United States is skin color. Consequently, I chose to focus my research on the assumptions Americans make about race and skin color.

Through this research project I wanted to test my hypothesis that the point on a continuum at which an individual labels skin color "white" or "black" is arbitrary and subjective, therefore supporting the idea that pigmentation does not translate into perceived races. I collected data from thirty individuals on the University of Missouri–St. Louis campus by means of surveys using thirty skin-tone color chips, from deep brown to pale cream. The chips were paint samples mounted on a white index card, randomly assigned a letter or symbol.

Each participant was asked to place the color chips in order from darkest to lightest and then identify where "black" ended and "white" began. By forcing individuals to choose a dividing point, I was able to evaluate hidden perceptions. They were also asked to select a color they thought most closely matched their own skin tone, where they placed their ancestry geographically, and where they would place their chosen skin color geographically.

Even though a person may intellectually accept that there are no biologically distinct races, it is my opinion that they will still evaluate every other person they encounter and attempt to assign them to one of a minimum of two groups. This illustrates how race is a socially constructed concept rather than one based in scientific fact. For the purpose of my research, I limited the group designations to African descent and European descent.

My research found considerable variability in color placement (no one placed the chips in the same order) and the point of division. My research sub-jects were asked to select the point on their constructed color continuum (the order in which they had placed the color chips) indicating where "white" skin color ended and "black" skin color began. The most commonly chosen division point was between positions 19 and 20 (smaller numbers indicate darker; larger numbers, lighter skin tone). This point was chosen by 9 of the 30 people I surveyed. The choices of the other 21 spanned between positions 15/16 and 26/27.

To prevent bias, I kept track of the colors by means of letters and symbols on the back of each chip. Letters were assigned randomly. On closer examination of the actual color chips chosen by the nine people who selected 19/20, I discovered that they had not chosen the same colors. Where one person had placed chip "Y" as number 19 (indicating s/he felt that was a black skin tone) and chip "X" as 20 (indicating s/he felt that was a white skin tone), the next had chosen different color chips—"J" and "R" (for example) for the same positions. There were even instances where the choices were complete reversals (one person chose "Y" as white and the next chose "Y" as black).

I plan to continue this research as my senior thesis (devoting a total of ten academic credit hours to the project), and expand my data collection to include individuals belonging to other ethnicities (e.g., Native American and Asian) to determine further the degree to which race is socially constructed.

See the Internet Exercises
at your OLC

mhhe.com/kottak

identify with particular qualities of either parent. It is troubling for many of them to have so important an identity as race dictated by the arbitrary rule of hypodescent. It may be especially discordant when racial identity doesn't parallel gender identity, for example, a boy with a white father and a black mother, or a girl with a white mother and a black father.

How does the Canadian census compare with the American census in its treatment of race? Rather than race, the Canadian census asks about "visible minorities." That country's Employment Equity Act defines such groups as "persons, other than Aboriginal peoples [aka First Nations in Canada, Native Americans in the United States], who are non-Caucasian in race or non-white in colour" (Statistics Canada 2001a). Table 5.4 shows that "Chinese" and "South Asian" are Canada's largest visible minorities. Note that Canada's total visible minority population of 13.4 percent (up from 11.2 percent in 1996) contrasts with a figure of about 25 percent for the United States in the 2000 Census. In particular, Canada's black 2.2 percent population contrasts with the American figure of 12.5 percent for African Americans, while Canada's Asian population is significantly higher than the U.S. figure of 3.7 percent on a percentage basis. Only a tiny fraction of the Canadian population (0.2 percent) claimed multiple visible minority affiliation, compared with 2.4 percent claiming "more than one race" in the United States in 2000.

**Bringing It
All Together**

For more on ethnic diversity in Canada, see the "Bringing It All Together" essay that immediately follows Chapter 6.

Canada's visible minority population has been increasing steadily. In 1981, 1.1 million visible minorities accounted for 4.7 percent of the total population, versus more than 13.4 percent today. Visible minorities are growing much faster than is Canada's total population. Between 1996 and 2001, the total population increased 4 percent, while visible minorities rose 25 percent. If recent immigration trends continue, by 2016, visible minorities will account for one-fifth of the Canadian population.

Not Us: Race in Japan

American culture ignores considerable diversity in biology, language, and geographic origin as it socially constructs race within the United States. North Americans also overlook diversity by seeing Japan as a nation that is homogeneous in race, ethnicity, language, and culture—an image the Japanese themselves cultivate. Thus in 1986, former Prime Minister Nakasone created an international furor by contrasting his country's supposed homogeneity (responsible, he suggested, for Japan's success in international business) with the ethnically mixed United States. To describe Japanese society, Nakasone used *tan'itsu minzoku,* an expression connoting a single ethnic-racial group (Robertson 1992).

Japan is hardly the uniform entity Nakasone described. Some dialects of the Japanese language are mutually unintelligible. Scholars estimate that

TABLE 5.4 Visible Minority Population of Canada, 2001 Census		
	Number	**Percent**
Total population	**29,639,030**	**100.0**
Total visible minority population	3,983,845	13.4
Chinese	1,029,395	3.5
South Asian	917,075	3.1
Black	662,210	2.2
Arab/West Asian	303,965	1.0
Filipino	308,575	1.0
Southeast Asian	198,880	0.7
Latin American	216,980	0.7
Korean	100,660	0.3
Japanese	73,315	0.2
Other visible minority	98,915	0.3
Multiple visible minority	73,875	0.2
Nonvisible minority	25,655,185	86.6

SOURCE: From Statistics Canada, 2001a, 2001 Census, http://www40.statcan.ca/101/cst01/demo50a.htm?sdi=visible.

10 percent of Japan's population are minorities of various sorts. These include aboriginal Ainu, annexed Okinawans, outcast *burakumin,* children of mixed marriages, and immigrant nationalities, especially Koreans, who number more than 700,000 (De Vos, Wetherall, and Stearman 1983; Lie 2001).

To describe racial attitudes in Japan, Jennifer Robertson (1992) uses Kwame Anthony Appiah's (1990) term *intrinsic racism*—the belief that a (perceived) racial difference is a sufficient reason to value one person less than another. In Japan, the valued group is majority ("pure") Japanese, who are believed to share "the same blood." Thus, the caption to a printed photo of a Japanese American model reads: "She was born in Japan but raised in Hawaii. Her nationality is American but no foreign blood flows in her veins" (Robertson 1992, p. 5). Something like hypodescent also operates in Japan, but less precisely than in the United States, where mixed offspring automatically become members of the minority group. The children of mixed marriages between majority Japanese and others (including Euro-Americans) may not get the same "racial" label as the minority parent, but they are still stigmatized for their non-Japanese ancestry (De Vos and Wagatsuma 1966).

How is race culturally constructed in Japan? The (majority) Japanese define themselves by opposition to others, whether minority groups in their own nation or outsiders—anyone who is "not us." The "not us" should stay that way; assimilation is generally discouraged. Cultural mechanisms, especially residential segregation and taboos on "interracial" marriage, work to keep minorities "in their place."

In its construction of race, Japanese culture regards certain ethnic groups as having a biological basis, when there is no evidence that they do. The best example is the *burakumin,* a stigmatized group of at least four million outcasts. They are sometimes compared to India's untouchables. The *burakumin* are physically and genetically indistinguishable from other Japanese. Many of them "pass" as (and marry) majority Japanese, but a deceptive marriage can end in divorce if *burakumin* identity is discovered (Aoki and Dardess, eds. 1981).

Burakumin are perceived as standing apart from majority Japanese. Through ancestry and descent (and thus, it is assumed, "blood," or genetics), *burakumin* are "not us." Majority Japanese try to keep their lineage pure by discouraging mixing. The *burakumin* are residentially segregated in neighborhoods (rural or urban) called *buraku,* from which the racial label is derived. Compared with majority Japanese, the *burakumin* are less likely to attend high school and college. When *burakumin* attend the same schools as majority Japanese, they face discrimination. Majority children and teachers may refuse to eat with them because *burakumin* are considered unclean.

Japan's stigmatized burakumin *are physically and genetically indistinguishable from other Japanese. In response to* burakumin *political mobilization, Japan has dismantled the legal structure of discrimination against* burakumin. *This Sports Day for* burakumin *children is one kind of mobilization.*

In applying for university admission or a job, and in dealing with the government, Japanese must list their address, which becomes part of a household or family registry. This list makes residence in a *buraku,* and likely *burakumin* social status, evident. Schools and companies use this information to discriminate. (The best way to pass is to move so often that the *buraku* address eventually disappears from the registry.) Majority Japanese also limit "race" mixture by hiring marriage mediators to check out the family histories of prospective spouses. They are especially careful to check for *burakumin* ancestry (De Vos et al. 1983).

The origin of the *burakumin* lies in a historic system of stratification (from the Tokugawa period: 1603–1868). The top four ranked categories were warrior-administrators (*samurai*), farmers, artisans, and merchants. The ancestors of the *burakumin* were below this hierarchy. An outcast group, they did unclean jobs, like animal slaughter and disposal of the dead. *Burakumin* still do related jobs, including work with animal products, like leather. The *burakumin* are more likely than majority Japanese to do manual labor (including farm work) and to belong to the national lower class. *Burakumin* and other Japanese minorities are also more likely to have careers in crime, prostitution, entertainment, and sports (De Vos et al. 1983).

Like blacks in the United States, the *burakumin* are class-stratified. Because certain jobs are reserved for the *burakumin,* people who are successful in those occupations (e.g., shoe factory owners) can be wealthy. *Burakumin* also have found jobs as government bureaucrats. Financially successful *burakumin* can temporarily escape their stigmatized status by travel, including foreign travel.

Discrimination against the *burakumin* is strikingly like the discrimination that blacks have faced in the United States. The *burakumin* often live in villages and neighborhoods with poor housing and sanitation. They have limited access to education, jobs, amenities, and health facilities. In response to *burakumin* political mobilization, Japan has dismantled the legal structure of discrimination against *burakumin* and has worked to improve conditions in the *buraku*. Still, Japan has not instituted American-style affirmative action programs for education and jobs. Discrimination against nonmajority Japanese is still the rule in companies. Some employers say that hiring *burakumin* would give their companies an unclean image and thus create a disadvantage in competing with other businesses (De Vos et al. 1983).

Phenotype and Fluidity: Race in Brazil

There are more flexible, less exclusionary ways of constructing social race than those used in the United States and Japan. Along with the rest of Latin America, Brazil has less exclusionary categories, which permit individuals to change their racial classification. Brazil shares a history of slavery with the United States, but it lacks the hypodescent rule. Nor does Brazil have racial aversion of the sort found in Japan.

Brazilians use many more racial labels—over 500 have been reported (Harris 1970)—than Americans or Japanese do. In northeastern Brazil I found 40 different racial terms in use in Arembepe, a village of only 750 people (Kottak 2006). Through their classification system Brazilians recognize and attempt to describe the physical variation that exists in their population. The system used in the United States, by recognizing only three or four races, blinds Americans to an equivalent range of evident physical contrasts. The system Brazilians use to construct social race has other special features. In the United States one's race is an ascribed status; it is assigned automatically by hypodescent and doesn't usually change. In Brazil racial identity is more flexible, more of an achieved status. Brazilian racial classification pays attention to phenotype. **Phenotype** refers to an organism's evident traits, its "manifest biology"—physiology and anatomy, including skin color, hair form, facial features, and eye color. A Brazilian's phenotype and racial label may change because of environmental factors, such as the tanning rays of the sun or the effects of humidity on the hair.

As physical characteristics change (sunlight alters skin color, humidity affects hair form), so do racial terms. Furthermore, racial differences may be so insignificant in structuring community life that people may forget the terms they have applied to others. Sometimes they even forget the ones they've used for themselves. In Arembepe, I made it a habit to ask the same person on different days to tell me the races of others in the village (and my own). In the United States I am always "white" or "Euro-American," but in Arembepe I got lots of terms besides *branco* ("white"). I could be *claro* ("light"), *louro* ("blond"), *sarará* ("light-skinned redhead"), *mulato claro* ("light mulatto"), or *mulato* ("mulatto"). The racial term used to describe me or anyone else varied from person to person, week to week, even day to day. My best informant, a man with very dark skin color, changed the term he used for himself all the time—from *escuro* ("dark") to *preto* ("black") to *moreno escuro* ("dark brunet").

The American and Japanese racial systems are creations of particular cultures, rather than scientific—or even accurate—descriptions of human biological differences. Brazilian racial classification is also a cultural construction, but Brazilians have developed a way of describing human biological diversity that is more detailed, fluid, and flexible than the systems used in most cultures. Brazil lacks Japan's racial aversion, and it also lacks a rule of descent like that which ascribes racial status in the United States (Degler 1970; Harris 1964).

For centuries the United States and Brazil have had mixed populations, with ancestors from Native America, Europe, Africa, and Asia. Although "races" have mixed in both countries, Brazilian and American cultures have constructed the results differently. The historical reasons for this contrast lie mainly in the different characteristics of the settlers of the two countries. The mainly English early settlers of the United States came as women, men, and families, but Brazil's Portuguese colonizers were mainly men—merchants and adventurers. Many of these Portuguese men married Native American women and recognized their "racially mixed" children as their heirs. Like their North American counterparts, Brazilian plantation owners had sexual relations with their slaves. But the Brazilian landlords more often freed the children that resulted—for demographic and economic reasons. (Sometimes these were their only children.) Freed offspring of master and slave became plantation overseers and foremen and filled many intermediate positions in the emerging Brazilian economy. They were not classed with the slaves, but were allowed to join a new intermediate category. No hypodescent rule developed in Brazil to ensure that whites and blacks remained separate (see Degler 1970; Harris 1964).

STRATIFICATION AND "INTELLIGENCE"

Over the centuries groups with power have used racial ideology to justify, explain, and preserve their privileged social positions. Dominant groups have declared minorities to be *innately*, that is, biologically, inferior. Racial ideas are used

■ These photos, taken in Brazil by the author in 2003 and 2004, give just a glimpse of the spectrum of phenotypical diversity encountered among contemporary Brazilians.

to suggest that social inferiority and presumed shortcomings (in intelligence, ability, character, or attractiveness) are immutable and passed across the generations. This ideology defends stratification as inevitable, enduring, and "natural"—based in biology rather than society. Thus the Nazis argued for the superiority of the "Aryan race," and European colonialists asserted the "white man's burden." South Africa institutionalized *apartheid*. Again and again, to justify exploitation of minorities and native peoples, those in control have proclaimed the innate inferiority of the oppressed. In the United States the supposed superiority of whites was once standard segregationist doctrine. Belief in the biologically based inferiority of Native Americans has been an argument for their slaughter, confinement, and neglect.

However, anthropologists know that most of the behavioral variation among contemporary human groups rests on culture rather than biology. The cultural similarities revealed through thousands of ethnographic studies leave no doubt that capacities for cultural evolution are equal in all human populations. There is also excellent evidence that within any **stratified** (class-based) society, differences in performance between economic, social, and ethnic groups reflect different experiences and opportunities rather than genetic makeup. (Stratified societies are those with marked differences in wealth, prestige, and power between social classes.)

Stratification, political domination, prejudice, and ignorance continue to exist. They propagate the mistaken belief that misfortune and poverty result from lack of ability. Occasionally doctrines of innate superiority are even set forth by scientists, who, after all, tend to come from the favored stratum of society. One example is Jensenism, named for the educational psychologist Arthur Jensen (Herrnstein 1971; Jensen 1969), its leading proponent. Jensenism is a highly questionable interpretation of the observation that African Americans, on average, perform less well on intelligence tests than Euro-Americans do. Jensenism asserts that blacks are hereditarily incapable of performing as well as whites do. Richard Herrnstein, writing with Charles Murray, makes a similar argument in the 1994 book *The Bell Curve,* to which the following critique also applies.

Environmental explanations for test scores are much more convincing than are the genetic tenets of Jensen, Herrnstein, and Murray (see Montagu, ed. 1999). An environmental explanation does not deny that some people may be smarter than others. In any society, for many reasons, genetic and environmental, the talents of individuals vary. An environmental explanation does deny, however, that these differences can be generalized to whole groups. Even when talking about individual intelligence, however, we have to decide which of several abilities is an accurate measure of intelligence.

Most intelligence tests are written by educated people in Europe and North America. They reflect the experiences of the people who devise them. It is not surprising that middle- and upper-class children do better since they are more likely to share the test makers' educational background and standards. Numerous studies have shown that performance on Scholastic Achievement Tests (SATs) can be improved by coaching and preparation. Parents who can afford $500 or more for an SAT preparation course enhance their kids' chances of getting high scores. Standardized college entrance exams are similar to IQ tests in that they purportedly measure intellectual aptitude. They may do this, but they also measure type and quality of high school education, linguistic and cultural background, and parental wealth. No test is free of class, ethnic, and cultural biases.

Tests invariably measure particular learning histories, not the potential for learning. They use middle-class performance as a standard for determining what should be known at a given chronological age. Furthermore, tests are usually administered by middle-class white people who give instructions in a dialect or language that may not be totally familiar to the child being tested. Test performance improves when the subcultural, socioeconomic, and linguistic backgrounds of subjects and test personnel are similar.

Links between social, economic, and educational environment and test performance show up in comparisons of American blacks and whites. At the beginning of World War I, intelligence tests were given to approximately 1 million American army recruits. Blacks from some northern states had higher average scores than did whites from some southern states. At that time northern blacks got a better public education than did many southern whites. Thus, their superior performance is not surprising. On the other hand, southern whites did better than southern blacks. This was also expectable, given the unequal school systems then open to whites and blacks in the South.

Racists tried to dismiss the environmental explanation for the superior performance of northern blacks compared with southern whites by suggesting selective migration—smarter blacks had moved north. However, it was possible to test this hypothesis, which turned out to be false. If smarter blacks had moved north, their superior intelligence should have been evident in their school records while they were still living in the South. It was not. Furthermore, studies in New York, Washington, and Philadelphia showed that as length of residence increased, test scores also rose.

Studies of identical twins raised apart also illustrate the impact of environment on identical heredity. In a study of nineteen pairs of twins, IQ scores varied directly with years in school. The average difference in IQ was only 1.5 points for the eight twin pairs with the same amount of schooling. It was 10 points for the eleven pairs with an average of five years' difference. One subject, with fourteen years more education than his twin, scored 24 points higher (Bronfenbrenner 1975).

These and similar studies provide overwhelming evidence that test performance measures education and social, economic, and cultural background rather than genetically determined intelligence. During the past 500 years Europeans and their descendants extended their political and economic control over most of the world. They colonized and occupied environments that they reached in their ships and conquered with their weapons. Most people in the most powerful contemporary nations—located in North America, Europe, and Asia—have light skin color. Some people in these currently powerful countries may incorrectly assert and believe that their world position has resulted from innate biological superiority. However, all contemporary human populations seem to have comparable learning abilities.

We are living in and interpreting the world at a particular time. In the past there were far different associations between centers of power and human physical characteristics. When Europeans lived in tribes, advanced civilizations thrived in the Middle East. When Europe was in the Dark Ages, there were civilizations in West Africa, on the East African coast, in Mexico, and in Asia. Before the Industrial Revolution, the ancestors of many white Europeans and Americans were living much more like precolonial Africans than like current members of the American middle class. Their average performance on 21st-century IQ tests would have been abominable.

ETHNIC GROUPS, NATIONS, AND NATIONALITIES

The term **nation** was once synonymous with "tribe" or "ethnic group"—what today we might call a cultural community. All these terms have been used to refer to a single ethnic unit, living together or apart, sharing perhaps a common language, religion, history, territory, ancestry, or genealogy. Thus, one could speak interchangeably of the Seneca (American Indian) nation, tribe, or ethnic group. Now, in our everyday language, nation has come to mean a **state**—an independent, centrally organized political unit—a government. Nation and state have become synonymous. Combined in **nation-state,** they refer to an autonomous political entity, a "country"—like the United States, "one nation, indivisible." "Nation" and "state" probably have become synonymous because of the prevalence of the idea of self-determination—that each group of people should have its own state (see Farnan 2004).

Because of migration, conquest, and colonialism, most nation-states are ethnically heterogeneous. Of 132 nation-states existing in 1971, Connor (1972) found only 12 (9 percent) to be ethnically homogeneous. In another 25 countries (19 percent), a single ethnic group accounted for more than 90 percent of the population. Forty percent of the countries had more than 5 significant ethnic groups. In a later study, Nielsson (1985) found that in only 45 of 164 states (27 percent) did a single ethnic group have more than 95 percent of the population.

Nationalities and Imagined Communities

Groups that now have, or wish to have or regain, autonomous political status (their own country) are called **nationalities.** In the words of Benedict Anderson (1991), nationalities are "imagined communities." Their members do not form an actual face-to-face community. They can only imagine that they all belong to and participate in the same group. Even when they become nation-states, they remain imagined communities, because most of their members, though feeling strong comradeship, will never meet (Anderson 1991, pp. 6–10).

Anderson traces Western European nationalism, which arose in imperial powers such as England, France, and Spain, back to the 18th century. He stresses that language and print played a crucial role in the growth of European national consciousness. (See "Interesting Issues" on pp. 110–111 for a modern illustration.) The novel and the newspaper were "two forms of imagining" communities that flowered in the 18th century (Anderson 1991, pp. 24–25). Such communities consisted of people who read the same sources and thus witnessed the same events.

Political upheavals and wars have divided many nationalities. The German and Korean homelands were artificially divided after wars, and according to socialist and capitalist ideologies. World War I split the Kurds, who form a majority in no state. They are a minority group in Turkey, Iran, Iraq, and Syria.

Migration is another reason certain nationally based ethnic groups now live in different nation-states. Massive migration in the decades before and after 1900 brought Germans, Poles, and Italians to Brazil, Canada, and the United States. Chinese, Senegalese, Lebanese, and Jews have spread all over the world. Some such people (e.g., descendants of Germans in Brazil and the United States) have assimilated to their host nations and no longer feel part of the imagined community of their origin. Such dispersed populations, which have spread out, voluntarily or not, from a common center or homeland, are called *diasporas*. The African diaspora, for example, encompasses descendants of Africans worldwide, such as in the United States, the Caribbean, and Brazil.

See the Internet Exercises at your OLC for information on ethnicity in Nigeria

mhhe.com/kottak

Ethnic Nationalism Runs Wild

The Socialist Federal Republic of Yugoslavia was a nonaligned country outside the former Soviet Union (U.S.S.R.). Like the U.S.S.R., Yugoslavia fell apart, mainly along ethnic and religious lines, in the early 1990s. Among Yugoslavia's ethnic groups were Roman Catholic Croats, Eastern Orthodox Serbs, Muslim Slavs, and ethnic Albanians. Citing ethnic and religious differences, several republics broke away from Yugoslavia in 1991–1992. These republics included

For more on Bosnia see the Virtual Exploration and the Internet Exercises at your OLC

mhhe.com/kottak

Slovenia, Croatia, and Bosnia-Herzegovina (see Figure 5.3). Serbia and Montenegro are the two remaining republics within Yugoslavia. In Kosovo, which is a province in Serbia, but one whose population is 90 percent ethnic Albanian, there has been a strong movement for independence, led by the Kosovo Liberation Army.

Much of the ethnic differentiation in Yugoslavia has been based on religion, culture, political and military history, and some differences involving

FIGURE 5.3 Former Yugoslavia, with Province and Republics.

The former Yugoslavia, although a socialist nation, was a nonaligned country outside the former Soviet Union. Like the U.S.S.R., Yugoslavia disintegrated in the early 1990s. The breakaway portions included Slovenia, Croatia, and Bosnia-Herzegovina.

language. Serbo-Croatian is a Slavic language spoken, with dialect variation, by Serbs, Croats, and Muslim Slavs alike. (Albanian is a separate language.) Croats and Serbs use different alphabets. The Croats have adopted the Roman alphabet, but the Serbs use the Cyrillic alphabet, which they share with Russia and Bulgaria. The two alphabets help promote ethnic differentiation and nationalism. Serbs and Croats, who share speech, are divided by writing—by literature, newsprint, and political manifestos.

The Yugoslav Serbs reacted violently—with military intervention—after a 1992 vote for the independence of Muslim-led Bosnia-Herzegovina, whose population is one-third Serbian. In Bosnia, the Serbs initiated a policy of forced expulsion—"ethnic purification"—against Croats, but mainly against Muslim Slavs. Serbs in Yugoslavia, who controlled the national army, lent their support to the Bosnian Serbs in their "ethnic-cleansing" campaign.

Backed by the Yugoslav army, Bosnian Serb militias rounded up Bosnian Muslims, killed groups of them, and burned and looted their homes. Thousands of Slavs fled. Hundreds of thousands of Muslims became involuntary refugees in tent camps, school gyms, and parks.

The Serbs had no use for the ethnic coexistence that the previous Yugoslav socialist government had encouraged. The Serbs also wished to avenge historic affronts by Muslims and Croats. In the 15th century, Muslim Turks had overthrown a Serbian ruler, persecuted the Serbs, and—eventually—converted

In creating multiethnic states, former colonial powers such as France and England often erected boundaries that corresponded poorly with preexisting cultural divisions. But colonial institutions also helped create new "imagined communities" beyond nations. One example is the idea of *négritude* ("black association and identity"). This concept was developed by dark-skinned intellectuals from the Francophone (French-speaking) colonies of West Africa and the Caribbean. (Günther Schlee, ed. [2002] provides cases illustrating the role of "imagined differences" in ethnic conflict—the dark side of imagining communities.)

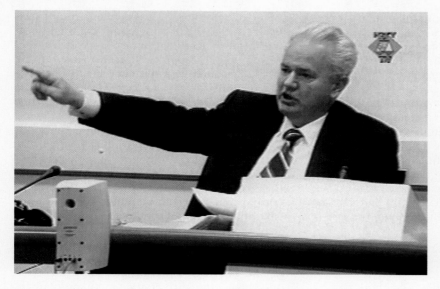

Former Yugoslav leader Slobodan Milosevic points across the court as he questions Croatian President Stipe Mesic at Milosevic's genocide trial at The Hague, Netherlands on October 2, 2002. Milosevic was allowed to defend himself during a trial that lasted two and a half years. Milosevic died on March 11, 2006, before his trial could be concluded.

many local people to Islam during their centuries of rule in this area. Bosnian Serbs still resent Muslims—including the descendants of the converts—for the Turkish conquest.

Bosnian Serbs claimed to be fighting to resist the Muslim-dominated government of Bosnia-Herzegovina. They feared that a policy of Islamic fundamentalism might arise and threaten the Serbian Orthodox Church and other expressions of Serbian identity. The Serbs' goal was to carve up Bosnia along ethnic lines, and they wanted two-thirds of it for themselves. A stated aim of Bosnia's ethnic purification was to ensure that the Serbs would never again be dominated by another ethnic group (Burns 1992*a*).

Although the Croats and the Muslim Slavs also carried out forced deportations in other parts of the former Yugoslavia, the Serbian campaign in Bosnia was the widest and the most systematic. More than 200,000 people were killed during the Bosnian conflict (Cohen 1995). With Bosnia's capital,

the multiethnic city of Sarajevo, under siege, the conflict was suspended after a December 1995 peace settlement was signed in Dayton, Ohio.

In spring 1999 NATO began a 78-day bombing campaign against Yugoslavia in retaliation for Serbian atrocities against ethnic Albanians in the separatist province of Kosovo. In May 1999 the then Yugoslav president, Slobodan Milosevic, was indicted for abuses against the Kosovar Albanian population by the war crimes tribunal in the Hague, Netherlands. By June 1999, accords ending 78 days of NATO bombing placed Kosovo under international control, enforced by NATO peacekeepers, who remain there as of this writing. In the year 2000 Yugoslavia itself took several steps toward democracy. In September 2000, Milosevic was voted out of office and replaced by a new president, Vajislav Kostinica. Parliamentary elections in December 2000 removed the last vestiges of power Milosevic had built up during

the previous decade. On June 28, 2001, Milosevic was transferred from a Belgrade jail to a prison cell in the Hague, Netherlands, for trial by the United Nations war crimes tribunal there. Before that trial could end, Milosevic died in his cell in March 2006.

How can we explain Yugoslavia's ethnic conflict? Ethnic distinctions represent people's perceptions of cultural differences, and people may overlook even very strong cultural similarities when circumstances make their differences more important. According to Fredrik Barth (see p. 112), ethnic differences are most secure and enduring in places where the groups occupy different ecological niches: They make their living in different ways or places, don't compete, and are mutually dependent. In Bosnia, the Serbs, the Croats, and the Muslim Slavs were more mixed than they were in any other former Yugoslav republic (Burns 1992*b*). Is it possible that the boundaries among the three groups were not sharp enough to keep them together by keeping them apart?

PEACEFUL COEXISTENCE

Ethnic diversity may be associated with positive group interaction and coexistence or with conflict—which is discussed in the next section. In many nations, multiple cultural groups live together in reasonable harmony. Three ways of realizing such peaceful coexistence are assimilation, the plural society, and multiculturalism.

Assimilation

Assimilation describes the process of change that a minority ethnic group may experience when it moves to a country where another culture dominates. By assimilating, the minority adopts the patterns and norms of its host culture. It is incorporated into the dominant culture to the point that it no longer exists as a separate cultural unit.

This is the "melting pot" model; ethnic groups give up their own cultural traditions as they blend into a common national stew. Some countries, such as Brazil, are more assimilationist than others are. Germans, Italians, Japanese, Middle Easterners, and East Europeans started migrating to Brazil late in the 19th century. These immigrants have assimilated to a common Brazilian culture, which has Portuguese, African, and Native American roots. The descendants of these immigrants speak the national language (Portuguese) and participate in the national culture. (During World War II, Brazil, which was on the Allied side, forced assimilation by banning instruction in any language other than Portuguese—especially in German.)

The Plural Society

Assimilation isn't inevitable, and there can be ethnic harmony without it. Ethnic distinctions can be maintained, rather than assimilated, despite decades, or even generations, of interethnic contact. Through a study of three ethnic groups in Swat, Pakistan, Fredrik Barth (1958/1968) challenged an old idea that interaction always leads to assimilation. He showed that ethnic groups can be in contact for generations without assimilating and that they can live in peaceful coexistence.

Barth (1958/1968, p. 324) defines a **plural society** as a society combining ethnic contrasts, ecological specialization (that is, use of different environmental resources by each ethnic group), and the economic interdependence of those groups. Consider his description of the Middle East (in the 1950s): "The 'environment' of any one ethnic group is not only defined by natural conditions, but also by the presence and activities of the other ethnic groups on which it depends. Each group exploits only part of the total environment, and leaves large parts of it open for other groups to exploit."

In Barth's view, ethnic boundaries are most stable and enduring when the groups occupy different ecological niches. That is, they make their living in different ways and don't compete. Ideally, they should depend on each other's activities and exchange with one another. Under such conditions, ethnic diversity can be maintained, although the specific cultural features of each group may change. By shifting the analytic focus from specific cultural practices and values to the *relations* between ethnic groups, Barth (1958/1968 and 1969) has made important contributions to ethnic studies.

Multiculturalism and Ethnic Identity

The view of cultural diversity in a country as something good and desirable is called **multiculturalism** (see Kottak and Kozaitis 2003). The multicultural model is the opposite of the assimilationist model, in which minorities are expected to abandon their cultural traditions and values, replacing them with those of the majority population. The multicultural view encourages the practice of cultural-ethnic traditions. A multicultural society socializes individuals not only into the dominant (national) culture but also into an ethnic culture. Thus in the United States millions of people speak both English and another language, eat both "American" (apple pie, steak, hamburgers) and "ethnic" foods, and celebrate both national (July 4, Thanksgiving) and ethnic-religious holidays.

In the United States and Canada multiculturalism is of growing importance. This reflects an awareness that the number and size of ethnic groups have grown dramatically in recent years. If this trend continues, the ethnic composition of the United States will change dramatically (see Figure 5.4).

Because of immigration and differential population growth, whites are now outnumbered by minorities in many urban areas. For example, of the 8,008,278 people living in New York City in 2000, 27 percent were black, 27 percent Hispanic, 10 percent Asian, and 36 percent other—including non-Hispanic whites. The comparable figures for Los Angeles (3,694,820 people) were 11 percent

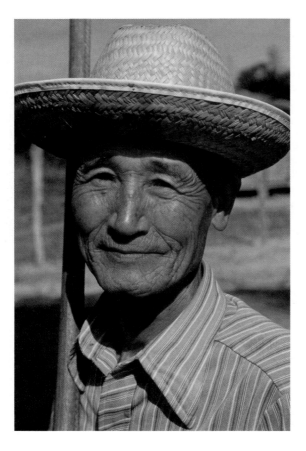

■ *German, Italian, Japanese, Middle Eastern, and Eastern European immigrants have assimilated, culturally and linguistically, to a common Brazilian culture. Shown here, a Brazilian farmer of Japanese ancestry in the Amazon. More than 220,000 people of Japanese descent live in Brazil, mostly in and around the southern city of São Paulo, Brazil's largest.*

black, 47 percent Hispanic, 9 percent Asian, and 33 percent other—including non-Hispanic whites (Census 2000, www.census.gov; see also Laguerre 2001).

One response to ethnic diversification and awareness has been for many whites to reclaim ethnic identities (Italian, Albanian, Serbian, Lithuanian, etc.) and to join ethnic associations (clubs, gangs). Some such groups are new. Others have existed for decades, although they lost members during the assimilationist years of the 1920s through the 1950s.

Multiculturalism seeks ways for people to understand and interact that don't depend on sameness but rather on respect for differences. Multiculturalism stresses the interaction of ethnic groups and their contribution to the country. It assumes that each group has something to offer and learn from the others.

Several forces have propelled North America away from the assimilationist model toward multiculturalism. First, multiculturalism reflects the fact of recent large-scale migration, particularly from the "less-developed countries" to the "developed" nations of North America and Western Europe. The global scale of modern migration introduces unparalleled ethnic variety to host nations. Multiculturalism is related to globalization: People use modern means of transportation to migrate to nations whose lifestyles they learn about through the media and from tourists who increasingly visit their own countries.

Migration is also fueled by rapid population growth, coupled with insufficient jobs (for both educated and uneducated people), in the less developed countries. As traditional rural economies decline or mechanize, displaced farmers move to cities, where they and their children are often unable to find jobs. As people in the less-developed countries get better educations, they seek more skilled employment. They hope to partake of an international culture of consumption that includes such modern amenities as refrigerators, televisions, and automobiles.

In a world with growing rural-urban and transnational migration, ethnic identities are used increasingly to form self-help organizations focused mainly on enhancing the group's economic competitiveness (Williams 1989). People claim and express ethnic identities for political and economic reasons. Michel Laguerre's (1984, 1998) studies of Haitian immigrants in the United States show that they mobilize to deal with the discriminatory structure (racist in this case, since Haitians tend to be black) of American society. Ethnicity (their common Haitian creole language and cultural background) is an evident basis for their mobilization. Haitian ethnicity then helps distinguish them from African Americans and other ethnic groups who may be competing for the same resources and recognition.

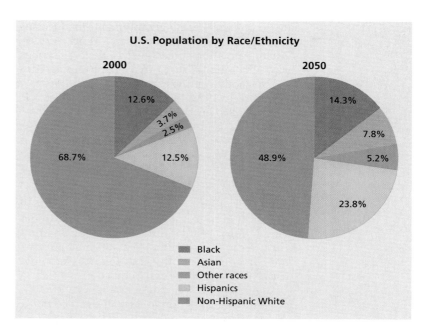

U.S. Population by Race/Ethnicity

2000: 12.6%, 3.7%, 2.5%, 12.5%, 68.7%

2050: 14.3%, 7.8%, 5.2%, 23.8%, 48.9%

Legend:
- Black
- Asian
- Other races
- Hispanics
- Non-Hispanic White

FIGURE 5.4 Ethnic Composition of the United States.
The proportion of the American population that is white and non-Hispanic is declining. The projection for 2050 shown here comes from a U.S. Census Bureau report issued in March 2004. Note especially the dramatic rise in the Hispanic portion of the American population between 2000 and 2050. SOURCE: Based on data from U.S. Census Bureau, International Data Base, Table 094, http://www.census.gov/ipc/www/idbprint.html.

In the United States and Canada, multiculturalism is of growing importance. Especially in large cities like Toronto (shown here), people of diverse backgrounds attend ethnic fairs and festivals and feast on ethnic foods. What are some other expressions of multiculturalism in your society?

In the face of globalization, much of the world, including the entire "democratic West," is experiencing an "ethnic revival." The new assertiveness of long-resident ethnic groups extends to the Basques and Catalans in Spain, the Bretons and Corsicans in France, and the Welsh and Scots in the United Kingdom. The United States and Canada

Bringing It All Together

For more on Canadian multiculturalism, see the "Bringing It All Together" essay that immediately follows Chapter 6.

are becoming increasingly multicultural, focusing on their internal diversity (see Laguerre 1999). "Melting pots" no longer, they are better described as ethnic "salads" (each ingredient remains distinct, although in the same bowl, with the same dressing). In 1992, then New York mayor David Dinkins called his city a "gorgeous mosaic."

ROOTS OF ETHNIC CONFLICT

Ethnicity, based on perceived cultural similarities and differences in a society or nation, can be expressed in peaceful multiculturalism or in discrimination or violent interethnic confrontation. Culture can be both adaptive and maladaptive. The perception of cultural differences can have disastrous effects on social interaction.

The roots of ethnic differentiation—and therefore, potentially, of ethnic conflict—can be political, economic, religious, linguistic, cultural, or "racial" (see Kuper 2005). Why do ethnic differences often lead to conflict and violence? The causes include a sense of injustice because of resource distribution, economic and/or political competition, and reaction to discrimination, prejudice, and other expressions of threatened or devalued identity (Ryan 1990, p. xxvii).

Prejudice and Discrimination

Ethnic conflict often arises in reaction to prejudice (attitudes and judgments) or discrimination (action). **Prejudice** means devaluing (looking

STUDENT CD-ROM LIVING ANTHROPOLOGY

The Return Home
Track 5

This clip focuses on ethnic diversity in Bosnia. The war described in this chapter's "Interesting Issues" box (pp. 110–111) may have ended, but ethnic animosity remains. In discussing the living arrangements of Croats and Muslims, the narrator of the clip describes a "checkerboard" settlement pattern that existed before the war. What does he mean by this? The clip shows that both Muslims and Croats were displaced by the war. Was the village of Bukovica, where the clip is mainly set, originally a Muslim or a Croat village? How is ethnic difference marked in everyday life, in such routine activities as buying things, talking on the phone, and driving an automobile? See "Interesting Issues" for aspects of ethnic diversity in Bosnia not addressed in the clip.

down on) a group because of its assumed behavior, values, capabilities, or attributes. People are prejudiced when they hold stereotypes about groups and apply them to individuals. (*Stereotypes* are fixed ideas—often unfavorable—about what the members of a group are like.) Prejudiced people assume that members of the group will act as they are "supposed to act" (according to the stereotype) and interpret a wide range of individual behaviors as evidence of the stereotype. They use this behavior to confirm their stereotype (and low opinion) of the group.

Discrimination refers to policies and practices that harm a group and its members. Discrimination may be *de facto* (practiced, but not legally sanctioned) or *de jure* (part of the law). An example of de facto discrimination is the harsher treatment that American minorities (compared with other Americans) tend to get from the police and the judicial system. This unequal treatment isn't legal, but it happens anyway. Segregation in the southern United States and *apartheid* in South Africa provide two examples of de jure discrimination, which are no longer in existence. In both systems, by law, blacks and whites had different rights and privileges. Their social interaction ("mixing) was legally curtailed.

Chips in the Mosaic

Although the multicultural model is increasingly prominent in North America, ethnic competition and conflict are just as evident. There is conflict between new arrivals, for instance, Central Americans and Koreans, and long-established ethnic groups, such as African Americans. Ethnic antagonism flared in South-Central Los Angeles in spring 1992 in rioting that followed the acquittal of four white police officers who were tried for the videotaped beating of Rodney King (see Abelmann and Lie 1995).

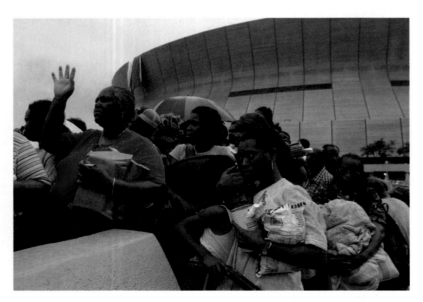

■ *In New Orleans, Louisiana, four family members wait in a hostile line for buses to take them to the Houston Astrodome on September 1, 2005, days after Hurricane Katrina flooded New Orleans. Discrimination refers to policies and practices that harm a group and its members. Does the fact that African Americans bore the brunt of the devastation caused by Hurricane Katrina in New Orleans constitute discrimination?*

Angry blacks attacked whites, Koreans, and Latinos. This violence expressed frustration by African Americans about their prospects in an increasingly multicultural society. A *New York Times*/CBS News Poll conducted May 8, 1992, just after the Los Angeles riots, found that blacks had a bleaker outlook than whites about the effects of immigration on their lives. Only 23 percent of the blacks felt they had more opportunities than recent immigrants, compared with twice that many whites (Toner 1992).

Korean stores were hard hit during the 1992 riots, and more than a third of the businesses destroyed were Latino-owned. A third of those who died in the riots were Latinos. These mainly recent migrants lacked deep roots to the neighborhood and, as Spanish speakers, faced language barriers (Newman 1992). Many Koreans also had trouble with English.

Koreans interviewed on ABC's *Nightline* on May 6, 1992, recognized that blacks resented them and considered them unfriendly. One man explained, "It's not part of our culture to smile." African Americans interviewed on the same program did complain about Korean unfriendliness. "They come into our neighborhoods and treat us like dirt." These comments suggest a shortcoming of the multicultural perspective: Ethnic groups (blacks here) expect other ethnic groups in the same nation-state to assimilate to some extent to a shared (national) culture. The African Americans' comments invoked a general American value system that includes friendliness, openness, mutual respect, community participation, and "fair play." Los Angeles blacks wanted their Korean neighbors to act more like generalized Americans—and good neighbors.

Aftermaths of Oppression

Fueling ethnic conflict are such forms of discrimination as genocide, forced assimilation, ethnocide, and cultural colonialism. *Genocide* refers to the physical destruction of an ethnic or religious group (e.g., Jews, Muslims) through mass murder. Examples include the Holocaust of Nazi Germany and "ethnic cleaning" in Bosnia, as described in "Interesting Issues" on pp. 110–111. A dominant group may try to destroy the cultures of certain ethnic groups (*ethnocide*) or force them to adopt the dominant culture (*forced assimilation*). Many countries have penalized or banned the language and customs of an ethnic group (including its religious observances). One example of forced assimilation is the anti-Basque campaign that the dictator Francisco Franco (who ruled between 1939 and 1975) waged in Spain. Franco banned Basque books, journals, newspapers, signs, sermons, and tombstones and imposed fines for using the Basque language in schools. His policies led to the formation of a Basque ter-

A refugee camp in Chad. Arab militias, called the Janjaweed, have forced black Africans off their land in the Darfur region of western Sudan, which borders Chad, through a campaign of killing, rape, and pillage. The Arab militias, equipped by the Sudanese government, are accused of killing up to 30,000 darker-skinned Africans in a campaign that United Nations officials say constitutes ethnic cleansing. Since the violence began in March 2003, more than one million people have fled to refugee camps in Sudan and Chad.

rorist group and spurred strong nationalist sentiment in the Basque region (Ryan 1990).

A policy of *ethnic expulsion* aims at removing groups that are culturally different from a country. There are many examples, including Bosnia-Herzegovina in the 1990s (see "Interesting Issues" on pp. 110–111). Uganda expelled 74,000 Asians in 1972. The neofascist parties of contemporary Western Europe advocate repatriation (expulsion) of immigrant workers (West Indians in England, Algerians in France, and Turks in Germany) (Ryan 1990, p. 9).

A policy of expulsion may create **refugees**— people who have been forced (involuntary refugees) or who have chosen (voluntary refugees) to flee a country, to escape persecution or war.

Colonialism, another form of oppression, refers to the political, social, economic, and cultural domination of a territory and its people by a foreign power for an extended time (Bell 1981). The British and French colonial empires are familiar examples of colonialism, but we can extend the term to the former Soviet empire, formerly known as the "Second World."

Using the labels "First World," "Second World," and "Third World" is a common, although clearly ethnocentric, way of categorizing nations (See Figure 5.5). The First World refers to the "democratic West"—traditionally conceived in opposition to a "Second World" ruled by "communism." The First World includes Canada, the United States, Western

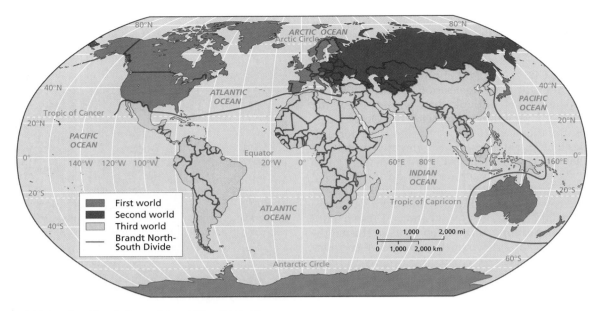

FIGURE 5.5   "First," "Second," and "Third" Worlds.

Use of "First World," "Second World," and "Third World" is a common, albeit ethnocentric, way of categorizing nations. "First World" refers to the "democratic West"—traditionally conceived in opposition to a "Second World" ruled by "communism." The "less-developed countries" or "developing nations" make up the "Third World." Another way of viewing the world in terms of differential economic and political influence is the Brandt North–South divide. This division classifies Australia and New Zealand as northern nations even though they are in the Southern Hemisphere. The map shows both divisions.

Europe, Japan, Australia, and New Zealand. The *Second World* refers to the Warsaw Pact nations, including the former Soviet Union and the Socialist and once-Socialist countries of Eastern Europe and Asia. Proceeding with this classification, the "less-developed countries" or "developing nations" make up the *Third World.*

The frontiers imposed by colonialism weren't usually based on, and often didn't reflect, preex-

isting cultural units. In many countries, colonial nation building left ethnic strife in its wake. Thus, over a million Hindus and Muslims were killed in the violence that accompanied the division of the Indian subcontinent into India and Pakistan. Problems between Arabs and Jews in Palestine began during the British mandate period.

Multiculturalism may be growing in the United States and Canada, but the opposite is

■ *Two faces of ethnic difference in the former Soviet empire. A propaganda poster depicts a happy mix of nationalities that make up the population of Kyrgyzstan, Central Asia (left). On September 3, 2004, in Beslan, Russia, two men carry young hostages who managed to escape after Russian special forces entered a school that had been occupied for three days by terrorists, who demanded that Russian troops pull out of Chechnya, a Russian republic with a large Islamic population.*

happening in the disintegrating Second World, where ethnic groups (nationalities) want their own nation-states. The flowering of ethnic feeling and conflict as the Soviet empire disintegrated illustrates that years of political repression and ideology provide insufficient common ground for lasting unity.

Cultural colonialism refers to internal domination—by one group and its culture/ideology over others. One example is the domination over the former Soviet empire by Russian people, language, and culture, and by communist ideology. The dominant culture makes itself the official culture. This is reflected in schools, the media, and public interaction. Under Soviet rule ethnic minorities had very limited self-rule in republics and regions controlled by Moscow.

All the republics and their peoples were to be united by the oneness of "socialist internationalism." One common technique in cultural colonialism is to flood ethnic areas with members of the dominant ethnic group. Thus, in the former Soviet Union, ethnic Russian colonists were sent to many areas, to diminish the cohesion and clout of the local people.

"The Commonwealth of Independent States" is all that remains of the Soviet Union (see Yurchak 2005). In this group of new nations, ethnic groups (nationalities) are seeking to establish separate and viable nation-states based on cultural boundaries. This celebration of ethnic autonomy is part of an ethnic florescence that—as surely as globalization and transnationalism—is a trend of the late 20th and early 21st centuries.

SUMMARY

1. An "ethnic group" refers to members of a particular culture in a nation or region that contains others. Ethnicity is based on actual, perceived, or assumed cultural similarities (among members of the same ethnic group) and differences (between that group and others). Ethnic distinctions can be based on language, religion, history, geography, kinship, or "race." A race is an ethnic group assumed to have a biological basis. Usually race and ethnicity are ascribed statuses; people are born members of a group and remain so all their lives.

2. Race is a cultural category, not a biological reality. "Races" derive from contrasts perceived in particular societies, rather than from scientific classifications based on common genes. In the United States "racial" labels such as "white" and "black" designate socially constructed races—categories defined by American culture. American racial classification, governed by the rule of hypodescent, is based neither on phenotype nor on genes. Children of mixed unions, no matter what their appearance, are classified with the minority-group parent.

3. Racial attitudes in Japan illustrate "intrinsic racism"—the belief that a perceived racial difference is a sufficient reason to value one person less than another. The valued group is majority ("pure") Japanese, who are believed to share "the same blood." Majority Japanese define themselves by opposition to others, such as Koreans and burakumin. These may be minority groups in Japan or outsiders—anyone who is "not us."

4. Such exclusionary racial systems are not inevitable. Although Brazil shares a history of slavery with the United States, it lacks the hypodescent rule. Brazilian racial identity is more of an achieved status. It can change during someone's lifetime, reflecting phenotypical changes. Given the correlation between poverty and dark skin, the class structure affects Brazilian racial classification. Someone with light skin who is poor will be classified as darker than a comparably colored person who is rich.

5. Some people assert genetic differences in the learning abilities of "races," classes, and ethnic groups. But environmental variables (particularly educational, economic, and social background) provide better explanations for performance on intelligence tests by such groups. Intelligence tests reflect the life experiences of those who develop and administer them. All tests are to some extent culture-bound. Equalized environmental opportunities show up in test scores.

6. The term nation was once synonymous with "ethnic group." Now nation has come to mean a state—a centrally organized political unit. Because of migration, conquest, and colonialism, most nation-states are not ethnically homogeneous. Ethnic groups that seek autonomous political status (their own country) are nationalities. Political upheavals, wars, and migrations have divided many imagined national communities.

7. Assimilation describes the process of change an ethnic group may experience when it moves to a country where another culture dominates. By assimilating, the minority adopts the patterns and norms of its host culture. Assimilation isn't inevitable, and there can be ethnic harmony without it. A plural society combines ethnic contrasts and economic interdependence between ethnic groups. The view of cultural diversity in a nation-state as good and desirable is multiculturalism. A multicultural society socializes individuals not only into the dominant (national) culture but also into an ethnic one.

8. Ethnicity can be expressed in peaceful multiculturalism, or in discrimination or violent confrontation. Ethnic conflict often arises in reaction to prejudice (attitudes and judgments) or discrimination (action). The most extreme form of ethnic discrimination is genocide, the deliberate elimination of a group through mass murder. A dominant group may try to destroy certain ethnic practices (ethnocide), or to force ethnic group members to adopt the dominant culture (forced assimilation). A policy of ethnic expulsion may create refugees. Colonialism is the political, social, economic, and cultural domination of a territory and its people by a foreign power for an extended time. Cultural colonialism refers to internal domination—by one group and its culture and/or ideology over others.

KEY TERMS

See the flash cards
mhhe.com/kottak

achieved status Social status that comes through talents, choices, actions, and accomplishments, rather than ascription.

ascribed status Social status (e.g., race or gender) that people have little or no choice about occupying.

assimilation The process of change that a minority group may experience when it moves to a country where another culture dominates; the minority is incorporated into the dominant culture to the point that it no longer exists as a separate cultural unit.

colonialism The political, social, economic, and cultural domination of a territory and its people by a foreign power for an extended time.

descent Rule assigning social identity on the basis of some aspect of one's ancestry.

discrimination Policies and practices that harm a group and its members.

ethnic group Group distinguished by cultural similarities (shared among members of that group) and differences (between that group and others); ethnic-group members share beliefs, customs, and norms, and, often, a common language, religion, history, geography, and kinship.

ethnicity Identification with, and feeling part of, an ethnic group, and exclusion from certain other groups because of this affiliation.

hypodescent Rule that automatically places the children of a union or mating between members of different socioeconomic groups in the less-privileged group.

multiculturalism The view of cultural diversity in a country as something good and desirable; a multicultural society socializes individuals not only into the dominant (national) culture but also into an ethnic culture.

nation Once a synonym for "ethnic group," designating a single culture sharing a language, religion, history, territory, ancestry, and kinship; now usually a synonym for *state* or *nation-state*.

nationalities Ethnic groups that once had, or wish to have or regain, autonomous political status (their own country).

nation-state An autonomous political entity; a country like the United States or Canada.

phenotype An organism's evident traits, its "manifest biology"—anatomy and physiology.

plural society A society that combines ethnic contrasts and economic interdependence of the ethnic groups.

prejudice Devaluing (looking down on) a group because of its assumed behavior, values, capabilities, attitudes, or other attributes.

race An ethnic group assumed to have a biological basis.

racism Discrimination against an ethnic group assumed to have a biological basis.

refugees People who have been forced (involuntary refugees) or who have chosen (voluntary refugees) to flee a country, to escape persecution or war.

social race A group assumed to have a biological basis but actually perceived and defined in a social context, by a particular culture rather than by scientific criteria.

state (nation-state) Complex sociopolitical system that administers a territory and populace with substantial contrasts in occupation, wealth, prestige, and power. An independent, centrally organized political unit; a government. A form of social and political organization with a formal, central government and a division of society into classes.

status Any position that determines where someone fits in society; may be ascribed or achieved.

stratified Class-structured; stratified societies have marked differences in wealth, prestige, and power between social classes.

CRITICAL
THINKING
QUESTIONS

For more self-testing,
see the self-quizzes
mhhe.com/kottak

1. What's the difference between a culture and an ethnic group? In what culture(s) do you participate? To what ethnic group(s) do you belong? What is the basis of your primary cultural identity?

2. Name five social statuses you currently occupy. Which of those statuses are ascribed, and which ones are achieved?

3. What kind of racial classification system operates in the community where you grew up or now live? Does it differ from the racial classification system described for American culture in this chapter?

4. If you had to devise an ideal system of racial categories, would it be more like the North American, the Japanese, or the Brazilian system? Why?

5. How does multiculturalism differ from assimilation? Which process do you favor for your country?

SUGGESTED ADDITIONAL READINGS

Abelmann, N., and J. Lie
  1995 *Blue Dreams: Korean Americans and the Los Angeles Riots.* Cambridge, MA: Harvard University Press. Some of the roots of ethnic conflict in Los Angeles today.

Anderson, B.
  1991 *Imagined Communities: Reflections on the Origin and Spread of Nationalism,* rev. ed. London: Verso. The origins of nationalism in Europe and its colonies, with special attention to the role of print, language, and schools.

Barth, F.
  1969 *Ethnic Groups and Boundaries: The Social Organization of Cultural Difference.* London: Allyn and Unwin. Classic discussion of the prominence of differentiation and boundaries (versus cultural features per se) in interethnic relations.

Friedman, J., ed.
  2002 *Globalization, the State, and Violence.* Walnut Creek, CA: AltaMira. Essays by prominent anthropologists focusing on violence in the context of globalization.

Gellner, E.
  1997 *Nationalism.* New York: New York University Press. Up-to-date comments from a long-time anthropological student of nationalism.

Harris, M.
  1964 *Patterns of Race in the Americas.* New York: Walker. Reasons for different racial and ethnic relations in North and South America and the Caribbean.

Hobsbawm, E. J.
  1992 *Nations and Nationalism since 1780: Programme, Myth, Reality,* 2nd ed. New York: Cambridge University Press. The making of modern nation-states.

Kottak, C. P., and K. A. Kozaitis
  2003 *On Being Different: Diversity and Multiculturalism in the North American Mainstream,* 2nd ed. New York: McGraw-Hill. Aspects of diversity in the United States and Canada, plus an original theory of multiculturalism.

Laguerre, M. S.
  1999 *The Global Ethnopolis: Chinatown, Japantown, and Manilatown in American Society.* New York: St. Martin's Press. Asian American urban enclaves, with a focus on San Francisco.

Maybury-Lewis, D.
  2002 *Indigenous Peoples, Ethnic Groups, and the State,* 2nd ed. Boston: Allyn & Bacon. Studies of cultural survival, ethnicity, and social change.

Molnar, S.
  2005 *Human Variation: Races, Types, and Ethnic Groups,* 6th ed. Upper Saddle River, NJ: Prentice Hall. Links between biological and social diversity.

Montagu, A., ed.
  1999 *Race and IQ,* expanded ed. New York: Oxford University Press. Revision of a classic volume of essays.

Ryan, S.
  1995 *Ethnic Conflict and International Relations,* 2nd ed. Brookfield, MA: Dartmouth. Crossnational review of the roots of ethnic conflict.

Schlee, G., ed.
  2002 *Imagined Differences: Hatred and the Construction of Identity.* New York: Palgrave. The dark side of imagining communities.

Scupin, R.
  2003 *Race and Ethnicity: An Anthropological Focus on the United States and the World.* Upper Saddle River, NJ: Prentice Hall. Broad survey of race and ethnic relations.

Spickard, P., ed.
  2004 *Race and Nation: Ethnic Systems in the Modern World.* New York: Routledge. Essays by 19 scholars on ethnic systems in various countries.

Wade, P.

2002 *Race, Nature, and Culture: An Anthropological Perspective.* Sterling, VA: Pluto Press. A processual approach to human biology and race.

Yurchak, A.

2005 *Everything Was Forever Until It Was No More: The Last Soviet Generation.* Princeton, NJ: Princeton University Press. Cultural paradoxes in the fall of the Soviet system.

INTERNET EXERCISES

1. Go to the U.S. Census page titled "Mapping Census 2000: The Geography of US Diversity," pp. 20–23 (**http://www.census.gov/population/cen2000/atlas/censr01-104.pdf**). Examine all four maps showing aspects of racial and ethnic diversity by county in the United States. Try to explain the historic processes that have produced, and are now producing, the patterns of diversity and density of specific groups.
   a. The first map shows the ethnic group with the highest percentage of population for all U.S. counties. What is the closest county to you with a high proportion of Native Americans? How about Hispanics?
   b. Examine Maps 1 and 2 for clusters of African Americans. Why are so many African Americans clustered in the southeastern part of the United States?
   c. Examine Map 2 for clusters of Hispanics. How do you explain high concentrations of Hispanics in the Pacific Northwest, in the Midwest, and on the East Coast?
   d. On Maps 1 and 2 determine where you find the highest concentrations of Asian Americans. Why are the concentrations of Asian Americans so different from those of other ethnic groups?
   e. Examine Map 3 to see which states were the most diverse in 2000. Examine Map 4 to see which states increased most in diversity between 1990 and 2000. Give a brief definition of the diversity index used in the map calculations.

2. Race and the Census: Read Gregory Rodriguez's article in Salon magazine titled "Do the Multiracial Count?" (**http://www.salon.com/news/feature/2000/02/15/census/index.html**).
   a. What was the problem that some people had with the original census? How does this reflect American notions of race as described in this chapter?
   b. What was the compromise that the Clinton administration presented? What are its ramifications?
   c. In this case what role does the federal government play in our society's notions of race? Is the federal government merely responding to changing conceptions of race of the American people, or is it trying to shape the way the American public thinks about race?
   d. Based on this chapter, how do you think this kind of question on the census form would be handled in Brazil? In Japan?

3. Ethnicity on the Border: Read Gregory Rodriguez's article "We're Patriotic Americans Because We're Mexicans" in *Salon* magazine, **http://archive.salon.com/news/feature/2000/ 02/24/laredo**.
   a. Who is participating in the celebration of George Washington's birthday?
   b. How does this celebration reflect the influence of Mexican and American cultures? Since it is a mixture, is this celebration any less "pure"?
   c. Do you think a multiethnic identity is incompatible with a single national identity?
   d. What factors would cause a border community to invest so much energy in recognizing a day such as Washington's birthday that so many other Americans ignore? Do you think it is more important for communities living on the border to assert their nationality than for communities living in the heartland?

See Chapter 5 at your McGraw-Hill Online Learning Center for additional review and interactive exercises.

Kottak, *Assault on Paradise,* **4th ed.**

Chapters 1, 3, and 10 contain information on race relations in Arembepe. Read Chapters 1 and 3 to see how Kottak conducted his microproject on racial terminology in 1962. What were his techniques and findings? Read Chapters 3 and 10 to see how race relations changed between the 1960s and the 1980s. What role did ethnicity play in Arembepe in the 1960s, and what role does it play today?

Peters-Golden, *Culture Sketches,* **4th ed.**

Read Chapter 5, "Hmong: Struggle and Perseverance." The text chapter you just read discussed ethnic pride, along with ethnic discrimination and violence. The Hmong are a tribal people who traditionally have lived in remote mountain villages throughout China, Laos, Thailand, and Vietnam. Their history is one of struggle, rebellion, and perseverance. For centuries, Hmong have suffered persecution by many groups, while fiercely defending their ethnic heritage. Despite war and resettlement, they continue to strive to maintain their traditions. Hmong in the United States have been criticized as unwilling to assimilate. Why might they be viewed this way? How might their long history of ethnic discrimination influence the way they think about themselves and their cultural heritage? How might you account for the clashes described in their adjustment to life in the United States?

Knauft, *The Gebusi,* **1st ed.**

Read Chapter 11. How is the ethnic difference between different peoples reflected in the Independence Day celebrations at Nomad? Describe an activity during the celebrations in which ethnic difference between Gebusi and Bedamini led to opposition and competition. Describe an activity during the celebrations in which ethnic difference led to appreciation and enjoyment between groups. Do you think relations between ethnic groups at Nomad in 1998 were mostly harmonious or mostly based on conflict? Support your answer. In what ways do you think this marks a change from indigenous relations between ethnic groups—for instance, indigenous relations between Gebusi and Bedamini?

6

Language and Communication

WHAT IS LANGUAGE?

Language, which may be spoken (*speech*) or written (*writing*), is our primary means of communication. Writing has existed for about 6,000 years. Language originated thousands of years before that, but no one can say exactly when. Like culture in general, of which language is a part, language is transmitted through learning, as part of enculturation. Language is based on arbitrary, learned associations between words and the things for which they stand. The complexity

Apes, such as these Congo chimpanzees, use call systems to communicate in the wild. Their vocal systems consist of a limited number of sounds—calls—that are produced only when particular environmental stimuli are encountered.

OVERVIEW

Linguistic anthropology shares anthropology's overall interest in diversity in time and space. Linguistic anthropology examines language structure and use, linguistic change, and the relations among language, society, and culture.

The call systems of our hominid ancestors eventually grew too complicated for genetic transmission. As hominids relied more and more on learning, their call systems evolved into language. But, like the other primates, humans also continue to use nonverbal communication, such as facial expressions and gestures. No language includes all the sounds the human vocal apparatus can make. Phonology, the study of speech sounds, focuses on sounds that make a difference in a given language.

Sociolinguistics investigates how linguistic variation is associated with social differences. Linguistic diversity reflects region, gender, social class, occupation, ethnicity, and other social variables. Also, people vary their speech on different occasions, shifting styles, dialects, and even languages.

Historical linguistics is useful for anthropologists interested in historical relationships. Linguistic clues can suggest past contacts between cultures. Relationships between languages don't necessarily mean there are biological ties between their speakers, because people can learn new languages.

of language—absent in the communication systems of other animals—allows humans to conjure up elaborate images, to discuss the past and the future, to share our experiences with others, and to benefit from their experiences.

Anthropologists study language in its social and cultural context. Linguistic anthropology illustrates anthropology's characteristic interest in comparison, variation, and change. A key feature of language is that it is always changing. Some linguistic anthropologists reconstruct ancient languages by comparing their contemporary descendants and in so doing make discoveries about history. Others study linguistic differences to discover the varied worldviews and patterns of thought in a multitude of cultures. Sociolinguists examine linguistic diversity in nation-states, ranging from multilingualism (see the "News Brief") to the varied dialects and styles used in a single language, to show how speech reflects social differences (Fasold 1990; Labov 1972a, 1972b). Linguistic anthropologists also explore the role of language in colonization and in the expansion of the world economy (Geis 1987).

NONHUMAN PRIMATE COMMUNICATION

Call Systems

Only humans speak. No other animal has anything approaching the complexity of language. The natural communication systems of other primates (monkeys and apes) are **call systems.** These vocal systems consist of a limited number of sounds—*calls*—that are produced only when particular environmental stimuli are encountered. Such calls may be varied in intensity and duration, but they are much less flexible than language because they are automatic and can't be combined. When primates encounter food and danger simultaneously, they can make only one call. They can't combine the calls for food and danger into a single utterance, indicating that both are present. At some point in human evolution, however, our ancestors began to combine calls and to understand the combinations. The number of calls also expanded, eventually becoming too great to be transmitted even partly through the genes. Communication came to rely almost totally on learning.

Although wild primates use call systems, the vocal tract of apes is not suitable for speech. Until the 1960s, attempts to teach spoken language to apes suggested that they lack linguistic abilities. In the 1950s, a couple raised a chimpanzee, Viki, as a member of their family and systematically tried to teach her to speak. However, Viki learned only four words ("mama," "papa," "up," and "cup").

Spanish At School Translates to Suspension

WASHINGTON POST NEWS BRIEF

by T. R. Reid
December 9, 2005

Linguistic diversity is a fact. Not even identical twins speak just alike. But we do share patterns of speech with other people, such as our parents, our peers, and people with the same ethnic, regional, educational, or occupational background. The United States is not famous for its appreciation of linguistic diversity or for its fostering of foreign language study. Compared with Europeans, Americans have under-developed foreign language skills. Why is that? How many languages do you speak fluently? This article describes a case of blatant sociolinguistic discrimination, in which a boy was suspended from school for speaking Spanish in the hallway. Consider how this account illustrates American atti-tudes about language, ethnicity, and even social class. Do you think the boy would have been suspended for speaking French to a French exchange student? But, then, what are the odds his French is good enough to permit such a conversation? This chapter focuses on how anthropologists and linguists study languages as formal systems, but also in their social and cultural contexts, including sociolinguistic diversity.

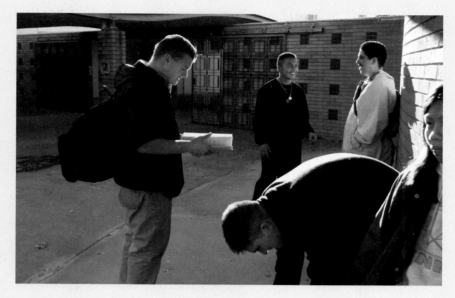

■ *On November 27, 2001, several students wait outside their drama classroom at multiethnic Luther Burbank High School in Sacramento, California. Anthropologists and linguists study linguistic diversity—languages and dialects—in its social and cultural context. What languages do you imagine are being spoken in the hallway?*

KANSAS CITY, Kan., Dec. 8—Most of the time, 16-year-old Zach Rubio converses in clear, unaccented American teen-speak, a form of English in which the three most common words are "like," "whatever" and "totally." But Zach is also fluent in his dad's native lan-guage, Spanish—and that's what got him suspended from school.

"It was, like, totally not in the classroom," the high school junior said, recalling the infraction. "We were in the, like, hall or whatever, on restroom break. This kid I know, he's like, 'Me prestas un dolar?' ['Will you lend me a dollar?'] Well, he asked in Spanish; it just seemed nat-ural to answer that way. So I'm like, 'No problema.'"

But that conversation turned out to be a big problem for the staff at the Endeavor Alternative School, a small public high school in an ethnically mixed blue-collar neighborhood. A teacher who overheard the two boys sent Zach to the office, where Princi-pal Jennifer Watts ordered him to call his father and leave the school.

Watts, whom students describe as a disciplinarian, said she can't discuss the case. But in a written "discipline referral" explaining her decision to suspend Zach for 1 1/2 days, she noted: "This is not the first time we have [asked] Zach and oth-ers to not speak Spanish at school."

Since then, the suspension of Zach Rubio has become the talk of the town in both English and Span-ish newspapers and radio shows. The school district has officially rescinded his punishment and said that speaking a foreign language is not grounds for suspension. Mean-while, the Rubio family has retained a lawyer, who says a civil rights law-suit may be in the offing.

The tension here surrounding that brief exchange in a high school hall reflects a broader national debate over the language Americans should speak amid a wave of Hispanic immigration.

The National Council of La Raza, a Hispanic advocacy group, says that 20 percent of the U.S. school–age population is Latino. For half of those Latino students, the native language is Spanish.

Conflicts are bursting out nation-wide over bilingual education, "English-only" laws, Spanish-language publications and advertis-ing, and other linguistic collisions. Language concerns have been a key aspect of the growing political movement to reduce immigration.

"There's a lot of backlash against the increasing Hispanic population," said D.C. school board member Victor A. Reinoso. "We've seen some of it in the D.C. schools. You see it in some cities, where people complain that their tax money shouldn't be used to print public notices in Spanish. And there have been cases where schools want to ban foreign languages."

Some advocates of an English-only policy in U.S. schools say that it is particularly important for students from immigrant families to use the nation's dominant language.

California Gov. Arnold Schwarzenegger (R) made that point this summer when he vetoed a bill authorizing various academic subjects to be tested in Spanish in the state's public schools. "As an immigrant," the Austrian-born governor said, "I know the importance of mastering English as quickly and as comprehensively as possible."

Hispanic groups generally agree with that, but they emphasize the value of a multilingual citizenry. "A fully bilingual young man like Zach Rubio should be considered an asset to the community," said Janet Murguia, national president of La Raza.

The influx of immigrants has reached every corner of the country—even here in Kansas City, which is about as far as a U.S. town can be from a border. Along Southwest Boulevard, a main street through some of the older neighborhoods, there are blocks where almost every shop and restaurant has signs written in Spanish.

"Most people, they don't care where you're from," said Zach's father, Lorenzo Rubio, a native of Veracruz, Mexico, who has lived in Kansas City for a quarter-century. "But sometimes, when they hear my accent, I get this, sort of, 'Why don't you go back home?'"

Rubio, a U.S. citizen, credits U.S. immigration law for his decision to fight his son's suspension.

"You can't just walk in and become a citizen," he said. "They make you take this government test. I studied for that test, and I learned that in America, they can't punish you unless you violate a written policy."

Rubio said he remembered that lesson on Nov. 28, when he received a call from Endeavor Alternative saying his son had been suspended.

"So I went to the principal and said, 'My son, he's not suspended for fighting, right? He's not suspended for disrespecting anyone. He's suspended for speaking Spanish in the hall?' So I asked her to show me the written policy about that. But they didn't have one."

Rubio then called the superintendent of the Turner Unified School District, which operates the school. The district immediately rescinded

Zach's suspension, local media reported. The superintendent did not respond to several requests to comment for this article.

Since then, the issue of speaking Spanish in the hall has not been raised at the school, Zach said. "I know it would be, like, disruptive if I answered in Spanish in the classroom. I totally don't do that. But outside of class now, the teachers are like, 'Whatever.'"

For Zach's father, and for the Hispanic organizations that have expressed concern, the suspension is not a closed case. "Obviously they've violated his civil rights," said Chuck Chionuma, a lawyer in Kansas City, Mo., who is representing the Rubio family. "We're studying what form of legal redress will correct the situation."

Said Rubio: "I'm mainly doing this for other Mexican families, where the legal status is kind of shaky and they are afraid to speak up. Punished for speaking Spanish? Somebody has to stand up and say: This is wrong."

_____

SOURCE: T. R. Reid, "Spanish At School Translates to Suspension," *Washington Post,* December 9, 2005, p. A03.

Sign Language

More recent experiments have shown that apes can learn to use, if not speak, true language (Miles 1983). Several apes have learned to converse with people through means other than speech. One such communication system is American Sign Language, or ASL, which is widely used by deaf and mute Americans. ASL employs a limited number of basic gesture units that are analogous to sounds in spoken language. These units combine to form words and larger units of meaning.

The first chimpanzee to learn ASL was Washoe, a female. Captured in West Africa, Washoe was acquired by R. Allen Gardner and Beatrice Gardner, scientists at the University of Nevada in Reno, in 1966, when she was a year old. Four years later, she moved to Norman, Oklahoma, to a converted farm that had become the Institute for Primate Studies. Washoe revolutionized the discussion of

the language-learning abilities of apes. At first she lived in a trailer and heard no spoken language. The researchers always used ASL to communicate with each other in her presence. The chimp gradually acquired a vocabulary of more than 100 signs representing English words (Gardner, Gardner, and Van Cantfort, eds. 1989). At the age of two, Washoe began to combine as many as five signs into rudimentary sentences such as "you, me, go out, hurry."

The second chimp to learn ASL was Lucy, Washoe's junior by one year. Lucy died, or was murdered by poachers, in 1986, after having been introduced to "the wild" in Africa in 1979 (Carter 1988). From her second day of life until her move to Africa, Lucy lived with a family in Norman, Oklahoma. Roger Fouts, a researcher from the nearby Institute for Primate Studies, came two days a week to test and improve Lucy's knowledge of ASL. During the rest of the week, Lucy used ASL to converse with her foster parents. After acquiring language, Washoe and Lucy exhibited several human traits: swearing, joking, telling lies, and trying to teach language to others (Fouts 1997).

When irritated, Washoe called her monkey neighbors at the institute "dirty monkeys." Lucy insulted her "dirty cat." On arrival at Lucy's place, Fouts once found a pile of excrement on the floor. When he asked the chimp what it was, she replied, "dirty, dirty," her expression for feces. Asked whose "dirty, dirty" it was, Lucy named Fouts's coworker, Sue. When Fouts refused to believe her about Sue, the chimp blamed the excrement on Fouts himself.

Cultural transmission of a communication system through learning is a fundamental attribute of language. Washoe, Lucy, and other chimps have tried to teach ASL to other animals, including their own offspring. Washoe has taught gestures to other institute chimps, including her son Sequoia, who died in infancy (Fouts, Fouts, and Van Cantfort 1989).

Because of their size and strength as adults, gorillas are less likely subjects than chimps for such experiments. Lean adult male gorillas in the wild weigh 400 pounds (180 kilograms), and full-grown females can easily reach 250 pounds (110 kilograms). Because of this, psychologist Penny Patterson's work with gorillas at Stanford University seems more daring than the chimp experiments. Patterson raised her now full-grown female gorilla, Koko, in a trailer next to a Stanford museum. Koko's vocabulary surpasses that of any chimp. She regularly employs 400 ASL signs and has used about 700 at least once.

Koko and the chimps also show that apes share still another linguistic ability with humans: **productivity.** Speakers routinely use the rules of their language to produce entirely new expressions that are comprehensible to other native speakers. I can, for example, create "baboonlet" to refer to a baboon infant. I do this by analogy with English words in which the suffix -*let* desig-

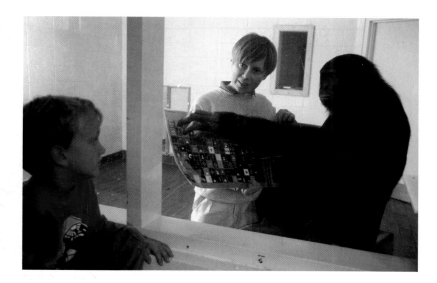

At the Language Research Center in Atlanta, Kanzi, the symboling bonobo, signals "Chase Kanzi" to a six-year-old boy. Kanzi points to a lexigram keyboard held by Sue Savage-Rumbaugh.

nates the young of a species. Anyone who speaks English immediately understands the meaning of my new word. Koko, Washoe, Lucy, and others have shown that apes also are able to use language productively. Lucy used gestures she already knew to create "drinkfruit" for watermelon. Washoe, seeing a swan for the first time, coined "waterbird." Koko, who knew the gestures for "finger" and "bracelet," formed "finger bracelet" when she was given a ring.

Chimps and gorillas have a rudimentary capacity for language. They may never have invented a meaningful gesture system in the wild. However, given such a system, they show many humanlike abilities in learning and using it. Of course, language use by apes is a product of human intervention and teaching. The experiments mentioned here do not suggest that apes can invent language (nor are human children ever faced with that task). However, young apes have managed to learn the basics of gestural language. They can employ it productively and creatively, although not with the sophistication of human ASL users.

Apes, like humans, also may try to teach their language to others. Lucy, not fully realizing the difference between primate hands and feline paws, once tried to mold her pet cat's paw into ASL signs. Koko taught gestures to Michael, a male gorilla six years her junior.

Apes also have demonstrated linguistic **displacement.** Absent in call systems, this is a key ingredient in language. Normally, each call is tied to an environmental stimulus such as food. Calls are uttered only when that stimulus is present. Displacement means that humans can talk about things that are not present. We don't have to see the objects before we say the words. Human conversations are not limited by place. We can discuss the past and future, share our experiences with others, and benefit from theirs.

 STUDENT CD-ROM LIVING ANTHROPOLOGY

Bonobos and Language

Track 6

This clip presents the work of Dr. Sue Savage-Rumbaugh of Georgia State University, who has been working with chimpanzees and bonobos for more than 20 years. The clip focuses on her work with Kanzi, a male bonobo, who has learned how to communicate through the manipulation of words and symbols. Like humans, but to a substantially lesser degree, apes can learn from observation, experience, and teaching. What did Kanzi learn that his mother could not learn? Why can't bonobos talk? Based on what you saw in the clip, would you say that Kanzi responds to spoken words or only to symbols?

"He says he wants a lawyer."

Patterson has described several examples of Koko's capacity for displacement (Patterson 1978). The gorilla once expressed sorrow about having bitten Penny three days earlier. Koko has used the sign "later" to postpone doing things she doesn't want to do. Table 6.1 summarizes the contrasts between language, whether sign or spoken, and the call systems that primates use in the wild.

Certain scholars doubt the linguistic abilities of chimps and gorillas (Sebeok and Umiker-Sebeok, eds. 1980; Terrace 1979). These people contend that Koko and the chimps are comparable to trained circus animals and don't really have linguistic ability. However, in defense of Patterson and the other researchers (Hill 1978; Van Cantfort and Rimpau 1982), only one of their critics has worked with an ape. This was Herbert Terrace, whose experience teaching a chimp sign language lacked the continuity and personal involvement that have contributed so much to Patterson's success with Koko.

No one denies the huge difference between human language and gorilla signs. There is a major gap between the ability to write a book or say a prayer and the few hundred gestures employed by

See the Internet Exercises at your OLC for more on primate language ability

mhhe.com/kottak

a well-trained chimp. Apes aren't people, but they aren't just animals either. Let Koko express it: When asked by a reporter whether she was a person or an animal, Koko chose neither. Instead, she signed "fine animal gorilla" (Patterson 1978).

The Origin of Language

The capacity to remember and combine linguistic expressions seems to be latent in the apes (Miles 1983). In human evolution, the same ability flowered into language. Language did not appear miraculously at a certain moment in human history. It developed over hundreds of thousands of years, as our ancestors' call systems were gradually transformed. Language offered a tremendous adaptive advantage to *Homo*. Language permits the information stored by a human society to exceed by far that of any nonhuman group. Language is a uniquely effective vehicle for learning. Because we can speak of things we have never experienced, we can anticipate responses before we encounter the stimuli. Adaptation can occur more rapidly in *Homo* than in the other primates because our adaptive means are more flexible.

NONVERBAL COMMUNICATION

Language is our principal means of communicating, but it isn't the only one we use. We communicate when we transmit information about ourselves to others and receive such information from them. Our facial expressions, bodily stances, gestures, and movements, even if unconscious, convey information and are part of our communication styles. Deborah Tannen (1990) discusses differences in the communication styles of American men and women, and her comments go beyond language. She notes that American girls and women tend to look directly at each other when they talk, whereas American boys and men do not. Males are more likely to look straight

TABLE 6.1 Language Contrasted with Call Systems	
Human Language	**Primate Call Systems**
Has the capacity to speak of things and events that are not present (displacement).	Are stimuli-dependent; the food call will be made only in the presence of food; it cannot be faked.
Has the capacity to generate new expressions by combining other expressions (productivity).	Consist of a limited number of calls that cannot be combined to produce new calls.
Is group specific in that all humans have the capacity for language, but each linguistic community has its own language, which is culturally transmitted.	Tend to be species specific, with little variation among communities of the same species for each call.

Some of our facial expressions reflect our primate heritage. We can see them in monkeys and especially in the apes. How "natural" and universal are the meanings conveyed by facial expressions? Throughout the world, smiles, laughs, frowns, and tears tend to have similar meanings, but culture does intervene. In some cultures, people smile less than in others. In a given culture, men may smile less than women; and adults, less than children. A lifetime of smiling and frowning marks the face, so that smile lines and frown furrows develop. In North America, smile lines may be more marked in women than in men. Margaret Mead focused on kinesics in her studies of infant care in different cultures. She noted differences in mother–child interactions, finding that patterns of holding, releasing, and playing varied from culture to culture. In some cultures, babies were held more securely than in others. Mead thought that patterns of infant and child care played an important role in forming adult personality.

American men and women differ in their phonology, grammar, and vocabulary, and in the body stances and movements that accompany speech. What differences do you note in the communication styles of the two women in the foreground, compared with the several men in the background?

ahead rather than turn and make eye contact with someone, especially another man, seated beside them. Also, in conversational groups, American men tend to relax and sprawl out. American women may adopt a similar relaxed posture in all-female groups, but when they are with men, they tend to draw in their limbs and adopt a tighter stance.

Kinesics is the study of communication through body movements, stances, gestures, and facial expressions. Related to kinesics is the examination of cultural differences in personal space and displays of affection discussed in the chapter "Culture." Linguists pay attention not only to what is said but to how it is said, and to features besides language itself that convey meaning. A speaker's enthusiasm is conveyed not only through words, but also through facial expressions, gestures, and other signs of animation. We use gestures, such as a jab of the hand, for emphasis. We use verbal and nonverbal ways of communicating our moods: enthusiasm, sadness, joy, regret. We vary our intonation and the pitch or loudness of our voices. We communicate through strategic pauses, and even by being silent. An effective communication strategy may be to alter pitch, voice level, and grammatical forms, such as declaratives ("I am . . ."), imperatives ("Go forth . . ."), and questions ("Are you . . . ?"). Culture teaches us that certain manners and styles should accompany certain kinds of speech. Our demeanor, verbal and non-

verbal, when our favorite team is winning would be out of place at a funeral, or when a somber subject is being discussed.

Culture always plays a role in shaping the "natural." Animals communicate through odors, using scent to mark territories, a chemical means of communication. Among modern North Americans, the perfume, mouthwash, and deodorant industries are based on the idea that the sense of smell plays a role in communication and social interaction. But different cultures are more tolerant of "natural" odors than ours is. Cross-culturally, nodding does not always mean affirmative, nor does head shaking from side to side always mean negative. Brazilians wag a finger to mean no. Americans say "uh huh" to affirm, whereas in Madagascar a similar sound is made to deny. Americans point with their fingers; the people of Madagascar point with their lips. Patterns of "lounging around" vary, too. Outside, when resting, some people may sit or lie on the ground; others squat; others lean against a tree.

Body movements communicate social differences. Lower-class Brazilians, especially women, offer limp handshakes to their social superiors. In many cultures, men have firmer handshakes than women do. In Japan, bowing is a regular part of social interaction, but different bows are used depending on the social status of the people who are interacting. In Madagascar and Polynesia, people of lower status should not hold their heads above those of people of higher status. When one approaches someone older or of higher status, one bends one's knees and lowers one's head as a sign of respect. In Madagascar, one always does this, for politeness, when passing between two people. Although our gestures, facial expressions, and body stances have roots in our primate heritage, and can be seen in the monkeys and the apes, they have not escaped the cultural shaping described in previous chapters. Language, which is so highly dependent on the use of symbols, is the domain of communication, in which culture plays the strongest role.

THE STRUCTURE OF LANGUAGE

The scientific study of a spoken language (*descriptive linguistics*) involves several interrelated areas of analysis: phonology, morphology, lexicon, and syntax. **Phonology,** the study of speech sounds, considers which sounds are present and significant in a given language. **Morphology** studies the forms in which sounds combine to form *morphemes*—words and their meaningful parts. Thus, the word *cats* would be analyzed as containing two morphemes: *cat,* the name for a kind of animal, and *-s,* a morpheme indicating plurality. A language's **lexicon** is a dictionary containing all its morphemes and their meanings. **Syntax** refers to the arrangement and order of words in phrases and sentences. Syntactic questions include whether nouns usually come before or after verbs, or whether adjectives normally precede or follow the nouns they modify.

Speech Sounds

From the movies and TV, and from actually meeting foreigners, we know something about foreign accents and mispronunciations. We know that someone with a marked French accent doesn't pronounce *r* the same way an American does. But at least someone from France can distinguish between "craw" and "claw," which someone from Japan may not be able to do. The difference between *r* and *l* makes a difference in English and in French, but it doesn't in Japanese. In linguistics, we say that the difference between *r* and *l* is *phonemic* in English and French but not in Japanese; that is, *r* and *l* are phonemes in English and French but not in Japanese. A **phoneme** is a sound contrast that makes a difference, that differentiates meaning.

We find the phonemes in a given language by comparing *minimal pairs,* words that resemble each other in all but one sound. The words have totally different meanings, but they differ in just one sound. The contrasting sounds are therefore phonemes in that language. An example in English is the minimal pair *pit/bit.* These two words are distinguished by a single sound contrast between /p/ and /b/ (we enclose phonemes in slashes). Thus /p/ and /b/ are phonemes in English. Another example is the different vowel sound of *bit* and *beat* (see Figure 6.1). This contrast serves to distinguish these two words and the two vowel phonemes written /I/ and /i/ in English.

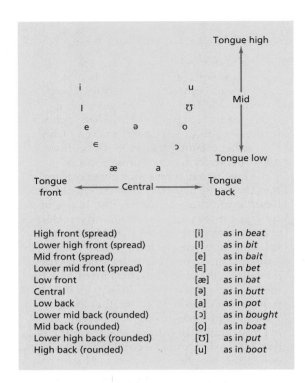

FIGURE 6.1 Vowel Phonemes in Standard American English.
The phonemes are shown according to height of tongue and tongue position at front, center, or back of mouth. Phonetic symbols are identified by English words that include them; note that most are minimal pairs. SOURCE: Adaptation of excerpt and figure 2–1 from Dwight L. Bolinger and Donald A. Sears, *Aspects of Language,* 3rd ed. (New York: Harcourt Brace Jovanovich, 1981).

Standard (American) English (SE), the "region-free" dialect of TV network newscasters, has about 35 phonemes: at least 11 vowels and 24 consonants. The number of phonemes varies from language to language—from 15 to 60, averaging between 30 and 40. The number of phonemes also varies between dialects of a given language. In American English, for example, vowel phonemes vary noticeably from dialect to dialect (see "Interesting Issues" on page 132). Readers should pronounce the words in Figure 6.1, paying attention to (or asking someone else) whether they distinguish each of the vowel sounds. Most Americans don't pronounce them all.

Phonetics is the study of speech sounds in general, what people actually say in various languages, like the differences in vowel pronunciation described in "Interesting Issues." **Phonemics** studies only the *significant* sound contrasts (phonemes) of a given language. In English, like /r/ and /l/ (remember *craw* and *claw*), /b/ and /v/ are also phonemes, occurring in minimal pairs like *bat* and *vat.* In Spanish, however, the contrast between [b] and [v] doesn't distinguish meaning, and they are therefore not phonemes (we enclose sounds that

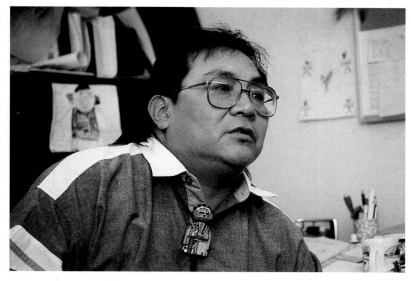

■ *Shown here (in 1995) is Leigh Jenkins, who was or is Director of Cultural Preservation for the Hopi tribal council. The Hopi language would not distinguish between* was *and* is *in the previous sentence. For the Hopi, present and past are real and are expressed grammatically in the same way while the future remains hypothetical and has a different grammatical expression.*

are not phonemic in brackets). Spanish speakers normally use the [b] sound to pronounce words spelled with either *b* or *v.*

In any language, a given phoneme extends over a phonetic range. In English, the phoneme /p/ ignores the phonetic contrast between the [pʰ] in *pin* and the [p] in *spin.* Most English speakers don't even notice that there is a phonetic difference: [pʰ] is aspirated, so that a puff of air follows the [p]; the [p] in *spin* is not. (To see the difference, light a match, hold it in front of your mouth, and watch the flame as you pronounce the two words.) The contrast between [pʰ] and [p] is phonemic in some languages, such as Hindi (spoken in India). That is, there are words whose meaning is distinguished only by the contrast between an aspirated and an unaspirated [p].

Native speakers vary in their pronunciation of certain phonemes, such as the /e/ phoneme discussed in "Interesting Issues." This variation is important in the evolution of language. With no shifts in pronunciation, there can be no linguistic change. The section on sociolinguistics below considers phonetic variation and its relationship to social divisions and the evolution of language.

LANGUAGE, THOUGHT, AND CULTURE

The well-known linguist Noam Chomsky (1955) has argued that the human brain contains a limited set of rules for organizing language, so that all languages have a common structural basis. (Chomsky calls this set of rules *universal grammar.*) The fact that people can learn foreign languages and that words and ideas can be translated from one language into another tends to

support Chomsky's position that all humans have similar linguistic abilities and thought processes. Another line of support comes from creole languages. Such languages develop from pidgins, languages that form in situations of acculturation, when different societies come into contact and must devise a system of communication. As mentioned in the "Culture" chapter, pidgins based on English and native languages developed in the context of trade and colonialism in China, Papua New Guinea, and West Africa. Eventually, after generations of being spoken, pidgins may develop into *creole languages.* These are more mature languages, with developed grammatical rules and native speakers (that is, people who learn the language as their primary means of communication during enculturation). Creoles are spoken in several Caribbean societies. Gullah, which is spoken by African Americans on coastal islands in South Carolina and Georgia, is also a creole language. Supporting the idea that creoles are based on universal grammar is the fact that such languages all share certain features. Syntactically, all use particles (e.g., will, was) to form future and past tenses and multiple negation to deny or negate (e.g., he don't got none). Also, all form questions by changing inflection rather than by changing word order. For example, "You're going home for the holidays?" (with a rising tone at the end) rather than "Are you going home for the holidays?"

The Sapir-Whorf Hypothesis

Other linguists and anthropologists take a different approach to the relation between language and thought. Rather than seeking universal linguistic structures and processes, they believe that different languages produce different ways of

Do Midwesterners Have Accents?

Depending on where we live, Americans have certain stereotypes about how people in other regions talk. Some stereotypes, spread by the mass media, are more generalized than others. Most Americans think they can imitate a "southern accent." We also have nationwide stereotypes about speech in New York City (the pronunciation of *coffee*, for example) and Boston ("I pahked the kah in Hahvahd Yahd").

Many Americans also believe that midwesterners don't have accents. This belief stems from the fact that midwestern dialects don't have many stigmatized linguistic variants—speech patterns that people in other regions recognize and look down on, such as *r*lessness and *dem*, *dese*, and *dere* (instead of *them*, *these*, and *there*).

Actually, regional patterns influence the way all Americans speak. Midwesterners do have a variety of detectable accents. College students from out of state easily recognize that their in-state classmates speak differently. In-state students, however, have difficulty hearing their own speech peculiarities, because they are accustomed to them and view them as normal.

Far from having no accents, midwesterners, even in the same high school, exhibit linguistic variation (see Eckert 1989, 2000). Furthermore, dialect differences are immediately obvious to people, like myself, who come from other parts of the country. One of the best examples of variable midwestern pronunciation, involving vowels, is the /e/ phoneme, which occurs in words like *ten, rent, French, section, lecture, effect, best,* and *test.* In southeastern Michigan, where I live and teach, there are four different ways of pronouncing this phoneme. Speakers of Black English and immigrants from Appalachia often pronounce *ten* as *tin*, just as southerners habitually do. Some Michiganders say *ten*, the correct pronunciation in Standard English. However, two other pronunciations are more common. Instead of *ten*, many Michiganders say *tan*, or *tun* (as though they were using the word *ton*, a unit of weight).

My students often astound me with their pronunciation. One day I met one of my Michigan-raised teaching assistants in the hall. She was deliriously happy. When I asked why, she replied, "I've just had the best suction."

"What?" I said.

"I've just had a wonderful suction," she repeated.

"What?" I still wasn't understanding.

She finally spoke more precisely. "I've just had the best saction." She considered this a clearer pronunciation of the word *section*.

Another TA complimented me, "You luctured to great effuct today." After an exam, a student lamented that she hadn't been able to do her "bust on the tust." Once I lectured about uniformity in fast-food restaurant chains. One of my students had just vacationed in Hawaii, where, she told me, hamburger prices were higher than they were on the mainland. It was, she said, because of the runt. Who, I wondered, was this runt? The very puny owner of Honolulu's McDonald's franchise? Perhaps he advertised on television, "Come have a hamburger with the runt." Eventually I figured out that she was talking about the high cost of *rent* on those densely packed islands.

---

thinking. This position is sometimes known as the **Sapir-Whorf hypothesis** after Edward Sapir (1931) and his student Benjamin Lee Whorf (1956), its prominent early advocates. Sapir and Whorf argued that the grammatical categories of different languages lead their speakers to think about things in particular ways. For example, the third-person singular pronouns of English (*he, she; him, her; his, hers*) distinguish gender, whereas those of the Palaung, a small tribe in Burma, do not (Burling 1970). Gender exists in English, although a fully developed noun-gender and adjective-agreement system, as in French and other Romance languages (*la belle fille, le beau fils*), does not. The Sapir-Whorf hypothesis therefore might suggest that English speakers can't help paying more attention to differences between males and females than do the Palaung and less than do French or Spanish speakers.

English divides time into past, present, and future. Hopi, a language of the Pueblo region of the Native American Southwest, does not. Rather, Hopi distinguishes between events that exist or

have existed (what we use present and past to discuss) and those that don't or don't yet (our future events, along with imaginary and hypothetical events). Whorf argued that this difference leads Hopi speakers to think about time and reality in different ways than English speakers do. A similar example comes from Portuguese, which employs a future subjunctive verb form, introducing a degree of uncertainty into discussions of the future. In English, we routinely use the future tense to talk about something we think will happen. We don't feel the need to qualify "The sun'll come out tomorrow," by adding "if it doesn't go supernova." We don't hesitate to proclaim "I'll see you next year," even when we can't be absolutely sure we will. The Portuguese future subjunctive qualifies the future event, recognizing that the future can't be certain. Our way of expressing the future as certain is so ingrained that we don't even think about it, just as the Hopi don't see the need to distinguish between present and past, both of which are real, while the future remains hypothetical. It would seem, however, that language does not tightly restrict thought, because cultural changes can produce changes in thought and in language, as we shall see in the next section.

Focal Vocabulary

A **lexicon** (or vocabulary) is a language's dictionary, its set of names for things, events, and ideas. Lexicon influences perception. Thus, Eskimos have several distinct words for different types of snow that in English are all called *snow*. Most English speakers never notice the differences between these types of snow and might have trouble seeing them even if someone pointed them out. Eskimos recognize and think about differences in snow that English speakers don't see because our language provides us with just one word.

Similarly, the Nuer of Sudan have an elaborate vocabulary to describe cattle. Eskimos have several words for snow and Nuer have dozens for cattle because of their particular histories, economies, and environments. When the need arises, English speakers also can elaborate their snow and cattle vocabularies. For example, skiers name varieties of snow with words that are missing from the lexicons of Florida retirees. Similarly, the cattle vocabulary of a Texas rancher is much more ample than that of a salesperson in a New York City department store. Such specialized sets of terms and distinctions that are particularly important to certain groups (those with particular foci of experience or activity) are known as **focal vocabulary.**

Vocabulary is the area of language that changes most readily. New words and distinctions, when needed, appear and spread. For example, who would have "faxed" or e-mailed anything a generation ago? Names for items get simpler as they become common and important. A television has become a *TV,* an automobile a *car,* and a digital video disc a *DVD.*

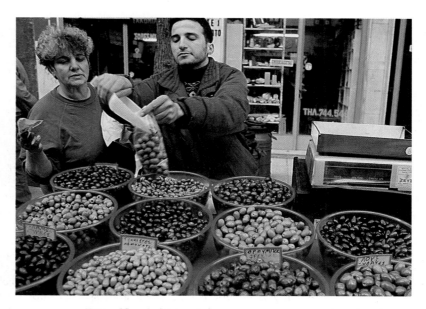

Olives, but what kinds? Undoubtedly the olive vendor has a more elaborate focal vocabulary for what he sells than you or I do.

Language, culture, and thought are interrelated. However, and in opposition to the Sapir-Whorf hypothesis, it might be more reasonable to say that changes in culture produce changes in language and thought than the reverse. Consider differences between female and male Americans in regard to the color terms they use (Lakoff 2004). Distinctions implied by such terms as *salmon, rust, peach, beige, teal, mauve, cranberry,* and *dusky orange* aren't in the vocabularies of most American men. However, many of them weren't even in American women's lexicons 50 years ago. These changes reflect changes in American economy, society, and culture. Color terms and distinctions have increased with the growth of the fashion and cosmetic industries. A similar contrast (and growth) in Americans' lexicons shows up in football, basketball, and hockey vocabularies. Sports fans, more often males than females, use more terms in reference to, and make more elaborate distinctions between, the games they watch, such as hockey (see Table 6.2). Thus, cultural contrasts and changes affect lexical distinctions (for instance, peach versus salmon) within semantic domains (for instance, color terminology). **Semantics** refers to a language's meaning system.

Meaning

Speakers of particular languages use sets of terms to organize, or categorize, their experiences and perceptions. Linguistic terms and contrasts encode (embody) differences in meaning that people perceive. **Ethnosemantics** studies such classification systems in various languages. Well-studied ethnosemantic *domains* (sets of related things, perceptions, or concepts named in a language) include kinship terminology and color terminology. When we study such domains, we

TABLE 6.2 Focal Vocabulary for Hockey	
Insiders have special terms for the major elements of the game.	
Element of Hockey	**Insiders' Term**
puck	biscuit
goal/net	pipes
penalty box	sin bin
hockey stick	twig
helmet	bucket
space between a goalie's leg pads	five hole

How would a hockey insider use focal vocabulary to describe the items shown in this photo of a Stanley Cup final? How would you describe them?

Bringing It All Together

For a more detailed look at the linguistic, cultural, and ethnic aspects of unity and diversity in a contemporary nation-state (Canada), see the "Bringing It All Together" essay that immediately follows this chapter.

are examining how those people perceive and distinguish between kin relationships or colors. Other such domains include ethnomedicine—the terminology for the causes, symptoms, and cures of disease (Frake 1961); ethnobotany—native classification of plant life (Berlin, Breedlove, and Raven 1974; Carlson and Maffi 2004; Conklin 1954); and ethnoastronomy (Goodenough 1953).

The ways in which people divide up the world—the contrasts they perceive as meaningful or significant—reflect their experiences (see Bicker, Sillitoe, and Pottier, eds. 2004). Anthropologists have discovered that certain lexical domains and vocabulary items evolve in a determined order. For example, after studying color terminology in more than 100 languages, Berlin and Kay (1991, 1999) discovered 10 basic color terms: *white, black, red, yellow, blue, green, brown, pink, orange,* and *purple* (they evolved in more or less that order). The number of terms varied with cultural complexity. Representing one extreme were Papua New Guinea cultivators and Australian hunters and gatherers, who used only two basic terms, which translate as *black* and *white* or *dark* and *light.* At the other end of the continuum were European and Asian languages with all the color terms. Color terminology was most developed in areas with a history of using dyes and artificial coloring.

SOCIOLINGUISTICS

No language is a uniform system in which everyone talks just like everyone else. Linguistic *performance* (what people actually say) is the concern of sociolinguists. The field of **sociolinguistics** investigates relationships between social and linguistic variation, or language in its social context (Eckert and Rickford, eds. 2001). How do different speakers use a given language? How do linguistic features correlate with social stratification, including class, ethnic, and gender differences (Tannen 1990; Tannen, ed. 1993)? How is language used to express, reinforce, or resist power (Geis 1987; Thomas 1999)?

Sociolinguists don't deny that the people who speak a given language share knowledge of its basic rules. Such common knowledge is the basis of mutually intelligible communication. However, sociolinguists focus on features that vary systematically with social position and situation. To study variation, sociolinguists must do fieldwork. They must observe, define, and measure variable use of language in real-world situations. To show that linguistic features correlate with social, economic, and political differences, the social attributes of speakers also must be measured and related to speech (Fasold 1990; Labov 1972a; Trudgill 2000).

Variation within a language at a given time is historic change in progress. The same forces that, working gradually, have produced large-scale linguistic change over the centuries are still at work today. Linguistic change doesn't occur in a vacuum but in society. When new ways of speaking are associated with social factors, they are imitated, and they spread. In this way, a language changes.

Linguistic Diversity

As an illustration of the linguistic variation that is encountered in all nations, consider the contemporary United States. Ethnic diversity is revealed by the fact that millions of Americans learn first languages other than English. Spanish is the most common. Most of those people eventually become bilinguals, adding English as a second language. In many multilingual (including colonized) nations, people use two languages on different occasions: one in the home, for example, and the other on the job or in public.

Whether bilingual or not, we all vary our speech in different contexts; we engage in **style shifts** (see Eckert and Rickford, eds. 2001). In certain parts of Europe, people regularly switch dialects. This phenomenon, known as **diglossia**, applies to "high" and "low" variants of the same language, for example, in German and Flemish (spoken in Belgium). People employ the "high" variant at universities and in writing, professions, and the mass media. They use the "low" variant for ordinary conversation with family members and friends.

Just as social situations influence our speech, so do geographic, cultural, and socioeconomic differences. Many dialects coexist in the United States with Standard (American) English (SE). SE itself is a dialect that differs, say, from "BBC English," which is the preferred dialect in Great Britain. According to the principle of *linguistic relativity*, all dialects are equally effective as systems of communication, which is language's main job. Our tendency to think of particular dialects as cruder or more sophisticated than others is a social rather than a linguistic judgment. We rank certain speech patterns as better or worse because we recognize that they are used by groups that

we also rank. People who say *dese, dem,* and *dere* instead of *these, them,* and *there* communicate perfectly well with anyone who recognizes that the *d* sound systematically replaces the *th* sound in their speech. However, this form of speech has become an indicator of low social rank. We call it, like the use of *ain't,* "uneducated speech." The use of *dem, dese,* and *dere* is one of many phonological differences that Americans recognize and look down on.

Gender Speech Contrasts

Comparing men and women, there are differences in phonology, grammar, and vocabulary, as well as in the body stances and movements that accompany speech (Baron 1986; Eckert and McConnell-Ginet 2003; Lakoff 2004; Tannen 1990). In phonology, American women tend to pronounce their vowels more peripherally ("rant," "rint"), whereas men tend to pronounce theirs more centrally ("runt"—in all cases when saying the word "rent"). In public contexts, Japanese women tend to adopt an artificially high voice, for the sake of politeness, according to their traditional culture. In North America and Great Britain, women's speech tends to be more similar to the standard dialect than men's is. Consider the data in Table 6.3, gathered in Detroit. In all social classes, but particularly in the working class, men were more apt to use double negatives (e.g., "I don't want none"). Women tend to be more careful about "uneducated speech." This trend shows up in both the United States and England. Men may adopt working-class speech because they associate it with masculinity. Perhaps women pay more attention to the media, where standard dialects are employed.

According to Robin Lakoff (2004), the use of certain types of words and expressions has been associated with women's traditional lesser power in American society (see also Coates 1986; Tannen 1990). For example, *Oh dear, Oh fudge,* and *Goodness!* are less forceful than *Hell* and *Damn.* Watch the lips of a disgruntled athlete in a televised competition, such as a football game. What's the likelihood he's saying "Phooey on you"? Women are more likely to use such adjectives as *adorable, charming, sweet, cute, lovely,* and *divine* than men are.

See the Internet Exercises at your OLC for information on the extinction of languages

mhhe.com/kottak

TABLE 6.3 Multiple Negation ("I don't want none") According to Gender and Class (in Percentages)				
	Upper Middle Class	**Lower Middle Class**	**Upper Working Class**	**Lower Working Class**
Male	6.3	32.4	40.0	90.1
Female	0.0	1.4	35.6	58.9

SOURCE: Peter Trudgill, *Sociolinguistics: An Introduction to Language and Society* (London: Penguin, 1974, revised edition 1983), p. 85.

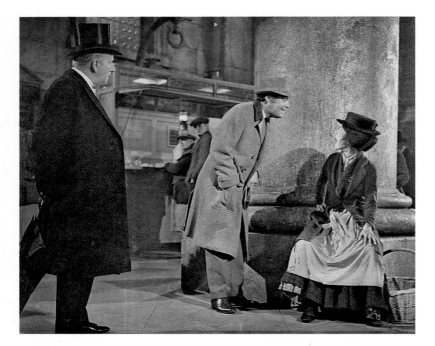

How does gender help us understand differences in communication styles? Differences in the linguistic strategies and behavior of American men and women are examined in several books by the well-known sociolinguist Deborah Tannen (1990, 1993). Tannen (1990) uses the terms "rapport" and "report" to contrast women's and men's overall linguistic styles. American women, says Tannen, typically use language and the body movements that accompany it to build rapport, social connections with others. American men, on the other hand, tend to make reports, reciting information that serves to establish a place for themselves in a hierarchy, as they also attempt to determine the relative ranks of their conversation mates.

■ *Certain dialects are stigmatized, not because of actual linguistic deficiencies, but because of a symbolic association between a certain way of talking and low social status. In this scene from* My Fair Lady, *Professor Henry Higgins (Rex Harrison) encounters Eliza Doolittle (Audrey Hepburn), a Cockney flower girl. Higgins will teach Doolittle how to speak like an English aristocrat.*

Let's return to the previously discussed domains of sports and color terminology for additional illustration of differences in lexical (vocabulary) distinctions that men and women make. Men typically know more terms related to sports, make more distinctions among them (e.g., runs versus points), and try to use the terms more precisely than women do. Correspondingly, influenced more by the fashion and cosmetics industries than men are, women use more color terms and attempt to use them more specifically than men do. Thus, when I lecture on sociolinguistics, and to make this point, I bring an off-purple shirt to class. Holding it up, I first ask women to say aloud what color the shirt is. The women rarely answer with a uniform voice, as they try to distinguish the actual shade (mauve, lilac, lavender, wisteria, or some other purplish hue). I then ask the men, who consistently answer as one, "PURPLE." Rare is the man who on the spur of the moment can imagine the difference between *fuchsia* and *magenta* or *grape* and *aubergine*.

Language and Status Position

Honorifics are terms used with people, often by being added to their names, to "honor" them. Such terms may convey or imply a status difference between the speaker and the person being referred to ("the good doctor") or addressed ("Professor Dumbledore"). Although Americans tend to be less formal than other nationalities, American English still has its honorifics. They include such terms as "Mr.," "Mrs.," "Ms.," "Dr.," "Professor," "Dean," "Senator," "Reverend," "Honorable," and "Presi-

dent." Often these terms are attached to names, as in "Dr. Wilson," "President Bush," and "Senator Clinton," but some of them can be used to address someone without using his or her name, such as "Dr.," "Mr. President," "Senator," and "Miss." The British have a more developed set of honorifics, corresponding to status distinctions based in class, nobility (e.g., Lord and Lady Trumble), and special recognition (e.g., knighthood—"Sir Elton" or "Dame Maggie").

The Japanese language has several honorifics, some of which convey more respect than others do. The suffix *-sama* (added to a name), showing great respect, is used to address someone of higher social status, such as a lord or a respected teacher. Women can use it to demonstrate love or respect for their husbands. The most common Japanese honorific, *-san*, attached to the last name, is respectful, but less formal than "Mr.," "Mrs.," or "Ms." in American English. Attached to a first name, *-san* denotes more familiarity. The honorific *-dono* shows more respect and is intermediate between *-san* and *-sama*.

Other Japanese honorifics don't necessarily honor the person being addressed. The term *-kun*, for example, conveys familiarity when addressing friends, like using *-san* attached to the first name. The term *-kun* is used also with younger or lower-ranking people. A boss might use *-kun* with employees, especially females. Here the honorific works in reverse; the speaker uses the term (somewhat like "boy" or "girl" in English) to address someone he or she perceives as having lower status. Japanese speakers use the very friendly and familiar term *-chan* with someone of the same age or younger, including close friends, siblings, and children (*Free Dictionary* 2004; Loveday 1986, 2001).

Kin terms also can be associated with gradations in rank and familiarity. "Dad" is a more familiar, less formal kin term than "Father," but it still shows more respect than would using the father's first name. Outranking their children, parents routinely use their kids' first names, nicknames, or baby names, rather than addressing them as "son" and "daughter." American English terms like "bro," "man," "dude," and "girl" (in some contexts) seem similar to the informal/familiar honorifics in Japanese. Southerners up to (and sometimes long past) a certain age routinely use "ma'am" and "sir" for older or higher-status women and men.

Stratification

We use and evaluate speech in the context of *extralinguistic* forces—social, political, and economic. Mainstream Americans evaluate the speech of low-status groups negatively, calling it "uneducated." This is not because these ways of speaking are bad in themselves but because they have come to symbolize low status. Consider variation in the pronunciation of *r*. In some parts of the United States, *r* is regularly pronounced, and in other (*r*less) areas, it is not. Originally, American *r*less speech was modeled on the fashionable speech of England. Because of its prestige, *r*lessness was adopted in many areas and continues as the norm around Boston and in the South.

New Yorkers sought prestige by dropping their *r*'s in the 19th century, after having pronounced them in the 18th. However, contemporary New Yorkers are going back to the 18th-century pattern of pronouncing *r*'s. What matters, and what governs linguistic change, is not the reverberation of a strong midwestern *r* but *social* evaluation, whether *r*'s happen to be "in" or "out."

Studies of *r* pronunciation in New York City have clarified the mechanisms of phonological change. William Labov (1972*b*) focused on whether *r* was pronounced after vowels in such words as *car, floor, card,* and *fourth.* To get data on how this linguistic variation correlated with social class, he used a series of rapid encounters with employees in three New York City department stores, each of whose prices and locations attracted a different socioeconomic group. Saks Fifth Avenue (68 encounters) catered to the upper middle class, Macy's (125) attracted middle-class shoppers, and S. Klein's (71) had predominantly lower-middle-class and working-class customers. The class origins of store personnel tended to reflect those of their customers.

Having already determined that a certain department was on the fourth floor, Labov approached ground-floor salespeople and asked where that department was. After the salesperson had answered, "Fourth floor," Labov repeated his "Where?" in order to get a second response. The second reply was more formal and emphatic,

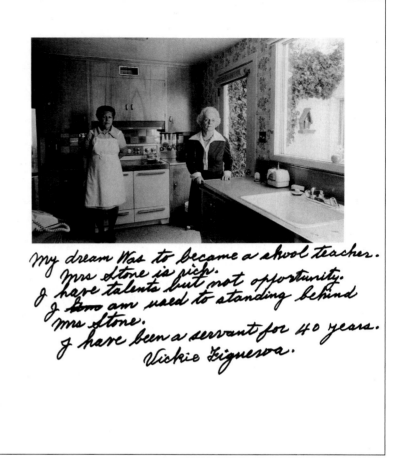

the salesperson presumably thinking that Labov hadn't heard or understood the first answer. For each salesperson, therefore, Labov had two samples of /r/ pronunciation in two words.

Labov calculated the percentages of workers who pronounced /r/ at least once during the interview. These were 62 percent at Saks, 51 percent at Macy's, but only 20 percent at S. Klein's. He also found that personnel on upper floors, where he asked "What floor is this?" (and where more expensive items were sold), pronounced /r/ more often than ground-floor salespeople did.

In Labov's study, summarized in Table 6.4, /r/ pronunciation was clearly associated with prestige. Certainly the job interviewers who had hired the salespeople never counted *r*'s before offering employment. However, they did use speech evaluations to make judgments about how effective certain people would be in selling particular kinds of merchandise. In other words, they practiced sociolinguistic discrimination, using linguistic features in deciding who got certain jobs.

Our speech habits help determine our access to employment and other material resources. Because of this, "proper language" itself becomes a strategic resource—and a path to wealth, pres-

■ *"Proper language" is a strategic resource, correlated with wealth, prestige, and power. How is linguistic (and social) stratification illustrated in the photo above, including the handwritten comments below it?*

TABLE 6.4 Pronunciation of *r* in New York City Department Stores		
Store	Number of Encounters	% *r* Pronunciation
Saks Fifth Avenue	68	62
Macy's	125	51
S. Klein's	71	20

tige, and power (Gal 1989; Thomas and Wareing, eds. 2004). Illustrating this, many ethnographers have described the importance of verbal skill and oratory in politics (Beeman 1986; Bloch, ed. 1975; Brenneis 1988; Geis 1987). Ronald Reagan, known as a "great communicator," dominated American society in the 1980s as a two-term president. Another twice-elected president, Bill Clinton, despite his southern accent, was known for his verbal skills in certain contexts (e.g., televised debates and town-hall meetings). Communications flaws may have helped doom the presidencies of Gerald Ford, Jimmy Carter, and George Bush (the elder) ("Couldn't do that; wouldn't be prudent").

The French anthropologist Pierre Bourdieu views linguistic practices as *symbolic capital* that properly trained people may convert into economic and social capital. The value of a dialect—its standing in a "linguistic market"—depends on the extent to which it provides access to desired positions in the labor market. In turn, this reflects its legitimation by formal institutions: educational institutions, state, church, and prestige media. Even people who don't use the prestige dialect accept its authority and correctness, its "symbolic domination" (Bourdieu 1982, 1984). Thus, linguistic forms, which lack power in themselves, take on the power of the groups they symbolize. The education system, however (defending its own worth), denies linguistic relativity, misrepresenting prestige speech as being inherently better. The linguistic insecurity often felt by lower-class and minority speakers is a result of this symbolic domination.

Black English Vernacular (BEV)

No one pays much attention when someone says "runt" instead of "rent." But some nonstandard speech carries more of a stigma. Sometimes stigmatized speech is linked to region, class, or educational background; sometimes it is associated with ethnicity or "race."

The sociolinguist William Labov and several associates, both white and black, have conducted detailed studies of what they call **Black English**

Vernacular (BEV). (*Vernacular* means ordinary, casual speech.) BEV is the "relatively uniform dialect spoken by the majority of black youth in most parts of the United States today, especially in the inner city areas of New York, Boston, Detroit, Philadelphia, Washington, Cleveland, . . . and other urban centers. It is also spoken in most rural areas and used in the casual, intimate speech of many adults" (Labov 1972*a*, p. xiii). This does not imply that all, or even most, African Americans speak BEV.

BEV isn't an ungrammatical hodgepodge. Rather, BEV is a complex linguistic system with its own rules, which linguists have described. The phonology and syntax of BEV are similar to those of southern dialects. This reflects generations of contact between southern whites and blacks, with mutual influence on each other's speech patterns. Many features that distinguish BEV from SE (Standard English) also show up in southern white speech, but less frequently than in BEV.

Linguists disagree about exactly how BEV originated (Rickford 1997). Smitherman (1986) calls it an Africanized form of English reflecting both an African heritage and the conditions of servitude, oppression, and life in America. She notes certain structural similarities between West African languages and BEV. African linguistic backgrounds no doubt influenced how early African Americans learned English. Did they restructure English to fit African linguistic patterns? Or did they quickly learn English from whites, with little continuing influence from the African linguistic heritage? Or, possibly, in acquiring English, did African slaves fuse English with African languages to make a pidgin or creole, which influenced the subsequent development of BEV? Creole speech may have been brought to the American colonies by the many slaves who were imported from the Caribbean during the 17th and 18th centuries. Some slaves may even have learned, while still in Africa, the pidgins or creoles spoken in West African trading forts (Rickford 1997).

Origins aside, there are phonological and grammatical differences between BEV and SE. One phonological difference between BEV and SE is that BEV speakers are less likely to pronounce *r* than SE speakers are. Actually, many SE speakers don't pronounce *r*'s that come right before a consonant (ca*r*d) or at the end of a word (car). But SE speakers do usually pronounce an *r* that comes right before a vowel, either at the end of a word (fou*r* o'clock) or within a word (Ca*r*ol). BEV speakers, by contrast, are much more likely to omit such intervocalic (between vowels) *r*'s. The result is that speakers of the two dialects have different *homonyms* (words that sound the same but have different meanings). BEV speakers who don't pronounce intervocalic *r*'s have the following homonyms: Carol/Cal; Paris/pass.

Observing different phonological rules, BEV speakers pronounce certain words differently than SE speakers do. Particularly in the elementary school context, the homonyms of BEV-speaking students typically differ from those of their SE-speaking teachers. To evaluate reading accuracy, teachers should determine whether students are recognizing the different meanings of such BEV homonyms as *passed, past,* and *pass.* Teachers need to make sure students understand what they are reading, which is probably more important than whether they are pronouncing words correctly according to the SE norm.

The phonological contrasts between BEV and SE speakers often have grammatical consequences. One of these is *copula deletion,* which means the absence of SE forms of the copula—the verb *to be.* For example, SE and BEV may contrast as follows:

SE	SE Contraction	BEV
you are tired	you're tired	you tired
he is tired	he's tired	he tired
we are tired	we're tired	we tired
they are tired	they're tired	they tired

In its deletion of the present tense of the verb *to be,* BEV is similar to many languages, including Russian, Hungarian, and Hebrew. BEV's copula deletion is simply a grammatical result of its phonological rules. Notice that BEV deletes the copula where SE has contractions. BEV's phonological rules dictate that *r*'s (as in *you're, we're,* and *they're*) and word-final *s*'s (as in *he's*) be dropped. However, BEV speakers do pronounce *m,* so that the BEV first-person singular is "I'm tired," just as in SE. Thus, when BEV omits the copula, it merely carries contraction one step further, as a result of its phonological rules.

Also, phonological rules may lead BEV speakers to omit *-ed* as a past-tense marker and *-s* as a marker of plurality. However, other speech contexts demonstrate that BEV speakers do understand the difference between past and present verbs, and between singular and plural nouns. Confirming this are irregular verbs (e.g., *tell, told*) and irregular plurals (e.g., *child, children*), in which BEV works the same as SE.

SE is not superior to BEV as a linguistic system, but it does happen to be the prestige dialect—the one used in the mass media, in writing, and in most public and professional contexts. SE is the dialect that has the most "symbolic capital." In areas of Germany where there is diglossia, speakers of Plattdeusch (Low German) learn the High German dialect to communicate appropriately in the national context. Similarly, upwardly mobile BEV-speaking students learn SE.

HISTORICAL LINGUISTICS

Sociolinguists study contemporary variation in speech—language change in progress. **Historical linguistics** deals with longer-term change. Historical linguists can reconstruct many features of past languages by studying contemporary **daughter languages.** These are languages that descend from the same parent language and that have been changing separately for hundreds or even thousands of years. We call the original language from which they diverge the **protolanguage.** Romance languages such as French and Spanish, for example, are daughter languages of Latin, their common protolanguage. German, English, Dutch, and the Scandinavian languages

are daughter languages of proto-Germanic. Latin and proto-Germanic were both Indo-European languages. Historical linguists classify languages according to their degree of relationship (see Figure 6.2).

Language changes over time. It evolves—varies, spreads, divides into **subgroups** (languages within a taxonomy of related languages that are most closely related). Dialects of a single parent language become distinct daughter languages, especially if they are isolated from one another. Some of them split, and new "granddaughter" languages develop. If people remain in the ancestral homeland, their speech patterns also change. The evolving speech in the ancestral homeland should be considered a daughter language like the others.

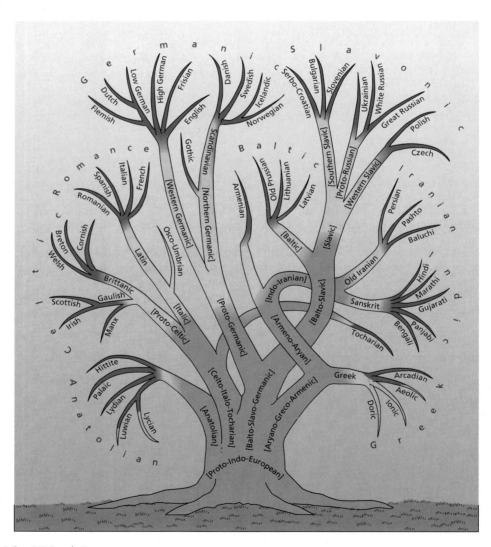

Map Atlas

Map 11 plots the distribution of the world's major language families, including Indo-European, whose languages are spoken now in areas far from its geographic origin.

FIGURE 6.2 PIE Family Tree.

This is a family tree of the Indo-European languages. All can be traced back to a protolanguage, Proto-Indo-European (PIE), spoken more than 6,000 years ago. PIE split into dialects that eventually evolved into separate languages, which, in turn, evolved into languages such as Latin and proto-Germanic, which are ancestral to dozens of modern daughter languages.

For more on PIE, see the Virtual Exploration

mhhe.com/kottak

BEYOND THE CLASSROOM

Cybercommunication in Collegespace

BACKGROUND INFORMATION

STUDENT:
Jason A. DeCaro

SUPERVISING PROFESSOR:
Robert Herbert

SCHOOL:
State University of New York
at Binghamton

YEAR IN SCHOOL/MAJOR:
Senior/Anthropology and
Biochemistry dual major

FUTURE PLANS:
Ph.D. in Biological Anthropology;
career in academics or public health

PROJECT TITLE:
Cybercommunication in
Collegespace: The Electronic/
Personal Juncture in a Campus
Living Community

How is online communication related to face-to-face communication and to social interaction? On the basis of this research, is electronic communication good or bad for community formation?

Why do people who live in face-to-face proximity communicate using their computers? What is the interaction between their social lives "on-" and "off-line"? How does this affect their sense of community? I conducted research to address these questions through an anthropological case study.

The Internet has been interpreted as personalizing or depersonalizing, as highly democratic or merely chaotic, and as vitalizing or damaging to American "community." Some theorists suppose that electronic communication extends the pool of individuals with whom one maintains contact. However, others suggest that this merely creates an electronic "pseudocommunity" with shifting membership and superficial social ties. If this "pseudocommunity" competes for members' time and energy, it may be detrimental to their face-to-face interaction. Despite the active theoretical debate, very few studies have examined the interaction between electronic and face-to-face community in a geographically local group of individuals.

I observed a group of students of mixed gender who live in close proximity on a college campus. These students chose their living arrangement on the basis of common interest in computers, robotics, and engineering. Not all are computer scientists; some pursue majors such as creative writing and chemistry. Roughly a dozen alumni, some of whom no longer live in the local area, remain integral to the organization.

I am an alumnus; thus, I have a personal as well as a professional interest. One of my most challenging jobs was to avoid unintentional manipulation—even distancing myself from the group would have changed it! Yet, by remaining an "insider," I received tremendous access, and had a great deal of fun.

Members maintain face-to-face social activity and a busy electronic mailing list. The "real" and "virtual" communities thus created have overlapping but nonidentical membership. Most members who communicate exclusively within the "virtual" electronic domain are alumni. Students vary with respect to the form of communication that they favor. A few shun the electronic medium entirely and thereby opt out of the "virtual" community.

I distributed questionnaires, analyzed one year's mailing list traffic, and remained a participant in face-to-face social life. I found that conversations sometimes flow on and off the mailing list, and members do organize face-to-face social activities on-line. However, most people segregate the electronic and face-to-face domains, and most messages serve no explicit organizational purpose. Messages in this latter category allow contact between people who are not local, or strengthen bonds between individuals who see each other regularly.

Those who dedicate considerable time and energy to the virtual community put the mailing list to its widest range of uses. However, there is little evidence that electronic communication detracts from face-to-face interaction. Most people who are highly social on-line are highly social off-line as well. I suspect that individuals supplement, rather than replace, their face-to-face social lives with electronic communication. This is particularly valuable to those who do not live locally, or are less than comfortable with face-to-face communication. Thus, on the whole, members are integrated far more than they are alienated by the mailing list.

A close relationship between languages does not necessarily mean that their speakers are closely related biologically or culturally, because people can adopt new languages. In the equatorial forests of Africa, "pygmy" hunters have discarded their ancestral languages and now speak those of the cultivators who have migrated to the area. Immigrants to the United States and Canada spoke many different languages on arrival, but their descendants now speak fluent English.

The Book of Kells, an illustrated manuscript, was created at Kells, an ancient Irish monastery. Shown here is the title page of the book, which now resides in the Trinity College library in Dublin, Ireland. Such documents provide historical linguists with information on how languages change.

Knowledge of linguistic relationships is often valuable to anthropologists interested in history, particularly events during the past 5,000 years. Cultural features may (or may not) correlate with the distribution of language families. Groups that speak related languages may (or may not) be more culturally similar to each other than they are to groups whose speech derives from different linguistic ancestors. Of course, cultural similarities aren't limited to speakers of related languages. Even groups whose members speak unrelated languages have contact through trade, intermarriage, and warfare. Ideas and inventions diffuse widely among human groups. Many items of vocabulary in contemporary English come from French. Even without written documentation of France's influence after the Norman Conquest of England in 1066, linguistic evidence in contemporary English would reveal a long period of important firsthand contact with France. Similarly, linguistic evidence may confirm cultural contact and borrowing when written history is lacking. By considering which words have been borrowed, we also can make inferences about the nature of the contact.

SUMMARY

1. Wild primates use call systems to communicate. Environmental stimuli trigger calls, which cannot be combined when multiple stimuli are present. Contrasts between language and call systems include displacement, productivity, and cultural transmission. Over time, our ancestral call systems grew too complex for genetic transmission, and hominid communication began to rely on learning. Humans still use nonverbal communication, such as facial expressions, gestures, and body stances and movements. But language is the main system humans use to communicate. Chimps and gorillas can understand and manipulate nonverbal symbols based on language.

2. No language uses all the sounds the human vocal tract can make. Phonology—the study of speech sounds—focuses on sound contrasts (phonemes) that distinguish meaning. The grammars and lexicons of particular languages can lead their speakers to perceive and think in certain ways. Studies of domains such as kinship, color terminologies, and pronouns show that speakers of different languages categorize their experiences differently.

3. Linguistic anthropologists share anthropology's general interest in diversity in time and space. Sociolinguistics investigates relationships between social and linguistic variation by focusing on the actual use of language. Only when features of speech acquire social meaning are they imitated. If they are valued, they will spread. People vary their speech, shifting styles, dialects, and languages. As linguistic systems, all languages and dialects are equally complex, rule-governed, and effective for communication. However, speech is used, is evaluated, and changes in the context of political, economic, and social forces. Often the linguistic traits of a low-status group are negatively evaluated. This devaluation is not because of *linguistic* features per se. Rather, it reflects the association of such features with low *social* status. One dialect, supported by the dominant institutions of the state, exercises symbolic domination over the others.

4. Historical linguistics is useful for anthropologists interested in historic relationships among populations. Cultural similarities and differences often correlate with linguistic ones. Linguistic clues can suggest past contacts between cultures. Related languages—members of the same language family—descend from an original protolanguage. Relationships between languages don't necessarily mean that there are biological ties between their speakers, because people can learn new languages.

Black English Vernacular (BEV) A rule-governed dialect of American English with roots in southern English. BEV is spoken by African American youth and by many adults in their casual, intimate speech.

call systems Systems of communication among nonhuman primates, composed of a limited number of sounds that vary in intensity and duration. Tied to environmental stimuli.

cultural transmission A basic feature of language; transmission through learning.

daughter languages Languages developing out of the same parent language; for example, French and Spanish are daughter languages of Latin.

diglossia The existence of "high" (formal) and "low" (informal, familial) dialects of a single language, such as German.

displacement A basic feature of language; the ability to speak of things and events that are not present.

ethnosemantics The study of lexical (vocabulary) contrasts and classifications in various languages.

focal vocabulary A set of words and distinctions that are particularly important to certain groups (those with particular foci of experience or activity), such as types of snow to Eskimos or skiers.

historical linguistics Subdivision of linguistics that studies languages over time.

honorific A term, such as "Mr." or "Lord," used with people, often by being added to their names, to "honor" them.

kinesics The study of communication through body movements, stances, gestures, and facial expressions.

language Human beings' primary means of communication; may be spoken or written; features productivity and displacement and is culturally transmitted.

lexicon Vocabulary; a dictionary containing all the morphemes in a language and their meanings.

morphology The study of form; used in linguistics (the study of morphemes and word construction) and for form in general—for example, biomorphology relates to physical form.

phoneme Significant sound contrast in a language that serves to distinguish meaning, as in minimal pairs.

phonemics The study of the sound contrasts (phonemes) of a particular language.

phonetics The study of speech sounds in general; what people actually say in various languages.

phonology The study of sounds used in speech.

productivity A basic feature of language; the ability to use the rules of one's language to create new expressions comprehensible to other speakers.

protolanguage Language ancestral to several daughter languages.

Sapir-Whorf hypothesis Theory that different languages produce different ways of thinking.

semantics A language's meaning system.

sociolinguistics Study of relationships between social and linguistic variation; study of language (performance) in its social context.

style shifts Variations in speech in different contexts.

subgroups Languages within a taxonomy of related languages that are most closely related.

syntax The arrangement and order of words in phrases and sentences.

KEY TERMS

See the flash cards

mhhe.com/kottak

1. Give some additional examples of nonverbal communication. Check out your classmates during a discussion and see what examples you notice.

2. During a class discussion, what examples do you notice of sociolinguistic variation—say, between men and women, the professor and students, and so forth?

3. List some stereotypes about how different sorts of people speak. Are those real differences, or just stereotypes? Are the stereotypes positive or negative? Why do you think those stereotypes exist?

4. Based on your own experience and observations, list five ways in which men and women differ in their use of language. Now classify these differences as kinesic, phonological, grammatical, lexical—or other.

5. Do you agree with the principle of linguistic relativity? If not, why not? What dialects and languages do you speak? Do you tend to use different dialects, languages, or speech styles in different contexts? Why?

CRITICAL THINKING QUESTIONS

For more self-testing, see the self-quizzes

mhhe.com/kottak

Bonvillain, N.
   2003 *Language, Culture, and Communication: The Meaning of Messages,* 4th ed. Upper Saddle River, NJ: Prentice Hall. Up-to-date text on language and communication in cultural context.

Eckert, P.
   2000 *Linguistic Variation as Social Practice: The Linguistic Construction of Identity in Belten High.* Malden, MA: Blackwell. How speech correlates with high school social networks and cliques.

SUGGESTED ADDITIONAL READINGS

Eckert, P., and S. McConnell-Ginet
2003 *Language and Gender.* New York: Cambridge University Press. The sociolinguistics of male and female speech.

Eckert, P., and J. R. Rickford, eds.
2001 *Style and Sociolinguistic Variation.* New York: Cambridge University Press. The social context of style shifts.

Foley, W. A.
1997 *Anthroplogical Linguistics: An Introduction.* Cambridge, MA: Blackwell. Language, society, and culture.

Fouts, R.
1997 *Next of Kin: What Chimpanzees Have Taught Me about Who We Are.* New York, William Morrow. A teacher of Washoe, Lucy, and other signing chimps tells what he's learned from them.

Geis, M. L.
1987 *The Language of Politics.* New York: Springer-Verlag. Thorough examination of political uses of speech and oratory and the manipulation of language in power relations.

Lakoff, R. T.
2000 *Language War.* Berkeley: University of California Press. Politics and language in the United States today.
2004 *Language and Woman's Place,* rev. ed. (M. Bucholtz, ed.). New York: Oxford University Press. Influential nontechnical discussion of how women use and are treated in Standard American English.

Rickford, J. R., and R. J. Rickford
2000 *Spoken Soul: The Story of Black English.* New York: Wiley. Readable account of the history and social meaning of BEV.

Romaine, S.
1999 *Communicating Gender.* Mahwah, NJ: Erlbaum. Gender and language.
2000 *Language in Society: An Introduction to Sociolinguistics,* 2nd ed. New York: Oxford University Press. An introduction to sociolinguistics.

Salzmann, Z.
2004 *Language, Culture, and Society: An Introduction to Linguistic Anthropology,* 3rd ed. Boulder, CO: Westview. The function of language in culture and society.

Tannen, D.
1990 *You Just Don't Understand: Women and Men in Conversation.* New York: Ballantine. Popular book on gender differences in speech and conversational styles.

Tannen, D., ed.
1993 *Gender and Conversational Interaction.* New York: Oxford University Press. Twelve papers about conversational interaction illustrate the complexity of the relationship between gender and language use.

Thomas, L., and S. Wareing, eds.
2004 *Language, Society and Power,* 2nd ed. New York: Routledge. Political dimensions and use of language.

Trudgill, P.
2000 *Sociolinguistics: An Introduction to Language and Society,* 4th ed. New York: Penguin. Readable short introduction to the role and use of language in society.

INTERNET EXERCISES

1. Politeness Strategies: Go and read Cyndi Patee's article "Politeness," **http://logos.uoregon.edu/ explore/socioling/ politeness.html**.
   a. What kind of strategy do you most often use? Do your strategies change when you are talking to different people (i.e., your friend, your parent, your professor)?
   b. What kind of politeness strategy do you like other people to use with you? Would you prefer people to sacrifice politeness for directness?
   c. Pay attention to what politeness strategies are being used around you in class, at home, and with friends. Can you identify any patterns in the way people select politeness strategies?

2. Urban Legends: Read the Urban Legends and Folklore information page at About.com, **http://urbanlegends.about.com/science/ urbanlegends/library/weekly/aa082497.htm**. Make sure to read some of the examples of urban legends that are provided.
   a. What constitutes an urban legend?
   b. Why are urban legends so popular? Many of them are not true, so why do they continue to be shared?
   c. What role does the Internet play in propagating urban legends?
   d. After reading this page, are you going to be more or less skeptical the next time a friend relates a story to you?

See Chapter 15 at your McGraw-Hill Online Learning Center for additional review and interactive exercises.

Kottak, *Assault on Paradise*, 4th ed.

Read Chapter 7, especially the section "The Hippie Handbook." How did language figure in the way Arembepeiros characterized hippies? Read Chapter 12. How has television affected the way Arembepeiros deal with outsiders? What's your reaction to the stories of Nadia and Olga in relation to the impact of television? Do Brazilian attitudes about reading and print surprise you? Why?

Knauft, *The Gebusi*, 1st ed.

Based on Chapter 1 of Knauft's *The Gebusi,* how *important* was it for the author to learn the Gebusi language during his fieldwork? How easy was it for the author to learn the Gebusi language during his fieldwork? How did the author go about learning the Gebusi language—and how well or poorly did his language abilities develop over time?

LINKAGES

Canada: Unity and Diversity in Culture and Language

See your OLC Bringing
It All Together links

mhhe.com/kottak

There are levels of culture, as was pointed out in the chapter titled "Culture." National culture consists of the beliefs, values, behavior patterns, and institutions that people share through growing up in a given nation. Cultures also can be smaller than nations. Such "subcultures" may originate in region, ethnicity, language, class, or religion. Thus, the religious backgrounds of American Jews, Baptists, Roman Catholics, and Muslims create subcultural differences among them. French-speaking Canadians contrast with English-speaking people in the same country.

Studying a modern nation, anthropologists may focus on either unity or diversity—on what is common or what is different. A focus on unity would examine themes, values, behavior, institutions, and experiences that transcend regions and social divisions. A focus on diversity would look at the cultures within the national culture.

The two approaches shouldn't be mutually exclusive. Despite diversity, we can still detect a series of nationally relevant institutions, norms, and expectations. As we saw in the chapter on "Ethnicity and Race," the pressure on members of an ethnic group to observe a set of common national values comes not only from the national culture, but also from other ethnic groups. For example, African Americans in Los Angeles, after that city's 1992 riots, complained about their Korean neighbors. In doing so they referred to such general American values as openness, mutual respect, community participation, and "fair play." They saw their Korean neighbors as deficient in these traits. The Koreans countered by stressing another set of American national

values, involving education, family unity, discipline, hard work, and achievement.

We focus now on unity and diversity in Canada. (American national culture is examined in Appendix 3.) One key feature of Canadian national consciousness is the contrast with the United States. Canadians, when traveling internationally, often are taken for Americans, which emphatically they are not. To be sure, Canada and the United States share many cultural traits. Some reflect the shared English-language heritage of most Canadians and Americans. Some reflect common experiences in the colonization of North America. Still others reflect participation in a global system, or diffusion of products and information across porous borders.

The media, especially television, have helped bring nationalism and its symbols, including cultural contrasts with the United States, to prominence in Canada. In spring 2000, a TV commercial produced in Toronto for Molson Canadian beer gained instantaneous national prominence. The ad featured the character Joe Canadian, delivering what came to be known as The Rant, soon to become a nationalist mantra for 30 million Canadians:

"I'm not a lumberjack or a fur trader; I don't live in an igloo, eat blubber or own a dogsled."

"I have a prime minister, not a president. I speak English and French, not American."

"I can proudly sew my country's flag on my backpack." (This refers to Canada's gender-neutral school curriculum, in which sewing is taught to both boys and girls.)

"I believe in peacekeeping, not policing; diversity, not assimilation."

Images of maple leaves and beavers flashed on the screen as Joe reached his climax:

"Canada is the second-largest land mass, the first nation of hockey and the best part of North America. My name is Joe and I am Canadian" (quoted in Brooke 2000).

The Rant spurred the government of Ontario, Canada's most populous province, to announce that starting in September 2000, each student would start the day by singing "O Canada," and pledging allegiance to the queen (since Canada is a member of the British Commonwealth). Although The Rant was recited by ordinary Canadians from Vancouver to Halifax, one province did not join in this affirmation of national identity. In French-

■ Jeff Douglas, who plays Joe Canadian, delivers "The Rant" in Ottawa, Ontario, on Canada Day—July 1, 2000.

speaking Quebec, which was governed by the separatist Parti Quebecois between 1994 and 2003, Canadian national symbols such as the flag and the anthem were officially ignored, and Molson Canadian beer was not even marketed (Brooke 2000).

The contrast between Quebec and the rest of Canada is the most dramatic, jarring, and politically problematic in a nation that prides itself on diversity in language and culture. Few countries rival Canada in cultivating a national image of a bilingual, multicultural society. According to a Government of Canada website:

> Canada's experience with diversity distinguishes it from most other countries. Our 30 million inhabitants reflect a cultural, ethnic and linguistic makeup found nowhere else on earth . . . Diversity has been a fundamental characteristic of Canada since its beginnings (http://www.pch.gc.ca/progs/multi/respect_e.cfm).

Unlike the United States, which is suspicious of linguistic difference, bilingualism (with English and French as official languages) lies at the root of the Canadian federation. When the Canadian Confederation was established in 1867, English and French were accorded official, constitutional status. Substantial powers were granted to Canada's constituent provinces. In one of those provinces, Quebec, French-speaking Canadians formed a large majority. They used their constitutional powers to protect and develop a regional culture based on French language and culture and French-Canadian heritage. Elsewhere in Canada, the French language was swamped by immigrants who either were of English origin or were encouraged to speak English. In 2001 86 percent of Canada's native French speakers (Francophones) lived in Quebec, where they made up 82 percent of the population.

The longest-standing test of Canada's capacity to balance unity and diversity is the challenge of linguistic duality. The national dominance of English is troubling to French Canadians. Illustrating a power imbalance that tilts toward English is the fact that there are five times as many bilingual Francophones as Anglophones (native English speakers). Francophones need to learn English more than Anglophones need to learn French.

Because of immigration, linguistic diversity in Canada is increasing. In 2001 (the date of the last census), 5.2 million Canadians, in a population of some 30 million people, reported a mother tongue (language learned in the home in childhood) other than English or French. Anglophone Canadians accounted for 59 percent of the population, versus 23 percent for Francophones. Eighteen percent of Canadians habitually spoke a language other than English or French. Chinese was the third most common, followed by Italian, German, Punjabi,

Spanish, Portuguese, Polish, Arabic, Tagalog (Filipino), Ukrainian, Dutch, Vietnamese, Greek, and aboriginal languages.

English-French bilingualism (people speaking both English and French) has increased. In 2001, 18 percent of the population could speak both official languages, compared with 13 percent in 1971. Note that both Canada and Canadians illustrate increased linguistic diversity.

In 1950, 92 percent of Canada's population growth was from births to Canadians. Today, with around 200,000 people moving to Canada each year, immigration accounts for over 55 percent of the overall population growth. Of Canada's population in 2001, 18.4 percent was foreign-born. Canada has been called "the global village in one country." Toronto, Canada's largest city, in its largest province, has become the world's most multicultural city, ahead of New York and London.

Canada has always relied on immigrants to supply settlers and labor. During the late 19th and early 20th centuries, Canada's immigration policy had as its primary objective supplying a labor pool, first for settlement and agriculture and then to support industrialization. In 1960, a Canadian Bill of Rights barred discrimination by federal agencies based on national origin, race, color, religion, or sex. In 1962 a revised Canadian Immigration Act stated that any qualified person from any part of the world could be considered for immigration. The mix of source countries soon shifted from northern Europe to southern Europe, Asia, the West Indies, and the Middle East.

■ Canada is officially bilingual, but French language and culture dominate in the province of Quebec. Shown here, Quebec Liberal Party leader Jean Charest speaks to supporters during a campaign stop on April 12, 2003. After this successful campaign, Charest became Premier of Quebec in 2003.

Despite its admirable ideology of respect, Canada hasn't totally avoided discrimination. Abuses of the rights of aboriginal peoples, for example, can be traced back to Canada's beginnings. Aboriginal Canadians still have more poverty, poorer health, higher death and suicide rates, and more unemployment than their fellow citizens do. To its credit, the Canadian government has taken many steps to correct past mistakes and to address the needs of aboriginal peoples. For example, in 1973 Canada's Supreme Court recognized land rights based on an aboriginal group's traditional use and occupancy of land. And in 1982, the government affirmed the treaty rights of aboriginal peoples to protect their cultures, customs, traditions and languages.

In 2001 some 975,000 Canadians (3.3 percent of the national population) claimed aboriginal identity as North American Indians (First Nations), *métis* (mixed), or Inuit. A fifth of the aboriginal population reported an aboriginal language as the mother tongue. At the time of European settlement, Canada had more than 56 aboriginal nations speaking more than 30 languages. Among aboriginal languages reported as mother tongues in 2001, the three largest were Cree (72,690 people), Inuktitut (spoken by Inuit—29,005), and Ojibway (20,890).

The chapter "Ethnicity and Race" discussed the social construction of race in the United States, Japan, and Brazil. Canada constructs race and ethnicity differently from any of those three countries, although there are similarities. For example, the classification of people who claim a *métis* (mixed) identity as Aboriginal People hints of the American hypodescent rule. Rather than race, the Canadian census asks about "visible minorities." That country's Employment Equity Act defines such groups as "persons, other than Aboriginal peoples, who are non-Caucasian in race or non-white in colour" (Statistics Canada 2001*a*). Unlike the United States, the Canadian census would seem to assume that racial differences lie in the minds (and eyes) of the beholder rather than being self-identified.

Canada's 1996 census was the first to gather systematic data on visible minorities—for the purpose of assessing employment equity. Like affirmative action in the United States, Canada's Employment Equity Act was a response to evidence of discrimination.

"Chinese" and "South Asian" are Canada's largest visible minorities. Note that Canada's total visible minority population of 13.4 percent contrasts with a comparable figure of about 25 percent for the United States in the 2000 census. In particular, Canada's 2.2 percent black population contrasts with the American figure of 12.5 percent for African Americans. Canada's Asian population is significantly higher than the U.S. figure of 3.7 percent. Only a tiny fraction of the Canadian population (0.2 percent) claimed multiple visible minority affiliations, compared with 2.4 percent claiming "more than one race" in the United States in 2000.

Having read this essay, think about the main similarities and differences between the United States and Canada in terms of racial classification, ethnicity and multiculturalism, and linguistic diversity. What are key symbols of Canadian national culture—and of the national culture of the United States?

7

Making a Living

ADAPTIVE STRATEGIES

Compared with hunting and gathering (foraging), the advent of *food production* (plant cultivation and animal domestication) fueled major changes in human life, such as the formation of larger social and political systems—eventually states. The pace of cultural transformation increased enormously. This chapter provides a framework for understanding a variety of human adaptive strategies and economic systems—ranging from hunting and gathering to farming and herding.

The anthropologist Yehudi Cohen (1974b) used the term *adaptive strategy* to describe a group's system of economic production. Cohen argued that the most important reason for similarities between two (or more) unrelated societies is their possession of a similar adaptive strategy. For example, there are clear similarities among societies that have a foraging (hunting and gathering) strategy. Cohen developed a typology of societies based on correlations between their economies and their social features. His typology includes these five adaptive strategies: foraging, horticulture, agriculture, pastoralism, and industrialism. Industrialism is discussed in the chapter "The Modern World System." The present chapter focuses on the first four adaptive strategies.

FORAGING

Until 10,000 years ago, people everywhere were foragers, also known as hunter-gatherers. However, environmental differences did create substantial contrasts among the world's foragers. Some, such as the people who lived in Europe during the ice ages, were big-game hunters. Today, hunters in the Arctic still focus on large animals and herd animals; they have much less vegetation and variety in their diets than do tropical foragers. In general, as one moves from colder to warmer areas, there is an increase in the

OVERVIEW

Nonindustrial adaptive strategies include foraging, horticulture, agriculture, and pastoralism. Ties of kinship and marriage link members of foraging bands, whose men usually hunt and fish, while the women usually gather.

Horticulture and agriculture stand at opposite ends of a continuum based on intensity of land and labor use. Horticulturalists always fallow their land. Agriculturalists farm the same piece of land year after year and use labor intensively, through irrigation, terracing, and caring for domesticated animals. Pastoralists (herders) have mixed economies. Nomadic pastoralists trade with farmers. Among transhumant pastoralists, part of the population farms, while another part pastures the herds.

Economic anthropologists, who study systems of production, distribution, and consumption cross-culturally, counter Western economic assumptions about the universality of scarcity and the profit motive. There are three main forms of exchange. Market exchange is based on purchase and sale, motivated by profit. With redistribution, goods are collected at a central place, with some eventually being given back to the people. Reciprocity governs exchanges between social equals. The primary exchange mode in a society is the one that allocates the means of production.

number of species. The tropics contain tremendous biodiversity, a great variety of plant and animal species, many of which have been used by human foragers. Tropical foragers typically hunt and gather a wide range of plant and animal life. The same may be true in temperate areas, such as the North Pacific Coast of North America, where Native American foragers could draw on a rich variety of land and sea resources, including salmon, other fish species, berries, mountain goats, seals, and sea mammals. Nevertheless, despite differences due to environmental variation, all foraging economies have shared one essential feature: People rely on available natural resources for their subsistence, rather than controlling the reproduction of plants and animals.

Such control came with the advent of animal domestication (initially of sheep and goats) and plant cultivation (of wheat and barley), which began 10,000 to 12,000 years ago in the Middle East. Cultivation based on different crops, such as maize, manioc (cassava), and potatoes, arose independently some 3,000 to 4,000 years later in the Americas. In both hemispheres the new economy spread rapidly. Most foragers eventually turned to food production. Today, almost all foragers have at least some dependence on food production or on food producers (Kent 1992).

The foraging way of life survived into modern times in certain environments (see Figure 7.1), including a few islands and forests, along with deserts and very cold areas—places where food production was not practicable with simple technology (see Lee and Daly 1999). In many areas, foragers had been exposed to the "idea" of food production but never adopted it because their own economies provided a perfectly adequate and nutritious diet—with a lot less work. In some areas, people reverted to foraging after trying food production and abandoning it. In most areas where hunter-gatherers did survive, foraging should be described as "recent" rather than "contemporary." All modern foragers live in nation-states, depend to some extent on government assistance, and have contacts with food-producing neighbors, as well as missionaries and other outsiders. We should not view contemporary foragers as isolated or pristine survivors of the Stone Age. Modern foragers are influenced by regional forces (e.g., trade and war), national and international policies, and political and economic events in the world system.

Although foraging is disappearing as a way of life, the outlines of Africa's two broad belts of recent foraging remain evident. One is the Kalahari Desert of southern Africa. This is the home of the *San* ("Bushmen"), who include the *Ju/'hoansi* (see Kent 1996; Lee 2003). The other main African foraging area is the equatorial forest of central and eastern Africa, home of the Mbuti, Efe, and other "pygmies" (Bailey et al. 1989; Turnbull 1965).

Reindeer Herders, at Home on a (Very Cold) Range

NEW YORK TIMES NEWS BRIEF

by Warren Hoge
March 26, 2001

This chapter surveys systems of production and exchange in nonindustrial economies. Some economic roles, such as hunting and herding, have been around for millennia. In Norway, Sweden, and Finland, the Samis (also known as Lapps or Laplanders) domesticated reindeer, which their ancestors used to hunt, in the 16th century. Like other herders, the Samis still follow their animals as they make an annual trek, in this case from the coast to the interior. Their environment may be harsher, but the Samis, like other contemporary herders, live in nation-states. They must deal with outsiders as they make their living through animal husbandry, trade, and sales. The Samis now use modern technology, including snowmobiles and four-wheel-drive vehicles, to follow their herds. In today's world, communities are being incorporated, at an accelerating rate, into larger systems (a trend that began with the advent of food production). The Samis face increased regulation of their economic adaptation—reindeer herding—by the government of Norway. In addition, the reindeer industry has been outflanked by the better organized and far larger commercial beef industry.

KAUTOKEINO, Norway—Johan Martin Eira stepped from his front door into the Arctic dawn and studied the snowbound valley dotted with cozy homes and cabins.

"When the smoke rises straight up from the chimneys like that," he said, "you know it's really cold."

Really cold this February morning meant minus 40 degrees, and presumably even the wind had gone into deep freeze . . .

Mr. Eira, 31, was born and raised in this town, 200 miles north of the Arctic Circle, and has spent his life with creatures who are as comfortable in polar climes as he and his fellow reindeer herders seem to be.

For the indigenous Samis, like Mr. Eira, reindeer can be everything. Samis, also known as Lapps or Laplanders, raise them, sell them, race them, eat them, capture their images in their art, make jewelry from their bones, decorate barn walls with their pelts and use their hides to make coats, boots, leggings, hats and gloves. Economic and cultural activity centers on reindeer . . .

Reindeer husbandry has existed here since the end of the Ice Age. Reindeer followed the ice as it receded, the story goes, and the people followed the reindeer.

These animals are so much a part of the landscape that hundreds huddle silently on a hillside several miles out of town, barely spottable, the pewter color of their skins camouflaging them against the gray sky, white birch and snowy fields. In this cold, they stand unmoving as statues, eager to conserve their energy.

"I can't say they really like it outside in this temperature, but they can survive it," Mr. Eira said. They have a natural interior heating system, warming air in their mouths and lungs and then spreading it through their bodies. Their hairs are hollow, providing insulation . . .

Norway has an estimated 190,000 reindeer, and about 40 percent of the country's land is used for grazing and calving. In the 16th century, there was a gradual transition from hunting wild reindeer to herding, and the Samis became a nomadic people in what is now Europe's last wilderness. Of the 80,000 Samis in Norway, Sweden and Finland, about 10 percent are still reindeer herders. The largest number, about 50,000, live in Norway, where laws passed the last 25 years have given them exclusive right to the trade.

Mr. Eira, his four brothers and their father all mind the family herd of 3,500 animals, and though they have traded in their sleds for snowmobiles, and their wagons for four-wheel-drive vehicles, their lives follow ancient traditions.

Throughout the winter, the herds move across the slopes and valleys,

In northern Norway a Sami herder uses a snow scooter to drive his migrating reindeer.

feeding on moss and lichen the animals dig from beneath the snow and shreds of bark from scrubby trees that poke above the drifts. In the spring they move to milder areas for calving and then to the coast, where they fatten up for the winter on grass, shrubs and mushrooms. They are beasts of rigid habit.

"They're patterned from ancient times," Mr. Eira said, "and when they decide they want to move, they just turn and go . . ." . . .

Each siida, a Sami family cooperative that owns and cares for its herd, has a distinguishing design that is cut into a reindeer's ear at birth to identify it . . .

Predators are by far the greatest worry: bear, wolves, wolverines, lynxes, eagles. An eagle can lift a 40-pound animal and spirit it away for the kill. Losses can approach 40 percent of the herd, and Samis are locked in a dispute over the issue with government conservationists who want to protect large carnivores

and see the wolf population grow. When a herder is not there to protect the herd, trained huskies mind the animals, intimidating them into remaining bunched together and trying to scare off tormentors.

In recent years the government has become more active in trying to regulate the reindeer industry, ending traditional slaughtering on the snow and directing it toward large government abattoirs, providing subsidies to herders who will sell at lower prices. The Samis complain that this interference has hurt their business. The quality of the meat has declined with the greater distances the animals have to be trucked to slaughter, prices have dropped by 50 percent and the reindeer folk have been outflanked by the better organized and far larger beef industry.

The supply has also fallen. Reindeer meat is scarce everywhere, from local food stores to Oslo restaurants, where it was long considered a delicacy. In addition, herders must

give the entire carcasses to the slaughterhouse and cannot put other parts of the animals to traditional uses, ranging from soup to clothing.

"Agricultural politics have hit the reindeer industry and ruined it," said Erik S. Reinert, an Oslo economist and anthropologist who negotiates for the Samis. "These are the last tribal people of Europe, and they have a unique thing going for them—they have a luxury product." Reindeer meat, aside from being tasty, is fat free.

Mr. Reinert argued that at a time when Europeans are panicked about the quality and safety of their food, meat from reindeer raised in unpolluted surroundings on natural feed ought to command a growing market . . .

———
SOURCE: Warren Hoge, "Kautokeino Journal; Reindeer Herders, at Home on a (Very Cold) Range," *New York Times*, March 26, 2001, late edition, final, section A, p. 4, col. 3.

People still do subsistence foraging in certain remote forests in Madagascar; in Southeast Asia, including Malaysia and the Philippines; and on certain islands off the Indian coast (Lee and Daly 1999). Some of the best-known recent foragers are the aborigines of Australia. Those Native Australians lived on their island continent for more than 50,000 years without developing food production.

The Western Hemisphere also had recent foragers. The Eskimos, or Inuit, of Alaska and Canada are well-known hunters. Like the Sami herders described in the "News Brief," these (and other) northern foragers now use modern technology, including rifles and snowmobiles, in their subsistence activities (Pelto 1973). The native populations of California, Oregon, Washington, British Columbia, and Alaska all were foragers, as were those of inland subarctic Canada and the Great Lakes. For many Native Americans, fishing, hunting, and gathering remain important subsistence (and sometimes commercial) activities.

Coastal foragers also lived near the southern tip of South America, in Patagonia. On the grassy plains of Argentina, southern Brazil, Uruguay, and Paraguay, there were other hunter-gatherers. The contemporary Aché of Paraguay are usually called "hunter-gatherers" even though they get

just a third of their livelihood from foraging. The Aché also grow crops, have domesticated animals, and live in or near mission posts, where they receive food from missionaries (Hawkes, O'Connell, and Hill 1982; Hill et al. 1987).

Throughout the world, foraging survived mainly in environments that posed major obstacles to food production. (Some foragers took refuge in such areas after the rise of food production, the state, colonialism, or the modern world system.) The difficulties of cultivating at the North Pole are obvious. In southern Africa, the Dobe Ju/'hoansi San area studied by Richard Lee is surrounded by a waterless belt 45 to 125 miles (70 to 200 kilometers) in breadth. The Dobe area is hard to reach even today, and there is no archaeological evidence of occupation of this area by food producers before the 20th century (Solway and Lee 1990). However, environmental limits to other adaptive strategies aren't the only reason foragers survived. Their niches have one thing in common: their marginality. Their environments haven't been of immediate interest to groups with other adaptive strategies.

The hunter-gatherer way of life did persist in a few areas that could be cultivated, even after contact with cultivators. Those tenacious foragers, such as indigenous foragers in what is now Cali-

FIGURE 7.1 Worldwide Distribution of Recent Hunter-Gatherers.

SOURCE: Adapted from a map by Ray Sim, in Göran Burenhult, ed., *Encyclopedia of Humankind: People of the Stone Age* (McMahons Point, NSW, Australia: Weldon Owen Pty Ltd., 1993), p. 193.

Historically Known Foragers (Hunter-gatherers)

1-Eskimos or Inuit
2-Subarctic Indians
3-Northwest Coast Indians
4-Plateau Indians
5-California Indians
6-Great Basin Indians
7-Plains Indians
8-Amazon Basin Hunter-gatherers
9-Gran Chaco Indians
10-Tehuelche

11-Fuegians
12-"Pygmies"
13-Okiek
14-Hadza
15-San
16-Native Australians
17-Maori
18-Toala
19-Agta
20-Punan

21-Kubu
22-Semang
23-Andaman Islanders
24-Mlabri
25-Vedda
26-Kadar
27-Chenchu
28-Birhor
29-Ainu
30-Chukchi

fornia, Oregon, Washington, and British Columbia, did not turn to food production because they were supporting themselves very adequately by hunting and gathering (see the section on the potlatch at the end of this chapter). As the modern world system spreads, the number of foragers continues to decline.

Correlates of Foraging

Typologies, such as Cohen's adaptive strategies, are useful because they suggest **correlations**—that is, association or covariation between two or more variables. (Correlated variables are factors that are linked and interrelated, such as food intake and body weight, such that when one increases or decreases, the other tends to change, too.) Ethnographic studies in hundreds of societies have revealed many correlations between the economy and social life. Associated (correlated) with each adaptive strategy is a bundle of particular cultural features. Correlations, however, are rarely perfect. Some foragers lack cultural features usually associated with foraging, and some of those features are found in groups with other adaptive strategies.

What, then, are some correlates of foraging? People who subsist by hunting, gathering, and fishing often live in band-organized societies.

Their basic social unit, the **band,** is a small group of fewer than a hundred people, all related by kinship or marriage. Band size varies between cultures and often from one season to the next in a given culture. In some foraging societies, band size stays about the same year-round. In others, the band splits up for part of the year. Families leave to gather resources that are better exploited by just a few people. Later, they regroup for cooperative work and ceremonies.

Several examples of seasonal splits and reunions are known from ethnography and archaeology. In southern Africa, some San aggregate around waterholes in the dry season and split up in the wet season, whereas other bands disperse in the dry season (Barnard 1979; Kent 1992). This reflects environmental variation. San who lack permanent water must disperse and forage widely for moisture-filled plants. In ancient Oaxaca, Mexico, before the advent of plant cultivation there around 4,000 years ago, foragers assembled in large bands in summer. They collectively harvested tree pods and cactus fruits. Then, in fall, they split into much smaller family groups to hunt deer and gather grasses and plants that were effectively foraged by small teams.

One typical characteristic of the foraging life is mobility. In many San groups, as among the

BEYOND THE CLASSROOM

Integrating Archaeological, Ethnographic, and Analytic Subsistence Data: A Case Study from Patagonia, South America

BACKGROUND INFORMATION

STUDENT:
Jennifer A. Kelly

SUPERVISING PROFESSOR:
Robert Tykot

SCHOOL:
University of South Florida

YEAR IN SCHOOL/MAJOR:
Senior/Archaeology

FUTURE PLANS:
Graduate school in archaeology

In this account, Jennifer Kelly uses various sources to reconstruct the subsistence strategies and diets of the aboriginal inhabitants of Patagonia, located at South America's southern tip. For her senior thesis, Kelly began by reading historic and ethnographic accounts of the region. Then she turned to archaeological data from sites in coastal and inland areas once occupied by different ethnic groups, such as the Ona, the Yamana, and the Tehuelche. Working with samples of human bone and tooth, she did isotope analysis, which demonstrates how specific dietary resources affect the skeleton. From her analysis she concludes there was more variation in subsistence economies and diets than the ethnographic accounts suggested. Classic ethnographies have a tendency to see human groups as culturally programmed to go after certain foods and to ignore others, which may be used by their neighbors. This account suggests that foragers are more opportunistic. Although there are certainly cultural preferences for certain foods and ways of getting them, humans are malleable, pursuing a range of resources as they become available and are needed.

Ethnohistoric, archaeological, and other scientific methods are integrated here to reconstruct prehistoric subsistence adaptations in Patagonia and Tierra del Fuego. Ethnohistoric data from the late 19th and early 20th centuries emphasize discrete dietary practices in coastal, inland, and Fuegan Patagonia. More recent archaeological evidence, however, suggests significant variations in subsistence strategies, each tailored to specific local resources.

At the time of European arrival, several indigenous groups inhabited Patagonia and Tierra del Fuego. The Onas (Haush and Selk'nam) lived in the wooded southern part of Tierra del Fuego. Archaeological evidence suggests that the Ona diet was based mainly on the guanaco (a wild grazing animal related to the llama). Other reports indicate that in some places the Onas did intensive shellfish collection and hunted fish in tidal pools. The Yamana lived along the southern and western coasts and island archipelagos of Tierra del Fuego. Early ethnographies report that they relied on marine mammals. Later accounts suggest a diet based on shellfish and seabirds.

Archaeological evidence indicates that the use of marine resources increased after 6000 B.P., and suggests non-specialized seasonal procurement of shellfish, fish, and mammals using simple hunting and gathering technology.

Carbon and nitrogen isotope analysis of human skeletal remains can differentiate between diets based on land and marine foods, as well as those based on plant foods that use different photosynthetic pathways. Bone collagen (a protein) and bone apatite (the mineral portion of bone) reveal the average diet over the last several years of an individual's life. Tooth enamel reflects diet only at the time of crown formation. As little as one gram of bone and a few milligrams of tooth enamel are sufficient for analysis. Samples of 40 individuals were obtained from coastal sites along the Straits of Magellan, and from sites located well inland. The sites range in age from 7000 B.P. through the early historic period.

For northern Patagonia, the results indicate that the northern Tehuelches who lived on the coast ate a lot of seafood in addition to guanaco. This conclusion is based on positive carbon and nitrogen isotope ratios in their bone collagen and apatite. Inland samples from this region have isotope ratios that suggest consumption of guanaco, which grazed on certain grasses.

Isotope data for coastal areas near the Straits of Magellan, homeland of the southern Tehuelches, also suggest diets dependent on both guanaco and marine resources, although the latter appear more important than in the north. The slightly enriched carbon isotope ratios of individuals from inland sites in this area may reflect their consumption of marine foods on a seasonal basis. In the Selk'nam area of Isla Grande, however, marine foods were less important than the guanaco, even along the coast, thus corroborating ethnohistoric descriptions of this area.

In the Haush region, however, marine foods of high trophic level (e.g. sea lions) accounted for most of the dietary protein. This finding contradicts ethnohistoric accounts, which describe the Haush as intermediate between the Selk'nam and the Yamana in their dependence on marine resources.

In conclusion, isotope analysis confirms some but not all of the ethnohistoric descriptions of subsistence patterns in Patagonia, while providing evidence of significant variation within each cultural group. A larger number of skeletal samples from dated archaeological contexts, and a better sampling of faunal and floral resources in each area, would allow for fuller understanding of dynamic, prehistoric Patagonian subsistence adaptations.

San-speaking "Bushmen" of Botswana's Kalahari Desert use ostrich eggs for drawing and carrying water. In what forms does foraging survive in our own society?

Mbuti of Congo, people shift band membership several times in a lifetime. One may be born, for example, in a band where one's mother has kin. Later, one's family may move to a band where the father has relatives. Because bands are exogamous (people marry outside their own band), one's parents come from two different bands, and one's grandparents may come from four. People may join any band to which they have kinship or marriage links. A couple may live in, or shift between, the husband's band and the wife's band.

One also may affiliate with a band through *fictive kinship*—personal relationships modeled on kinship, such as that between godparents and godchildren. San, for example, have a limited number of personal names. People with the same name have a special relationship; they treat each other like siblings. San expect the same hospitality in bands where they have *namesakes* as they do in a band in which a real sibling lives. Namesakes share a strong identity. They call everyone in a namesake's band by the kin terms the namesake uses. Those people reply as if they were addressing a real relative. Kinship, marriage, and fictive kinship permit San to join several bands, and nomadic (regularly on-the-move) foragers do change bands often. Band membership therefore can change tremendously from year to year.

All human societies have some kind of division of labor based on gender (see the chapter on gender for much more on this). Among foragers, men typically hunt and fish while women gather and collect, but the specific nature of the work varies among cultures. Sometimes women's work contributes most to the diet. Sometimes male hunting and fishing predominate. Among foragers in tropical and semitropical areas, gather-

How do we use fictive kinship? Although most of us are born in families, most of the people in our lives are nonrelatives. This is a major contrast with a kin-based society, such as that of the San. There is a human tendency to be social, to seek friends, to make alliances, and to convert nonrelatives to whom we are especially close into something more—something like kin. Do you have godparents? Often godparents are close friends of one's parents. Or they may be actual relatives to whom one's parents felt especially close, and so they sought to strengthen the relationship. Adoptive parents and siblings are fictive kin who become legal kin. Fraternities and sororities have fictive kin including "brothers," "sisters," and house "mothers." Priests are addressed as "father"; nuns, as "sister." What other fictive kin can you think of? In our society how is fictive kinship like and unlike the San namesake system?

ing tends to contribute more to the diet than hunting and fishing do—even though the labor costs of gathering tend to be much higher than those of hunting and fishing.

All foragers make social distinctions based on age. Often old people receive great respect as guardians of myths, legends, stories, and traditions. Younger people value the elders' special knowledge of ritual and practical matters. Most foraging societies are *egalitarian*. This means that contrasts in prestige are minor and are based on age and gender.

When considering issues of "human nature," we should remember that the egalitarian band was a basic form of human social life for most of our history. Food production has existed less than 1 percent of the time *Homo* has spent on earth. However, it has produced huge social differences. We now consider the main economic features of food-producing strategies.

CULTIVATION

In Cohen's typology, the three adaptive strategies based on food production in nonindustrial societies are horticulture, agriculture, and pastoralism. In non-Western cultures, as is also true in modern nations, people carry out a variety of economic activities. Each adaptive strategy refers to the main economic activity. Pastoralists (herders), for example, consume milk, butter, blood, and meat from their animals as mainstays of their diet. However, they also add grain to the diet by doing some cultivating or by trading with neighbors. Food producers also may hunt or gather to supplement a diet based on domesticated species.

■ In slash-and-burn horticulture, the land is cleared by cutting down (slashing) and burning trees and bush, using simple technology. After such clearing this woman uses a digging stick to plant mountain rice in Madagascar. What might be the environmental effects of slash-and-burn cultivation?

Horticulture

Horticulture and agriculture are two types of cultivation found in nonindustrial societies. Both differ from the farming systems of industrial nations like the United States and Canada, which use large land areas, machinery, and petrochemicals. According to Cohen, **horticulture** is cultivation that makes intensive use of *none* of the factors of production: land, labor, capital, and machinery. Horticulturalists use simple tools such as hoes and digging sticks to grow their crops. Their fields are not permanently cultivated and lie fallow for varying lengths of time.

Horticulture often involves *slash-and-burn techniques.* Here, horticulturalists clear land by cutting down (slashing) and burning forest or bush or by setting fire to the grass covering a plot. The vegetation is broken down, pests are killed, and the ashes remain to fertilize the soil. Crops are then sown, tended, and harvested. Use of the plot is not continuous. Often it is cultivated for only a year. This depends, however, on soil fertility and weeds, which compete with cultivated plants for nutrients.

When horticulturalists abandon a plot because of soil exhaustion or a thick weed cover, they clear another piece of land, and the original plot reverts to forest. After several years of fallowing (the duration varies in different societies), the cultivator returns to farm the original plot again. Horticulture is also called *shifting cultivation.* Such shifts from plot to plot do not mean that whole villages must move when plots are abandoned. Horticulture can support large permanent villages. Among the Kuikuru of the South American tropical forest, for example, one village of 150 people remained in the same place for 90 years (Carneiro 1956). Kuikuru houses are large and well made. Because the work involved in building them is great, the Kuikuru would rather walk farther to their fields than construct a new village. They shift their plots rather than their settlements. On the other hand, horticulturalists in the montaña (Andean foothills) of Peru live in small villages of about 30 people (Carneiro 1961/1968). Their houses are small and simple. After a few years in one place, these people build new villages near virgin land. Because their houses are so simple, they prefer rebuilding to walking even a half-mile to their fields.

Agriculture

Agriculture is cultivation that requires more labor than horticulture does, because it uses land intensively and continuously. The greater labor demands associated with agriculture reflect its common use of domesticated animals, irrigation, or terracing.

Domesticated Animals

Many agriculturalists use animals as means of production—for transport, as cultivating machines, and for their manure. Asian farmers typically incorporate cattle and/or water buffalo into agricultural economies based on rice production. Rice farmers may use cattle to trample pretilled flooded fields, thus mixing soil and water, prior to transplanting. Many agriculturalists attach animals to plows and harrows for field preparation before planting or transplanting. Also, agriculturalists typically collect manure from their animals, using it to fertilize their plots, thus increasing yields. Animals are attached to carts for transport, as well as to implements of cultivation.

Irrigation

While horticulturalists must await the rainy season, agriculturalists can schedule their planting in advance, because they control water. Like other irrigation experts in the Philippines, the Ifugao (Figure 7.2) irrigate their fields with canals from rivers, streams, springs, and ponds. Irrigation makes it possible to cultivate a plot year after year. Irrigation enriches the soil because the irrigated field is a unique ecosystem with several species of plants and animals, many of them minute organisms, whose wastes fertilize the land.

An irrigated field is a capital investment that usually increases in value. It takes time for a field to start yielding; it reaches full productivity only after several years of cultivation. The Ifugao, like other irrigators, have farmed the same fields for generations. In some agricultural areas, including the Middle East, however, salts carried in the irrigation water can make fields unusable after 50 or 60 years.

Terracing

Terracing is another agricultural technique the Ifugao have mastered. Their homeland has small valleys separated by steep hillsides. Because the population is dense, people need to farm the hills. However, if they simply planted on the steep hillsides, fertile soil and crops would be washed away during the rainy season. To prevent this, the Ifugao cut into the hillside and build stage after stage of terraced fields rising above the valley floor. Springs located above the terraces supply their irrigation water. The labor necessary to build and maintain a system of terraces is great. Terrace walls crumble each year and must be partially rebuilt. The canals that bring water down through the terraces also demand attention.

Costs and Benefits of Agriculture

Agriculture requires human labor to build and maintain irrigation systems, terraces, and other

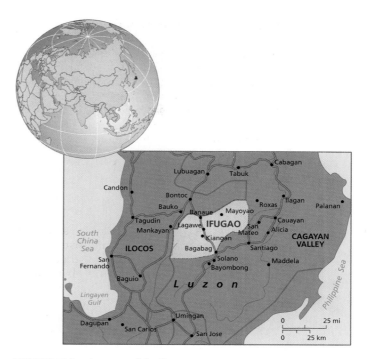

FIGURE 7.2 Location of the Ifugao.

works. People must feed, water, and care for their animals. Given sufficient labor input and management, agricultural land can yield one or two crops annually for years or even generations. An agricultural field does not necessarily produce a higher single-year yield than does a horticultural plot. The first crop grown by horticulturalists on long-idle land may be larger than that from an agricultural plot of the same size. Furthermore, because agriculturalists work harder than horticulturalists do, agriculture's yield relative to the labor invested is also lower. Agriculture's main advantage is that the long-term yield per area is far greater and more dependable. Because a single field sustains its owners year after year, there is no need to maintain a reserve of uncultivated land as horticulturalists do. This is why agricultural societies tend to be more densely populated than are horticultural ones.

The Cultivation Continuum

Because nonindustrial economies can have features of both horticulture and agriculture, it is useful to discuss cultivators as being arranged along a **cultivation continuum.** Horticultural systems stand at one end—the "low-labor, shifting-plot" end. Agriculturalists are at the other—the "labor-intensive, permanent-plot" end.

We speak of a continuum because there are today intermediate economies, combining horticultural and agricultural features—more intensive than annually shifting horticulture but less

Agriculture requires more labor than horticulture does and uses land intensively and continuously. Labor demands associated with agriculture reflect its use of domesticated animals, irrigation, and terracing. The rice farmers of Luzon in the Philippines, such as the Ifugao, are famous for their irrigated and terraced fields.

Map Atlas

Map 12 displays the kinds of economies that existed throughout the world at the start of the European age of discovery and conquest—250 years before the Industrial Revolution.

intensive than agriculture. These recall the intermediate economies revealed by archaeological sequences leading from horticulture to agriculture in the Middle East, Mexico, and other areas of early food production. Unlike nonintensive horticulturalists, who farm a plot just once before fallowing it, the South American Kuikuru grow two or three crops of *manioc*, or cassava—an edible tuber—before abandoning their plots. Cultivation is even more intense in certain densely populated areas of Papua New Guinea, where plots are planted for two or three years, allowed to rest for three to five, and then recultivated. After several of these cycles, the plots are abandoned for a longer fallow period. Such a pattern is called *sectorial fallowing* (Wolf 1966). Besides Papua New Guinea, such systems occur in places as distant as West Africa and highland Mexico. Sectorial fallowing is associated with denser populations than is simple horticulture.

The key difference between horticulture and agriculture is that horticulture always uses a fallow period whereas agriculture does not. The earliest cultivators in the Middle East and in Mexico were rainfall-dependent horticulturalists. Until recently, horticulture was the main form of cultivation in several areas, including parts of Africa, Southeast Asia, the Pacific islands, Mexico, Central America, and the South American tropical forest.

Intensification: People and the Environment

The range of environments available for food production has widened as people have increased their control over nature. For example, in arid areas of California, where Native Americans once foraged, modern irrigation technology now sustains rich agricultural estates. Agriculturalists live in many areas that are too arid for nonirrigators or too hilly for nonterracers. Many ancient civilizations in arid lands arose on an agricultural base. Increasing labor intensity and permanent land use have major demographic, social, political, and environmental consequences.

Thus, because of their permanent fields, intensive cultivators are sedentary. People live in larger and more permanent communities located closer to other settlements. Growth in population size and density increases contact between individuals and groups. There is more need to regulate interpersonal relations, including conflicts of interest. Economies that support more people usually require more coordination in the use of land, labor, and other resources.

Intensive agriculture has significant environmental effects. Irrigation ditches and paddies (fields with irrigated rice) become repositories for organic wastes, chemicals (such as salts), and disease microorganisms. Intensive agriculture typically spreads at the expense of trees and forests, which are cut down to be replaced by fields. Accompanying such deforestation is loss of environmental diversity (see Srivastava, Smith, and Forno 1999). Agricultural economies grow increasingly specialized—focusing on one or a few caloric staples, such as rice, and on the animals that are raised and tended to aid the agricultural economy. Because tropical horticulturalists typically cultivate dozens of plant species simultaneously, a horticultural plot tends to mirror the botanical diversity that is found in a tropical forest. Agricultural plots, by contrast, reduce ecological diversity by cutting down trees and concentrating on just a few staple foods. Such crop specialization is true of agriculturalists both in the tropics (e.g., Indonesian paddy farmers) and outside the tropics (e.g., Middle Eastern irrigated farmers).

At least in the tropics, the diets of both foragers and horticulturalists are typically more diverse, although under less secure human control, than the diets of agriculturalists. Agriculturists attempt to reduce risk in production by favoring stability in the form of a reliable annual harvest and long-term production. Tropical foragers and horticulturalists, by contrast, attempt to reduce risk by relying on multiple species and benefiting from ecological diversity. The agricultural strategy is to put all one's eggs in one big and very dependable basket. Of course, even with agriculture, there is a possibility that the single staple crop may fail, and famine may result. The strategy of tropical foragers and horticulturalists is to have several smaller baskets, a few of which may fail without endangering subsistence. The agricultural strategy makes sense when there are lots of children to raise and adults to be fed. Foraging and horticulture, of course, are associated with smaller, sparser, and more mobile populations.

Agricultural economies also pose a series of regulatory problems—which central governments often have arisen to solve. How is water to be managed—along with disputes about access to and distribution of water? With more people living closer together on more valuable land, agriculturalists are more likely to come into conflict than foragers and horticulturalists are. Agriculture paved the way for the origin of the state, and most agriculturalists live in *states:* complex sociopolitical systems that administer a territory and populace with substantial contrasts in occupation, wealth, prestige, and power. In such societies, cultivators play their role as one part of a differentiated, functionally specialized, and tightly integrated sociopolitical system. The social and political implications of food production and intensification are examined more fully in the next chapter, "Political Systems."

PASTORALISM

Pastoralists live in North Africa, the Middle East, Europe, Asia, and sub-Saharan Africa. These herders are people whose activities focus on such domesticated animals as cattle, sheep, goats, camels, and yak. East African pastoralists, like many others, live in symbiosis with their herds. (*Symbiosis* is an obligatory interaction between groups—here humans and animals—that is beneficial to each.) Herders attempt to protect their animals and to ensure their reproduction in return for food and other products, such as leather. Herds provide dairy products, meat, and blood. Animals are killed at ceremonies, which occur throughout the year, and so beef is available regularly.

People use livestock in a variety of ways. Natives of North America's Great Plains, for example, didn't eat, but only rode, their horses. (Europeans reintroduced horses to the Western Hemisphere; the native American horse had become extinct thousands of years earlier.) For Plains Indians, horses served as "tools of the trade," means of production used to hunt buffalo, a main target of their economies. So the Plains Indians were not true pastoralists but *hunters* who used horses—as many agriculturalists use animals—as means of production.

Unlike the use of animals merely as productive machines, pastoralists, including the Samis discussed in the "News Brief" at the beginning of this chapter, typically make direct use of their herds for food. They consume their meat, blood, and milk, from which they make yogurt, butter, and cheese. Although some pastoralists rely on their herds more completely than others do, it is impossible to base subsistence solely on animals.

■ Pastoralists may be nomadic or transhumant, but they don't typically live off their herds alone. They either trade or cultivate. The photo at the top shows female shepherds in Morocco's Drâa Valley. The photo at the bottom shows a male Alpine shepherd in Germany. This man accompanies his flocks to highland meadows each year.

Most pastoralists therefore supplement their diet by hunting, gathering, fishing, cultivating, or trading. To get crops, pastoralists either trade with cultivators or do some cultivating or gathering themselves.

Unlike foraging and cultivation, which existed throughout the world before the Industrial Revolution, pastoralism was confined almost totally to the Old World. Before European conquest, the only pastoralists in the Americas lived in the Andean region of South America. They used their llamas and alpacas for food and wool and in agriculture and transport. Much more recently, Navajo of the southwestern United States developed a pastoral economy based on sheep, which were brought to North America by Europeans. The populous Navajo are now the major pastoral population in the Western Hemisphere.

TABLE 7.1 Yehudi Cohen's Adaptive Strategies (Economic Typology) Summarized

Adaptive Strategy	Also Known As	Key Features/Varieties
Foraging	Hunting-gathering	Mobility, use of nature's resources
Horticulture	Slash-and-burn, shifting cultivation, swiddening, dry farming	Fallow period
Agriculture	Intensive farming	Continuous use of land, intensive use of labor
Pastoralism	Herding	Nomadism and transhumance
Industrialism	Industrial production	Factory production, capitalism, socialist production

For more on pastoralism, see the Internet Exercises at your OLC

mhhe.com/kottak

Two patterns of movement occur with pastoralism: nomadism and transhumance. Both are based on the fact that herds must move to use pasture available in particular places in different seasons. In **pastoral nomadism,** the entire group—women, men, and children—moves with the animals throughout the year. The Middle East and North Africa provide numerous examples of pastoral nomads. In Iran, for example, the Basseri and the Qashqai ethnic groups traditionally followed a nomadic route more than 300 miles (480 kilometers) long. Starting each year near the coast, they took their animals to grazing land 17,000 feet (5,400 meters) above sea level (see Salzman 2004).

With **transhumance,** part of the group moves with the herds, but most people stay in the home village. There are examples from Europe and Africa. In Europe's Alps, it is just the shepherds and goatherds—not the whole village—who accompany the flocks to highland meadows in summer. Among the Turkana of Uganda, men and boys accompany the herds to distant pastures, while much of the village stays put and does some horticultural farming. Villages tend to be located in the best-watered areas, which have the longest pasture season. This permits the village population to stay together during a large chunk of the year.

During their annual trek, pastoral nomads trade for crops and other products with more sedentary people. Transhumants don't have to trade for crops. Because only part of the population accompanies the herds, transhumants can maintain year-round villages and grow their own crops. Table 7.1 summarizes the main features of Cohen's adaptive strategies.

Bringing It All Together

For more on herding in Europe—and the transfer of a herding pattern from Europe to the United States—see the "Bringing It All Together" essay on the Basques that immediately follows the chapter on gender.

MODES OF PRODUCTION

See the Interactive Exercises for a quiz on economics

mhhe.com/kottak

An **economy** is a system of production, distribution, and consumption of resources; *economics* is the study of such systems. Economists tend to focus on modern nations and capitalist systems, while anthropologists have broadened understanding of economic principles by gathering data on nonindustrial economies. Economic anthropology studies economics in a comparative perspective (see Gudeman, ed. 1998; Plattner, ed. 1989; Sahlins 2004; Wilk 1996).

A **mode of production** is a way of organizing production—"a set of social relations through which labor is deployed to wrest energy from nature by means of tools, skills, organization, and knowledge" (Wolf 1982, p. 75). In the capitalist mode of production, money buys labor power, and there is a social gap between the people (bosses and workers) involved in the production process. By contrast, in nonindustrial societies, labor is not usually bought but is given as a social obligation. In such a *kin-based* mode of production, mutual aid in production is one among many expressions of a larger web of social relations.

Societies representing each of the adaptive strategies just discussed (e.g., foraging) tend to have a similar mode of production. Differences in the mode of production within a given strategy may reflect the differences in environments, target resources, or cultural traditions (Kelly 1995). Thus, a foraging mode of production may be based on individual hunters or teams, depending on whether the game is a solitary or a herd animal. Gathering is usually more individualistic than hunting, although collecting teams may assemble when abundant resources ripen and must be harvested quickly. Fishing may be done alone (as in ice or spear fishing) or in crews (as with open sea fishing and hunting of sea mammals).

Production in Nonindustrial Societies

Although some kind of division of economic labor related to age and gender is a cultural universal, the specific tasks assigned to each sex and to people of different ages vary. Many horticultural societies assign a major productive role to women, but some make men's work primary (see the chapter on gender for more on this). Similarly, among pastoralists, men generally tend large animals, but in some cultures women do the milking. Jobs accomplished through teamwork in some cultivating societies are done by smaller groups or individuals working over a longer period of time in others.

The Betsileo of Madagascar have two stages of teamwork in rice cultivation: transplanting and harvesting. Team size varies with the size of the field. Both transplanting and harvesting feature a traditional division of labor by age and gender that is well known to all Betsileo and is repeated across the generations. The first job in transplanting is the trampling of a previously tilled flooded field by young men driving cattle, in order to mix earth and water. They bring cattle to trample the fields just before transplanting. The young men yell at and beat the cattle, striving to drive them into a frenzy so that they will trample the fields properly. Trampling breaks up clumps of earth and mixes irrigation water with soil to form a smooth mud into which women transplant seedlings. Once the tramplers leave the field, older men arrive. With their spades, they break up the clumps that the cattle missed. Meanwhile, the owner and other adults uproot rice seedlings and bring them to the field.

At harvest time, four or five months later, young men cut the rice off the stalks. Young women carry it to the clearing above the field. Older women arrange and stack it. The oldest men and women then stand on the stack, stomping and compacting it. Three days later, young men thresh the rice, beating the stalks against a rock to remove the grain. Older men then attack the stalks with sticks to make sure all the grains have fallen off.

Most of the other tasks in Betsileo rice cultivation are done by individual owners and their immediate families. All household members help weed the rice field. It's a man's job to till the fields with a spade or a plow. Individual men repair the irrigation and drainage systems and the earth walls that separate one plot from the next. Among other agriculturalists, however, repairing the irrigation system is a task involving teamwork and communal labor.

Means of Production

In nonindustrial societies, there is a more intimate relationship between the worker and the means of production than there is in industrial nations. **Means, or factors, of production** include land (territory), labor, and technology.

Land

Among foragers, ties between people and land are less permanent than they are among food producers. Although many bands have territories,

Women transplant rice seedlings in Banjar Negara, Indonesia. Transplanting and weeding are arduous tasks that especially strain the back.

the boundaries usually are not marked, and there is no way they can be enforced. The hunter's stake in an animal that is being stalked or has been hit with a poisoned arrow is more important than where the animal finally dies. A person acquires the rights to use a band's territory by being born in the band or by joining it through a tie of kinship, marriage, or fictive kinship. In Botswana in southern Africa, Ju/'hoansi San women, whose work provides over half the food, habitually use specific tracts of berry-bearing trees. However, when a woman changes bands, she immediately acquires a new gathering area.

Among food producers, rights to the means of production also come through kinship and marriage. Descent groups (groups whose members claim common ancestry) are common among nonindustrial food producers, and those who descend from the founder share the group's territory and resources. If the adaptive strategy is horticulture, the estate includes garden and fallow land for shifting cultivation. As members of a descent group, pastoralists have access to animals to start their own herds, to grazing land, to garden land, and to other means of production.

Labor, Tools, and Specialization

Like land, labor is a means of production. In nonindustrial societies, access to both land and labor comes through social links such as kinship, marriage, and descent. Mutual aid in production is merely one aspect of ongoing social relations that are expressed on many other occasions.

Nonindustrial societies contrast with industrial nations in regard to another means of production: technology. In bands and tribes, manufacturing is often linked to age and gender. Women may weave and men may make pottery or vice versa. Most people of a particular age and gender share the technical knowledge associated with that age and gender. If married women customarily make baskets, all or most married women know how to make baskets. Neither technology nor technical knowledge is as specialized as it is in states.

However, some tribal societies do promote specialization. Among the Yanomami of Venezuela and Brazil (Figure 7.3), for instance, certain villages manufacture clay pots and others make hammocks. They don't specialize, as one might suppose, because certain raw materials happen to be available near particular villages. Clay suitable for pots is widely available. Everyone knows how to make pots, but not everybody does so. Craft specialization reflects the social and political environment rather than the natural environment. Such specialization promotes trade, which is the first step in creating an alliance with enemy villages (Chagnon 1997). Specialization contributes to keeping the peace, although it has not prevented intervillage warfare.

FIGURE 7.3 Location of the Yanomami.

Alienation in Industrial Economies

There are some significant contrasts between industrial and nonindustrial economies. When factory workers produce for sale and for their employer's profit, rather than for their own use, they may be alienated from the items they make. Such alienation means they don't feel strong pride in or personal identification with their products. They see their product as belonging to someone else, not to the man or woman whose labor actually produced it. In nonindustrial societies, by contrast, people usually see their work through from start to finish and have a sense of accomplishment in the product. The fruits of their labor are their own, rather than someone else's.

In nonindustrial societies, the economic relation between coworkers is just one aspect of a more general social relation. They aren't just coworkers but kin, in-laws, or celebrants in the same ritual. In industrial nations, people don't usually work with relatives and neighbors. If coworkers are friends, the personal relationship usually develops out of their common employment rather than being based on a previous association.

Thus, industrial workers have impersonal relations with their products, coworkers, and employers. People sell their labor for cash, and the economic domain stands apart from ordinary social life. In nonindustrial societies, however, the relations of production, distribution, and consumption are *social relations with economic aspects*.

Economy is not a separate entity but is *embedded* in the society.

A Case of Industrial Alienation

For decades, the government of Malaysia has promoted export-oriented industry, allowing transnational companies to install labor-intensive manufacturing operations in rural Malaysia. The industrialization of Malaysia is part of a global strategy. In search of cheaper labor, corporations headquartered in Japan, Western Europe, and the United States have been moving labor-intensive factories to developing countries. Malaysia has hundreds of Japanese and American subsidiaries, which mainly produce garments, foodstuffs, and electronics components. In electronics plants in rural Malaysia, thousands of young women from peasant families now assemble microchips and microcomponents for transistors and capacitors. Aihwa Ong (1987) did a study of electronics assembly workers in an area where 85 percent of the workers were young unmarried females from nearby villages.

Ong found that, unlike village women, female factory workers had to cope with a rigid work routine and constant supervision by men. The discipline that factories value was being taught in local schools, where uniforms helped prepare girls for the factory dress code. Village women wear loose, flowing tunics, sarongs, and sandals, but factory workers had to don tight overalls and heavy rubber gloves, in which they felt constrained. Assembling electronics components requires precise, concentrated labor. Demanding and depleting, labor in these factories illustrates the separation of intellectual and manual activity—the alienation that Karl Marx considered the defining feature of industrial work. One woman said about her bosses, "They exhaust us very much, as if they do not think that we too are human beings" (Ong 1987, p. 202). Nor does factory work bring women a substantial financial reward, given low wages, job uncertainty, and family claims on wages. Young women typically work just a few years. Production quotas, three daily shifts, overtime, and surveillance take their toll in mental and physical exhaustion.

One response to factory relations of production has been spirit possession (factory women are possessed by spirits). Ong interprets this phenomenon as the women's unconscious protest against labor discipline and male control of the industrial setting. Sometimes possession takes the form of mass hysteria. Spirits have simultaneously invaded as many as 120 factory workers. Weretigers (the Malay equivalent of the werewolf) arrive to avenge the construction of a factory on aboriginal burial grounds. Disturbed earth and grave spirits swarm on the shop floor. First the women see the spirits; then their bodies are invaded. The women become violent and

scream abuses. The weretigers send the women into sobbing, laughing, and shrieking fits. To deal with possession, factories employ local medicine men, who sacrifice chickens and goats to fend off the spirits. This solution works only some of the time; possession still goes on. Factory women continue to act as vehicles to express their own frustrations and the anger of avenging ghosts.

Ong argues that spirit possession expresses anguish at, and resistance to, capitalist relations of production. By engaging in this form of rebellion, however, factory women avoid a direct confrontation with the source of their distress. Ong concludes that spirit possession, while expressing repressed resentment, doesn't do much to modify factory conditions. (Other tactics, such as unionization, would do more.) Spirit possession may even help maintain the current system by operating as a safety valve for accumulated tensions.

■ *Employees working in a Celestica factory outside Penang, Malaysia. Celestica, which is based in Toronto, Canada, makes electronics for other companies. In Malaysia, thousands of young women from peasant families now assemble electronic components. Unlike village women, female factory workers often face a rigid work routine and constant supervision by men.*

ECONOMIZING AND MAXIMIZATION

Economic anthropologists have been concerned with two main questions:

1. How are production, distribution, and consumption organized in different societies? This question focuses on *systems* of human behavior and their organization.

2. What motivates people in different cultures to produce, distribute or exchange, and consume? Here the focus is not on systems of behavior but on the motives of the *individuals* who participate in those systems.

Anthropologists view both economic systems and motivations in a cross-cultural perspective. Motivation is a concern of psychologists, but it

Scarcity and the Betsileo

In the late 1960s my wife and I lived among the Betsileo people of Madagascar, studying their economy and social life (Kottak 1980). Soon after our arrival we met two well-educated schoolteachers (first cousins) who were interested in our research. The woman's father was a congressman who became a cabinet minister during our stay. Their family came from a historically important and typical Betsileo village called Ivato, which they invited us to visit with them.

We had traveled to many other Betsileo villages, where we often were displeased with our reception. As we drove up, children would run away screaming. Women would hurry inside. Men would retreat to doorways, where they lurked bashfully. This behavior expressed the Betsileo's great fear of the *mpakafo*. Believed to cut out and devour his victim's heart and liver, the mpakafo is the Malagasy vampire. These cannibals are said to have fair skin and to be very tall. Because I have light skin and stand over six feet tall, I was a natural suspect. The fact that such creatures were not known to travel with their wives helped convince the Betsileo that I wasn't really a mpakafo.

When we visited Ivato, its people were different—friendly and hospitable. Our very first day there we did a brief census and found out who lived in which households. We learned people's names and their relationships to our schoolteacher friends and to each other. We met an excellent informant who knew all about the local history. In a few afternoons I learned much more than I had in the other villages in several sessions.

Ivatans were so willing to talk because we had powerful sponsors, village natives who had made it in the outside world, people the Ivatans knew would protect them. The schoolteachers vouched for us, but even more significant was the cabinet minister, who was like a grandfather and benefactor to everyone in town. The Ivatans had no reason to fear us because their more influential native son had asked them to answer our questions.

Once we moved to Ivato, the elders established a pattern of visiting us every evening. They came to talk, attracted by the inquisitive foreigners but also by the wine, tobacco, and food we offered. I asked questions about their customs and beliefs. I eventually developed interview schedules about various subjects, including rice production. I used these forms in Ivato and in two other villages I was studying less intensively. Never have I interviewed as easily as I did in Ivato.

As our stay neared its end, our Ivatan friends lamented, saying, "We'll miss you. When you leave, there won't be any more cigarettes, any more wine, or any more questions." They wondered what it would be like for us back in the United States. They knew we had an automobile and that we regularly purchased things, including the wine, cigarettes, and food we shared with them. We could afford to buy products they would never have. They commented, "When you go back to your country, you'll need a lot of money for things like cars, clothes, and food. We don't need to buy those things. We make almost everything we use. We don't need as much money as you, because we produce for ourselves."

The Betsileo weren't unusual for nonindustrial people. Strange as it may seem to an American consumer, those rice farmers actually believed *they had all they needed*. The lesson from the Betsileo of the 1960s is that scarcity, which economists view as universal, is variable. Although shortages do arise in nonindustrial societies, the concept of scarcity (insufficient means) is much less developed in stable subsistence-oriented societies than in the societies characterized by industrialism, particularly as the reliance on consumer goods increases.

But, over the past several decades, significant changes have affected the Betsileo—and most nonindustrial peoples. On my last visit to Ivato, in

---

also has been, implicitly or explicitly, a concern of economists and anthropologists. Economists tend to assume that producers and distributors make decisions rationally by using the *profit motive*, as do consumers when they shop around for the best value. Although anthropologists know that the profit motive is not universal, the assumption that individuals try to maximize profits is basic to the capitalist world economy and to much of Western economic theory. In fact, the subject matter of economics is often defined as **economizing,** or the rational allocation of scarce means (or resources) to alternative ends (or uses).

What does that mean? Classical economic theory assumes that our wants are infinite and that our means are limited. Since means are limited, people must make choices about how to use their scarce resources: their time, labor, money, and capital. (The "Interesting Issues" box "Scarcity and the Betsileo" disputes the idea that people always make economic choices based on scarcity.) Economists assume that when confronted with choices and decisions, people tend to make the one that maximizes profit. This is assumed to be the most rational (reasonable) choice.

The idea that individuals choose to maximize profit was a basic assumption of the classical economists of the 19th century and one that is held by many contemporary economists. However, certain economists now recognize that individuals in Western cultures, as in others, may be motivated by many other goals. Depending on the society and the situation, people may try to maximize profit, wealth, prestige, pleasure, com-

1990, the effects of cash and of rapid population increase were evident there—and throughout Madagascar—where the national growth rate has been about 3 percent per year. Madagascar's population doubled between 1966 and 1991—from 6 to 12 million people. Today it stands near 18 million (Kottak 2004). One result of population pressure has been agricultural intensification. In Ivato, farmers who formerly had grown only rice in their rice fields now were using the same land for commercial crops, such as carrots, after the annual rice harvest. Another change affecting Ivato in 1990 was the breakdown of social and political order, fueled by increasing demand for cash.

Cattle rustling was a growing threat. Cattle thieves (sometimes from neighboring villages) were terrorizing peasants who previously had felt secure in their villages. Some of the rustled cattle were being driven to the coasts for commercial export to nearby islands. Prominent among the rustlers were relatively well-educated young men who had studied long enough to be comfortable negotiating with outsiders, but who had been unable to find formal work, and who were unwilling to work the rice fields like their peasant ancestors. The formal education system had familiarized them with external institutions and norms, including the need for cash. The concepts of scarcity, commerce, and negative reciprocity (see p. 373) now thrived among the Betsileo.

Women hull rice in a Betsileo village. In the village of Ivato, farmers who traditionally grew only rice in their rice fields now use the same land for commercial crops, such as carrots, after the annual rice harvest.

I witnessed other striking evidence of the new addiction to cash during my 1990 visit to Betsileo country. Near Ivato's county seat, we met men selling precious stones—tourmalines, which had been found by chance in a local rice field. Around the corner we saw an amazing site—dozens of villagers destroying an ancestral resource, digging up a large rice field, seeking tourmalines—clear evidence of the encroachment of cash on the local subsistence economy.

Throughout the Betsileo homeland, population growth and density were propelling emigration. Locally, land, jobs, and money were all scarce. One woman with ancestors from Ivato, herself now a resident of the national capital (Antananarivo), remarked that half the children of Ivato now lived in that city. Although she was exaggerating, a census of all the descendants of Ivato would surely reveal a substantial emigrant and urban population.

Ivato's recent history is one of increasing participation in a cash economy. That history, combined with the pressure of a growing population on local resources, has made scarcity not just a concept but a reality for Ivatans and their neighbors.

fort, or social harmony. Individuals may want to realize their personal or family ambitions or those of another group to which they belong (see Sahlins 2004).

Alternative Ends

To what uses do people in various societies put their scarce resources? Throughout the world, people devote some of their time and energy to building up a *subsistence fund* (Wolf 1966). In other words, they have to work to eat, to replace the calories they use in their daily activity. People also must invest in a *replacement fund*. They must maintain their technology and other items essential to production. If a hoe or plow breaks, they must repair or replace it. They also must obtain and replace items that are essential not to production but to everyday life, such as clothing and shelter.

People also have to invest in a *social fund*. They have to help their friends, relatives, in-laws, and neighbors. It is useful to distinguish between a social fund and a *ceremonial fund*. The latter term refers to expenditures on ceremonies or rituals. To prepare a festival honoring one's ancestors, for example, requires time and the outlay of wealth.

Citizens of nonindustrial states also must allocate scarce resources to a *rent fund*. We think of rent as payment for the use of property. However, rent fund has a wider meaning. It refers to resources that people must render to an individual or agency that is superior politically or economically. Tenant farmers and sharecroppers, for example, either pay rent or give some of

Bringing It All Together

For some effects of marketing and product manipulation on consumption patterns in the United States, see the "Bringing It All Together" essay that immediately follows the last chapter in this book.

What motivates us? Do we have the same motives our parents had? People must choose among alternatives, and economists think such choices are guided mainly by the desire for economic gain. Do you agree? Such an assumption isn't evident among the Betsileo of Madagascar. Is it true of individual Americans? Think about the choices your parents have made. Did they make decisions that maximized their incomes, their lifestyles, their individual happiness, family benefits, or what? What about you? What factors were involved when you chose to apply to and attend a college? Did you want to stay close to home, to attend college with friends, or to maintain a romantic attachment (all social reasons)? Did you seek the lowest tuition and college costs—or get a generous scholarship (economic decisions)? Did you choose prestige, or perhaps the likelihood that one day you would earn more money because of the reputation of your alma mater (maximizing prestige and future wealth)? The profit motive may predominate in contemporary North America, but different individuals, like different cultures, may choose to pursue other goals.

is a profit motive, people are often prevented from rationally maximizing self-interest by factors beyond their control.

DISTRIBUTION, EXCHANGE

The economist Karl Polanyi (1968) stimulated the comparative study of exchange, and several anthropologists followed his lead. To study exchange cross-culturally, Polanyi defined three principles orienting exchanges: the market principle, redistribution, and reciprocity. These principles can all be present in the same society, but in that case they govern different kinds of transactions. In any society, one of them usually dominates. The principle of exchange that dominates in a given society is the one that allocates the means of production.

The Market Principle

In today's world capitalist economy, the **market principle** dominates. It governs the distribution of the means of production: land, labor, natural resources, technology, and capital. "Market exchange refers to the organizational process of purchase and sale at money price" (Dalton, ed. 1967; Madra 2004). With market exchange, items are bought and sold, using money, with an eye to maximizing profit, and value is determined by the *law of supply and demand* (things cost more the scarcer they are and the more people want them).

Bargaining is characteristic of market-principle exchanges. The buyer and seller strive to maximize—to get their "money's worth." In bargaining, buyers and sellers don't need to meet personally. But their offers and counteroffers do need to be open for negotiation over a fairly short time period.

Redistribution

Redistribution operates when goods, services, or their equivalent move from the local level to a center. The center may be a capital, a regional collection point, or a storehouse near a chief's residence. Products often move through a hierarchy of officials for storage at the center. Along the way, officials and their dependents may consume some of them, but the exchange principle here is *re*distribution. The flow of goods eventually reverses direction—out from the center, down through the hierarchy, and back to the common people.

One example of a redistributive system comes from the Cherokee, the original owners of the Tennessee Valley. Productive farmers who subsisted on maize, beans, and squash, supplemented by hunting and fishing, the Cherokee had chiefs. Each of their main villages had a central plaza, where

their produce to their landlords, as peasants did under feudalism.

Peasants are small-scale agriculturalists who live in nonindustrial states and have rent fund obligations (see Kearney 1996). They produce to feed themselves, to sell their produce, and to pay rent. All peasants have two things in common:

1. They live in state-organized societies.

2. They produce food without the elaborate technology—chemical fertilizers, tractors, airplanes to spray crops, and so on—of modern farming or agribusiness.

In addition to paying rent to landlords, peasants must satisfy government obligations, paying taxes in the form of money, produce, or labor. The rent fund is not simply an *additional* obligation for peasants. Often it becomes their foremost and unavoidable duty. Sometimes, to meet the obligation to pay rent, their own diets suffer. The demands of paying rent may divert resources from subsistence, replacement, social, and ceremonial funds.

Motivations vary from society to society, and people often lack freedom of choice in allocating their resources. Because of obligations to pay rent, peasants may allocate their scarce means toward ends that are not their own but those of government officials. Thus, even in societies where there

See the Virtual Exploration for ways in which redistribution and reciprocity can change over time

mhhe.com/kottak

meetings of the chief's council took place, and where redistributive feasts were held. According to Cherokee custom, each family farm had an area where the family could set aside a portion of its annual harvest for the chief. This supply of corn was used to feed the needy, as well as travelers and warriors journeying through friendly territory. This store of food was available to all who needed it, with the understanding that it "belonged" to the chief and was dispersed through his generosity. The chief also hosted the redistributive feasts held in the main settlements (Harris 1978).

Reciprocity

Reciprocity is exchange between social equals, who are normally related by kinship, marriage, or another close personal tie. Because it occurs between social equals, it is dominant in the more egalitarian societies—among foragers, cultivators, and pastoralists. There are three degrees of reciprocity: generalized, balanced, and negative (Sahlins 1968, 2004; Service 1966). These may be imagined as areas of a continuum defined by these questions:

1. How closely related are the parties to the exchange?

2. How quickly and unselfishly are gifts reciprocated?

Generalized reciprocity, the purest form of reciprocity, is characteristic of exchanges between closely related people. In *balanced reciprocity,* social distance increases, as does the need to reciprocate. In *negative reciprocity,* social distance is greatest and reciprocation is most calculated.

With **generalized reciprocity,** someone gives to another person and expects nothing concrete or immediate in return. Such exchanges (including parental gift giving in contemporary North America) are not primarily economic transactions but expressions of personal relationships. Most parents don't keep accounts of every penny they spend on

 STUDENT CD-ROM LIVING ANTHROPOLOGY

Insurance Policies for Hunter-Gatherers?

Track 7

This clip features Polly Wiesnner, an ethnologist (cultural anthropologist) who has worked among the San ("Bushmen") for 25 years. The clip contrasts the foraging way of life with other economies in terms of storage, risk, and insurance against lean times. Industrial nations have banks, refrigerators, and insurance policies. Pastoralists have herds, which store meat and wealth on the hoof. Farmers have larders and granaries. How do the San anticipate and deal with hard times? What form of insurance do they have? What was it, according to Wiesnner, that allowed *Homo sapiens* to "colonize so many niches in this world"?

■ *Sharing the fruits of production, a keystone of many nonindustrial societies, also has been a goal of socialist nations, such as China. These workers in Yunnan province strive for an equal distribution of meat.*

their children. They merely hope that the children will respect their culture's customs involving love, honor, loyalty, and other obligations to parents.

Among foragers, generalized reciprocity tends to govern exchanges. People routinely share with other band members (Bird-David 1992; Kent 1992). A study of the Ju/'hoansi San (Figure 7.4) found that 40 percent of the population contributed little to the food supply (Lee 1968/1974). Children, teenagers, and people over 60 depended on other people for their food. Despite the high proportion of dependents, the average worker hunted or gathered less than half as much (12 to 19 hours a week) as the average American works. Nonetheless, there was always food because different people worked on different days.

So strong is the ethic of reciprocal sharing that most foragers lack an expression for "thank you." To offer thanks would be impolite because it would imply that a particular act of sharing, which is the keystone of egalitarian society, was unusual. Among the Semai, foragers of central Malaysia (Dentan 1979), to express gratitude would suggest surprise at the hunter's generosity or success (Harris 1974).

Balanced reciprocity applies to exchanges between people who are more distantly related than are members of the same band or household. In a horticultural society, for example, a man presents a gift to someone in another village. The recipient may be a cousin, a trading partner, or a brother's fictive kinsman. The giver expects something in return. This may not come immediately, but the social relationship will be strained if there is no reciprocation.

Exchanges in nonindustrial societies also may illustrate **negative reciprocity,** mainly in dealing with people outside or on the fringes of their social systems. To people who live in a world of close personal relations, exchanges with outsiders are full of ambiguity and distrust. Exchange is one way of establishing friendly rela-

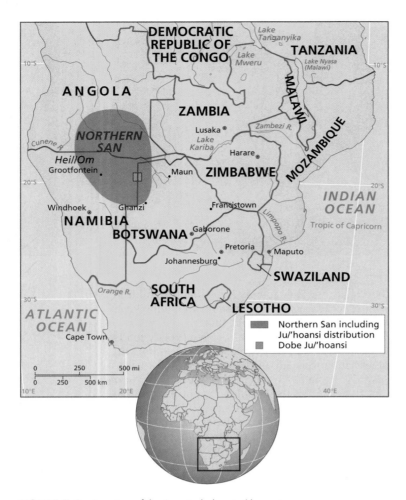

FIGURE 7.4 Location of the San, including Ju/'hoansi.

tions with outsiders, but especially when trade begins, the relationship is still tentative. Often, the initial exchange is close to being purely economic; people want to get something back immediately. Just as in market economies, but without using money, they try to get the best possible immediate return for their investment.

Generalized and balanced reciprocity are based on trust and a social tie. But negative reciprocity involves the attempt to get something for as little as possible, even if it means being cagey or deceitful or cheating. Among the most extreme and "negative" examples of negative reciprocity was 19th-century horse thievery by North American Plains Indians. Men would sneak into camps and villages of neighboring tribes to steal horses. A similar pattern of cattle raiding continues today in East Africa, among tribes like the Kuria (Fleisher 2000). In these cases, the party that starts the raiding can expect reciprocity—a raid on their own village—or worse. The Kuria hunt down cattle thieves and kill them. It's still reciprocity, governed by "Do unto others as they have done unto you."

One way of reducing the tension in situations of potential negative reciprocity is to engage in "silent trade." One example is the silent trade of the Mbuti "pygmy" foragers of the African equatorial forest and their neighboring horticultural villagers. There is no personal contact during their exchanges. A Mbuti hunter leaves game, honey, or another forest product at a customary site. Villagers collect it and leave crops in exchange. Often the parties bargain silently. If one feels the return is insufficient, he or she simply leaves it at the trading site. If the other party wants to continue trade, it will be increased.

Coexistence of Exchange Principles

In today's North America, the market principle governs most exchanges, from the sale of the means of production to the sale of consumer goods. We also have redistribution. Some of our tax money goes to support the government, but some of it also comes back to us in the form of social services, education, health care, and road building. We also have reciprocal exchanges. Generalized reciprocity characterizes the relationship between parents and children. However, even here the dominant market mentality surfaces in comments about the high cost of raising children and in the stereotypical statement of the disappointed parent: "We gave you everything money could buy."

Exchanges of gifts, cards, and invitations exemplify reciprocity, usually balanced. Everyone has heard remarks like "They invited us to their daughter's wedding, so when ours gets married, we'll have to invite them" and "They've been here for dinner three times and haven't invited us yet. I don't think we should ask them back until they do." Such precise balancing of reciprocity would be out of place in a foraging band, where resources are communal (common to all) and daily sharing based on generalized reciprocity is an essential ingredient of social life and survival.

POTLATCHING

One of the most thoroughly studied cultural practices known to ethnography is the **potlatch,** a festive event within a regional exchange system among tribes of the North Pacific Coast of North America, including the Salish and Kwakiutl of Washington and British Columbia and the Tsimshian of Alaska (Figure 7.5). Some tribes still practice the potlatch, sometimes as a memorial to the dead (Kan 1986, 1989). At each such event, assisted by members of their communities, potlatch sponsors traditionally gave away food, blankets, pieces of copper, or other items. In return for this, they got prestige. To give a potlatch enhanced one's reputation. Prestige increased with the lavishness of the potlatch, the value of the goods given away in it.

The potlatching tribes were foragers, but atypical ones. They were sedentary and had chiefs. And unlike the environments of most other recent foragers, theirs was not marginal. They had access to a wide variety of land and sea resources. Among their most important foods were salmon, herring, candlefish, berries, mountain goats, seals, and porpoises (Piddocke 1969).

According to classical economic theory, the profit motive is universal, with the goal of maximizing material benefits. How then does one explain the potlatch, in which substantial wealth is given away (and even destroyed—see below)? Christian missionaries considered potlatching to be wasteful and antithetical to the Protestant work ethic. By 1885, under pressure from Indian Agents, missionaries, and Indian converts to Christianity, both Canada and the United States had outlawed potlatching. Between 1885 and 1951 the custom went underground. By 1951 both countries had discreetly dropped the antipotlatching laws from the books (Miller n.d.).

Some scholars seized on this view of the potlatch as a classic case of economically wasteful behavior. The economist and social commentator Thorstein Veblen cited potlatching as an example of conspicuous consumption in his influential book *The Theory of the Leisure Class* (1934), claiming that potlatching was based on an economically irrational drive for prestige. This interpretation stressed the lavishness and supposed wastefulness, especially of the Kwakiutl displays, to support the contention that in some societies people strive to maximize prestige at the expense of their material well-being. This interpretation has been challenged.

Ecological anthropology, also known as *cultural ecology,* is a theoretical school in anthropology that attempts to interpret cultural practices, such as the potlatch, in terms of their long-term role in helping humans adapt to their environments. A different interpretation of the potlatch has been offered by the ecological anthropologists Wayne Suttles (1960) and Andrew Vayda (1961/1968). These scholars see potlatching not in terms of its apparent wastefulness, but in terms of its long-term role as a cultural adaptive mechanism. This view not only helps us understand potlatching, it also has comparative value because it helps us understand similar patterns of lavish feasting in many other parts of the world. Here is the ecological interpretation: *Customs like the potlatch are cultural adaptations to alternating periods of local abundance and shortage.*

How does this work? The overall natural environment of the North Pacific Coast is favorable, but resources fluctuate from year to year and place to place. Salmon and herring aren't equally abundant every year in a given locality. One vil-

FIGURE 7.5 Location of potlatching groups.

lage can have a good year while another is experiencing a bad one. Later their fortunes reverse. In this context, the potlatch cycle of the Kwakiutl and Salish had adaptive value, and the potlatch was not a competitive display that brought no material benefit.

A village enjoying an especially good year had a surplus of subsistence items, which it could trade for more durable wealth items, like blankets, canoes, or pieces of copper. Wealth, in turn, by being distributed, could be converted into prestige. Members of several villages were invited to any potlatch and got to take home the resources that were given away. In this way, potlatching linked villages together in a regional economy—an exchange system that distributed food and wealth from wealthy to needy communities. In return, the potlatch sponsors and their villages got prestige. The decision to potlatch was determined by the health of the local economy. If there had been subsistence surpluses, and thus a buildup of wealth over several good years, a village could afford a potlatch to convert its food and wealth into prestige.

See the Internet Exercises at your OLC for information about feasting among the Hoploi of Papua New Guinea

mhhe.com/kottak

The historic photo (above) shows the amassing of blankets to be given away at a Kwakiutl potlatch. The man in the foreground is making a speech praising the generosity of the potlatch host. The photo below shows a modern potlatch, lasting four days, celebrated by Alaska's Tsimshian Indians. Nowadays, the gifts to be distributed are piled at the center of the large room where the event is taking place. Have you ever partaken in anything like a potlatch?

The long-term adaptive value of intercommunity feasting becomes clear when we consider what happened when a formerly prosperous village had a run of bad luck. Its people started accepting invitations to potlatches in villages that were doing better. The tables were turned as the temporarily rich became temporarily poor and vice versa. The newly needy accepted food and wealth items. They were willing to receive rather than bestow gifts and thus to relinquish some of their stored-up prestige. They hoped their luck would eventually improve so that resources could be recouped and prestige regained.

The potlatch linked local groups along the North Pacific Coast into a regional alliance and exchange network. Potlatching and intervillage exchange had adaptive functions, regardless of the motivations of the individual participants. The anthropologists who stressed rivalry for prestige were not wrong. They were merely emphasizing motivations at the expense of an analysis of economic and ecological systems.

The use of feasts to enhance individual and community reputations and to redistribute wealth is not peculiar to populations of the North Pacific Coast. Competitive feasting is widely characteristic of nonindustrial food producers. But among most foragers, who live, remember, in marginal areas, resources are too meager to support feasting on such a level. In such societies, sharing rather than competition prevails.

Like many other cultural practices that have attracted considerable anthropological attention, the potlatch does not, and did not, exist apart from larger world events. For example, within the spreading world capitalist economy of the 19th century, the potlatching tribes, particularly the Kwakiutl, began to trade with Europeans (fur for blankets, for example). Their wealth increased as a result. Simultaneously, a huge proportion of the Kwakiutl population died from previously unknown diseases brought by the Europeans. As a result, the increased wealth from trade flowed into a drastically reduced population. With many of the traditional sponsors dead (such as chiefs and their families), the Kwakiutl extended the right to give a potlatch to the entire population. This stimulated very intense competition for prestige. Given trade, increased wealth, and a decreased population, the Kwakiutl also started converting wealth into prestige by destroying wealth items such as blankets, pieces of copper, and houses (Vayda 1961/1968). Blankets and houses could be burned, and coppers could be buried at sea. Here, with dramatically increased wealth and a drastically reduced population, Kwakiutl potlatching changed its nature. It became much more destructive than it had been previously and than potlatching continued to be among tribes that were less affected by trade and disease.

In any case, note that potlatching also served to prevent the development of socioeconomic stratification, a system of social classes. Wealth relinquished or destroyed was converted into a nonmaterial item: prestige. Under capitalism, we reinvest our profits (rather than burning our cash), with the hope of making an additional profit. However, the potlatching tribes were content to relinquish their surpluses rather than use them to widen the social distance between themselves and their fellow tribe members.

1. Cohen's adaptive strategies include foraging (hunting and gathering), horticulture, agriculture, pastoralism, and industrialism. Foraging was the only human adaptive strategy until the advent of food production (farming and herding) 10,000 years ago. Food production eventually replaced foraging in most places. Almost all modern foragers have at least some dependence on food production or food producers.

2. Horticulture and agriculture stand at opposite ends of a continuum based on labor intensity and continuity and land use. Horticulture doesn't use land or labor intensively. Horticulturalists cultivate a plot for one or two years and then abandon it. Further along the continuum, horticulture becomes more intensive, but there is always a fallow period. Agriculturalists farm the same plot of land continuously and use labor intensively. They use one or more of the following: irrigation, terracing, domesticated animals as means of production and manuring.

3. The pastoral strategy is mixed. Nomadic pastoralists trade with cultivators. Part of a transhumant pastoral population cultivates while another part takes the herds to pasture. Except for some Peruvians and the Navajo, who are recent herders, the New World lacks native pastoralists.

4. Economic anthropology is the cross-cultural study of systems of production, distribution, and consumption. In nonindustrial societies, a kin-based mode of production prevails. One acquires rights to resources and labor through membership in social groups, not impersonally through purchase and sale. Work is just one aspect of social relations expressed in varied contexts.

5. Economics has been defined as the science of allocating scarce means to alternative ends. Western economists assume that the notion of scarcity is universal—which it isn't—and that in making choices, people strive to maximize personal profit. In nonindustrial societies, indeed as in our own, people often maximize values other than individual profit.

6. In nonindustrial societies, people invest in subsistence, replacement, social, and ceremonial funds. States add a rent fund: People must share their output with social superiors. In states, the obligation to pay rent often becomes primary.

7. Besides production, economic anthropologists study and compare exchange systems. The three principles of exchange are the market principle, redistribution, and reciprocity. The market principle, based on supply and demand and the profit motive, dominates in states. With redistribution, goods are collected at a central place, but some of them are eventually given back, or redistributed, to the people. Reciprocity governs exchanges between social equals. It is the characteristic mode of exchange among foragers and horticulturists. Reciprocity, redistribution, and the market principle may coexist in a society, but the primary exchange mode is the one that allocates the means of production.

8. Patterns of feasting and exchanges of wealth among villages are common among nonindustrial food producers, as among the potlatching cultures of North America's North Pacific Coast. Such systems help even out the availability of resources over time.

---

agriculture   Nonindustrial systems of plant cultivation characterized by continuous and intensive use of land and labor.

balanced reciprocity   See *generalized reciprocity.*

band   Basic unit of social organization among foragers. A band includes fewer than 100 people; it often splits up seasonally.

correlation   An association between two or more variables such that when one changes (varies), the other also changes (covaries); for example, temperature and sweating.

cultivation continuum   A continuum based on the comparative study of nonindustrial cultivating societies in which labor intensity increases and fallowing decreases.

economizing   The rational allocation of scarce means (or resources) to alternative ends (or uses); often considered the subject matter of economics.

economy   A population's system of production, distribution, and consumption of resources.

generalized reciprocity   Principle that characterizes exchanges between closely related individuals. As social distance increases, reciprocity becomes balanced and finally negative.

horticulture   Nonindustrial system of plant cultivation in which plots lie fallow for varying lengths of time.

market principle   Profit-oriented principle of exchange that dominates in states, particularly industrial states. Goods and services are bought and sold, and values are determined by supply and demand.

means (or factors) of production   Land, labor, technology, and capital—major productive resources.

mode of production   Way of organizing production—a set of social relations through which labor is deployed to wrest energy from nature by means of tools, skills, and knowledge.

negative reciprocity   See *generalized reciprocity.*

nomadism, pastoral   Movement throughout the year by the whole pastoral group (men, women, and children) with their animals; more generally, such constant movement in pursuit of strategic resources.

pastoralists   People who use a food-producing strategy of adaptation based on care of herds of domesticated animals.

peasant   Small-scale agriculturalist living in a state with rent fund obligations.

potlatch   Competitive feast among Indians on the North Pacific Coast of North America.

reciprocity   One of the three principles of exchange; governs exchange between social equals; major exchange mode in band and tribal societies.

redistribution   Major exchange mode of chiefdoms, many archaic states, and some states with managed economies.

transhumance   One of two variants of pastoralism; part of the population moves seasonally with the herds while the other part remains in home villages.

CRITICAL THINKING QUESTIONS

For more self-testing, see the self-quizzes

mhhe.com/kottak

1. What are some of the main advantages and disadvantages of living in a foraging society? How about horticulture? Agriculture? Pastoralism? In which one would you want to live, and why?

2. What do you see as the main differences and similarities between ancient and modern hunter-gatherers?

3. What are your scarce means? How do you make decisions about allocating them?

4. What do you attempt to maximize? Does that vary depending on the situation?

5. Give examples from your own exchanges of different degrees of reciprocity.

SUGGESTED ADDITIONAL READINGS

Bates, D. G.
   2005   *Human Adaptive Strategies: Ecology, Culture, and Politics*, 3rd ed. Boston: Pearson/Allyn & Bacon. Recent discussion of the different adaptive strategies and their political correlates.

Cohen, Y.
   1974   *Man in Adaptation: The Cultural Present*, 2nd ed. Chicago: Aldine. Presents Cohen's economic typology of adaptive strategies and uses it to organize a valuable set of essays on culture and adaptation.

Gudeman, S.
   2001   *The Anthropology of Economy: Community, Market, and Culture.* Malden, MA: Blackwell. Economic aspects of globalization in relation to economic anthropology.

Gudeman, S., ed.
   1998   *Economic Anthropology.* Northhampton, MA: E. Elgar. Reference essays in economic anthropology.

Ingold, T., D. Riches, and J. Woodburn
   1991   *Hunters and Gatherers.* New York: Berg (St. Martin's). Volume I examines history and social change among foragers. Volume II looks at their property, ideology, and power relations. These broad regional surveys illuminate current issues and debates.

Kearney, M.
   1996   *Reconceptualizing the Peasantry: Anthropology in Global Perspective.* Boulder, CO: Westview. How peasants live today, in post–Cold War nation-states.

Kelly, R. L.
   1995   *The Foraging Spectrum: Diversity in Hunter-Gatherer Lifeways.* Washington, DC: Smithsonian Institution Press. Survey of foragers in varied environments.

Kent, S.
   1996   *Cultural Diversity among Twentieth-Century Foragers: An African Perspective.* New York: Cambridge University Press. Africa's hunter-gatherers, their adaptations, social life, and variety.

Lee, R. B.
   2003   *The Dobe Ju/'hoansi*, 3rd ed. Belmont, CA: Wadsworth. Account of well-known San foragers, by one of their principal ethnographers.

Lee, R. B., and R. H. Daly
   1999   *The Cambridge Encyclopedia of Hunters and Gatherers.* New York: Cambridge University Press. Indispensable reference work on foragers.

Plattner, S., ed.
   1989   *Economic Anthropology.* Stanford, CA: Stanford University Press. Articles on economic features of foraging, tribal, peasant, state, and industrial societies.

Sahlins, M. D.
   2004   *Stone Age Economics.* New York: Routledge. A reprinted classic, with a new preface.

Salzman, P. C.
   2004   *Pastoralists: Equality, Hierarchy, and the State.* Boulder, CO: Westview. What we can learn from pastoralists about equality, freedom, and democracy.

Salzman, P. C., and J. G. Galaty, eds.
 1990 *Nomads in a Changing World.* Naples: Istituto Universitario Orientale. Pastoral nomads in varied contemporary settings.
Srivastava, J., N. J. H. Smith, and D. A. Forno
 1999 *Integrating Biodiversity in Agricultural Intensification: Toward Sound Practices.* Washington, DC: World Bank. Environmentally and socially sustainable agriculture in today's world.
Wilk, R. R.
 1996 *Economies and Cultures: An Introduction to Economic Anthropology.* Boulder, CO: Westview. A thorough introduction to economic anthropology.

INTERNET EXERCISES

1. Reciprocity: Go to the Living Link's video collection at Emory University's Center for the Advanced Study of Ape and Human Evolution page, **http://www.emory.edu/LIVING_LINKS/AV_Library.html**, and watch the Chimpanzee Food Sharing Movie.
  a. What is an example in this film of generalized reciprocity?
  b. What is an example of balanced reciprocity?
  c. What is an example of negative reciprocity?
  d. What inferences can be made from the observation that humans and chimpanzees exhibit similar capacities for reciprocity? Even when humans and chimpanzees enact similar behaviors (i.e., generalized reciprocity), are there important differences?

2. Subsistence and Settlement: Go to the Ethnographic Atlas Cross-tabulations page, **http://lucy.ukc.ac.uk/cgi-bin/uncgi/Ethnoatlas/atlas.vopts**. This site has compiled ethnographic information on many different groups, and you can use the tools provided to cross-tabulate the prevalence of certain traits. Under "Select Row Category" choose "subsistence economy," and under "Select Column Category" select "settlement patterns." Press the Submit Query button. The table that appears shows the frequency with which groups of different subsistence systems use certain mobility strategies.

  a. Notice that a high number of groups with agriculture use "Compact and relatively permanent settlements." Is this what you would expect?
  b. What kinds of subsistence strategies are used by groups that are the most mobile (have "Migratory or nomadic," "Seminomadic," or "Semisedentary" settlement patterns)?
  c. Now let's focus on the groups that are exceptional and do not combine subsistence and settlement strategies in the most usual or common way. There is a single group that uses intensive agriculture and is seminomadic. Click on the number at that location. What is the name of that group, and where are they found?
  d. There are a few groups that are in permanent settlements and use hunting, gathering, or fishing. What region of the world are most of these groups from?
  e. Feel free to explore many of the other variables listed in the table. We suggest you check "mean size of local communities," "settlement patterns," and "subsistence economy" against each other. What patterns do you see?

See Chapter 7 at your McGraw-Hill Online Learning Center for additional review and interactive exercises.

LINKAGES

Kottak, *Assault on Paradise*, 4th ed.

In Chapter 4, "The Spirit of Fishermen," Arembepe's value system is characterized with reference to two classic formulations in social science: Max Weber's *The Protestant Ethic and the Spirit of Capitalism* (1904/1958) and George Foster's "image of limited good." How were Arembepe's fishermen like the early Protestant entrepreneurs described by Weber? Indicate, too, how the image of limited good, which Foster considers characteristic of peasant societies, showed up in Arembepe. What is the "riddle of the spots," and how did it fit within Arembepe's basically egalitarian social structure?

Peters-Golden, *Culture Sketches*, 4th ed.

This text chapter has examined systems of production, distribution, and consumption among societies with various adaptive strategies. In *Culture Sketches*, read the chapter "Basseri: Pastoral Nomads on the il-Rah." What are some ways in which the Basseri's adaptive strategy—pastoral nomadism—influences their other social institutions and relationships? How might Basseri life change with increasing sedentism?

Knauft, *The Gebusi*, 1st ed.

Based on information in Chapter 2 of *The Gebusi*, what food-related activities of the Gebusi are similar to those of foragers or hunter-gatherers? What food-related activities of Gebusi are similar to those of horticulturalists? List the ways in which Gebusi pigs are domesticated and the ways in which they are still wild. What examples does the author provide concerning the following types of subsistence: (a) intensive foraging that allows for the development of large villages; (b) intensive agriculture paired with intensive animal husbandry? What accounts for such differences in subsistence orientation? Describe some features of Gebusi residence that are "sedentary" and others that are "seminomadic."

8

Political Systems

WHAT IS "THE POLITICAL"?

Anthropologists and political scientists share an interest in political systems and organization, but the anthropological approach is global and comparative, and includes nonstates as well as the states and nation-states usually studied by political scientists. Anthropological studies have revealed substantial variation in power (formal and informal), authority, and legal systems in different societies and communities. (Power is the ability to exercise one's will over others; authority is the socially approved use of power.) (See Cheater, ed. 1999; Gledhill 2000; Kurtz 2001; Wolf with Silverman 2001.)

■ *Citizens routinely use collective action to influence public policy. Shown here, members of Citizens for Responsible Growth in Clemson, South Carolina, have mobilized against the construction of a Wal-Mart Super Center on this 35-acre site. Have your own actions ever influenced public policy?*

Recognizing that political organization is sometimes just an aspect of social organization, Morton Fried offered this definition:

Political Organization comprises those portions of social organization that specifically relate to the individuals or groups that manage the affairs of public policy or seek to control the appointment or activities of those individuals or groups. (Fried 1967, pp. 20–21)

OVERVIEW

Politicians lead, manage public policy, make decisions, and try to implement them. Political anthropology is the cross-cultural study of political systems and institutions. Not all societies have had law—in the sense of a formal legal code, judiciary, and enforcement—but all societies have means of social control. Some political systems have informal or temporary leaders with limited local authority. Others have strong and permanent political institutions that prevail over entire regions.

The terms *band, tribe, chiefdom,* and *state* describe forms of social and political organization. Bands are small, mobile, kin-based groups with little differential power. Tribes have villages and/or descent groups but lack a formal government. Chiefdoms, although kin-based, have differential access to resources and a permanent political structure. The state is an autonomous political entity encompassing many communities. Its government can collect taxes, draft people for work or war, and decree and enforce laws. All states have a central government and socioeconomic stratification. The concept of social control is broader than the political and encompasses all beliefs and practices that work to maintain norms, ensure compliance, and regulate conflict.

This definition certainly fits contemporary North America. Under "individuals or groups that manage the affairs of public policy" come federal, state (provincial), and local (municipal) governments. Those who seek to control the activities of the groups that manage public policy include such interest groups as political parties, unions, corporations, consumers, activists, action committees, religious groups, and nongovernmental organizations (NGOs).

Fried's definition is much less applicable to nonstates, where it was often difficult to detect any "public policy." For this reason, I prefer to speak of *socio*political organization in discussing the regulation or management of interrelations among groups and their representatives. In a general sense, regulation is the process that ensures that variables stay within their normal ranges, corrects deviations from the norm, and thus maintains a system's integrity. In the case of political regulation, this includes such things as decision making, social control, and conflict resolution. The study of political regulation draws our attention to those who make decisions and resolve conflicts (are there formal leaders?).

Ethnographic and archaeological studies in hundreds of places have revealed many correlations between economy and social and political organization.

TYPES AND TRENDS

Decades ago, the anthropologist Elman Service (1962) listed four types, or levels, of political organization: band, tribe, chiefdom, and state. Today, none of these political entities (*polities*) can be

Chat Rooms, Bedouin Style

CHRISTIAN SCIENCE MONITOR NEWS BRIEF

by Ilene R. Prusher
April 26, 2000

When we think of politics, we think of government, of federal and state institutions, of Washington, Ottawa, or perhaps our state capital, city hall, or courthouse. We hear discussions of public service, political offices, and elections—and maybe the economic and political power that goes along with holding office, or with influencing those who hold office. Binding decisions are made at the top levels of government. There are also informal political institutions, which aren't part of the governmental apparatus, but which may substantially influence it. Described here are the diwaniyas *of Kuwait—informal, local-level meeting places where informal discussions can have formal consequences. Much of Kuwait's decision making, networking, and influence peddling takes place in these* diwaniyas. *What do you see as the advantages and disadvantages of the* diwaniya *system? Do we have anything like it in our society?*

The process of deliberation and decision making that goes on within—and then beyond—Kuwait's diwaniya *system illustrates a political process. Anthropologists share with political scientists an interest in political processes, systems, and organization, but the anthropological approach is characteristically global and comparative, including nonstates as well as states. Anthropological studies have revealed substantial variation in power, authority, and legal systems among the world's cultures.*

In the historical fabric of Kuwait, *diwaniyas* have been men-only political salons—a local equivalent of neighborhood pub and town-hall meeting combined. They serve not only as parlors for chit-chats, but governance, too. *Diwaniyas* are so integral to Kuwaiti culture that during election season, candidates don't go door to door, but *diwaniya* to *diwaniya*. This is where business deals are made and marriages arranged . . .

Traditionally, most men have an open invitation to attend a *diwaniya* on any given night, and wealthy families have a large, long room adjacent to their homes expressly for their *diwaniya*. Some neighborhoods have a common *diwaniya*, much like a community center.

At a typical men-only *diwaniya* . . . the attendees lounge among the partitions of a never-ending couch that follow the contours of the room in one giant U. They usually gather once a week, starting at 8 in the evening and sometimes going past midnight.

As they discuss issues . . . they twirl smoothly polished beads around their fingers and worry aloud whether change has come to Kuwait too fast. The presence of malls and movies, they fret, is breaking down social norms like the taboo against premarital dating . . .

At the Al-Fanar Center, with its bevy of Body Shops and Benettons, teenage boys say they also have no interest in chattering the night away when they could be flirting. "We like to follow around girls without hijab [veil]," says teenager Abdul Rahman Al-Tarket, roaming the mall with his two friends . . .

Mixed [male and female] *diwaniyas* are still an anomaly. "For me, the *diwaniya* is a very comfortable place to have people come and see me," says artist Thoraya al-Baqsami, who co-hosts one mixed gathering. "I know many people don't like it, but we are in the 21st century now," she says as she gives a tour of her adjacent gallery . . .

Many women here say they're happy to leave the *diwaniya* to the domain of men. But more problematic is that it is the *diwaniya* at which much of the country's decision-making and networking takes place. It is also a forum where a constituent can meet his parliamentary representative and consult him about major problems or minor potholes.

■ *A Kuwaiti* diwaniya.

studied as a self-contained form of political organization, since all exist within nation-states and are subject to state control. There is archaeological evidence for early bands, tribes, and chiefdoms that existed before the first states appeared. However, since anthropology came into being long after the origin of the state, anthropologists have never been able to observe "in the flesh" a band, tribe, or chiefdom outside the influence of some state. All the bands, tribes, and chiefdoms known to ethnography have been within the borders of a state. There still may be local political leaders (e.g., village heads) and regional figures (e.g., chiefs) of the sort discussed in this chapter, but all exist and function within the context of state organization.

A *band* refers to a small *kin-based* group (all the members are related to each other by kinship or marriage ties) found among foragers. **Tribes** had economies based on nonintensive food production (horticulture and pastoralism). Living in villages and organized into kin groups based on common descent (clans and lineages), tribes lacked a formal government and had no reliable means of enforcing political decisions. **Chiefdom** refers to a form of sociopolitical organization intermediate between the tribe and the state. In chiefdoms, social relations were based mainly on kinship, marriage, descent, age, generation, and gender—just as they were in bands and tribes. Although chiefdoms were kin-based, they featured differential access to resources (some people had more wealth, prestige, and power than others) and a permanent political structure. The **state** is a form of sociopolitical organization based on a formal government structure and socioeconomic stratification.

The four labels in Service's typology are much too simple to account for the full range of political diversity and complexity known to archaeology and ethnography. We'll see, for instance, that tribes have varied widely in their political systems and institutions. Nevertheless, Service's typology does highlight some significant contrasts in political organization, especially those between states and nonstates. For example, in bands and tribes—unlike states, which have clearly visible governments—political organization did not stand out as separate and distinct from the total social order. In bands and tribes, it was difficult to characterize an act or event as political rather than merely social.

Service's labels "band," "tribe," "chiefdom," and "state" are categories or types within a *sociopolitical typology*. These types are correlated with the adaptive strategies (economic typology) discussed in Chapter 7, "Making a Living." Thus, foragers (an economic type) tended to have band organization (a sociopolitical type). Similarly, many horticulturalists and pastoralists lived in tribal societies (or, more simply, tribes). Although most chiefdoms had farming economies, herding was important in some Middle Eastern chiefdoms. Nonindustrial states usually had an agricultural base.

With food production came larger, denser populations and more complex economies than was the case among foragers. These features posed new regulatory problems, which gave rise to more complex relations and linkages. Many sociopolitical trends reflect the increased regulatory demands associated with food production. Archaeologists have studied these trends through time, and cultural anthropologists have observed them among contemporary groups.

BANDS AND TRIBES

This chapter examines a series of societies with different political systems. A common set of questions will be addressed for each one. What kinds of social groups does the society have? How do people affiliate with those groups? How do the groups link up with larger ones? How do the groups represent themselves to each other? How are their internal and external relations regulated? To answer these questions, we begin with bands and tribes and then move on to chiefdoms and states.

Foraging Bands

Modern hunter-gatherers should not be seen as representative of Stone Age peoples, all of whom also were foragers. Anthropologists wonder just how much contemporary foragers can tell us about the economic and social relations that characterized humanity before food production. Modern foragers, after all, live in nation-states and an interlinked world. For generations, the pygmies of Congo have shared a social world with their neighbors who are cultivators. They exchange forest products (e.g., honey and meat) for crops (e.g., bananas and manioc). All foragers now trade with food producers. Most contemporary hunter-gatherers rely on governments and on missionaries for at least part of what they consume.

The San

The San speakers ("Bushmen") of southern Africa have been influenced by Bantu speakers (farmers and herders) for 2,000 years and by Europeans for centuries. Edwin Wilmsen (1989) sees the San as a rural underclass in a larger political and economic system dominated by Europeans and Bantu food producers. Many San now tend cattle for wealthier Bantu rather than foraging independently. Wilmsen also argues that many San descend from herders who were pushed into the desert by poverty or oppression.

Susan Kent (1992, 1996) notes a tendency to stereotype foragers, to treat them all as alike. They used to be stereotyped as isolated, primitive survivors of the Stone Age. A new stereotype sees them as culturally deprived people forced by states, colonialism, or world events into marginal environments. Although this view often is exaggerated, it probably is more accurate than the former one. Modern foragers differ substantially from Stone Age hunter-gatherers.

Kent (1996) stresses variation among foragers, focusing on diversity in time and space among the San. The nature of San life has changed considerably since the 1950s and 1960s, when a series of anthropologists from Harvard University, including Richard Lee, embarked on a systematic study of life in the Kalahari. Lee and others have doc-

STUDENT CD-ROM LIVING ANTHROPOLOGY

Insurance Policies for Hunter-Gatherers?
Track 7

This clip features Polly Wiessner, an ethnologist (cultural anthropologist) who has studied the San ("Bushmen") for 25 years. As the clip makes clear, Wiessner is well aware that the San are not an isolated people, or a relic population left over from the Stone Age. If there are limitations to what the San can tell us about our past, what, according to Wiessner, is the value of studying them?

umented many of the changes in various publications (Lee 1979, 1984, 2003; Silberbauer 1981; Tanaka 1980). Such longitudinal research monitors variation in time, while fieldwork in many San areas has revealed variation in space. One of the most important contrasts is between settled (sedentary) and nomadic groups (Kent and Vierich 1989). Sedentism is increasing, but some San groups (along rivers) have been sedentary for generations. Others, including the Dobe Ju/'hoansi San studied by Lee (1984, 2003) and the Kutse San that Kent studied, have retained more of the hunter-gatherer lifestyle.

Modern foragers are not Stone Age relics, living fossils, lost tribes, or noble savages. Still, to the extent that foraging is the basis of their subsistence, modern hunter-gatherers can illustrate links between a foraging economy and other aspects of society and culture. For example, San groups that still are mobile, or that were so until recently, emphasize social, political, and gender equality. A social system based on kinship, reciprocity, and sharing is appropriate for an economy with few people and limited resources. The nomadic pursuit of wild plants and animals tends to discourage permanent settlement, wealth accumulation, and status distinctions. In this context families and bands are adaptive social units. People have to share meat when they get it; otherwise it rots.

Foraging bands, which were nomadic or seminomadic, formed seasonally when component nuclear families got together. The particular families in a band varied from year to year. Marriage and kinship created ties between members of different bands. Because one's parents and grandparents came from different bands, a person had relatives in several of those groups. Trade and visiting also linked local groups, as did fictive kinship, such as the San namesake system described in the last chapter.

■ Among tropical foragers, women make an important economic contribution through gathering, as is true among the San shown here in Namibia. What evidence do you see in this photo that contemporary foragers participate in the modern world system?

For a discussion of relative affluence among foragers, see the Internet Exercises at your OLC

mhhe.com/kottak

Foraging bands tended to be egalitarian in terms of power and authority, although particular talents did lead to special respect. For example, someone could sing or dance well, was an especially good storyteller, or could go into a trance and communicate with spirits. Band leaders were leaders in name only. They were first among equals. Sometimes they gave advice or made decisions, but they had no way to enforce their decisions.

The Inuit

Foragers lacked formal **law** in the sense of a legal code with trial and enforcement, but they did have methods of social control and dispute settlement. The absence of law did not entail total anarchy. The aboriginal Inuit (Hoebel 1954, 1954/1968) provide a good example of methods of settling disputes in stateless societies. As described by E. A. Hoebel (1954) in a study of Inuit conflict resolution, a sparse population of some 20,000 Inuit spanned 6,000 miles (9,500 kilometers) of the Arctic region (Figure 8.1). The most significant social groups were the nuclear family and the band. Personal relationships linked the families and bands. Some bands had headmen. There were also shamans (part-time religious specialists). However, these positions conferred little power on those who occupied them.

Hunting and fishing by men were the primary Inuit subsistence activities. The diverse and abundant plant foods available in warmer areas, where female labor in gathering is important, were absent in the Arctic. Traveling on land and sea in a bitter environment, Inuit men faced more dangers than women did. The traditional male role took its toll in lives. Adult women would have outnumbered men substantially without occasional female infanticide (killing of a baby), which Inuit culture permitted.

Despite this crude (and to us unthinkable) means of population regulation, there were still more adult women than men. This permitted some men to have two or three wives. The ability to support more than one wife conferred a certain amount of prestige, but it also encouraged envy. (*Prestige* is esteem, respect, or approval for culturally valued acts or qualities.) If a man seemed to be taking additional wives just to enhance his reputation, a rival was likely to steal one of them. Most disputes were between men and originated over women, caused by wife stealing or adultery. If a man discovered that his wife had been having sexual relations without his permission, he considered himself wronged.

Although public opinion would not let the husband ignore the matter, he had several options. He could try to kill the wife stealer. However, if he succeeded, one of his rival's kinsmen would surely try to kill him in retaliation. One dispute could escalate into several deaths as relatives avenged a succession of murders. No government existed to intervene and stop such a *blood feud* (a murderous feud between families). However, one also could challenge a rival to a song battle. In a public setting, contestants made up insulting songs about each other. At the end of the match, the audience judged one of them the winner. However, if a man whose wife had been stolen won, there was no guarantee she would return. Often she would decide to stay with her abductor.

Thefts are common in societies with marked property differentials, like our own, but thefts are uncommon among foragers. Each Inuit had access to the resources needed to sustain life. Every man could hunt, fish, and make the tools necessary for subsistence. Every woman could obtain the materials needed to make clothing, prepare food, and do domestic work. Inuit men could even hunt and fish in the territories of other local groups. There was no notion of private ownership of territory or animals. However, certain minor personal items were associated with a specific person. In various societies, such items include things such as arrows, a tobacco pouch, clothing, and personal ornaments. One of the most basic Inuit beliefs was that "all natural resources are free or common goods" (Hoebel 1954/1968). Band-organized societies usually lack differential access to strategic resources. If people want something from someone else, they ask for it, and usually it is given.

Tribal Cultivators

As is true with foraging bands, there are no totally autonomous tribes in today's world. Still, there are societies, for example, in Papua New Guinea and in South America's tropical forests, in which tribal principles still operate. Tribes typically have a horticultural or pastoral economy and are organized by village life and/or membership in *descent groups* (kin groups whose members trace descent from a common ancestor). Tribes lack socioeconomic stratification (i.e., a class structure) and a formal government of their own. A few tribes still conduct small-scale warfare, in the form of intervillage raiding. Tribes have more effective regulatory mechanisms than foragers do, but tribal societies have no sure means of enforcing political decisions. The main regulatory officials are village heads, "big men," descent-group leaders, village councils, and leaders of pantribal associations. All these figures and groups have limited authority.

Like foragers, horticulturalists tend to be egalitarian, although some have marked gender stratification: an unequal distribution of resources, power, prestige, and personal freedom between men and women. Horticultural villages are usu-

FIGURE 8.1 Location of the Inuit.

ally small, with low population density and open access to strategic resources. Age, gender, and personal traits determine how much respect people receive and how much support they get from others. Egalitarianism diminishes, however, as village size and population density increase. Horticultural villages usually have headmen—rarely, if ever, headwomen.

The Village Head

The Yanomami (Chagnon 1997) are Native Americans who live in southern Venezuela and the adjacent part of Brazil. Their tribal society has about 20,000 people living in 200 to 250 widely scattered villages, each with a population between 40 and 250. The Yanomami are horticulturalists who also hunt and gather. Their staple crops are bananas and plantains (a bananalike crop). There are more significant social groups among the Yanomami than exist in a foraging

society. The Yanomami have families, villages, and descent groups. Their descent groups, which span more than one village, are patrilineal (ancestry is traced back through males only) and exogamous (people must marry outside their own descent group). However, local branches of two different descent groups may live in the same village and intermarry.

As has been true in many village-based tribal societies, the only leadership position among the Yanomami is that of **village head** (always a man). His authority, like that of a foraging band's leader, is severely limited. If a headman wants something done, he must lead by example and persuasion. The headman lacks the right to issue orders. He can only persuade, harangue, and try to influence public opinion. For example, if he wants people to clean up the central plaza in preparation for a feast, he must start sweeping it himself, hoping that his covillagers will take the hint and relieve him.

STUDENT CD-ROM LIVING ANTHROPOLOGY

Leadership among the Canela
Track 8

This clip features ethnographer Bill Crocker, who has worked among the Canela for more than 40 years, and Raimundo Roberto, a respected ceremonial chief, who has been Crocker's key cultural consultant during that entire time. Raimundo discusses his role in Canela society, mentioning the values of generosity, sharing, and comforting words. How does this clip illustrate differences between leadership in a tribal society and leadership in our own? Does Raimundo have formal authority? Compare him to the Yanomami village head and the band leader discussed in this chapter. The clip also shows a mending ceremony celebrating the healing of a rift that once threatened Canela society.

When conflict erupts within the village, the headman may be called on as a mediator who listens to both sides. He will give an opinion and advice. If a disputant is unsatisfied, the headman can do nothing. He has no power to back his decisions and no way to impose punishments. Like the band leader, he is first among equals.

A Yanomami village headman also must lead in generosity. Because he must be more generous than any other villager, he cultivates more land. His garden provides much of the food consumed when his village holds a feast for another village. The headman represents the village in its dealings with outsiders. Sometimes he visits other villages to invite people to a feast. The way a person acts as headman depends on his personal traits and the number of supporters he can muster. One village headman, Kaobawa, intervened in a dispute between a husband and a wife and kept him from killing her (Chagnon 1968). He also guaranteed safety to a delegation from a village with which a covillager of his wanted to start a war. Kaobawa was a particularly effective headman. He had demonstrated his fierceness in battle, but he also knew how to use diplomacy to avoid offending other villagers. No one in the village had a better personality for the headmanship. Nor (because Kaobawa had many brothers) did anyone have more supporters. Among the Yanomami, when a group is dissatisfied with a village headman, its members can leave and found a new village; this is done from time to time.

Yanomami society, with its many villages and descent groups, is more complex than a band-organized society. The Yanomami also face more regulatory problems. A headman sometimes can prevent a specific violent act, but there is no government to maintain order. In fact, intervillage raiding in which men are killed and women are captured has been a feature of some areas of Yanomami territory, particularly those studied by Chagnon (1997).

We also must stress that the Yanomami are not isolated from outside events, including missionization (although there still may be uncontacted villages). The Yanomami live in two nation-states, Venezuela and Brazil, and external warfare waged by Brazilian ranchers and miners increasingly has threatened them (Chagnon 1997; *Cultural Survival Quarterly* 1989; Ferguson 1995). During a Brazilian gold rush between 1987 and 1991, one Yanomami died each day, on average, from external attacks (including biological warfare—introduced diseases to which the Indians lack resistance). By 1991, there were some 40,000 Brazilian miners in the Yanomami homeland. Some Indians were killed outright. The miners introduced new diseases, and the swollen population ensured that old diseases became epidemic. In 1991, a commission of the American Anthropological Association reported on the plight of the Yanomami. Brazilian Yanomami were dying at a rate of 10 percent annually, and their fertility rate had dropped to zero. Since then, both the Brazilian and the Venezuelan governments have intervened to protect the Yanomami. One Brazilian president declared a huge Yanomami territory off-limits to outsiders. Unfortunately, by mid-1992, local politicians, miners, and ranchers were increasingly evading the ban. The future of the Yanomami remains uncertain.

The "Big Man"

In many areas of the South Pacific, particularly the Melanesian Islands and Papua New Guinea, native cultures had a kind of political leader that we call the big man. The **big man** (almost always a male) was an elaborate version of the village head, but with one significant difference. The village head's leadership is within one village; the big man had supporters in several villages. The big man therefore was a regulator of regional political organization. Here we see the trend toward expansion in the scale of sociopolitical regulation—from village to region.

The Kapauku Papuans live in Irian Jaya, Indonesia (which is on the island of New Guinea) (Figure 8.2). Anthropologist Leopold Pospisil (1963) studied the Kapauku (45,000 people), who grow crops (with the sweet potato as their staple) and raise pigs. Their economy is too complex to be described as simple horticulture. The only political figure among the Kapauku was the big man, known as a *tonowi*. A tonowi achieved his status through hard work, amassing wealth in the form of pigs and other native riches. Characteristics that distinguished a big man from his fellows included wealth, generosity, eloquence, physical fitness, bravery, and supernatural powers. Men became big men because they had certain personalities. They had amassed resources during their own lifetimes, as they did not inherit their wealth or position.

A man who was determined enough could become a big man, creating wealth through hard work and good judgment. Wealth resulted from successful pig breeding and trading. As a man's pig herd and prestige grew, he attracted supporters. He sponsored ceremonial pig feasts in which pigs were slaughtered, and their meat distributed to guests.

Unlike the Yanomami village head, a big man's wealth exceeded that of his fellows. His supporters, recognizing his past favors and anticipating future rewards, recognized him as a leader and accepted his decisions as binding. The big man was an important regulator of regional events in Kapauku life. He helped determine the dates for feasts and markets. He persuaded people to sponsor feasts, which distributed pork and wealth. He initiated economic projects requiring the cooperation of a regional community.

The Kapauku big man again exemplifies a generalization about leadership in tribal societies: If someone achieves wealth and widespread respect and support, he or she must be generous. The big man worked hard not to hoard wealth but to be able to give away the fruits of his labor, to convert wealth into prestige and gratitude. A stingy big man would lose his support, his reputation plummeting. The Kapauku might take even more extreme measures against big men who hoarded wealth. Selfish and greedy men sometimes were murdered by their fellows.

Political figures such as the big man emerge as regulators both of demographic growth and of economic complexity. Kapauku cultivation has used varied techniques for specific kinds of land. Labor-intensive cultivation in valleys involves mutual aid in turning the soil before planting. The digging of long drainage ditches is even more complex. Kapauku plant cultivation supports a larger and denser population than does the simpler horticulture of the Yanomami. Kapauku society could not survive in its current form without collective cultivation and political regulation of the more complex economic tasks.

Pantribal Sodalities and Age Grades

Big men could forge regional political organization—albeit temporarily—by mobilizing people from different villages. Other social and political mechanisms in tribal societies, such as a belief in common ancestry, kinship, or descent, could be used to link local groups within a region. The same descent group, for example, might span several villages, and its dispersed members might follow a descent-group leader.

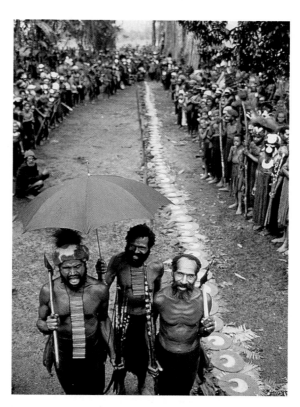

■ The "big man" persuades people to organize feasts, which distribute pork and wealth. Shown here is such a regional event, drawing on several villages, in Papua New Guinea. Big men owe their status to their individual personalities rather than to inherited wealth or position. Does our society have equivalents of big men?

FIGURE 8.2 Location of the Kapauku.

Many factors contribute to political success in a modern nation such as the United States. They include personality, kin connections, and inherited status. Politically valuable attributes of a Melanesian big man included wealth, generosity, eloquence, physical fitness, bravery, and supernatural powers. How do such characteristics influence contemporary political careers? Americans routinely use their own wealth to finance campaigns. Big men get their loyalists to produce and deliver wealth in the form of pigs, just as modern politicians persuade their supporters to make campaign contributions. And, like big men, successful American politicians try to be generous with their supporters. Payback may take the form of a night in the Lincoln bedroom, an invitation to a strategic dinner, an ambassadorship, or largesse to a place that was particularly supportive. Big men amass wealth and then give away pigs. Successful American politicians give away "pork."

As with the big man, eloquence and communication skills contribute to political success (e.g., Bill Clinton and Ronald Reagan), although lack of such skills isn't necessarily fatal (e.g., either President Bush). What about physical fitness? Hair, height, and health are still political advantages. Bravery, for example, as demonstrated through distinguished military service, may help political careers, but it certainly isn't required. Supernatural powers? Candidates who proclaim themselves atheists are as rare as self-identified witches. Almost all political candidates claim to belong to a mainstream religion. Some even present their candidacies as promoting divine wishes. However, contemporary politics isn't just about personality, as it is in big man systems. We live in a state-organized, stratified society with inherited wealth, power, and privilege, all of which have political implications. As is typical of states, inheritance and kin connections play a role in political success. Just think of Kennedys, Bushes, Gores, Clintons, and Doles.

Principles other than kinship also can link local groups. In a modern nation, a labor union, national sorority or fraternity, political party, or religious denomination may provide such a non-kin-based link. In tribes, nonkin groups called associations or sodalities may serve the same linking function. Often, sodalities are based on common age or gender, with all-male sodalities more common than all-female ones.

Pantribal sodalities (those that extend across the whole tribe, spanning several villages) sometimes arose in areas where two or more different cultures came into regular contact. Such sodalities were especially likely to develop in the presence of warfare between tribes. Drawing their membership from different villages of the same tribe, pantribal sodalities could mobilize men in many local groups for attack or retaliation against another tribe.

In the cross-cultural study of nonkin groups, we must distinguish between those that are confined to a single village and those that span several local groups. Only the latter, the pantribal groups, are important in general military mobilization and regional political organization. Localized men's houses and clubs, limited to particular villages, are found in many horticultural societies in tropical South America, Melanesia, and Papua New Guinea. These groups may organize village activities and even intervillage raiding, but their leaders are similar to village heads and their political scope is mainly local. The following discussion, which continues our examination of the growth in scale of regional sociopolitical organization, concerns pantribal groups.

The best examples of pantribal sodalities come from the Central Plains of North America and from tropical Africa. During the 18th and 19th centuries, native populations of the Great Plains of the United States and Canada experienced a rapid growth of pantribal sodalities. This development reflected an economic change that followed the spread of horses, which had been reintroduced to the Americas by the Spanish, to the states between the Rocky Mountains and the Mississippi River. Many Plains Indian societies changed their adaptive strategies because of the horse. At first, they had been foragers who hunted bison (buffalo) on foot. Later, they adopted a mixed economy based on hunting, gathering, and horticulture. Finally, they changed to a much more specialized economy based on horseback hunting of bison (eventually with rifles).

As the Plains tribes were undergoing these changes, other Indians also adopted horseback hunting and moved into the Plains. Attempting to occupy the same area, groups came into conflict. A pattern of warfare developed in which the members of one tribe raided another, usually for horses. The new economy demanded that people follow the movement of the bison herds. During the winter, when the bison dispersed, a tribe fragmented into small bands and families. In the summer, as huge herds assembled on the Plains, members of the tribe reunited. They camped together for social, political, and religious activities, but mainly for communal bison hunting.

Natives of the Great Plains of North America originally hunted bison (buffalo) on foot, using the bow and arrow. The introduction of horses and rifles fueled a pattern of horse raiding and warfare. How far had the change gone, as depicted in this painting?

Only two activities in the new adaptive strategy demanded strong leadership: organizing and carrying out raids on enemy camps (to capture horses) and managing the summer bison hunt. All the Plains cultures developed pantribal sodalities, and leadership roles within them, to police the summer hunt. Leaders coordinated hunting efforts, making sure that people did not cause a stampede with an early shot or an ill-advised action. Leaders imposed severe penalties, including seizure of a culprit's wealth, for disobedience.

Some of the Plains sodalities were **age sets** of increasing rank. Each set included all the men—from that tribe's component bands—born during a certain time span. Each set had its distinctive dance, songs, possessions, and privileges. Members of each set had to pool their wealth to buy admission to the next higher level as they moved up the age hierarchy. Most Plains societies had pantribal warrior associations whose rituals celebrated militarism. As noted previously, the leaders of these associations organized bison hunting and raiding. They also arbitrated disputes during the summer, when large numbers of people came together.

Many of the tribes that adopted this Plains strategy of adaptation had once been foragers for whom hunting and gathering had been individual or small-group affairs. They never had come together previously as a single social unit. Age and gender were available as social principles that could quickly and efficiently forge unrelated people into pantribal groups.

Raiding of one tribe by another, this time for cattle rather than horses, also was common in eastern and southeastern Africa, where pantribal sodalities, including age sets, also developed.

Among the pastoral Masai of Kenya and Tanzania (Figure 8.3), men born during the same four-year period were circumcised together and belonged to the same named group, an age set, throughout their lives. The sets moved through grades, the most important of which was the warrior grade. Members of the set who wished to enter the warrior grade were at first discouraged by its current occupants, who eventually vacated the warrior grade and married. Members of a set felt a strong allegiance to one another and eventually had sexual rights to each other's wives. Masai women lacked comparable set organization, but they also passed through culturally recognized age grades: the initiate, the married woman, and the postmenopausal woman.

To understand the difference between an age set and an age grade, think of a college class, the Class of 2011, for example, and its progress through the university. The age set would be the group of people constituting the Class of 2011, while the first ("freshman"), sophomore, junior, and senior years would represent the age grades.

Not all cultures with age grades also have age sets. When there are no sets, men can enter or leave a particular grade individually or collectively, often by going through a predetermined ritual. The grades most commonly recognized in Africa are these:

1. Recently initiated youths.

2. Warriors.

3. One or more grades of mature men who play important roles in pantribal government.

4. Elders, who may have special ritual responsibilities.

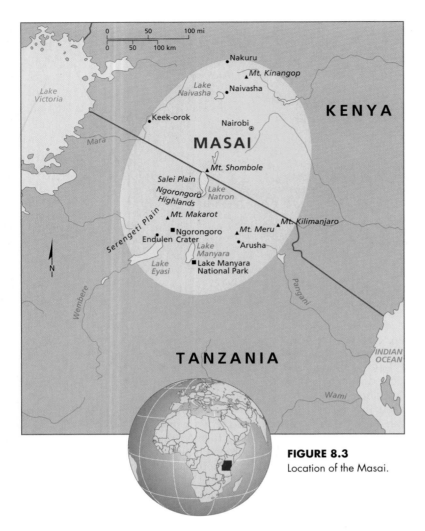

FIGURE 8.3
Location of the Masai.

■ *Among the Masai of Kenya and Tanzania, men born during the same four-year period were circumcised together. They belonged to the same named group, an age set, throughout their lives. The sets moved through grades, of which the most important was the warrior grade. Here we see the warrior (ilmurran) age grade dancing with a group of girls of a lower age grade (intoyie). Do we have any equivalents of age sets or grades in our own society?*

In certain parts of West Africa and Central Africa, the pantribal sodalities are *secret societies*, made up exclusively of men or women. Like our college fraternities and sororities, these associations have secret initiation ceremonies. Among the Mende of Sierra Leone, men's and women's secret societies are very influential. The men's group, the Poro, trains boys in social conduct, ethics, and religion and supervises political and economic activities. Leadership roles in the Poro often overshadow village headship and play an important part in social control, dispute management, and tribal political regulation. Like descent, then, age, gender, and ritual can link members of different local groups into a single social collectivity in tribal society and thus create a sense of ethnic identity, of belonging to the same cultural tradition.

Nomadic Politics

Although many pastoralists, such as the Masai, had tribal sociopolitical organization, a range of demographic and sociopolitical diversity occurs with pastoralism. A comparison of pastoralists shows that as regulatory problems increase, political hierarchies become more complex. Political organization becomes less personal, more formal, and less kinship-oriented. The pastoral strategy of adaptation does not dictate any particular political organization. A range of authority structures manage regulatory problems associated with specific environments. Some pastoralists have traditionally existed as well-defined ethnic groups in nation-states. This reflects pastoralists' need to interact with other populations—a need that is less characteristic of the other adaptive strategies.

The scope of political authority among pastoralists expands considerably as regulatory problems increase in densely populated regions. Consider two Iranian pastoral nomadic tribes: the Basseri and the Qashqai (Salzman 1974). Starting each year from a plateau near the coast, these groups took their animals to grazing land 17,000 feet (5,400 meters) above sea level. The Basseri and the Qashqai shared this route with one another and with several other ethnic groups (Figure 8.4).

Use of the same pasture land at different times was carefully scheduled. Ethnic-group movements were tightly coordinated. Expressing this schedule is *il-rah*, a concept common to all Iranian nomads. A group's *il-rah* is its customary path in time and space. It is the schedule, different for each group, of when specific areas can be used in the annual trek.

Each tribe had its own leader, known as the *khan* or *il-khan*. The Basseri *khan*, because he dealt with a smaller population, faced fewer problems in coordinating its movements than did the leaders of the Qashqai. Correspondingly, his rights, privileges, duties, and authority were weaker.

Nevertheless, his authority exceeded that of any political figure we have discussed so far. However, the *khan*'s authority still came from his personal traits rather than from his office. That is, the Basseri followed a particular *khan* not because of a political position he happened to fill but because of their personal allegiance and loyalty to him as a man. The *khan* relied on the support of the heads of the descent groups into which Basseri society was divided.

In Qashqai society, however, allegiance shifts from the person to the office. The Qashqai had multiple levels of authority and more powerful chiefs or *khans*. Managing 400,000 people required a complex hierarchy. Heading it was the *il-khan*, helped by a deputy, under whom were the heads of constituent tribes, under each of whom were descent-group heads.

A case illustrates just how developed the Qashqai authority structure was. A hailstorm prevented some nomads from joining the annual migration at the appointed time. Although everyone recognized that they were not responsible for their delay, the *il-khan* assigned them less favorable grazing land, for that year only, in place of their usual pasture. The tardy herders and other Qashqai considered the judgment fair and didn't question it. Thus, Qashqai authorities regulated the annual migration. They also adjudicated disputes between people, tribes, and descent groups.

These Iranian cases illustrate the fact that pastoralism is often just one among many specialized economic activities within complex nation-states and regional systems. As part of a larger whole, pastoral tribes are constantly pitted against other ethnic groups. In these nations, the state becomes a final authority, a higher-level regulator that attempts to limit conflict between ethnic groups. State organization arose not just to manage agricultural economies but also to regulate the activities of ethnic groups within expanding social and economic systems.

CHIEFDOMS

Having looked at bands and tribes, we turn to more complex forms of sociopolitical organization: chiefdoms and states. The first states emerged in the Old World about 5,500 years ago. The first chiefdoms developed perhaps a thousand years earlier, but few survive today. In many parts of the world the chiefdom was a transitional form of organization that emerged during the evolution of tribes into states. State formation began in Mesopotamia (currently Iran and Iraq). It next occurred in Egypt, the Indus Valley of Pakistan and India, and northern China. A few thousand years later, states also arose in two parts of the Western Hemisphere: Mesoamerica (Mexico, Guatemala,

Political organization is well developed among the Qashqai, who share their nomadic route and strategic resources with several other tribes. Here, Qashqai nomads cross a river in Iran's Fars province.

FIGURE 8.4 Location of the Basseri and Qashqai.

Perspectives on Group Membership

BACKGROUND INFORMATION

STUDENT:
Abigail Dreibelbis

SUPERVISING PROFESSOR:
Miriam Chaiken

SCHOOL:
Indiana University of Pennsylvania

YEAR IN SCHOOL/MAJOR:
Senior/Anthropology

FUTURE PLANS:
Seeking positions
in resource management
and environmental protection

PROJECT TITLE:
Delta, Delta, Delta, Can I Help Ya,
Help Ya, Help Ya

This research examines reasons why college women do or don't join sororities. Does the achieved status of sorority membership differ significantly from the mainly ascribed group memberships discussed in this chapter? Do you think that men join fraternities for the same reasons women join sororities? What relation do you see between the Greek system on college campuses and politics?

There is a human need for belonging, for affiliation. Identification with a group that has common norms and roles helps fulfill this need for security and creates social bonds that establish and assure companionship and personal identification.

This understanding has come from the study I did on members and nonmembers of social sororities at Indiana University of Pennsylvania. Since I started college, I had noticed a dichotomy between these two groups. I wanted to find out the real and perceived differences between them. My hypothesis was that there was a higher level of need for group identity and involvement in sorority members, and conversely more independence in nonmembers. I formed a survey for both groups, with questions about demographics and activities and I used open-ended questions to elicit their views and followed up with in-depth interviews to get a more personal response.

I found that participation in high school student government had been three times higher for members of sororities. This showed the great importance of social identity for Greeks, as student government members have prestige as a minority segment of the student body. Membership is competitive and based on peer acceptance. Conversely, activity in the arts was twice as high in the independent (nonsorority) group. This is a more aesthetic, personal activity, done for the act itself (singing or performing) rather than to gain the acceptance of peers.

The affinity for group identity is reflected in the expressed reasons for joining a sorority. Members found a "sense of belonging" and "self-confidence." Independents cited these same as reasons for joining, yet they saw this need as negative, and leading to a "group identity [that] is their identity." They did not like the "controlling" qualities of the sorority. The sorority member acknowledges the search for social and personal identification in a group as well as the resulting gratification in joining.

It has been hypothesized that the eldest child is the most independent. I found that twice as many nonsorority women were the oldest siblings in their family. Independents "just weren't the type" for a sorority. Nonmembers seem to find identity or belonging through other groups (volunteering, sports, honors societies) more for personal interest than social merit. This statistic seemed to support the idea that women who join sororities have a higher value of social involvement and acceptance for security and identity.

Everyone finds support and identity in groups. Groups provide safety along with a sense of personal worth and common identity with at least a few people in this vast world. Through my research I found that this need varies in degree among individuals. Those with a higher level of need find fulfillment in a social group such as a sorority. Non-Greeks do not value and are less dependent on such a social identity. These personality differences may create a sense of separation between the two groups and result in the dichotomy observed on campus.

It was fulfilling to challenge my hypothesis through questions of my own making and to come to an understanding of how and why people function. By gaining these insights on aspects of personality that underlie culture, I have developed a broader view of the intangible differences that affect our daily interactions.

Belize) and the central Andes (Peru and Bolivia). Early states are known as *archaic states,* or nonindustrial states, in contrast to modern industrial nation-states. Robert Carneiro defines the state as "an autonomous political unit encompassing many communities within its territory, having a centralized government with the power to collect taxes, draft men for work or war, and decree and enforce laws" (Carneiro 1970, p. 733).

The chiefdom and the state, like many categories used by social scientists, are *ideal types.* That is, they are labels that make social contrasts seem sharper than they really are. In reality, there is a continuum from tribe to chiefdom to state. Some societies have many attributes of chiefdoms but retain tribal features. Some advanced chiefdoms have many attributes of archaic states and thus are difficult to assign to either category. Recognizing this "continuous change" (Johnson and Earle, eds. 2000), some anthropologists speak of "complex chiefdoms" (Earle 1987), which are almost states.

Political and Economic Systems in Chiefdoms

State formation did not occur, and only chiefdoms emerged in several areas, including the circum-Caribbean (e.g., Caribbean islands, Panama, Colombia), lowland Amazonia, what is now the southeastern United States, and Polynesia. Between the emergence and spread of food production and the expansion of the Roman empire, much of Europe was organized at the chiefdom level, to which it reverted for centuries after the fall of Rome in the fifth century AD. Chiefdoms created the megalithic cultures of Europe, such as the one that built Stonehenge. Bear in mind that chiefdoms and states can fall (disintegrate) as well as rise.

Much of our ethnographic knowledge about chiefdoms comes from Polynesia (Kirch 2000), where they were common at the time of European exploration. In chiefdoms, social relations are mainly based on kinship, marriage, descent, age, generation, and gender—as they are in bands and tribes. This is a basic difference between chiefdoms and states. States bring nonrelatives together and oblige them to pledge allegiance to a government.

Unlike bands and tribes, however, chiefdoms are characterized by *permanent political regulation* of the territory they administer. Chiefdoms might include thousands of people living in many villages and/or hamlets. Regulation was carried out by the chief and his or her assistants, who occupied political offices. An **office** is a permanent position, which must be refilled when it is vacated by death or retirement. Because offices were systematically refilled, the structure of a chiefdom endured across the generations, ensuring permanent political regulation.

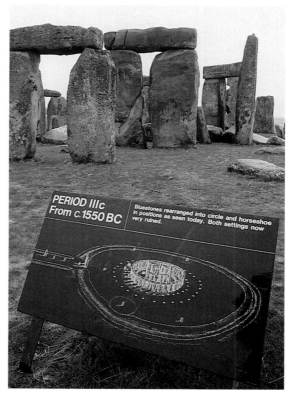

■ Stonehenge, England, and an educational display designed for tourists and visitors. Chiefdoms created the megalithic cultures of Europe, such as the one that built Stonehenge over 5,000 years ago. Between the emergence and spread of food production and the expansion of the Roman empire, much of Europe was organized at the chiefdom level, to which it reverted after the fall of Rome.

In the Polynesian chiefdoms, the chiefs were full-time political specialists in charge of regulating the economy—production, distribution, and consumption. Polynesian chiefs relied on religion to buttress their authority. They regulated production by commanding or prohibiting (using religious taboos) the cultivation of certain lands and crops. Chiefs also regulated distribution and consumption. At certain seasons—often on a ritual occasion such as a first-fruit ceremony— people would offer part of their harvest to the chief through his or her representatives. Products moved up the hierarchy, eventually reaching the chief. Conversely, illustrating obligatory sharing with kin, chiefs sponsored feasts at which they gave back much of what they had received.

Such a flow of resources to and then from a central office is known as *chiefly redistribution.* Redistribution offers economic advantages. If the different areas specialized in particular crops, goods, or services, chiefly redistribution made those products available to the whole society. Chiefly redistribution also played a role in risk management. It stimulated production beyond the immediate subsistence level and provided a central storehouse for goods that might become scarce at times of famine (Earle 1987, 1991). Chiefdoms and archaic states had similar economies, often based on intensive cultivation, and both administered systems of regional trade or exchange.

For more on prehistoric chiefdoms in the southeastern U.S., see the Internet Exercises at your OLC **mhhe.com/kottak**

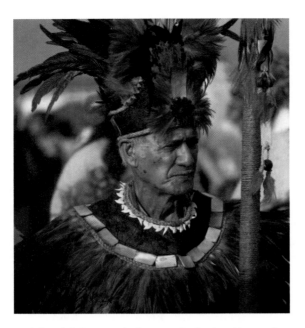

A French Polynesian chief wears a feather headdress at the Pacific Arts festival. How do chiefs differ from ordinary people? What kind of status do you imagine this chief has today?

Social Status in Chiefdoms

Social status in chiefdoms was based on seniority of descent. Because rank, power, prestige, and resources came through kinship and descent, Polynesian chiefs kept extremely long genealogies. Some chiefs (without writing) managed to trace their ancestry back 50 generations. All the people in the chiefdom were thought to be related to each other. Presumably, all were descended from a group of founding ancestors.

The chief (usually a man) had to demonstrate seniority in descent. Degrees of seniority were calculated so intricately on some islands that there were as many ranks as people. For example, the third son would rank below the second, who in turn would rank below the first. The children of an eldest brother, however, would all rank above the children of the next brother, whose children would in turn outrank those of younger brothers. However, even the lowest-ranking person in a chiefdom was still the chief's relative. In such a kin-based context, everyone, even a chief, had to share with his or her relatives.

Because everyone had a slightly different status, it was difficult to draw a line between elites and common people. Although other chiefdoms calculated seniority differently and had shorter genealogies than did those in Polynesia, the concern for genealogy and seniority and the absence of sharp gaps between elites and commoners were features of all chiefdoms.

Status Systems in Chiefdoms and States

The status systems of chiefdoms and states are similar in that both are based on **differential access** to resources. This means that some men and women had privileged access to power, prestige, and wealth. They controlled strategic resources such as land and water. Earle characterizes chiefs as "an incipient aristocracy with advantages in wealth and lifestyle" (1987, p. 290). Nevertheless, differential access in chiefdoms was still very much tied to kinship. The people with privileged access were generally chiefs and their nearest relatives and assistants.

Compared with chiefdoms, archaic states drew a much firmer line between elites and masses, distinguishing at least between nobles and commoners. Kinship ties did not extend from the nobles to the commoners because of *stratum endogamy*— marriage within one's own group. Commoners married commoners; elites married elites.

Such a division of society into socioeconomic strata contrasts strongly with bands and tribes, whose status systems are based on prestige, rather than on differential access to resources. The prestige differentials that do exist in bands reflect special qualities and abilities. Good hunters get respect from their fellows as long as they are generous. So does a skilled curer, dancer, storyteller—or anyone else with a talent or skill that others appreciate.

In tribes, some prestige goes to descent-group leaders, to village heads, and especially to the big man, a regional figure who commands the loyalty and labor of others. However, all these figures must be generous. If they accumulate more resources—that is, property or food—than others in the village, they must share them with the others. Since strategic resources are available to everyone, social classes based on the possession of unequal amounts of resources can never exist.

In many tribes, particularly those with patrilineal descent, men have much greater prestige and power than women do. The gender contrast in rights could diminish in chiefdoms, where prestige and access to resources were based on seniority of descent, so that some women were senior to some men. Unlike big men, chiefs were exempt from ordinary work and had rights and privileges that were unavailable to the masses. However, like big men, they still gave back much of the wealth they took in.

The Emergence of Stratification

The status system in chiefdoms, although based on differential access, differed from the status system in states because the privileged few were always relatives and assistants of the chief. However, this type of status system didn't last very long. Chiefs would start acting like kings and try to erode the kinship basis of the chiefdom. In Madagascar, they would do this by demoting their more distant relatives to commoner status and banning marriage between nobles and commoners (Kottak 1980). Such moves, *if accepted by the society,* created separate social strata—*unrelated* groups that differ in their access to wealth, prestige, and power. (A *stratum* is one of two or more groups that contrast in regard to social status and access to strategic resources. Each stratum includes people of both sexes and all ages.) The creation of separate social strata is called **stratification,** and its emergence signified the transition from chiefdom to state. *The presence and acceptance of stratification is one of the key distinguishing features of a state.*

The influential sociologist Max Weber (1922/1968) defined three related dimensions of social stratification: (1) Economic status, or **wealth,** encompasses all a person's material assets, including income, land, and other types of property. (2) **Power,** the ability to exercise one's will over others—to do what one wants—is the basis of political status. (3) **Prestige**—the basis of social status—refers to esteem, respect, or approval for acts, deeds, or qualities considered exemplary. Prestige, or "cultural capital" (Bourdieu 1984), provides people with a sense of worth and respect, which they may often convert into economic and political advantage (Table 8.1).

In archaic states—for the first time in human evolution—there were contrasts in wealth, power, and prestige between entire groups (social strata) of men and women. Each stratum included people of both sexes and all ages. The **superordinate** (the higher or elite) stratum had privileged access to wealth, power, and other valued resources. Access to resources by members of the **subordinate** (lower or underprivileged) stratum was limited by the privileged group.

Socioeconomic stratification continues as a defining feature of all states, archaic or industrial. The elites control a significant part of the means of production, for example, land, herds, water, capital, farms, or factories. Those born at the bottom of the hierarchy have reduced chances of social mobility. Because of elite ownership rights, ordinary people lack free access to resources.

■ *Shown here in Cleveland, Ohio, in January, 2004, Rebecca Jemison meets the media after being announced as the winner of Ohio's first ($162 million) "Mega Millions" lottery. Wealth and prestige are not always correlated. Do you think Jemison's prestige will rise as a result of winning the lottery?*

Only in states do the elites get to keep their differential wealth. Unlike big men and chiefs, they don't have to give it back to the people whose labor has built and increased it.

STATES

Table 8.2 summarizes the information presented so far on bands, tribes, chiefdoms, and states. States, remember, are autonomous political units with social classes and a formal government, based on law. States tend to be large and populous, compared to bands, tribes, and chiefdoms. Certain statuses, systems, and subsystems with specialized functions are found in all states. They include the following:

1. *Population control:* fixing of boundaries, establishment of citizenship categories, and the taking of a census.

2. *Judiciary:* laws, legal procedure, and judges.

3. *Enforcement:* permanent military and police forces.

4. *Fiscal:* taxation.

In archaic states, these subsystems were integrated by a ruling system or government composed of civil, military, and religious officials (Fried 1960).

Population Control

To know whom they govern, all states conduct censuses. States demarcate boundaries that separate them from other societies. Customs agents, immigration officers, navies, and coast guards patrol frontiers. Even nonindustrial states have

TABLE 8.1 Max Weber's Three Dimensions of Stratification		
wealth	=>	economic status
power	=>	political status
prestige	=>	social status

TABLE 8.2   Economic Basis of and Political Regulation in Bands, Tribes, Chiefdoms, and States

Sociopolitical Type	Economic Type	Examples	Type of Regulation
Band	Foraging	Inuit, San	Local
Tribe	Horticulture, pastoralism	Yanomami, Kapauku, Masai	Local, temporary regional
Chiefdom	Productive horticulture, pastoral nomadism, agriculture	Qashqai, Polynesia, Cherokee	Permanent regional
State	Agriculture, industrialism	Ancient Mesopotamia, contemporary United States and Canada	Permanent regional

To see how states are created, see the Virtual Exploration

mhhe.com/kottak

boundary-maintenance forces. In Buganda, an archaic state on the shores of Lake Victoria in Uganda, the king rewarded military officers with estates in outlying provinces. They became his guardians against foreign intrusion.

States also control population through administrative subdivision: provinces, districts, "states," counties, subcounties, and parishes. Lower-level officials manage the populations and territories of the subdivisions.

In nonstates, people work and relax with their relatives, in-laws, fictive kin, and agemates—people with whom they have a personal relationship. Such a personal social life existed throughout most of human history, but food production spelled its eventual decline. After millions of years of human evolution, it took a mere 4,000 years for the population increase and regulatory problems spawned by food production to lead from tribe to chiefdom to state. With state organization, kinship's pervasive role diminished. Descent groups may continue as kin groups within states, but their importance in political organization declines.

States foster geographic mobility and resettlement, severing long-standing ties among people, land, and kin. Population displacements have increased in the modern world. War, famine, and job seeking across national boundaries churn up migratory currents. People in states come to identify themselves by new statuses, both ascribed and achieved, including ethnic background, place of birth or residence, occupation, party, religion, and team or club affiliation, rather than only as members of a descent group or extended family.

States also manage their populations by granting different rights and obligations to citizens and noncitizens. Status distinctions among citizens are also common. Many archaic states granted different rights to nobles, commoners, and slaves. Unequal rights within state-organized societies persist in today's world. In recent American history, before the Emancipation Proclamation, there

were different laws for slaves and free people. In European colonies, separate courts judged cases involving only natives and those that involved Europeans. In contemporary America, a military code of justice and court system continue to coexist alongside the civil judiciary.

Judiciary

States have *laws* based on precedent and legislative proclamations. Without writing, laws may be preserved in oral tradition, with justices, elders, and other specialists responsible for remembering them. Oral traditions as repositories of legal wisdom have continued in some nations with writing, such as Great Britain. Laws regulate relations between individuals and groups.

Crimes are violations of the legal code, with specified types of punishment. However, a given act, such as killing someone, may be legally defined in different ways (e.g., as manslaughter, justifiable homicide, or first-degree murder). Furthermore, even in contemporary North America, where justice is supposed to be "blind" to social distinctions, the poor are prosecuted more often and more severely than are the rich.

To handle disputes and crimes, all states have courts and judges. Precolonial African states had subcounty, county, and district courts, plus a high court formed by the king or queen and his or her advisers. Most states allow appeals to higher courts, although people are encouraged to solve problems locally.

A striking contrast between states and nonstates is intervention in family affairs. In states, aspects of parenting and marriage enter the domain of public law. Governments step in to halt blood feuds and regulate previously private disputes. States attempt to curb *internal* conflict, but they aren't always successful. About 85 percent of the world's armed conflicts since 1945 have begun within states—in efforts to overthrow a rul-

Map Atlas

Map 13 shows the global distribution of organized states and chiefdoms on the eve of European colonization.

ing regime or as disputes over tribal, religious, and ethnic minority issues. Only 15 percent have been fights across national borders (Barnaby 1984). Rebellion, resistance, repression, terrorism, and warfare continue. Indeed, recent states have perpetrated some of history's bloodiest deeds.

Enforcement

All states have agents to enforce judicial decisions. Confinement requires jailers, and a death penalty calls for executioners. Agents of the state collect fines and confiscate property. These officials wield real power.

As a relatively new form of sociopolitical organization, states have competed successfully with less-complex societies throughout the world. Military organization helps states subdue neighboring nonstates, but this is not the only reason for the spread of state organization. Although states impose hardships, they also offer advantages. More obviously, they provide protection from outsiders and preserve internal order. By promoting internal peace, states enhance production. Their economies support massive, dense populations, which supply armies and colonists to promote expansion.

Fiscal Systems

A financial or **fiscal** system is needed in states to support rulers, nobles, officials, judges, military personnel, and thousands of other specialists. As in the chiefdom, the state intervenes in production, distribution, and consumption. The state may decree that a certain area will produce certain things or forbid certain activities in particular places. Although, like chiefdoms, states also have redistribution (through taxation), generosity and sharing are played down. A smaller proportion of what comes in flows back to the people.

In nonstates, people customarily share with relatives, but residents of states face added obligations to bureaucrats and officials. Citizens must turn over a substantial portion of what they produce to the state. Of the resources that the state collects, it reallocates part for the general good and uses another part (often larger) for the elite.

The state does not bring more freedom or leisure to the common people, who usually work harder than do the people in nonstates. They may be called on to build monumental public works. Some of these projects, such as dams and irrigation systems, may be economically necessary. However, people also build temples, palaces, and tombs for the elites.

Markets and trade are usually under at least some state control, with officials overseeing distribution and exchange, standardizing weights and measures, and collecting taxes on goods passing into or through the state. Taxes support

To handle disputes and crimes, all states, including Bermuda, shown here, have courts and judges. Does this photo say anything about cultural diffusion and/or colonialism?

government and the ruling class, which is clearly separated from the common people in regard to activities, privileges, rights, and obligations. Taxes also support the many specialists: administrators, tax collectors, judges, lawmakers, generals, scholars, and priests. As the state matures, the segment of the population freed from direct concern with subsistence grows.

The elites of archaic states reveled in the consumption of *sumptuary goods*: jewelry, exotic food and drink, and stylish clothing reserved for, or affordable only by, the rich. Peasants' diets suffered as they struggled to meet government demands. Commoners might perish in territorial wars that had little relevance to their own needs. Are any of these observations true of contemporary states?

SOCIAL CONTROL

Previous sections of this chapter have focused more on formal political organization than on political process. We've considered political regulation in various types of societies, using such convenient labels as *bands*, *tribes*, *chiefdoms*, and *states*. We've seen how the scale and strength of political systems have expanded over time and in relation to major economic changes, such as the origin and spread of food production. We've examined reasons why disputes arise and how they are settled in various types of society. We've looked at political decision making, including leaders and their limits. We've also recognized that all contemporary humans have been affected by states, colonialism, and the spread of the modern world system.

In this section we'll see that political systems have their more subtle and informal aspects along with their public and formal dimensions. In

Bringing It All Together

The "Bringing It All Together" essay that immediately follows the chapter on gender discusses the Basques, a minority population and imagined community split between, and subject to the governments of, two nation-states—France and Spain. States have to deal with the conflicting interests of diverse groups within their borders.

studying systems of domination—whether political, economic, religious, or cultural—we must pay attention not only to the formal institutions but to other forms of social control as well. Broader than the political is the concept of **social control,** which refers to "those fields of the social system (beliefs, practices, and institutions) that are most actively involved in the maintenance of any norms and the regulation of any conflict" (N. Kottak 2002, p. 290). (*Norms* are cultural standards or guidelines that enable individuals to distinguish between appropriate and inappropriate behavior.)

Hegemony

Antonio Gramsci (1971) developed the concept of **hegemony** for a stratified social order in which subordinates comply with domination by internalizing their rulers' values and accepting the "naturalness" of domination (this is the way things were meant to be). According to Pierre Bourdieu (1977, p. 164), every social order tries to make its own arbitrariness (including its mechanisms of control and oppression) seem natural. All hegemonic ideologies offer explanations about why the existing order is in everyone's interest. Often promises are made (things will get better if you're patient). Gramsci and others use the idea of hegemony to explain why people conform even when they are not forced to do so.

■ *Because of its costumed anonymity, Carnaval is an excellent arena for expressing normally suppressed speech. Here a man peeks out of the mouth of a giant mask during the parade of the São Clemente Samba school in Rio de Janeiro, Brazil, on March 1, 2003. Is there anything like Carnaval in your society?*

Both Bourdieu (1977) and Michel Foucault (1979) argue that it is easier and more effective to dominate people in their minds than to try to control their bodies. Besides, and often replacing, gross physical violence, industrial societies have devised more insidious forms of social control. These include various techniques of persuading and managing people and of monitoring and recording their beliefs, activities, and contacts. Can you think of some contemporary examples?

Hegemony, the internalization of a dominant ideology, is one way in which elites curb resistance and maintain power. Another way is to make subordinates believe they eventually will gain power—as young people usually foresee when they let their elders dominate them. Another way of curbing resistance is to separate or isolate people while supervising them closely, as is done in prisons. According to Foucault (1979), describing control over prisoners, solitary confinement is one effective way to get them to submit to authority.

Weapons of the Weak

The analysis of political systems also should consider the behavior that lies beneath the surface of evident, public behavior. In public, the oppressed may seem to accept their own domination, even as they question it offstage in private. James Scott (1990) uses **"public transcript"** to describe the open, public interactions between superordinates and subordinates—the outer shell of power relations. He uses **"hidden transcript"** to describe the critique of power that goes on offstage, where the power holders can't see it. In public, the elites and the oppressed observe the etiquette of power relations. The dominants act like haughty masters while their subordinates show humility and defer.

Often, situations that seem to be hegemonic do have active resistance, but it is individual and disguised rather than collective and defiant. James Scott (1985) uses Malay peasants, among whom he did field work, to illustrate small-scale acts of resistance—which he calls "weapons of the weak." The Malay peasants used an indirect strategy to resist an Islamic tithe (religious tax). Peasants were expected to pay the tithe, usually in the form of rice, which was sent to the provincial capital. In theory, the tithe would come back as charity, but it never did. Peasants didn't resist the tithe by rioting, demonstrating, or protesting. Instead they used a "nibbling" strategy, based on small acts of resistance. For example, they failed to declare their land or lied about the amount they farmed. They underpaid or delivered rice contaminated with water, rocks, or mud, to add weight. Because of this resistance, only 15 percent of what was due actually was paid (Scott 1990, p. 89).

Subordinates also use various strategies to resist *publicly,* but, again, usually in disguised form. Discontent may be expressed in public rituals and language, including metaphors, euphemisms, and folk tales. For example, trickster tales (like the Brer Rabbit stories told by slaves in the southern United States) celebrate the wiles of the weak as they triumph over the strong.

Resistance is most likely to be expressed openly when people are allowed to assemble. The hidden transcript may be publicly revealed on such occasions. People see their dreams and anger shared by others with whom they haven't been in direct contact. The oppressed may draw courage from the crowd, from its visual and emotional impact and its anonymity. Sensing danger, the elites discourage such public gatherings. They try to limit and control holidays, funerals, dances, festivals, and other occasions that might unite the oppressed. Thus, in the pre–Civil War era southern United States, gatherings of five or more slaves were forbidden unless a white person was present.

Factors that interfere with community formation—such as geographic, linguistic, and ethnic separation—also work to curb resistance. Consequently, southern U.S. plantation owners sought slaves with diverse cultural and linguistic backgrounds. Despite the measures used to divide them, the slaves resisted, developing their own popular culture, linguistic codes, and religious vision. The masters taught portions of the Bible that stressed compliance, but the slaves seized on the story of Moses, the promised land, and deliverance. The cornerstone of slave religion became the idea of a reversal in the conditions of whites and blacks. Slaves also resisted directly, through sabotage and flight. In many New World areas, slaves managed to establish free communities in the hills and other isolated areas (Price 1973).

Hidden transcripts tend to be expressed publicly at certain times (festivals and *Carnavals*) and in certain places (for example, markets). Because of its costumed anonymity, Carnaval is an excellent arena for expressing normally suppressed speech and aggression—antihegemonic discourse. (*Discourse* includes talk, speeches, gestures, and actions.) Carnavals celebrate freedom through immodesty, dancing, gluttony, and sexuality (DaMatta 1991). Carnaval may begin as a playful outlet for frustrations built up during the year. Over time, it may evolve into a powerful annual critique of stratification and domination and thus a threat to the established order (Gilmore 1987). (Recognizing that ceremonial license could turn into political defiance, the Spanish dictator Francisco Franco outlawed Carnaval.)

Politics, Shame, and Sorcery

We turn now to a case study of sociopolitical process, viewing it as part of a larger system of social control experienced by individuals in their everyday lives. No one today lives in an isolated band, tribe, chiefdom, or state. All groups studied by ethnographers, like the Makua to be discussed below, live in nation-states, where individuals have to deal with various levels and types of political authority, and experience other forms of social control.

Nicholas Kottak (2002) did an ethnographic field study of political systems, and social control more generally, among the rural Makua of northern Mozambique (Figure 8.5). He focused on three fields of social control: political, religious, and reputational systems. (Reputational systems have to do with the way various people are considered in the community—their reputations.) The significance of these fields emerged through conversations about social norms and crimes. Makua revealed their own ideas about social control most clearly in a discussion about stealing a neighbor's chicken.

Most Makua villagers have a makeshift chicken coop in a corner of the home. Chickens leave the coop before sunrise each day and wander in the surrounding area in search of scraps. Chickens usually return to their coop at dusk, but sometimes the chickens, often recently purchased ones, settle in

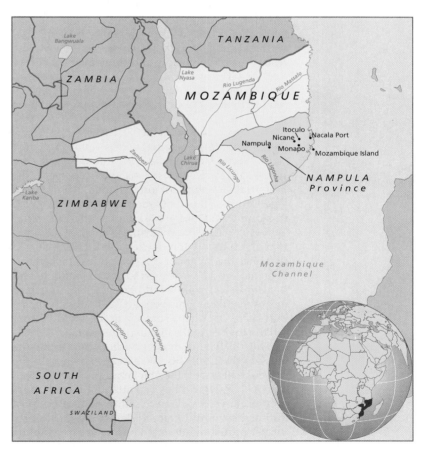

FIGURE 8.5 Location of the Makua and the village of Nicane in northern Mozambique. The province of Nampula shown here is Makua territory.

Nicholas Kottak (back center) attends a village meeting among the Makua of northern Mozambique. Two chiefs have called the meeting to renegotiate the boundaries of their political jurisdictions.

another villager's coop. Villagers worry about their chickens as mobile assets. Owners can't always be sure where their birds are roaming. Villagers may be tempted to steal a neighbor's chicken when its owner seems oblivious to its whereabouts.

The Makua have few material possessions and a meat-poor diet, making wandering chickens a temptation. As the Makua identified chicken wandering and the occasional chicken theft as community problems, Kottak began to draw out their ideas about social control—about why people did *not* steal their neighbor's chickens. The Makua responses coalesced around three main disincentives or sanctions: *ehaya* (shame), *enretthe* (sorcery attack), and *cadeia* (jail). (As used here, a *sanction* refers to a kind of punishment that follows a norm violation.)

According to Kottak (2002), each of these terms (jail, sorcery, and shame) refers to an imagined "social script," culminating in an undesirable consequence. *Cadeia* (jail), for instance, represents the potential last phase of an extended political and legal process (most violations are resolved before this point). When the Makua responded *enretthe* (sorcery), they were referring to another sequence that might follow the chicken theft. They believed that once the neighbor discovered his chicken had been stolen, he would go to a traditional healer (*mukulukhana*), who would direct a sorcery attack (*opaka enretthe*) on his behalf. The Makua believed that such a punitive sorcery attack would either kill the thief or make him extremely ill.

The third and most popular answer to the chicken theft question was *ehaya* (shame). In the *ehaya* social script, the chicken thief, having been discovered, would have to attend a formal, publicly organized village meeting, where political authorities would meet to determine the appropriate punishment and compensation. Makua were concerned not so much with the fine as with the intense shame or embarrassment they would feel as a confirmed chicken thief in the village

spotlight. The chicken thief also would experience an extended feeling of disgrace, also described as *ehaya*, from his or her knowledge of his or her now spoiled social identity or community reputation.

Living in a nation-state, the Makua have access to several types and levels of potential conflict resolution. A dispute between two people can quickly become a broader conflict between their respective matrilineal descent groups. (In a matrilineal descent group, kinship is calculated through females only—see the next chapter.) The heads of the disputing descent groups meet to resolve the matter. If they can't settle it (e.g., through financial compensation), the conflict moves to a state political authority. Intervention by this official can prevent the individual dispute from escalating into ongoing conflict between the descent groups (e.g., a blood feud, as described earlier in this chapter).

Mozambique has a history of colonialism (under Portugal), independence (achieved late, in 1975), and bloody civil war (1984–1992). Because of this history, its formal authorities have been split into two opposing political fields: the state-appointed and the more "traditional" authorities. Shortly after Mozambique's independence from Portugal, its ruling Marxist political party, *Frelimo*, handpicked a village secretary (*secretário*) for each village. Frelimo had launched a program of villagization, in which rural people were required to move from hamlets dispersed throughout the countryside into nucleated villages. Much of the rural Makua population was upset with both the forced villagization program and the new set of authorities. This resentment helped sustain Mozambique's civil war. After the war, Frelimo made significant efforts to work with the traditional authorities (*regulo, cabo,* and *capitão*)—political leaders whom Frelimo had initially accused of being "colonial collaborators" and alienated. The *regulo* is a territorial chief and succeeds to his political office through matrilineal descent (mother's brother to sister's son). Below him are *cabos,* and below them are *capitães.*

Few village conflicts go beyond the jurisdiction of the locality administrator (*ensatoro*)—an even higher political office that, according to the Makua, originated early in the colonial era. It is this locality administrator (*ensatoro*) who dispatches the police and periodically detains villagers. Thus, he explicitly has control over the state's use of force. Although *regulos* (traditional chiefs) increasingly meet directly with the *ensatoro, secretários* (recently appointed state officials) have even better relations with the *ensatoro.* Since access to force strengthens political authority, the *secretário*'s closer link to the *ensatoro* confers a degree of legitimacy. However, most villagers still rank the *regulo* higher in the political hierarchy than the *secretário* and prefer that he handle their conflicts and problems. The *regulo*'s legitimacy derives from the sanctity of the matrilineal principle of descent through which he holds office.

This combination of newer and more traditional offices constitutes the Makua's formal political system. This system, despite its duality, includes legitimate positions and officials and represents formal social control. This "political" part of the Makua social system has been explicitly or "formally" designated to handle conflict and crime. As has been discussed in previous sections of this chapter, anthropologists have tended to focus on the formal aspects of social control (i.e., the political field). But, like the Makua, anthropologists also recognize the importance of other fields of social control. When Nicholas Kottak asked Makua in one rural community about deterrents to theft, only 10 percent mentioned jail (the formal system), compared with the 73 percent who listed *ehaya* (shame) as the reason not to steal a neighbor's chicken.

Shame can be a powerful social sanction. Bronislaw Malinowski (1927) described how Trobriand Islanders might climb to the top of a palm tree and dive to their deaths because they couldn't tolerate the shame associated with public knowledge of some stigmatizing action, especially incest. Makua tell the story of a man rumored to have fathered a child with his stepdaughter. The political authorities imposed no formal sanctions (e.g., a fine or jail time) on this man, but gossip about the affair circulated widely. The gossip crystallized in the lyrics of a song that groups of young women would perform. When the man heard his name and alleged incestuous behavior mentioned in that song, he told a few people he was going to take a trip to the district capital. He was found a few hours later hanging by the neck from a mango tree on the village periphery. The reason for the man's suicide was self-evident to the Makua—"he felt too much *ehaya* (shame)." (Previously we saw the role of song in the social control system of the Inuit.)

Many anthropologists cite the importance of "informal" processes of social control, which include gossip, stigma, and shame, especially in small-scale societies such as the Makua (see Freilich, Raybeck, and Savishinsky 1991). Gossip, which can lead to shame, sometimes is used when a direct or formal sanction is risky or impossible (Herskovits 1937). Margaret Mead (1937) and Ruth Benedict (1946) distinguished between *shame* as an external sanction (i.e., forces set in motion by others) and *guilt* as an internal sanction, psychologically generated by the individual. They regarded shame as a more prominent form of social control in non-Western societies and guilt as a dominant emotional sanction in Western societies.

Of course, to be effective as a sanction, the prospect of being shamed or of shaming oneself must be internalized by the individual. For the Makua, potential shame is a powerful deterrent. Rural Makua tend to remain in or around one community for their entire lives. Such communities usually have fewer than a thousand people, so that residents can keep track of most community members' identities and reputations. According to Kottak (2002), the rural Makua monitor, transmit, and memorize the details of each other's identities with remarkable precision. Tight clustering of homes, markets, and schools facilitates the monitoring process. In this social environment, people try to avoid behavior that might spoil their reputations and alienate them from their native community.

Beliefs in sorcery also facilitate social control. (Religion as social control is discussed further in the chapter on religion.) Although the Makua constantly discuss the existence of sorcerers (*nikwiri*) and sorcery (*opaka enretthe*), they aren't explicit about who the sorcerers are. This identity ambiguity is coupled with a local theory of sorcery that strongly implicates malice, which everyone feels at some point. Having felt malice themselves, individual Makua probably experience moments of self-doubt about their own potential status as a sorcerer. And they recognize that others have similar feelings.

Beliefs in sorcery trigger anxieties about death, since the Makua think that a chicken thief will be the inevitable target of a vengeance sorcery attack. Local theories presume that sickness, social misfortune, and death are directly caused by malicious sorcery. Life expectancy is relatively short and infant mortality very high in a Makua village. Relatives drop dead suddenly from infectious diseases. Health, life, and existence are far more problematic than they are for most Westerners. Such uncertainty heightens the dramatic stakes associated with sorcery. Not just theft, but any conflict, is inherently dangerous because it could trigger a sorcery attack.

The following dialogue reported by Kottak (2002, p. 312) highlights the Makua's recognition of sorcery as a social control process.

Ethnographer: Why don't you steal your neighbor's chicken?

Informant: Huh? My neighbor's not short a chicken.

Ethnographer: No. I know. Your neighbor has a chicken. That chicken is always walking on your land. Sometimes it sleeps in your coop at night. Why don't you just take that chicken? What do you think is stopping you?

Informant: *Enretthe. Akwa.* (Sorcery. Death.)

The efficacy of social control depends on how clearly people envision the sanctions that an antisocial act might trigger. The Makua are well informed about norm violations, conflicts, and the sanctions that follow them. As we have seen, jail (*cadeia*), shame (*ehaya*), and sorcery (*enretthe*) are the main sanctions anticipated by the rural Makua.

This chapter began by quoting Fried's definition of political organization as comprising "those portions of social organization that specifically relate to the individuals or groups that manage the affairs of public policy" (Fried 1967, pp. 20–21). As I noted there, Fried's definition works nicely for nation-states but not so well for nonstate societies, where "public policy" is much harder to detect. For this reason, I claimed it was better to focus on sociopolitical organization in discussing the regulation of interrelations among individuals, groups, and their representatives. (Regulation, remember, is the process that corrects deviations from the norm, and thus maintains a system's integrity.) Such regulation, we have learned, is a process that extends beyond the political to other fields of social control, including religion and reputational systems, which involve an interplay of public opinion with social norms and sanctions internalized by the individual.

SUMMARY

1. One sociopolitical typology classifies societies as bands, tribes, chiefdoms, and states. Foragers tended to live in egalitarian band-organized societies. Personal networks linked individuals, families, and bands. Band leaders were first among equals, with no sure way to enforce decisions. Disputes rarely arose over strategic resources, which were open to all. Political authority and power tend to increase along with population and the scale of regulatory problems. More people mean more relations among individuals and groups to regulate. Increasingly complex economies pose further regulatory problems.

2. Heads of horticultural villages are local leaders with limited authority. They lead by example and persuasion. Big men have support and authority beyond a single village. They are regional regulators, but temporary ones. In organizing a feast, they mobilize labor from several villages. Sponsoring such events leaves them with little wealth but with prestige and a reputation for generosity.

3. Age and gender also can be used for regional political integration. Among North America's Plains Indians, men's associations (pantribal sodalities) organized raiding and buffalo hunting. Such men's associations tend to emphasize the warrior grade. They serve for offense and defense when there is intertribal raiding for animals. Among pastoralists, the degree of authority and political organization reflects population size and density, interethnic relations, and pressure on resources.

4. The state is an autonomous political unit that encompasses many communities. Its government collects taxes, drafts people for work and war, and decrees and enforces laws. The state is defined as a form of sociopolitical organization based on central government and social stratification—a division of society into classes. Early states are known as archaic, or nonindustrial, states, in contrast to modern industrial nation-states.

5. Unlike tribes, but like states, chiefdoms had permanent regional regulation and differential access to resources. But chiefdoms lacked stratification. Unlike states, but like bands and tribes, chiefdoms were organized by kinship, descent, and marriage. State formation did not occur, and only chiefdoms emerged in several areas, including the circum-Caribbean, lowland Amazonia, the southeastern United States, and Polynesia.

6. Weber's three dimensions of stratification are wealth, power, and prestige. In early states—for the first time in human history—contrasts in wealth, power, and prestige between entire groups of men and women came into being. A socioeconomic stratum includes people of both sexes and all ages. The superordinate—higher or elite—stratum enjoys privileged access to resources.

7. Certain systems are found in all states: population control, judiciary, enforcement, and fiscal. These are integrated by a ruling system or government composed of civil, military, and religious officials. States conduct censuses and demarcate boundaries. Laws are based on precedent and legislative

proclamations. Courts and judges handle disputes and crimes. A police force maintains internal order, and a military defends against external threats. A financial or fiscal system supports rulers, officials, judges, and other specialists.

8. *Hegemony* describes a stratified social order in which subordinates comply with domination by internalizing its values and accepting its "naturalness." Often, situations that appear hegemonic have resistance that is individual and disguised rather than collective and defiant. "Public transcript" refers to the open, public interactions between the dominators and the oppressed. "Hidden transcript" describes the critique of power that goes on offstage, where the power holders can't see it. Discontent also may be expressed in public rituals and language.

9. Broader than the political is the concept of social control—those fields of the social system most actively involved in the maintenance of norms and the regulation of conflict. Among the Makua of northern Mozambique, three such fields stand out: the political system (formal authority), religion (mainly involving fear of sorcery), and the reputational system (mainly involving avoidance of shame). Social control works best when people can clearly envision the sanctions that an antisocial act might trigger. The Makua are well informed about norm violations, conflicts, and the sanctions that follow them. Jail, shame, and sorcery attacks are the main sanctions anticipated by the rural Makua.

KEY TERMS

See the flash cards

mhhe.com/kottak

age set   Group uniting all men or women born during a certain time span; this group controls property and often has political and military functions.

big man   Regional figure found among tribal horticulturalists and pastoralists. The big man occupies no office but creates his reputation through entrepreneurship and generosity to others. Neither his wealth nor his position passes to his heirs.

chiefdom   Form of sociopolitical organization intermediate between the tribe and the state; kin-based with differential access to resources and a permanent political structure.

differential access   Unequal access to resources; basic attribute of chiefdoms and states. Superordinates have favored access to such resources, while the access of subordinates is limited by superordinates.

fiscal   Pertaining to finances and taxation.

head, village   A local leader in a tribal society who has limited authority, leads by example and persuasion, and must be generous.

hegemony   As used by Antonio Gramsci, a stratified social order in which subordinates comply with domination by internalizing its values and accepting its "naturalness."

hidden transcript   As used by James Scott, the critique of power by the oppressed that goes on offstage—in private—where the power holders can't see it.

law   A legal code, including trial and enforcement; characteristic of state-organized societies.

office   Permanent political position.

power   The ability to exercise one's will over others—to do what one wants; the basis of political status.

prestige   Esteem, respect, or approval for acts, deeds, or qualities considered exemplary.

public transcript   As used by James Scott, the open, public interactions between dominators and oppressed—the outer shell of power relations.

social control   Those fields of the social system (beliefs, practices, and institutions) that are most actively involved in the maintenance of norms and the regulation of conflict.

sodality, pantribal   A non-kin-based group that exists throughout a tribe, spanning several villages.

state   Sociopolitical organization based on central government and socioeconomic stratification—a division of society into classes.

stratification   Characteristic of a system with socioeconomic strata—groups that contrast in regard to social status and access to strategic resources. Each stratum includes people of both sexes and all ages.

subordinate   The lower, or underprivileged, group in a stratified system.

superordinate   The upper, or privileged, group in a stratified system.

tribe   Form of sociopolitical organization usually based on horticulture or pastoralism. Socioeconomic stratification and centralized rule are absent in tribes, and there is no means of enforcing political decisions.

wealth   All a person's material assets, including income, land, and other types of property; the basis of economic status.

CRITICAL THINKING QUESTIONS

For more self-testing, see the self-quizzes

mhhe.com/kottak

1. What's the rationale for using the term "socio-political organization" instead of "political organization"?

2. How do the political roles of village head and big man differ? Does your own society have figures comparable to big men?

3. What are sodalities? Does your society have them? Do you belong to any?

4. What conclusions do you draw from this chapter about the relationship between population density and political hierarchy?

5. What are the advantages and disadvantages of the state from the ordinary citizen's perspective?

SUGGESTED ADDITIONAL READINGS

Arnold, B., and B. Gibson, eds.
  1995 *Celtic Chiefdom, Celtic State.* New York: Cambridge University Press. This collection of articles examines the structure and development of Europe's prehistoric Celtic societies and debates whether they were chiefdoms or states.

Borneman, J.
  1998 *Subversions of International Order: Studies in the Political Anthropology of Culture.* Albany: State University of New York Press. Political culture, international relations, world politics, and national characteristics.

Chagnon, N. A.
  1997 *Yanomamö,* 5th ed. Fort Worth: Harcourt Brace. Most recent revision of a well-known account of the Yanomami, including their social organization, politics, warfare, and cultural change, and the crisis they now confront.

Cheater, A. P., ed.
  1999 *The Anthropology of Power: Empowerment and Disempowerment in Changing Structures.* New York: Routledge. Overcoming social marginality through participation and political mobilization in today's world.

Cohen, R., and E. R. Service, eds.
  1978 *Origins of the State: The Anthropology of Political Evolution.* Philadelphia: Institute for the Study of Human Issues. Several articles on state formation in many areas.

Earle, T. K.
  1997 *How Chiefs Come to Power: The Political Economy in Prehistory.* Stanford, CA: Stanford University Press. Political succession and the economic basis of power in chiefdoms.

Ferguson, R. B.
  1995 *Yanomami Warfare: A Political History.* Santa Fe, NM: School of American Research. From village raiding to incursions from nation-states.
  2002 *State, Identity, and Violence: Political Disintegration in the Post–Cold War Era.* New York: Routledge. Political relations, the state, ethnic relations, and violence.

Fry, D. P.
  2006 *The Human Potential for Peace: An Anthropological Challenge to Assumptions about War and Violence.* New York: Oxford University Press. Is war inevitable?

Gledhill, J.
  2000 *Power and Its Disguises: Anthropological Perspectives on Politics.* Sterling, VA: Pluto Press. The anthropology of power.

Heider, K. G.
  1997 *Grand Valley Dani: Peaceful Warriors,* 3rd ed. Fort Worth: Harcourt Brace. Comprehensive and readable account of a tribal group on the island of New Guinea, now under Indonesian rule.

Kelly, R. C.
  2000 *Warless Societies and the Origin of War.* Ann Arbor, MI: University of Michigan Press. An anthropologist looks at stateless societies in Papua New Guinea to reconstruct the origins of warfare.

Kirch, P. V.
  1984 *The Evolution of the Polynesian Chiefdoms.* Cambridge: Cambridge University Press. Diversity and sociopolitical complexity in native Oceania.

Kurtz, D. V.
  2001 *Political Anthropology: Power and Paradigms.* Boulder, CO: Westview. Up-to-date treatment of the field of political anthropology.

Otterbein, K.
  2005 *How War Began.* College Station: Texas A&M University Press. The origins of war discussed in terms of human evolution, prehistory, and cross-cultural comparison.

Vincent, J., ed.
  2002 *The Anthropology of Politics: A Reader in Ethnography, Theory, and Critique.* Malden, MA: Blackwell. Basic and classic articles in political anthropology.

Wolf, E. R., with S. Silverman
  2001 *Pathways of Power: Building an Anthropology of the Modern World.* Berkeley: University of California Press. Political and social identity and power in the modern world.

1. Subsistence and Status: Go to the Ethnographic Atlas Cross-tabulations page, **http://lucy.ukc. ac.uk/cgi-bin/uncgi/Ethnoatlas/atlas.vopts**. This site has compiled ethnographic information on many different groups, and you can use the tools provided to cross-tabulate the prevalence of certain traits. Under "Select Row Category" choose "subsistence economy," and under "Select Column Category" select "class stratification, prevailing type." Press the Submit Query button. This table shows the frequency of class stratification among groups with different subsistence strategies.
   a. What kinds of subsistence strategies are most common among groups with "Complex" class stratification? Do any of these groups use hunting, gathering, or fishing as the primary means of feeding themselves?
   b. Is any one subsistence strategy predominant among groups with "Absence among freemen" class stratification (egalitarian)?
   c. Looking at the table, which of the following statements is (are) true: All societies with complex class stratification are agriculturalists. All agriculturalists have complex class stratification. No societies that practice hunting, fishing, and gathering have complex class stratification. All hunting, fishing, and gathering societies have class stratification absent among freemen (egalitarian).

2. Read the Mesa Community College page on "A Look at a Bigman: Bougainville," **http://www. mc.maricopa.edu/dept/d10/asb/anthro2003/ glues/bigman/mumi.html**, and the "35 Key Rules for Bougainville Bigmen," **http://www. mc.maricopa.edu/dept/d10/asb/anthro2003/ glues/bigman/rules.html**.

a. Where is Bougainville? What is the environment like? What are the main sources of food?
b. What is a *mumi*? How does one become a *mumi*? What role do feasts play in determining who is a *mumi*? How important are friends and family for an aspiring *mumi*?
c. What other statuses exist in Bougainville society for men?
d. After reading the rules for a bigman, does the life of a bigman appear to be a life of leisure or does it involve a lot of work?

3. In the year 2000, the field of anthropology was jolted by the announcement of the publication of a book called *Darkness in El Dorado* by the journalist Patrick Tierney (New York: W. W. Norton, 2000). The book contained accusations of inappropriate, unethical, and perhaps even criminal behavior by scientists who had studied the Yanomami Indians of Brazil and Venezuela since the late 1960s.
   a. For a brief account of the controversy, check out **dir.salon.com/books/feature/2000/09/ 28/yanomamo/index.html**.
   b. Visit the website "The Anthropological Niche of Douglas W. Hume," **http://members.aol. com/archaeodog/darkness_in_el_dorado/ index.htm**. This website is dedicated to providing one place to find all information about Patrick Tierney's *Darkness in El Dorado*. Follow its various links for different accounts of the controversy.
   c. What do you make of the controversy? Is it possible to choose sides from the information you have examined?
   d. What are the larger ethical issues raised by the furor surrounding Tierney's book?

See Chapter 8 at your McGraw-Hill Online Learning Center for additional review and interactive exercises.

INTERNET EXERCISES

Kottak, *Assault on Paradise*, 4th ed.

Read Chapters 5, 9, and 14 for changes in Arembepe's political organization and orientation from the 1960s through the present. What have been the major changes? Has anything remained the same? Describe Arembepe's patronage system during the 1960s. As discussed in Chapter 5, how does patron-clientship differ from patron-dependency? Have there been leaders in Arembepe? If so, describe their roles and spheres of influence and compare them with the band and tribal leaders discussed in this chapter of the text.

Peters-Golden, *Culture Sketches*, 4th ed.

This text chapter has discussed the formal and informal leadership roles found in various societies, among them that of the "big man." In *Culture Sketches* read Chapter 8, "Kapauku: New Guinea 'Capital-

ists.'" An important role in Kapauku society is that of the *tonowi*, a "big man." How is this leadership role related to the other key features of Kapauku society, such as individualism and economics?

Knauft, *The Gebusi*, 1st ed.

Based on information in Chapter 3 of *The Gebusi*, who was the person most responsible for organizing and orchestrating the community's response to the death of Daguwa? How did this person exert influence or authority, and in what ways did he or did he not serve as a political leader? How does the Gebusi political structure differ from that in societies that have formal leaders, chiefs, and/or class stratification? Although Gebusi politics are decentralized, important status inequalities still remain. What are the greatest social inequalities in Gebusi society? Who has more power, and who has less?

LINKAGES

Families, Kinship, and Descent

FAMILIES

The kinds of societies anthropologists have studied traditionally, such as the Barí discussed in the "News Brief," have stimulated a strong interest in families, along with larger systems of kinship, descent, and marriage. Cross-culturally, the social construction of kinship illustrates considerable diversity. Understanding kinship systems has become an essential part of anthropology because of the importance of those systems to the people we study. We are ready to take a closer look at the systems of kinship and descent that have organized human life during much of our history.

Ethnographers quickly recognize social divisions—groups—within any society they study. During field work, they learn about significant groups by observing their activities and composition. People often live in the same village or neighborhood or work, pray, or celebrate together because they are related in some way. To understand the social structure, an ethnographer must investigate such kin ties. For example, the most significant local groups may consist of descendants of the same grandfather. These people may live in neighboring houses, farm adjoining fields, and help each other in everyday tasks. Other sorts of groups, based on different or more distant kin links, get together less often.

The nuclear family is one kind of kin group that is widespread in human societies. The nuclear family consists of parents and children, normally living together in the same household. Other kin groups include extended families (families consisting of three or more generations) and descent groups—lineages and clans. Such groups are not usually residentially based as the nuclear family is. Extended family members get together from time to time, but they don't necessarily live together. Branches of a given descent group may reside in several villages and rarely assemble for common activity. Descent groups, which are composed of people claiming common ancestry, are basic units in the social organization of nonindustrial food producers.

Nuclear and Extended Families

A nuclear family lasts only as long as the parents and children remain together. Most people belong to at least two nuclear families at different times in their lives. They are born into a family consisting of their parents and siblings. When they reach adulthood, they may marry and establish a nuclear family that includes the spouse and eventually the children. Since most societies permit divorce, some people establish more than one family through marriage.

Anthropologists distinguish between the **family of orientation** (the family in which one is born and grows up) and the **family of procreation** (formed when one marries and has children). From the individual's point of view, the critical relationships are with parents and siblings in the family of orientation and with spouse and children in the family of procreation.

In most societies, relations with nuclear family members (parents, siblings, and children) take precedence over relations with other kin. Nuclear family organization is very widespread but not universal, and its significance in society differs greatly from one place to another. In a few societies, such as the classic Nayar case described below, nuclear families are rare or nonexistent. In others, the nuclear family plays no special role in social life. The nuclear family is not always the

■ Siblings play a prominent role in child rearing in many societies. Here, in China's Yunnan province, two sisters give their younger brother a drink of water from a folded leaf. Do your siblings belong to your family of orientation or your family of procreation?

OVERVIEW

Especially in nonindustrial societies, kinship, descent, and marriage are basic social building blocks, linking individuals and groups in a common social system. Kin groups, such as families and descent groups, are social units whose members can be identified and whose residence patterns and activities can be observed. A nuclear family, for instance, consists of a married couple and their children, living together. Although nuclear families are widespread among the world's societies, other social forms, such as extended families and descent groups, can complement, overshadow, or even replace the nuclear family. Contemporary industrial North America features diverse and changing family, household, and living arrangements, including nuclear families, single-parent households, and expanded family households. Descent groups, typically found among nonindustrial food producers, have perpetuity—they last for generations. Descent groups include lineages and clans, with patrilineal or matrilineal membership rules. Kinship terminologies are ways of classifying one's relatives based on perceived differences and similarities. Worldwide, there are four basic systems for classifying kin on the parental generation.

When Are Two Dads Better Than One?
When the Women Are in Charge

UNIVERSITY OF EAST LONDON NEWS BRIEF

by Patrick Wilson

June 12, 2002

The kinds of societies that anthropologists have studied traditionally, such as the Barí of Venezuela described in this news story, have stimulated a strong interest in families, along with larger systems of kinship, descent, and marriage. This chapter surveys the varied kinship systems that have organized human life for much of our history. Like race, kinship is socially constructed. Cultures develop their own explanations for biological processes, such as the role of insemination in the creation and growth of a human embryo. Scientifically informed people know that fertilization of an ovum by a single sperm is responsible for conception. But other cultures, including the Barí and their neighbors, hold different views about procreation. In some societies it is believed that spirits, rather than men, place babies in women's wombs. In others it is believed that a fetus must be nourished by continuing insemination during pregnancy. In the societies discussed here people believe that multiple men can create the same fetus. When a baby is born, the Barí mother names the men she recognizes as fathers, and they assist her in raising the child. The realm of cultural diversity contains much more than contemporary North American notions of marriage and the family. In the United States, having two dads may be the result of divorce, remarriage, stepparenthood, or a same-sex union. In the societies discussed here, multiple (partible) paternity is a common and beneficial social fact.

[A mong] the Barí people of Venezuela, . . . multiple paternity is the norm . . . In such societies, children with more than one official father are more likely to survive to adulthood than those with just one Dad . . . The findings have . . . been published in a book, *Cultures of Multiple Fathers: The Theory and Practice of Partible Paternity in Lowland South America* [Beckerman and Valentine 2002], that questions accepted theories about social organization, the balance of power between the sexes and human evolution.

[The book] . . . draws on more than two decades of fieldwork among South American tribal peoples. The central theme . . . is the concept of partible paternity—the widespread belief that fertilization is not a one-time event and that more than one father can contribute to the developing embryo . . .

The authors have discovered a strong correlation between the status of women in the society and the benefits of multiple paternity . . . Among the Barí, 80% of children with two or more official dads survive to adulthood, compared with 64% with one father. This contrasts with male-dominated cultures such as the neighboring Curripaco, where children of doubtful parentage are outcast and frequently die young.

Explaining the significance of this discovery, Paul Valentine said: "The conventional view of the male-

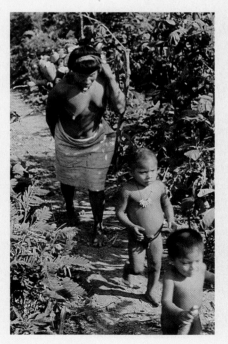

■ *The Barí of Venezuela believe that a child can have multiple fathers.*

female bargain is that a man will provide food and shelter for a woman and her children if he can be assured that the children are biologically his. Our research turns this idea on its head . . . In societies where women control marriages and other aspects of social life, both men and women have multiple partners and spread the responsibilities of child rearing." It is of course scientifically impossible to have more than one biological father, but aboriginal peoples in South America, Africa and Australasia [Australia and Asia] believe that it takes more than one act of intercourse to make a baby. In some of these societies, nearly all children have multiple fathers. In others, while partible paternity is accepted, socially the child has only one father. However, in the middle are groups where some children do have multiple fathers and some do not. In this case, the children can be compared to see how having more than one father benefits the children—and generational studies show that the children do benefit from the extra care.

When a child is born among the Barí, the mother publicly announces the names of the one or more men she believes to be the fathers, who, if they accept paternity, are expected to provide care for the mother and child . . . "In small egalitarian societies, women's interests are best served if mate choice is a non-binding, female decision; if a network of multiple females to aid or substitute for a woman in her mothering responsibilities exists; if multiple men support a woman and her children; and if a woman is shielded from the effects of male sexual jealousy." . . .

In cultures where women choose their mates, women have broad sexual freedom and partible paternity is accepted, women clearly have the upper hand. In Victorian-style societies where women's sexual activity is controlled by men, marriage is exclusive and male sexual jealousy is a constant threat, men have the upper hand. In between is a full range of combinations and options, all represented in the varying South American cultures . . .

Robert Carneiro, curator at the American Museum of Natural History, said: "Rarely does a book thrust open a door, giving us a striking new view. It has long been known that . . . peoples around the world believe that one act of sexual intercourse is not enough for a child to be born. Now for the first time we

have a volume that deals with the consequences and ramifications of this belief, and it does so in exhaustive and fascinating detail." . . .

SOURCE: AlphaGalileo: the Internet Press Center for European Science and the Arts. http://www.alphagalileo.org/index.cfm?f useaction=readRelease&Releaseid=9918.

---

basis of residence or authority organization. Other social units—most notably descent groups and extended families—can assume many of the functions otherwise associated with the nuclear family.

Consider an example from the former Yugoslavia. Traditionally, among the Muslims of western Bosnia (Lockwood 1975), nuclear families lacked autonomy. Several such families were embedded in an extended family household called a *zadruga*. The *zadruga* was headed by a male household head and his wife, the senior woman. It also included married sons and their wives and children, and unmarried sons and daughters. Each nuclear family had a sleeping room, decorated and partly furnished from the bride's trousseau. However, possessions—even clothing items—were freely shared by *zadruga*

members. Even trousseau items were appropriated for use elsewhere. Such a residential unit is known as a *patrilocal* extended family, because each couple resides in the husband's father's household after marriage.

The *zadruga* took precedence over its component units. Social interaction was more usual among women, men, or children than between spouses or between parents and children. Larger households ate at three successive settings: for men, women, and children. Traditionally, all children over 12 slept together in boys' or girls' rooms. When a woman wished to visit another village, she sought the permission of the male *zadruga* head. Although men usually felt closer to their own children than to those of their brothers, they were obliged to treat them equally. Children were disciplined by any adult in the household. When a nuclear family broke up, children under seven went with the mother. Older children could choose between their parents. Children were considered part of the household where they were born even if their mother left. One widow who remarried had to leave her five children, all over seven, in their father's *zadruga*, now headed by his brother.

Another example of an alternative to the nuclear family is provided by the Nayars (or Nair), a large and powerful caste on the Malabar

This just-married Khasi couple poses (in 1997) in India's northeastern city of Shillong. The Khasis are matrilineal, tracing descent through women and taking their maternal ancestors' surnames. Women choose their husbands; family incomes are pooled, and extended family households are managed by older women.

 STUDENT CD-ROM LIVING ANTHROPOLOGY

Tradition Meets Law: Families of China
Track 9

This clip exposes the conflict between traditional family structures and beliefs in China and the governmental policy allowing only one child per family. The Chinese view that boys are more valuable than girls has led to a widespread pattern of aborting females or abandoning them as infants. This has produced a sharp imbalance in the number of males and females. How large is the imbalance in Hunan province? Why are boys so valuable? What happens to people who choose to have more than one child? Do you think Chinese women will become more valued as the new generation reaches marriageable age?

Coast of southern India (Figure 9.1). Their traditional kinship system was matrilineal (descent traced only through females). Nayar lived in matrilineal extended family compounds called *tarawads*. The *tarawad* was a residential complex with several buildings, its own temple, granary, water well, orchards, gardens, and land holdings. Headed by a senior woman, assisted by her brother, the *tarawad* housed her siblings, sisters' children, and other matrikin—matrilineal relatives (Gough 1959; Shivaram 1996).

Traditional Nayar marriage seems to have been hardly more than a formality—a kind of coming of age ritual. A young woman would go through a marriage ceremony with a man, after which they might spend a few days together at her *tarawad*. Then the man would return to his own *tarawad*, where he lived with his sisters, aunts, and other matrikin. Nayar men belonged to a warrior class, who left home regularly for military expeditions, returning permanently to their *tarawad* on retirement. Nayar women could have multiple sexual partners. Children became members of the mother's *tarawad*; they were not considered to be relatives of their biological father. Indeed, many Nayar children didn't even know who their genitor was. Child care was the responsibility of the *tarawad*. Nayar society therefore reproduced itself biologically without the nuclear family.

Industrialism and Family Organization

For many Americans and Canadians, the nuclear family is the only well-defined kin group. Family isolation arises from geographic mobility, which is associated with industrialism, so that a nuclear family focus is characteristic of many modern nations. Born into a family of orientation, North Americans leave home for work or college, and the break with parents is under way. Eventually most North Americans marry and start a family of procreation. Because less than 3 percent of the U.S. population now farms, most people aren't tied to the land. Selling our labor on the market, we often move to places where jobs are available.

Many married couples live hundreds of miles from their parents. Their jobs have determined where they live. Such a postmarital residence pattern is called **neolocality:** Married couples are expected to establish a new place of residence—a "home of their own." Among middle-class North Americans, neolocal residence is both a cultural preference and a statistical norm. Most middle-class Americans eventually establish households and nuclear families of their own.

Within stratified nations, value systems vary to some extent from class to class, and so does kinship. There are significant differences between middle-class and poorer North Americans. For example, in the lower class the incidence of

FIGURE 9.1 Location of the Nayars in India's Kerala province.

■ An extended Navajo family outside a traditional hogan on a Navajo reservation in Arizona.

expanded family households (those that include non-nuclear relatives) is greater than it is in the middle class. When an expanded family household includes three or more generations, it is an **extended family household,** such as the *zadruga*. Another type of expanded family is the *collateral household*, which includes siblings and their spouses and children.

In contemporary North America, single-parent families are increasing at a rapid rate. In 1960, 88 percent of American children lived with both parents, compared with 68 percent today. This divorced mom, Valerie Jones, is enjoying a candlelight dinner with her kids. What do you see as the main differences between nuclear families and single-parent families?

The higher proportion of expanded family households among poorer Americans has been explained as an adaptation to poverty (Stack 1975). Unable to survive economically as nuclear family units, relatives band together in an expanded household and pool their resources. Adaptation to poverty causes kinship values and attitudes to diverge from middle-class norms. Thus, when North Americans raised in poverty achieve financial success, they often feel obligated to provide financial help to a wide circle of less fortunate relatives (see "Interesting Issues" on p. 216).

Changes in North American Kinship

Although the nuclear family remains a cultural ideal for many Americans, Table 9.1 and Figure 9.2 show that nuclear families accounted for just 23 percent of American households in 2003–2004. Other domestic arrangements now outnumber the "traditional" American household more than four to one. There are several reasons for this changing household composition. Women increasingly are joining men in the cash work force. This often removes them from their family of orientation while making it economically feasible to delay marriage. Furthermore, job demands compete with romantic attachments. The median age at first marriage for American women rose from 21 years in 1970 to 25 in 2003. For men the comparable ages were 23 and 27 (Fields 2004).

Also, the U.S. divorce rate has risen, making divorced Americans much more common today than they were in 1970. Between 1970 and 2003 the number of divorced Americans quintupled—some 22 million in 2003 versus 4.3 million in 1970. (Note, however, that each divorce creates two divorced people.) Table 9.2 shows the ratio of divorces to marriages in the United States for selected years between 1950 and 2003. The major jump in the American divorce rate took place between 1960 and 1980. During that period the ratio of divorces to marriage doubled. Since 1980 the ratio has stayed the same, around 50 percent. That is, each year there are about half as many new divorces as there are new marriages.

The rate of growth in single-parent families also has outstripped population growth, quadrupling from fewer than 4 million in 1970 to more than 16 million in 2003. (The overall American population in 2003 was 1.4 times its size in 1970.) The percentage of children living in fatherless (mother-headed, no resident dad) households in 2003 was more than

TABLE 9.1   Changes in Family and Household Organization in the United States: 1970 versus 2004

	1970	2004
Numbers:		
Total number of households	63 million	112 million
Number of people per household	3.1	2.6
Percentages:		
Married couples with children	40%	23%
Family households	81%	68%
Households with five or more people	21%	10%
People living alone	17%	26%
Percentage of single-mother families	5%	12%
Percentage of single-father families	0%	4%
Households with own children under 18	45%	32%

SOURCES: From U.S. Census data in J. M. Fields, "America's Families and Living Arrangements: 2003," *Current Population Reports*, P20-553, November 2004. http://www.census.gov/prod/2004pubs/p20-553.pdf, p. 4; J. M. Fields and L. M. Casper, "America's Families and Living Arrangements: Population Characteristics, 2000," *Current Population Reports*, P20-537, June 2001. http://www.census.gov/prod/2001pubs/p20-537.pdf; U.S. Census Bureau, *Statistical Abstract of the United States 2006*, Tables 55, 56, and 65. http://www.census.gov/prod/www/statistical_abstract.html.

Americans are supposed to love their parents, their siblings, their spouse, and especially their children. Many, perhaps most, of us would agree that "family" is very important, but just how important is kinship in our lives? How might one answer such a question? In nonindustrial societies, people are with their kin *all the time*—at home, at work, at play, in the village, in the fields, with the herds. Contemporary North Americans, by contrast, typically spend our days—weekdays at least—with people we don't love, and may not even like. We have to do balancing acts to be with our families as we also fulfill work demands. How different were TV's leisured Harriet Nelson and Carol Brady from the harried physicians of NBC's medical drama *ER* and all the other TV parents who struggle to maintain family responsibilities even as work demands compete for their time.

How did your parents manage their work/family responsibilities? It's statistically probable that both of your parents worked outside the home at least part of the time you were growing up. It's also likely that your mother, even if she had the higher-paying job, spent more time on child care and home care than your father did. Did your family of orientation illustrate the rule, or was it an exception to it? Do you think it will be different in your household if you form a family of procreation? Why or why not?

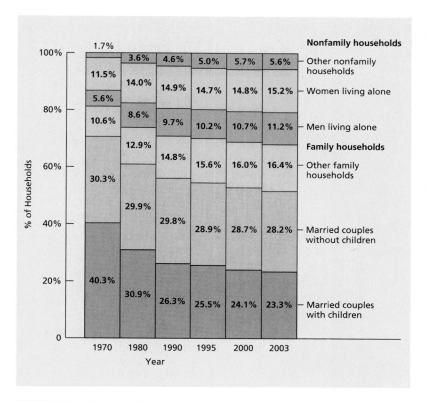

FIGURE 9.2 Households by Type: Selected Years, 1970 to 2003 (percent distribution).

SOURCE: U.S. Census Bureau, *Current Population Survey,* March and Annual Social and Economic Supplements: 1970 to 2003; J. M. Fields, "America's Families and Living Arrangements: 2003," *Current Population Reports,* P20-553, November 2004. http://www.census.gov/prod/2004pubs/p20-553.pdf, p. 4.

TABLE 9.2 Ratio of Divorces to Marriages per 1,000 U.S. Population, Selected Years, 1950–2003

1950	1960	1970	1980	1990	2000	2003
23%	26%	33%	50%	48%	49%	51%

SOURCES: U.S. Census Bureau, *Statistical Abstract of the United States 2006,* Tables 71, p. 64. http://www.census.gov/prod/www/statistical_abstract.html.

twice the 1970 rate, while the percentage in motherless (father-headed, no resident mom) homes increased fivefold. About 57 percent of American women and 60 percent of American men were currently married in 2004, versus 60 and 65 percent, respectively, in 1970 (Fields 2004; Fields and Casper 2001). To be sure, contemporary Americans maintain social lives through work, friendship, sports, clubs, religion, and organized social activities. However, the growing isolation from kin that these figures suggest may well be unprecedented in human history.

Table 9.3 documents similar changes in family and household size in the United States and Canada between 1975 and 2003. Those figures confirm a general trend toward smaller families and living units in North America. This trend is also detectable in Western Europe and other industrial nations.

The entire range of kin attachments is narrower for North Americans, particularly those in the middle class, than it is for nonindustrial peoples. Although we recognize ties to grandparents, uncles, aunts, and cousins, we have less contact with, and depend less on, those relatives than people in other cultures do. We see this when we answer a few questions: Do we know exactly how we are related to all our cousins? How much do we know about our ancestors, such as their full names and where they lived? How many of the people with whom we associate regularly are our relatives?

Differences in the answers to these questions by people from industrial and those from nonindustrial societies confirm the declining importance of kinship in contemporary nations. Immigrants are often shocked by what they perceive as weak kinship bonds and lack of proper

TABLE 9.3 Household and Family Size in the United States and Canada, 1980 versus 2004

	1980	2004
Average family size:		
United States	3.3	3.1
Canada	3.4	3.0
Average household size:		
United States	2.9	2.6
Canada	2.9	2.6

SOURCES: J. M. Fields, "America's Families and Living Arrangements: 2003," *Current Population Reports*, P20-553, November 2004. http://www.census.gov/prod/2004pubs/p20-553.pdf, pp. 3–4. U.S. Census Bureau, *Statistical Abstract of the United States, 2004–5*; Statistics Canada, 2001 Census. http://www.statcan.ca/english/Pgdb/famil53a.htm, http://www.statcan.ca/english/Pgdb/famil40a.htm.

respect for family in contemporary North America. In fact, most of the people whom middle-class North Americans see every day are either nonrelatives or members of the nuclear family. On the other hand, Stack's (1975) study of welfare-dependent families in a ghetto area of a midwestern city showed that sharing with non-nuclear relatives is an important strategy that the urban poor use to adapt to poverty.

One of the most striking contrasts between the United States and Brazil, the two most populous nations of the Western Hemisphere, is in the meaning and role of the family. Contemporary North American adults usually define their families as consisting of their husbands or wives and their children. However, when middle-class Brazilians talk about their families, they mean their parents, siblings, aunts, uncles, grandparents, and cousins. Later they add their children, but rarely the husband or wife, who has his or her own family. The children are shared by the two families. Because middle-class Americans lack an extended family support system, marriage assumes more importance. The husband–wife relationship is supposed to take precedence over either spouse's relationship with his or her own parents. This places a significant strain on North American marriages.

Living in a less mobile society, Brazilians stay in closer contact with their relatives, including members of the extended family, than North Americans do. Residents of Rio de Janeiro and São Paulo, two of South America's largest cities, are reluctant to leave those urban centers to live away from family and friends. Brazilians find it hard to imagine, and unpleasant to live in, social worlds without relatives. Contrast this with a characteristic American theme: learning to live with strangers.

The Family among Foragers

Populations with foraging economies are far removed from industrial societies in terms of social complexity, but they do feature geographic mobility, which is associated with nomadic or seminomadic hunting and gathering. Here again the nuclear family is often the most significant kin group, although in no foraging society is the nuclear family the only group based on kinship. The two basic social units of traditional foraging societies are the nuclear family and the band.

Unlike middle-class couples in industrial nations, foragers don't usually reside neolocally. Instead, they join a band in which either the husband or the wife has relatives. However, couples and families may move from one band to another several times. Although nuclear families are ultimately as impermanent among foragers as they are in any other society, they are usually more stable than bands are.

Many foraging societies lacked year-round band organization. The Native American Shoshoni of the Great Basin in Utah, Nevada, Idaho, and Wyoming (Figure 9.3) provide an example. The resources available to the Shoshoni were so meager that for most of the year families traveled alone through the countryside hunting and gathering. In certain seasons families assembled to hunt cooperatively as a band; after just a few months together they dispersed.

In neither industrial nor foraging societies are people tied permanently to the land. The mobility and the emphasis on small, economically self-sufficient family units promote the nuclear family as a basic kin group in both types of societies.

DESCENT

We've seen that the nuclear family is important in industrial nations and among foragers. The analogous group among nonindustrial food producers is the descent group. A **descent group** is a permanent social unit whose members say they have ancestors in common. Descent-group members believe they share, and descend from, those common ancestors. The group endures even though its membership changes, as members are born and die, move in and move out. Often, descent-group membership is determined at birth and is lifelong. In this case, it is an ascribed status.

Descent Groups

Descent groups frequently are exogamous (members must seek their mates from other descent groups). Two common rules serve to admit certain people as descent-group members while excluding others. With a rule of **matrilineal descent**, people join the mother's group automatically at birth and stay members throughout life. Matrilineal descent groups therefore include only the children of the group's women. (For a discussion of the prominence of matrilineal descent in early anthropological theory, see Appendix 1.) With **patrilineal descent,** people automatically have lifetime membership in the father's group. The children of all the group's men join the group, but the children of the female members of that group are excluded. (In Figures 9.4 and 9.5, which show matrilineal and patrilineal descent groups, respectively, the triangles stand for males and the circles for females.) Matrilineal and patrilineal descent are types of **unilineal descent.** This means the descent rule uses one line only, either the male or the female line. Patrilineal descent is much more common than is matrilineal descent. In a sample of 564 societies (Murdock 1957), about three times as many were found to be patrilineal (247 to 84).

Descent groups may be **lineages** or **clans.** Common to both is the belief that members descend from the same *apical ancestor.* That person stands at the apex, or top, of the common genealogy. For example, Adam and Eve, according to the Bible, are the apical ancestors of all humanity. Since Eve is said to have come from Adam's rib, Adam stands as the original apical ancestor for the patrilineal genealogies laid out in the Bible.

How do lineages and clans differ? A lineage uses *demonstrated descent.* Members can recite the names of their forebears in each generation from the apical ancestor through the present. (This doesn't mean their recitations are accurate, only that lineage members think they are.) In the Bible the litany of men who "begat" other men is a demonstration of genealogical descent for a large patrilineage that ultimately includes Jews and Arabs (who share Abraham as their last common apical ancestor).

Unlike lineages, clans use *stipulated descent.* Clan members merely say they descend from the apical ancestor. They don't try to trace the actual genealogical links between themselves and that ancestor. The Betsileo of Madagascar have both clans and lineages. Descent may be demonstrated for the most recent 8 to 10 generations, then stipulated for the more remote past—sometimes with mermaids and vaguely defined foreign royalty mentioned among the founders (Kottak 1980). Like the Betsileo, many societies have both lineages and clans. In such a case, clans have more members and cover a larger geographic area than lineages do. Sometimes a clan's apical ancestor is not a human at all but an animal or plant (called a *totem*). Whether human or not, the ancestor symbolizes the social unity and identity of the members, distinguishing them from other groups.

The economic types that usually have descent group organization are horticulture, pastoralism,

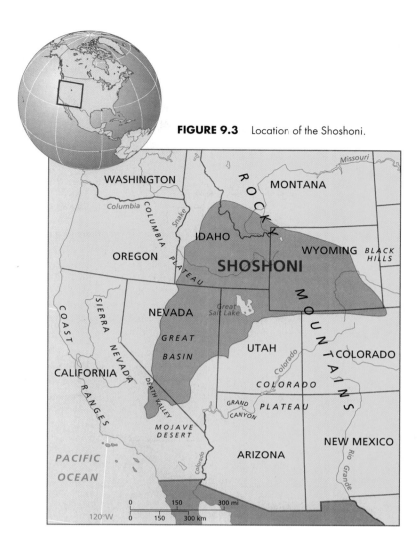

FIGURE 9.3 Location of the Shoshoni.

and agriculture, as discussed in Chapter 16 "Making a Living." Such societies tend to have several descent groups. Any one of them may be confined to a single village, but they usually span more than one village. Any branch of a descent group that lives in one place is a *local descent group.* Two or more local branches of different descent groups may live in the same village. Descent groups in the same village or different villages may establish alliances through frequent intermarriage.

Lineages, Clans, and Residence Rules

As we've seen, descent groups, unlike nuclear families, are permanent and enduring units, with new members added in every generation. Members have access to the lineage estate, where some of them must live, in order to benefit from and manage that estate across the generations. To endure, descent groups need to keep at least some of their members at home, on the ancestral estate. An easy way to do this is to have a rule

Bringing It All Together

For information on kinship in a European peasant society, see the "Bringing It All Together" essay on the Basques that immediately follows the chapter on gender.

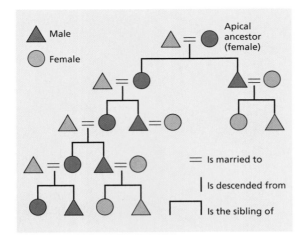

FIGURE 9.4 A Matrilineage Five Generations Deep.
Matrilineages are based on demonstrated descent from a female ancestor. Only the children of the group's women (blue) belong to the matrilineage. The children of the group's men are excluded; they belong to their mother's matrilineage.

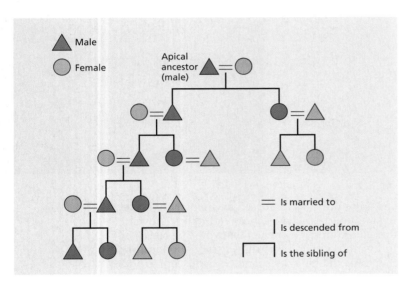

FIGURE 9.5 A Patrilineage Five Generations Deep.
Lineages are based on demonstrated descent from a common ancestor. With patrilineal descent, children of the group's men (blue) are included as descent-group members. Children of the group's female members are excluded; they belong to their father's patrilineage. Also notice lineage exogamy.

about who belongs to the descent group and where they should live after they get married. Patrilineal and matrilineal descent, and the postmarital residence rules that usually accompany them, ensure that about half the people born in each generation will live out their lives on the ancestral estate. Neolocal residence, which is the rule for most middle-class Americans, isn't very common outside modern North America, Western Europe, and the European-derived cultures of Latin America.

Much more common is **patrilocality:** When a couple marries, it moves to the husband's father's community, so that their children will grow up in their father's village. Patrilocality is associated with patrilineal descent. This makes sense. If the group's male members are expected to exercise their rights in the ancestral estate, it's a good idea to raise them on that estate and to keep them there after they marry. This can be done by having wives move to their husband's village, rather than vice versa.

A less common postmarital residence rule, associated with matrilineal descent, is **matrilocality:** Married couples live in the wife's mother's community, and their children grow up in their mother's village. This rule keeps related women together. Together, patrilocality and matrilocality are known as *unilocal* rules of postmarital residence.

Ambilineal Descent

The descent rules examined so far admit certain people as members while excluding others. A unilineal rule uses one line only, either the female or the male. Besides the unilineal rules, there is another descent rule called nonunilineal or **ambilineal** descent. As in any descent group, membership comes through descent from a common ancestor. However, ambilineal groups differ from unilineal groups in that they do not *automatically* exclude either the children of sons or those of daughters. People can choose the descent group they join (for example, that of their father's father, father's mother, mother's father, or mother's mother). People also can change their descent-group membership, or belong to two or more groups at the same time.

Unilineal descent is a matter of ascribed status; ambilineal descent illustrates achieved status. With unilineal descent, membership is automatic; no choice is permitted. People are born members of their father's group in a patrilineal society or of their mother's group in a matrilineal society. They are members of that group for life. Ambilineal descent permits more flexibility in descent-group affiliation.

Before 1950, descent groups were generally described simply as patrilineal or matrilineal. If the society tended toward patrilineality, the anthropologist classified it as a patrilineal rather than an ambilineal group. The treatment of ambilineal descent as a separate category was a formal recognition that many descent systems are flexible—some more so than others.

Family versus Descent

There are rights, duties, and obligations associated with kinship and descent. Many societies have both families and descent groups. Obligations to one may conflict with obligations to the other—more so in matrilineal than in patrilineal societies. In the latter, a woman typically leaves home when she marries and raises her children in her husband's community. After leaving home, she has no primary or substantial obligations to her own descent group. She can invest fully in her children, who will become members of her husband's group. In a matrilineal society things are different. A man has strong obligations both to his family of procreation (his wife and children) and to his closest matrikin (his sisters and their children). The continuity of his descent group depends on his sisters and her children, since descent is carried by females, and he has descent-based obligations to look out for their welfare. He also has obligations to his wife and children. If a man is sure his wife's children are his own, he has more incentive to invest in them than is the case if he has doubts.

Compared with patrilineal systems, matrilineal societies tend to have higher divorce rates and greater female promiscuity (Schneider and Gough, eds. 1961). According to Nicholas Kottak (2002), among the matrilineal Makua of northern Mozambique, a husband is concerned about his wife's potential promiscuity. A man's sister also takes an interest in her brother's wife's fidelity; she doesn't want her brother wasting time on children who may not be his, thus diminishing his investment as an uncle (mother's brother) in her children. A confessional ritual that is part of the Makua birthing process demonstrates the sister's allegiance to her brother. When a wife is deep in labor, the husband's sister, who attends her, must ask, "Who is the real father of this child?" If the wife lies, the Makua believe the birth will be difficult, often ending in the death of the woman and/or the baby. This ritual serves as an important social paternity test. It is in both the husband's and his sister's interest to ensure that his wife's children are indeed his own.

KINSHIP CALCULATION

In addition to studying kin groups, anthropologists are interested in **kinship calculation:** the system by which people in a society reckon kin relationships. To study kinship calculation, an ethnographer must first determine the word or words for different types of "relatives" used in a particular language and then ask questions such as, "Who are your relatives?" Kinship, like race and gender (discussed in other chapters), is culturally constructed. This means that some genealogical kin are considered to be relatives whereas others are not. As we saw in the account of the Barí of Venezuela in the "News Brief" at the beginning of this chapter, even people who aren't genealogical relatives can be constructed socially as kin. The Barí recognize

■ *Most societies have a prevailing opinion about where a couple should live after they marry; this is called a postmarital residence rule. A common rule is patrilocality: the couple lives with the husband's relatives, so that children grow up in their father's community. In the top image, a bride on horseback is escorted to her husband in the Macedonian village of Galicnik in 2004. Her new father-in-law and the marriage witnesses lead the procession. In the bottom image, in Lendak, Slovakia, women transport part of the bride's dowry to the groom's house.*

multiple fathers, even though biologically there can be only one actual genitor. Through questioning, the ethnographer discovers the specific genealogical relationships between "relatives" and the person who has named them—the **ego.** *Ego* means *I* (or *me*) in Latin. It's who you, the

Social Security, Kinship Style

My book *Assault on Paradise*, 4th edition (Kottak 2006), describes social relations in Arembepe, the Brazilian fishing community I've studied since the 1960s. When I first studied Arembepe, I was struck by how similar its social relations were to those in the egalitarian, kin-based societies anthropologists have studied traditionally. The twin assertions "We're all equal here" and "We're all relatives here" were offered repeatedly as Arembepeiros' summaries of the nature and basis of local life. Like members of a clan (who claim to share common ancestry, but who can't say exactly how they are related), most villagers couldn't trace precise genealogical links to their distant kin. "What difference does it make, as long as we know we're relatives?"

As in most nonindustrial societies, close personal relations were either based or modeled on kinship. A degree of community solidarity was promoted, for example, by the myth that everyone was kin. However, social solidarity was actually much *less* developed in Arembepe than in societies with clans and lineages—which use genealogy to include some people, and *exclude* others, from membership in a given descent group. Intense social solidarity demands that some people be excluded. By asserting they all were related—that is, by excluding no one—Arembepeiros were actually weakening kinship's potential strength in creating and maintaining group solidarity.

Rights and obligations always are associated with kinship and marriage. In Arembepe, the closer the kin connection and the more formal the marital tie, the greater the rights and obligations. Couples could be married formally or informally. The most common union was a stable common-law marriage. Less common, but with more prestige, was legal (civil) marriage, performed by a justice of the peace and conferring inheritance rights. The union with the most prestige combined legal validity with a church ceremony.

The rights and obligations associated with kinship and marriage constituted the local social security system, but people had to weigh the benefits of the system against its costs. The most obvious cost was this: Villagers had to share in proportion to their success. As ambitious men climbed the local ladder of success, they got more dependents. To maintain their standing in public opinion, and to guarantee that they could depend on others in old age, they had to share. However, sharing was a powerful leveling mechanism. It drained surplus wealth and restricted upward mobility.

How, specifically, did this leveling work? As is often true in stratified nations, Brazilian national cultural norms are set by the upper classes. Middle- and upper-class Brazilians usually marry legally and in church. Even Arembepeiros knew this was the only "proper" way to marry. The most successful and ambitious local men copied the behavior of elite Brazilians. By doing so, they hoped to acquire some of their prestige.

However, legal marriage drained individual wealth, for example, by creating a responsibility to help one's in-laws financially. Such obligations could be regular and costly. Obligations to kids also increased with income, because successful people tended to have more living children. Children were valued as companions and as an eventual economic benefit to their parents. Boys especially were prized because their economic prospects were so much brighter than those of girls.

Children's chances of survival surged dramatically in wealthier households with better diets. The normal household diet included fish—usually in a stew with tomatoes, onions, palm oil, vinegar, and lemon. Dried beef replaced fish once a week. Roasted manioc flour was the main source of calories and was eaten at all meals. Other daily staples included coffee, sugar, and salt. Fruits and vegetables were eaten in season. Diet was one of the main contrasts between households. The poorest people didn't eat fish regularly; often they subsisted on manioc flour, coffee, and sugar. Better-off households supplemented the staples with milk, butter, eggs, rice, beans, and more ample portions of fresh fish, fruits, and vegetables.

Adequate incomes bought improved diets and provided the means and confidence to seek out better medical attention than was locally available. Most of the children born in the wealthier households survived. But this meant more mouths to feed, and (since the heads of such households usually wanted a better education for their children) it meant increased expenditures on schooling. The correlation between economic success and large families was a siphoner of wealth that restricted individual economic advance. Tomé, a fishing entrepreneur, envisioned a life of constant hard work if he was to feed, clothe, and educate his growing family. Tomé and his wife had never lost a child. But he recognized that his growing family would, in the short run, be a drain on his resources. "But in the end, I'll have successful sons to help their mother and me, if we need it, in our old age."

Arembepeiros knew who could afford to share with others; success can't be concealed in a small community. Villagers based their expectations of others on this knowledge. Successful people had to share with more kin and in-laws, and with more distant kin, than did poorer people. Successful captains and boat owners were expected to buy beer for ordinary fishermen; store owners had to sell on credit. As in bands and tribes, any well-off person was expected to exhibit a corresponding generosity. With increasing wealth, people were also asked more frequently to enter ritual kin relationships. Through baptism—which took place twice a year when a priest visited, or which could be done outside—a child acquired two godparents. These people became the coparents (*compadres*) of the baby's parents. The fact that ritual kinship obligations increased with wealth was another factor limiting individual economic advance.

We see that kinship, marriage, and ritual kinship in Arembepe had costs and benefits. The costs were limits on the economic advance of individuals. The primary benefit was social security—guaranteed help from kin, in-laws, and ritual kin in times of need. Benefits, however, came only after costs had been paid—that is, only to those who had lived "proper" lives, not deviating too noticeably from local norms, especially those about sharing.

reader, are in the kin charts that follow. It's your perspective looking out on your kin. By posing the same questions to several local people, the ethnographer learns about the extent and direction of kinship calculation in that society. The ethnographer also begins to understand the relationship between kinship calculation and kin groups: how people use kinship to create and maintain personal ties and to join social groups. In the kinship charts that follow, the black square labeled "ego" identifies the person whose kinship calculation is being examined.

Genealogical Kin Types and Kin Terms

At this point, we may distinguish between *kin terms* (the words used for different relatives in a particular language) and *genealogical kin types*. We designate genealogical kin types with the letters and symbols shown in Figure 9.6. *Genealogical kin type* refers to an actual genealogical relationship (e.g., father's brother) as opposed to a kin term (e.g., *uncle*).

Kin terms reflect the social construction of kinship in a given culture. A kin term may (and usually does) lump together several genealogical relationships. In English, for instance, we use *father* primarily for one kin type: the genealogical father. However, *father* can be extended to an adoptive father or stepfather—and even to a priest. *Grandfather* includes mother's father and father's father. The term *cousin* lumps together several kin types. Even the more specific *first cousin* includes mother's brother's son (MBS), mother's brother's daughter (MBD), mother's sister's son (MZS), mother's sister's daughter (MZD), father's brother's son (FBS), father's brother's daughter (FBD), father's sister's son (FZS), and father's sister's daughter (FZD). *First cousin* thus lumps together at least eight genealogical kin types.

Uncle encompasses mother's and father's brothers, and *aunt* includes mother's and father's sisters. We also used *uncle* and *aunt* for the spouses of our "blood" aunts and uncles. We use the same term for mother's brother and father's brother because we perceive them as being the same sort of relative. Calling them *uncles*, we distinguish between them and another kin type, F, whom we call *Father, Dad,* or *Pop.* In many societies, however, it is common to call a father and a father's brother by the same term. Later we'll see why.

In the United States and Canada, the nuclear family continues to be the most important group based on kinship. This is true despite an increased incidence of single parenthood, divorce, and re-marriage. The nuclear family's relative isolation from other kin groups in modern nations reflects geographic mobility within an industrial economy with sale of labor for cash.

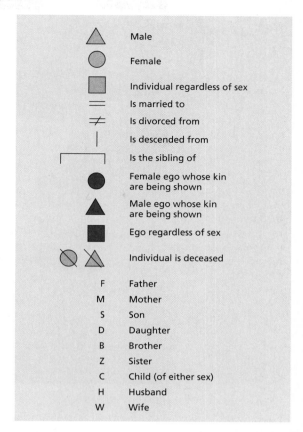

FIGURE 9.6 Kinship Symbols and Genealogical Kin Type Notation.

It's reasonable for North Americans to distinguish between relatives who belong to their nuclear families and those who don't. We are more likely to grow up with our parents than with our aunts and uncles. We tend to see our parents more often than we see our uncles and aunts, who may live in different towns and cities. We often inherit from our parents, but our cousins have first claim to inherit from our aunts and uncles. If our marriage is stable, we see our children daily as long as they remain at home. They are our heirs. We feel closer to them than to our nieces and nephews.

American kinship calculation and kin terminology reflect these social features. Thus, the term *uncle* distinguishes between the kin types MB and FB on the one hand and the kin type F on the other. However, this term also lumps kin types together. We use the same term for MB and FB, two different kin types. We do this because American kinship calculation is **bilateral**—traced equally through males and females, for example, father and mother. Both kinds of uncle are brothers of one of our parents. We think of both as roughly the same kind of relative.

"No," you may object, "I'm closer to my mother's brother than to my father's brother."

A Canadian nuclear family at play in a campsite in Quebec on August 14, 2003.

Bringing It All Together

For a description of unity and diversity in Canada, see the "Bringing It All Together" essay that immediately follows the chapter "Language and Communication."

That may be. However, in a representative sample of American students, we would find a split, with some favoring one side and some favoring the other. We'd actually expect a bit of *matrilateral skewing*—a preference for relatives on the mother's side. This occurs for many reasons. When contemporary children are raised by just one parent, it's much more likely to be the mother than the father. Also, even with intact marriages, the wife tends to play a more active role in managing family affairs, including family visits, reunions, holidays, and extended family relations, than the husband does. This would tend to reinforce her kin network over his and thus favor matrilateral skewing.

Bilateral kinship means that people tend to perceive kin links through males and females as being similar or equivalent. This bilaterality is expressed in interaction with, living with or near, and rights to inherit from relatives. We don't usually inherit from uncles, but if we do, there's about as much chance that we'll inherit from the father's brother as from the mother's brother. We don't usually live with either aunt, but if we do, the chances are about the same that it will be the father's sister as the mother's sister.

KINSHIP TERMINOLOGY

For a review and quiz on kinship terminology, see the Virtual Exploration

mhhe.com/kottak

People perceive and define kin relations differently in different cultures. In any culture, kinship terminology is a classification system, a taxonomy or typology. It is a *native taxonomy*, developed over generations by the people who live in a particular society. A native classification system is based on how people perceive similarities and differences in the things being classified.

However, anthropologists have discovered that there are a limited number of patterns in which people classify their kin. People who speak very different languages may use exactly the same system of kinship terminology. This section examines the four main ways of classifying kin on the parental generation: lineal, bifurcate merging, generational, and bifurcate collateral. We also consider the social correlates of these classification systems. (Note that each of the systems described here applies to the parental generation. There are also differences in kin terminology on ego's generation. These systems involve the classification of siblings and cousins. There are six such systems, called Eskimo, Iroquois, Hawaiian, Crow, Omaha, and Sudanese cousin terminology, after societies that traditionally used them. You can see them diagrammed and discussed at the following websites: http://anthro.palomar.edu/kinship/kinship_5.htm; http://anthro.palomar.edu/kinship/kinship_6.htm; http://www.umanitoba.ca/anthropology/tutor/kinterms/index.html.)

A **functional explanation** will be offered for each system of kinship terminology, such as lineal, bifurcate merging, and generational terminology. Functional explanations attempt to relate particular customs (such as the use of kin terms) to other features of a society, such as rules of descent and postmarital residence. Certain aspects of a culture are *functions* of others. That is, they are correlated variables, so that when one of them changes, the others inevitably change too. For certain terminologies, the social correlates are very clear.

Kinship terms provide useful information about social patterns. If two relatives are designated by the same term, we can assume that they are perceived as sharing socially significant attributes. Several factors influence the way people interact with, perceive, and classify relatives. For instance, do certain kinds of relatives customarily live together or apart? How far apart? What benefits do they derive from each other, and what are their obligations? Are they members of the same descent group or of different descent groups? With these questions in mind, let's examine systems of kinship terminology.

Lineal Terminology

Our own system of kinship classification is called the *lineal system* (Figure 9.7). The number 3 and the color light blue stand for the term *uncle,* which we apply both to FB and to MB. **Lineal kinship terminology** is found in societies such as the United States and Canada in which the nuclear family is the most important group based on kinship.

Lineal kinship terminology has absolutely nothing to do with lineages, which are found in very different social contexts. (What contexts are those?) Lineal kinship terminology gets its name from the fact that it distinguishes lineal relatives from collateral relatives. What does that mean? A **lineal relative** is an ancestor or descendant, anyone on the direct line of descent that leads to and from ego (Figure 9.8). Thus, lineal relatives are one's parents, grandparents, great-grandparents, and other direct forebears. Lineal relatives also include children, grandchildren, and great-grandchildren. **Collateral relatives** are all other kin. They include siblings, nieces and nephews, aunts and uncles, and cousins (Figure 9.8). **Affinals** are relatives by marriage, whether of lineals (e.g., son's wife) or of collaterals (sister's husband).

Bifurcate Merging Terminology

Bifurcate merging kinship terminology (Figure 9.9) *bifurcates,* or splits, the mother's side and the father's side. But it also *merges* same-sex siblings of each parent. Thus, mother and mother's sister are merged under the same term (1), while father and father's brother also get a common term (2). There are different terms for mother's brother (3) and father's sister (4).

People use this system in societies with unilineal (patrilineal and matrilineal) descent rules and unilocal (patrilocal and matrilocal) postmarital residence rules. When the society is unilineal and unilocal, the logic of bifurcate merging terminol-

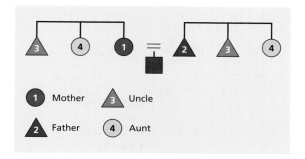

FIGURE 9.7 Lineal Kinship Terminology.

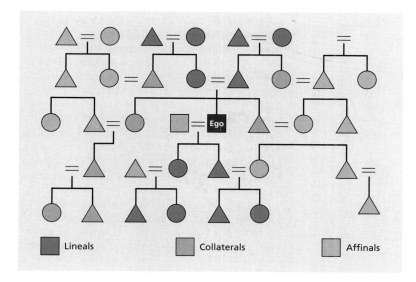

FIGURE 9.8 The Distinctions among Lineals, Collaterals, and Affinals as Perceived by Ego.

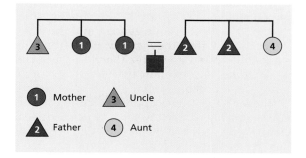

FIGURE 9.9 Bifurcate Merging Kinship Terminology.

ogy is fairly clear. In a patrilineal society, for example, father and father's brother belong to the same descent group, gender, and generation. Since patrilineal societies usually have patrilocal residence, the father and his brother live in the same local group. Because they share so many attributes that are socially relevant, ego regards them as social equivalents and calls them by the same kinship term—2. However, the mother's

The nuclear family still dominates in our society, ideologically if not statistically. Imagine a society where someone doesn't know for sure, and doesn't care much about, who his actual mother was. Consider Joseph Rabe, a Betsileo man who was my field assistant in Madagascar. One of the villages where I worked was his village of origin, where Rabe had been raised by his father's sister. How and why did that happen? I asked him. Rabe told me about two sisters, one of whom was his mother and the other was his mother's sister. He knew their names, but he didn't know which was which. Illustrating a pattern of child fosterage and adoption that is common among the Betsileo, Rabe was given to his father's childless sister to raise when he was a toddler. His mother and her sister lived far away and died in his childhood, and so he didn't really know them. But he was very close to his father's sister, for whom he used the term for mother. Indeed, he had to call her that, because the Betsileo have generational kinship terminology. They call mother, mother's sister, and father's sister by the same term, *reny*. The Betsileo live in an ambilineal society (albeit with a patrilineal tilt), and they use generational kin terms, which are associated with ambilineality. Since the Betsileo socially construct kinship, and encourage fosterage (typically by childless

relatives), in these ways, the difference between "real" and socially constructed kinship did not matter to Rabe, or to many others like him.

Contrast the Betsileo case with Americans' attitudes about kinship and adoption. On family-oriented radio talk shows, I've heard hosts who are "helping professionals" distinguish between "birth mothers" and adoptive mothers, and between "sperm daddies" and "daddies of the heart." The latter may be adoptive fathers, or stepfathers who have "been like fathers" to someone. American culture tends to promote the view that kinship is, and should be, biological. Americans have some trouble with the social construction of kinship. Less and less are we warned against searching for our birth parents (which was formerly discouraged as disruptive), even if we've had a perfectly satisfactory upbringing with our adoptive parents. One common reason an adopted person might give for trying to track down his or her birth parents is based in biology—to discover family health history, including inherited diseases. The American emphasis on biology for kinship is also seen in the recent proliferation of DNA testing. Understanding ourselves through cross-cultural comparison helps us see that kinship and biology don't always converge, nor do they need to.

brother belongs to a different descent group, lives elsewhere, and has a different kin term—3.

What about mother and mother's sister in a patrilineal society? They belong to the same descent group, the same gender, and the same generation. Often they marry men from the same village and go to live there. These social similarities help explain the use of the same term—1—for both.

Similar observations apply to matrilineal societies. Consider a society with two matrilineal clans, the Ravens and the Wolves. Ego is a member of his mother's clan, the Raven clan. Ego's father is a member of the Wolf clan. His mother and her sister are female Ravens of the same generation. If there is matrilocal residence, as there often is in matrilineal societies, they will live in the same village. Because they are so similar socially, ego calls them by the same kin term—1.

The father's sister, however, belongs to a different group, the Wolves; lives elsewhere; and has a different kin term—4. Ego's father and father's brother are male Wolves of the same generation. If they marry women of the same clan and live in the same village, this creates additional social similarities that reinforce this usage.

For a quiz on kinship systems, see the Interactive Exercise
mhhe.com/kottak

Generational Terminology

Like bifurcate merging kinship terminology, **generational kinship terminology** uses the same term for parents and their siblings, but the lumping is more complete (Figure 9.10). With generational terminology, there are only two terms for the parental *generation*. We may translate them as "father" and "mother," but more accurate translations would be "male member of the parental generation" and "female member of the parental generation."

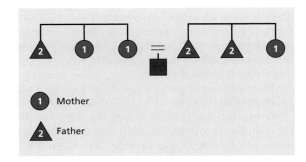

FIGURE 9.10 Generational Kinship Terminology.

TABLE 9.4 The Four Systems of Kinship Terminology, with Their Social and Economic Correlates

Kinship Terminology	Kin Group	Residence Rule	Economy
Lineal	Nuclear family	Neolocal	Industrialism, foraging
Bifurcate merging	Unilineal descent group—patrilineal or matrilineal	Unilocal—patrilocal or matrilocal	Horticulture, pastoralism, agriculture
Generational	Ambilineal descent group, band	Ambilocal	Agriculture, horticulture, foraging
Bifurcate collateral	Varies	Varies	Varies

Generational kinship terminology does not distinguish between the mother's and father's sides. It does not bifurcate, but it certainly does merge. It uses just one term for father, father's brother, and mother's brother. In a unilineal society, these three kin types would never belong to the same descent group. Generational kinship terminology also uses a single term for mother, mother's sister, and father's sister. Nor, in a unilineal society, would these three ever be members of the same group.

Nevertheless, generational terminology suggests closeness between ego and his or her aunts and uncles—much more closeness than exists between Americans and these kin types. How likely would you be to call your uncle "Dad" or your aunt "Mom"? We'd expect to find generational terminology in cultures in which kinship is much more important than it is in our own but in which there is no rigid distinction between the father's side and the mother's side.

It's logical, then, that generational kin terminology is typical of societies with ambilineal descent. In such contexts, descent-group membership is not automatic. People may choose the group they join, change their descent-group membership, or belong to two or more descent groups simultaneously. Generational terminology fits these conditions. The use of intimate kin terms signals that people have close personal relations with all their relatives of the parental generation. People exhibit similar behavior toward their aunts, uncles, and parents. Someday they'll have to choose a descent group to join. Furthermore, in ambilineal societies, postmarital residence is usually ambilocal. This means that the married couple can live with either the husband's or the wife's group.

Significantly, generational terminology also characterizes certain foraging bands, including Kalahari San groups and several native societies of North America. Use of this terminology reflects certain similarities between foraging bands and ambilineal descent groups. In both societies, people have a choice about their kin-group affiliation. Foragers always live with kin, but they often shift band affiliation and so may be members of several different bands during their lifetimes. Just as in food-producing societies with ambilineal descent, generational terminology among foragers helps maintain close personal relationships with several parental-generation relatives whom ego may eventually use as a point of entry into different groups. Table 9.4 summarizes the types of kin group, the postmarital residence rule, and the economy associated with the four types of kinship terminology.

Bifurcate Collateral Terminology

Of the four kin classification systems, **bifurcate collateral kinship terminology** is the most specific. It has separate terms for each of the six kin types of the parental generation (Figure 9.11). Bifurcate collateral terminology isn't as common as the other types. Many of the societies that use it are in North Africa and the Middle East, and many of them are offshoots of the same ancestral group.

Bifurcate collateral terminology also may be used when a child has parents of different ethnic backgrounds and uses terms for aunts and uncles derived from different languages. Thus, if you have a mother who is Latina and a father who is Anglo, you may call your aunts and uncles on your mother's side "tia" and "tio," while calling those on your father's side "aunt" and "uncle." And your mother and father may be "Mom" and "Pop." That's a modern form of bifurcate collateral kinship terminology.

FIGURE 9.11 Bifurcate Collateral Kinship Terminology.

SUMMARY

1. In nonindustrial societies, kinship, descent, and marriage organize social and political life. In studying kinship, we must distinguish between kin groups, whose composition and activities can be observed, and kinship calculation—how people identify and designate their relatives.

2. One widespread kin group is the nuclear family, consisting of a married couple and their children. There are functional alternatives to the nuclear family. That is, other groups may assume functions usually associated with the nuclear family. Nuclear families tend to be especially important in foraging and industrial societies. Among farmers and herders, other kinds of kin groups often overshadow the nuclear family.

3. In contemporary North America, the nuclear family is the characteristic kin group for the middle class. Expanded households and sharing with extended family kin occur more frequently among the poor, who may pool their resources in dealing with poverty. Today, however, even in the American middle class, nuclear family households are declining as single-person households and other domestic arrangements increase.

4. The descent group is a basic kin group among nonindustrial food producers (farmers and herders). Unlike families, descent groups have perpetuity—they last for generations. Descent-group members share and manage a common estate: land, animals, and other resources. There are several kinds of descent groups. Lineages are based on demonstrated descent; clans, on stipulated descent. Descent rules may be unilineal or ambilineal. Unilineal (patrilineal and matrilineal) descent is associated with unilocal (respectively, patrilocal and matrilocal) postmarital residence. Obligations to one's descent group and to one's family of procreation may conflict, especially in matrilineal societies.

5. A kinship terminology is a classification of relatives based on perceived differences and similarities. Comparative research has revealed a limited number of ways of classifying kin. Because there are correlations between kinship terminology and other social practices, we often can predict kinship terminology from other aspects of culture. The four basic kinship terminologies for the parental generation are lineal, bifurcate merging, generational, and bifurcate collateral. Many foraging and industrial societies use lineal terminology, which is associated with nuclear family organization. Cultures with unilocal residence and unilineal descent tend to have bifurcate merging terminology. Generational terminology correlates with ambilineal descent and ambilocal residence.

KEY TERMS

See the flash cards
mhhe.com/kottak

affinals Relatives by marriage, whether of lineals (e.g., son's wife) or collaterals (e.g., sister's husband).

ambilineal Principle of descent that does not automatically exclude the children of either sons or daughters.

bifurcate collateral kinship terminology Kinship terminology employing separate terms for M, F, MB, MZ, FB, and FZ.

bifurcate merging kinship terminology Kinship terminology in which M and MZ are called by the same term, F and FB are called by the same term, and MB and FZ are called by different terms.

bilateral kinship calculation A system in which kinship ties are calculated equally through both sexes: mother and father, sister and brother, daughter and son, and so on.

clan Unilineal descent group based on stipulated descent.

collateral relative A genealogical relative who is not in ego's direct line, such as B, Z, FB, or MZ.

descent group A permanent social unit whose members claim common ancestry; fundamental to tribal society.

ego Latin for *I*. In kinship charts, the point from which one views an egocentric genealogy.

extended family household Expanded household including three or more generations.

family of orientation Nuclear family in which one is born and grows up.

family of procreation Nuclear family established when one marries and has children.

functional explanation Explanation that establishes a correlation or interrelationship between social customs. When customs are functionally interrelated, if one changes, the others also change.

generational kinship terminology Kinship terminology with only two terms for the parental generation, one designating M, MZ, and FZ and the other designating F, FB, and MB.

kinship calculation The system by which people in a particular society reckon kin relationships.

lineage Unilineal descent group based on demonstrated descent.

lineal kinship terminology Parental generation kin terminology with four terms: one for M, one for F, one for FB and MB, and one for MZ and FZ.

lineal relative Any of ego's ancestors or descendants (e.g., parents, grandparents, children, grandchildren) on the direct line of descent that leads to and from ego.

matrilineal descent Unilineal descent rule in which people join the mother's group automatically at birth and stay members throughout life.

matrilocality   Customary residence with the wife's relatives after marriage, so that children grow up in their mother's community.

neolocality   Postmarital residence pattern in which a couple establishes a new place of residence rather than living with or near either set of parents.

patrilineal descent   Unilineal descent rule in which people join the father's group automatically at birth and stay members throughout life.

patrilocality   Customary residence with the husband's relatives after marriage, so that children grow up in their father's community.

unilineal descent   Matrilineal or patrilineal descent.

---

1. Why is kinship so important to anthropologists? How might the study of kinship be useful for research in fields of anthropology other than cultural anthropology?

2. To what sorts of family or families do you belong? Have you belonged to other kinds of families? When you were growing up, how did you feel about your family compared with those of your friends?

3. Choose two of your friends who have families of orientation that differ from your own. How do they differ?

4. What do "family" and "family values" mean to you?

5. How do the kin terms you use compare with the four classification systems discussed in this chapter? What's the strangest use of kin terms you've ever heard (among your friends or acquaintances)?

CRITICAL THINKING QUESTIONS

For more self-testing, see the self-quizzes
mhhe.com/kottak

SUGGESTED ADDITIONAL READINGS

Carsten, J.
   2004   *After Kinship.* New York: Cambridge University Press. Rethinking anthropological approaches to kinship for the modern world.

Collier, J. F., and S. J. Yanagisako, eds.
   1987   *Gender and Kinship: Essays toward a Unified Analysis.* Stanford, CA: Stanford University Press. Consideration of kinship in the context of gender issues.

Finkler, K.
   2000   *Experiencing the New Genetics: Family and Kinship on the Medical Frontier.* Philadelphia: University of Pennsylvania Press. Examines some medical and genetic aspects of kinship, along with social dimensions of contemporary medical/genetics debates.

Hansen, K. V.
   2004   *Not-So-Nuclear Families: Class, Gender, and Networks of Care.* New Brunswick, NJ: Rutgers University Press. Support networks based in class, gender, and kinship.

Hansen, K. V., and A. I. Garey, eds.
   1998   *Families in the U.S.: Kinship and Domestic Politics.* Philadelphia: Temple University Press. Families, family policy, and diversity in the contemporary United States.

Netting, R. M. C., R. R. Wilk, and E. J. Arnould, eds.
   1984   *Households: Comparative and Historical Studies of the Domestic Groups.* Berkeley: University of California Press. Excellent collection of articles on household research.

O'Dougherty, M.
   2002   *Consumption Intensified: The Politics of Middle-Class Daily Life in Brazil.* Durham, NC: Duke University Press. Families and consumption in contemporary Brazil.

Parkin, R.
   1997   *Kinship: An Introduction to Basic Concepts.* Cambridge, MA: Blackwell. The basics of kinship study.

Parkin, R., and L. Stone, eds.
   2004   *Kinship and Family: An Anthropological Reader.* Malden, MA: Blackwell. Up-to-date reader.

Pasternak, B., C. R. Ember, and M. Ember
   1997   *Sex, Gender, and Kinship: A Cross-Cultural Perspective.* Upper Saddle River, NJ: Prentice Hall. Sex roles, kinship, and marriage in comparative perspective.

Radcliffe-Brown, A. R., and D. Forde, eds.
   1994   *African Systems of Kinship and Marriage.* New York: Columbia University Press. Reissue of a classic work, indispensable to understanding kinship, descent, and marriage.

Stacey, J.
   1998   *Brave New Families: Stories of Domestic Upheaval in Late Twentieth Century America.* Berkeley: University of California Press. Contemporary family life in the United States, based on field work in California's Silicon Valley.

Stone, L.
   2001   *New Directions in Anthropological Kinship.* Lanham, MD: Rowman and Littlefield. How contemporary anthropologists think about kinship.

Willie, C. V.
   2003   *A New Look at Black Families,* 5th ed. Walnut Creek, CA: AltaMira. Family experience in relation to socioeconomic status, presented through case studies.

Yanagisako, S. J.
   2002   *Producing Culture and Capital: Family Firms in Italy.* Princeton, NJ: Princeton University Press. Families making money.

INTERNET EXERCISES

1. Kinship and Conflict: Go to the Yanamamo Interactive: Understanding the Ax Fight page, **http://www.anth.ucsb.edu/projects/axfight/index.html**, and go to the Web version of the CD-ROM, **http://www.anth.ucsb.edu/projects/axfight/prep.html**. View the film of the Ax Fight and read the text titled "Chagnon's Voice-Over Narration from the 1975 *The Ax Fight*." The questions below ask you to interpret the fight, and it may be necessary to view the film or read the text more than once to understand it.
   a. What is the cause of the fight?
   b. Who are the aggressors? Whom are they attacking?
   c. As the fight escalates, more people join in. What is their relationship to the people who start the fight? Why is that important?
   d. How is kinship important for understanding this conflict? Can you think of examples from your own society where kinship served to escalate or diffuse conflict?

2. Descent and Subsistence: Go to the Ethnographic Atlas Cross-tabulations page, **http://lucy.ukc.ac.uk/cgi-bin/uncgi/Ethnoatlas/atlas.vopts**. This site has compiled ethnographic information on many different groups, and you can use the tools provided to cross-tabulate the prevalence of certain traits. Under "Select Row Category" choose "region," and under "Select Column Category" select "descent." Press the Submit Query button. The table that appears shows the frequency of descent patterns from regions around the world.
   a. Look at the total row for descent. Which forms of descent are most common worldwide? What is the *most* common? Is that the system with which you are most familiar in your own society?
   b. Where are most of the patrilineal societies found? Where are most of the bilateral societies found? In the Insular Pacific, is any one descent system predominant?
   c. Now go back to the Ethnographic Atlas Cross-tabulations page and change the "Select Row Category" from "region" to "subsistence economy" and press the Submit Query button. What kind of subsistence economy do most patrilineal societies practice? Are matrilineal societies more likely to use hunting, gathering, or fishing or to use agriculture? Is the pattern as strong as with patrilineal groups? Are there any strong patterns for the type of subsistence economy practiced by bilateral groups?

3. Kinship Terminologies: Go to the website created by Professor Brian Schwimmer of the Department of Anthropology at the University of Manitoba, **http://www.umanitoba.ca/faculties/arts/anthropology/kintitle.html**. Click on "Begin Tutorial." Next click on topic 3—Kinship Terminology. Press "Continue" at the bottom left of the next two pages until you reach a page titled "Systematic Kinship Terminologies." Scroll down the page to the diagram labeled "Eskimo Kin Terms."
   a. To what parental generation kin terminology discussed in the book (lineal, bifurcate merging, generational, or bifurcate collateral) do the Eskimo cousin terms correspond?
   b. Answer the same question for Iroquois, Hawaiian, and Sudanese terms.
   c. Do you see any logic in the relation between the terms used on the parental generation (for parents, aunts, and uncles) and those used on ego's own generation (for siblings and cousins)?
   d. How do these associated sets of kin terms fit with particular kinds of kin groups, for example, the nuclear family, a unilineal descent group, an ambilineal descent group?
   e. At the bottom of the web page, can you see how Omaha kin terms might fit with patrilineal descent, and Crow terms with matrilineal descent?

See Chapter 9 at your McGraw-Hill Online Learning Center for additional review and interactive exercises.

Kottak, *Assault on Paradise,* **4th ed.**

Read Chapters 3 and 11 and comment on the role of kinship and ritual kinship for Dora and Fernando. Why, unlike Alberto and Tomé, did Fernando have to rely so heavily on ritual kinship? To which of her kin did Dora look for present and future support? See Chapter 3 for others like Dora, their status, and how they used the local kinship system.

Peters-Golden, *Culture Sketches,* **4th ed.**

Read Chapter 10, "Nuer: Cattle and Kinship in Sudan." The traditional descent system of the Nuer, called segmentary lineage organization (SLO), offered an effective way of resolving disputes and of mobilizing support among kin groups. In recent years, however, civil war and ethnic clashes in Sudan have led to widespread resettlement and a contemporary refugee crisis. Also, thousands of Nuer have migrated to the United States. This chapter on the Nuer demonstrates the potential political significance of kinship alliances. For Nuer emigrants, what might be some challenges in creating social ties without the political ties and village links that underlie traditional Nuer solidarity?

Knauft, *The Gebusi,* **1st ed.**

Based on information in Chapter 4 of *The Gebusi,* why is kinship important for understanding Gebusi social life? How do Gebusi trace descent? What difference is there in the way Gebusi trace descent in lineages as opposed to in clans? What is Omaha kinship terminology, and how is it important among Gebusi?

10

Marriage

CHAPTER OUTLINE

WHAT IS MARRIAGE?

"Love and marriage," "marriage and the family": These familiar phrases show how we link the romantic love of two individuals to marriage and how we link marriage to reproduction and family creation. But marriage is an institution with significant roles and functions in addition to reproduction. What is marriage, anyway?

No definition of marriage is broad enough to apply easily to all societies and situations. A commonly quoted definition comes from *Notes and Queries on Anthropology:*

> Marriage is a union between a man and a woman such that the children born to the woman are recognized as legitimate offspring of both partners. (Royal Anthropological Institute 1951, p. 111)

This definition isn't universally valid for several reasons. In many societies, marriages unite more than two spouses, as we see in the "News Brief" about Kenya. Here we speak of *plural marriages,* as when a man weds two (or more) women, or a woman weds a group of brothers—an arrangement called *fraternal polyandry* that is characteristic of certain Himalayan cultures. In the Brazilian community of Arembepe, people can choose among various forms of marital union. Most people live in long-term "common-law" domestic partnerships that are not legally sanctioned. Some have civil marriages, which are licensed and legalized by a justice of the peace. Still others go through religious ceremonies, so that they are united in "holy matrimony," although not legally. And some have both civil and religious ties. The different forms of union permit someone to have multiple spouses (e.g., one common-law, one civil, one religious) without ever getting divorced.

Some societies recognize various kinds of same-sex marriages. In Sudan, a Nuer woman can marry a woman if her father has only daughters but no male heirs, who are necessary if his patrilineage is to survive. He may ask his daughter to stand as a son in order to take a bride. This daughter will become the socially recognized husband of another woman (the wife). This is a symbolic and social relationship rather than a sexual one. The "wife" has sex with a man or men (whom her female "husband" must approve) until she gets pregnant. The children born to the wife are accepted as the offspring of both the female husband and the wife. Although the female husband is not the actual **genitor,** the biological father, of the children, she is their **pater,** or socially recognized father. What's important in this Nuer case is *social* rather than *biological paternity.* We see again how kinship is socially constructed. The bride's children are considered the legitimate offspring of her female "husband," who is biologically a woman but socially a man, and the descent line continues.

INCEST AND EXOGAMY

In many nonindustrial societies, a person's social world includes two main categories: kin and strangers. Strangers are potential or actual enemies. Marriage is one of the primary ways of converting strangers into kin, of creating and maintaining personal and political alliances, relationships of affinity (*affinal* relationships). **Exogamy,** the practice of seeking a husband or wife outside one's own group, has adaptive value because it links people into a wider social network that nurtures, helps, and protects them in times of need.

Incest refers to sexual relations with someone considered to be a close relative. All cultures have taboos against it. However, although the taboo is a cultural universal, cultures define incest differently. As an illustration, consider some implications of the distinction between two kinds of first cousins: cross cousins and parallel cousins (see Ottenheimer 1996).

The children of two brothers or two sisters are **parallel cousins.** The children of a brother and a sister are **cross cousins.** Your mother's sister's children and your father's brother's children are your parallel cousins. Your father's sister's children and your mother's brother's children are your cross cousins.

The American kin term *cousin* doesn't distinguish between cross and parallel cousins, but in many societies, especially those with unilineal descent, the distinction is essential. As an example, consider a community with only two descent groups. This exemplifies what is known as *moiety* organization—from the French *moitié,* which means "half." Descent bifurcates the community so that everyone belongs to one half or the other. Some societies have patrilineal moieties; others have matrilineal moieties.

In Figures 10.1 and 10.2, notice that cross cousins are always members of the opposite moiety and parallel cousins always belong to your (ego's) own moiety. With patrilineal descent (Figure 10.1), people take the father's descent-group affiliation; in a matrilineal society (Figure 10.2), they take the mother's affiliation. You can see from these diagrams that your mother's sister's children (MZC) and your father's brother's children (FBC) always belong to your group. Your

Nairobi Journal; Is Polygamy Confusing, or Just a Matter of Family Values?

NEW YORK TIMES NEWS BRIEF

by Marc Lacey
December 16, 2003

In nonindustrial societies, marriage is an important means of creating or maintaining alliances beyond one's own kin group. Many societies, such as Kenya, described here, permit plural marriage. This news story reports on polygyny, the form of polygamy (plural marriage) in which a man has more than one wife. Anthropologists also have studied the rarer custom of polyandry, in which a woman has more than one husband. Marriage is usually a domestic partnership, but the secondary wife, who sometimes is chosen by the first wife, may or may not reside near the first wife. In this Kenyan case the president's second wife has her own residence (his ranch) and appears very discreetly at public events that the senior wife also attends. For thousands of years the rich and powerful, especially rulers, have used marriage to build and maintain alliances, to acquire territory, and to guarantee their power base. Monogamy creates an alliance with one group; polygamy, with many.

NAIROBI, Kenya, Dec. 15— When President Mwai Kibaki of Kenya arrived at the White House recently for a state visit, his wife, Lucy Kibaki, was at his side, resplendent in a flowing gown.

Perhaps fortunately for the White House protocol office, which has little experience with polygamous relationships, Mr. Kibaki left his second wife, Wambui Kibaki, back home.

Mr. Kibaki's multiple marriage has been known for decades among close friends and family in his native village of Othaya, near Mount Kenya. But most Kenyan voters first learned of it on Sunday morning, nearly a year into Mr. Kibaki's presidency, when a local newspaper, *The East African Standard*, splashed a profile of Mr. Kibaki's second wife on its front page.

Such a complicated family life is not uncommon here. By no means limited to Muslims, polygamy is widely practiced in Africa, particularly among the well-off members of Mr. Kibaki's generation who can afford multiple dowries [bridewealth] and the expense of keeping more than one home.

But polygamy is also falling from favor, according to social scientists and women's rights advocates, especially among younger Kenyans, and Mr. Kibaki has not sought to publicize his living arrangements. His official campaign Web site, for example, mentioned only one Mrs. Kibaki. "I don't believe in sharing husbands," said Rose Nganga, 20, a Nairobi college student. "If my husband were to bring another wife, he would have to either divorce her or me. Why should I be the second wheel to a man?" For polygamy to work peacefully, the wives must buy into the tradition. Sometimes an older wife will actually assist her husband in choosing a younger bride, typically to provide some assistance with all the work at the homestead. But Kenya's newspapers are rife with stories of disputes between wives of the same husband. They frequently scheme against each other and sometimes come to blows . . .

Mr. Kibaki's home life is, by all accounts, a calm one. Lucy Kibaki, a former schoolteacher whom Mr. Kibaki married in the 1960's, lives with the president. Wambui Kibaki, who was also a schoolteacher before meeting Mr. Kibaki in the 1970's, occupies the presidential ranch.

It is Lucy Kibaki who typically appears at Mr. Kibaki's side at ceremonial functions and acts as first lady. But Wambui Kibaki is often just a few rows behind the first couple, as she was last Friday at a 40th anniversary celebration of Kenya's independence from Britain.

Wambui Kibaki has her own security detail and more access to the presidential office compound than many ministers. Parliament is debating whether the government ought to provide benefits should a retired president have more than one spouse.

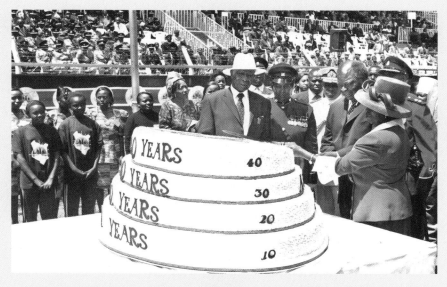

■ *Lucy Kibaki, the first lady of Kenya, and her polygynous husband, President Mwai Kibaki, at a state celebration.*

In the only interview she has given since her husband took over the presidency a year ago, Wambui Kibaki said she was comfortable with her arrangement. "I do not feel restricted," she told *The Standard*. "I have my time with him, just as before he became president. I go to State House when I want, and I can't complain. I am his wife, and not being made public does not bother me."

Mr. Kibaki is not the first polygamous politician here. Kenya's first president, Jomo Kenyatta, had several wives, although only one of them took on the official role of first lady.

A recently retired member of Parliament, Dickson Kihaika Kimani, has more than a dozen wives. Last fall he sought to have two of them join him in Parliament, but voters rejected their candidacies—and his as well. Supporters of the practice say that in the AIDS era, polygamy is a far healthier arrangement than another one favored by many men: one wife and one or more mistresses, or even prostitutes . . .

But polygamous relationships, too, are blamed for helping spread AIDS. The more sexual partners involved, critics say, even under the cloak of marriage, the greater risk of the disease spreading, particularly as some men take on multiple wives and still have affairs on the side. In an advertising campaign aimed at reducing the spread of AIDS, Mr. Kibaki urges Kenyans to "be faithful." He avoids the ticklish question of how much faithfulness he thinks that Kenyan men ought to spread around.

SOURCE: Marc Lacey, "Nairobi Journal; Is Polygamy Confusing, or Just a Matter of Family Values?" *New York Times*, December 16, 2003, late edition, final, section A, p. 4, col. 3.

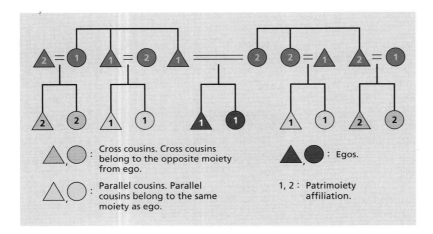

FIGURE 10.1 Parallel and Cross Cousins and Patrilineal Moiety Organization.

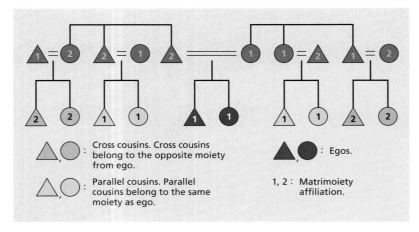

FIGURE 10.2 Matrilineal Moiety Organization.

cross cousins—that is, FZC and MBC—belong to the other moiety.

Parallel cousins belong to the same generation and the same descent group as ego does, and they are like ego's brothers and sisters. They are called by the same kin terms as brother and sister are. Defined as close relatives, parallel cousins are tabooed as sex or marriage partners. They fall within the incest taboo, but cross cousins don't.

In societies with unilineal moieties, cross cousins always belong to the opposite group. Sex with cross cousins isn't incestuous, because they aren't considered relatives. In fact, in many unilineal societies, people must marry either a cross cousin or someone from the same descent group as a cross cousin. A unilineal descent rule ensures that the cross cousin's descent group is never one's own. With moiety exogamy, spouses must belong to different moieties.

Among the Yanomami of Venezuela and Brazil (Chagnon 1997), men anticipate eventual marriage to a cross cousin by calling her "wife." They call their male cross cousins "brother-in-law." Yanomami women call their male cross cousins "husband" and their female cross cousins "sister-in-law." Among the Yanomami, as in many societies with unilineal descent, sex with cross cousins is proper but sex with parallel cousins is considered incestuous.

A custom that is much rarer than cross-cousin marriage also illustrates that people define their kin, and thus incest, differently in different societies. When unilineal descent is very strongly developed, the parent who does not belong to one's own descent group isn't considered a relative. Thus, with strict patrilineality, the mother is not a relative but a kind of in-law who has married a member of ego's group—ego's father. With strict matrilineality, the father isn't a relative, because he belongs to a different descent group.

The Lakher of Southeast Asia (Figure 10.3) are strictly patrilineal (Leach 1961). Using the male ego in Figure 10.4, let's suppose that ego's father and mother get divorced. Each remarries and has a daughter by a second marriage. A Lakher always belongs to his or her father's group, all the members of which (one's *agnates*, or patrikin) are considered too closely related to marry because they are members of the same patrilineal descent group. Therefore, ego can't marry his father's daughter by the second marriage, just as in contemporary North America it's illegal for half-siblings to marry.

However, in contrast to our society, where all half-siblings are tabooed, the Lakher permit ego to marry his mother's daughter by a different father. She is not a forbidden relative because she belongs to her own father's descent group rather than ego's. The Lakher illustrate clearly that definitions of forbidden relatives, and therefore of incest, vary from culture to culture.

We can extend these observations to strict matrilineal societies. If a man's parents divorce and his father remarries, ego may marry his pater-

nal half-sister. By contrast, if his mother remarries and has a daughter, the daughter is considered ego's sister, and sex between them is taboo. Cultures therefore have different definitions and expectations of relationships that are biologically or genetically equivalent.

Among the Yanomami of Brazil and Venezuela (shown here), sex with (and marriage to) cross cousins is proper, but sex with parallel cousins is considered incestuous. With unilineal descent, sex with cross cousins isn't incestuous because cross cousins never belong to ego's descent group.

FIGURE 10.3 Location of the Lakher.

For a quiz on marriage patterns, see the Interactive Exercise
mhhe.com/kottak

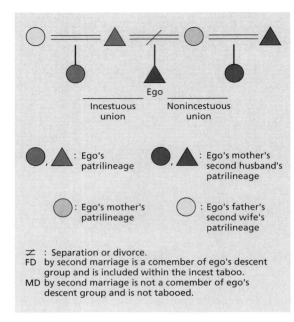

Ego

| Incestuous union | Nonincestuous union |

● , ▲ : Ego's patrilineage

● , ▲ : Ego's mother's second husband's patrilineage

● : Ego's mother's patrilineage

○ : Ego's father's second wife's patrilineage

⊄ : Separation or divorce.
FD by second marriage is a comember of ego's descent group and is included within the incest taboo.
MD by second marriage is not a comember of ego's descent group and is not tabooed.

FIGURE 10.4 Patrilineal Descent-Group Identity and Incest among the Lakher.

EXPLAINING THE TABOO

Although Tabooed, Incest Does Happen

There is no simple or universally accepted explanation for the fact that all cultures ban incest. Do primate studies offer any clues? Research with primates does show that adolescent males (among monkeys) or females (among apes) often move away from the group in which they were born (Rodseth et al. 1991). This emigration reduces the frequency of incestuous unions, but it doesn't eliminate them. DNA testing of wild chimps has confirmed incestuous unions between adult sons and their mothers, who reside in the same group. Human behavior with respect to mating with close relatives may express a generalized primate tendency, in which we see both urges and avoidance.

A cross-cultural study of 87 societies (Meigs and Barlow 2002) revealed that incest did occur in several of them. For example, among the Yanomami, Chagnon reported that "incest, far from being feared, is widely practiced" (1967, p. 66). Meyer Fortes observed about the Ashanti: "In the old days it [incest] was punished by death. Nowadays the culprits are heavily fined" (Fortes 1950, p. 257). Among 24 Ojibwa individuals from whom he obtained information about incest, A. Irving Hallowell found 8 cases of parent–child incest and 10 cases of brother–sister incest (Hallowell 1955, pp. 294–295).

In ancient Egypt, sibling marriage apparently was allowed not just for royalty (see below), but for commoners as well, in at least some districts. Based on official census records from Roman Egypt (first to third centuries A.D.) preserved on papyrus, 24 percent of all documented marriages in the Arsinoites district were between brothers and sisters. In the second century A.D., the rates were 37 percent for the city of Arsinoe and 19 percent for the surrounding villages. These figures are much higher than any other documented levels of inbreeding among humans (Scheidel 1997).

According to Anna Meigs and Kathleen Barlow (2002), for Western societies with nuclear family organization, statistics show a significant risk of father–daughter incest under certain conditions (Russell 1986). Father–daughter incest is most common with stepfathers and nonbiological male household members, but it also happens with biological fathers, especially those who were absent or did little caretaking of their daughters in childhood (Williams and Finkelhor 1995). In a carefully designed study, Linda M. Williams and David Finkelhor (1995) found father–daughter incest to be least likely when there was substantial paternal parenting of daughters who were four to five years old. This experience enhanced the father's parenting skills and his feelings of nurturance, protectiveness, and identification with his daughter, thus reducing the risk of incest.

Cross-cultural findings show that incest and its avoidance are shaped by kinship structures. Meigs and Barlow (2002) suggest that a cultural focus on risks and avoidance of father–daughter incest correlates with a patriarchal nuclear family structure, whereas the cultural focus is on avoiding brother–sister incest in societies that have such nonnuclear structures as lineages and clans.

■ *Discovered in Egypt's Valley of the Kings, a gold and silver inlaid throne from the tomb of Tutankhamun is now on display in Cairo's Egyptian Museum. Sibling marriage was allowed not only for ancient Egyptian royalty but also for commoners in some regions.*

Instinctive Horror

It has been argued (Hobhouse 1915; Lowie 1920/1961) that the incest taboo is universal because incest horror is instinctive: Humans have a genetically programmed disgust toward incest. Because of this feeling, early humans banned it. However, cultural universality doesn't necessarily entail an instinctual basis. Fire making, for example, is a cultural universal, but it certainly isn't an ability transmitted by the genes. Furthermore, if people really did have an instinctive horror of mating with blood relatives, a formal incest taboo would be unnecessary. No one would do it. However, as we have just seen, and as social workers, judges, psychiatrists, and psychologists know, incest is more common than we might suppose.

A final objection to the instinctive horror theory is that it can't explain why in some societies people can marry their cross cousins but not their parallel cousins. Nor does it tell us why the Lakher can marry their maternal, but not their paternal, half-siblings. No known instinct can distinguish between parallel and cross cousins.

The specific kin types included within the incest taboo—and the taboo itself—have a cultural rather than a biological basis. Even among nonhuman primates, there is no definite evidence for an instinct against incest. Adolescent dispersal does not prevent—but merely limits the frequency of—incestuous unions. Among humans, cultural traditions determine the specific relatives with whom sex is considered incestuous. They also deal with the people who violate prohibited relationships in different ways. Banishment, imprisonment, death, and threats of supernatural retaliation are some of the punishments imposed.

Biological Degeneration

Another theory is that the taboo emerged because early *Homo* noticed that abnormal offspring were born from incestuous unions (Morgan 1877/1963). To prevent this, our ancestors banned incest. The human stock produced after the taboo originated was so successful that it spread everywhere.

What is the evidence for this theory? Laboratory experiments with animals that reproduce faster than humans do (such as mice and fruit flies) have been used to investigate the effects of inbreeding: A decline in survival and fertility does accompany brother–sister mating across several generations. However, despite the potentially harmful biological results of systematic inbreeding, human marriage patterns are based on specific cultural beliefs rather than universal concerns about biological degeneration several generations in the future. Neither instinctive horror nor fear of biological degeneration explains the very widespread custom of marrying cross cousins. Nor can fears about degeneration explain why breeding with parallel cousins but not cross cousins is so often tabooed.

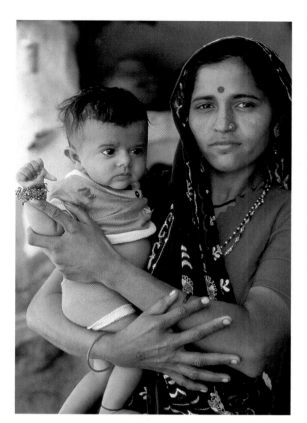

How many fingers do this Indian woman and her child have? Such genetically determined traits as polydactylism (extra fingers) may show up when there is a high incidence of endogamy. Despite the biological effects of inbreeding, marriage preferences and prohibitions are based on specific cultural beliefs rather than universal concerns about future biological degeneration.

Attempt and Contempt

Sigmund Freud is the most famous advocate of the theory that children have sexual feelings toward their parents, which they eventually repress or resolve. Other scholars have looked to the dynamics of growing up for an explanation of the incest taboo. Bronislaw Malinowski believed that children would naturally seek to express their sexual feelings, particularly as they increased in adolescence, with members of their nuclear family, because of preexisting intimacy and affection. Yet, he thought, sex was too powerful a force to unleash in the family. It would threaten existing family roles and ties; it could destroy the family. Malinowski proposed that the incest taboo originated to direct sexual feeling outside—to avoid disruption of—existing family structure and relations.

The opposite theory is that children are not likely to be sexually attracted to those with whom they have grown up (Westermarck 1894). This is related to the idea of instinctive horror, but without assuming a biological (instinctual) basis. The notion here is that a lifetime of living together in particular, nonsexual relationships would make the idea of sex with a family member less desirable. The two opposed theories are sometimes characterized as "familiarity breeds attempt" versus "familiarity breeds contempt." One bit of evidence to support the contempt theory comes from Joseph Shepher's (1983) study of Israeli *kibbutzim*.

He found that unrelated people who had been raised in the same *kibbutz* (domestic community) avoided intermarriage. They tended to choose their mates from outside—not because they were related, but because their prior residential histories and roles made sex and marriage unappealing. Again, there is no final answer to the question of whether people who grow up together, related or unrelated, are likely to be sexually attracted to one another. Usually they aren't; sometimes they are. Incest is universally tabooed, but it does happen.

Marry Out or Die Out

One of the most accepted explanations for the incest taboo is that it arose in order to ensure exogamy, to force people to marry outside their kin groups (Lévi-Strauss 1949/1969; Tylor 1889; White 1959). In this view, the taboo originated early in human evolution because it was adaptively advantageous. Marrying a close relative, with whom one is already on peaceful terms, would be counterproductive. There is more to gain by extending peaceful relations to a wider network of groups. (See Appendix 1 for a discussion of the contributions of Tylor, Malinowski, White, and Lévi-Strauss to the development of anthropological theory.)

This view emphasizes the role of marriage in creating and maintaining alliances. By forcing members to marry out, a group increases its allies. Marriage within the group, by contrast, would isolate that group from its neighbors and their resources and social networks, and might ultimately lead to the group's extinction. Exogamy and the incest taboo that propels it help explain human adaptive success. Besides the sociopolitical function, exogamy ensures genetic mixture between groups and thus maintains a successful human species.

ENDOGAMY

The practice of exogamy pushes social organization outward, establishing and preserving alliances among groups. In contrast, rules of **endogamy** dictate mating or marriage within a group to which one belongs. Formal endogamic rules are less common but are still familiar to anthropologists. Indeed, most societies *are* endogamous units, although they usually do not need a formal rule requiring people to marry someone from their own society. In our own society, classes and ethnic groups are quasi-endogamous groups. Members of an ethnic or religious group often want their children to marry within that group, although many of them do not do so. The outmarriage rate varies among such groups, with some more committed to endogamy than others are.

Homogamy means to marry someone similar, as when members of the same social class intermarry. There's a correlation between socioeconomic status (SES) and education. People with similar SES tend to have similar educational aspirations, to attend similar schools, and to aim at similar careers. For example, people who meet at an elite private university are likely to have similar backgrounds and career prospects. Homogamous marriage may work to concentrate wealth in social classes and to reinforce the system of social stratification. In the United States, for example, the rise in female employment, especially in professional careers, when coupled with homogamy, has dramatically increased household incomes in the upper classes. This pattern has been one factor in sharpening the contrast in household income between the richest and poorest quintiles (top and bottom 20 percent) of Americans.

Caste

An extreme example of endogamy is India's caste system, which was formally abolished in 1949, although its structure and effects linger. Castes are stratified groups in which membership is ascribed at birth and is lifelong. Indian castes are grouped into five major categories, or *varna*. Each is ranked relative to the other four, and these categories extend throughout India. Each *varna* includes a large number of subcastes (*jati*), each of which includes people within a region who may intermarry. All the *jati* in a single *varna* in a given region are ranked, just as the *varna* themselves are ranked.

Occupational specialization often sets off one caste from another. A community may include castes of agricultural workers, merchants, artisans, priests, and sweepers. The untouchable *varna*, found throughout India, includes subcastes whose ancestry, ritual status, and occupations are considered so impure that higher-caste people consider even casual contact with untouchables to be defiling.

The belief that intercaste sexual unions lead to ritual impurity for the higher-caste partner has been important in maintaining endogamy. A man who has sex with a lower-caste woman can restore his purity with a bath and a prayer. However, a woman who has intercourse with a man of a lower caste has no such recourse. Her defilement cannot be undone. Because the women have the babies, these differences protect the purity of the caste line, ensuring the pure ancestry of high-caste children. Although Indian castes are endogamous groups, many of them are internally subdivided into exogamous lineages. Traditionally this meant that Indians had to marry a member of another descent group from the same caste.

Royal Endogamy

Royal endogamy, based in a few societies on brother–sister marriage, is similar to caste endogamy. Inca Peru, ancient Egypt, and traditional Hawaii all allowed royal brother–sister marriages. In ancient Peru and Hawaii, such marriages were permitted despite the sibling incest taboo that applied to commoners in those societies.

Manifest and Latent Functions

To understand royal brother–sister marriage, it is useful to distinguish between the manifest and latent functions of customs and behavior. The *manifest function* of a custom refers to the reasons people in that society give for it. Its *latent function* is an effect the custom has on the society that its members don't mention or may not even recognize. (See Appendix 1 for a discussion of the theoretical school in anthropology known as *functionalism*.)

Royal endogamy illustrates this distinction. Hawaiians and other Polynesians believed in an impersonal force called *mana*. Mana could exist in things or people, in the latter case marking them off from other people and making them sacred. The Hawaiians believed that no one had as much mana as the ruler. Mana depended on genealogy. The person whose own mana was exceeded only by the king's was his sibling. The most appropriate wife for a king was his own full sister. Notice that the brother–sister marriage also meant that royal heirs would be as manaful, or sacred, as possible. The manifest function of royal endogamy in ancient Hawaii was part of that culture's beliefs about mana and sacredness.

Royal endogamy also had latent functions—political repercussions. The ruler and his wife had the same parents. Since mana was believed to be inherited, they were almost equally sacred. When the king and his sister married, their children indisputably had the most mana in the land. No one could question their right to rule. But if the king had taken as a wife someone with less mana than his sister, his sister's children eventually could cause problems. Both sets of children could assert their sacredness and right to rule. Royal sibling marriage therefore limited conflicts about succession by reducing the number of people with claims to rule. The same result would be true in ancient Egypt and Peru.

Other kingdoms, including European royalty, also have practiced endogamy, but based on cousin marriage rather than sibling marriage. In many cases, as in Great Britain, it is specified that the eldest child (usually the son) of the reigning monarch can succeed. This custom is called *primogeniture*. Commonly, rulers have banished or killed claimants who rival the chosen heir.

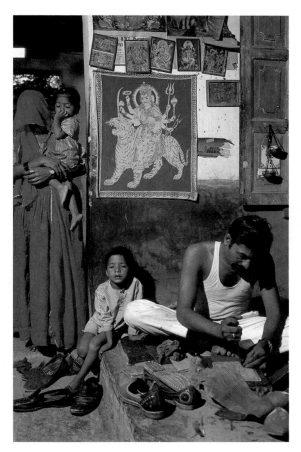

An extreme example of endogamy is India's caste system, which was formally abolished in 1949, although its structure and effects linger. In Gadwada village, cobblers still make shoes in a traditional style. Here, Devi-Lal sits with his child as his wife looks on. In the traditional caste system, such cobblers had a higher status than did sweepers and tanners, whose work is considered so smelly and dirty that they live at the far end of the village.

Royal endogamy also had a latent economic function. If the king and his sister had rights to inherit the ancestral estate, their marriage to each other, again by limiting the number of heirs, kept it intact. Power often rests on wealth, and royal endogamy tended to ensure that royal wealth remained concentrated in the same line.

MARITAL RIGHTS AND SAME-SEX MARRIAGE

The British anthropologist Edmund Leach (1955) observed that, depending on the society, several different kinds of rights are allocated by marriage. According to Leach, marriage can, but doesn't always, accomplish the following:

1. Establish the legal father of a woman's children and the legal mother of a man's.

2. Give either or both spouses a monopoly in the sexuality of the other.

3. Give either or both spouses rights to the labor of the other.

4. Give either or both spouses rights over the other's property.

On December 21, 2005, Sir Elton John (right) married his long-time domestic partner, David Furnish. The ceremony took place in the town chapel in Windsor, England, where, eight months earlier, Prince Charles had married Camilla Parker-Bowles. The John-Furnish union took place on the first day on which same-sex couples were allowed a legal status comparable to marriage—including the same social security, pension, tax and inheritance rights—in England and Wales. (The law took effect earlier that week in Northern Ireland and Scotland.)

For more on laws affecting same-sex marriage, see the Internet Exercises at your OLC

mhhe.com/kottak

5. Establish a joint fund of property—a partnership—for the benefit of the children.

6. Establish a socially significant "relationship of affinity" between spouses and their relatives.

The discussion of same-sex marriage that follows will serve to illustrate the six rights just listed by seeing what happens in their absence. What if same-sex marriages, which by and large are illegal in the United States, were legal? Could a same-sex marriage establish legal parentage of children born to one or both partners after the partnership is formed? In the case of a different-sex marriage, children born to the wife after the marriage takes place usually are legally defined as her husband's regardless of whether he is the genitor.

Nowadays, of course, DNA testing makes it possible to establish paternity, just as modern reproductive technology makes it possible for a lesbian couple to have one or both partners artificially inseminated. If same-sex marriages were legal, the social construction of kinship could easily make both partners parents. If a Nuer woman married to a woman can be the pater of a child she did not father, why can't two lesbians be the **maters** (socially recognized mothers) of a child one of them did not father? And if a married different-sex couple can adopt a child and have it be theirs through the social and legal construction of kinship, the same logic could be applied to a gay male or lesbian couple.

Continuing with Leach's list of the rights transmitted by marriage, same-sex marriage could certainly give each spouse rights to the sexuality of the other. Unable to marry legally, gay men and lesbians have used various devices, such as mock weddings, to declare their commitment and desire for a monogamous sexual relationship. In April 2000, Vermont passed a bill allowing same-sex

couples to unite legally, with virtually all the benefits of marriage. In June 2003 a court ruling established same-sex marriages as legal in the province of Ontario, Canada. On June 28, 2005, Canada's House of Commons voted to guarantee full marriage rights to same-sex couples throughout that nation. On May 17, 2004, Massachusetts became the first state in the United States to allow same-sex couples to marry. In reaction to same-sex marriage, voters in 18 U.S. states have approved measures in their state constitutions defining marriage as an exclusively heterosexual union.

Legal same-sex marriages could easily give each spouse rights to the other spouse's labor and its products. Some societies have allowed marriage between members of the same biological sex, who may, however, be considered to belong to a different, socially constructed, gender. Several Native American groups had figures known as *berdaches*, representing a third gender (Murray and Roscoe 1998). These were biological men who assumed many of the mannerisms, behavior patterns, and tasks of women. Sometimes *berdaches* married men, who shared the products of their labor from hunting and traditional male roles, as the *berdache* fulfilled the traditional wifely role. Also, in some Native American cultures, a marriage of a "manly-hearted woman" (a third or fourth gender) to another woman brought the traditional male–female division of labor to their household. The manly woman hunted and did other male tasks, while the wife played the traditional female role.

There's no logical reason why same-sex marriage could not give spouses rights over the other's property. But in the United States, the same inheritance rights that apply to male–female couples do not apply to same-sex couples. For instance, even in the absence of a will, property can pass to a widow or a widower without going through probate. The wife or husband pays no inheritance tax. This benefit is not available to gay men and lesbians.

What about Leach's fifth right—to establish a joint fund of property—to benefit the children? Here again, gay and lesbian couples are at a disadvantage. If there are children, property is separately, rather than jointly, transmitted. Some organizations do make staff benefits, such as health and dental insurance, available to same-sex domestic partners.

Finally, there is the matter of establishing a socially significant "relationship of affinity" between spouses and their relatives. In many societies, one of the main roles of marriage is to establish an alliance between groups, in addition to the individual bond. Affinals are relatives through marriage, such as a brother-in-law or mother-in-law. For same-sex couples in contemporary North America, affinal relations are problematic. In an unofficial union, terms like "daughter-in-law"

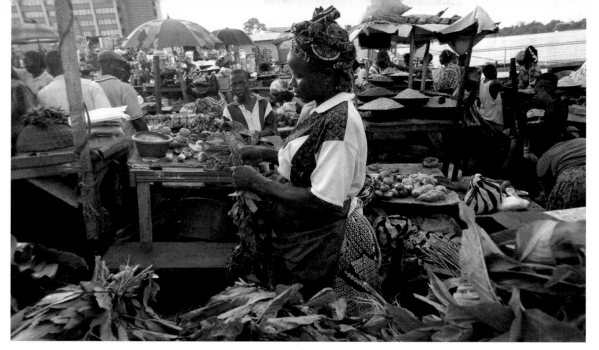

In Lagos, Nigeria, women work with green vegetables in a bayside market. In parts of Nigeria, prominent market women may take a wife. Such marriage allows wealthy women to strengthen their social status and the economic importance of their households.

and "mother-in-law" may sound strange. Many parents are suspicious of their children's sexuality and lifestyle choices and may not recognize a relationship of affinity with a child's partner of the same sex.

This discussion of same-sex marriage has been intended to illustrate the different kinds of rights that typically accompany marriage by seeing what may happen when there is a permanent pair bond without legal sanction. In the United States, with the fleeting exception of Hawaii, which flirted with the legalization of same-sex marriage, Vermont, and Massachusetts, as mentioned previously, such unions are illegal. As we have seen, same-sex marriages have been recognized in different historical and cultural settings. In certain African cultures, including the Igbo of Nigeria and the Lovedu of South Africa, women may marry other women. In situations in which women, such as prominent market women in West Africa, are able to amass property and other forms of wealth, they may take a wife. Such marriage allows the prominent woman to strengthen her social status and the economic importance of her household (Amadiume 1987).

MARRIAGE AS GROUP ALLIANCE

Outside industrial societies, marriage is often more a relationship between groups than one between individuals. We think of marriage as an individual matter. Although the bride and groom usually seek their parents' approval, the final choice (to live together, to marry, to divorce) lies with the couple. The idea of romantic love symbolizes this individual relationship.

In nonindustrial societies, although there can be romantic love, as we see in "Interesting Issues" (on pp. 240–241), marriage is a group concern. People don't just take a spouse; they assume obligations to a group of in-laws. When residence is patrilocal, for example, a woman often must leave the community where she was born. She faces the prospect of spending the rest of her life in her husband's village, with his relatives. She may even have to transfer her major allegiance from her own group to her husband's.

Bridewealth and Dowry

In societies with descent groups, people enter marriage not alone but with the help of the descent group. Descent-group members often have to contribute to the **bridewealth,** a customary gift before, at, or after the marriage from the husband and his kin to the wife and her kin. Another word for bridewealth is *brideprice,* but this term is inaccurate because people with the custom don't usually regard the exchange as a sale. They don't think of marriage as a commercial relationship between a man and an object that can be bought and sold.

Bridewealth compensates the bride's group for the loss of her companionship and labor. More important, it makes the children born to the woman full members of her husband's descent group. For this reason, the institution is also called **progeny price.** Rather than the woman herself, it is her children, or progeny, who are permanently transferred to the husband's group. Whatever we call it, such a transfer of wealth at marriage is common in patrilineal groups. In matrilineal societies, children are members of the mother's group, and there is no reason to pay a progeny price.

For more information about marriage among the Hmong, see the Internet Exercises at your OLC

mhhe.com/kottak

Human Mate Preference in Matrimonial Advertisements from Gujarat, India

BACKGROUND INFORMATION

STUDENT:
Kim Shah

SCHOOL:
Rutgers University

SUPERVISING PROFESSOR:
Lee Kronk

YEAR IN SCHOOL/MAJOR:
Senior/Anthropology

FUTURE PLANS:
Graduate study of nutritional anthropology and public health

This study suggests that Indian marriage customs are changing, and particularly that women may have a stronger role in marital choices than has been thought traditionally (see the section "Bridewealth and Dowry"). It's also true that marriage customs and the roles of men and women vary by region in a country as large and populous as India, which contains considerable cultural diversity. Still, this account also demonstrates that caste still matters and that parents play a significant role in arranging marriages.

Human mate preferences have been studied in many settings, among them newspaper ads, often termed lonely-hearts personal advertisements. In these ads, people describe their own attributes and those they seek in potential mates. The ad might look something like this, "Tall, handsome, intelligent investment banker seeks smart, slim, fun-loving woman."

Most studies of mate preference theory using such advertisements have been done in western settings. My research involved the study of non-western advertisements, specifically from the state of Gujarat in India. These ads were taken from the matrimonial section of a Gujarati newspaper. A typical one looked something like this: "For marriage: vaisshnav, vanik (caste designation) man, 34 years old, owns his own home and car, makes 75,000Rs. per year, (seeks) pretty, smart, lady."

The purpose of my project was to test hypotheses of mate preference based on evolutionary theory. I did this by content analysis focusing on the characteristics sought and offered by advertisers. For this task I took advantage of the cultural diversity of my university (Rutgers) and hired international students from Gujarat to help me in this procedure.

A total of 142 advertisements, 20 seeking wives and 122 seeking husbands, were studied. Under "physical attractiveness" I coded for looks, stature/weight, and fairness. I hypothesized that advertisers seeking wives would look for physical attractiveness more than advertisers seeking husbands would. In turn, women seeking husbands would mention their own physical attractiveness more often than men seeking wives would. These hypotheses were confirmed with the data on good looks and stature/weight.

Yet cultural differences were also apparent. Compared with similar studies done elsewhere, the male preference for good looks was de-emphasized in my results. Only 14% of wife-seeking advertisers requested good looks, significantly fewer than in other studies. An explanation may be that parental involvement in writing and/or answering these ads affects the male request for good looks. Indeed, on re-analysis, I found that 46% of all advertisers sought responses not from the prospective mate himself or herself, but from the parents of the prospective mate. Thus de-emphasis of the male preference for physical attractiveness may reflect the advertisers' awareness of parental involvement.

Male advertisers were on average 4 years older than female advertisers. The content analysis also revealed that advertisers seeking wives offered information about financial resources more than advertisers seeking husbands did. In other words, prospective husbands were more likely to include information about their salary or possessions than prospective wives were. Logically, advertisers seeking husbands made more inquiries about the prospective mate's financial situation.

Throughout this project it was apparent that cultural and social forces played a significant role. Gujarati society displayed strong adherence to maintaining caste integrity. I also learned that the advertisers had above average educations, so I must view the results of my project as representative of this particular group only. I was able to understand many aspects of Gujarati culture, language, and religion because my own family is from the state of Gujarat. I presented this project at the 14th annual meeting of the Human Evolution and Behavior Society in 2002. Future work on this project will include a study of response rates.

It's hard to make the transition from the family of orientation to the family of procreation. Unlike people in nonindustrial societies, most of us get a head start by "leaving home" long before we marry. We go off to college or find a job that enables us to support ourselves so that we can live independently, or with roommates. In nonindustrial societies people, especially women, may have to leave home abruptly when they marry. In patrilocal societies a woman must leave her home village and her own kin and move in with her husband and his relatives. This can be an unpleasant and alienating transition. Many women complain about feeling isolated when they first arrive in the husband's village. Later they may be mistreated by their husband or in-laws, including the mother-in-law. However, things will be brighter if women from village or descent group A typically marry men from village or descent group B. If this is the case, a woman can be sure to find some of her own relatives, such as her sister or aunt (father's sister), living as wives in her husband's village, and she will feel more at home.

In contemporary North America, neither women nor men typically have to adjust to in-laws living close at hand. But we do have to learn to live with our spouses. Marriage always raises issues of accommodation and adjustment. Initially the married couple is just that, unless there are children from a previous marriage. If there are, adjustment issues will involve stepparenthood—and a prior spouse—as well as the new marital relationship. Once a couple has its own child, the family-of-procreation mentality takes over. In the United States family loyalty shifts, but not completely, from the family of orientation to the family that includes spouse and child(ren). Given our bilateral kinship system, we maintain relations with our sons and daughters after they marry, and grandchildren theoretically are as close to one set of grandparents as to the other. In a patrilineal society there would be a closer bond with the paternal grandparents. What about in a matrilineal society?

Dowry is a marital exchange in which the wife's group provides substantial gifts to the husband's family. Dowry, best known from India, correlates with low female status. Women are perceived as burdens. When husbands and their families take a wife, they expect to be compensated for the added responsibility.

Gift-giving customs are associated with marriage throughout the world. In this photo, guests bring presents in baskets to a wedding in Wenjiang, China.

Although India passed a law in 1961 against compulsory dowry, the practice continues. When the dowry is considered insufficient, the bride may be harassed and abused. Domestic violence can escalate to the point where the husband or his family burn the bride, often by pouring kerosene on her and lighting it, usually killing her. It should be pointed out that dowry doesn't necessarily lead to domestic abuse. In fact, Indian dowry murders seem to be a fairly recent phenomenon. It also has been estimated that the rate of spousal murders in the contemporary United States may rival the incidence of India's dowry murders (Narayan 1997).

Sati was the very rare practice through which widows were burned alive, voluntarily or forcibly, on the husband's funeral pyre (Hawley 1994). Although it has become well known, *sati* was mainly practiced in a particular area of northern India by a few small castes. It was banned in 1829. Dowry murders and *sati* are flagrant examples of *patriarchy,* a political system ruled by men in which women have inferior social and political status, including basic human rights.

Bridewealth exists in many more cultures than dowry does, but the nature and quantity of transferred items differ. In many African societies, cattle constitute bridewealth, but the number of cattle given varies from society to society. *As the value of bridewealth increases, marriages become more stable.* Bridewealth is insurance against divorce.

Imagine a patrilineal society in which a marriage requires the transfer of about 25 cattle from the groom's descent group to the bride's. Michael, a member of descent group A, marries Sarah from group B. His relatives help him assemble the bridewealth. He gets the most help from his close agnates (patrilineal relatives): his older brother, father, father's brother, and closest patrilineal cousins.

The distribution of the cattle once they reach Sarah's group mirrors the manner in which they were assembled. Sarah's father, or her oldest

Love and Marriage

Love and marriage, the song says, go together like a horse and carriage. But the link between love and marriage, like the horse–carriage combination, isn't a cultural universal. Described here is a cross-cultural survey, published in the anthropological journal Ethnology, *which found romantic ardor to be widespread, perhaps universal. Previously anthropologists had tended to ignore evidence for romantic love in other cultures, probably because arranged marriages were so common. Today, diffusion, mainly via the mass media, of Western ideas about the importance of love for marriage appears to be influencing marital decisions in other cultures.*

Some influential Western social historians have argued that romance was a product of European medieval culture that spread only recently to other cultures. They dismissed romantic tales from other cultures as representing the behavior of just the elites. Under the sway of this view, Western anthropologists did not even look for romantic love among the peoples they studied. But they are now beginning to think that romantic love is universal . . .

"For decades anthropologists and other scholars have assumed romantic love was unique to the modern West," said Dr. Leonard Plotnicov, an anthropologist at the University of Pittsburgh and editor of the journal *Ethnology.* "Anthropologists came across it in their field work, but they rarely mentioned it because it wasn't supposed to happen."

"Why has something so central to our culture been so ignored by anthropology?" asked Dr. William Jankowiak, an anthropologist at the University of Nevada.

The reason, in the view of Dr. Jankowiak and others, is a scholarly bias throughout the social sciences that viewed romantic love as a luxury in human life, one that could be indulged only by people in Westernized cultures or among the educated elites of other societies. For example it was assumed in societies where life is hard that romantic love has less chance to blossom, because higher economic standards and more leisure time create more opportunity for dalliance. That also contributed to the belief that

romance was for the ruling class, not the peasants.

But, said Dr. Jankowiak, "There is romantic love in cultures around the world." [In 1991] Dr. Jankowiak, with Dr. Edward Fischer, an anthropologist at Tulane University, published in *Ethnology* the first cross-cultural study, systematically comparing romantic love in many cultures.

In the survey of ethnographies from 166 cultures, they found what they considered clear evidence that romantic love was known in 147 of them—89 percent. And in the other 19 cultures, Dr. Jankowiak said, the absence of conclusive evidence seemed due more to anthropologists' oversight than to a lack of romance.

Some of the evidence came from tales about lovers, or folklore that offered love potions or other advice on making someone fall in love.

Another source was accounts by informants to anthropologists. For example, Nisa, a !Kung woman among the Bushmen of the Kalahari, made a clear distinction between the affection she felt for her husband, and that she felt for her lovers, which was "passionate and

brother if the father is dead, receives her bridewealth. He keeps most of the cattle to use as bridewealth for his sons' marriages. However, a share also goes to everyone who will be expected to help when Sarah's brothers marry.

When Sarah's brother David gets married, many of the cattle go to a third group: C, which is David's wife's group. Thereafter, they may serve as bridewealth to still other groups. Men constantly use their sisters' bridewealth cattle to acquire their own wives. In a decade, the cattle given when Michael married Sarah will have been exchanged widely.

In such societies, marriage entails an agreement between descent groups. If Sarah and Michael try to make their marriage succeed but fail to do so, both groups may conclude that the marriage can't last. Here it becomes especially obvious that such marriages are relationships between groups as well as between individuals. If Sarah has a younger sister or niece (her older

brother's daughter, for example), the concerned parties may agree to Sarah's replacement by a kinswoman.

However, incompatibility isn't the main problem that threatens marriage in societies with bridewealth. Infertility is a more important concern. If Sarah has no children, she and her group have not fulfilled their part of the marriage agreement. If the relationship is to endure, Sarah's group must furnish another woman, perhaps her younger sister, who can have children. If this happens, Sarah may choose to stay with her husband. Perhaps she will someday have a child. If she does stay on, her husband will have established a plural marriage.

Most nonindustrial food-producing societies, unlike most foraging societies and industrial nations, allow **plural marriages,** or *polygamy.* There are two varieties; one is common, and the other is very rare. The more common variant is **polygyny,** in which a man has more than one wife. The rare

See the Virtual Exploration for bridewealth traditions of the Nenetsi of Siberia

mhhe.com/kottak

exciting," though fleeting. Of these extramarital affairs, she said: "When two people come together their hearts are on fire and their passion is very great. After a while the fire cools and that's how it stays." . . .

While finding that romantic love appears to be a human universal, Dr. Jankowiak allows that it is still an alien idea in many cultures that such infatuation has anything to do with the choice of a spouse.

"What's new in many cultures is the idea that romantic love should be the reason to marry someone," said Dr. Jankowiak. "Some cultures see being in love as a state to be pitied. One tribe in the mountains of Iran ridicules people who marry for love."

Of course, even in arranged marriages, partners may grow to feel romantic love for each other. For example, among villagers in the Kangra valley of northern India, "people's romantic longings and yearnings ideally would become focused on the person they're matched with by their families," said Dr. Kirin Narayan, an anthropologist at the University of Wisconsin.

But that has begun to change, Dr. Narayan is finding, under the influence of popular songs and movies. "In these villages the elders are worried

that the younger men and women are getting a different idea of romantic love, one where you choose a partner yourself," said Dr. Narayan. "There are starting to be elopements, which are absolutely scandalous."

The same trend toward love matches, rather than arranged marriages, is being noted by anthropologists in many other cultures. Among aborigines in Australia's Outback, for example, marriages had for centuries been arranged when children were very young.

That pattern was disrupted earlier in the last century by missionaries, who urged that marriage not occur until children reached adolescence. Dr. Victoria Burbank, an anthropologist at the University of California at Davis, said that in pre-missionary days, the average age of a girl at marriage was always before menarche, sometimes as young as 9 years. Today the average age at marriage is 17; girls are more independent by the time their parents try to arrange a marriage for them.

"More and more adolescent girls are breaking away from arranged marriages," said Dr. Burbank. "They prefer to go off into the bush for a 'date' with someone they like, get pregnant, and use that pregnancy to get parental approval for the match."

Even so, parents sometimes are adamant that the young people should not get married. They prefer, instead, that the girls follow the traditional pattern of having their mothers choose a husband for them.

"Traditionally among these people, you can't choose just any son-in-law," said Dr. Burbank. "Ideally, the mother wants to find a boy who is her maternal grandmother's brother's son, a pattern that insures partners are in the proper kin group."

Dr. Burbank added: "These groups have critical ritual functions. A marriage based on romantic love, which ignores what's a proper partner, undermines the system of kinship, ritual, and obligation."

Nevertheless, the rules for marriage are weakening. "In the grandmothers' generation, all marriages were arranged. Romantic love had no place, though there were a few stories of a young man and woman in love running off together. But in the group I studied, in only one recent case did the girl marry the man selected for her. All the rest are love matches." . . .

SOURCE: Daniel Goleman, "Anthropology Goes Looking in All the Old Places," *New York Times*, November 24, 1992, p. B1.

variant is **polyandry,** in which a woman has more than one husband. If the infertile wife remains married to her husband after he has taken a substitute wife provided by her descent group, this is polygyny. Reasons for polygyny other than infertility will be discussed shortly.

Durable Alliances

It is possible to exemplify the group-alliance nature of marriage by examining still another common practice: continuation of marital alliances when one spouse dies.

Sororate

What happens if Sarah dies young? Michael's group will ask Sarah's group for a substitute, often her sister. This custom is known as the **sororate** (Figure 10.5). If Sarah has no sister or if all her sisters are already married, another woman

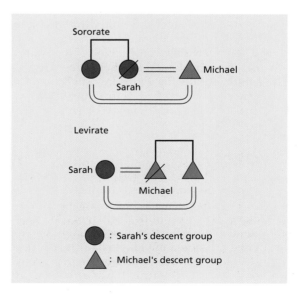

FIGURE 10.5 Sororate and Levirate.

STUDENT CD-ROM LIVING ANTHROPOLOGY

Courtship among the Dinka
Track 10

This clip shows courtship practices among the Dinka, pastoralists of southern Sudan. It describes the importance of brideprice or bridewealth, customarily given by the family of the groom to the family of the bride. We also see why bridewealth is sometimes called progeny price. According to the Dinka, why are cattle and children (progeny) similar? The narrator claims there is no room for romance in Dinka courtship. Based on the "Interesting Issues" feature titled "Love and Marriage" and on what you see in this clip, do you believe this claim to be true? The clip also illustrates the text's point that marriage in such societies is as much a relation between groups as one between individuals. The Dinka have descent groups. Do you think they are patrilineal or matrilineal? Why? Among the Dinka, what are the barriers to marriage—and to polygyny?

from her group may be available. Michael marries her, there is no need to return the bridewealth, and the alliance continues. The sororate exists in both matrilineal and patrilineal societies. In a matrilineal society with matrilocal postmarital residence, a widower may remain with his wife's group by marrying her sister or another female member of her matrilineage (Figure 10.5).

Levirate

What happens if the husband dies? In many societies, the widow may marry his brother. This custom is known as the **levirate** (Figure 10.5). Like the sororate, it is a continuation marriage that maintains the alliance between descent groups, in this case by replacing the husband with another member of his group. The implications of the levirate vary with age. One study found that in African societies, the levirate, though widely permitted, rarely involves cohabitation of the widow and her new husband. Furthermore, widows don't automatically marry the husband's brother just because they are allowed to. Often, they prefer to make other arrangements (Potash 1986).

DIVORCE

Ease of divorce varies across cultures. What factors work for and against divorce? As we've seen, marriages that are political alliances between groups are more difficult to dissolve than are marriages that are more individual affairs, of concern mainly to the married couple and their children. We've seen that substantial bridewealth may decrease the divorce rate for individuals and that replacement marriages (levirate and sororate) also work to preserve group alliances. Divorce tends to

be more common in matrilineal than in patrilineal societies. When residence is matrilocal (in the wife's place), the wife may simply send off a man with whom she's incompatible.

Among the Hopi of the American Southwest, houses were owned by matrilineal clans, with matrilocal postmarital residence. The household head was the senior woman of that household, which also included her daughters and their husbands and children. A son-in-law had no important role there; he returned to his own mother's home for his clan's social and religious activities. In this matrilineal society, women were socially and economically secure, and the divorce rate was high. Consider the Hopi of Oraibi (Orayvi) pueblo, northeastern Arizona (Levy with Pepper 1992; Titiev 1992). In a study of the marital histories of 423 Oraibi women, Mischa Titiev found that 35 percent had been divorced at least once. Jerome Levy found that 31 percent of 147 adult women had been divorced and remarried at least once. For comparison, of all ever-married women in the United States, only 4 percent had been divorced in 1960, 10.7 percent in 1980, and 11.5 percent in 2004. Titiev characterizes Hopi marriages as unstable. Part of this brittleness was due to conflicting loyalties to matrikin versus spouse. Most Hopi divorces appear to have been matters of personal choice. Levy generalizes that, cross-culturally, high divorce rates are correlated with a secure female economic position. In Hopi society women were secure in their home and land ownership and in the custody of their children. In addition, there were no formal barriers to divorce.

Divorce is harder in a patrilineal society, especially when substantial bridewealth would have to be reassembled and repaid if the marriage failed. A woman residing patrilocally (in her husband's household and community) might be reluctant to leave him. Unlike the Hopi, where the kids stay with the mother, in patrilineal, patrilocal societies, the children of divorce would be expected to remain with their father, as members of his patrilineage. From the women's perspective this is a strong impediment to divorce.

Political and economic factors complicate the divorce process. Among foragers, different factors tend to favor and oppose divorce. What factors work against durable marriages? Since foragers tend to lack descent groups, the political alliance functions of marriage are less important to them than they are to food producers. Foragers also tend to have minimal material possessions. The process of dissolving a joint fund of property is less complicated when spouses do not hold substantial resources in common. What factors favor marital stability among foragers? In societies where the family is an important year-round unit with a gender-based division of labor, ties between spouses tend to be durable. Also, sparse populations mean few alternative spouses if a marriage doesn't work out. But in band-organized societies, foragers can always find a band to join or rejoin if a marriage doesn't work. And food producers can always draw on their descent-group estate if a marriage fails. With patriliny, a woman often can return home, albeit without her children, and with matriliny, a man can do the same. Descent-group estates are not transferred through marriages, although movable resources such as bridewealth cattle certainly are.

In contemporary Western societies, we do stress the idea that romantic love is necessary for a good marriage (see "Interesting Issues," pp. 240–241). When romance fails, so may the marriage. Or it may not fail, if the other rights associated with marriage, as discussed previously in this chapter, are compelling. Economic ties and obligations to kids, along with other factors, such as concern about public opinion, or simple inertia, may keep marriages intact after sex, romance, and/or companionship fade. Also, even in modern societies, royalty, leaders, and other elites may have political marriages similar to the arranged marriages of nonindustrial societies.

In the United States, divorce figures have been kept since 1860. Divorces tend to increase after wars and to decrease when times are bad economically. But with more women working outside the home, economic dependence on the husband as breadwinner is weaker, which no doubt facilitates a decision to divorce when a marriage has major problems.

TABLE 10.1 Changing Divorce Rates (Number per Year) in the United States, 1940 through 2000

Year	Divorce Rate per 1,000 Population	Divorce Rate per 1,000 Women Aged 15 and Older
1940	2.0	8.8
1950	2.6	10.3
1960	2.2	9.2
1970	3.5	14.9
1980	5.2	22.6
1990	4.7	20.9
2000	4.2	19.5
2005	3.6	NA

SOURCES: S. C. Clarke, "Advance Report of Final Divorce Statistics, 1989 and 1990," *Monthly Vital Statistics Report* 43(8, 9). Hyattsville, MD: National Center for Health Statistics; R. Hughes, Jr., "Demographics of Divorce," 1996. http://www.hec.ohio-state.edu/famlife/divorce/demo.htm; *National Vital Statistics Reports* 54(12), 2006. http://www.cdc.gov/nchs/data/nvsr/nvsr54_12.pdf.

Table 10.1 is based on two measures of the divorce rate. The left column shows the rate per 1,000 people per year in the overall population. The right column shows the annual rate per 1,000 married women over the age of 15, which is the best measure of divorce. In either case, comparing 2000 with 1960, the divorce rate more than doubled. Note that the rate rose slightly after World War II (1950), then declined a decade later (1960). The most notable rate rise occurred between 1960 and 1980. The rate actually has been falling since 1980, and continued to fall between 2000 and 2005.

Among nations, the United States has one of the world's highest divorce rates. There are several probable causes: economic, cultural, and religious among them. Economically, the United States has a larger percentage of gainfully employed women than most nations. Work outside the home provides a cash basis for independence, as it also places strains on marriage and social life for both partners. Culturally, Americans tend to value independence and its modern form, self-actualization. Also, Protestantism (in its various guises) is the most common form of religion in the United States. Of the two major religions in the United States and Canada (where Catholicism predominates), Protestantism has been less stringent in denouncing divorce than has Catholicism.

PLURAL MARRIAGES

In contemporary North America, where divorce is fairly easy and common, polygamy (marriage to more than one spouse at the same time) is against the law. Marriage in industrial nations joins individuals, and relationships between individuals can be severed more easily than can those between groups. As divorce grows more common, North Americans practice *serial monogamy:* Individuals have more than one spouse but never, legally, more than one at the same time. As stated earlier, the two forms of polygamy are polygyny and polyandry. Polyandry is practiced in only a few cultures, notably among certain groups in Tibet, Nepal, and India. Polygyny is much more common.

Polygyny

We must distinguish between the social approval of plural marriage and its actual frequency in a particular society. Many cultures approve of a man having more than one wife. However, even when polygyny is encouraged, most men are monogamous, and polygyny characterizes only a fraction of the marriages. Why is this true?

One reason is equal sex ratios. In the United States, about 105 males are born for every 100 females. In adulthood, the ratio of men to women equalizes, and eventually it reverses. The average North American woman outlives the average

Bringing It All Together

For a description of unity and diversity in Canada, see the "Bringing It All Together" essay that immediately follows the chapter "Language and Communication."

■ *Members of the Uighur ethnic group, this polygynous family includes two wives, six children, and one husband. They sit in front of their house at the Buzak Commune, near Khotan, Xinjiang Province, People's Republic of China. Would you expect most marriages to be polygynous in a society that allows polygyny?*

man. In many nonindustrial societies as well, the male-biased sex ratio among children reverses in adulthood.

The custom of men marrying later than women promotes polygyny. Among the Kanuri people of Bornu, Nigeria (Figure 10.6), men got married between the ages of 18 and 30; women, between 12 and 14 (Cohen 1967). The age difference between spouses meant that there were more widows than widowers. Most of the widows remarried, some in polygynous unions. Among the Kanuri of Bornu and in other polygynous societies, widows made up a large number of the women involved in plural marriages (Hart, Pilling, and Goodale 1988). In many societies, including the Kanuri, the number of wives is an indicator of a man's household productivity, prestige, and social position. The more wives, the more workers. Increased productivity means more wealth. This wealth in turn attracts additional wives to the household. Wealth and wives bring greater prestige to the household and head.

If a plural marriage is to work, there needs to be some agreement among the existing spouses when another one is to be added, especially if they are to share the same household. In certain societies, the first wife requests a second wife to help with household chores. The second wife's status is lower than that of the first; they are senior and junior wives. The senior wife sometimes chooses the junior one from among her close kinswomen. Among the Betsileo of Madagascar, the different wives always lived in different villages. A man's first and senior wife, called "Big Wife," lived in the village where he cultivated his best rice field and spent most of his time. High-status men with several rice fields and multiple wives had households near each field. They spent most of their time with the senior wife but visited the others throughout the year.

Plural wives can play important political roles in nonindustrial states. The king of the Merina, a society with more than one million people in the highlands of Madagascar, had palaces for each of his 12 wives in different provinces. He stayed with them when he traveled through the kingdom. They were his local agents, overseeing and reporting on provincial matters. The king of

FIGURE 10.6 Location of Bornu, home of the Kanuri, in Nigeria.

Buganda, the major precolonial state of Uganda, took hundreds of wives, representing all the clans in his nation. Everyone in the kingdom became the king's in-law, and all the clans had a chance to provide the next ruler. This was a way of giving the common people a stake in the government.

These examples show that there is no single explanation for polygyny. Its context and function vary from society to society and even within the same society. Some men are polygynous because they have inherited a widow from a brother (the levirate). Others have plural wives because they seek prestige or want to increase household productivity. Still others use marriage as a political tool or a means of economic advancement. Men and women with political and economic ambitions cultivate marital alliances that serve their aims. In many societies, including the Betsileo of Madagascar and the Igbo of Nigeria, women arrange the marriages.

Polyandry

Polyandry is rare and is practiced under very specific conditions. Most of the world's polyandrous peoples live in South Asia—Tibet, Nepal, India, and Sri Lanka. In some of these areas, polyandry seems to be a cultural adaptation to mobility associated with customary male travel for trade, commerce, and military operations. Polyandry ensures there will be at least one man at home to accomplish male activities within a gender-based division of labor. Fraternal polyandry is also an effective strategy when resources are scarce. Brothers with limited resources (in land) pool their resources in expanded (polyandrous) households. They take just one wife. Polyandry restricts the number of wives and heirs. Less competition among heirs means that land can be transmitted with minimal fragmentation.

SUMMARY

1. Marriage, which is usually a form of domestic partnership, is hard to define. All societies have some kind of incest taboo. Human behavior with respect to mating with close relatives may express a generalized primate tendency, illustrating both urges and avoidance. But types, risks, and avoidance of incest also reflect specific kinship structures. A cultural focus on father–daughter incest may correlate with a patriarchal nuclear family structure, whereas the cultural focus is on avoiding brother–sister incest in societies with lineages and clans.

2. The following are some of the explanations that have been offered for the incest taboo: (1) It codifies instinctive horror of incest, (2) it expresses concern about the biological effects of incestuous unions, (3) it reflects feelings of attraction or aversion that develop as one grows up in a household, and (4) it has an adaptive advantage because it promotes exogamy, thereby increasing networks of friends and allies.

3. Exogamy extends social and political ties outward. This is confirmed by a consideration of endogamy—marriage within the group. Endogamic rules are common in stratified societies. One extreme example is India, where castes are the endogamous units. Castes are subdivided into exogamous descent groups. The same culture can therefore have both endogamic and exogamic rules. Certain ancient kingdoms encouraged royal incest while condemning incest by commoners.

4. The discussion of same-sex marriage, which, by and large, is illegal in contemporary North America, illustrates the various rights that go along with different-sex marriages. Marriage establishes the legal parents of children. It gives spouses rights to the sexuality, labor, and property of the other. And it establishes a socially significant "relationship of affinity" between spouses and each other's relatives. Some of these rights may be established by same-sex domestic partnerships.

5. In societies with descent groups, marriages are relationships between groups as well as between spouses. With the custom of bridewealth, the groom and his relatives transfer wealth to the bride and her relatives. As the bridewealth's value increases, the divorce rate declines. Bridewealth customs show that marriages among nonindustrial food producers create and maintain group alliances. So do the sororate, by which a man marries the sister of his deceased wife, and the levirate, by which a woman marries the brother of her deceased husband.

6. The ease and frequency of divorce vary across cultures. Political, economic, social, cultural, and religious factors affect the divorce rate. When marriage is a matter of intergroup alliance, as is typically true in societies with descent groups, divorce is less common. A large fund of joint property also complicates divorce.

7. Many societies permit plural marriages. The two kinds of polygamy are polygyny and polyandry. The former involves multiple wives; the latter, multiple husbands. Polygyny is much more common than is polyandry.

KEY TERMS

See the flash cards
mhhe.com/kottak

bridewealth   See *progeny price.*

cross cousins   Children of a brother and a sister.

dowry   A marital exchange in which the wife's group provides substantial gifts to the husband's family.

endogamy   Rule or practice of marriage between people of the same social group.

exogamy   Rule requiring people to marry outside their own group.

genitor   Biological father of a child.

incest   Forbidden sexual relations with a close relative.

levirate   Custom by which a widow marries the brother of her deceased husband.

mater   Socially recognized mother of a child.

parallel cousins   Children of two brothers or two sisters.

pater   Socially recognized father of a child; not necessarily the genitor.

plural marriage   Any marriage with more than two spouses, aka polygamy.

polyandry   Variety of plural marriage in which a woman has more than one husband.

polygyny   Variety of plural marriage in which a man has more than one wife.

progeny price   A gift from the husband and his kin to the wife and her kin before, at, or after marriage; legitimizes children born to the woman as members of the husband's descent group.

sororate   Custom by which a widower marries the sister of his deceased wife.

CRITICAL
THINKING
QUESTIONS

For more self-testing,
see the self-quizzes
mhhe.com/kottak

1. Try to come up with a definition of marriage that fits all the cases examined in this chapter. What problems do you encounter in doing this?

2. What is bridewealth? What else is it called, and why? Do we have anything like it in our own society? Why or why not?

3. What is the difference between sororate and levirate? What do they have in common? Do these customs make sense to you?

4. If you had to live in a society with plural marriage, would you prefer polygyny or polyandry? Why?

5. What general conclusions do you draw about the differences between marriage in your society and marriage in nonindustrial societies?

Collier, J. F., ed.
1988 *Marriage and Inequality in Classless Societies.* Stanford, CA: Stanford University Press. Marriage and issues of gender stratification in bands and tribes.

Goody, J., and S. T. Tambiah
1973 *Bridewealth and Dowry.* Cambridge, England: Cambridge University Press. Marital exchanges in comparative perspective.

Hart, C. W. M., A. R. Pilling, and J. C. Goodale
1988 *The Tiwi of North Australia,* 3rd ed. Fort Worth: Harcourt Brace. Latest edition of classic case study of Tiwi marriage arrangements, including polygyny, and social change over 60 years of anthropological study.

Ingraham, C.
1999 *White Weddings: Romancing Heterosexuality in Popular Culture.* New York: Routledge. Love and marriage, including the ceremony, in today's United States.

Levine, N. E.
1988 *The Dynamics of Polyandry: Kinship, Domesticity, and Population in the Tibetan Border.* Chicago: University of Chicago Press. Case study of fraternal polyandry and household organization in northwestern Nepal.

Malinowski, B.
2001 (orig. 1927). *Sex and Repression in Savage Society.* New York: Routledge. Classic study of sex, marriage, and kinship among the matrilineal Trobrianders.

Murray, S. O., and W. Roscoe, eds.
1998 *Boy-Wives and Female Husbands: Studies in African Homosexualities.* New York: St. Martin's. Same-sex sex and marriage in Africa.

Ottenheimer, M.
1996 *Forbidden Relatives: The American Myth of Cousin Marriage.* Champaign–Urbana: University of Illinois Press. Incest laws and cousin marriage in the United States and Europe.

Shepher, J.
1983 *Incest, a Biosocial View.* New York: Academic Press. A view from Israel, based on a case study in the kibbutz.

Simpson, B.
1998 *Changing Families: An Ethnographic Approach to Divorce and Separation.* New York: Berg. Current marriage and divorce trends in Great Britain.

SUGGESTED
ADDITIONAL
READINGS

1. Weddings: Here are some websites that sell wedding supplies for couples from different nationalities and traditions. Pick three of these websites and answer the questions below: Indian, **http:// www.weddingsutra.com/**; Jewish, **http://www. mazornet.com/jewishcl/jewishwd.htm**; African American, **http://www.africanweddingguide. com/**; Mormon, **http://www.askginka.com/ religions/mormon.htm**; Eastern Orthodox, **http://www.askginka.com/religions/eastern_ orthodox.htm**; Muslim, **http://www.askginka. com/religions/muslim.htm**; Roman Catholic, **http://www.askginka.com/religions/catholic. htm**.

a. What kinds of clothes are worn by the bride and the groom? To what degree are the clothes dictated by tradition or modern style? How much choice do the wedding planners have in the clothing that is worn?
b. What kind of locations are popular for the weddings?
c. What aspects of each of these weddings is most different from your own? What aspects are similar?
d. Why do you think wedding traditions vary so much by culture and religion?

INTERNET
EXERCISES

2. Descent and Postmarital Residence Rules: Go to the Ethnographic Atlas Cross-Tabulations page, **http://lucy.ukc.ac.uk/cgi-bin/uncgi/Ethnoatlas/atlas.vopts**. This site has compiled ethnographic information on many different groups, and you can use the tools provided to cross-tabulate the prevalence of certain traits. Under "Select Row Category" choose "descent," and under "Select Column Category" select "transfer of residence at marriage: prevalent form." Press the Submit Query button. The table that appears shows the frequency of postmarital residence rules for groups with different descent systems.

   a. What postmarital residence rules are most common for patrilineal groups? For matrilineal groups? Is this what you would expect?

   b. Based on your observations in section a, what postmarital residence practice would you least expect to find in patrilineal societies? How many groups in this chart practice such a pattern? Click on the number at that location to find out which groups those are and where they are located. What postmarital residence pattern would you least expect to find in matrilineal societies? Which groups practice that pattern?

   c. What is the most common form of descent for groups with an "Optional for couple" (ambilocal) postmarital residence pattern? Does this make sense?

See Chapter 10 at your McGraw-Hill Online Learning Center for additional review and interactive exercises.

LINKAGES

Kottak, *Assault on Paradise*, 4th ed.

Chapters 3 and 9 discuss types of marriage and domestic partnership in Arembepe. Chapter 3 describes the arrangements during the 1960s, and Chapter 9 shows how ideas and behavior concerning marriage had changed by the 1980s. What was the main incentive to marry formally in the 1960s? What were the main reasons for the changes described? Have there been significant changes in your own society in ideas about marriage and marital behavior over the last few years?

Peters-Golden, *Culture Sketches*, 4th ed.

In *Culture Sketches*, read Chapter 13, "Tiwi: Tradition in Australia." A tradition, no longer practiced, that all Tiwi females had to be married led to the betrothal of baby girls and the mandatory remarriage of all widows. This practice served several social ends. How do Tiwi marriage customs illustrate the social functions of marriage, as discussed in this text chapter? How do Tiwi customs compare with the rules and functions of marriage in your own society? Have those changed over time? If so, what might be the reason?

Knauft, *The Gebusi*, 1st ed.

Based on information in Chapters 4 and 10 of *The Gebusi*, what is the ideal form of marriage in Gebusi society? How much influence do women have in determining such marriages? Based on Chapter 4, what form of reciprocity do Gebusi practice between the bride's and the groom's groups? What is likely to happen when reciprocity cannot be arranged? What kinds of violence are related to marriage patterns in Gebusi society, and who is most likely to be attacked or killed? Based on Chapter 10 of *The Gebusi*, how did Gebusi marriage patterns change between 1980 and 1998? What benefits and what costs have been experienced by young Gebusi men and women as marriage patterns have changed?

11

Gender

SEX AND GENDER

Because anthropologists study biology, society, and culture, they are in a unique position to comment on nature (biological predispositions) and nurture (environment) as determinants of human behavior. Human attitudes, values, and behavior are limited not only by our genetic predispositions—which are often difficult to identify—but also by our experiences during enculturation. Our attributes as adults are determined both by our genes and by our environment during growth and development.

Questions about nature and nurture emerge in the discussion of human sex-gender roles and sexuality. Men and women differ genetically. Women have two X chromosomes, and men have an X and a Y. The father determines a baby's sex because only he has the Y chromosome to transmit. The mother always provides an X chromosome.

The chromosomal difference is expressed in hormonal and physiological contrasts. Humans are sexually dimorphic, more so than some primates, such as gibbons (small tree-living Asiatic apes), and less so than others, such as gorillas and orangutans. **Sexual dimorphism**

■ The realm of cultural diversity contains richly different social constructions and expressions of gender roles, as is illustrated by these Wodaabe male celebrants in Niger. (Look closely for suggestions of diffusion.) For what reasons do men decorate their bodies in our society?

refers to differences in male and female biology besides the contrasts in breasts and genitals. Women and men differ not just in primary (genitalia and reproductive organs) and secondary (breasts, voice, hair distribution) sexual characteristics but in average weight, height, strength, and longevity. Women tend to live longer than men and have excellent endurance capabilities. In a given population, men tend to be taller and to weigh more than women do. Of course, there is a considerable overlap between the sexes in terms of height, weight, and physical strength, and there has been a pronounced reduction in sexual dimorphism during human biological evolution.

OVERVIEW

Gender refers to the cultural construction of sexual difference. Male and female are biological sexes that differ in their X and Y chromosomes. Gender roles are the activities a culture assigns to each sex. Gender stratification describes an unequal distribution of rights and resources between the genders. Sometimes a distinction between extradomestic and domestic labor reinforces a contrast between males perceived as being publicly active and females seen as being domestic and less valuable. Patriarchy describes a system in which women have inferior social and political status. Although anthropologists know of no society in which women as a group dominate men as a group, women in many societies wield power and serve as leaders. In North America, female cash labor has increased, promoting greater autonomy for many women. But also increasing, globally, is the feminization of poverty: the rise in poor families headed by women. Despite individual variation in sexual orientation within a society, culture always plays a role in molding individual sexual urges toward a collective norm. Such norms vary widely from culture to culture.

Just how far, however, do such genetically and physiologically determined differences go? What effects do they have on the way men and women act and are treated in different societies? Anthropologists have discovered both similarities and differences in the roles of men and women in different cultures. The predominant anthropological position on sex-gender roles and biology may be stated as follows:

The biological nature of men and women [should be seen] not as a narrow enclosure limiting the human organism, but rather as a broad base upon which a variety of structures can be built. (Friedl 1975, p. 6)

Although in most societies men tend to be somewhat more aggressive than women are, many of the behavioral and attitudinal differences between the sexes emerge from culture rather than biology. Sex differences are biological, but gender encompasses all the traits that a culture assigns to and inculcates in males and females. "Gender," in other words, refers to the cultural construction of male and female characteristics (Rosaldo 1980b).

Given the "rich and various constructions of gender" within the realm of cultural diversity, Susan Bourque and Kay Warren (1987) note that the same images of masculinity and femininity do not always apply. Anthropologists have gathered systematic ethnographic data about similarities and differences involving gender in many cultural settings (Bonvillain 2001; Brettell and Sargent 2005; Gilmore 2001; Mascia-Lees and Black 2000; Nanda 2000; Ward and Edelstein 2006). Anthropologists can detect recurrent themes and patterns involving gender differences. They also can observe that gender roles vary with environment, economy, adaptive strategy, and type of political system. Before we examine the cross-cultural data, some definitions are in order.

Gender roles are the tasks and activities a culture assigns to the sexes. Related to gender roles are **gender stereotypes,** which are oversimplified

 STUDENT CD-ROM LIVING ANTHROPOLOGY

The Human Animal: Woman and Man
Track 11

This clip emphasizes how culture molds masculinity and femininity. It shows how different social treatment received by girls and boys (including male and female styles of play) influences gender differences. The clip notes how sex (involving biological differences) serves as a basis for gender, which emerges through a process of socialization and enculturation. What are some of the differences noted between male and female children? Based on what you have read in the text chapter, does a cross-cultural perspective help you evaluate this clip?

Indonesia's Matriarchal Minangkabau Offer an Alternative Social System

EUREKALERT NEWS BRIEF

by Pam Kosty
May 9, 2002

Cross-culturally, anthropologists have described tremendous variation in the roles of men and women, and the power differentials between them. If a patriarchy is a political system ruled by men, what would a matriarchy be? Would a matriarchy be a political system ruled by women, or a political system in which women play a much more prominent role than men do in social and political organization? This news account reports on Peggy Sanday's conclusion that matriarchies exist, but not as mirror images of patriarchies. The superior power that men typically have in a patriarchy isn't matched by women's equally disproportionate power in a matriarchy. Many societies, like the Minangkabau described here, lack the substantial power differentials that usually accompany patriarchal systems. In reading this account, pay attention to the centrality of Minangkabau women in social, economic, and ceremonial life and as key symbols. Matrilineality is uncommon as an organizing principle in nation-states, such as Indonesia, where the Minangkabau live. But political systems operate at different levels. We see here that matriliny and matriarchy are expressed locally, at the village level, and regionally, where seniority of matrilineal descent serves as a way to rank villages.

For the last century, . . . scholars have searched both human history and the continents to find a matriarchy—a society where the power was in the hands of women, not men. Most have concluded that a genuine matriarchy does not exist, perhaps may never have existed.

Anthropologist Peggy Reeves Sanday, Consulting Curator, University of Pennsylvania Museum of Archaeology and Anthropology, disagrees. After years of research among the Minangkabau people of West Sumatra, Indonesia, she has accepted that group's own self-labeling, as a "matriarchate," or matriarchy. The problem, she asserts, lies in Western cultural notions of what a matriarchy "should" look like—patriarchy's female-twin.

"Too many anthropologists have been looking for a society where women rule the affairs of everyday life, including government," she said. "That template—and a singular, Western perspective on power—doesn't fit very well when you're looking at non-Western cultures like the Minangkabau of West Sumatra, Indonesia, where males and females are partners for the common good rather than competitors ruled by self-interest. Social prestige accrues to those who promote good relations by following the dictates of custom and religion."

The four million Minangkabau, one of Indonesia's largest ethnic groups, live in the highlands of the province of West Sumatra. Their society is founded on the coexistence of matrilineal custom and a nature-based philosophy called adat. More recently, Islam has been incorporated into the foundation . . .

The key to Minangkabau matriarchy, according to Sanday, is found in the ever-present adat idea [that] "One must nurture growth in humans, animals, and plants so that society will be strong." . . .

The emphasis on nurturing growth yields a unique emphasis on the maternal in daily life. The Minangkabau glorify their mythical Queen Mother and cooperation. In village social relations senior women are associated with the central pillar of the traditional house, which is the oldest pillar because it is the first erected. The oldest village in a group of villages is referred to as the "mother village." When they stage ceremonies in their full ceremonial regalia, women are addressed by the same term reserved for the mythical Queen. Such practices suggest that matriarchy in this society is about making the maternal the center, origin, and foundation, not just of life but of the social order as well.

The power of Minangkabau women extends to the economic and social realms. Women control land inheritance, and husbands move into the households of their wives . . . During the wedding ceremony the wife collects her husband from his household and, with her female relatives, brings him back to her household to live. In the event of a divorce

■ *A Minangkabau bride and groom in West Sumatra, Indonesia, where anthropologist Peggy Reeves Sanday has conducted several years of ethnographic field work.*

the husband collects his clothes and leaves. Yet, despite the special position women are accorded in the society, the Minangkabau matriarchy is not the equivalent of female rule.

"Neither male nor female rule is possible because of the Minangkabau belief that decision-making should be by consensus," Dr. Sanday said. "In answer to my persistent questions about 'who rules,' I was often told that I was asking the wrong question. Neither sex rules, it was explained to me, because males and females complement one another."

Today, according to Dr. Sanday, while the Minangkabau matriarchy is based largely on adat, Islam also

plays a role. Islam arrived in West Sumatra sometime in the 16th century, long after adat customs and philosophy had been established. At first there was an uneasy relationship between adat and Islam and, in the 19th century, a war between adherents of adat customs and fundamentalist beliefs imported from Mecca. The conflict was resolved by both sides making accommodations. Today, matrilineal adat and Islam are accepted as equally sacred and inviolate.

Resurgent Islamic fundamentalism, nationalism, and expanding capitalism may erode the Minangkabau's nature-based matriarchal

culture and the adat that infuses meaning into their lives. [Sanday] remains optimistic that their culture has the innate flexibility to adapt to a changing world. "Had the Minangkabau chosen to fight rather than to accommodate the numerous influences that impinged on their world over the centuries, had they chosen to assert cultural purity, no doubt their 'adat' would have long ago succumbed. The moral of the Minangkabau story is that accommodating differences can preserve a world."

―――――

SOURCE: http://www.eurekalert.org/pub_releases/2002-05/uop-imm050902.php.

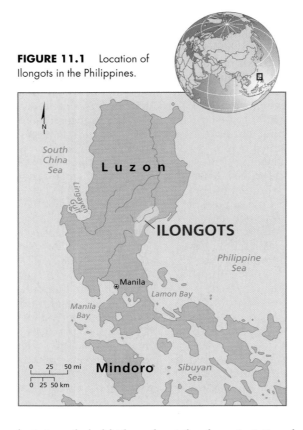

FIGURE 11.1 Location of Ilongots in the Philippines.

For information on multiple genders among Native Americans, see the Internet Exercises at your OLC

mhhe.com/kottak

but strongly held ideas about the characteristics of males and females. **Gender stratification** describes an unequal distribution of rewards (socially valued resources, power, prestige, human rights, and personal freedom) between men and women, reflecting their different positions in a social hierarchy. According to Ann Stoler (1977), the "economic determinants of gender status" include

freedom or autonomy (in disposing of one's labor and its fruits) and social power (control over the lives, labor, and produce of others).

In stateless societies, gender stratification is often more obvious in regard to prestige than it is in regard to wealth. In her study of the Ilongots of northern Luzon in the Philippines (Figure 11.1), Michelle Rosaldo (1980a) described gender differences related to the positive cultural value placed on adventure, travel, and knowledge of the external world. More often than women, Ilongot men, as headhunters, visited distant places. They acquired knowledge of the external world, amassed experiences there, and returned to express their knowledge, adventures, and feelings in public oratory. They received acclaim as a result. Ilongot women had inferior prestige because they lacked external experiences on which to base knowledge and dramatic expression. On the basis of Rosaldo's study and findings in other stateless societies, Ong (1989) argues that we must distinguish between prestige systems and actual power in a given society. High male prestige may not entail economic or political power held by men over their families.

RECURRENT GENDER PATTERNS

Remember from previous chapters that ethnologists compare ethnographic data from several cultures (i.e., cross-cultural data) to discover and explain differences and similarities. Data relevant to the cross-cultural study of gender can be drawn from the domains of economics, politics, domestic activity, kinship, and marriage. Table 11.1 shows cross-cultural data from 185 randomly selected societies on the division of labor by gender.

Remembering the discussion, in Chapter 3 on "Culture," of universals, generalities, and particularities, the findings in Table 11.1 about the division of labor by gender illustrate generalities rather than universals. That is, among the societies known to ethnography, there is a very strong tendency for men to build boats, but there are exceptions. One was the Hidatsa, a Native American group in which the women made the boats used to cross the Missouri River. (Traditionally, the Hidatsa were village farmers and bison hunters on the North American Plains; they now live in North Dakota.) Another exception: Pawnee women worked wood; this is the only Native American group that assigned this activity to women. (The Pawnee, also traditionally Plains farmers and bison hunters, originally lived in what is now central Nebraska and central Kansas; they now live on a reservation in north central Oklahoma.) Among the Mbuti "pygmies" of Africa's Ituri forest, women hunt by catching small, slow animals, using their hands or a net (Murdock and Provost 1973).

Exceptions to cross-cultural generalizations may involve societies or individuals. That is, a society like the Hidatsa can contradict the cross-cultural generalization that men build boats by assigning that task to women. Or, in a society where the cultural expectation is that only men build boats, a particular woman or women can contradict that expectation by doing the male activity. Table 11.1 shows that in a sample of 185 societies, certain activities ("swing activities") are assigned to either or both men and women.

TABLE 11.1	Generalities in the Division of Labor by Gender, Based on Data from 185 Societies	
Generally Male Activities	**Swing (Male or Female) Activities**	**Generally Female Activities**
Hunting large aquatic animals (e.g., whales, walrus)	Making fire	Gathering fuel (e.g., firewood)
Smelting ores	Body mutilation	Making drinks
Metalworking	Preparing skins	Gathering wild vegetal foods
Lumbering	Gathering small land animals	Dairy production (e.g., churning)
Hunting large land animals	Planting crops	Spinning
Working wood	Making leather products	Doing the laundry
Hunting fowl	Harvesting	Fetching water
Making musical instruments	Tending crops	Cooking
Trapping	Milking	Preparing vegetal food (e.g., processing cereal grains)
Building boats	Making baskets	
Working stone	Carrying burdens	
Working bone, horn, and shell	Making mats	
Mining and quarrying	Caring for small animals	
Setting bones	Preserving meat and fish	
Butchering*	Loom weaving	
Collecting wild honey	Gathering small aquatic animals	
Clearing land	Clothing manufacture	
Fishing	Making pottery	
Tending large herd animals		
Building houses		
Preparing the soil		
Making nets		
Making rope		

*All the activities above "butchering" are almost always done by men; those from "butchering" through "making rope" usually are done by men.

SOURCE: Adapted from G. P. Murdock and C. Provost, "Factors in the Division of Labor by Sex: A Cross-Cultural Analysis," *Ethnology* 12(2):202–225.

In many societies women routinely do hard physical labor, as is illustrated by these women carrying bricks inside a kiln in Adlaj, India in March 2006. Anthropologists have described both commonalities and differences in gender roles and activities among the world's societies.

What's missing from Table 11.1? Notice that there's no mention of trade and market activity, in which either or both men and women are active. Is Table 11.1 somewhat androcentric in detailing more tasks for men than for women? More than men, women do child care, but the study on which Table 11.1 is based (Murdock and Provost 1973) does not break down domestic activities to the same extent that it details extradomestic activities.

Both women and men have to fit their activities into 24-hour days. Based on cross-cultural data, Table 11.2 shows that the time and effort spent in subsistence activities by men and women tend to be about equal. If anything, men do slightly less subsistence work than women do. Think about how female domestic activities could have been specified in greater detail in Table 11.1. The original coding of the data in Table 11.1 probably illustrates a male bias in that extradomestic activities received much more prominence than domestic activities did. For example, is collecting wild honey (listed in Table 11.1) more necessary and/or time-consuming than cleaning a baby's bottom (absent from Table 11.1)? Think about Table 11.1 in terms of today's home and job roles and with respect to the activities done by contemporary women and men. Men still do most of the hunting; either gender can collect the honey from a supermarket, even as most baby bottom wiping continues to be in female hands.

Among the most important of such activities are planting, tending, and harvesting crops. We'll see below that some societies customarily assign more farming chores to women, whereas others call on men to be the main farm laborers. Among the tasks almost always assigned to men (Table 11.1), some (e.g., hunting large animals on land and sea) seem clearly related to the greater average size and strength of males. Others, such as working wood and making musical instruments, seem more culturally arbitrary. And women, of course, are not exempt from arduous and time-consuming physical labor, such as gathering firewood and fetching water. In Arembepe, Bahia, Brazil, women routinely transport water in five-gallon tins, balanced on their heads, from wells and lagoons located at long distances from their homes.

Cross-culturally the subsistence contributions of men and women are roughly equal (Table 11.2). But in domestic activities and child care, female labor predominates, as we see in Tables 11.3 and 11.4. Table 11.3 shows that in about half the societies studied, men did virtually no domestic work. Even in societies where men did

some domestic chores, the bulk of such work was done by women. Adding together their subsistence activities and their domestic work, women tend to work more hours than men do. Has this changed in the contemporary world?

What about child care? Women tend to be the main caregivers in most societies, but men often play a role. Again there are exceptions, both within and between societies. Table 11.4 uses cross-cultural data to answer the question "Who—men or women—has final authority over the care, handling, and discipline of children younger than four years?" Although women have primary authority over infants in two-thirds of the societies, there are still societies (18 percent of the total) in which men have the major say. In the United States and Canada today, some men are primary child caregivers despite the cultural fact that the female role in child care remains more prominent in both countries. Given the critical role of breast-feeding in ensuring infant survival,

TABLE 11.2 Time and Effort Expended on Subsistence Activities by Men and Women*	
More by men	16
Roughly equal	61
More by women	23

*Percentage of 88 randomly selected societies for which information was available on this variable.

SOURCE: M. F. Whyte, "Cross-Cultural Codes Dealing with the Relative Status of Women," *Ethnology* 17(2):211–239.

TABLE 11.3 Who Does the Domestic Work?*	
Males do virtually none	51
Males do some, but mostly done by females	49

*Percentage of 92 randomly selected societies for which information was available on this variable.
SOURCE: M. F. Whyte, "Cross-Cultural Codes Dealing with the Relative Status of Women," *Ethnology* 17(2):211–239.

TABLE 11.4 Who Has Final Authority over the Care, Handling, and Discipline of Infant Children (under Four Years Old)?*	
Males have more say	18
Roughly equal	16
Females have more say	66

*Percentage of 67 randomly selected societies for which information was available on this variable.
SOURCE: M. F. Whyte, "Cross-Cultural Codes Dealing with the Relative Status of Women," *Ethnology* 17(2):211–239.

TABLE 11.5 Does the Society Allow Multiple Spouses?*	
Only for males	77
For both, but more commonly for males	4
For neither	16
For both, but more commonly for females	2

*Percentage of 92 randomly selected societies.
SOURCE: M. F. Whyte, "Cross-Cultural Codes Dealing with the Relative Status of Women," *Ethnology* 17(2):211–239.

TABLE 11.6 Is There a Double Standard with Respect to PREMARITAL Sex*	
Yes—females are more restricted	44
No—equal restrictions on males and females	56

*Percentage of 73 randomly selected societies for which information was available on this variable.
SOURCE: M. F. Whyte, "Cross-Cultural Codes Dealing with the Relative Status of Women," *Ethnology* 17(2):211–239.

TABLE 11.7 Is There a Double Standard with Respect to EXTRAMARITAL Sex*	
Yes—females are more restricted	43
Equal restrictions on males and females	55
Males punished more severely for transgression	3

*Percentage of 75 randomly selected societies for which information was available on this variable.
SOURCE: M. F. Whyte, "Cross-Cultural Codes Dealing with the Relative Status of Women," *Ethnology* 17(2):211–239.

it makes sense, for infants especially, for the mother to be the primary caregiver.

There are differences in male and female reproductive strategies. Women give birth, breast-feed, and assume primary responsibility for infant care. Women ensure that their progeny will survive by establishing a close bond with each baby. It's also advantageous for a woman to have a reliable mate to ease the child-rearing process and ensure the survival of her children. (Again, there are exceptions, for example, the matrilineal Nayars discussed in the chapter "Families, Kinship, and Descent.") Women can have only so many babies during the course of their reproductive years, which begin after menarche (the advent of first menstruation) and end with menopause (cessation of menstruation). Men, in contrast, have a longer reproductive period, which can last into the elder years. If they choose to do so, men can enhance their reproductive success by impregnating several women over a longer time period. Although men do not always have multiple mates, they do have a greater tendency to do so than women do (see Tables 11.5, 11.6, and 11.7). Among the societies known to ethnography, polygyny is much more common than polyandry is (see Table 11.5).

Men mate, within and outside marriage, more than women do. Table 11.6 shows cross-cultural data on premarital sex, and Table 11.7 summarizes the data on extramarital sex. In both cases men are less restricted than women are, although

the restrictions are equal in about half the societies studied.

Double standards that restrict women more than men illustrate gender stratification. Several studies have shown that economic roles affect gender stratification. In one cross-cultural study, Sanday (1974) found that gender stratification decreased when men and women made roughly equal contributions to subsistence. She found that gender stratification was greatest when the women contributed either much more or much less than the men did.

■ *Among foragers, gender stratification tends to increase when men contribute much more to the diet than women do—as has been true among the Inuit and other northern hunters and fishers. Shown here, Mikile, an Inuit hunter, opens up a narwhal he hunted and killed near Qeqertat in Northwest Greenland.*

GENDER AMONG FORAGERS

In foraging societies, gender stratification was most marked when men contributed much more to the diet than women did. This was true among the Inuit and other northern hunters and fishers. Among tropical and semitropical foragers, by contrast, gathering usually supplies more food than hunting and fishing do. Gathering is generally women's work. Men usually hunt and fish, but women also do some fishing and may hunt small animals. When gathering is prominent, gender status tends to be more equal than it is when hunting and fishing are the main subsistence activities.

Gender status is also more equal when the domestic and public spheres aren't sharply separated. (*Domestic* means within or pertaining to the home.) Strong differentiation between the home and the outside world is called the **domestic–public dichotomy** or the *private–public contrast*. The outside world can include politics, trade, warfare, or work. Often when domestic and public spheres are clearly separated, public activities have greater prestige than domestic ones do. This can promote gender stratification, because men are more likely to be active in the public domain than women are. Cross-culturally, women's activities tend to be closer to home than men's are. Thus, another reason hunter-gatherers have less gender stratification than food producers do is that the domestic–public dichotomy is less developed among foragers.

We've seen that certain gender roles are more sex-linked than others. Men are the usual hunters and warriors. Given such tools and weapons as spears, knives, and bows, men make better hunters and fighters because they are bigger and stronger on the average than are women in the same population (Divale and Harris 1976). The male hunter-fighter role also reflects a tendency toward greater male mobility.

In foraging societies, women are either pregnant or lactating during most of their childbearing period. Late in pregnancy and after childbirth, carrying a baby limits a woman's movements, even her gathering. However, among the Agta of the Philippines (Griffin and Estioko-Griffin, eds. 1985) women not only gather, they also hunt with dogs while carrying their babies with them. Still, given the effects of pregnancy and breast-feeding on mobility, it is rarely feasible for women to be the primary hunters (Friedl 1975). Warfare, which also requires mobility, is not found in most foraging societies, nor is interregional trade well developed. Warfare and trade are two public arenas that can contribute to status inequality of males and females among food producers.

The Ju/'hoansi San illustrate the extent to which the activities and spheres of influence of men and women may overlap among foragers (Draper 1975). Traditional Ju/'hoansi gender roles were interdependent. During gathering, women discovered information about game animals, which they passed on to the men. Men and women spent about the same amount of time away from the camp, but neither worked more than three days a week. Between one-third and one-half of the band stayed home while the others worked.

The Ju/'hoansi saw nothing wrong in doing the work of the other gender. Men often gathered food and collected water. A general sharing ethos dictated that men distribute meat and that women share the fruits of gathering. Boys and girls of all ages played together. Fathers took an active role in raising children. Resources were adequate, and competition and aggression were discouraged. Exchangeability and interdependence of roles are adaptive in small groups.

Patricia Draper's field work among the Ju/'hoansi is especially useful in showing the relationships between economy, gender roles, and stratification because she studied both foragers and a group of former foragers who had become sedentary. Just a few thousand Ju/'hoansi continue their culture's traditional foraging pattern. Most are now sedentary, living near food producers or ranchers (see Kent 1992; Solway and Lee 1990; Wilmsen 1989).

Draper studied sedentary Ju/'hoansi at Mahopa, a village where they herded, grew crops, worked for wages, and did a small amount of gathering. Their gender roles were becoming more rigidly defined. A domestic–public dichotomy was developing as men traveled farther than women did. With less gathering, women were confined more to the home. Boys could gain mobility through herding, but girls' movements were more limited. The equal and communal world of the bush was yielding to the social features of sedentary life. A differential ranking of men according to their herds, houses, and sons began to replace sharing. Males came to be seen as more valuable producers.

If there is some degree of male dominance in virtually every contemporary society, it may be because of changes such as those that have drawn the Ju/'hoansi into wage work, market sales, and thus the world capitalist economy. A historic interplay between local, national, and international forces influences systems of gender stratification (Ong 1989). In traditional foraging cultures, however, egalitarianism extended to the relations between the sexes. The social spheres, activities, rights, and obligations of men and women overlapped. Foragers' kinship systems tend to be bilateral (calculated equally through males and females) rather than favoring either the mother's side or the father's side. Foragers may live with either the husband's or the wife's kin and often shift between one group and the other.

One last observation about foragers: It is among them that the public and private spheres are least separate, hierarchy is least marked, aggression and competition are most discouraged, and the rights, activities, and spheres of influence of men and women overlap the most. Our ancestors lived entirely by foraging until 10,000 years ago. If there is any most "natural" form of human society, it is best, although imperfectly, represented by foragers. Despite the popular stereotype of the club-wielding caveman dragging his mate by the hair, relative gender equality is a much more likely ancestral pattern.

GENDER AMONG HORTICULTURALISTS

Gender roles and stratification among cultivators vary widely, depending on specific features of the economy and social structure. Demonstrating this, Martin and Voorhies (1975) studied a sample of 515 horticultural societies, representing all parts of the world. They looked at several variables, including descent and postmarital residence, the percentage of the diet derived from cultivation, and the productivity of men and women.

Women were found to be the main producers in horticultural societies. In 50 percent of those societies, women did most of the cultivating. In 33 percent, contributions to cultivation by men and women were equal. In only 17 percent did men do most of the work. Women tended to do a bit more cultivating in matrilineal compared with patrilineal societies. They dominated horticulture in 64 percent of the matrilineal societies versus 50 percent of the patrilineal ones.

Many jobs that men do in some societies are done by women in others, and vice versa. In West Africa, women play a prominent role in trade and marketing. In Togo, shown here, women dominate textile sales. Is there a textile shop near you? Who runs it?

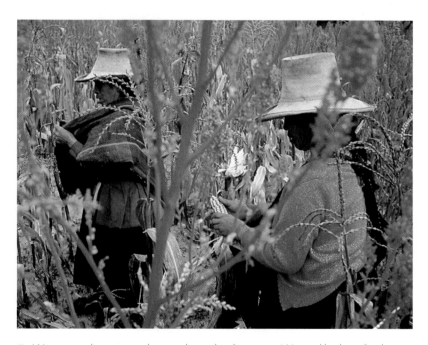

Women are the main producers in horticultural societies. Women like these South American corn farmers do most of the cultivating in such societies. What kinds of roles do women play in contemporary North American farming?

Reduced Gender Stratification—Matrilineal, Matrilocal Societies

Cross-cultural variation in gender status is related to rules of descent and postmarital residence (Friedl 1975; Martin and Voorhies 1975). Among horticulturalists with matrilineal descent and *matrilocality* (residence after marriage with the

See the Virtual Exploration for more on how gender roles can change

mhhe.com/kottak

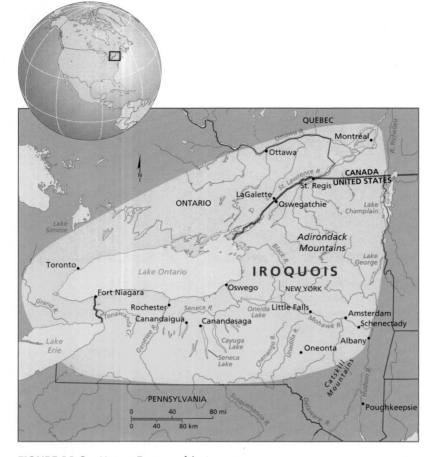

FIGURE 11.2 Historic Territory of the Iroquois.

societies, including the *Iroquois* (Brown 1975), a confederation of tribes in aboriginal New York, show that women's economic, political, and ritual influence can rival that of men (Figure 11.2).

Iroquois women played a major subsistence role, while men left home for long periods to wage war. As is usual in matrilineal societies, *internal* warfare was uncommon. Iroquois men waged war only on distant groups; this could keep them away for years.

Iroquois men hunted and fished, but women controlled the local economy. Women did some fishing and occasional hunting, but their major productive role was in horticulture. Women owned the land, which they inherited from matrilineal kinswomen. Women controlled the production and distribution of food.

Iroquois women lived with their husbands and children in the family compartments of a communal longhouse. Women born in a longhouse remained there for life. Senior women, or *matrons,* decided which men could join the longhouse as husbands, and they could evict incompatible men. Women therefore controlled alliances between descent groups, an important political job in tribal society.

Iroquois women thus managed production and distribution. Social identity, succession to office and titles, and property all came through the female line, and women were prominent in ritual and politics. Related tribes made up a confederacy, the League of the Iroquois, with chiefs and councils.

A council of male chiefs managed military operations, but chiefly succession was matrilineal. That is, succession went from a man to his brother, his sister's son, or another matrilineal relative. The matrons of each longhouse nominated a man as their representative. If the council rejected their first nominee, the women proposed others until one was accepted. Matrons constantly monitored the chiefs and could impeach them. Women could veto war declarations, withhold provisions for war, and initiate peace efforts. In religion, too, women shared power. Half the tribe's religious practitioners were women, and the matrons helped select the others.

Reduced Gender Stratification— Matrifocal Societies

Nancy Tanner (1974) also found that the combination of male travel and a prominent female economic role reduced gender stratification and promoted high female status. She based this finding on a survey of the **matrifocal** (mother-centered, often with no resident husband-father) organization of certain societies in Indonesia, West Africa, and the Caribbean. Matrifocal societies are not necessarily matrilineal. A few are even patrilineal.

wife's relatives, so that children grow up in their mother's village), female status tends to be high (see Blackwood 2000). Matriliny and matrilocality disperse related males, rather than consolidating them. By contrast, patriliny and *patrilocality* (residence after marriage with the husband's kin) keep male relatives together, an advantage given warfare. Matrilineal-matrilocal systems tend to occur in societies where population pressure on strategic resources is minimal and warfare is infrequent.

As we saw in the "News Brief" that opened this chapter, women tend to have high status in matrilineal, matrilocal societies for several reasons. Descent-group membership, succession to political positions, allocation of land, and overall social identity all come through female links. In Negeri Sembilan, Malaysia (Peletz 1988), matriliny gave women sole inheritance of ancestral rice fields. Matrilocality created solidarity clusters of female kin. Women had considerable influence beyond the household (Swift 1963). In such matrilineal contexts, women are the basis of the entire social structure. Although public authority may be (or may appear to be) assigned to the men, much of the power and decision making may actually belong to the senior women. Some matrilineal

For example, Tanner (1974) found matrifocality among the Igbo of eastern Nigeria, who are patrilineal, patrilocal, and polygynous (men have multiple wives). Each wife had her own house, where she lived with her children. Women planted crops next to their houses and traded surpluses. Women's associations ran the local markets, while men did the long-distance trading.

In a case study of the Igbo, Ifi Amadiume (1987) noted that either sex could fill male gender roles. Before Christian influence, successful Igbo women used wealth to take titles and acquire wives. Wives freed husbands (male and female) from domestic work and helped them accumulate wealth. Female husbands were not considered masculine but preserved their femininity. Igbo women asserted themselves in women's groups, including those of lineage daughters, lineage wives, and a communitywide women's council led by titled women. The high status and influence of Igbo women rested on the separation of males from local subsistence and on a marketing system that encouraged women to leave home and gain prominence in distribution and—through these accomplishments—in politics.

■ A significant number of female-centered, or matrifocal, households characterize many Caribbean societies, such as the Bahamas, shown here. As men travel, women pursue such economic activities as handicraft production and sales. This Cat Island beach scene shows a female-run basketry shop.

Increased Gender Stratification—Patrilineal-Patrilocal Societies

The Igbo are unusual among patrilineal-patrilocal societies, many of which have marked gender stratification. Martin and Voorhies (1975) link the decline of matriliny and the spread of the **patrilineal-patrilocal complex** (consisting of patrilineality, patrilocality, warfare, and male supremacy) to pressure on resources. Faced with scarce resources, patrilineal-patrilocal cultivators such as the Yanomami often wage warfare against other villages. This favors patrilocality and patriliny, customs that keep related men together in the same village, where they make strong allies in battle. Such societies tend to have a sharp domestic–public dichotomy, and men tend to dominate the prestige hierarchy. Men may use their public roles in warfare and trade and their greater prestige to symbolize and reinforce the devaluation or oppression of women.

The patrilineal-patrilocal complex characterizes many societies in highland Papua New Guinea. Women work hard growing and processing subsistence crops, raising and tending pigs (the main domesticated animal and a favorite food), and doing domestic cooking, but they are isolated from the public domain, which men control. Men grow and distribute prestige crops, prepare food for feasts, and arrange marriages. The men even get to trade the pigs and control their use in ritual.

In densely populated areas of the Papua New Guinea highlands, male–female avoidance is associated with strong pressure on resources (Lindenbaum 1972). Men fear all female contacts, including

■ In some parts of Papua New Guinea, the patrilineal-patrilocal complex has extreme social repercussions. Regarding females as dangerous and polluting, men may segregate themselves in men's houses (such as this one, located near the Sepik River), where they hide their precious ritual objects from women. Are there places like this in your society?

sex. They think that sexual contact with women will weaken them. Indeed, men see everything female as dangerous and polluting. They segregate themselves in men's houses and hide their precious ritual objects from women. They delay marriage, and some never marry.

By contrast, the sparsely populated areas of Papua New Guinea, such as recently settled areas, lack taboos on male–female contacts. The image of woman as polluter fades, heterosexual intercourse is valued, men and women live together, and reproductive rates are high.

GENDER AMONG AGRICULTURALISTS

When the economy is based on agriculture, women typically lose their role as primary cultivators. Certain agricultural techniques, particularly plowing, have been assigned to men because of their greater average size and strength (Martin and Voorhies 1975). Except when irrigation is used, plowing eliminates the need for constant weeding, an activity usually done by women.

Cross-cultural data illustrate these contrasts in productive roles. Women were the main workers in 50 percent of the horticultural societies surveyed but in only 15 percent of the agricultural groups. Male subsistence labor dominated 81 percent of the agricultural societies but only 17 percent of the horticultural ones (Martin and Voorhies 1975) (see Table 11.8).

With the advent of agriculture, women were cut off from production for the first time in human history. Perhaps this reflected the need for women to stay closer to home to care for the larger numbers of children that typify agriculture, compared with less labor-intensive economies. Belief systems started contrasting men's valuable extradomestic labor with women's domestic role, now viewed as inferior. (**Extradomestic** means outside the home, within or pertaining to the public domain.) Changes in kinship and postmarital residence patterns also hurt women. Descent groups and polygyny declined with agriculture, and the nuclear family became more common. Living with her husband and children, a woman was isolated from her kinswomen and cowives. Female sexuality is carefully supervised in agricultural economies; men have easier access to divorce and extramarital sex, reflecting a "double standard."

Still, female status in agricultural societies is not inevitably bleak. Gender stratification is associated with plow agriculture rather than with intensive cultivation per se. Studies of peasant gender roles and stratification in France and Spain (Harding 1975; Reiter 1975), which have plow agriculture, show that people think of the house as the female sphere and the fields as the male domain. However, such a dichotomy is not inevitable, as my own research among Betsileo agriculturalists in Madagascar shows.

Betsileo women play a prominent role in agriculture, contributing a third of the hours invested in rice production. They have their customary tasks in the division of labor, but their work is more seasonal than men's is. No one has much to do during the ceremonial season, between mid-June and mid-September. Men work in the rice fields almost daily the rest of the year. Women's cooperative work occurs during transplanting (mid-September through November) and harvesting (mid-March through early May). Along with other members of the household, women do daily weeding in December and January. After the harvest, all family members work together winnowing the rice and then transporting it to the granary.

If we consider the strenuous daily task of husking rice by pounding (a part of food preparation rather than production per se), women actually contribute slightly more than 50 percent of the labor devoted to producing and preparing rice before cooking.

Not just women's prominent economic role but traditional social organization enhances female status among the Betsileo. Although postmarital residence is mainly patrilocal, descent rules permit married women to keep membership in and a strong allegiance to their own descent groups. Kinship is broadly and bilaterally calculated (on both sides—as in contemporary North America). The Betsileo exemplify Aihwa Ong's (1989) generalization that bilateral (and matrilineal) kinship systems, combined with subsistence economies in which the sexes have complementary roles in food production and distribution, are characterized by reduced gender stratification. Such societies are common among South Asian peasants (Ong 1989).

Bringing It All Together

See the "Bringing It All Together" essay that immediately follows this chapter.

TABLE 11.8   *Male and Female Contributions to Production in Cultivating Societies*

	Horticulture (Percentage of 104 Societies)	Agriculture (Percentage of 93 Societies)
Women are primary cultivators	50	15
Men are primary cultivators	17	81
Equal contributions to cultivation	33	3

SOURCE: K. Martin and B. Voorhies, *Female of the Species* (New York: Columbia University Press, 1975), p. 283.

Traditionally, Betsileo men participate more in politics, but the women also hold political office. Women sell their produce and products in markets, invest in cattle, sponsor ceremonials, and are mentioned during offerings to ancestors. Arranging marriages, an important extradomestic activity, is more women's concern than men's. Sometimes Betsileo women seek their own kinswomen as wives for their sons, reinforcing their own prominence in village life and continuing kin-based female solidarity in the village.

The Betsileo illustrate the idea that intensive cultivation does not necessarily entail sharp gender stratification. We can see that gender roles and stratification reflect not just the type of adaptive strategy but also specific cultural attributes. Betsileo women continue to play a significant role in their society's major economic activity, rice production.

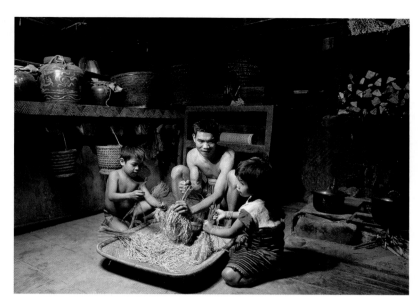

PATRIARCHY AND VIOLENCE

Patriarchy describes a political system ruled by men in which women have inferior social and political status, including basic human rights. Barbara Miller (1997), in a study of systematic neglect of females, describes women in rural northern India as "the endangered sex." Societies that feature a full-fledged patrilineal-patrilocal complex, replete with warfare and intervillage raiding, also typify patriarchy. Such practices as dowry murders, female infanticide, and clitoridectomy exemplify patriarchy, which extends from tribal societies such as the Yanomami to state societies such as India and Pakistan.

Although more prevalent in certain social settings than in others, family violence and domestic abuse of women are worldwide problems. Domestic violence certainly occurs in neolocal–nuclear family settings, such as Canada and the United States. Cities, with their impersonality and isolation from extended kin networks, are breeding grounds for domestic violence.

We've seen that gender stratification is typically reduced in matrilineal, matrifocal, and bilateral societies in which women have prominent roles in the economy and social life. When a woman lives in her own village, she has kin nearby to look after and protect her interests. Even in patrilocal polygynous settings, women often count on the support of their cowives and sons in disputes with potentially abusive husbands. Such settings, which tend to provide a safe haven for women, are retracting rather than expanding in today's world, however. Isolated families and patrilineal social forms have spread at the expense of matrilineality. Many nations have declared polygyny illegal. More and more women, and men, find themselves cut off from extended kin and families of orientation.

With the spread of the women's rights movement and the human rights movement, attention to domestic violence and abuse of women has increased. Laws have been passed, and mediating institutions established. Brazil's female-run police stations for battered women provide an example, as do shelters for victims of domestic abuse in the United States and Canada. But patriarchal institutions do persist in what should be a more enlightened world.

Bilateral kinship systems, combined with subsistence economies in which the sexes have complementary roles in food production and distribution, have reduced gender stratification. Such features are common among Asian rice cultivators, such as the Ifugao of the Philippines (shown here).

GENDER AND INDUSTRIALISM

The domestic–public dichotomy, which is developed most fully among patrilineal-patrilocal food producers and plow agriculturalists, also has affected gender stratification in industrial societies, including the United States and Canada. However, gender roles have been changing rapidly in North America. The "traditional" idea that "a woman's place is in the home" developed among middle- and upper-class Americans as industrialism spread after 1900. Earlier, pioneer women in the Midwest and West had been recognized as fully productive workers in farming and home industry. Under industrialism, attitudes about gendered work came to vary with class and region. In early industrial Europe, men, women, and children had flocked to factories as wage laborers. Enslaved Americans of both sexes had done grueling work in cotton fields. After abolition, southern African American women continued working as field hands and domestics. Poor white women labored in the South's early cotton mills. In the 1890s, more than one million American women held menial, repetitious, and

Sure, ideas about gender are changing along with the employment patterns of men and women. We see this in the media, as shows like *Sex and the City*, featuring characters who display nontraditional gender behavior and sexual behavior, attract significant audiences. But old beliefs, cultural expectations, and gender stereotypes linger. Thus, American culture expects women to be meeker than men. This poses a challenge for women, since our culture also values decisiveness and "standing up for your beliefs." When American men and women display certain behavior—speaking up for their ideas, for example—they are judged differently. A man's assertive behavior may be admired and rewarded, but a women's similar behavior may be labeled "aggressive"—or worse. Women must constantly negotiate this conundrum.

Both men and women are constrained by their cultural training, stereotypes, and expectations. For example, American culture stigmatizes male crying. It's okay for little boys to cry, but becoming a man discourages this natural expression of joy and sadness. Why shouldn't men cry when they feel emotions? American men are trained to make decisions and stick to them. Politicians routinely criticize their opponents for being indecisive, for waffling or flip-flopping on issues. What a strange idea—that people shouldn't change their positions if they've discovered there's a better way. Males, females, and humanity may be equally victimized by aspects of cultural training.

unskilled factory positions (Margolis 1984, 2000; Martin and Voorhies 1975). Poor, immigrant, and African American women continued to work throughout the 20th century.

After 1900, European immigration produced a male labor force willing to work for wages lower than those of American-born men. Those immigrant men moved into factory jobs that previously had gone to women. As machine tools and mass production further reduced the need for female labor, the notion that women were biologically unfit for factory work began to gain ground (Martin and Voorhies 1975).

Maxine Margolis (1984, 2000) has shown how gendered work, attitudes, and beliefs have varied in response to American economic needs. For example, wartime shortages of men have promoted the idea that work outside the home is women's patriotic duty. During the world wars,

the notion that women are biologically unfit for hard physical labor faded. Inflation and the culture of consumption have also spurred female employment. When prices and/or demand rises, multiple paychecks help maintain family living standards.

The steady increase in female paid employment since World War II also reflects the baby boom and industrial expansion. American culture has traditionally defined clerical work, teaching, and nursing as female occupations. With rapid population growth and business expansion after World War II, the demand for women to fill such jobs grew steadily. Employers also found that they could increase their profits by paying women lower wages than they would have to pay returning male war veterans.

Woman's role in the home has been stressed during periods of high unemployment, although when wages fall or inflation occurs simultaneously, female employment may still be accepted. Margolis (1984, 2000) contends that changes in the economy lead to changes in attitudes toward and about women. Economic changes paved the way for the contemporary women's movement, which also was spurred by the publication of Betty Friedan's book *The Feminine Mystique* in 1963 and the founding of NOW, the National Organization of Women, in 1966. The movement in turn promoted expanded work opportunities for women, including the goal of equal pay for equal work. Between 1970 and 2003, the female percentage of the American work force rose from 38 to 47 percent. In other words, almost half of all Americans who work outside the home are women. Over 71 million women now have paid jobs, compared with 80 million men. Women now fill more than half (57 percent) of all professional jobs (*Statistical Abstract of the United States 2006*, p. 429). And it's not mainly single women working, as once was the case. Table 11.9 presents figures on the ever-increasing cash employment of American wives and mothers.

Note in Table 11.9 that the cash employment of American married men has been falling while that of American married women has been rising. There has been a dramatic change in behavior and attitudes since 1960, when 89 percent of all married men worked, compared with just 32 percent of married women. The comparable figures in 2004 were 77 percent and 61 percent. Ideas about the gender roles of males and females have changed. Compare your grandparents and your parents. Chances are you have a working mother, but your grandmother was more likely a stay-at-home mom. Your grandfather is more likely than your father to have worked in manufacturing and to have belonged to a union. Your father is more likely than your grandfather to have shared child care and domestic responsibilities. Age at marriage has been delayed for both men and women.

Bringing It All Together

See the "Bringing It All Together" essay that immediately follows the chapter "Language and Communication" for information on Canada's gender-neutral public school curriculum.

College educations and professional degrees have increased. What other changes do you associate with the increase in female employment outside the home?

Table 11.10 details employment in the United States in 2002 by gender, income, and job type for year-round full-time workers. Overall, the ratio of female to male income rose from 68 percent in 1989 to 76 percent in 2003.

Today's jobs aren't especially demanding in terms of physical labor. With machines to do the heavy work, the smaller average body size and lesser average strength of women are no longer impediments to blue-collar employment. The main reason we don't see more modern-day Rosies working alongside male riveters is that the U.S. work force itself is abandoning heavy-goods manufacture. In the 1950s, two-thirds of American jobs were blue-collar, compared with less than 15 percent today. The location of those jobs has shifted within the world capitalist economy. Third World countries with cheaper labor produce steel, automobiles, and other heavy goods less expensively than the United States can, but the United States excels at services. The American mass education system has many inadequacies, but it does train millions of people for service- and information-oriented jobs, from sales clerks to computer operators.

The Feminization of Poverty

Alongside the economic gains of many American women stands an opposite extreme: the feminization of poverty. This refers to the increasing representation of women (and their children) among America's poorest people. Women head over half of U.S. households with incomes below the poverty line. Feminine poverty has been a trend in the United States since World War II, but it has

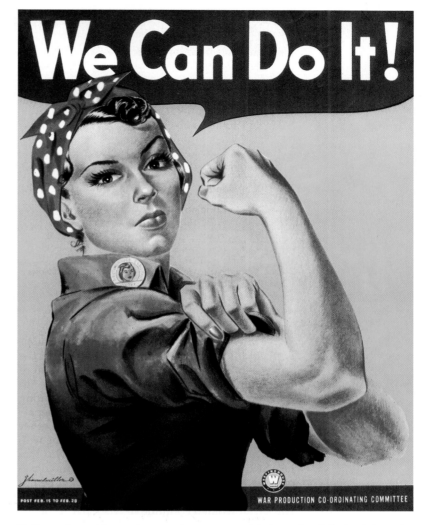

■ During the world wars, the notion that women were biologically unfit for hard physical labor faded. World War II's Rosie the Riveter—a strong, competent woman dressed in overalls and a bandanna—was introduced as a symbol of patriotic womanhood. Is there a comparable poster woman today? What does her image say about modern gender roles?

TABLE 11.9	Cash Employment of American Mothers, Wives, and Husbands, 1960–2002*		
Year	Percentage of Married Women, Husband Present with Children under 6	Percentage of All Married Women[a]	Percentage of All Married Men[b]
1960	19	32	89
1970	30	40	86
1980	45	50	81
1990	59	58	79
2004	59	61	77

*Civilian population 16 years of age and older.

[a]Husband present.

[b]Wife present.

SOURCE: *Statistical Abstract of the United States 2006*, Table 584, p. 392; Table 587, p. 393. http://www.census.gov/prod/www/statistical_abstract.html.

TABLE 11.10 Earnings in the United States by Gender and Job Type for Year-Round Full-Time Workers, 2003*

	Median Annual Salary		Ratio of Earnings Female/Male	
	Women	Men	2003	1989
Median earnings	$30,724	$40,668	76	68
By Job Type				
Management/business/financial	$42,064	$60,447	70	61
Professional	40,298	58,867	68	71
Sales and office	27,803	39,491	70	54
Service	19,970	26,447	76	62

*By occupation of longest job held.

SOURCE: Based on data in *Statistical Abstract of the United States 2006*, Table 633, p. 429. http://www.census.gov/prod/www/statistical_abstract.html.

For more on gender differences and poverty, see the Internet Exercises at your OLC

mhhe.com/kottak

accelerated recently. In 1959, female-headed households accounted for just one-fourth of the American poor. Since then, that figure has more than doubled. About half the female poor are "in transition." These are women who are confronting a temporary economic crisis caused by the departure, disability, or death of a husband. The other half are more permanently dependent on the welfare system or on friends or relatives who live nearby. The feminization of poverty and its consequences in regard to living standards and health are widespread even among wage earners. Many American women continue to work part time for low wages and meager benefits.

Married couples are much more secure economically than single mothers are. The data in Table 11.11 demonstrate that the average income for married-couple families is more than twice that of families maintained by a woman. The average one-earner family maintained by a woman had an annual income of $29,307 in 2003. This was less than one-half the mean income ($62,405) of a married-couple household.

The feminization of poverty isn't just a North American trend. The percentage of female-headed households has been increasing worldwide. In Western Europe, for example, it rose from 24 percent in 1980 to 30 percent in 2000. The figure ranges from below 20 percent in certain South Asian and Southeast Asian countries to almost 50 percent in certain African countries and the Caribbean (Buvinic 1995).

Why must so many women be solo household heads? Where are the men going, and why are they leaving? Among the causes are male migration, civil strife (men off fighting), divorce, abandonment, widowhood, unwed adolescent parenthood, and, more generally, the idea that children are women's responsibility.

Globally, households headed by women tend to be poorer than are those headed by men. In one study, the percentage of single-parent families considered poor was 18 percent in Britain, 20 percent in Italy, 25 percent in Switzerland, 40 percent in Ireland, 52 percent in Canada, and 63 percent in the United States. Poverty, of course, has health consequences. Studies in Brazil, Zambia, and the Philippines show the survival rates of children from female-headed households to be inferior to those of other children (Buvinic 1995).

In the United States, the feminization of poverty is a concern of the National Organization of Women. NOW still exists, alongside many newer women's organizations. The women's movement has become international in scope and membership. And its priorities have shifted from mainly job-oriented to more broadly social issues. These include poverty, homelessness, women's health care, day care, domestic violence, sexual assault, and reproductive rights (Calhoun, Light, and Keller 1997). These issues and others that particularly affect women in the developing countries were addressed at the United Nations' Fourth World Conference on Women held in 1995 in Beijing. In attendance were women's groups from all over the world. Many of these were national and international NGOs (nongovernmental organizations), which work with women at the local level to augment productivity and improve access to credit.

It is widely believed that one way to improve the situation of poor women is to encourage them to organize. New women's groups can in some cases revive or replace traditional forms of social

Map Atlas

Map 14 shows inequalities in cash employment and secondary education among countries of the world.

TABLE 11.11 Median Annual Income of U.S. Households, by Household Type, 2003

	Number of Households (1000s)	Median Annual Income (Dollars)	Percentage of Median Earnings Compared with Married-Couple Households
All households	112,000	$43,318	69
Family households	76,217	53,991	87
Married-couple households	57,719	62,405	100
Male earner, no wife	4,717	41,959	67
Female earner, no husband	13,781	29,307	47
Nonfamily households	35,783	25,741	41
Single male	16,136	31,928	51
Single female	19,647	21,313	34

SOURCE: *Statistical Abstract of the United States 2006*, Table 675, p. 461. http://www.census.gov/prod/www/statistical_abstract.html.

organization that have been disrupted. Membership in a group can help women to mobilize resources, to rationalize production, and to reduce the risks and costs associated with credit. Organization also allows women to develop self-confidence and to decrease dependence on others. Through such organization, poor women throughout the world are working to determine their own needs and priorities, and to change things so as to improve their social and economic situation (Buvinic 1995).

SEXUAL ORIENTATION

Sexual orientation refers to a person's habitual sexual attraction to, and sexual activities with, persons of the opposite sex, *heterosexuality;* the same sex, *homosexuality;* or both sexes, *bisexuality. Asexuality,* indifference toward or lack of attraction to either sex, is also a sexual orientation. All four of these forms are found in contemporary North America, and throughout the world. But each type of desire and experience holds different meanings for individuals and groups. For example, an asexual disposition may be acceptable in some places but may be perceived as a character flaw in others. Male–male sexual activity may be a private affair in Mexico, rather than public, socially sanctioned, and encouraged as it was among the Etoro (see below) of Papua New Guinea (see also Blackwood and Wieringa, eds. 1999; Herdt 1981, Kottak and Kozaitis 2003; Lancaster and Di Leonardo, eds. 1997; Nanda 2000).

Recently in the United States there has been a tendency to see sexual orientation as fixed and biologically based. There is not enough information at this time to determine the extent to which sexual orientation is based on biology. What we can say is that, to some extent at least, all human activities and preferences, including erotic expression, are learned, malleable, and culturally constructed.

In any society, individuals will differ in the nature, range, and intensity of their sexual interests and urges. No one knows for sure why such individual sexual differences exist. Part of the answer may be biological, reflecting genes or hormones. Another part may have to do with experiences during growth and development. But whatever the reasons for individual variation, culture always plays a role in molding individual sexual urges toward a collective norm. And such sexual norms vary from culture to culture.

What do we know about variation in sexual norms from society to society, and over time? A classic cross-cultural study (Ford and Beach 1951) found wide variation in attitudes about masturbation, bestiality (sex with animals), and homosexuality. Even in a single society, such as the United States, attitudes about sex differ over time and with socioeconomic status, region, and rural versus urban residence. However, even in the 1950s, prior to the "age of sexual permissiveness" (the pre-HIV period from the mid-1960s through the 1970s), research showed that almost all American men (92 percent) and more than half of American women (54 percent) admitted to masturbation. In the famous Kinsey report (Kinsey, Pomeroy, and Martin 1948), 37 percent of the men surveyed admitted having had at least one sexual experience leading to orgasm with another male. In a later study of 1,200 unmarried women, 26 percent

Hidden Women, Public Men—Public Women, Hidden Men

For several years, one of Brazil's top sex symbols was Roberta Close, whom I first saw in a furniture commercial. Roberta ended her pitch with an admonition to prospective furniture buyers to accept no substitute for the advertised product. "Things," she warned, "are not always what they seem."

Nor was Roberta. This petite and incredibly feminine creature was actually a man. Nevertheless, despite the fact that he—or she (speaking as Brazilians do)—is a man posing as a woman, Roberta won a secure place in Brazilian mass culture. Her photos decorated magazines. She was a panelist on a TV variety show and starred in a stage play in Rio with an actor known for his supermacho image. Roberta even inspired a well-known, and apparently heterosexual, pop singer to make a video honoring her. In it, she pranced around Rio's Ipanema Beach in a bikini, showing off her ample hips and buttocks.

The video depicted the widespread male appreciation of Roberta's beauty. As confirmation, one heterosexual man told me he had recently been on the same plane as Roberta and had been struck by her looks. Another man said he wanted to have sex with her. These comments, it seemed to me, illustrated striking cultural contrasts about gender and sexuality. In Brazil, a Latin American country noted for its machismo, heterosexual men did not feel that attraction toward a transvestite blemished their masculine identities.

Roberta Close can be understood in relation to a gender-identity scale that jumps from extreme femininity to extreme masculinity, with little in between. Masculinity is stereotyped as active and public, femininity as passive and domestic. The male–female contrast in rights and behavior is much stronger in Brazil than it is in North America. Brazilians confront a more rigidly defined masculine role than North Americans do.

The active–passive dichotomy also provides a stereotypical model for male–male sexual relations. One man

is supposed to be the active, masculine (inserting) partner, whereas the other is the passive, effeminate one. The latter man is derided as a *bicha* (intestinal worm), but little stigma attaches to the inserter. Indeed, many "active" (and married) Brazilian men like to have sex with transvestite prostitutes, who are biological males.

If a Brazilian man is unhappy pursuing either active masculinity or passive effeminacy, there is one other choice—active femininity. For Roberta Close and others like her, the cultural demand of ultramasculinity has yielded to a performance of ultrafemininity. These men-women form a third gender in relation to Brazil's polarized male–female identity scale.

Transvestites like Roberta are particularly prominent in Rio de Janeiro's annual Carnaval, when an ambience of inversion rules the city. In the culturally accurate words of the American popular novelist Gregory McDonald, who sets one of his books in Brazil at Carnaval time:

> Everything goes topsy-turvy . . .
> Men become women; women
> become men; grown-ups become
> children; rich people pretend
> they're poor; poor people, rich;
> sober people become drunkards;
> thieves become generous. Very
> topsy-turvy. (McDonald 1984,
> p. 154)

Most notable in this costumed inversion (DaMatta 1991), men dress as women. Carnaval reveals and expresses normally hidden tensions and conflicts as social life is turned upside down. Reality is illuminated through a dramatic presentation of its opposite.

This is the final key to Roberta's cultural meaning. She emerged in a setting in which male–female inversion is part of the year's most popular festival. Transvestites are the pièces de résistance at Rio's Carnaval balls, where they dress as scantily as the real women do. They wear postage-stamp bikinis, sometimes with no tops. Photos of real women and transformed

Roberta Close, in her prime.

ones vie for space in the magazines. It is often impossible to tell the born women from the hidden men. Roberta Close is a permanent incarnation of Carnaval—a year-round reminder of the spirit of Carnavals past, present, and yet to come.

Roberta emerged from a Latin culture whose gender roles contrast strongly with those of the United States. From small village to massive city, Brazilian males are public and Brazilian females are private creatures. Streets, beaches, and bars belong to the men. Although bikinis adorn Rio's beaches on weekends and holidays, there are many more men than women there on weekdays. The men revel in their ostentatiously sexual displays. As they sun themselves and play soccer and volleyball, they regularly stroke their genitals to keep them firm. They are living publicly, assertively, and sexually in a world of men.

Brazilian men must work hard at this public image, constantly acting out their culture's definition of masculine behavior. Public life is a play whose strong roles go to men. Roberta Close, of course, was a public figure. Given that Brazilian culture defines the public world as male, we can perhaps better understand now why the nation's number one sex symbol has been a man who excels at performing in public as a woman.

reported same-sex sexual activities. (Because Kinsey's research relied on nonrandom samples, it should be considered merely illustrative, rather than a statistically accurate representation of, sexual behavior at the time.)

Sex acts involving people of the same sex were absent, rare, or secret in only 37 percent of 76 societies for which data were available in the Ford and Beach study (1951). In the others, various forms of same-sex sexual activity were considered normal and acceptable. Sometimes sexual relations between people of the same sex involved transvestism on the part of one of the partners, like the *berdaches* discussed in the last chapter (see "Interesting Issues" on p. 268).

Transvestism did not characterize male–male sex among the Sudanese Azande, who valued the warrior role (Evans-Pritchard 1970). Prospective warriors—young men aged 12 to 20—left their families and shared quarters with adult fighting men, who paid bridewealth for, and had sex with, them. During this apprenticeship, the young men did the domestic duties of women. Upon reaching warrior status, these young men took their own younger male brides. Later, retiring from the warrior role, Azande men married women. Flexible in their sexual expression, Azande males had no difficulty shifting from sex with older men (as male brides), to sex with younger men (as warriors), to sex with women (as husbands) (see Murray and Roscoe, eds. 1998).

An extreme example of tension involving male–female sexual relations in Papua New Guinea is provided by the Etoro (Kelly 1976), a group of 400 people who subsist by hunting and horticulture in the Trans-Fly region (Figure 11.3). The Etoro illustrate the power of culture in molding human sexuality. The following account, based on ethnographic field work by Raymond C. Kelly in the late 1960s, applies only to Etoro males and their beliefs. Etoro cultural norms prevented the male anthropologist who studied them from gathering comparable information about female attitudes. Note, also, that the activities described have been discouraged by missionaries. Since there has been no restudy of the Etoro specifically focusing on these activities, the extent to which these practices continue today is unknown. For this reason, I'll use the past tense in describing them.

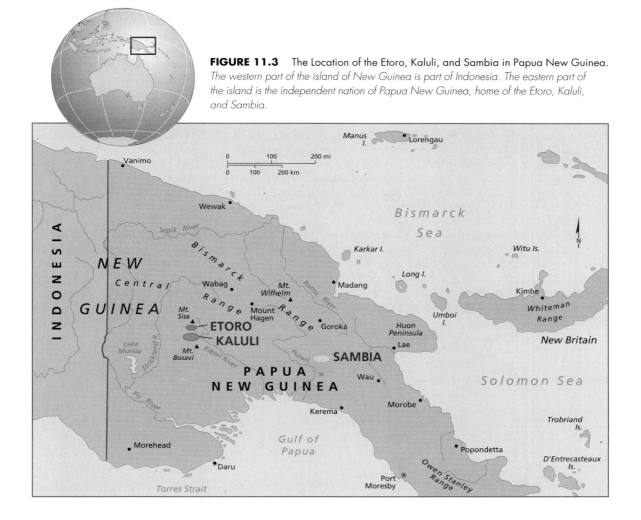

FIGURE 11.3 The Location of the Etoro, Kaluli, and Sambia in Papua New Guinea. *The western part of the island of New Guinea is part of Indonesia. The eastern part of the island is the independent nation of Papua New Guinea, home of the Etoro, Kaluli, and Sambia.*

Do the taboos that have surrounded homosexuality in our own society remind you of Etoro taboos? Homosexual activity has been stigmatized in Western industrial societies. Indeed, sodomy laws continue to make it illegal in many U.S. states. Among the Etoro, male–female sex is banned from the social center and moved to the fringes or margins of society (the woods, filled with dangerous snakes). In our own society, homosexual activity has traditionally been hidden, furtive, and secretive—also moved to the margins of society rather than its valued center. Imagine what our own sex lives would be like if we had been raised with Etoro beliefs and taboos.

Etoro opinions about sexuality were linked to their beliefs about the cycle of birth, physical growth, maturity, old age, and death. Etoro men believed that semen was necessary to give life force to a fetus, which was, they believed, implanted in a woman by an ancestral spirit. Sexual intercourse during pregnancy nourished the growing fetus. The Etoro believed that men had a limited lifetime supply of semen. Any sex act leading to ejaculation was seen as draining that supply, and as sapping a man's virility and vitality. The birth of children, nurtured by semen, symbolized a necessary sacrifice that would lead to the husband's eventual death. Heterosexual intercourse, required only for reproduction, was discouraged. Women who wanted too much sex were viewed as witches, hazardous to their husbands' health. Etoro culture allowed heterosexual intercourse only about 100 days a year. The rest of the time it was tabooed. Seasonal birth clustering shows the taboo was respected.

So objectionable was male–female sex that it was removed from community life. It could occur neither in sleeping quarters nor in the fields. Coitus could happen only in the woods, where it was risky because poisonous snakes, the Etoro claimed, were attracted by the sounds and smells of male–female sex.

Although coitus was discouraged, sex acts between men were viewed as essential. Etoro believed that boys could not produce semen on their own. To grow into men and eventually give life force to their children, boys had to acquire semen orally from older men. From the age of 10 until adulthood, boys were inseminated by older men. No taboos were attached to this. Such oral insemination could proceed in the sleeping area or garden. Every three years, a group of boys around the age of 20 was formally initiated into manhood. They went to a secluded mountain lodge, where they were visited and inseminated by several older men.

Male–male sex among the Etoro was governed by a code of propriety. Although sexual relations between older and younger males were considered culturally essential, those between boys of the same age were discouraged. A boy who took semen from other youths was believed to be sapping their life force and stunting their growth. A boy's rapid physical development might suggest that he was getting semen from other boys. Like a sex-hungry wife, he might be shunned as a witch.

These sexual practices among the Etoro rested not on hormones or genes but on cultural beliefs and traditions. The Etoro were an extreme example of a male–female avoidance pattern that has been widespread in Papua New Guinea and in patrilineal-patrilocal societies. The Etoro shared a cultural pattern, which Gilbert Herdt (1984) calls "ritualized homosexuality," with some 50 other tribes in Papua New Guinea, especially in that country's Trans-Fly region. These societies illustrate one extreme of a male–female avoidance pattern that is widespread in Papua New Guinea and indeed in many patrilineal-patrilocal societies.

Flexibility in sexual expression seems to be an aspect of our primate heritage. Both masturbation and same-sex sexual activity exist among chimpanzees and other primates. Male bonobos (pygmy chimps) regularly engage in a form of mutual masturbation known as "penis fencing." Females get sexual pleasure from rubbing their genitals against those of other females (de Waal 1997). Our primate sexual potential is molded by culture, the environment, and reproductive necessity. Heterosexual coitus is practiced in all human societies—which, after all, must reproduce themselves—but alternatives are also widespread (Rathus, Nevid, and Fichner-Rathus 2005). Like gender roles and attitudes more generally, the sexual component of human personality and identity—just how we express our "natural" sexual urges—is a matter that culture and environment direct and limit.

1. *Gender roles* are the tasks and activities that a culture assigns to each sex. *Gender stereotypes* are oversimplified ideas about attributes of males and females. *Gender stratification* describes an unequal distribution of rewards by gender, reflecting different positions in a social hierarchy. Cross-cultural comparison reveals some recurrent patterns involving the division of labor by gender and gender-based differences in reproductive strategies. Gender roles and gender stratification also vary with environment, economy, adaptive strategy, level of social complexity, and degree of participation in the world economy.

2. When gathering is prominent, gender status is more equal than it is when hunting or fishing dominates the foraging economy. Gender status is more equal when the domestic and public spheres aren't sharply separated. Foragers lack two public arenas that contribute to higher male status among food producers: warfare and organized interregional trade.

3. Gender stratification also is linked to descent and residence. Women's status in matrilineal societies tends to be high because descent-group membership, political succession, land allocation, and overall social identity come through female links. Women in many societies wield power and make decisions. Scarcity of resources promotes intervillage warfare, patriliny, and patrilocality. The localization of related males is adaptive for military solidarity. Men may use their warrior role to symbolize and reinforce the social devaluation and oppression of women.

4. With the advent of plow agriculture, women were removed from production. The distinction between women's domestic work and men's "productive" labor reinforced the contrast between men as public and valuable and women as homebound and inferior. Patriarchy describes a political system ruled by men in which women have inferior social and political status, including basic human rights. Some expressions of patriarchy include female infanticide, dowry murders, domestic abuse, and forced genital operations.

5. Americans' attitudes toward gender vary with class and region. When the need for female labor declines, the idea that women are unfit for many jobs increases, and vice versa. Factors such as war, falling wages, and inflation help explain female cash employment and Americans' attitudes toward it. Countering the economic gains of many American women is the feminization of poverty. This has become a global phenomenon, as impoverished female-headed households have increased worldwide.

6. There has been a recent tendency to see sexual orientation as fixed and biologically based. But to some extent, at least, all human activities and preferences, including erotic expression, are influenced by culture. Sexual orientation stands for a person's habitual sexual attraction to, and activities with, persons of the opposite sex, *heterosexuality*; the same sex, *homosexuality*; or both sexes, *bisexuality*. Sexual norms vary widely from culture to culture.

KEY TERMS

See the flash cards
mhhe.com/kottak

domestic–public dichotomy Contrast between women's role in the home and men's role in public life, with a corresponding social devaluation of women's work and worth.

extradomestic Outside the home; within or pertaining to the public domain.

gender roles The tasks and activities that a culture assigns to each sex.

gender stereotypes Oversimplified but strongly held ideas about the characteristics of males and females.

gender stratification Unequal distribution of rewards (socially valued resources, power, prestige, and personal freedom) between men and women, reflecting their different positions in a social hierarchy.

matrifocal Mother-centered; often refers to a household with no resident husband-father.

patriarchy Political system ruled by men in which women have inferior social and political status, including basic human rights.

patrilineal-patrilocal complex An interrelated constellation of patrilineality, patrilocality, warfare, and male supremacy.

sexual dimorphism Marked differences in male and female biology besides the contrasts in breasts and genitals.

sexual orientation A person's habitual sexual attraction to, and activities with, persons of the opposite sex, heterosexuality; the same sex, homosexuality; or both sexes, bisexuality.

CRITICAL THINKING QUESTIONS

For more self testing,
see the self quizzes

mhhe.com/kottak

1. What characteristics of men and women do you see as most directly linked to biological differences between the sexes? What kinds of characteristics are most influenced by culture?

2. Using your own society, give an example of a gender role, a gender stereotype, and gender stratification.

3. What do you see as the main factor that has changed North American gender roles since World War II? How do you expect gender roles to change in the next generation?

4. If you had to pick three factors that play a role in determining cross-cultural variation in gender roles, what would they be?

5. What lessons about human sexuality do you draw from the Etoro? How fixed is human sexual orientation, in your opinion?

SUGGESTED ADDITIONAL READINGS

Behar, R., and D. A. Gordon, eds.
  1995 *Women Writing Culture.* Berkeley: University of California Press. Feminist scholars reflect on identity and difference.

Blackwood, E., and S. Wieringa, eds.
  1999 *Female Desires: Same-Sex Relations and Transgender Practices across Cultures.* New York: Columbia University Press. Lesbianism and male homosexuality in cross-cultural perspective.

Bonvillain, N.
  2001 *Women and Men: Cultural Constructions of Gender,* 3rd ed. Upper Saddle River, NJ: Prentice Hall. A cross-cultural study of gender roles and relationships, from bands to industrial societies.

Brettell, C. B., and C. F. Sargent, eds.
  2005 *Gender in Cross-Cultural Perspective.* Upper Saddle River, NJ: Pearson/Prentice Hall. Articles on variation in gender systems across cultures.

Dahlberg, F., ed.
  1981 *Woman the Gatherer.* New Haven, CT: Yale University Press. Female roles and activities among prehistoric and contemporary foragers.

Kimmel, M., and R. Plante
  2004 *Sexualities: Identities, Behaviors, and Society.* New York: Oxford University Press.

Kimmel, M., J. Hearn, and R. W. Connell
  2005 *Handbook of Studies on Men and Masculinities.* Thousand Oaks, CA: Sage.

Kimmel, M. S., and M. A. Messner, eds.
  2007 *Men's Lives,* 7th ed. Boston: Pearson/Allyn & Bacon. The study of men in society and concepts of masculinity in the United States.

Lamphere, L., H. Ragone, and P. Zavella, eds.
  1997 *Situated Lives: Gender and Culture in Everyday Life.* New York: Routledge. Essays on gender and culture as illustrated by everyday social interaction.

Lancaster, R. N., and M. Di Leonardo, eds.
  1997 *The Gender/Sexuality Reader: Culture, History, Political Economy.* New York: Routledge. Gender and sexuality in history and in the modern social context.

Mascia-Lees, F., and N. J. Black
  2000 *Gender and Anthropology.* Prospect Heights, Il: Waveland. History of gender studies in anthropology.

Nanda, S.
  2000 *Gender Diversity: Crosscultural Variations.* Prospect Heights, Il: Waveland. Sexuality, gender, and genders in various societies.

Nelson, S. N., and M. Rosen-Ayalon, eds.
  2002 *In Pursuit of Gender: Worldwide Archaeological Approaches.* Social archaeology, history of gender roles, and women in prehistory.

Rathus, S. A., J. S. Nevid, and J. Fichner-Rathus
  2005 *Human Sexuality in a World of Diversity,* 6th ed. Boston: Pearson/Allyn & Bacon. Multicultural and ethnic perspectives.

Reiter, R., ed.
  1975 *Toward an Anthropology of Women.* New York: Monthly Review Press. Classic anthology, with a particular focus on peasant societies.

Rosaldo, M. Z., and L. Lamphere, eds.
  1974 *Woman, Culture, and Society.* Stanford, CA: Stanford University Press. Another classic anthology, covering many areas of the world.

Sinnott, M. J.
  2004 *Toms and Dees: Transgender Identity and Female Same-Sex Relationships in Thailand.* Honolulu: University of Hawaii Press. An ethnography about non-Western female same-sex sexuality and transgenderism.

Ward, M. C., and M. Edelstein
  2006 *A World Full of Women,* 4th ed. Boston: Allyn & Bacon. A global and comparative approach to the study of women.

---

1. Gender in the Classroom: Read the article "Student Ratings of Professors Are Not Gender Blind" by Susan Basow, **http://eserver.org/ feminism/workplace/fces-not-gender-blind.txt**.

    a. How much difference is there between male and female students who are rating a male professor? How much difference is there between male and female students in rating a female professor?

    b. What are the added expectations students have for female professors? What do you think is the source of those expectations? Do you think the expectations discussed in this article hold true for female teachers all over the world?

    c. Do you think the findings of this study are consistent with the way you and your friends rate professors?

2. Gender on the Internet: Read the paper by Amy Bruckman titled "Gender Swapping on the Internet," **http://www.inform.umd.edu/EdRes/ Topic/WomensStudies/Computing/Articles+ ResearchPapers/gender-swapping**.

    a. Do gender roles exist on the Internet, such as in the MUDs described in this article, or in chat rooms, or e-mail? Do gender roles belong on the Internet? Would it be possible for people to remain gender-neutral on the Internet indefinitely?

    b. Imagine you are using a MUD. You encounter a character with a gender-neutral name (like Pat) and description. What clues would you use to identify the gender of Pat and Pat's user? Do you think this detective work would be more or less difficult if Pat's user was also from a different culture than your own?

    c. Do the cases described in this paper say more about the person swapping genders or about the other users?

See Chapter 11 at your McGraw-Hill Online Learning Center for additional review and interactive exercises.

Kottak, *Assault on Paradise*, 4th ed.

Compare the discussions of gender and female status in Chapters 3 and 9. How did gender issues change over time in Arembepe? How does Dora's case, in Chapter 10, illustrate some of these changes? Chapter 12 considers the impact of television on Arembepeiros. Did it affect gender roles? Pay attention to the description of Nadia in Chapter 12 as you think about this question.

Peters-Golden, *Culture Sketches*, 4th ed.

Read Chapter 9, "Minangkabau: Merantau and Matriliny." Among the Minangkabau, also discussed in the text chapter, what are some ways in which matrilineality influences, and is reflected in, aspects of their lives other than kinship?

Knauft, *The Gebusi*, 1st ed.

Read Chapters 1, 5, and 10. Based on Chapter 1, what are the biggest inequalities in Gebusi gender relations? How do Gebusi women seem to view these inequities? Based on Chapter 5, describe sexual relations that traditionally have taken place between Gebusi men. What is the relation between male–male sexuality and the sexual relationship of Gebusi men to Gebusi women, including in marriage? What is the attitude of Gebusi women to the male–male sexual practices, and how does this compare or contrast with attitudes in Western societies? Based on Chapter 10 of *The Gebusi*, described how gender and sex practices among Gebusi have changed over time. What are the primary reasons for these changes? Based on Chapters 5 and 10, what personal tensions do ethnographers face in studying issues of gender and sexuality during fieldwork? Despite these difficulties, why does the cross-cultural study of gender and of sexuality remain important?

The Basques

The Basque people of Spain and France, and their diaspora, including their migration to the United States, have attracted the attention of anthropology's four subfields. Having maintained a strong ethnic identity, perhaps for millennia, the Basques are linguistically unique in that their language is unrelated to any other known language. Genetic differences also set them off from neighboring European populations.

Their homeland lies in the western Pyrenees mountains, straddling the French–Spanish border. Seven traditional provinces within Basque country (three in France and four in Spain) are distinguished by dialect differences. Basques refer to their homeland as Euskal-Herria ("Land of the Basques") or Euskadi ("Country of the Basques"). Although their seven regions have not been unified politically for nearly a millennium, the Basques remain one of Europe's most distinctive ethnic groups.

Romans, Goths, Franks, and Moors all controlled parts of Basque country without ever totally subduing it. For the last thousand years the Basque territory has been influenced by European polities. Yet for much of this time the Basques have managed to retain significant autonomy in their affairs.

The French Revolution of 1789 ended the political autonomy of the three Basque provinces in France. During the 19th century in Spain the Basques fought on the losing side in two internal wars, yielding much of their political autonomy in defeat. When the Spanish Civil War broke out in 1936, the Basques remained loyal to the republic, opposing the eventual Spanish dictator, Francisco Franco, who eventually defeated them. Under Franco's rule (1936–1975), Basques were executed, imprisoned, and exiled, and Basque culture was systematically repressed.

In the late 1950s disaffected Basque youths founded ETA (Euskadi Ta Azkatasuna, or "Basque Country and Freedom"). Its goal was complete independence from Spain (Zulaika 1988). The ETA's opposition to Franco escalated into violence, which continued thereafter, diminishing in recent years. Effective March 24, 2006, the leaders of ETA announced a cease-fire. They planned thereafter to seek full independence from Spain through the political process.

Franco's death in 1975 had ushered in an era of democracy in Spain. Mainline Basque nationalists collaborated in framing a new constitution which gave considerable autonomy to the Basque regions (Trask 1996). Since 1979 the three Spanish Basque

The prolific Spanish painter Pablo Picasso portrayed the destruction of a Basque town in his famous painting Guernica (1937).

provinces of Vizcaya, Guipuzcoa, and Alava have been united as the Basque Autonomous Region, which governs the Basque homeland. The Basque language is co-official with Spanish in this territory. Spain's fourth Basque province, Navarra, formed its own autonomous region, where the Basque language has a degree of official standing. In France, Basque, like other regional languages, has been victimized for centuries by laws hostile to languages other than French (Trask 1996).

The ancestral form of the Basque language reached Western Europe thousands—perhaps even tens of thousands—of years ago, from where we cannot say. All the other modern languages of Western Europe arrived much later. Spreading across Europe from the east, the Indo-European languages, such as Latin, Germanic, and Celtic, gradually displaced all but one of the indigenous languages. When the Romans invaded Gaul (France), an early form of Basque, known as Aquitanian, was the only non-Indo-European language that survived there. In Spain, several pre-Indo-European languages were still spoken, including Aquitanian and Iberian. Latin replaced them all, with the sole exception of Aquitanian (ancestral Basque) (Trask 1996).

After generations of decline, the number of Basque speakers is increasing today. Much education, publishing, and broadcasting now proceeds in Basque in the Autonomous Region. Still, Basque faces the same pressures that all other minority languages do: Knowledge of the national language (Spanish or French) is essential, and most education, publishing, and broadcasting is in the national language (Trask 1996).

How long have the Basques been in their homeland? Some scholars believe the Basques may be direct descendants of the Upper Paleolithic cave painters active in southwestern Europe 15,000 years ago. Archaeological evidence suggests that a single group of people lived in the Basque country continuously from late Paleolithic times through the Bronze Age (about 3,000 years ago). There is no evidence to suggest that any new population entered the area after that. However, such an intrusion cannot be ruled out (La Fraugh n.d.).

We've seen that linguistically the Basques are absolutely distinct. To an extent, they also contrast biologically with other Europeans. For example, Basques have the highest proportion of RH-negative blood in Europe (25 percent), and one of the highest percentages of type O blood (55 percent). The geneticist Luigi Cavalli-Sforza (2000), who developed a gene map of Europe, found the Basques to be strikingly different from their neighbors.

However, a recent genetic study involving the Y chromosome, which is passed exclusively from father to son, establishes links between the Basques and the Celts of Wales and Ireland. In

Location of the Basque homeland.

terms of the Y chromosome, the researchers found Celts and Basques to be statistically indistinguishable (Wade 2001).

Historically the Basques have been herders, fishers, and farmers. (Today most of them work in business and industry.) Through the Middle Ages they were mainly herders. As Europe's earliest and most efficient whalers, Basques may have reached North America before Columbus did. There is documentation of Basque whaling and cod fishing along Canada's Labrador coast by 1500. Some Atlantic coastal Native American languages in Canada have Basque loan words. Canadian archivists and archaeologists have discovered a 16th-century Basque whaling station (used seasonally) and a sunken whaling ship at Red Bay, Labrador. Basque activity in Canadian coastal waters lasted into the 19th century (Douglass 1992).

The Basque homeland contains major cities, along with coastal fishing communities and farming (peasant) villages. The typical peasant village

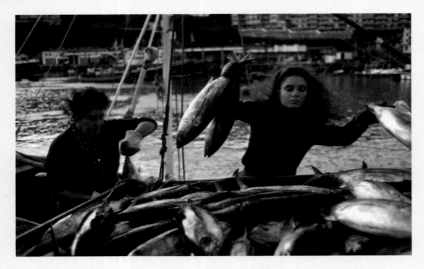

■ *Women unload the catch in Bermeo, a Basque fishing village in Spain. Fishing, farming, and herding are mainstays of the Basque economy.*

■ *The herding of sheep, shown here in the Basque homeland (Pyrenees), remained a primary occupation of Basque men who started migrating to the American West in the 19th century.*

includes a river valley, where the village is seated, and the surrounding hillsides, which have *baserriak*, or farmsteads. These houses are large stone structures, often three stories tall. The ground floor is for animal stables; the second floor is living space, while the third is used to store hay and other crops (Douglass 1992).

The Basque *basseria* (family farm) once thrived as a mixed-farming unit emphasizing self-sufficiency. The farm family grew wheat, corn, vegetables, fruits, and nuts and raised poultry, rabbits, pigs, cows, and sheep. Subsistence pursuits have become increasingly commercialized,

with the production of vegetables, dairy products, and fish aimed at urban markets (Greenwood 1976).

On the family farm, the stem family was the basic social unit. This included an older couple, their heir (usually male), and his wife and children. Unmarried siblings of the heir could reside in their natal households until death, but they had to respect the authority of the male and female heads. The household had to approve the selection of the spouse of the designated heir. Ownership of the farm was transferred to the newlyweds as part of the marital arrangements— to a single heir(ess) in each generation. By custom, male primogeniture was preferred. Siblings who married and moved away received dowries. Because only one child was socialized into the role of the heir(ess), his or her siblings were raised anticipating that they would leave. This system has made the rural Basque country a font of emigration (Douglass 1975, 1992).

BASQUE AMERICANS

Basque immigrants originally entered North America as either Spanish or French nationals. Basque Americans, numbering some 50,000, now invoke Basqueness as their primary ethnic identity. They are concentrated in California, Idaho, and Nevada. First-generation immigrants are usually fluent in Basque. They are more likely to be bilingual in Basque and English than to have their parents' fluency in Spanish or French (Douglass 1992).

Building on a traditional occupation in Basque country, Basques in the United States are notable for their identification with sheep herding (see Ott 1981). Most of them settled and worked in the open-range livestock districts of the 13 states of the American West. Basques first entered the western United States as agents of Spanish colonialism. They numbered among the Spanish soldiers, explorers, missionaries, and administrators in the American Southwest and Spanish California. More Basques came during the California gold rush, many from southern South America, where they were established sheep herders. In the 1870s Basque shepherds spread throughout California's central valleys and expanded into Arizona, New Mexico, and western Nevada (Douglass 1992).

Restrictive immigration laws enacted in the 1920s, which had an anti–southern European bias, limited Basque immigration to the United States. During World War II, with the country in need of shepherds, the U.S. government exempted Basque herders from immigration quotas. Between 1950 and 1975, several thousand Basques entered the United States on three-year contracts. Later, the decline of the U.S. sheep industry would slow Basque immigration dramatically (Douglass 1992).

With that decline, many Basque herders returned to Europe; others converted sheep ranches to cattle. Many more moved to nearby small towns where they did construction work or established small businesses (bars, bakeries, motels, gasoline stations). Wherever jai alai (words which mean "happy festival" in Basque) is legal, Basque players are recruited from Europe. They play part of the year in Basque country and the rest in the United States (Douglass 1992).

Catering to Basque sheep herders, most western towns in the open-range country had one or more Basque boardinghouses. The typical one had a bar and a dining room, where meals were served family-style at long tables. A second floor of sleeping rooms was reserved for permanent boarders. Also lodged were herders in town for a brief visit, vacation, or employment layoff or in transit to an employer (Echeverria 1999).

Both traditionally and in the United States, Basque culture has promoted a degree of equality between men and women. In farming, women and men have shared many tasks, including working together in the fields. In Basque cities, where women are increasingly employed in industry and services, there is a income gender gap comparable to the one that exists in the United States. Although domestic tasks remain largely the domain of women, they are not regarded as demeaning for men. Also, whether running a ranching operation, a boardinghouse, or a town business, Basque American women work alongside men and perform virtually any task (Douglass 1992).

The social glue that holds Basque Americans together includes extended bilateral kinship and affinal ties. Basque men recruited their brothers and cousins to herd sheep in the American West. Basque American colonies often included family clusters, with local endogamy increasing the degree of interrelatedness. Even today, extended Basque American families maintain close ties, as they gather for baptisms, graduations, weddings, and funerals (Douglass 1992).

Initially, few Basques came to the United States intending to stay. Most early immigrants were young, unmarried men. The transhumant sheep herding pattern, with solitary summers in the mountains, did not fit well with family life. Eventually, Basque men came with the intent to stay. They either sent back or went back to Europe for brides (few married non-Basques). Many brides, of the "mail order" sort, were sisters or cousins of an acquaintance made in the United States. Basque boardinghouses also became a source of spouses. The boardinghouse owners sent back to Europe for women willing to

Basque-American folk dancers at a Cultural Festival in San Francisco. Basques settled in several western states, including California and Nevada. What was their main occupation?

come to America as domestics. Few remained single for long (Douglass 1992). In these ways Basque Americans drew on their homeland society and culture in establishing the basis of their family and community life in North America.

Among the homeland patterns that the Basques transferred from the Old World to the New were transhumant herding, a blurred division of labor by gender in farming and industry, ethnic endogamy, and strong family ties. Yet another is the role of unrelated neighbors, who traditionally played an important role in rural Basque society (Douglass 1992). After the family, the most important social institution for Basque Americans has been the boardinghouse, where Basques could again draw on the support of their neighbors. The boardinghouse was a multifunctional institution that served as a town address, a bank, an employment agency, an ethnic haven, a source of help and advice, a place to leave one's possessions, a possible source of a bride, and a potential retirement home. For the Basque American, it was a place to recharge ethnic batteries, practice one's rusty Basque, learn something about traditional culture, dance to Basque music, eat Basque cuisine, hire help, and hold baptisms, weddings, and wakes (Douglass 1992; Echeverria 1999).

Basques have not escaped discrimination in the United States. In the American West, sheep herding is an occupation that carries some stigma. Mobile sheep herders competed with settled livestock interests for access to the range. These were some of the sources of anti-Basque sentiment and even legislation. More recently, newspaper coverage of conflict in the Basque country, particularly the activities of the ETA, has made Basque Americans sensitive to the possible charge of being terrorist sympathizers (Douglass 1992; see also Zulaika 1988).

12

Religion

WHAT IS RELIGION?

The anthropologist Anthony F. C. Wallace defined **religion** as "belief and ritual concerned with supernatural beings, powers, and forces" (1966, p. 5). The supernatural is the extraordinary realm outside (but believed to impinge on) the observable world. It is non-empirical and inexplicable in ordinary terms. It must be accepted "on faith." Supernatural beings—gods and goddesses, ghosts, and souls—are not of the material world. Nor are supernatural forces, some of which may be wielded by beings. Other sacred forces are impersonal; they simply exist. In many societies, however, people believe they can benefit from, become imbued with, or manipulate supernatural forces (see Bowie 2006; Crapo 2003).

Another definition of religion (Reese 1999) focuses on bodies of people who gather together regularly for worship. These congregants or adherents subscribe to and internalize a common system of meaning. They accept (adhere to or believe in) a set of doctrines involving the relationship between the individual and divinity, the supernatural, or whatever is taken to be the ultimate nature of reality. Anthropologists have stressed the collective, shared, and enacted nature of religion, the emotions it generates, and the meanings it embodies. Émile Durkheim (1912/2001), an early scholar of religion, stressed religious *effervescence*, the bubbling up of collective emotional intensity generated by worship. Victor Turner (1969/1995) updated Durkheim's notion, using the term *communitas*, an intense community spirit, a feeling of great social solidarity, equality, and togetherness. The word *religion* derives from the Latin *religare*, "to tie, to bind," but it is not necessary for all the members of a given religion to meet together as a common body. Subgroups meet regularly at local congregation sites. They may attend occasional meetings with adherents representing a wider region. And they may form an imagined community with people of similar faith throughout the world.

Like ethnicity and language, religion also is associated with social divisions within and between societies and nations, such as those countries into which Islam has diffused, as described in the "News Brief." Religion both unites and divides. Participation in common rites may affirm, and thus maintain, the social solidarity of one religion's adherents. However, as we know from daily headlines, religious difference also may be associated with bitter enmity.

In studying religion cross-culturally, anthropologists pay attention to the social nature and roles of religion as well as to the nature, content, and meaning to people of religious doctrines, acts, events, settings, practitioners, and organizations. We also consider such verbal manifestations of religious beliefs as prayers, chants, myths, texts, and statements about ethics and morality. Religion, by either definition offered here, exists in all human societies. It is a cultural universal. However, we'll see that it isn't always easy to distinguish the supernatural from the natural and that different societies conceptualize divinity, supernatural entities, and ultimate realities very differently.

ORIGINS, FUNCTIONS, AND EXPRESSIONS OF RELIGION

When did religion begin? No one knows for sure. There are suggestions of religion in Neandertal burials and on European cave walls, where painted stick figures may represent shamans, early religious specialists. Nevertheless, any statement about when, where, why, and how religion arose, or any description of its original nature, can only be speculative. However, although such speculations are inconclusive, many have revealed important functions and effects of religious behavior. Several theories will be examined now.

Animism

The founder of the anthropology of religion was the Englishman Sir Edward Burnett Tylor (1871/1958). Religion was born, Tylor thought, as people tried to understand conditions and events they could not explain by reference to daily experience. Tylor believed that our ancestors—and contemporary nonindustrial peoples—were particularly intrigued with death, dreaming, and trance. In dreams and trances, people see images they may remember when they wake up or come out of the trance state.

Tylor concluded that attempts to explain dreams and trances led early humans to believe that two entities inhabit the body: one active during the day and the other—a double or soul—active during sleep and trance states. Although they never meet, they are vital to each other.

OVERVIEW

Religion is a cultural universal—manifest in a body of people with similar beliefs who gather together regularly for worship. Cross-cultural studies have revealed many expressions, meanings, and functions of religion. Religion provides comfort and security in times of uncertainty and crisis. Rituals are formal, invariant, earnest acts that require people to join actively in a social collectivity. Rites of passage may mark any change in social status, age, place, or social condition. Collective rituals often are cemented by communitas, a feeling of intense fellowship and solidarity. Religion achieves social control through moral and ethical beliefs, along with real and imagined rewards and punishments. Religion also can promote change. Religious movements aimed at the revitalization of society have helped people cope with changing conditions. Contemporary religious trends include both rising secularism and a resurgence of religious fundamentalism. Some of today's new religions are inspired by science and technology; others, by spiritualism. Rituals can be secular as well as religious.

Islam Expanding Globally, Adapting Locally

NATIONAL GEOGRAPHIC NEWS BRIEF

by Brian Handwerk
October 24, 2003

One well-known anthropological definition of religion stresses beliefs and behavior concerned with supernatural beings, powers, and forces. Another definition focuses on congregants—a body of people who gather together regularly for worship, and who accept a set of doctrines involving the relationship between the individual and divinity. Some religions, and the beliefs, affirmations, and forms of worship they promote, have spread widely. This news brief describes how Islam, the world's fastest-growing religion, has adapted locally to various nations and cultures. In this process, although certain fundamentals endure, there is also room for considerable diversity. Local people always assign their own meanings to the messages and social forms, including religion, they receive from outside. Such meanings reflect their cultural backgrounds and experiences. This news story describes how Islam has adapted successfully to many cultural differences, including linguistic practices, building styles, and the presence of other religions, such as Hinduism, already established in that area.

One in every five people worldwide is a Muslim, some 1.3 billion believers. Islam is the world's fastest growing religion and it has spread across the globe.

Muslims everywhere agree on the Shahadah, the profession of faith: "There is no God but Allah; Mohammed is the prophet of Allah." But Islam is far from homogeneous—the faith reflects the increasingly diverse areas in which it is practiced.

"Islam is a world religion," said Ali Asani, a Harvard professor of Indo-Muslim Languages and Culture. "If you think about doctrine and theology, when these sets of religious ideas and concepts are transferred to different parts of the world—and Muslims live in many cultures and speak many different languages—the expressions of those doctrines and theology will necessarily be influenced by local culture."

Sometimes such regional distinctions are obvious to even casual observers. Mosques, for example, all share common features—they face Mecca and have a mihrab, or niche, that indicates that direction. Yet they also boast unique architectural elements and decor that suggest whether their location is Iran, Africa, or China. The houses of worship provide what Asani calls "a visual reminder of cultural diversity." Other easily grasped regional distinctions have their origins at the level of language. While Arabic is Islam's liturgical language, used for prayer, most Muslims' understanding of their faith occurs in their local language.

"Languages are really windows into culture," Asani explains. "So very often what you find is that theological Islamic concepts get translated into local idioms." . . .

Some Islamic fundamentalists might frown upon the diversity caused by local characteristics, but such are the predominant forms of Islam. "Rather than discussing Islam, we might more accurately talk about 'Islams' in different cultural contexts," Asani said. "We have Muslim literature from China, for example, where Islamic concepts are understood within a Confucian framework."

In the region of Bengal, now part of the nation of Bangladesh and the Indian state of West Bengal, a popular literary tradition created a context for the arrival of Islam. The concept of the avatar is important to the Hindu tradition, in which these deities become incarnate and descend to Earth to guide the righteous and fight evil.

"What you find in 16th century Bengal is the development of what you might call 'folk literature' where the Islamic idea of the prophet becomes understood within the framework of the avatar," Asani said. "So you have bridges being built between religious traditions as concepts resonate against each other."

■ *Muslims before an Islamic mosque in Kano, northern Nigeria.*

This example is quite different from conditions in pre-Islam Arabia, at the time of Mohammed, where the poet held a special place in society. "If you consider the Koran, the word means 'recitation' in Arabic, and it's primarily an oral scripture, intended to be recited aloud and heard; to be performed," Asani said. "Viewed from a literary perspective, its form and structure relate very well to the poetic traditions of pre-Islamic Arabia. It's an example where the format of revelation was determined by the culture. In pre-Islamic Arabia the poet was often considered to be inspired in his poetic compositions by jinn from another world. So when the Prophet Muhammed began receiving revelations which were eventually compiled into the Koran, he was accused of being a poet, to which he responded 'I'm not a poet but a prophet.'" . . .

Islam came to Indonesia with merchants who were not theologians but simply practicing Muslims who people looked to as an example. There were also Sufi teachers who were quite willing to create devotional exercises that fit the way people in Sumatra or Java already practiced their faith. The two largest Muslim groups in Indonesia today, and perhaps in the world, are Muhammadyya and Nahdlatul Ulama. Each of them has over 30 million members, and each began as local reform movement rooted in the promotion of a more modern education within the framework of Islam . . .

A large number of Muslims, of course, don't live in Islamic nations at all but as minorities in other countries. The emergence of some minority Muslim communities has been an interesting and important development of the last 25 to 30 years.

Some relatively small communities can have a large impact. The European Muslim populations, for example, have a high component of refugee intellectuals. They've had an effect on their adopted countries, and also on the rest of the Islamic world . . .

In South Africa the Muslim community is less than three percent of the population—but it's highly visible and highly educated. In the days of apartheid they had the advantage of being an intermediary, a community that was neither black nor white. By the 1980s the younger Muslim leadership became very opposed to apartheid on Islamic grounds and on basic human rights grounds. Muslims became quite active in the African National Congress (ANC). Though they were only a small minority when apartheid was destroyed, a number of Muslims became quite visible in the new South African regime—and throughout the larger Muslim world. Encompassing both Islamic states and minority communities, Islam is the world's fastest growing religion and an increasingly common topic of global conversation. Yet much of the discourse paints the faith with a single brush. As more people become familiar with Islam around the world it may be well for them to first ask, as Professor Asani suggests: "Whose Islam? Which Islam?"

SOURCE: Brian Handwerk, "Islam Expanding Globally, Adapting Locally," *National Geographic News,* October 24, 2003. http://news.nationalgeographic. com/news/2003/10/1022_031022_ islamdiversity.html.

■ *Ancient Greek polytheism is illustrated by this image of Apollo, with a lyre, and Artemis, sacrificing over an altar fire. The red-figured terra-cotta vessel dates to 490–480 B.C.E.*

When the double permanently leaves the body, the person dies. Death is departure of the soul. From the Latin for soul, *anima,* Tylor named this belief animism. The soul was one sort of spiritual entity; people remembered various images from their dreams and trances—other spirits. For Tylor, **animism,** the earliest form of religion, was a belief in spiritual beings.

Tylor proposed that religion evolved through stages, beginning with animism. *Polytheism* (the belief in multiple gods) and then *monotheism* (the belief in a single, all-powerful deity) developed later. Because religion originated to explain things people didn't understand, Tylor thought it would decline as science offered better explanations. To an extent, he was right. We now have scientific explanations for many things that religion once elucidated. Nevertheless, because religion persists, it must do something more than explain the mysterious. It must, and does, have other functions and meanings. (For more on Durkheim, Turner, and Tylor, see Appendix 1.)

Mana and Taboo

Besides animism—and sometimes coexisting with it in the same society—is a view of the supernatural as a domain of raw impersonal power, or *force,* that people can control under certain conditions. (You'd be right to think of *Star Wars.*) Such a conception of the supernatural is particularly prominent in Melanesia, the area of the South Pacific that includes Papua New Guinea and adjacent islands. Melanesians believed in **mana,** a sacred impersonal force existing in the universe. Mana can reside in people, animals, plants, and objects.

Melanesian mana was similar to our notion of efficacy or luck. Melanesians attributed success to mana, which people could acquire or manipulate in different ways, such as through magic. Objects with mana could change someone's luck. For example, a charm or amulet belonging to a successful hunter might transmit the hunter's mana to the next person who held or wore it. A woman might put a rock in her garden, see her yields improve dramatically, and attribute the change to the force contained in the rock.

Beliefs in manalike forces are widespread, although the specifics of the religious doctrines vary. Consider the contrast between mana in Melanesia and Polynesia (the islands included in a triangular area marked by Hawaii to the north, Easter Island to the east, and New Zealand to the southwest). In Melanesia, one could acquire mana by chance, or by working hard to get it. In Polynesia, however, mana wasn't potentially available to everyone but was attached to political offices. Chiefs and nobles had more mana than ordinary people did.

So charged with mana were the highest chiefs that contact with them was dangerous to the commoners. The mana of chiefs flowed out of their bodies wherever they went. It could infect the ground, making it dangerous for others to walk in the chief's footsteps. It could permeate the containers and utensils chiefs used in eating. Contact between chief and commoners was dangerous because mana could have an effect like an electric shock. Because high chiefs had so much mana, their bodies and possessions were **taboo** (set apart as sacred and off-limits to ordinary people). Contact between a high chief and commoners was forbidden. Because ordinary people couldn't bear as much sacred current as royalty could, when commoners were accidentally exposed, purification rites were necessary.

One role of religion is to explain (see Horton 1993). A belief in souls explains what happens in sleep, trance, and death. Melanesian mana explains differential success that people can't understand in ordinary, natural terms. People fail at hunting, war, or gardening not because they are lazy, stupid, or inept but because success comes—or doesn't come—from the supernatural world.

The beliefs in spiritual beings (e.g., animism) and supernatural forces (e.g., mana) fit within the definition of religion given at the beginning of this chapter. Most religions include both spirits and impersonal forces. Likewise, the supernatural beliefs of contemporary North Americans include beings (gods, saints, souls, demons) and forces (charms, talismans, crystals, and sacred objects).

Magic and Religion

Magic refers to supernatural techniques intended to accomplish specific aims. These techniques include spells, formulas, and incantations used with deities or with impersonal forces. Magicians use *imitative magic* to produce a desired effect by imitating it. If magicians wish to injure or kill someone, they may imitate that effect on an image of the victim. Sticking pins in "voodoo dolls" is an example. With *contagious magic,* whatever is done to an object is believed to affect a person who once had contact with it. Sometimes practitioners of contagious magic use body products from prospective victims—their nails or hair, for example. The spell performed on the body product is believed to reach the person eventually and work the desired result.

We find magic in cultures with diverse religious beliefs. It can be associated with animism, mana, polytheism, or monotheism. Magic is neither simpler nor more primitive than animism or the belief in mana.

Anxiety, Control, Solace

Religion and magic don't just explain things and help people accomplish goals. They also enter the

Illustrating baseball magic, Los Angeles Dodgers first baseman Nomar Garciaparra goes through his glove adjustment ritual between pitches during the first inning of a spring training game against the New York Mets Sunday, March 5, 2006, in Vero Beach, Florida. Such rituals are most common in batting and pitching.

Trobriand Islanders prepare a traditional trading canoe for use in the Kula, which is a regional exchange system. The woman's basket contains trade goods, while the men prepare the long canoe to set sail. Magic is often associated with uncertainty, such as sailing in unpredictable waters.

For information on Ecuadorian curers, see the Internet Exercises at your OLC

mhhe.com/kottak

For information on spiritual beliefs among Native Australians, see the Internet Exercises at your OLC

mhhe.com/kottak

Bringing It All Together

The "Bringing It All Together" essay that follows the last chapter in this book describes ritual behavior in an unlikely setting—a fast-food restaurant.

realm of human feelings. In other words, they serve emotional needs as well as cognitive (e.g., explanatory) ones. For example, supernatural beliefs and practices can help reduce anxiety. Magical techniques can dispel doubts that arise when outcomes are beyond human control. Similarly, religion helps people face death and endure life crises.

Although all societies have techniques to deal with everyday matters, there are certain aspects of people's lives over which they lack control. When people face uncertainty and danger, according to Malinowski, they turn to magic.

> [H]owever much knowledge and science help man in allowing him to obtain what he wants, they are unable completely to control chance, to eliminate accidents, to foresee the unexpected turn of natural events, or to make human handiwork reliable and adequate to all practical requirements. (Malinowski 1931/1978, p. 39)

Malinowski found that the Trobriand Islanders used magic when sailing, a hazardous activity. He proposed that because people can't control matters such as wind, weather, and the fish supply, they turn to magic. People may call on magic when they come to a gap in their knowledge or powers of practical control yet have to continue in a pursuit (Malinowski 1931/1978).

Malinowski noted that it was only when confronted by situations they could not control that Trobrianders, out of psychological stress, turned from technology to magic. Despite our improving technical skills, we can't still control every outcome, and magic persists in contemporary societies. Magic is particularly evident in baseball, where George Gmelch (1978, 2001) describes a series of rituals, taboos, and sacred objects. Like Trobriand sailing magic, these behaviors serve to reduce psychological stress, creating an illusion of magical control when real control is lacking. Even

the best pitchers have off days and bad luck. Examples of pitchers' magic include tugging one's cap between pitches, touching the resin bag after each bad pitch, and talking to the ball. Gmelch's conclusions confirm Malinowski's that magic is most prevalent in situations of chance and uncertainty. All sorts of magical behavior surrounded pitching and batting, where uncertainty is rampant, but few rituals involved fielding, where players have much more control. (Batting averages of .350 or higher are very rare after a full season, but a fielding percentage below .900 is a disgrace.)

According to Malinowski, magic is used to establish control, but religion "is born out of . . . the real tragedies of human life" (1931/1978, p. 45). Religion offers emotional comfort, particularly when people face a crisis. Malinowski saw tribal religions as concerned mainly with organizing, commemorating, and helping people get through such life events as birth, puberty, marriage, and death. (For more on Malinowski, see Appendix 1.)

Rituals

Several features distinguish rituals from other kinds of behavior (Rappaport 1974). **Rituals** are formal—stylized, repetitive, and stereotyped. People perform them in special (sacred) places and at set times. Rituals include *liturgical orders*—sequences of words and actions invented prior to the current performance of the ritual in which they occur.

These features link rituals to plays, but there are important differences. Plays have audiences rather than participants. Actors merely *portray* something, but ritual performers—who make up congregations—are in earnest. Rituals convey information about the participants and their traditions. Repeated year after year, generation after generation, rituals translate enduring messages, values, and sentiments into action.

Rituals are *social* acts. Inevitably, some participants are more committed than others are to the beliefs that lie behind the rites. However, just by taking part in a joint public act, the performers signal that they accept a common social and moral order, one that transcends their status as individuals.

Rites of Passage

Magic and religion, as Malinowski noted, can reduce anxiety and allay fears. Ironically, beliefs and rituals also can *create* anxiety and a sense of insecurity and danger (Radcliffe-Brown 1962/1965). Anxiety may arise *because* a rite exists. Indeed, participation in a collective ritual may build up stress, whose common reduction, through the completion of the ritual, enhances the solidarity of the participants.

Rites of passage, for example, the collective circumcision of teenagers, can be very stressful. The traditional vision quests of Native Americans, particularly the Plains Indians, illustrate **rites of passage** (customs associated with the transition from one place or stage of life to another), which are found throughout the world. Among the Plains Indians, to move from boyhood to manhood, a youth temporarily separated from his community. After a period of isolation in the wilderness, often featuring fasting and drug consumption, the young man would see a vision, which would become his guardian spirit. He would then return to his community as an adult.

The rites of passage of contemporary cultures include confirmations, baptisms, bar and bat mitzvahs, and fraternity hazing. Passage rites involve changes in social status, such as from boyhood to manhood and from nonmember to sorority sister. There are also rites and rituals in our business and corporate lives. Examples include promotion and retirement parties. More generally, a rite of passage may mark any change in place, condition, social position, or age.

All rites of passage have three phases: separation, liminality, and incorporation. In the first phase, people withdraw from the group and begin moving from one place or status to another. In the third phase, they reenter society, having completed the rite. The *liminal* phase is the most interesting. It is the period between states, the limbo during which people have left one place or state but haven't yet entered or joined the next (Turner 1969/1995).

Liminality always has certain characteristics. Liminal people occupy ambiguous social positions. They exist apart from ordinary distinctions and expectations, living in a time out of time. They are cut off from normal social contacts. A variety of contrasts may demarcate liminality from regular social life. For example, among the Ndembu of Zambia, a chief underwent a rite of passage before taking office. During the liminal period, his past and future positions in society were ignored, even reversed. He was subjected to a variety of insults, orders, and humiliations.

Passage rites are often collective. Several individuals—boys being circumcised, fraternity or sorority initiates, men at military boot camps, football players in summer training camps, women becoming nuns—pass through the rites together as a group. Table 12.1 summarizes the contrasts or oppositions between liminality and normal social life. Most notable is a social aspect of *collective liminality* called **communitas** (Turner 1967), an intense community spirit, a feeling of great social solidarity, equality, and togetherness. People experiencing liminality together form a

TABLE 12.1 Oppositions between Liminality and Normal Social Life	
Liminality	**Normal Social Structure**
Transition	State
Homogeneity	Heterogeneity
Communitas	Structure
Equality	Inequality
Anonymity	Names
Absence of property	Property
Absence of status	Status
Nakedness or uniform dress	Dress distinctions
Sexual continence or excess	Sexuality
Minimization of sex distinctions	Maximization of sex distinctions
Absence of rank	Rank
Humility	Pride
Disregard of personal appearance	Care for personal appearance
Unselfishness	Selfishness
Total obedience	Obedience only to superior rank
Sacredness	Secularity
Sacred instruction	Technical knowledge
Silence	Speech
Simplicity	Complexity
Acceptance of pain and suffering	Avoidance of pain and suffering

SOURCE: Adapted from Victor W. Turner, *The Ritual Process: Structure and Anti-structure* (New York: Aldine de Gruyter, 1969/1995), p. 106.

Passage rites are often collective. A group—such as these initiates in Togo or these Navy trainees in San Diego—passes through the rites as a unit. Such liminal people experience the same treatment and conditions and must act alike. They share communitas, an intense community spirit, a feeling of great social solidarity or togetherness.

In a variety of contexts, liminal features signal the sacredness or distinctiveness of groups, persons, settings, and events. Liminal symbols mark entities and circumstances as extraordinary—outside and beyond ordinary social space and routine social events. In the case of cults, group identity typically is expected to transcend individuality. Cult members often wear uniform clothing. They may try to reduce distinctions based on age and gender by using a common hairstyle (shaved head, short hair, or long hair). The Heaven's Gate cult, whose mass suicide garnered headlines in 1997, even used castration to increase androgyny (similarity between males and females). In such cults, the individual, so important in American culture, is submerged in the collective. This is one reason Americans are so fearful and suspicious of "cults." (Note, however, that all the distinction-reducing features of cults described here [uniform clothing, short hair, elimination of sexuality] also are true of the military and of such mainstream religious institutions as monasteries and convents.)

community of equals. The social distinctions that have existed before or will exist afterward are temporarily forgotten. Liminal people experience the same treatment and conditions and must act alike. Liminality may be marked ritually and symbolically by reversals of ordinary behavior. For example, sexual taboos may be intensified, or, conversely, sexual excess may be encouraged.

Liminality is a basic part of every passage rite. Furthermore, in certain societies, including our own, liminal symbols may be used to set off one (religious) group from another, and from society as a whole. Such "permanent liminal groups" (e.g., sects, brotherhoods, and cults) are found most characteristically in complex societies—nation-states. Liminal features such as humility, poverty, equality, obedience, sexual abstinence, and silence may be required for all sect or cult

members. Those who join such a group agree to abide by its rules. As if they were undergoing a passage rite—but in this case a never-ending one—they may rid themselves of their previous possessions and cut themselves off from former social links, including those with family members.

Totemism

Rituals serve the social function of creating temporary or permanent solidarity among people—forming a social community. We see this also in practices known as totemism. Totemism has been important in the religions of Native Australians. *Totems* can be animals, plants, or geographic features. In each tribe, groups of people have particular totems. Members of each totemic group believe themselves to be descendants of their totem. Traditionally they customarily neither killed nor ate a totemic animal, but this taboo was lifted once a year, when people assembled for ceremonies dedicated to the totem. These annual rites were believed to be necessary for the totem's survival and reproduction.

Totemism uses nature as a model for society. The totems are usually animals and plants, which are part of nature. People relate to nature through their totemic association with natural species. Because each group has a different totem, social differences mirror natural contrasts. Diversity in the natural order becomes a model for diversity in the social order. However, although totemic plants and animals occupy different niches in nature, on another level they are united because they all are part of nature. The unity of the human social order is enhanced by symbolic association with and imitation of the natural order (Durkheim 1912/2001; Lévi-Strauss 1963; Radcliffe-Brown 1962/1965).

One role of religious rites and beliefs is to affirm, and thus maintain, the solidarity of a religion's adherents. Totems are sacred emblems symbolizing common identity. This is true not just among Native Australians, but also among Native American groups of the North Pacific coast of North America, whose totem poles are well known. Their totemic carvings, which commemorate, and tell visual stories about, ancestors, animals, and spirits, also are associated with ceremonies. In totemic rites, people gather together to honor their totem. In so doing, they use ritual to maintain the social oneness that the totem symbolizes.

In contemporary nations, too, totems continue to mark groups, such as states and universities (e.g., Badgers, Buckeyes, and Wolverines), professional teams (Lions, Tigers, and Bears), and political parties (donkeys and elephants). Although the modern context is more secular, one can still witness, in intense college football rivalries, some of the effervescence Durkheim noted in Australian totemic religion.

RELIGION AND CULTURAL ECOLOGY

Another domain in which religion plays a prominent role is cultural ecology. Behavior motivated by beliefs in supernatural beings, powers, and forces may help people survive in their material environment. In this section, we will see how beliefs and rituals may function as part of a group's cultural adaptation to its environment.

Sacred Cattle in India

The people of India revere zebu cattle, which are protected by the Hindu doctrine of *ahimsa*, a principle of nonviolence that forbids the killing of animals generally. Western economic development experts occasionally (and erroneously) cite the Hindu cattle taboo to illustrate the idea that religious beliefs can stand in the way of rational economic decisions. Hindus might seem to be irrationally ignoring a valuable food (beef) because of their cultural or religious traditions. The economic developers also comment that Indians don't know how to raise proper cattle. They point to the scraggly zebus that wander about town and country. Western techniques of animal

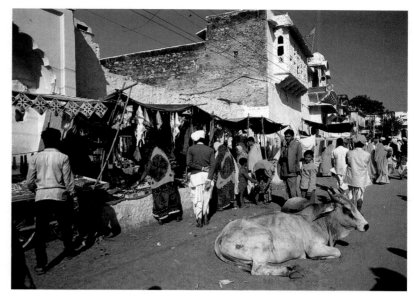

India's zebu cattle are protected by the doctrine of ahimsa, a principle of nonviolence that forbids the killing of animals generally. This Hindu doctrine puts the full power of organized religion behind the command not to destroy a valuable resource even in times of extreme need. What kinds of animal avoidance taboos do you observe? Is their origin religious or secular?

husbandry grow bigger cattle that produce more beef and milk. Western planners lament that Hindus are set in their ways. Bound by culture and tradition, they refuse to develop rationally.

However, these assumptions are both ethnocentric and wrong. Sacred cattle actually play an important adaptive role in an Indian ecosystem that has evolved over thousands of years (Harris 1974, 1978). Peasants' use of cattle to pull plows and carts is part of the technology of Indian agriculture. Indian peasants have no need for large, hungry cattle of the sort that economic developers, beef marketers, and North American cattle ranchers prefer. Scrawny animals pull plows and carts well enough but don't eat their owners out of house and home. How could peasants with limited land and marginal diets feed supersteers without taking food away from themselves?

Indians use cattle manure to fertilize their fields. Not all the manure is collected, because peasants don't spend much time watching their cattle, which wander and graze at will during certain seasons. In the rainy season, some of the manure that cattle deposit on the hillsides washes down to the fields. In this way, cattle also fertilize the fields indirectly. Furthermore, in a country where fossil fuels are scarce, dry cattle dung, which burns slowly and evenly, is a basic cooking fuel.

Far from being useless, as the development experts contend, sacred cattle are essential to Indian cultural adaptation. Biologically adapted to poor pasture land and a marginal environment, the scraggly zebu provides fertilizer and fuel, is indispensable in farming, and is affordable for peasants. The Hindu doctrine of *ahimsa* puts the full power of organized religion behind the command not to destroy a valuable resource even in times of extreme need.

BEYOND THE CLASSROOM

Ewe Traditional and Biomedical Healing Practices in Ghana's Volta Region

STUDENT:
(Lauren) Charlie Graham

SUPERVISING PROFESSOR:
Kara Hoover

SCHOOL:
Georgia State University

YEAR IN SCHOOL/MAJOR:
Fourth year/Anthropology (Medical)

FUTURE PLANS:
Internship/Graduate School

PROJECT TITLE:
Ewe Traditional and Biomedical Healing Practices in Ghana's Volta Region

In summer 2004 Charlie Graham initiated a preliminary study of traditional and biomedical healing among the Ewe of Ghana's Volta region. She plans to continue this work as a graduate student in medical anthropology. Unlike our own society, where medicine is a separate and distinct field, it is common in nonindustrial societies for medicine to be intertwined with religion. The Ewe, like the Makua discussed in Chapter 8 on "Political Systems," and many other cultures believe that sorcery can cause mental and physical unrest, which traditional healers can treat.

In summer 2004 I began fieldwork in Ghana which I plan on continuing in graduate school. Ghana's Volta Region is home to the Ewe, a historically migrant tribe who also reside in Togo and Benin. My research compares and contrasts traditional herbal healing with biomedical treatment methods among the Ewe. The cultural synthesis of traditional and British/Western imposed customs makes for a particularly interesting perspective.

Ghana gained independence from British rule in 1957, making it the first self-governing country in Africa. Since then, it has remained a democratic nation, enjoying peaceful relations with neighboring countries and among its several tribes. Divided into 10 regions, Ghana's tribal leaders share political power with elected officials. Ghanaians practice traditional religions, although Islam and Christianity dominate the North and South respectively, due in large part to missionary influence.

For nine weeks I lived in Ho, the Volta Region's capital, volunteering part time at the Ho District Hospital. I observed various units, including Psychiatric, Maternity, Diabetic, Family Planning, Children's, Male and Female wards. I shadowed the doctor on her rounds and learned alongside third-year nursing students in the midst of their residencies. I also worked with and learned from local medicine men. I traveled to different areas of the Volta Region to visit high priests, observing and surveying their medicinal diversity. I conducted extensive formal and informal interviews of patients, healers, and third parties; observed diagnostic and treatment procedures; and even served as the patient, receiving assorted treatments from both doctors and traditional healers.

Although Ghana's biomedical system bears a fundamental likeness to Britain's, I routinely encountered disparities in medical practices. From doctor-patient relations to disease etiologies to administrative protocol, the differences stood out as opportunities

SOCIAL CONTROL

Religion has meaning for people. It helps men and women cope with adversity and tragedy. It offers hope that things will get better. Lives can be transformed through spiritual healing or rebirth. Sinners can repent and be saved—or they can go on sinning and be damned. If the faithful truly internalize a system of religious rewards and punishments, their religion becomes a powerful means of controlling their beliefs, their behavior, and what they teach their children.

Many people engage in religious activity because it seems to work. Prayers get answered. Faith healers heal. Sometimes it doesn't take much to convince the faithful that religious actions are efficacious. Many American Indian people in southwestern Oklahoma use faith healers at high monetary costs, not just because it makes them feel better about the uncertain but because it works (Lassiter 1998). Each year legions of Brazilians visit a church, Nosso Senhor do Bomfim, in the city of Salvador, Bahia. They vow to repay "Our Lord" (Nosso Senhor) if healing happens. Showing that the vows work, and are repaid, are the thousands of ex votos, plastic impressions of every conceivable body part, that adorn the church, along with photos of people who have been cured.

Religion can work by getting inside people and mobilizing their emotions—their joy, their wrath, their righteousness. We've seen how Émile Durkheim (1912/2001), a prominent French social theorist and scholar of religion (see Appendix 1), described the collective "effervescence" that can develop in religious contexts. Intense emotion bubbles up. People feel a deep sense of shared joy, meaning, experience, communion, belonging, and commitment to their religion.

The power of religion affects action. When religions meet, they can coexist peacefully, or their differences can be a basis for enmity and dishar-

288 PART 2 Cultural Diversity

for cultural exchange and theoretical application. One unique aspect of my research was the incorporation of traditional etiological beliefs, like *juju*, into biomedical practice. *Juju* refers to interpersonally imposed evil forces that create physical and mental unrest (sorcery). Although the majority of Southern Ghanaians practice Christianity, they incorporate traditional beliefs such as this.

In the hospital, language barriers caused miscommunication. Because many Ghanaian doctors leave the country to work in private or better-paying hospitals, many government hospitals employ Spanish-speaking doctors from Cuba who speak basic English and little Ewe. Moreover, although English is Ghana's official language, most patients speak only Ewe. Thus as a Spanish speaker, I often served as a translator. Nurses interviewed patients in Ewe, roughly conveyed the information to me in English, and in Spanish, I reported to the doctor. Due to this linguistic disparity, the healthcare system is inefficient, and patient recovery is often stunted.

My background in medical anthropology and the research I conducted prior to arrival enabled me to recognise the traditional healing practices I encountered. Medicine men train for three years and rank from herbalist to

■ *Charlie Graham with village children in Ghana.*

high priest or sorcerer. I encountered practitioners in each year of study during my time in Ghana. Treatment ranges from preventative to curative, and revolves around belief in patients' physical or spiritual unrest. Relief comes from spiritual penitence via the healer. I sat in on sessions with first-time and regular clients with complaints of behavioral to epidermal abnormalities. Some sorcerers performed ceremonies specifically for me,

communicating with their spirits on my behalf. All communication was in Ewe, for which I had a translator.

It was an honor to learn first-hand from healers on both ends of the medical spectrum, and my fieldwork thrived with rich and intricate data collection. I had the unique opportunity to engage in and scrutinize two different medical realms, struggling to find and maintain their complementary balance in a developing country.

mony, even battle. Religious fervor has inspired Christians on crusades against the infidel and has led Muslims to wage holy wars against non-Islamic peoples. Throughout history, political leaders have used religion to promote and justify their views and policies.

By late September 1996, the Taliban movement had firmly imposed an extreme form of social control in the name of religion on Afghanistan (Figure 12.1) and its people. Led by Muslim clerics, the Taliban attempted to create their version of an Islamic society modeled on the teachings of the Koran (Burns 1997). Various repressive measures were instituted. The Taliban barred women from work and girls from school. Females past puberty were prohibited from talking to unrelated men. Women needed an approved reason, such as shopping for food, to leave their homes. Men, who were required to grow bushy beards, also faced an array of bans—against playing cards, listening to music, keeping pigeons, and flying kites.

To enforce their decrees, the Taliban sent armed enforcers throughout the country. Those agents took charge of "beard checks" and other forms of scrutiny on behalf of a religious police force known as the General Department for the Preservation of Virtue and the Elimination of Vice (Burns 1997). By late fall 2001 the Taliban had been overthrown, with a new interim government established in Kabul, the Afghani capital, on December 22. The collapse of the Taliban followed American bombing of Afghanistan in response to the September 11, 2001, attacks on New York's World Trade Center and Washington's Pentagon. As the Taliban yielded Kabul to victorious Northern Alliance forces, local men flocked to barbershops to have their beards trimmed or shaved. They were using a key Taliban symbol to celebrate the end of religious repression.

Note that in the case of the Taliban, forms of social control were used to support a strict religious orthodoxy. This wasn't repression in

■ *Kite flying, traditionally a popular sport in Afghanistan, was banned by the Taliban. Shown here, on Fridays, after prayers, hundreds of men and boys come to a hilltop overlooking Kabul to fly kites in the windy skies. A kite flyer's goal is to maneuver his kite so as to cut the strings of other kite flyers around him, causing their kites to fall from the sky. The fallen kite belongs to the boy who runs for and finds it first.*

religion's name, but repressive religion. In other countries, secular leaders use religion to justify social control. Seeking power, they use religious rhetoric to get it. The Saudi Arabian government, for example, can be seen as using religion to divert attention from a repressive social policy.

How may leaders mobilize communities and, in so doing, gain support for their own policies? One way is by persuasion; another is by instilling hatred or fear. As we saw in the chapter "Political Systems," fears about and accusations of witchcraft and sorcery can be powerful means of social control by creating a climate of danger and insecurity that affects everyone.

Witchcraft accusations often are directed at socially marginal or anomalous individuals. Among the Betsileo of Madagascar, for example, who prefer patrilocal postmarital residence, men living in the wife's or the mother's village violate a

FIGURE 12.1   Location of Afghanistan.

cultural norm. Linked to their anomalous social position, just a bit of unusual behavior (e.g., staying up late at night) on their part is sufficient for them to be called witches and avoided as a result. In tribes and peasant communities, people who stand out economically, especially if they seem to be benefiting at the expense of others, often face accusations of witchcraft, leading to social ostracism or punishment. In this case witchcraft accusation becomes a **leveling mechanism,** a custom or social action that operates to reduce differences in wealth and thus to bring standouts in line with community norms—another form of social control.

To ensure proper behavior, religions offer rewards, such as the fellowship of the religious community, and punishments, such as the threat of being cast out or excommunicated. Many religions promise rewards for the good life and punishment for the bad. Your physical, mental, moral, and spiritual health, now and forever, may depend on your beliefs and behavior. For example, if you don't pay enough attention to the ancestors, they may snatch your kids from you.

Religions, especially the formal organized ones typically found in state societies, often prescribe a code of ethics and morality to guide behavior. The Judaic Ten Commandments lay down a set of prohibitions against killing, stealing, adultery, and other misdeeds. Crimes are breaches of secular laws, just as sins are breaches of religious strictures. Some rules (e.g., the Ten Commandments) proscribe or prohibit behavior; others prescribe behavior. The Golden Rule, for instance, is a religious guide to do unto others as you would have them do unto you. Moral codes are ways of maintaining order and stability. Codes of morality and ethics are repeated constantly in religious sermons, catechisms, and the like. They become internalized psychologically. They guide behavior and produce regret, guilt, shame, and the need for forgiveness, expiation, and absolution when they are not followed.

Religions also maintain social control by stressing the temporary and fleeting nature of this life. They promise rewards (and/or punishment) in an afterlife (Christianity) or reincarnation (Hinduism and Buddhism). Such beliefs serve to reinforce the status quo. People accept what they have now, knowing they can expect something better in the afterlife or the next life if they follow religious guidelines. Under slavery in the American South, the masters taught portions of the Bible, such as the story of Job, that stressed compliance. The slaves, however, seized on the story of Moses, the promised land, and deliverance.

KINDS OF RELIGION

Religion is a cultural universal. But religions are parts of particular cultures, and cultural differences show up systematically in religious beliefs and practices. For example, the religions of stratified, state societies differ from those of cultures with less marked social contrasts and power differentials.

Considering several cultures, Wallace (1966) identified four types of religion: shamanic, communal, Olympian, and monotheistic (Table 12.2). Unlike priests, the **shamans** of a shamanic religion aren't full-time religious officials but part-time religious figures who mediate between people and supernatural beings and forces. All cultures have medico-magico-religious specialists. *Shaman* is the general term encompassing curers ("witch doctors"), mediums, spiritualists, astrologers, palm readers, and other diviners. Wallace found shamanic religions to be most characteristic of foraging societies, particularly those found in the northern latitudes, such as the Inuit and the native peoples of Siberia.

Although they are only part-time specialists, shamans often set themselves off symbolically

For more on shamans, see the Virtual Exploration
mhhe.com/kottak

For a quiz on types of religion, see the Interactive Exercise
mhhe.com/kottak

TABLE 12.2	Anthony F. C. Wallace's Typology of Religions		
Type of Religion (Wallace)	**Type of Practitioner**	**Conception of Supernatural**	**Type of Society**
Monotheistic	Priests, ministers, etc.	Supreme being	States
Olympian	Priesthood	Hierarchical pantheon with powerful deities	Chiefdoms and archaic states
Communal	Part-time specialists; occasional community-sponsored events, including rites of passage	Several deities with some control over nature	Food-producing tribes
Shamanic	Shaman = part-time	Zoomorphic practitioner	Foraging bands (plants and animals)

FIGURE 12.2 Location of Chukchee in Siberia.

We'wha, a Zuni berdache, in 1885. In some Native American societies, certain ritual duties were reserved for berdaches, *men who rejected the male role and joined a third gender.*

from ordinary people by assuming a different or ambiguous sex or gender role. (In nation-states, priests, nuns, and vestal virgins do something similar by taking vows of celibacy and chastity.) Transvestism is one way of being sexually ambiguous. Among the Chukchee of Siberia (Figure 12.2), where coastal populations fished and interior groups hunted, male shamans copied the dress, speech, hair arrangements, and life styles of women (Bogoras 1904). These shamans took other men as husbands and sex partners and received respect for their supernatural and curative expertise. Female shamans could join a fourth gender, copying men and taking wives.

Among the Crow of the North American Plains, certain ritual duties were reserved for *berdaches,* men who rejected the male role of bison hunter, raider, and warrior and joined a third gender. The fact that certain key rituals could be conducted only by *berdaches* indicates their regular and normal place in Crow social life (Lowie 1935).

Communal religions have, in addition to shamans, community rituals such as harvest ceremonies and rites of passage. Although communal religions lack *full-time* religious specialists, they believe in several deities (**polytheism**) who control aspects of nature. Although some hunter-gatherers, including Australian totemites, have communal religions, these religions are more typical of farming societies.

Olympian religions, which arose with state organization and marked social stratification, add full-time religious specialists—professional *priesthoods.* Like the state itself, the priesthood is hierarchically and bureaucratically organized. The term *Olympian* comes from Mount Olympus, home of the classical Greek gods. Olympian religions are polytheistic. They include powerful anthropomorphic gods with specialized functions, for example, gods of love, war, the sea, and death. Olympian *pantheons* (collections of supernatural beings) were prominent in the religions of many nonindustrial nation-states, including the Aztecs of Mexico, several African and Asian kingdoms, and classical Greece and Rome. Wallace's fourth type—**monotheism**—also has priesthoods and notions of divine power, but it views the supernatural differently. In monotheism, all supernatural phenomena are manifestations of, or are under the control of, a single eternal, omniscient, omnipotent, and omnipresent supreme being.

RELIGION IN STATES

Robert Bellah (1978) coined the term "world-rejecting religion" to describe most forms of Christianity, including Protestantism. World-rejecting religions arose in ancient civilizations, along with literacy and a specialized priesthood. These religions are so named because of their tendency to reject the natural (mundane, ordinary, material, secular) world and to focus instead on a higher (sacred, transcendent) realm of reality. The divine is a domain of exalted morality to which humans can only aspire. Salvation through fusion with the supernatural is the main goal of such religions.

Protestant Values and the Rise of Capitalism

Notions of salvation and the afterlife dominate Christian ideologies. However, most varieties of Protestantism lack the hierarchical structure of earlier monotheistic religions, including Roman Catholicism. With a diminished role for the priest (minister), salvation is directly available to individuals. Regardless of their social status, Protestants have unmediated access to the supernatural. The individualistic focus of Protestantism offers a close fit with capitalism and with American culture.

In his influential book *The Protestant Ethic and the Spirit of Capitalism* (1904/1958), the social theorist Max Weber linked the spread of capitalism to the values preached by early Protestant leaders. Weber saw European Protestants (and eventually their American descendants) as more successful financially than Catholics. He attributed this difference to the values stressed by their religions. Weber saw Catholics as more concerned with immediate happiness and security. Protestants were more ascetic, entrepreneurial, and future-oriented, he thought.

Capitalism, said Weber, required that the traditional attitudes of Catholic peasants be replaced by values fitting an industrial economy based on capital accumulation. Protestantism placed a premium on hard work, an ascetic life, and profit seeking. Early Protestants saw success on earth as a sign of divine favor and probable salvation. According to some Protestant credos, individuals could gain favor with God through good works. Other sects stressed predestination, the idea that only a few mortals have been selected for eternal life and that people cannot change their fates. However, material success, achieved through hard work, could be a strong clue that someone was predestined to be saved.

Weber also argued that rational business organization required the removal of industrial production from the home, its setting in peasant societies. Protestantism made such a separation possible by emphasizing individualism: individuals, not families or households, would be saved or not. Interestingly, given the connection that is usually made with morality and religion in contemporary American discourse about family values, the family was a secondary matter for Weber's early Protestants. God and the individual reigned supreme.

Today, of course, in North America as throughout the world, people of many religions and with diverse worldviews are successful capitalists. Furthermore, traditional Protestant values often have little to do with today's economic maneuvering. Still, there is no denying that the individualistic focus of Protestantism was compatible with the severance of ties to land and kin that industrialism demanded. These values remain prominent in the religious background of many of the people of the United States.

WORLD RELIGIONS

Information on the world's major religions is provided in Table 12.3 (number of adherents) and Figure 12.3 (percentage of world population). Based on people's claimed religions, Christianity is the world's largest, with some 2.1 billion adherents. Islam, with some 1.3 billion practitioners, is next, followed by Hinduism, then Chinese traditional religion (also known as Chinese folk religion or Confucianism), and Buddhism. More than a billion people claim no official religion, but only about a fifth of them are self-proclaimed atheists. Worldwide, Islam is growing at a rate of about 2.9 percent annually, versus 2.3 percent for Christianity, whose overall growth rate is the same as the rate of world population increase (Adherents.com 2002; Ontario Consultants 2001).

Within Christianity, there is variation in the growth rate. There were an estimated 680 million "born-again" Christians (e.g., Pentecostals and Evangelicals) in the world in 2001, with an annual worldwide growth rate of 7 percent, versus just 2.3 percent for Christianity overall. (This would translate into 954 million Pentecostals and Evangelicals in 2006.) The global growth rate of

Map 15 shows the distribution of the world's major religions, also summarized in Table 12.3.

TABLE 12.3 Religions of the World, by Estimated Number of Adherents, 2005

Christianity	2.1 billion
Islam	1.3 billion
Secular/Nonreligious/Agnostic/Atheist	1.1 billion
Hinduism	900 million
Chinese traditional religion	394 million
Buddhism	376 million
Primal-indigenous	300 million
African traditional and diasporic	100 million
Sikhism	23 million
Juche	19 million
Spiritism	15 million
Judaism	14 million
Baha'i	7 million
Jainism	4.2 million
Shinto	4 million
Cao Dai	4 million
Zoroastrianism	2.6 million
Tenrikyo	2 million
Neo-Paganism	1 million
Unitarian-Universalism	800 thousand
Rastafarianism	600 thousand
Scientology	500 thousand

SOURCE: Adherents.com. 2005. http//www.adherents.com/Religions_By_Adherents.html.

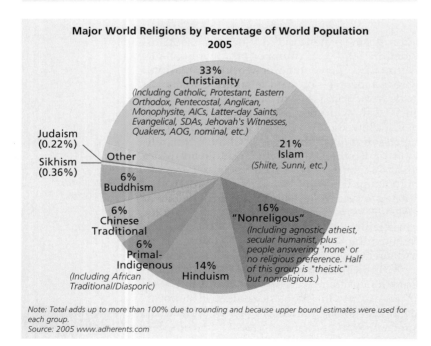

Major World Religions by Percentage of World Population 2005

- 33% Christianity (Including Catholic, Protestant, Eastern Orthodox, Pentecostal, Anglican, Monophysite, AICs, Latter-day Saints, Evangelical, SDAs, Jehovah's Witnesses, Quakers, AOG, nominal, etc.)
- Judaism (0.22%)
- Sikhism (0.36%)
- Other
- 21% Islam (Shiite, Sunni, etc.)
- 6% Buddhism
- 6% Chinese Traditional
- 6% Primal-Indigenous (Including African Traditional/Diasporic)
- 14% Hinduism
- 16% "Nonreligous" (Including agnostic, atheist, secular humanist, plus people answering 'none' or no religious preference. Half of this group is "theistic" but nonreligious.)

Note: Total adds up to more than 100% due to rounding and because upper bound estimates were used for each group.
Source: 2005 www.adherents.com

FIGURE 12.3 Major World Religions by Percentage of World Population, 2005. SOURCE: Adherents.com. 2005. http//www.adherents.com/Religions_By_Adherents.html.

Roman Catholics has been estimated at only 1.3 percent, compared with a Protestant growth rate of 3.3 percent per year (Winter 2001). Much of this explosive growth, especially in Africa, is of a type of Protestantism that would be scarcely recognizable to most Americans, given its incorporation of many animistic elements.

Table 12.4 classifies 11 world religions according to their degree of internal unity and diversity. Listed first are the most cohesive/unified groups. Listed last are the religions with the most internal diversity. The list is based mainly on the degree of doctrinal similarity among the various subgroups. To a lesser extent it reflects diversity in practice, ritual, and organization. (The list includes the majority manifestations of each religion, as well as subgroups that the larger branches may label "heterodox.") How would you decide whether a value judgment is implied by this list? Is it better for a religion to be highly unified, cohesive, monolithic, and lacking in internal diversity, or to be fragmented, schismatic, multifaceted, and abounding in variations on the same theme? Over time such diversity can give birth to new religions; for example, Christianity arose from Judaism, Buddhism from Hinduism, Baha'i from Islam, and Sikhism from Hinduism. Within Christianity, Protestantism developed out of Roman Catholicism.

RELIGION AND CHANGE

Fundamentalists seek order based on strict adherence to purportedly traditional standards, beliefs, rules, and customs. Christian and Islamic fundamentalists recognize, decry, and attempt to redress change, yet they also contribute to change. In a worldwide process, new religions challenge established churches. In the United States, conservative Christian TV hosts have become influential broadcasters and opinion shapers. In Latin America, evangelical Protestantism is winning millions of converts from Roman Catholicism.

Like political organization, religion helps maintain social order. And, like political mobilization, religious energy can be harnessed not just for change, but also for revolution. Reacting to conquest or to actual or perceived foreign domination, for instance, religious leaders may seek to alter or revitalize their society. In an "Islamic Revolution," for example, Iranian ayatollahs marshaled religious fervor to create national solidarity and radical change. We call such movements nativistic movements (Linton 1943) or revitalization movements (Wallace 1956).

Revitalization Movements

Revitalization movements are social movements that occur in times of change, in which religious leaders emerge and undertake to alter or revital-

TABLE 12.4 Classical World Religions Ranked by Internal Religious Similarity

Most unified

Baha'i

Zoroastrianism

Sikhism

Islam

Jainism

Judaism

Taoism

Shinto

Christianity

Buddhism

Hinduism

Most diverse

SOURCE: Adherents.com. 2001. http//www.adherents.com/Religions_By_Adherents.html.

ize a society. Christianity originated as a revitalization movement. Jesus was one of several prophets who preached new religious doctrines while the Middle East was under Roman rule. It was a time of social unrest, when a foreign power ruled the land. Jesus inspired a new, enduring, and major religion. His contemporaries were not so successful.

The Handsome Lake religion arose around 1800 among the Iroquois of New York State (Wallace 1970). Handsome Lake, the founder of this revitalization movement, was a leader of one of the Iroquois tribes. The Iroquois had suffered because of their support of the British against the American colonials (and for other reasons). After the colonial victory and a wave of immigration to their homeland, the Iroquois were dispersed on small reservations. Unable to pursue traditional horticulture and hunting in their homeland, they became heavy drinkers and quarreled among themselves.

Handsome Lake was a heavy drinker who started having visions from heavenly messengers. The spirits warned him that unless the Iroquois changed their ways, they would be destroyed. His visions offered a plan for coping with the new order. Witchcraft, quarreling, and drinking would end. The Iroquois would copy European farming techniques, which, unlike traditional Iroquois horticulture, stressed male rather than female labor. Handsome Lake preached that the Iroquois should also abandon their communal longhouses and matrilineal descent groups for more permanent marriages and individual family households. The teachings of Handsome Lake produced a new

church and religion, one that still has members in New York and Ontario. This revitalization movement helped the Iroquois adapt to and survive in a modified environment. They eventually gained a reputation among their non-Indian neighbors as sober family farmers.

Syncretisms

Especially in today's world, religious expressions emerge from the interplay of local, regional, national, and international cultural forces. **Syncretisms** are cultural mixes, including religious blends, that emerge from acculturation—the exchange of cultural features when cultures come into continuous firsthand contact. One example of religious syncretism is the mixture of African, Native American, and Roman Catholic saints and deities in Caribbean *vodun,* or "voodoo," cults. This blend also is present in Cuban *santeria* and in *candomblé,* an "Afro-Brazilian" cult. Another syncretism is the blend of Melanesian and Christian beliefs in cargo cults.

Like the Handsome Lake religion just discussed, cargo cults are revitalization movements. Such movements may emerge when natives have regular contact with industrial societies but lack their wealth, technology, and living standards. Some such movements attempt to explain European domination and wealth and to achieve similar success magically by mimicking European behavior and manipulating symbols of the desired lifestyle. The syncretic **cargo cults** of Melanesia and Papua New Guinea weave Christian doctrine with aboriginal beliefs (Figure 12.4). They take their name from their focus on cargo: European goods of the sort natives have seen unloaded from the cargo holds of ships and airplanes.

In one early cult, members believed that the spirits of the dead would arrive in a ship. These ghosts would bring manufactured goods for the natives and would kill all the whites. More recent cults replaced ships with airplanes (Worsley 1959/1985). Many cults have used elements of European culture as sacred objects. The rationale is that Europeans use these objects, have wealth, and therefore must know the "secret of cargo." By mimicking how Europeans use or treat objects, natives hope also to come upon the secret knowledge needed to gain cargo.

For example, having seen Europeans' reverent treatment of flags and flagpoles, the members of one cult began to worship flagpoles. They believed the flagpoles were sacred towers that could transmit messages between the living and the dead. Other natives built airstrips to entice planes bearing canned goods, portable radios, clothing, wristwatches, and motorcycles. Near the airstrips they made effigies of towers, airplanes, and radios. They talked into the cans in a magical attempt to establish radio contact with the gods.

FIGURE 12.4 Location of Melanesia.

A cargo cult in Vanuatu. Boys and men march with spears, imitating British colonial soldiers. Does anything in your own society remind you of a cargo cult?

As syncretisms, cargo cults blend aboriginal and Christian beliefs. Melanesian myths told of ancestors shedding their skins and changing into powerful beings and of dead people returning to life. Christian missionaries, who had been in Melanesia since the late 19th century, also spoke of resurrection. The cults' preoccupation with cargo is related to traditional Melanesian big-man systems. In the chapter "Political Systems," we saw that a Melanesian big man had to be generous. People worked for the big man, helping him amass wealth, but eventually he had to give a feast and give away all that wealth.

Because of their experience with big-man systems, Melanesians believed that all wealthy people eventually had to give their wealth away. For decades, they had attended Christian missions and worked on plantations. All the while they expected Europeans to return the fruits of their labor as their own big men did. When the Europeans refused to distribute the wealth or even to let natives know the secret of its production and distribution, cargo cults developed.

Like arrogant big men, Europeans would be leveled, by death if necessary. However, natives lacked the physical means of doing what their traditions said they should do. Thwarted by well-armed colonial forces, natives resorted to magical leveling. They called on supernatural beings to intercede, to kill or otherwise deflate the European big men and redistribute their wealth.

Some cargo cult prophets proclaimed that success would come through a reversal of European domination and native subjugation. The day was near, they preached, when natives, aided by God, Jesus, or native ancestors, would turn the tables. Native skins would turn white, and those of Europeans would turn brown; Europeans would die or be killed.

Cargo cults are religious responses to the expansion of the world capitalist economy. However, this religious mobilization had political and economic results. Cult participation gave Melanesians a basis for common interests and activities and thus helped pave the way for political parties and economic interest organizations. Previously separated by geography, language, and customs, Melanesians started forming larger groups as members of the same cults and followers of the same prophets. The cargo cults paved the way for political action through which the indigenous peoples eventually regained their autonomy.

Antimodernism and Fundamentalism

Antimodernism describes the rejection of the modern in favor of what is perceived as an earlier, purer, and better way of life. This viewpoint grew out of disillusionment with Europe's Industrial Revolution and subsequent developments in science, technology, and consumption patterns. Antimodernists typically consider technology's use today to be misguided, or think technology should have a lower priority than religious and cultural values.

The modern and the antimodern are key ingredients in Benjamin R. Barber's (1992, 1995) contention that tribalism and globalism are the two key—and opposed—principles of our age. Tribalism, which Barber sums up with the term "Jihad" (borrowed loosely from Islam, where it means quest or struggle), is an antimodern force pitting culture against culture, tribe against tribe, and religion against religion. For Jihad's enemy, Barber coins the term "McWorld," which subsumes the modern forces that promote global integration and uniformity, including the diffusion of music, computers, and fast food—MTV, Macintosh, and McDonald's. Barber argues that Jihad and McWorld operate today with equal force in opposite directions. Jihad is driven by parochial hatreds; McWorld, by universalizing markets.

Jihad resists McWorld, which spans nations, cultures, and ideologies. Groups like Al Qaeda exist in perpetual rebellion against McWorld and its perceived values and consumption patterns. To its warriors and adherents, Jihad offers an identity and a sense of community. But that social solidarity is grounded in exclusion, separation, opposition, and anger. Solidarity is achieved through war against outsiders. In places like Afghanistan under Taliban rule, solidarity might entail submission to an arbitrary hierarchy, fanaticism in beliefs, and the absorption or destruction of the individual self for the goals of the group.

Religious fundamentalism, a form of contemporary antimodernism, can be compared to the revitalization movements discussed previously. **Fundamentalism** describes antimodernist movements in various religions. Ironically, religious fun-

damentalism is itself a modern phenomenon, based on a strong feeling among its adherents of alienation from the surrounding (modern) culture. Fundamentalists assert an identity separate from the larger religious group from which they arose. Their separation reflects their belief that the founding principles on which the larger religion is based have been corrupted, neglected, compromised, forgotten, or replaced with other principles. Fundamentalists advocate strict fidelity to the "true" religious principles of the larger religion.

Fundamentalists also seek to rescue religion from absorption into modern, Western culture, which they see as already having corrupted the mainstream version of their religion—and others. Fundamentalists establish a "wall of virtue" against alien religions, as well as against the modernized, compromised version of their own religion. In Christianity, fundamentalists are "born again," as opposed to "mainline," "liberal," or "modernist" Protestants. In Islam they are *jama'at* (in Arabic, enclaves based on close fellowship) engaged in *jihad* (struggle) against a Western culture hostile to Islam and the God-given (*shariah*) way of life. In Judaism they are *Haredi*, "Torah-true" Jews. All such groups see a sharp divide between themselves and other religions, and between a "sacred" view of life and the "secular" world and "nominal religion" (see Antoun 2001).

Fundamentalists strive to protect a distinctive doctrine and way of life and of salvation. A strong sense of community is created, focused on a clearly defined religious way of life. The prospect of joining such a community may appeal to people who find little that is distinctive or vital in their previous religious identity. Fundamentalists get their converts, mainly from their larger religion, by convincing them of its inauthenticity.

Many fundamentalists are politically aware citizens of nation-states. Often they believe that government processes and policies must recognize

A Pentecostal church service in Brooklyn, New York. Pentecostalism is a rapidly expanding Christian religious movement that emphasizes the "gifts of the Holy Spirit," traditionally first bestowed on the day of Pentecost (50 days after Easter). There is considerable diversity among Pentecostals, who are not necessarily fundamentalists.

TABLE 12.5 Religious Composition (in Percentages) of the Populations of the United States, 1990 and 2001, and Canada, 1991 and 2001

| | United States | | Canada | |
	1990	2001	1991	2001
Protestant	60%	52%	36%	29%
Catholic	26	24	46	44
Jewish	2	1	1	1
Other	5	10	4	9
None given	7	13	12	17

SOURCE: *Statistical Abstract of the United States 2003*, Table 79, p. 67. http://www.census.gov/statab/www/; *Census of Canada*, 2001. http://www40.statcan.ca/l01/cst01/demo30a.htm?sdi=religion.

the way of life set forth in scripture. In their eyes, the state should be subservient to God. The governments of many Muslim countries, such as Afghanistan, Iran, and Saudi Arabia, are Islamic, and include people with fundamentalist beliefs, as is also true of many countries where Christians predominate.

A New Age

Fundamentalists may or may not be correct in seeing a rise in secularism in contemporary North America. Between 1990 and 2001, the number of Americans giving no religious preference grew from 7 to 13 percent. In Canada the comparable figure rose from 12 to 17 percent in that period (Table 12.5). Of course, people who lack a religious preference aren't necessarily atheists. Many of them are believers who don't belong to a church. According to U.S. Census Bureau figures for 2001, about two million Americans (just 1 percent of the population) self-identified as atheists or agnostics. Even fewer (less than 100,000 in 2001) called themselves "secular" or "humanists." Still, atheists and secular humanists do exist, and they, too, are organized.

Like members of religious groups, they use varied media, including print and the Internet, to communicate among themselves. Just as Buddhists can peruse *Tricycle: The Buddhist Review*, secular humanists can find their views validated in *Free Inquiry*, a quarterly identifying itself as "the international secular humanist magazine." Secular humanists speak out against organized religion and its "dogmatic pronouncements" and "supernatural or spiritual agendas" and the "obscurantist views" of religious leaders who presume "to inform us of God's views" by appealing to sacred texts (Steinfels 1997).

Is American society really growing more secular? A considerable body of sociological research

suggests that levels of American religiosity haven't changed much over the past century (see Finke and Stark 2005). To be sure, there are new religious trends and forms of spiritualism. Some Americans have turned to charismatic Christianity. In the United States and Australia, respectively, some people who are not Native Americans or Native Australians have appropriated the symbols, settings, and purported religious practices of Native Americans and Native Australians, for New Age religions. Many natives have strongly protested the use of their sacred symbols and places by such groups.

New religious movements have varied origins. Some have been influenced by Christianity, others by Eastern (Asian) religions, still others by mysticism and spiritualism. Religion also evolves in tandem with science and technology. For example, the Raelian Movement, a religious group centered in Switzerland and Montreal, promotes cloning as a way of achieving "eternal life." Raelians believe that extraterrestrials called "Elohim" artificially created all life on earth. The group has established a company called Valiant Venture Ltd., which offers infertile and homosexual couples the opportunity to have a child cloned from one of the spouses (Ontario Consultants 1996).

In the United States, the official recognition of a religion entitles it to a modicum of respect, and certain benefits, such as exemption from taxation on its income and property (as long as it does not engage in political activity). Not all would-be religions receive official recognition. For example, Scientology is recognized as a church in the United States but not in Germany. In 1997, United States government officials spoke out against Germany's persecution of Scientologists as a form of "human rights abuse." Germans protested vehemently, calling Scientology a dangerous nonreligious political movement, with between 30,000 and 70,000 German members.

SECULAR RITUALS

In concluding this discussion of religion, we may recognize some problems with the definition of religion given at the beginning of this chapter. The first problem: If we define religion with reference to supernatural beings, powers, and forces, how do we classify ritual-like behavior that occurs in secular contexts? Some anthropologists believe there are both sacred and secular rituals. Secular rituals include formal, invariant, stereotyped, earnest, repetitive behavior and rites of passage that take place in nonreligious settings.

A second problem: If the distinction between the supernatural and the natural is not consistently made in a society, how can we tell what is religion and what isn't? The Betsileo of Madagascar, for example, view witches and dead ancestors as real people who play roles in ordinary life. However, their occult powers are not empirically demonstrable.

A third problem: The behavior considered appropriate for religious occasions varies tremendously from culture to culture. One society may consider drunken frenzy the surest sign of faith, whereas another may inculcate quiet reverence. Who is to say which is "more religious"?

Many Americans believe that recreation and religion are separate domains. From my fieldwork in Brazil and Madagascar and my reading about other societies, I believe that this separation is both ethnocentric and false. Madagascar's tomb-centered ceremonies are times when the living and the dead are joyously reunited, when people get drunk, gorge themselves, and enjoy sexual license. Perhaps the gray, sober, ascetic, and moralistic aspects of many religious events in the United States, in taking the "fun" out of religion, force us to find our religion in fun. Many Americans seek in such apparently secular contexts as amusement parks, rock concerts, and sporting events what other people find in religious rites, beliefs, and ceremonies (see Appendix 3).

SUMMARY

1. Religion, a cultural universal, consists of belief and behavior concerned with supernatural beings, powers, and forces. Religion also encompasses the feelings, meanings, and congregations associated with such beliefs and behavior. Anthropological studies have revealed many aspects and functions of religion.

2. Tylor considered animism—the belief in spirits or souls—to be religion's earliest and most basic form. He focused on religion's explanatory role, arguing that religion would eventually disappear as science provided better explanations. Besides animism, yet another view of the supernatural also occurs in nonindustrial societies. This sees the supernatural as a domain of raw, impersonal power or force (called mana in Polynesia and Melanesia). People can manipulate and control mana under certain conditions.

3. When ordinary technical and rational means of doing things fail, people may turn to magic. Often they use magic when they lack control over outcomes. Religion offers comfort and psychological security at times of crisis. However, rites also can create anxiety. Rituals are formal, invariant, stylized, earnest acts in which people subordinate their particular beliefs to a social collectivity. Rites of passage have three stages: separation, liminality, and incorporation. Such rites can mark any change in social status, age, place, or social condition. Collective rites often are cemented by communitas, a feeling of intense solidarity.

4. Besides their psychological and social functions, religious beliefs and practices play a role in the adaptation of human populations to their environments. The Hindu doctrine of ahimsa, which prohibits harm to living things, makes cattle sacred and beef a tabooed food. The taboo's force stops peasants from killing their draft cattle even in times of extreme need.

5. Religion establishes and maintains social control through a series of moral and ethical beliefs, and real and imagined rewards and punishments, internalized in individuals. Religion also achieves social control by mobilizing its members for collective action.

6. Wallace defines four types of religion: shamanic, communal, Olympian, and monotheistic. Each has its characteristic ceremonies and practitioners. Religion helps maintain social order, but it also can promote change. Revitalization movements blend old and new beliefs and have helped people adapt to changing conditions.

7. Protestant values have been important in the United States, as they were in the rise and spread of capitalism in Europe. The world's major religions vary in their growth rates, with Islam expanding more rapidly than Christianity. There is growing religious diversity in the United States and Canada. Fundamentalists are antimodernists who claim an identity separate from the larger religious group from which they arose; they advocate strict fidelity to the "true" religious principles on which the larger religion was founded. Religious trends in contemporary North America include rising secularism and new religions, some inspired by science and technology, some by spiritism. There are secular as well as religious rituals.

KEY TERMS

See the flash cards
mhhe.com/kottak

animism   Belief in souls or doubles.

antimodernism   The rejection of the modern in favor of what is perceived as an earlier, purer, and better way of life.

cargo cults   Postcolonial, acculturative religious movements, common in Melanesia, that attempt to explain European domination and wealth and to achieve similar success magically by mimicking European behavior.

communal religions   In Wallace's typology, these religions have, in addition to shamanic cults, communal cults in which people organize community rituals such as harvest ceremonies and rites of passage.

communitas Intense community spirit, a feeling of great social solidarity, equality, and togetherness; characteristic of people experiencing liminality together.

fundamentalism Describes antimodernist movements in various religions. Fundamentalists assert an identity separate from the larger religious group from which they arose; they advocate strict fidelity to the "true" religious principles on which the larger religion was founded.

leveling mechanism A custom or social action that operates to reduce differences in wealth and thus to bring standouts in line with community norms.

liminality The critically important marginal or in-between phase of a rite of passage.

magic Use of supernatural techniques to accomplish specific aims.

mana Sacred impersonal force in Melanesian and Polynesian religions.

monotheism Worship of an eternal, omniscient, omnipotent, and omnipresent supreme being.

Olympian religions In Wallace's typology, develop with state organization; have full-time religious specialists—professional priesthoods.

polytheism Belief in several deities who control aspects of nature.

religion Belief and ritual concerned with supernatural beings, powers, and forces.

revitalization movements Movements that occur in times of change, in which religious leaders emerge and undertake to alter or revitalize a society.

rites of passage Culturally defined activities associated with the transition from one place or stage of life to another.

ritual Behavior that is formal, stylized, repetitive, and stereotyped, performed earnestly as a social act; rituals are held at set times and places and have liturgical orders.

shaman A part-time religious practitioner who mediates between ordinary people and supernatural beings and forces.

syncretisms Cultural mixes, including religious blends, that emerge from acculturation—the exchange of cultural features when cultures come into continuous firsthand contact.

taboo Set apart as sacred and off-limits to ordinary people; prohibition backed by supernatural sanctions.

CRITICAL THINKING QUESTIONS

For more self-testing, see the self-quizzes

mhhe.com/kottak

1. Do you see any problem in talking about religion in terms of its functions?

2. What's an example of a religious ritual in which you've engaged? How about a nonreligious ritual?

3. Describe a rite of passage you, or a friend, have been through. How did it fit the three-stage model given in the text?

4. From the news or your own knowledge, can you provide additional examples of revitalization movements, new religions, or liminal cults?

5. How are shamans similar to and different from priests? Are there shamans in your society? Who are they?

SUGGESTED ADDITIONAL READINGS

Bowie, F.
　2006　*The Anthropology of Religion: An Introduction.* Malden, MA: Blackwell. Surveys classic and recent work in the anthropology of religion, including the politics of religious identity.

Brown, K. M.
　2001　*Mama Lola: A Vodou Priestess in Brooklyn,* rev. ed. Berkeley: University of California Press. Ethnographic study of a religious community and its leader.

Child, A. B., and I. L. Child
　1993　*Religion and Magic in the Life of Traditional Peoples.* Englewood Cliffs, NJ: Prentice Hall. A cross-cultural study.

Crapo, R. H.
　2003　*Anthropology of Religion: The Unity and Diversity of Religions.* Boston: McGraw-Hill. Examines religious universals and variation.

Cunningham, G.
　1999　*Religion and Magic: Approaches and Theories.* New York: New York University Press. A survey of approaches to magic and religion, ancient and modern.

Durkheim, E.
　2001　(orig. 1912). *The Elementary Forms of the Religious Life.* Translated by Carol Cosman. Abridged with an introduction and notes by Mark S. Cladis. New York: Oxford University Press. Shortened edition of a classic work.

Hicks, D., ed.
　2001　*Ritual and Belief: Readings in the Anthropology of Religion,* 2nd ed. Boston: McGraw-Hill. Up-to-date reader, with useful annotation.

Klass, M.
　1995　*Ordered Universes: Approaches to the Anthropology of Religion.* Boulder, CO: Westview. Wide-ranging overview of key issues in the anthropology of religion.
　2003　*Mind over Mind: The Anthropology and Psychology of Spirit Possession.* Lanham, MD: Rowman and Littlefield. Understanding a mysterious process.

Klass, M., and M. Weisgrau, eds.
　1999　*Across the Boundaries of Belief: Contemporary Issues in the Anthropology of Religion.* Boulder, CO: Westview. Up-to-date collection of articles.

Lehmann, A. C., J. E. Meyers, and P. A. Moro, eds.
2005 *Magic, Witchcraft, and Religion: An Anthropological Study of the Supernatural,* 6th ed. Boston: McGraw-Hill. A comparative reader covering Western and non-Western cultures.

Lessa, W. A., and E. Z. Vogt, eds.
1979 *Reader in Comparative Religion: An Anthropological Approach,* 4th ed. New York: Harper & Row. Excellent collection of major articles on the origins, functions, and expressions of religion in comparative perspective.

Rappaport, R. A.
1999 *Holiness and Humanity: Ritual in the Making of Religious Life.* New York: Cambridge University Press. The nature, meaning, and functions of ritual in religion.

Stein, R. L., and P. L. Stein
2005 *The Anthropology of Religion, Magic, and Witchcraft.* Boston: Pearson/Allyn & Bacon. Religion and culture.

Turner, V. W.
1995 (orig. 1969). *The Ritual Process.* Hawthorne, NY: Aldine de Gruyter. Liminality among the Ndembu discussed in a comparative perspective.

INTERNET EXERCISES

1. Go to the anthropology tutorials at Palomar College in San Marcos, California, at the website **http://anthro.palomar.edu/religion/rel_2.htm**, and read the section titled "Common Elements of Religion."
   a. What's the difference between animatism and animism? Which is related to the idea of mana discussed in this chapter?
   b. How do European and Chinese cultures differ in their attitudes about ancestral spirits?
   c. What is an otiose god, and does your religion have one?
   d. Bugs Bunny is likened here to what kind of minor spiritual being?

2. Read the article by Robert Hefner titled "September 11 and the Struggle for Islam," **http://www.ssrc.org/sept11/essays/hefner.htm**.
   a. How might the rise of "hardline" Islam be viewed as a revitalization movement? How is it different?
   b. Where is the "real struggle," according to this author? Do you agree? Why or why not?
   c. How can anthropology contribute to an understanding of September 11 and its aftermath? What questions should anthropologists now look at to achieve this understanding?

See Chapter 12 at your McGraw-Hill Online Learning Center for additional review and interactive exercises.

LINKAGES

Kottak, *Assault on Paradise*, 4th ed.

Chapter 4 discusses the rise and role of *candomblé*, Afro-Brazilian religion, in Arembepe between the 1960s and 1973. In Chapter 10, the section "The Birth of Religion" describes an increase in *candomblé* activity and other religious changes in Arembepe from the 1960s to the 1980s. Chapter 13 reports on further changes, including the growing importance of evangelical Protestantism. What kinds of people were initially attracted to *candomblé*? How had religious activity become a social role in Arembepe by the 1980s? Why were Carolina, as described in Chapter 4, and Fernando, as described in Chapter 11, attracted to *candomblé*?

Peters-Golden, *Culture Sketches*, 4th ed.

This text chapter has discussed ways in which religious beliefs may serve to establish social control and to provide comfort and answers in times of crisis. Read Chapter 1, "Azande: Witchcraft and Oracles in Africa." Witchcraft among the Azande traditionally served as an effective means of social control. What are the major institutions and beliefs in your own culture that function similarly? Think about the ways in which members of your society are compelled to behave in socially acceptable ways. Is religion among them? There is a "logic" to the Azande belief in witchcraft and the causality of misfortune. Do you employ logic that is similar or different when explaining negative events? Are there several different "systems of logic" that may be invoked, depending on the circumstances?

Knauft, *The Gebusi*, 1st ed.

Read Chapters 3, 5–6, and 8. Based on Chapter 3, describe how Gebusi have contacted traditional spirits and how spiritual communications have influenced Gebusi actions. Describe how spiritual beliefs relate to Gebusi practices concerning death and violence. Based on Chapters 5 and 6, describe how spiritual influence is related to growth and maturity in Gebusi society. In Gebusi initiation rituals, what in-between stages and traumas are initiates subjected to? What values of Gebusi culture are emphasized to the initiates, and how does their costuming and etiquette reflect these spiritual and social values? Based on Chapter 8, describe the biggest changes that have taken place in Gebusi religion. Why did Yuway decide to change his religion, and what wider forces and changes are reflected in his religious conversion? How does contemporary Christianity among Gebusi compare to and contrast with what you know of Christianity in North America? How would you assess the costs and benefits of Gebusi conversions to Christianity?

13

The Arts

WHAT IS ART?

The **arts** include music, theater arts, visual arts, and storytelling and literature (oral and written). These manifestations of human creativity sometimes are called **expressive culture.** People express themselves in dance, music, song, painting, sculpture, pottery, cloth, storytelling, verse, prose, drama, and comedy. Many cultures lack terms that can be translated easily as "art" or "the arts." Yet even without a word for art, people everywhere do associate an aesthetic experience—a sense of beauty, appreciation, harmony, pleasure—with sounds, patterns, objects, and events that have certain qualities. The Bamana people of Mali have a word (like "art") for something that attracts your attention and directs your thoughts (Ezra 1986). Among the Yoruba of Nigeria, the word for art, *ona*, encompasses the designs made on objects, the art objects themselves, and the profession of the creators of such patterns and works. For two Yoruba lineages of leather workers, Otunisona and Osiisona, the suffix *-ona* in their names denotes art (Adepegba 1991).

A dictionary defines **art** as "the quality, production, expression, or realm of what is beautiful or of more than ordinary significance; the

For cross-cultural meanings of art, see the Virtual Exploration

mhhe.com/kottak

■ *Art serving religion. This photo was taken in Phnom Penh, Cambodia, in 1988. On the grounds of a Buddhist temple, artisans make religious artifacts. We see a young man carving a Buddha, along with several completed Buddha statues.*

class of objects subject to aesthetic criteria" (*The Random House College Dictionary* 1982, p. 76). Drawing on the same dictionary, **aesthetics** involves "the qualities perceived in works of art . . .; the . . . mind and emotions in relation to the sense of beauty" (p. 22). However, it is possible for a work of art to attract our attention, direct our thoughts, and have more than ordinary significance without being judged as beautiful by most people who experience that work. Pablo Picasso's *Guernica,* a famous

OVERVIEW

People everywhere associate an aesthetic experience—a sense of beauty, appreciation, harmony, pleasure—with certain sounds, patterns, objects, and events. The arts are part of culture, and aesthetic judgments reflect cultural background. Experiencing art involves feelings as well as appreciation of form. The arts, sometimes called "expressive culture," include the visual arts, literature, music, and theater arts. Students of non-Western art have been criticized for ignoring individual artists, and for focusing too much on the social nature and context of art. Many non-Western societies do recognize the achievements of individual artists. Folk art, music, and lore refer to the expressive culture of ordinary people. Myths, legends, tales, and storytelling play important roles in transmitting culture and preserving traditions. The arts go on changing, although certain art forms have survived for thousands of years. In today's world, a huge "arts and leisure" industry links Western and non-Western art forms in an international network with both aesthetic and commercial dimensions.

painting of the Spanish Civil War (see p. 146), comes to mind as a scene that, while not beautiful, is indisputably moving, and thus is a work of art.

George Mills (1971) notes that in many cultures, the role of art lover lacks definition because art isn't viewed as a separate activity. But this doesn't stop individuals from being moved by sounds, patterns, objects, and events in a way that we would call aesthetic. Our own society does provide a fairly well-defined role for the connoisseur of the arts, as well as sanctuaries—concert halls, theaters, museums—where people can retreat to be aesthetically pleased and emotionally moved by objects and performances.

This chapter will not attempt to do a systematic survey of all the arts, or even their major subdivisions. Rather, the general approach will be to examine topics and issues that apply to expressive culture generally. "Art" will be used to encompass all the arts, including the print and film narratives discussed in the "News Brief," not just the visual ones. In other words, the observations to be made about "art" are intended to apply to music, theater, film, television, books, stories, and lore, as well as to painting and sculpture.

That which is aesthetically pleasing is perceived with the senses. Usually, when we think of art, we have in mind something that can be seen or heard. But others might define art more broadly to include things that can be smelled (scents, fragrances), tasted (recipes), or touched (cloth textures). How enduring must art be? Visual works and written works, including musical compositions, may last for centuries. Can a single noteworthy event, such as a feast, which is not in the least eternal, except in memory, be a work of art?

Art and Religion

Some of the issues raised in the discussion of religion also apply to art. Definitions of both art and religion mention the "more than ordinary" or the "extraordinary." Religious scholars may distinguish between the sacred (religious) and the profane (secular). Similarly, art scholars may distinguish between the artistic and the ordinary.

If we adopt a special attitude or demeanor when confronting a sacred object, do we display something similar when experiencing a work of art? According to the anthropologist Jacques Maquet (1986), an artwork is something that stimulates and sustains contemplation. It compels attention and reflection. Maquet stresses the importance of the object's form in producing such artistic contemplation. But other scholars stress feeling and meaning in addition to form. The experience of art involves feeling, such as being moved, as well as appreciation of form, such as balance or harmony.

Narratives of Social Class and the Social Gap

NEW YORK TIMES NEWS BRIEF

by Charles McGrath
June 8, 2005

All cultures express imagination—in dreams, fantasies, songs, myths, and stories. The arts allow us to imagine a set of possible lives beyond our own. One very important source for this imagining has been the mass media, including television, movies, and the popular press. In this news story we see how American popular culture has moved from a preoccupation with class differences to a tendency to deny or ignore their existence. Although the media continue to celebrate the lifestyles of the rich and famous, what is gone is the preoccupation with difference. The narratives we see on screen and in print today often present a homogenized upper-middle-class lifestyle in which social differences are minimized and the economic underpinnings of class are ignored. An anthropological approach to the arts recognizes that they exist in society and can be understood in relation to sociocultural change.

On television and in the movies now, and even in the pages of novels, people tend to dwell in a classless, homogenized American Never-Never Land. This place is an upgrade, but not a drastic one, from the old neighborhood where Beaver, Ozzie and Harriet, and Donna Reed used to live; it's those yuppified city blocks where the friends on "Friends" and the "Seinfeld" gang had their apartments, or in the now more fashionable version, it's part of the same exurb as One Tree Hill and Wisteria Lane—those airbrushed suburbs where all the cool young people hang out and where the pecking order of sex and looks has replaced the old hierarchy of jobs and money . . .

In the years before World War II, you couldn't go to the movies or get very far in a novel without being reminded that ours was a society where some were much better off than others, and where the class divide—especially the gap separating middle from upper—was an inescapable fact of life. The yearning to bridge this gap is most persistently and most romantically evoked in [F. Scott] Fitzgerald, of course, in characters like the former Jay Gatz of Nowhere, N.D. (*The Great Gatsby*), staring across Long Island Sound at that distant green light, and all those moony young men standing in the stag line at the country club, hoping to be noticed by the rich girls.

But there is also a darker version, the one that turns up in Dreiser's "American Tragedy" (1925), for example, where class envy . . . causes Clyde Griffiths to drown his hopelessly proletarian sweetheart, and where the impossibility of transcending his lot leads him inevitably to the electric chair. (In the upstate New York town of Lycurgus, where the story takes place, Dreiser reminds us that "the line of demarcation and stratification between the rich and the poor was as sharp as though cut by a knife or divided by a high wall.")

Some novels trade on class anxiety to evoke not the dream of betterment but the great American nightmare: the dread of waking up one day and finding yourself at the bottom. Frank Norris's "McTeague" is about a San Francisco dentist who, unmasked as a fraud, sinks to a life of crime and degradation . . . These books . . . suggested that the worst thing that could possibly happen to an American was to topple from his perch on the class ladder . . .

The poor are noticeably absent, however, in the great artistic flowering of the American novel at the turn of the 19th century, in the work of writers like Henry James, William Dean Howells and Edith Wharton, who are almost exclusively concerned with the rich or the aspiring middle classes: their marriages, their houses, their money and their stuff. Not accidentally, these novels coincided with America's Gilded Age, the era of overnight fortunes and conspicuous spending that followed in the wake of the Civil War . . .

One of the messages of the novel is that in America new money very

■ *What's the class status of these "Desperate Housewives," who reside on TV's Wisteria Lane? From what do they derive this class status?*

quickly, in a generation or less, takes on the patina of old; another is that the class structure is necessarily propped up by deceit and double standards . . .

What was the appeal? Vouyerism, in part . . . Fiction back then had a kind of documentary function; it was one of the places Americans went to learn about how other Americans lived. In time novels ceased to be so reportorial . . .

Novels these days take place in a kind of all-purpose middle-class America, in neighborhoods that could be almost anyplace, and where the burdens are more psychic than economic, with people too busy tending to their faltering relationships to pay much attention to keeping up with the neighbors.

It's a place where everyone fits in, more or less, but where, if you look hard enough, nobody feels really at home.

Novel reading is a middle-class pastime, which is another reason that novels have so often focused on the middle and upper classes. Mass entertainment is another matter, and when Hollywood took up the class theme, which it did in the 1930's, it made a crucial adjustment. During the Depression, the studios, which were mostly run by immigrant Jews, turned out a string of formulaic fantasies about life among the Gentile upper crust.

These movies were essentially twin variations on a single theme: either a rich young man falls for a working girl . . . or an heiress takes up with a young man who has to work for a living . . .

The upper-class person is thawed and humanized by the poorer one, but in every case the exchange is seen as fair and equitable, with the lower-class character giving as much as he or she gets in return. Unlike the novels of class, with their anxieties and sense of unbridgeable gaps, these are stories of harmony and inclusion, and they added what proved to be an enduring twist on the American view of class: the notion that wealth and privilege are somewhat crippling conditions . . .

Television used to be fascinated with blue-collar life, in shows like "The Honeymooners," "All in the Family," "Sanford and Son" and "Roseanne," but lately it too has turned its attention elsewhere. The only people who work on televison now are cops, doctors and lawyers, and they're so busy they seldom get to go home. The one vestige of the old curiosity about how other people live is in so-called reality television, when Paris Hilton and Nicole Richie drop in on rubes in "The Simple Life," or when upper- and middle-class families trade moms on "Wife Swap" and experience a week of culture shock.

But most reality television trades in a fantasy of sorts, based on the old game-show formula: the idea that you can be plucked out of ordinary life and anointed the new super-model, the new diva, the new survivor, the new assistant to Donald Trump. You get an instant infusion of wealth and are simultaneously vested with something far more valuable: celebrity, which has become a kind of super-class in America, and one that renders all the old categories irrelevant.

Celebrities, in fact, have inherited much of the glamour and sexiness that used to attach itself to the aristocracy. If Gatsby were to come back today, he would come back as Donald Trump and would want a date not with Daisy [Buchanan] but with Britney Spears.

But if the margins have shifted, and if fame, for example, now counts for more than breeding, what persists is the great American theme of longing, of wanting something more, or other, than what you were born with—the wish not to rise in class so much as merely to become classy. If you believe the novels of Dickens or Thackeray, say, the people who feel most at home in Britain are those who know their place, and that has seldom been the case in this country, where the boundaries of class seem just elusive and permeable enough to sustain both the fear of falling and the dream of escape.

SOURCE: Charles McGrath, "In Fiction, a Long History of Fixation on the Social Gap," *New York Times*, June 8, 2005, final, Section E, p. 1.

Bringing It All Together

See the "Bringing It All Together" essay that immediately follows the chapter "Gender" for *Guernica* and its political context.

Such an artistic attitude can be combined with and used to bolster a religious attitude. Much art has been done in association with religion. Many of the high points of Western art and music had religious inspiration, or were done in the service of religion, as a visit to a church or a large museum will surely illustrate. Bach and Handel are as well known for their church music as Michelangelo is for his religious painting and sculpture. The buildings (churches and cathedrals) in which religious music is played and in which visual art is displayed may themselves be works of art. Some of the major architectural achievements of Western art are religious structures. Examples include the Amiens, Chartres, and Notre Dame cathedrals in France.

Art may be created, performed, or displayed outdoors in public, or in special indoor settings, such as a theater, concert hall, or museum. Just as churches demarcate religion, museums and theaters set art off from the ordinary world, making it special, while inviting spectators in. Buildings dedicated to the arts help create the artistic atmosphere. Architecture may accentuate the setting as a place for works of art to be presented.

The settings of rites and ceremonies, and of art, may be temporary or permanent. State societies have permanent religious structures: churches and temples. So, too, may state societies have buildings and structures dedicated to the arts. Nonstate societies tend to lack such permanently demarcated settings. Both art and religion are more "out there" in society. Still, in bands and tribes, religious settings can be created without churches. Similarly, an artistic atmosphere can be created without museums. At particular times of the year, ordinary space can be set aside for a visual art display or a musical performance. Such special occasions parallel the times set aside for religious ceremonies. In fact, in tribal performances, the arts and religion often mix. For example, masked and costumed performers may imitate spirits. Rites of passage often feature special music, dance, song, bodily adornment, and other manifestations of expressive culture.

In the chapter "Making a Living," we looked at the potlatching tribes of the North Pacific Coast of North America. Erna Gunther (1971) shows how various art forms combined among those tribes to create the visual aspects of ceremonialism. During the winter, spirits were believed to pervade the atmosphere. Masked and costumed dancers represented the spirits. They dramatically reenacted spirit encounters with human beings, which are part of the origin myths of villages, clans, and lineages. In some areas, dancers devised intricate patterns of choreography. Their esteem was measured by the number of people who followed them when they danced.

In any society, art is produced for its aesthetic value as well as for religious purposes. According to Schildkrout and Keim (1990), non-Western art is usually, but wrongly, assumed to have some kind of connection to ritual. Non-Western art may be, but isn't always, linked with religion. Westerners have trouble accepting the idea that non-Western societies have art for art's sake just as Western societies do. There has been a tendency for Westerners to ignore the individuality of non-Western artists and their interest in creative expression. According to Isidore Okpewho (1977), an oral literature specialist, scholars have tended to see religion in all traditional African arts. Even when acting in the service of religion, there is room for individual creative expression. In the oral arts, for example, the audience is much more interested in the delivery and performance of the artist than in the particular god for whom the performer may be speaking.

Locating Art

Aesthetic value is one way of distinguishing art. Another way is to consider placement. The special places where we find art include museums, concert halls, opera houses, and theaters. If something is displayed in a museum, or in another socially accepted artistic setting, someone at least

■ Space transformed into art. "The Gates," by the experimental artist Christo and his wife, Jeanne-Claude, was unveiled in 2005 in New York City's Central Park. Long, billowy saffron ribbons meandered through the park. An army of paid helpers gradually released the panels of colored fabric from atop 7,500 gates standing 16-feet tall.

must think it's art. Although tribal societies typically lack museums, they may maintain special areas where artistic expression takes place. One example, discussed below, is the separate space in which ornamental burial poles are manufactured among the Tiwi of North Australia.

Will we know art if we see it? Art has been defined as involving that which is beautiful and of more than ordinary significance. But isn't beauty in the eye of the beholder? Don't reactions to art differ among spectators? And, if there can be secular ritual, can there also be ordinary art? The boundary between what's art and what's not is blurred. The American artist Andy Warhol is famous for transforming Campbell's soup cans, Brillo pads, and images of Marilyn Monroe into art. Many recent artists, such as Christo (see the photo above) have tried to erase the distinction between art and ordinary life by converting the everyday into a work of art.

If something is mass produced or industrially modified, can it be art? Prints made as part of a series certainly may be considered art. Sculptures that are created in clay, then fired with molten metal, such as bronze, at a foundry, also are art. But how does one know if a film is art? Is *Star Wars* art? How about *Citizen Kane*? When a book wins a National Book Award, is it immediately elevated to the status of art? What kinds of prizes make art? Objects never intended as art, such as an Olivetti typewriter, may be transformed into art by being placed in a museum, such as New York's Museum of Modern Art. Jacques Maquet (1986) distinguishes such "art by transformation" from art created and intended to be art, which he calls "art by destination."

In state societies, we have come to rely on critics, judges, and experts to tell us what's art and what isn't. A play titled *Art* is about conflict that arises among three friends when one of them buys an all-white painting. They disagree, as people often do, about the definition and value of a work of art. Such variation in art appreciation is especially common in contemporary society, with its professional artists and critics and great cultural diversity. We'd expect more uniform standards and agreement in less-diverse, less-stratified societies.

To be culturally relativistic, we need to avoid applying our own standards about what art is to the products of other cultures. Sculpture is art, right? Not necessarily. Previously, we challenged the view that non-Western art always has some kind of connection to religion. The Kalabari case to be discussed now makes the opposite point: that religious sculpture is not always art.

Among the Kalabari of southern Nigeria (Figure 13.1), wooden sculptures are not carved for aesthetic reasons, but to serve as "houses" for spirits (Horton 1963). These sculptures are used to control the spirits of Kalabari religion. The Kalabari place such a carving, and thus localize a spirit, in a cult house into which the spirit is invited. Here, sculpture is done not for art's sake but as a means of manipulating spiritual forces. The Kalabari do have standards for the carvings, but beauty isn't one of them. A sculpture must be sufficiently complete to represent its spirit. Carvings judged too crude are rejected by cult members. Also, carvers must base their work on past models. Particular spirits have particular images associated with them. It's considered dangerous to produce a carving that deviates too much from a previous image of the spirit or that resembles another spirit. Offended spirits may retaliate. As long as they observe these standards of completeness and established images, carvers are free to express themselves. But these images are considered repulsive rather than beautiful. And they are not manufactured for artistic but for religious reasons.

Art and Individuality

Those who work with non-Western art have been criticized for ignoring the individual and focusing too much on the social nature and context of art. When art objects from Africa or Papua New Guinea are displayed in museums, generally only the name of the tribe and of the Western donor are given, rather than that of the individual artist. It's as though skilled individuals don't exist in non-Western societies. The impression is that art is collectively produced. Sometimes it is; sometimes it isn't.

To some extent, there *is* more collective production of art in non-Western societies than in the United States and Canada. According to Hackett (1996), African artworks (sculpted figures, textiles, paintings, or pots) generally are enjoyed, critiqued, and used by communities or groups, rather than being the prerogative of the individual alone. The artist may receive more feedback during the creative process than the individual artist typically encounters in our own society. Here, the feedback often comes too late, after the product is complete, rather than during production, when it can still be changed.

During his field work among Nigeria's Tiv people, Paul Bohannan (1971) concluded that the

See the Internet Exercises at your OLC for Kalabari masks

mhhe.com/kottak

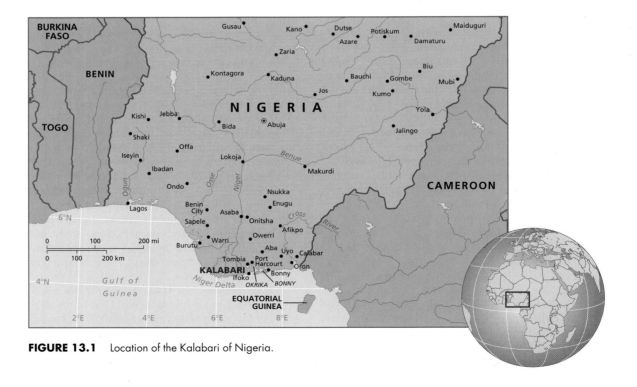

FIGURE 13.1   Location of the Kalabari of Nigeria.

308   PART 2   Cultural Diversity

proper study of art there should pay less attention to artists and more attention to art critics and products. There were few skilled Tiv artists, and such people avoided doing their art publicly. However, mediocre artists would work in public, where they routinely got comments from onlookers (critics). Based on critical suggestions, an artist often changed a design, such as a carving, in progress. There was yet another way in which Tiv artists worked socially rather than individually. Sometimes, when an artist put his work aside, someone else would pick it up and start working on it. The Tiv clearly didn't recognize the same kind of connection between individuals and their art that we do. According to Bohannan, every Tiv was free to know what he liked and to try to make it if he could. If not, one or more of his fellows might help him out.

In Western societies, artists of many sorts (e.g., writers, painters, sculptors, actors, classical and rock musicians) have reputations for being iconoclastic and antisocial. Social acceptance may be more important in the societies anthropologists have traditionally studied. Still, there are well-known individual artists in non-Western societies. They are recognized as such by other community members and perhaps by outsiders as well. Their artistic labor may even be conscripted for special displays and performances, including ceremonies, or palace arts and events.

To what extent can a work of art stand apart from its artist? Philosophers of art commonly regard works of art as autonomous entities, independent of their creators (Haapala 1998). Haapala argues the contrary, that artists and their works are inseparable. "By creating works of art a person creates an artistic identity for himself. He creates himself quite literally into the pieces he puts into his art. He exists in the works he has created." In this view, Picasso created many Picassos, and exists in and through those works of art.

Sometimes little is known or recognized about the individual artist responsible for an enduring art work. We are more likely to know the name of the recording artist than that of the writer of the songs we most commonly remember and perhaps sing. Sometimes we fail to acknowledge art individually because the artwork was collectively created. To whom should we attribute a pyramid or a cathedral? Should it be the architect, the ruler or leader who commissioned the work, or the master builder who implemented the design? A thing of beauty may be a joy forever even if and when we do not credit its creator(s).

The Work of Art

Some may see art as a form of expressive freedom, as giving free range to the imagination and the human need to create or to be playful. But consider the word *opera*. It is the plural of *opus*,

which means a work. For the artist, at least, art is work, albeit creative work. In nonstate societies, artists may have to hunt, gather, herd, fish, or farm in order to eat, but they still manage to find time to work on their art. In state societies, at least, artists have been defined as specialists—professionals who have chosen careers as artists, musicians, writers, or actors. If they manage to support themselves from their art, they may be full-time professionals. If not, they do their art part time, while earning a living from another activity. Sometimes artists associate in professional groups such as medieval guilds or contemporary unions. Actors Equity in New York, a labor union, is a modern guild, designed to protect the interests of its artist members.

Just how much work is needed to make a work of art? In the early days of French impressionism, many experts viewed the paintings of Claude Monet and his colleagues as too sketchy and spontaneous to be true art. Established artists and critics were accustomed to more formal and classic studio styles. The French impressionists got their name from their sketches—*impressions* in French—of natural and social settings. They took advantage of technological innovations, particularly the availability of oil paints in tubes, to take their palettes, easels, and canvases into the field. There they captured the images of changing light and color that hang today in so many museums, where they are now fully recognized as art. But before impressionism became an officially recognized "school" of art, its works were perceived by its critics as crude and unfinished. In terms of community standards, the first impressionist paintings were evaluated as harshly as were the overly crude and incomplete Kalabari wood carvings of spirits, as discussed previously.

To what extent does the artist—or society—make the decision about completeness? For familiar genres, such as painting or music, societies tend to have standards by which they judge whether an art work is complete or fully realized. Most people would doubt, for instance, that an all-white painting could be a work of art. Standards may be maintained informally in society, or by specialists, such as art critics. It may be difficult for unorthodox or renegade artists to innovate. But, like the impressionists, they may eventually succeed. Some societies tend to reward conformity, an artist's skill with traditional models and techniques. Others encourage breaks with the past, innovation.

ART, SOCIETY, AND CULTURE

More than 70,000 years ago, some of the world's first artists occupied Blombos Cave, located in a high cliff facing the Indian Ocean at the tip of what is now South Africa. They hunted game and ate

This musician living in the Central African Republic carved this instrument himself.

also confirm artistic expression throughout the Upper Paleolithic.

Art usually is more public than the cave paintings. Typically, it is exhibited, evaluated, performed, and appreciated in society. It has spectators or audiences. It isn't just for the artist.

Ethnomusicology

Ethnomusicology is the comparative study of the musics of the world and of music as an aspect of culture and society. The field of ethnomusicology thus unites music and anthropology. The music side involves the study and analysis of the music itself and the instruments used to create it. The anthropology side views music as a way to explore a culture, to determine the role—historic and contemporary—that music plays in that society, and the specific social and cultural features that influence how music is created and performed.

Ethnomusicology studies non-Western music, traditional and folk music, even contemporary popular music from a cultural perspective. To do this there has to be fieldwork—firsthand study of particular forms of music, their social functions and cultural meanings, within particular societies. Ethnomusicologists talk with local musicians, make recordings in the field, and learn about the place of musical instruments, performances, and performers in a given society (Kirman 1997). Nowadays, given globalization, diverse cultures and musical styles easily meet and mix. Music that draws on a wide range of cultural instruments and styles is called World Fusion, World Beat, or World Music—another topic within contemporary ethnomusicology

Because music is a cultural universal, and because musical abilities seem to run in families, it has been suggested that a predisposition for music may have a genetic basis (Crenson 2000). Could a "music gene" that arose tens, or hundreds, of thousands of years ago have conferred an evolutionary advantage on those early humans who possessed it? The fact that music has existed in all known cultures suggests that it arose early in human history. Providing direct evidence for music's antiquity is an ancient carved bone flute from a cave in Slovenia. This "Divje babe flute," the world's oldest known musical instrument, dates back more than 43,000 years.

Exploring the possible biological roots of music, Sandra Trehub (2001) notes striking similarities in the way mothers worldwide sing to their children—with a high pitch, a slow tempo, and a distinctive tone. All cultures have lullabies, which sound so much alike they cannot be mistaken for anything else (Crenson 2000). Trehub speculates that music might have been adaptive in human evolution because musically talented

fish from the waters below them. In terms of body and brain size, these ancient Africans were anatomically modern humans. They also were turning animal bones into finely worked tools and weapon points. Furthermore, they were engraving artifacts with symbolic marks—manifestations of abstract and creative thought and, presumably, communication through language (Wilford 2002*b*).

A group led by Christopher Henshilwood of South Africa has analyzed 28 bone tools and other artifacts from Blombos Cave, along with the mineral ocher, which may have been used for body painting. The most impressive bone tools are three sharp instruments. The bone appears first to have been shaped with a stone blade, then finished into a symmetrical shape and polished for hours. According to Henshilwood (quoted in Wilford 2002*b*), "It's actually unnecessary for projectile points to be so carefully made. It suggests to us that this is an expression of symbolic thinking. The people said, 'Let's make a really beautiful object . . .' Symbolic thinking means that people are using something to mean something else. The tools do not have to have only a practical purpose. And the ocher might be used to decorate their equipment, perhaps themselves."

In Europe, art goes back more than 30,000 years, to the Upper Paleolithic period in Western Europe (see Conkey et al. 1997). The earliest musical instrument, the "Divje babe flute," was made more than 43,000 years ago. Cave paintings, the best-known examples of Upper Paleolithic art, were separated from ordinary life and everyday social space. Those images were painted in true caves, located deep in the bowels of the earth. They may have been painted as part of some kind of rite of passage involving retreat from society. Portable art objects carved in bone and ivory, along with musical whistles and flutes, mothers had an easier time calming their babies. Calm babies who fell asleep easily and rarely made a fuss might well have been more likely to survive to adulthood. Their cries would not attract predators; they and their mothers would get more rest; and they would be less likely to be mistreated. If a gene conferring musical ability appeared early in human evolution, given a selective advantage, musical adults would pass their genes to their children.

Music would seem to be among the most social of the arts. Usually it unites people in groups. Indeed, music is all about groups—choirs, symphonies, ensembles, and bands. Could it be that early humans with a biological penchant for music were able to live more effectively in social groups—another possible adaptive advantage? Even master pianists and violinists are frequently accompanied by orchestras or singers. Alan Merriam (1971) describes how the Basongye people of the Kasai province of Congo (Figure 13.2) use three features to distinguish between music and other sounds, which are classified as "noise." First, music always involves humans. Sounds emanating from nonhuman creatures, such as birds and animals, are not music. Second, musical sounds must be organized. A single tap on the drum isn't music, but drummers playing together in a pattern is. Third, music must continue. Even if several drums are struck together simultaneously, it isn't music. They must go on playing to establish some kind of sound pattern. For the Basongye, then, music is inherently cultural (distinctly human) and social (dependent on cooperation).

Originally coined for European peasants, **"folk"** art, music, and lore refer to the expressive culture of ordinary people, as contrasted with the "high" art or "classic" art of the European elites. When European folk music is performed (see photo on p. 312), the combination of costumes, music, and often song and dance is supposed to say something about local culture and about tradition. Tourists and other outsiders often perceive rural and folk life mainly in terms of such performances. Community residents themselves often use such performances to display and enact their local culture and traditions for outsiders.

In Planinica, a Muslim village in (prewar) Bosnia, Yvonne Lockwood (1983) studied folksong, which could be heard there day or night. The most active singers were unmarried females age 16 to 26 (maidens). Lead singers, those who customarily began and led songs, had strong, full, clear voices with a high range. Like some of their counterparts in contemporary North America (but in a much milder fashion), some lead singers acted unconventionally. One was regarded as immodest because of her risqué lyrics. Another

FIGURE 13.2 Location of the Basongye of the Democratic Republic of Congo.

smoked (usually a man's habit) and liked to wear men's trousers. Local criticism aside, she was thought to be witty and to improvise songs better than others did.

The social transition from girl to maiden (marriageable female) was signaled by active participation in public song and dance. Adolescent girls were urged to join in by women and performing maidens. This was part of a rite of passage by which a little girl (*dite*) became a maiden (*cura*). Marriage, in contrast, moved most women from the public to the private sphere; public singing generally stopped. Married women sang in their own homes or among other women. Only occasionally would they join maidens in public song, but they never called attention to themselves by taking the lead. After age 50 wives tended to stop singing, even in private.

For women, singing thus signaled a series of transitions between age grades: girl to maiden (public singing), maiden to wife (private singing), and wife to elder (no more singing). Lockwood describes how one recently married woman

Musicians in folk outfits play violins in a town square in Ljubljana, Slovenia. For whose pleasure do you suppose this performance is being given? Nowadays, such performances attract tourists as well as local people.

made her ritual first visit after marriage to her family of origin. (Postmarital residence was patrilocal.) Then, as she was leaving to return to her husband's village, for "old times' sake" she led the village maidens in song. She used her native daughter status to behave like a maiden this one last time. Lockwood calls it a nostalgic and emotional performance for all who attended.

Singing and dancing were common at *prelos* attended by males and females. In Planinica the Serbo-Croatian word *prelo*, usually defined as "spinning bee," meant any occasion for visiting. *Prelos* were especially common in winter. During the summer, villagers worked long hours, and *prelos* were few. The *prelo* offered a context for play, relaxation, song, and dance. All gatherings of maidens, especially *prelos*, were occasions for song. Married women encouraged them to sing, often suggesting specific songs. If males were also present, a singing duel might occur, in which maidens and young men teased each other. A successful *prelo* was well attended, with much singing and dancing.

Public singing was traditional in many other contexts among prewar Bosnian Muslims. After a day of cutting hay on mountain slopes, parties of village men would congregate at a specific place on the trail above the village. They formed lines according to their singing ability, with the best singers in front and the less talented ones behind. They proceeded to stroll down to the village together, singing as they went, until they reached the village center, where they dispersed. According to Lockwood, whenever an activity of work or leisure brought together a group of maidens or young men, it rarely ended without public song. It would not be wrong to trace the inspiration for parts of *Snow White* and *Shrek* (the movies) back to the European countryside.

Representations of Art and Culture

Art can stand for tradition, even when traditional art is removed from its original (rural) context. As will be seen in Chapter 16 titled "Cultural Exchange and Survival," the creative products and images of folk, rural, and non-Western cultures are increasingly spread—and commercialized—by the media and tourism. A result is that many Westerners have come to think of "culture" in terms of colorful customs, music, dancing, and adornments: clothing, jewelry, and hairstyles.

A bias toward the arts and religion, rather than more mundane, less photogenic, economic and social tasks, shows up on TV's Discovery Channel, and even in many anthropological films. Many ethnographic films start off with music, often drum beats: "Bonga, bonga, bonga, bonga. Here in (supply place name), the people are very religious." We see in such presentations the previously critiqued assumption that the arts of nonindustrial societies usually have a link with religion. The (usually unintended) message is that non-Western peoples spend much of their time wearing colorful clothes, singing, dancing, and practicing religious rituals. Taken to an extreme, such images portray culture as recreational and ultimately unserious, rather than as something that ordinary people live every day of their lives—not just when they have festivals.

Art and Communication

Art also functions in society as a form of communication between artist and community or audience. Sometimes, however, there are intermediaries between the artist and the audience. Actors, for example, are artists who translate the works and ideas of other artists (writers and directors) into the performances that audiences see and appreciate. Musicians play and sing compositions of other people along with music they themselves have composed. Using music written by others, choreographers plan and direct patterns of dance, which dancers then execute for audiences.

How does art communicate? We need to know what the artist intends to communicate and how the audience reacts. Often, the audience communicates right back to the artist. Live performers, for instance, get immediate feedback, as may writers and directors by viewing a performance of their own work. Artists expect at least some variation in reception. In contemporary societies, with increasing diversity in the audience, uniform reactions are rare. Contemporary artists, like businesspeople, are well aware that they have target audiences. Certain segments of the population are more likely to appreciate certain forms of art than other segments are.

One key development in North American culture since the 1970s, especially evident in the media, is a general shift from "massification" to "segmental appeal." An increasingly differentiated nation celebrates diversity. The mass media—print and electronic—join the trend, measuring various "demographics." The media aim their products and messages at particular segments—*target audiences*—rather than at an undifferentiated mass audience. Television, films, radio, music, magazines, and Internet forums all gear their topics, formats, and styles toward particular homogeneous segments of the population. In particular, cable and satellite TV, along with VCR and DVD players, have helped direct television, the most important mass medium, away from the networks' cherished mass audiences of the 1950s and 1960s and toward particular viewing segments. Special-interest audiences can now choose from a multiplicity of targeted channels. Those channels specialize in music (country, pop, rock, Latin, or Black Entertainment), sports (financial, weather, headline), comedy, science fiction, gossip, movies (commercial, foreign, "art," "classic"), cartoons, old TV sitcoms, Spanish language, nature, travel, adventure, history, biography, and home shopping. The Super Bowl, Academy Awards, and Olympics still manage to capture large national and international audiences. But in 1998, the final episode of *Seinfeld,* though hugely popular, could not rival the mass audience shares of *Roots,* Lucy Ricardo's childbirth, or the final episode of *M*A*S*H.*

Art can transmit several kinds of messages. It can convey a moral lesson or tell a cautionary tale. It can teach lessons the artist, or society, wants told. Like the rites that induce, then dispel, anxiety, the tension and resolution of drama can lead to **catharsis,** intense emotional release, in the audience. Art can move emotions, make us laugh, cry, feel up or down. Art appeals to the intellect as well as to the emotions. We may delight in a well-constructed, nicely balanced, well-realized work of art.

Often, art is meant to commemorate and to last, to carry an enduring message. Like a ceremony, art may serve a mnemonic function, making people remember. Art may be designed to make people remember either individuals or events, such as the AIDS epidemic that has proved so lethal in many world areas, or the cataclysmic events of September 11, 2001.

Art and Politics

What is art's social role? To what extent should art serve society? Art can be self-consciously prosocial. It can be used either to express or challenge community sentiment and standards. Art enters the political arena. Decisions about what counts as a work of art, or about how to display art, may be political and controversial. Museums have to balance concern over community standards with a wish to be as creative and innovative as the artists and works they display.

Much art that is valued today was received with revulsion in its own time. New York's Brooklyn Museum of Art has documented how art that shocks or offends when it is new becomes accepted and valued over time. Children were prohibited from seeing paintings by Matisse, Braque, and Picasso when those works first were displayed in New York in the Armory Show of 1913. The *New York Times* called that Armory Show "pathological." Almost a century later, the City of New York and then Mayor Rudolph Giuliani took the Brooklyn Museum to court over its 1999–2000 "Sensation" show. After religious groups protested Chris Ofili's *Holy Virgin Mary,* a collage that included elephant dung, Giuliani deemed the work sacrilegious. The ensuing court trial prompted anticensorship groups and art advocates to speak out against the mayor's actions. The museum won the case, but Ofili's work again came under attack when a man smuggled paint inside the Brooklyn exhibition and tried to smear it on the *Virgin* (University of Virginia, n.d.). According to art professor Michael Davis, Ofili's collage is "shocking" because it

Appreciation for the arts must be learned. Here, three American boys seem intrigued by the painting Paris on a Rainy Day at the Chicago Art Institute. How does the placement of art in museums affect art appreciation?

deliberately provokes and intends to jolt viewers into an expanded frame of reference. The mayor's reactions may have been based on the narrow definition that art must be beautiful and an equally limited vision of a Virgin Mary as depicted in Italian Renaissance paintings (Mount Holyoke College 1999).

Today, no museum director can mount an exhibit without worrying that it will offend some politically organized segment of society. In the United States there has been an ongoing battle between liberals and conservatives involving the National Endowment for the Arts. Artists have been criticized as aloof from society, as creating only for themselves and for elites, as out of touch with conventional and traditional aesthetic values, even as mocking the values of ordinary people.

The Cultural Transmission of the Arts

Because art is part of culture, appreciation of the arts depends on cultural background. Watch Japanese tourists in a Western art museum trying to interpret what they are seeing. Conversely, the form and meaning of a Japanese tea ceremony, or a demonstration of origami (Japanese paper folding), will be alien to a foreign observer. Appreciation for the arts must be learned. It is part of

enculturation, as well as of more formal education. Robert Layton (1991) suggests that whatever universal principles of artistic expression may exist, they have been put into effect in a diversity of ways in different cultures.

What is aesthetically pleasing depends to some extent on culture. Based on familiarity, music with certain tonalities and rhythm patterns will please some people and alienate others. In a study of Navajo music, McAllester (1954) found that it reflected the overall culture of that time in three main ways: First, individualism is a key Navajo cultural value. Thus, it's up to the individual to decide what to do with his or her property—whether it be physical property, knowledge, ideas, or songs. Second, McAllester found that a general Navajo conservatism also extended to music. The Navajo saw foreign music as dangerous and rejected it as not part of their culture. (This second point is no longer true; there are now Navajo rock bands.) Third, a general stress on proper form applied to music. There is, in Navajo belief, a right way to sing every kind of song (see Figure 13.3 for the location of the Navajo).

People learn to listen to certain kinds of music and to appreciate particular art forms, just as they learn to hear and decipher a foreign language. Unlike Londoners and New Yorkers, Parisians don't flock to musicals. Despite its multiple French origins, even the musical *Les Miserables*, a huge hit in London, New York, and dozens of cities worldwide, bombed in Paris. Humor, too, a form of verbal art, depends on cultural background and setting. What's funny in one culture may not translate as funny in another. When a joke doesn't

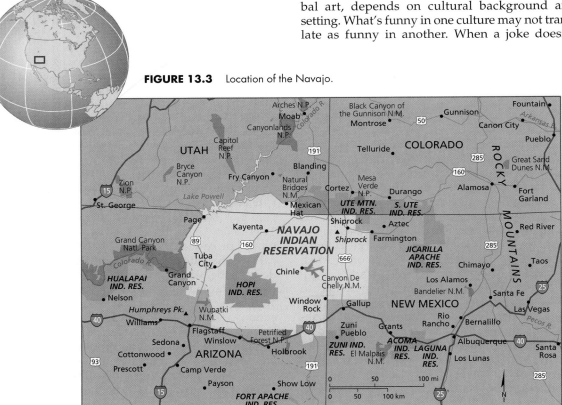

FIGURE 13.3 Location of the Navajo.

For art on the Web, see the Internet Exercises at your OLC

mhhe.com/kottak

▨ A violin class for a large group of four-year-old children at a Korean music school.

work, an American may say, "Well, you had to be there at the time." Jokes, like aesthetic judgments, depend on context.

At a smaller level of culture, certain artistic traditions may be transmitted in families. In Bali, for example, there are families of carvers, musicians, dancers, and mask makers. Among the Yoruba of Nigeria, two lineages of leatherworkers are entrusted with important bead embroidery works, such as for the king's crown and the bags and bracelets of priests. The arts, like other professions, often "run" in families. The Bachs, for example, produced not only Johann Sebastian, but several other noted composers and musicians.

In Chapter 1, anthropology's approach to the arts was contrasted with a traditional humanities focus on "fine arts" and elite expressions. Anthropology has extended the definition of "cultured" well beyond the elitist meaning of "high" art and culture. For anthropologists, everyone acquires culture through enculturation. In academia, growing acceptance of the anthropological definition of culture has helped broaden the study of the humanities from fine art and elite art to popular and folk art and the creative expressions of the masses and of many cultures.

In many societies, myths, legends, tales, and the art of storytelling play important roles in the transmission of culture and the preservation of tradition. In the absence of writing, oral traditions may preserve details of history and genealogy, as in many parts of West Africa. Art forms often go together. For example, music and storytelling may be combined for drama and emphasis (see the bottom photo on this page), much as they are in films and theater.

At what age do children start learning the arts? In some cultures, they start early. Contrast the photo of the Korean violin class above right with the photo of the Aleut gathering below. The

▨ This photo was taken on St. Paul Island, on the Bering Sea coast of Alaska. A traditional Aleut storyteller uses a drum to tell his tale to young Aleut people. Who are the storytellers of your society? How do their narrative techniques and styles differ from the one shown here?

Korean scene shows formal instruction. The teachers take the lead in showing the kids how to play the violin. The Aleut photo shows a more informal local scene in which children are learning about the arts as part of their overall enculturation. Presumably, the Korean children are learning the arts because their parents want them to, not necessarily because they have an artistic temperament that they need or wish to express. Sometimes children's participation in arts or performance, including sports, exemplifies forced enculturation. It may be pushed by parents rather than by kids themselves. In the United States, performance, usually associated with schools, has a strong social, and usually competitive, component. Kids perform with their peers.

I'll Get You, My Pretty, and Your Little R2

Techniques that anthropologists have used to analyze myths and folktales can be extended to two fantasy films that most of you have seen. *The Wizard of Oz* has been telecast annually for decades. The original *Star Wars* remains one of the most popular films of all time. Both are familiar and significant cultural products with obvious mythic qualities. The contributions of the French structuralist anthropologist Claude Lévi-Strauss (1967) and the neo-Freudian psychoanalyst Bruno Bettelheim (1975) to the study of myths and fairy tales permit the following analysis of visual fairy tales that contemporary Americans know well.

Examining the myths and tales of different cultures, Lévi-Strauss determined that one tale could be converted into another through a series of simple operations, for example, by doing the following:

1. Converting the positive element of a myth into its negative.
2. Reversing the order of the elements.
3. Replacing a male hero with a female hero.
4. Preserving or repeating certain key elements.

Through such operations, two apparently dissimilar myths can be shown to be variations on a common structure, that is, to be transformations of each other.

We'll see now that *Star Wars* is a systematic structural transformation of *The Wizard of Oz*. We may speculate about how many of the resemblances were conscious and how many simply reflect a process of enculturation that *Star Wars* writer and director George Lucas shares with other Americans.

The Wizard of Oz and *Star Wars* both begin in arid country, the first in Kansas and the second on the desert planet Tatooine (Table 13.1). *Star Wars* converts *The Wizard*'s female hero into a boy, Luke Skywalker. Fairytale heroes usually have short, common first names and second names that describe their origin or activity. Thus Luke, who travels aboard spaceships, is a Skywalker, while Dorothy Gale is swept off to Oz by a cyclone (a gale of wind). Dorothy leaves home with her dog, Toto, who is pursued by and has managed to escape from a woman who in Oz becomes the Wicked Witch of the West. Luke follows his "Two-Two" (R2D2), who is fleeing Darth Vader, the witch's structural equivalent.

Dorothy and Luke each start out living with an uncle and an aunt. However, because of the gender change of the hero, the primary relationship is reversed and inverted. Thus, Dorothy's relationship with her aunt is primary, warm, and loving, whereas Luke's relationship with his uncle, though primary, is strained and distant. Aunt and uncle are in the tales for the same reason. They represent home (the nuclear family of orientation), which children (according to American culture norms) must eventually leave to make it on their own. As Bettelheim (1975) points out, fairy tales often disguise parents as uncle and aunt, and this establishes social distance. The child can deal with the hero's separation (in *The Wizard of Oz*) or the aunt's and uncle's deaths (in *Star Wars*) more easily than with the death of or separation from real parents. Furthermore, this permits the child's strong feelings toward his or her real parents to be represented in different, more central characters, such as the Wicked Witch of the West and Darth Vader.

Both films focus on the child's relationship with the parent of the same sex, dividing that parent into three parts. In *The Wizard*, the mother is split into two parts bad and one part good. They are the Wicked Witch of the East, dead at the beginning of the movie; the Wicked Witch of the West, dead at the end; and Glinda, the good mother, who survives. The original *Star Wars* reversed the proportion of good and bad, giving Luke a good father (his own), the Jedi knight who is proclaimed dead at the film's beginning. There is another good father, Ben Kenobi, who is ambiguously dead when the movie ends. Third is the evil father figure, Darth Vader. As the good-mother third survives *The Wizard of Oz*, the bad-father third lives on after *Star Wars*, to strike back in the sequel.

The child's relationship with the parent of the opposite sex also is represented in the two films. Dorothy's father figure is the Wizard of Oz, an initially terrifying figure who later is proved to be a fake. Bettelheim notes that the typical fairy-tale father is disguised as a monster or giant. Or else, when preserved as a human, he is weak, distant, or ineffective. Dorothy counts on the wizard to save her but finds that he makes seemingly impossible demands and in the end is just an ordinary man. She succeeds on her own, no longer relying on a father who offers no more than she herself possesses.

In *Star Wars* (although emphatically not in the later films), Luke's mother figure is Princess Leia. Bettelheim notes that boys commonly fantasize their mothers to be unwilling captives of their fathers. Fairy tales often disguise mothers as princesses whose freedom the boy-hero must obtain. In graphic Freudian imagery, Darth Vader threatens Princess Leia with a needle the size of the witch's broomstick. By the end of the film, Luke has freed Leia and defeated Vader.

There are other striking parallels in the structure of the two films. Fairy-tale heroes often are accompanied on their adventures by secondary characters who personify the virtues needed in a successful quest. Such characters often come in threes. Dorothy takes along wisdom (the Scarecrow), love (the Tin Woodman), and courage (the Lion). *Star Wars* includes a structurally equivalent trio—Han Solo, C3PO, and Chewbacca—but their association with particular qualities isn't as precise. The minor characters are also structurally parallel: Munchkins and Jawas, Apple Trees and Sand People, Flying Monkeys and Stormtroopers. And compare settings—the witch's castle and the Death Star, the Emerald City and the rebel base. The endings are also parallel. Luke accomplishes his objective on his own, using the Force (mana, magical power). Dorothy's goal is to return to Kansas. She does that by tapping her shoes together and drawing on the Force in her ruby slippers.

All successful cultural products blend old and new, drawing on familiar themes. They may rearrange them in novel ways and thus win a lasting place in the imaginations of the culture that creates or accepts them. *Star Wars* successfully used old cultural themes in novel ways. It did that by drawing on *the* American fairy tale, one that had been available in book form since the turn of the 20th century.

TABLE 13.1 *Star Wars* as a Structural Transformation of *The Wizard of Oz*	
Star Wars	**The Wizard of Oz**
Male hero (Luke Skywalker)	Female hero (Dorothy Gale)
Arid Tatooine	Arid Kansas

Luke follows R2D2:
   R2D2 flees Vader
	Dorothy follows Toto:
	   Toto flees witch

Luke lives with uncle and aunt:
   Primary relationship with uncle
   (same sex as hero)
   Strained, distant relationship with uncle
	Dorothy lives with uncle and aunt:
	   Primary relationship with aunt
	   (same sex as hero)
	   Warm, close relationship with aunt

Tripartite division of same-sex parent:
   2 parts good, 1 part bad father
   Good father dead at beginning
   Good father dead (?) at end
   Bad father survives
	Tripartite division of same-sex parent:
	   2 parts bad, 1 part good mother
	   Bad mother dead at beginning
	   Bad mother dead at end
	   Good mother survives

Relationship with parent of opposite sex
   (Princess Leia Organa):
   Princess is unwilling captive
   Needle
   Princess is freed
	Relationship with parent of opposite sex
	   (Wizard of Oz):
	   Wizard makes impossible demands
	   Broomstick
	   Wizard turns out to be sham

Trio of companions:
   Han Solo, C3PO, Chewbacca
	Trio of companions:
	   Scarecrow, Tin Woodman, Cowardly Lion

Minor characters:
   Jawas
   Sand People
   Stormtroopers
	Minor characters:
	   Munchkins
	   Apple Trees
	   Flying Monkeys

Settings:
   Death Star
   Verdant Tikal (rebel base)
	Settings:
	   Witch's castle
	   Emerald City

Conclusion:
   Luke uses magic to accomplish goal
   (destroy Death Star)
	Conclusion:
	   Dorothy uses magic to accomplish goal
	   (return to Kansas)

In the process, they learn to compete, whether for a first place finish in a sports event or a first chair in the school orchestra or band.

The Artistic Career

In nonindustrial societies, artists tend to be part-time specialists. In states, there are more ways for artists to practice their craft full time. The number of positions in "arts and leisure" has mushroomed in contemporary societies, especially in North America. Many non-Western societies also offer career tracks in the arts: For example, a child born into a particular family or lineage may discover that he or she is destined for a career in leather working or weaving. Some societies are noted for particular arts, such as dance, wood carving, or weaving.

An artistic career also may involve some kind of a calling. Individuals may discover they have a particular talent and find an environment in which that talent is nourished. Separate career paths for artists usually involve special training and apprenticeship. Such paths are more likely in a complex society, where there are many separate career tracks, than in band or tribal societies, where expressive culture is less formally separated from daily life.

Artists need support if they are to devote full time to creative activity. They find support in their families or lineages if there is specialization in the arts involving kin groups. State societies often have patrons of the arts. Usually members of the elite class, patrons offer various kinds of support to aspiring and talented artists, such as court and palace painters, musicians, or sculptors. In some cases, an artistic career may entail a lifetime of dedication to religious art.

Goodale and Koss (1971) describe the manufacture of ornamental burial poles among the Tiwi of North Australia. Temporary separation and detachment from other social roles allowed burial pole artists to devote themselves to their work. The pole artists were ceremonially commissioned as such after a death. They were granted temporary freedom from the daily food quest. Other community members agreed to serve as their patrons. They supplied the artists with hard-to-get materials needed for their work. The burial pole artists were sequestered in a work area near the grave. That area was taboo to everyone else.

The arts usually are defined as neither practical nor ordinary. They rely on talent, which is individual, but which must be channeled and shaped in socially approved directions. Inevitably, artistic talent and production pull the artist away from the practical need to make a living. The issue of how to support artists and the arts arises again and again. We've all heard the phrase "struggling artist." But how should society support the arts? If there is state or religious support, something is typically expected in return. There is inevitably some limitation of the artist's "free" expression. Patronage and sponsorship also may result in the creation of art works that are removed from public display. Art commissioned for elites often is displayed only in their homes, perhaps finding its way into museums after their deaths. Church-commissioned art may be closer to the people. Artistic expressions of popular culture, intended for public rather than elite consumption, are discussed further in the chapter "Cultural Exchange and Survival."

Continuity and Change

The arts go on changing, although certain art forms have survived for thousands of years. The Upper Paleolithic cave art that has survived for more than 30,000 years was itself a highly developed manifestation of human creativity and symbolism, with an undoubtedly long evolutionary history. Monumental architecture, along with sculpture, reliefs, ornamental pottery, and written music, literature, and drama, have survived from early civilizations.

Countries and cultures are known for particular contributions, including art. The Balinese are known for dance; the Navajo for sand paintings, jewelry, and weaving; and the French for making cuisine an art form. We still read Greek tragedies and comedies in college, as we also read Shakespeare and Milton, and view the works of Michelangelo. Greek theater is among the most enduring of the arts. The words of Aeschylus,

In Athens, Greece, ancient Greek theater is being staged for a contemporary audience. Theater is typically a multimedia experience, with visual, aural, and often musical attributes.

Capoeira: The Afro-Brazilian Art of Unity and Survival

BACKGROUND INFORMATION

STUDENT:
Anne Haggerson

SUPERVISING PROFESSOR:
Rudi Colloredo-Mansfeld

SCHOOL:
University of Iowa

YEAR IN SCHOOL/MAJOR:
Senior/Anthropology and Spanish

FUTURE PLANS:
Internship in Washington, D.C.;
Ph.D.

PROJECT TITLE:
Capoeira: The Afro-Brazilian
Art of Unity and Survival

Which of the features and functions of art are illustrated by this account? Can you think of parallels to capoeira in form and/or function in your own society?

For two months, I lived in a small, concrete apartment in Mangueira, an inner-city shantytown constructed over trash and swamps in Salvador, Bahia. I was doing a fieldwork project for my senior thesis while working as an English teacher for GRUCON (Grupo de União e Consciência Negra), the local black consciousness movement that had been actively involved in community mobilization and youth-based consciousness raising projects for 30 years. My research focused on institutions that helped children and families overcome the forces of poverty, unemployment, racism, and failing schools.

Thus, I set out to investigate capoeira, an Afro-Brazilian martial art that assumes metaphors of slavery, liberation, and survival. The capoeira academy in the neighborhood was a subset of GRUCON and was grounded in a shared historical identity, fighting against economic oppression and political exclusion through music, dance, and African pride.

To prepare for this work, I researched problems of street children, took advanced Portuguese language courses, and worked out a research design that included interviews and participant observation. I trained formally with a local capoeira group for five months before going to Brazil, familiarizing myself with the key movements and game etiquette. Joining a capoeira academy in Brazil was one of the most challenging aspects of my research since I was a white, American woman participating in an activity dominated by Afro-Brazilian men. However, my active participation in the art was a crucial part of my fieldwork, allowing me to enter into the physical and psychological space of my informants, experience the power of symbolic movement, and access the sense of friendship, unity, and commitment among the players.

The practices were held in a small, humble concrete room and were administered with a high level of discipline and seriousness. The mestre served as the teacher, role model, and mediator of the 40 team members and created meaning and stability in their lives, encouraging them to pass physical limits, harness leadership roles on the team, proudly display their skills in the roda or performance circle, and research the history of capoeira in their free time.

Beyond participant observation, I also recorded important events and interviewed participants. I witnessed a spectacular annual community event called a batizado or baptism, where the students graduate to a higher-level capoeira belt. By observing and photographing this yearly initiation, it became clear that capoeira was much more than a pastime; it was a survival strategy, an educational tool, and a microcosmic social hierarchy that was maintained by a complex web of community political leaders and organizers.

Associated with rich memories of embarrassment and accomplishment, I proudly wear the capoeira warrior name the mestre gave me, "Serpente" or Snake, which, to me, is a symbolic tattoo that represents the dynamic beauty of doing anthropological fieldwork at the base level of urban society and thereby unleashing important insight on the resilient spirit of a vital civil society and the importance of building robust community institutions that spark political change and cultural solidarity.

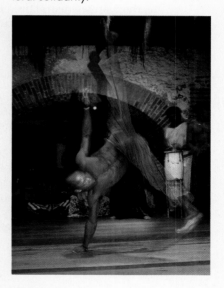

■ *A Brazilian* capoeira *dancer.*

Sophocles, Euripides, and Aristophanes have been captured in writing and live on. Who knows how many great preliterate creations and performances have been lost?

Classic Greek theater survives throughout the world. It is read in college courses, seen in the movies, and performed live on stages from Athens to New York. In today's world, the dramatic arts are part of a huge "arts and leisure" industry, which links Western and non-Western art forms in an international network that has both aesthetic and commercial dimensions (see

A synthesis of new and old theater techniques, including puppetry, is used in the Broadway production of Disney's The Lion King. What artistic influences have inspired the images shown in this photo?

worldwide. At least one store in Amsterdam, the Netherlands, specializes in didgeridoos, the only item it carries. Dozens of stores in any world capital hawk "traditional" arts, including musical instruments, from a hundred Third World countries. The commodification of non-Western art and the contemporary use of the arts to forge and redefine group identities are discussed further in the last chapter in this book.

We've seen that the arts typically draw in multiple media. Given the richness of today's media world, multimedia are even more marked. As ingredients and flavors from all over the world are combined in modern cuisine, so, too, are elements from many cultures and epochs woven into contemporary art and performance.

Our culture values change, experimentation, innovation, and novelty. But creativity also may be based on tradition. The Navajo, remember, can be at once individualistic, conservative, and attentive to proper form. In some cases and cultures, it's not necessary for artists to be innovative as they are being creative. Creativity can be expressed in variations on a traditional form. We see an example of this in "Interesting Issues" on pages 316–317, in which *Star Wars*, despite its specific story and innovative special effects, is shown to share its narrative structure with a previous film and fairy tale. It isn't always necessary for artists, in their work, to make a statement separating themselves from the past. Often, artists pay fealty to the past, associating with and building on, rather than rejecting, the work of their predecessors.

Marcus and Myers, eds. 1995; Root 1996). For example, non-Western musical traditions and instruments have joined the modern world system. We've seen that local musicians perform for outsiders, including tourists who increasingly visit their villages. And "tribal" instruments such as the Native Australian didgeridoo, a very long wooden wind instrument, are now exported

SUMMARY

1. Even if they lack a word for "art," people everywhere do associate an aesthetic experience with objects and events having certain qualities. The arts, sometimes called "expressive culture," include the visual arts, literature (written and oral), music, and theater arts. Some issues raised about religion also apply to art. If we adopt a special attitude or demeanor when confronting a sacred object, do we display something similar with art? Much art has been done in association with religion. In tribal performances, the arts and religion often mix. But non-Western art isn't always linked to religion.

2. The special places where we find art include museums, concert halls, opera houses, and theaters. However, the boundary between what's art and what's not may be blurred. Variation in art appreciation is especially common in contemporary society, with its professional artists and critics and great cultural diversity.

3. Those who work with non-Western art have been criticized for ignoring individual artists and for focusing too much on the social context and collective artistic production. Art is work, albeit creative work. In state societies, some people manage to support themselves as full-time artists. In nonstates artists are normally part time. Community standards judge the mastery and completion displayed in a work of art. Typically, the arts are exhibited, evaluated, performed, and appreciated in society. Music, which is often performed in groups, is among the most social of the arts. "Folk" art, music, and lore refer to the expressive culture of ordinary, usually rural, people.

4. Art can stand for tradition, even when traditional art is removed from its original context. Art can express community sentiment, with political goals, used to call attention to social issues. Often, art is meant to commemorate and to last. Growing acceptance of the anthropological definition of culture has guided the humanities beyond fine art,

elite art, and Western art to the creative expressions of the masses and of many cultures. Myths, legends, tales, and the art of storytelling often play important roles in the transmission of culture. Many societies offer career tracks in the arts; a child born into a particular family or lineage may discover that he or she is destined for a career in leatherworking or weaving.

5. The arts go on changing, although certain art forms have survived for thousands of years. Countries and cultures are known for particular contributions. Today, a huge "arts and leisure" industry links Western and non-Western art forms in an international network with both aesthetic and commercial dimensions.

aesthetics Appreciation of the qualities perceived in works of art; the mind and emotions in relation to a sense of beauty.

art An object or event that evokes an aesthetic reaction—a sense of beauty, appreciation, harmony, and/or pleasure; the quality, production, expression, or realm of what is beautiful or of more than ordinary significance; the class of objects subject to aesthetic criteria.

arts The arts include the visual arts, literature (written and oral), music, and theater arts.

catharsis Intense emotional release.

ethnomusicology The comparative study of the musics of the world and of music as an aspect of culture and society.

expressive culture The arts; people express themselves creatively in dance, music, song, painting, sculpture, pottery, cloth, storytelling, verse, prose, drama, and comedy.

folk Of the people; originally coined for European peasants; refers to the art, music, and lore of ordinary people, as contrasted with the "high" art or "classic" art of the European elites.

CRITICAL THINKING QUESTIONS

For more self-testing, see the self-quizzes

mhhe.com/kottak

1. Think of something visual that you consider to be art, but whose status as art is debatable. How would you convince someone else that it is art? What kinds of arguments against your position would you expect to hear?

2. Think of a musical composition or performance you consider to be art, but whose status as such is debatable. How would you convince someone else that it is art? What kinds of arguments against your position would you expect to hear?

3. Where did you last witness art? In what kind of a setting was it? Did people go there to appreciate the arts, or for some other reason?

4. Based on your own experience, how may the arts be used to buttress religion?

5. Can you think of a political dispute involving art or the arts? What were the different positions being debated?

SUGGESTED ADDITIONAL READINGS

Anderson, R.
    1989 *Art in Small-Scale Societies.* Upper Saddle River, NJ: Prentice Hall. Introduction to non-Western art, with a focus on the visual arts.
    2004 *Calliope's Sisters: A Comparative Study of Philosophies of Art,* 2nd ed. Upper Saddle River, NJ: Prentice Hall. A comparative study of aesthetics in 10 cultures.
Anderson, R., and K. Field, eds.
    1993 *Art in Small-Scale Societies: Contemporary Readings.* Upper Saddle River, NJ: Prentice Hall. An anthology of studies of non-Western art, with a focus on the visual arts.
Askew, K. M.
    2001 *Performing the Nation: Swahili Music and Cultural Politics in Tanzania.* Chicago: University of Chicago Press. Field-based study of music and politics in Tanzania.

Conkey, M., O. Soffer, D. Stratmann, and N. Jablonski
    1997 *Beyond Art: Pleistocene Image and Symbol.* San Francisco: Memoirs of the California Academy of Sciences, no. 23. A consideration of the symbolic basis and nature of prehistoric art.
Coote, J., and A. Shelton, eds.
    1992 *Anthropology, Art, and Aesthetics.* New York: Oxford University Press. Useful collection of essays.
Dublin, M.
    2001 *Native America Collected: The Culture of an Art World.* Albuquerque: University of New Mexico Press. Indians in art, tourism, and popular culture.
Hatcher, E. P.
    1999 *Art as Culture: An Introduction to the Anthropology of Art,* 2nd ed. Westport, CT: Bergin & Garvey. Up-to-date introduction.

Layton, R.
  1991   *The Anthropology of Art,* 2nd ed. New York: Cambridge University Press. Survey of the major issues, with a focus on visual art.

Marcus, G. E., and F. R. Myers, eds.
  1995   *The Traffic in Culture: Refiguring Art and Anthropology.* Berkeley: University of California Press. Art, society, and the marketing of culture in global perspective.

Moisala, P., and B. Diamond, eds.
  2000   *Music and Gender.* Champaign–Urbana: University of Illinois Press. Studies of the musical roles and performances of men and women in several societies.

Myers, F. R.
  2002   *Painting Culture: The Making of an Aboriginal High Art.* Durham, NC: Duke University Press. Artistic transformation in Australia's western desert.

Napier, A. D.
  1992   *Foreign Bodies: Performance, Art, and Symbolic Anthropology.* Berkeley: University of California Press. Focuses on the performing arts and symbols of society.

Root, D.
  1996   *Cannibal Culture: Art, Appropriation, and the Commodification of Difference.* Boulder, CO: Westview. How Western art and commerce classify, co-opt, and commodify "native" experiences, creations, and products.

Urban, Greg
  2001   *Metaculture: How Culture Moves through the World.* Minneapolis: University of Minnesota Press. Patterns, images, and cultural evaluation, with contemporary examples.

INTERNET EXERCISES

1. Body Art: Visit the National Museum of Natural History's online exhibit of "Canela body adornment," **http://www.nmnh.si.edu/naa/canela/canela1.htm**. Read all three pages of the exhibit and answer the questions below:

   a. In this example, how interrelated are art and worldview? How is art being used by the Canela?

   b. What individuals among the Canela get their ears pierced, and what does it signify? Who participates in the piercing? How does this practice compare to ear piercing in Western society?

   c. Cultures can change through time. What kinds of changes have occurred in the Canela practices of ear piercing since the 1950s? In the same way, what kinds of changes have occurred in ear piercing practices in Western society? What do these changes signify?

2. Comparing Art: Go to the Metropolitan Museum of Art's Collections page, **http://www.metmuseum.org/collections/index.asp** and browse the collections of Egyptian Art, **http://www.metmuseum.org/collections/department.asp?dep=10**, European Paintings, **http://www.metmuseum.org/collections/department.asp?dep=11**, and Modern Art, **http://www.metmuseum.org/Works_Of_Art/department.asp?dep=21**. For each of these collections, address the following questions:

   a. By whom is this art produced, and for whom is it produced?

   b. For what purpose is this art being produced (e.g., religious, aesthetic, political, monetary)?

   c. What themes and subjects are portrayed in the art?

   d. By just looking at the art, what can you learn about the culture that produced it?

See Chapter 13 at your McGraw-Hill Online Learning Center for additional review and interactive exercises.

Kottak, *Assault on Paradise,* **4th ed.**

Read Chapter 12, which discusses, among other aspects of globalization, television and its impact on Arembepe and Arembepeiros. What kind of TV programs do Arembepeiros habitually watch? What influence has television had on how Arembepeiros stage their festivals and performances?

Peters-Golden, *Culture Sketches,* **4th ed.**

This chapter has discussed the uses and places of arts in social life, describing music as one of the most social forms of expressive culture. In *Culture Sketches,* read Chapter 7, "Kaluli: Story, Song, and Ceremony." How does Kaluli music reflect central cultural ideas? What aspects of Kaluli life and society are represented in their music? How is the Kaluli relationship to music similar to, or different from, your own society's relationship to music? Several American and European musicians have joined to produce a recording of Bosavi music, *Voices of the Rainforest* (see "Interesting Issues" in Chapter 16). Profits from its sale benefit the Bosavi People's Fund, set up to provide financial aid to maintain Kaluli cultural survival in the face of threats to their rainforest environment. Why might it be that music, in particular, was chosen to raise money for the Kaluli?

Knauft, *The Gebusi,* **1st ed.**

Read Chapters 5, 6, and 11. Based on Chapters 5 and 6, what forms of artistic display and colorful performance are most developed among Gebusi? What symbols are reflected and encoded in Gebusi dance and initiation costuming? How does the art of Gebusi initiation costuming reflect social relations on the bodies of the initiates? Based on Chapter 11, what are the biggest changes in Gebusi artistic performances between 1980 and 1998? During Independence Day celebrations, are Gebusi exposed to more or to less artistic variety than they used to be? What do bodily art and performance during Independence Day celebrations reflect about changing social relations between Gebusi and other people?

14

The Modern World System

CHAPTER OUTLINE

THE EMERGENCE OF THE WORLD SYSTEM

Travel, trade, and murder may be as old as humanity. However, there is no doubt, as the "News Brief" confirms, that contact with Europe increased the scale of trade, interethnic contact, and violence in the Americas—and throughout the world. These trends continue today. Thus, although field work in small communities is anthropology's hallmark, isolated groups are impossible to find today and probably never have existed. For thousands of years, human groups have been in contact with one another. Local societies always have participated in a larger system, which today has global dimensions. We call it the *modern world system,* by which we mean a world in which nations are economically and politically interdependent. (Some earlier systems that controlled and blended large areas included the Roman empire, imperial China, and the spice trade.)

City, nation, and world increasingly invade local communities. Today, if anthropologists want to study a fairly isolated society, they must journey to the highlands of Papua New Guinea or the tropical forests of South America. Even in those places, they probably will encounter missionaries, prospectors, and tourists. In contemporary Australia, sheep owned by people who speak English graze where totemic ceremonies once were held. Farther in the outback, some descendants of those totemites may be working for a TV crew filming

325

■ *December 26, 2003: Illustrating a process of indigenizing offerings of the modern world system, children dress as Colonel Sanders to promote egg tarts (a local dish now offered by an international restaurant chain) at a KFC store in Shanghai, China.*

a new *Survivor* program. A Hilton hotel stands in the capital of faraway Madagascar, and a paved highway now has an exit for Arembepe, the Brazilian fishing village I have been studying since 1962. When and how did the modern world system begin?

The world system and the relations among the countries within that system are shaped by the world capitalist economy. World-system theory can be traced to the French social historian Fernand Braudel. In his three-volume work *Civilization and Capitalism, 15th–18th Century* (1981, 1982, 1992), Braudel argued that society consists of

OVERVIEW

The modern world system refers to a global system in which nations are economically and politically interdependent. The world economy is based on production for sale, guided by the profit motive. This capitalist world economy has political and economic specialization based on three positions: core, semiperiphery, and periphery. These positions have existed since the 16th century, although the particular countries filling them have changed.

Starting around 1750, industrialization increased production in farming and manufacturing. Workers moved from homes to factories, from rural areas to industrial cities. Today's world system maintains the distinction between those who own the means of production and those who don't. But the division is now worldwide. A middle class of skilled and professional workers has been added to the class structure. There is a marked contrast between capitalists and workers in the core nations and workers on the periphery. One effect of industrial expansion has been the destruction of indigenous peoples, cultures, and resources. For the last 500 years, the main forces influencing cultural interaction have been commercial expansion and the differential power of core nations.

interrelated parts assembled into a system. Societies are subsystems of bigger systems, with the world system as the largest.

As Europeans took to ships, developing a transoceanic trade-oriented economy, people throughout the world entered Europe's sphere of influence. In the 15th century, Europe established regular contact with Asia, Africa, and eventually the New World (the Caribbean and the Americas). Christopher Columbus's first voyage from Spain to the Bahamas and the Caribbean in 1492 was soon followed by additional voyages. These journeys opened the way for a major exchange of people, resources, diseases, and ideas, as the Old and New Worlds were forever linked (Crosby 1986, 2003; Diamond 1997; Viola and Margolis 1991). Led by Spain and Portugal, Europeans extracted silver and gold, conquered the natives (taking some as slaves), and colonized their lands.

Previously in Europe as throughout the world, rural people had produced mainly for their own needs, growing their own food and making clothing, furniture, and tools from local products. Production beyond immediate needs was undertaken to pay taxes and purchase trade items such as salt and iron. As late as 1650, the English diet, like diets in most of the world today, was based on locally grown starches (Mintz 1985). However, in the 200 years that followed, the English became extraordinary consumers of imported goods. One of the earliest and most popular of those goods was sugar (Mintz 1985).

Sugarcane was originally domesticated in Papua New Guinea, and sugar was first processed in India. Reaching Europe via the Middle East and the eastern Mediterranean, it was carried to the New World by Columbus (Mintz 1985). The climate of Brazil and the Caribbean proved ideal for growing sugarcane, and Europeans built plantations there to supply the growing demand for sugar. This led to the development in the 17th century of a plantation economy based on a single cash crop—a system known as monocrop production.

The demand for sugar in a growing international market spurred the development of the transatlantic slave trade and New World plantation economies based on slave labor. By the 18th century, an increased English demand for raw cotton led to rapid settlement of what is now the southeastern United States and the emergence there of another slave-based monocrop production system. Like sugar, cotton was a key trade item that fueled the growth of the world system.

The increasing dominance of trade led to the **capitalist world economy** (Wallerstein 1982, 2004*b*), a single world system committed to production for sale or exchange, with the object of maximizing profits rather than supplying domestic needs. **Capital** refers to wealth or resources invested in business, with the intent of using the means of production to produce a profit.

Bones Reveal Some Truth in "Noble Savage Myth"

WASHINGTON POST NEWS BRIEF

by Jack Lucentini
April 15, 2002

This "News Brief" reports on research demonstrating how contact with Europe increased the scale of trade, interethnic contact, and violence in the Americas. The research brings into focus an anthropological debate about the origin and nature of warfare and the role of European contact in fostering conflicts among indigenous peoples. The study shows that violence among Native Americans increased after contact. As the article begins, it suggests, mistakenly, that Native Americans lived in prehistory and lacked "civilization." In fact, Native Americans developed states and "civilizations" (e.g., Aztec, Maya, Inca) comparable to those of the Old World (e.g., ancient Mesopotamia and Egypt). Native Americans, most notably the Maya, also developed writing, which they used to

■ *The encounter between Hernán Cortés (1485–1547) and Montezuma II (1466–1520) was the subject of this 1820 painting by Gallo Gallina of Milan, Italy. Cortés went on to conquer Montezuma's Aztec empire.*

record their history—rendering the label prehistory *inaccurate. As you read, to understand why violence increased after contact, pay attention to the role of trade, disease, and slave raiding.*

A romantic-sounding notion dating back more than 200 years has it that people in prehistory, such as Native Americans, lived in peace and harmony.

Then "civilization" showed up, sowing violence and discord. Some see this claim as naive. It even has a derisive nickname, the "noble savage myth." But new research seems to suggest the "myth" contains at least some truth. Researchers examined thousands of Native American skeletons and found that those from after Christopher Columbus landed in the New World showed a rate of traumatic injuries more than 50 percent higher than those from before the Europeans arrived.

"Traumatic injuries do increase really significantly," said Philip L. Walker, an anthropology professor at the University of California at Santa Barbara, who conducted the study with Richard H. Steckel of Ohio State University.

The findings suggest "Native Americans were involved in more violence after the Europeans arrived than before," Walker said. But he emphasized there was also widespread violence before the Europeans came. Nevertheless, he said, "probably we're just seeing the tip of the iceberg" as far as the difference between violence levels before and after. That's because as many as half of bullet wounds miss the skeleton. Thus, the study couldn't detect much firearm violence, though some tribes wiped each other out using European-supplied guns.

The findings shed light on a controversy that has stirred not only living room discussions, but also an intense, sometimes ugly debate among anthropologists.

It involves two opposing views of human nature: Are we hard-wired for violence, or pushed into it?

Anthropologists who believe the latter seized on the findings as evidence for their view. "What it all says to me is that humans aren't demonic. Human males don't have an ingrained propensity for war . . . They can learn to be very peaceful, or terribly violent," said R. Brian Ferguson, a professor of anthropology at Rutgers University in Newark. Ferguson contends that before about 10,000 years ago, war was virtually nonexistent. But experts on the opposing side also said the findings fit their views.

"A 50 percent increase is the equivalent of moving from a suburb to the city, in terms of violence," said Charles Stanish, a professor of anthropology at the University of California at Los Angeles. "This shows the Native Americans were like us. Under stress, they fought more." Both sides called the study, which was presented Friday at the annual meeting of the American Association of Physical Anthropologists in Buffalo, a valuable contribution . . .

Walker and colleagues examined the skeletons of 3,375 pre-Columbian and 1,165 post-Columbian Native Americans, from archaeological sites throughout North and Central America.

The North Americans came mostly from the coasts and the Great Lakes region, Walker said.

Pre-Columbian skeletons showed an 11 percent incidence of traumatic injuries, he said, compared with almost 17 percent for the post-Columbians.

Walker said his findings surprised him. "I wasn't really expecting it," he said. Yet it undeniably suggests violence, he added. Most of the increase consisted of head injuries in young males, "which conforms pretty closely to the pattern you see today in homicides."

The researchers defined "traumatic injury" as anything leaving a mark on the skeleton, such as a skull fracture, a healed broken arm, or an embedded arrow point or bullet.

Walker said that although part of the increased injury rate doubtless stems from violence by whites themselves, it probably reflects mostly native-on-native violence. "In a lot of cases, such as in California, there weren't that many Europeans around—just a few priests, and thousands of Indians," he said.

Walker said the higher injury rate could have many explanations. Increased violence is normally associated with more densely populated, settled life, which Native Americans experienced in modernity, he said. Disease could also touch off war, he said.

"Here in California, there was a lot of inter-village warfare associated with the introduction of European diseases. People would attribute the disease to evil shamanic activity in another village," he said. Ferguson cited other factors. The Europeans often drew natives into their imperial wars, he said.

"Sometimes, the Europeans would enable someone to pursue a preexisting fight more aggressively, by backing one side," he added. Other times, he said, Europeans got natives to conduct slave raids on one another. Natives also fought over control of areas around trading outposts, to become middlemen, he said. "Sometimes that was a life-or-death matter, since it meant the difference between who would get guns or not." Stanish agreed. "Obviously, having an expanding imperial power coming at you is going to exacerbate tensions," he said . . . They're going to push you somewhere—into other groups."

"You're also going to get competition over access to the Europeans, who are a form of wealth," he added. Native Americans fought over areas rich in fur, which the whites would buy.

Yet Native American warfare was widespread long before that, Stanish said . . .

Keith F. Otterbein, an anthropology professor at the State University of New York at Buffalo, said the skeleton findings contribute to a balanced, middle-of-the-road view.

"The folks who are saying there was no early warfare—they're wrong, too. There is, in fact, a myth of the peaceful savage," he said. Otterbein said the controversy won't end here; both sides are too ideologically entrenched.

"Underlying the 'noble savage' myth," Stanish said, "is a political agenda by both the far right and far left. The right tries to turn the 'savages' into our little brown brothers, who need to be pulled up . . . On the left, they have another agenda, that the Western world is bad."

SOURCE: http://www.washingtonpost.com/ac2/wp-dyn?pagename=article&node=&contentId=A48 202-2002Apr14; in newspaper on p. A09.

The key claim of world-system theory is that an identifiable social system, based on wealth and power differentials, extends beyond individual states and nations. That system is formed by a set of economic and political relations that have characterized much of the globe since the 16th century, when the Old World established regular contact with the New World.

According to Wallerstein (1982, 2004b), the nations within the world system occupy three different positions of economic and political power: core, periphery, and semiperiphery. There is a geographic center or **core,** the dominant position in the world system, consisting of the strongest and most powerful nations. In core nations, "the complexity of economic activities and the level of capital accumulation is [sic] the greatest" (Thompson 1983, p. 12). With its sophisticated technologies and mechanized means of production, the core produces capital-intensive high-technology goods. Most of those products flow to other core nations, but some also go to the periphery and semiperiphery. According to Arrighi (1994), the core monopolizes the most profitable activities, especially the control of world finance.

Semiperiphery and **periphery** nations have less power, wealth, and influence. The semiperiphery is intermediate between the core and the periphery. Contemporary nations of the semiperiphery are industrialized. Like core nations, they export both industrial goods and commodities, but they lack the power and economic dominance of core nations. Thus Brazil, a semiperiphery nation, exports automobiles to Nigeria (a periphery nation) and auto engines, orange juice extract, coffee, and shrimp to the United States (a core nation).

Economic activities in the periphery are less mechanized than are those in the semiperiphery. The periphery produces raw materials, agricultural commodities, and, increasingly, human labor for export to the core and the semiperiphery. Today, although some degree of industrialization has reached even peripheral nations, the relationship between the core and the periphery remains fundamentally exploitative. Trade and other economic relations between core and periphery disproportionately benefit capitalists in the core (Shannon 1996).

In the United States and Western Europe today, immigrants, legal and illegal, supply cheap labor for agriculture in core countries. U.S. states as far-flung as California, Michigan, and South Carolina make significant use of farm labor from Mexico. The availability of relatively cheap workers from noncore nations such as Mexico (in the United States) and Turkey (in Germany) benefits farmers and business owners in core countries, while also supplying remittances to families in the semiperiphery and periphery. As a result of 21st-century telecommunications technology, cheap labor doesn't even need to migrate to the United States. Thousands of families in India are being supported as American companies "outsource" jobs—from telephone assistance to software engineering—to nations outside the core.

Consider recent moves by IBM, the world's largest information technology company. On June 24, 2005, the *New York Times* reported that IBM was planning to hire more than 14,000 additional workers in India, while laying off some 13,000 workers in Europe and the United States (Lohr 2005). These figures illustrate the ongoing globalization of work and the migration of even skilled jobs to low-wage countries. Its critics accuse IBM of shopping the globe for the cheapest labor to enhance corporate profits at the expense of wages, benefits, and job security in the United States and other developed countries. In explaining the hiring in India, an IBM senior vice president (quoted in Lohr 2005) cited a surging demand for technology services in India's thriving economy and the opportunity to tap the many skilled Indian software engineers to work on projects around the world. Skilled Western workers must compete now against well-educated workers in such low-wage countries as India, where an experienced software programmer earns one-fifth the average salary of a comparable American worker ($15,000 versus $75,000) (Lohr 2005).

INDUSTRIALIZATION

By the 18th century, the stage had been set for the **Industrial Revolution**—the historic transformation (in Europe, after 1750) of "traditional" into "modern" societies through industrialization of the economy. Industrialization required capital for investment. The established system of transoceanic trade and commerce supplied this capital from the enormous profits it generated. Wealthy people sought investment opportunities and eventually found them in machines and engines to drive machines. Industrialization increased production in both farming and manufacturing, as capital and scientific innovation fueled invention.

European industrialization developed from (and eventually replaced) the domestic system (cottage industry or home-handicraft system)

of manufacture. In this system, an organizer-entrepreneur supplied the raw materials to workers in their homes and collected the finished products from them. The entrepreneur, whose sphere of operations might span several villages, owned the materials, paid for the work, and arranged the marketing.

Causes of the Industrial Revolution

The Industrial Revolution began in the cotton products, iron, and pottery trades. These were widely used goods whose manufacture could be broken down into simple routine motions that machines could perform. When manufacturing moved from home to factory, where machinery replaced handwork, agrarian societies evolved into industrial ones. As factories produced cheap staple goods, the Industrial Revolution led to a dramatic increase in production. Industrialization

■ From producer to consumer, in the modern world system. The top photo, taken in the Caribbean nation of Dominica, shows the hard labor required to extract sugar using a manual press. In the bottom photo, an English middle-class family enjoys afternoon tea, sweetened with imported sugar. Which of the ingredients in your breakfast today were imported?

FIGURE 14.1 Location of England (United Kingdom) and France.

fueled urban growth and created a new kind of city, with factories crowded together in places where coal and labor were cheap.

The Industrial Revolution began in England rather than in France (Figure 14.1). Why? Unlike the English, the French didn't have to transform their domestic manufacturing system by industrializing. Faced with an increased need for products, with a late-18th-century population twice that of Great Britain, France could simply extend its domestic system of production by drawing in new homes. The French were able to increase production without innovating—they could enlarge the existing system rather than adopt a new one. However, to meet mounting demand for staples— at home and in its colonies—England, with fewer workers, had to industrialize.

As its industrialization proceeded, Britain's population began to increase dramatically. It doubled during the 18th century (especially after 1750) and did so again between 1800 and 1850. This demographic explosion fueled consumption, but British entrepreneurs couldn't meet the increased demand with the traditional production methods. This spurred experimentation, innovation, and rapid technological change.

English industrialization drew on national advantages in natural resources. Great Britain was rich in coal and iron ore and had navigable waterways and easily negotiated coasts. It was a seafaring island-nation located at the crossroads of international trade. These features gave Britain a favored position for importing raw materials and exporting manufactured goods. Another factor in England's industrial growth was the fact that much of its 18th-century colonial empire was occupied by English settler families who looked to the mother country as they tried to replicate European civilization in the New World. These colonies bought large quantities of English staples.

It also has been argued that particular cultural values and religion contributed to industrialization. Thus, many members of the emerging English middle class were Protestant nonconformists. Their beliefs and values encouraged industry, thrift, the dissemination of new knowledge, inventiveness, and willingness to accept change (Weber 1904/1958). Weber's ideas about Protestant values and capitalism were discussed in the chapter on "Religion."

STRATIFICATION

The socioeconomic effects of industrialization were mixed. English national income tripled between 1700 and 1815 and increased 30 times more by 1939. Standards of comfort rose, but prosperity was uneven. At first, factory workers got wages higher than those available in the domestic system. Later, owners started recruiting labor in places where living standards were low and labor (including that of women and children) was cheap.

Social ills increased with the growth of factory towns and industrial cities, with conditions like those Charles Dickens described in *Hard Times.* Filth and smoke polluted the 19th-century cities. Housing was crowded and unsanitary, with insufficient water and sewage disposal facilities and rising disease and death rates. This was the world of Ebenezer Scrooge, Bob Cratchit, Tiny Tim—and Karl Marx.

Industrial Stratification

The social theorists Karl Marx and Max Weber focused on the stratification systems associated with industrialization. From his observations in England and his analysis of 19th-century industrial capitalism, Marx (Marx and Engels 1848/1976) saw socioeconomic stratification as a sharp and simple division between two opposed classes: the bourgeoisie (capitalists) and the proletariat (propertyless workers). The bourgeoisie traced its origins to overseas ventures and the world capitalist economy, which had transformed the social structure of northwestern Europe, creating a wealthy commercial class.

Industrialization shifted production from farms and cottages to mills and factories, where mechanical power was available and where workers could be assembled to operate heavy machinery. The **bourgeoisie** were the owners of the factories, mines, large farms, and other means of production. The **working class,** or proletariat, was made up of people who had to sell their labor to survive. With the decline of subsistence production and with the rise of urban migration and the possibility

The Art of STOCKING-FRAME-WORK-KNITTING.

Engrav'd for the Universal Magazine 1750 for J. Hinton at the Kings Arms in S.t Pauls Church Yard LONDON.

of unemployment, the bourgeoisie came to stand between workers and the means of production.

Industrialization hastened the process of *proletarianization*—the separation of workers from the means of production. The bourgeoisie also came to dominate the means of communication, the schools, and other key institutions. Marx viewed the nation-state as an instrument of oppression and religion as a method of diverting and controlling the masses.

Class consciousness (recognition of collective interests and personal identification with one's economic group) was a vital part of Marx's view of class. He saw bourgeoisie and proletariat as socioeconomic divisions with radically opposed interests. Marx viewed classes as powerful collective forces that could mobilize human energies to influence the course of history. On the basis of their common experience, workers would develop class consciousness, which could lead to revolutionary change. Although no proletarian revolution was to occur in England, workers did develop organizations to protect their interests and increase their share of industrial profits. During the 19th century, trade unions and socialist parties emerged to express a rising anticapitalist spirit.

The concerns of the English labor movement were to remove young children from factories and limit the hours during which women and children could work. The profile of stratification in industrial core nations gradually took shape. Capitalists controlled production, but labor was organizing for better wages and working conditions. By 1900, many governments had factory legislation and social-welfare programs. Mass living standards in core nations rose as population grew.

■ In the home-handicraft, or domestic, system of production, an organizer supplied raw materials to workers in their homes and collected their products. Family life and work were intertwined, as in this English scene. Is there a modern equivalent to the domestic system of production?

In today's capitalist world system the class division between owners and workers is now worldwide. However, publicly traded companies complicate the division between capitalists and workers in industrial nations. Through pension plans and personal investments, many American workers now have some proprietary interest in the means of production. They are part-owners rather than propertyless workers. The key difference is that the wealthy have *control* over these means. The key capitalist now is not the factory owner, who may have been replaced by thousands of stockholders, but the CEO or the chair of the board of directors, neither of whom may actually own the corporation.

Modern stratification systems aren't simple and dichotomous. They include (particularly in core and semiperiphery nations) a middle class of skilled and professional workers. Gerhard Lenski (1966) argues that social equality tends to increase in advanced industrial societies. The masses improve their access to economic benefits and political power. In Lenski's scheme, the shift of political power to the masses reflects the growth of the middle class, which reduces the polarization between owning and working classes. The proliferation of middle-class occupations creates opportunities for social mobility. The stratification system grows more complex (Giddens 1973).

Faulting Marx for an overly simple and exclusively economic view of stratification, Weber (1922/1968) defined three dimensions of social stratification: wealth (economic status), power (political status), and prestige (social status). Although, as Weber showed, wealth, power, and prestige are separate components of social ranking, they do tend to be correlated. Weber also believed that social identities based on ethnicity, religion, race, nationality, and other attributes could take priority over class (social identity based on economic status). In addition to class contrasts, the modern world system is cross-cut by status groups, such as ethnic and religious groups and nations (Shannon 1996). Class conflicts tend to occur within nations, and nationalism has prevented global class solidarity, particularly of proletarians.

Although the capitalist class dominates politically in most countries, growing wealth has made it easier for core nations to grant higher wages to their own citizens (Hopkins and Wallerstein 1982). However, the improvement in core workers' living standards wouldn't have occurred without the world system. The added surplus and cheaper labor that come from the semiperiphery and the periphery allow core capitalists to maintain their profits while satisfying the demands of core workers. In the periphery, wages and living standards are much lower. The current *world stratification system* features a substantial contrast between both capitalists and workers in the core nations and workers on the periphery.

Asian Factory Women

Nike, the world's leading manufacturer of athletic shoes, has relied heavily on Asian labor in shoe manufacture, which Nike subcontracts to factories in Vietnam, Indonesia, China, Thailand, and Pakistan. Most of the factory workers are women between the ages of 15 and 28. The practices of Nike's Asian subcontractors, and of Nike itself, have been questioned by international media, labor, and human rights groups. Publicity centered on the fact that the shoes were being produced by very cheap Asian labor, then being sold in North America for up to $100 a pair. A group of Vietnamese Americans organized to form a new NGO (nongovernmental organization), Vietnam Labor Watch. With Nike's cooperation, this group carried out a study of Nike's Vietnamese operations—eventually suggesting changes, which Nike and its subcontractors agreed to implement (see Figure 14.2).

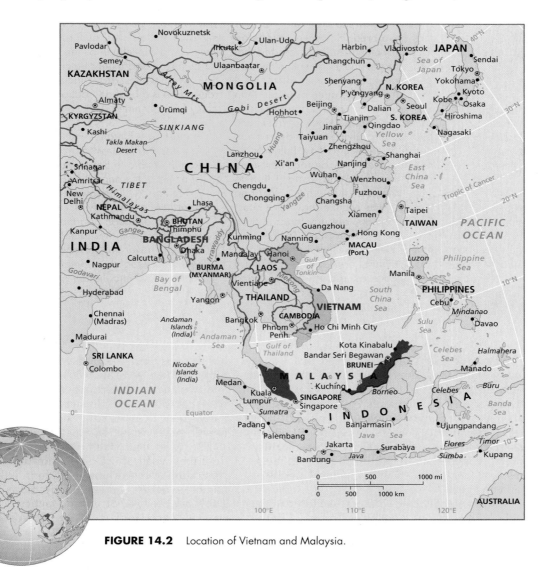

FIGURE 14.2   Location of Vietnam and Malaysia.

The Residue of Apartheid in Southern Africa

BACKGROUND INFORMATION

STUDENT:
Chanelle Mac Nab

SUPERVISING PROFESSOR:
Les Field

SCHOOL:
University of New Mexico

YEAR IN SCHOOL/MAJOR:
Senior/Anthropology (Ethnology)

FUTURE PLANS:
Graduate or medical school

PROJECT TITLE:
The Residue of Apartheid
in Southern Africa

Pay attention to the author's use of a personal perspective and personal vignettes in describing an experience abroad. How would you react in the author's situation? Are you surprised that the legacy of apartheid lingers in Southern Africa?

I spent six months in Botswana, Africa, on an international youth exchange program. I lived in six different villages and gained insight into the rural life of these pastoral people. During this time, I traveled to South Africa, Namibia, and Zimbabwe and witnessed varying degrees of racism. The color of my skin as a Caucasian allowed me to review both the white and black perspectives on racism.

Apartheid, which is an Afrikaans word that literally means "separateness," was a policy of racial segregation that was implemented in South Africa in 1948 when the Nationalist Party came to power. Apartheid resulted in one of the most unabashed forms of racism in the world.

Prior to going to southern Africa, like most of my American counterparts, I could see little good in the Afrikaners because of all the hate and violence they have bred. However, once I had lived in southern Africa, I realized that I too was passing judgment. In my own personal experience with Afrikaners, I found them to be quite opposite than their stereotypes had described them. To me they were a kindly and humane people, often giving me a ride, a meal, and a free place to stay. It is unfortunate that their view on race has separated them from the world. I had to stop blaming the whites for one moment and realize that the whites, like the blacks, are a product of their own cultural conditioning. They are victims of their own cultural constructions. Yes, the whites are capable of taking a new stance on racism. South Africa must move beyond their issues of race and strive for cohesion if they wish to build an equitable future for both whites and blacks in all of Africa.

Why did the supposed nonracial governments of the neighboring South African countries such as Botswana and Namibia also allow whites to come in and implement their racist laws? This answer lies in the history of Africa. Colonial powers drew lines across the African continent and divided it into pieces. With colonial rule controlling Africa throughout most of the 20th century, I assume that racism was adopted and implemented in all countries where whites were the minority in an effort to maintain power.

The greatest obstacle during my stay in Africa was overcoming the numerous confrontations I had with the whites in regards to race. Every day my own beliefs and cultural norms were being challenged by this unfamiliar culture. I had extensive conversations with whites and blacks about race. Here is a brief description of one of my journal entries.

August 14—Tonight I went with Rey (the Afrikaner who drove me from Namibia to Botswana) to the opening of the annual Agricultural Trade Fair . . . I am aware that apartheid ended only in 1994, and that, although apartheid is physically gone, it is latently present, but never did those words seem more real than tonight . . . As we drove into the fair grounds,

Vietnam Labor Watch confirmed that wages and working conditions were problematic. Across Asia, the wages paid to Nike workers averaged $1.84 per day. In Vietnam's Ho Chi Minh City, where the cost of three simple meals was $2.10 per day, Nike factory workers made only $1.60 per day. Health was also a concern, as was factory safety. Workers had to endure overheated factories with bad air filled with chemical smells of paint and glue.

Nike's young female workers, like those in the Malaysian electronics factories discussed in the chapter "Making a Living," had to wear uniforms. Adding to their regimentation was a military boot camp atmosphere. Workers were bullied, insulted, and subjected to harsh discipline. Workers were allowed only one toilet break and two chances to drink per eight hours. There were complaints of physical abuse and sexual harassment by male supervisors and insults by foreign supervisors (Koreans).

The Malaysian factory women previously described used spirit possession to vent their frustration over working conditions. Nike's Vietnamese workers did something more effective. They adopted labor union tactics, including strikes, work stoppages, and slowdowns. The Vietnamese workers also enlisted the support of NGOs, international labor organizations, and concerned Vietnamese Americans. Through such

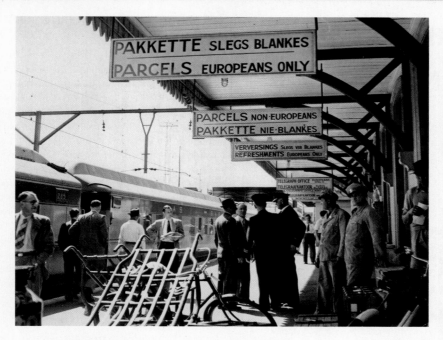

South Africa's segregationist policy known as apartheid lasted from 1948 until 1994. This historical image shows a train station with separate windows for parcels and refreshments for white and nonwhite people.

they did not know who I was on the inside. Yes, I was white but I was not one of them . . . I felt guilty, as if I were betraying all of my black friends and my black host family . . . As hard as it was, I kept my calm and I told Rey I would never be able to see it the way he does because of my different upbringing. Rey admitted that perhaps his children's children would one day see it the way I do. As Rey and I left the party to go home, I dared him to go with me to the "other side" so that we could dance. He responded with two words: "I cannot." Our conversation ended and we drove home in silence.

Today, the ideology of racism has seeped across borders and across imaginary lines like an oil spill and is ever present throughout the world's social, political, and economic systems. It is important to understand that apartheid is not isolated in South Africa. Apartheid has permeated all of the borders of southern Africa. Hence, racism is not exclusively a South African problem.

This research has attempted to shed light on the serious issue of racism, with its emphasis on the continuing effects of the apartheid regime in southern Africa. I hope that more people will come to understand apartheid and use this knowledge to understand why racism denies and oppresses people all around the world.

I could see the silhouettes of hundreds of black people dancing against the dimness of the lantern lights. The loud African music was familiar to me . . . [I]nstead of continuing forward to where the blacks were, we took a sharp left turn to the white sector of the fair. The whites were standing around a fire drinking while their black servants stoked the fire and prepared the food. I was stunned to be standing on segregated soil. I could not believe that I was in Botswana and not in South Africa. Every moment that I was with the whites I felt uncomfortable . . . I could not identify with these people . . . I was furious underneath my skin because

efforts and actions they managed to improve their working conditions and salaries.

Open and Closed Class Systems

Inequalities, which are built into the structure of state societies, tend to persist across the generations. The extent to which they do or don't is a measure of the openness of the stratification system, the ease of social mobility it permits. Within the world capitalist economy, stratification has taken many forms, including caste, slavery, and class systems.

Caste systems are closed, hereditary systems of stratification that often are dictated by religion.

Hierarchical social status is ascribed at birth, so that people are locked into their parents' social position. Caste lines are clearly defined, and legal and religious sanctions are applied against those who seek to cross them.

The world's best-known caste system is associated with Hinduism in traditional India. As described by Gargan (1992), despite the formal abolition of the caste system in 1949, caste-based stratification remains important in modern India. An estimated 5 million adults and 10 million children are bonded laborers. These people live in complete servitude, working to repay real or imagined debts. Most of them are untouchables, impoverished and powerless people at the bottom of the

Slavery is the most extreme, coercive, and abusive form of legalized inequality. Although proletarians, such as these "white slaves of England," also lacked control over the means of production, they did have some control over where they worked. In what other ways do proletarians differ from slaves?

See your OLC Internet Exercises
mhhe.com/kottak

caste hierarchy. Some families have been bonded for generations; people are born into servitude because their parents or grandparents were sold previously. Bonded workers toil unpaid in stone quarries, brick kilns, and rice paddies.

Another castelike system, *apartheid*, existed until recently in South Africa (see "Beyond the Classroom"). In that legally maintained hierarchy, blacks, whites, and Asians had their own separate (and unequal) neighborhoods, schools, laws, and punishments.

In **slavery,** the most inhumane and degrading form of stratification, people are treated as property. In the Atlantic slave trade, millions of human beings were treated as commodities. The plantation systems of the Caribbean, the southeastern United States, and Brazil were based on forced slave labor. Slaves lacked control over the means of production. They were like proletarians in this respect. But proletarians at least are legally free. Unlike slaves, they have some control over where they work, how much they work, for whom they work, and what they do with their wages. Slaves, in contrast, were forced to live and work at their master's whim. Defined as lesser human beings, slaves lacked legal rights. They could be sold and resold; their families, split apart. Slaves had nothing to sell—not even their own labor (Mintz 1985).

This clip draws parallels between the 1890s and today, mentioning advances in technology that took place through the discoveries and efforts of Bell, Edison, Carnegie, and Morgan. A century ago, laissez-faire economic policies allowed the barons of industry to increase profits and grow wealthy. The United States moved from semiperiphery to core. The clip mentions sweatshops, child labor, and low wages as the downside of capitalism. Today, transnational corporations increasingly operate internationally, beyond the boundaries of uniform national laws. This creates new business opportunities but also new legal, ethical, and moral challenges. What's the technological basis of the global village described in the clip? Because the world is so tightly integrated, the clip suggests that events in Asia can have immediate ripple effects in the West. Can you think of any examples?

Slavery is the most extreme, coercive, and abusive form of legalized inequality.

Vertical mobility is an upward or downward change in a person's social status. A truly **open class system** would facilitate mobility. Individual achievement and personal merit would determine social rank. Hierarchical social statuses would be achieved on the basis of people's efforts. Ascribed statuses (family background, ethnicity, gender, religion) would be less important. Open class systems would have blurred class lines and a wide range of status positions.

Compared with nonindustrial states and contemporary peripheral and semiperipheral nations, core industrial nations tend to have more open class systems. Under industrialism, wealth is based to some extent on **income**—earnings from wages and salaries. Economists contrast such a return on labor with interest, dividends, rent, and profits, which are *returns on property* or capital.

THE WORLD SYSTEM TODAY

We will see in "Interesting Issues: The American Periphery" (pp. 338–339) that the world economy also can create peripheral regions within core nations, such as rural areas of the American South. World-system theory stresses the existence of a global culture. It emphasizes historic contacts, linkages, and power differentials between local people and international forces. The major forces influencing cultural interaction during the past 500 years have been commercial expansion, industrial capitalism, and the differential power of colonial and core nations (Wallerstein 1982, 2004b; Wolf 1982). As state formation had done

Most Americans think they belong to, and claim identity with, the middle class, which they tend to perceive as a vast undifferentiated group. However, the American class system isn't as open or undifferentiated as most Americans assume it to be. There are substantial differences in income and wealth between the richest and the poorest Americans, and the gap is widening. According to U.S. Census data, from 1967 to 2000 the top (richest) fifth, or quintile, of American households increased their share of national income by 13.5 percent, while the shares of all the other quintiles fell. The percentage share of the lowest fifth fell most dramatically—17.6 percent. In 2003 the highest fifth of American households got about 48 percent of all national income, while the share of the lowest fifth was 4 percent. The richest fifth of American households, with a mean annual income of $141,621, had become 14 times wealthier than the poorest fifth, with a mean annual income of $10,188 (U.S. Census Bureau 2004), and the trend continues today. When we consider wealth (investments, property, possessions, etc.) rather than income, the contrast is even more striking: 1 percent of American families hold one-third of the nation's wealth (Calhoun, Light, and Keller 1997). Understanding ourselves means recognizing that our ideology about class doesn't accord with socioeconomic reality.

duce and in which market exchanges occur with profit as the primary motive (Bodley 2001).

After 1870, European business initiated a concerted search for markets in Asia, Africa, and other less-developed areas. This process led to European imperialism in Africa, Asia, and Oceania. **Imperialism** refers to a policy of extending the rule of a nation or empire, such as the British empire, over foreign nations and of taking and holding foreign colonies. *Colonialism* refers to the political, social, economic, and cultural domination of a territory and its people by a foreign power for an extended time. European imperial expansion was aided by improved transportation, which brought huge new areas within easy reach. Europeans also colonized vast areas of previously unsettled or sparsely settled lands in the interior of North and South America and Australia. The new colonies purchased masses of goods from the industrial centers and shipped back wheat, cotton, wool, mutton, beef, and leather. Thus began the second phase of colonialism (the first had been in the New World after Columbus) as European nations competed for colonies between 1875 and 1914, a process that helped cause World War I.

Industrialization spread to many other nations in a process that continues today (Table 14.1). By 1900, the United States had become a core nation within the world system. It had overtaken Great Britain in iron, coal, and cotton production. In a few decades (1868–1900), Japan changed from a medieval handicraft country to an industrial one, joining the semiperiphery by 1900 and moving to the core between 1945 and 1970. Figure 14.4 is a map showing the modern world system.

Twentieth-century industrialization added hundreds of new industries and millions of new jobs. Production increased, often beyond immediate demand. This spurred strategies such as advertising to sell everything that industry could churn out. Mass production gave rise to a culture of overconsumption, which valued acquisitiveness and conspicuous consumption (Veblen 1934). Industrialization entailed a shift from reliance on renewable resources to the use of fossil fuels, such

previously, industrialization accelerated local participation in larger networks. According to Bodley (2001), perpetual expansion (whether in population or consumption) is the distinguishing feature of industrial economic systems. Bands and tribes are small, self-sufficient, subsistence-based systems. Industrial economies, by contrast, are large, highly specialized systems in which local areas don't consume the products they pro-

---

TABLE 14.1   Ascent and Decline of Nations within the World System

Periphery to Semiperiphery	Semiperiphery to Core	Core to Semiperiphery
United States (1800–1860)	United States (1860–1900)	Spain (1620–1700)
Japan (1868–1900)	Japan (1945–1970)	
Taiwan (1949–1980)	Germany (1870–1900)	
S. Korea (1953–1980)		

SOURCE: Thomas Richard Shannon, *An Introduction to the World-System Perspective*, 2nd ed. (Boulder, CO: Westview Press, 1996), p. 147.

The American Periphery

The effects of the world economy also can create peripheral regions within core nations, such as areas of the rural South in the United States. In a comparative study of two counties at opposite ends of Tennessee (Figure 14.3), Thomas Collins (1989) reviewed the effects of industrialization on poverty and unemployment. Hill County, with an Appalachian white population, is on the Cumberland Plateau in eastern Tennessee. Delta County, which is predominantly African American, is 60 miles from Memphis in western Tennessee's lower Mississippi region. Both counties once had economies based on agriculture and timber, but jobs in those sectors declined sharply with the advent of mechanization. Both counties have unemployment rates more than twice that of Tennessee as a whole. More than a third of the people in each county live below the poverty level. Such poverty pockets represent a slice of the world periphery within modern America. Given very restricted job opportunities, the best-educated local youths have migrated to northern cities for three generations.

To increase jobs, local officials and business leaders have tried to attract industries from outside. Their efforts exemplify a more general rural southern strategy, which began during the 1950s, of courting industry by advertising "a good business climate"—which means low rents, cheap utilities, and a nonunion labor pool. However, few firms are attracted to an impoverished and poorly educated work force. All the industries that have come to such areas have very limited market power and a narrow profit margin. Such firms

FIGURE 14.3 Location of Cumberland Plateau and Memphis Vicinity (Delta County) in Tennessee.

survive by offering low wages and minimal benefits, with frequent layoffs. These industries tend to emphasize traditional female skills such as sewing and mostly attract women.

The garment industry, which is highly mobile, is Hill County's main employer. The knowledge that a garment plant can be moved to another locale very rapidly tends to reduce employee demands. Management can be as arbitrary and authoritarian as it

wishes. The unemployment rate and low educational level ensure that many women will accept sewing jobs for a bit more than the minimum wage.

In neither county has new industry brought many jobs for men, who have a higher unemployment rate than do women (as do blacks, compared with whites). Collins found that many men in Hill County had never been permanently employed; they had just done temporary jobs, always for cash.

Biocultural Case Study

The "Bringing It All Together" essay that immediately follows the last chapter in this book discusses "supersizing" and overconsumption in the contemporary United States.

as oil. Energy from fossil fuels, which have been stored over millions of years, is being depleted rapidly to support a previously unknown and probably unsustainable level of consumption (Bodley 2001).

Table 14.2 compares energy consumption in various types of cultures. Americans are the world's foremost consumers of nonrenewable resources. In terms of energy consumption, the average American is about 35 times more expen-

sive than the average forager or tribesperson. Since 1900, the United States has tripled its per capita energy use. It also has increased its total energy consumption 30-fold.

Table 14.3 compares energy consumption, per capita and total, in the United States and selected other countries. The United States represents 23.7 percent of the world's annual energy consumption, compared with China's 10.5 percent, but the average American consumes 10 times the energy

The effects of industrialization in Delta County have been similar. That county's recruitment efforts also have drawn only marginal industries. The largest is a bicycle seat and toy manufacturer, which employs 60 percent women. Three other large plants, which make clothing and auto seat covers, employ 95 percent women. Egg production was once significant in Delta County but folded when the market for eggs fell in response to rising national concern over the effects of cholesterol.

In both counties, the men, ignored by industrialization, maintain an informal economy. They sell and trade used goods through personal networks. They take casual jobs, such as operating farm equipment on a daily or seasonal basis. Collins found that maintaining an automobile was the most important and prestigious contribution these men made to their families. Neither county has public transportation; Hill County even lacks school buses. Families need cars to get women to work and kids to school. Men who keep an old car running longest get special respect.

Reduced opportunities for men to do well at work—to which American culture attributes great importance—lead to a feeling of lowered self-worth, which is expressed in physical violence. The rate of domestic violence in Hill County exceeds the state average. Spousal abuse arises from men's demands to control women's paychecks. (Men regard the cash they earn themselves as their own, to spend on male activities.)

One important difference between the two counties involves unionization. In Delta County, organizers have waged successful campaigns for unionization. Attitudes toward workers' rights in Tennessee correlate with race.

Poverty pockets of the rural South, illustrated by this scene from the Mississippi delta region, represent a slice of the world periphery within modern America. Through mechanization, industrialization, and other changes promoted by larger systems, local people have been deprived of land and jobs. Emigration of educated and talented locals continues as the opportunities shrink.

Rural southern whites usually don't vote for unions when they have a chance to do so, whereas African Americans are more likely to challenge management about pay and work rules. Local blacks view their work situation in terms of black against white rather than from a position of working-class solidarity. They are attracted to unions because they see only whites in managerial positions and resent differential advancement of white factory workers. One manager expressed to Collins that "once the work force of a plant becomes more than one-third black, you can expect to have union representation within a year" (Collins 1989, p. 10). Responding to this probability of unionization, core capitalists from Japan don't build plants in the primarily African American counties of the lower Mississippi. The state's Japanese factories cluster in eastern and central Tennessee.

Poverty pockets of the rural South (and other regions) represent a slice of the world periphery within modern America. Through mechanization, industrialization, and the other changes promoted by larger systems, local people have been deprived of land and jobs. After years of industrial development, a third of the people of Hill and Delta counties remain below the poverty level. Emigration of educated and talented locals continues as the opportunities shrink. Collins concluded that rural poverty would not be reduced by attracting additional peripheral industries because these firms lack the market power to improve wages and benefits. Different development schemes are needed for these counties and the rural South generally.

used by the average Chinese, and 26 times the energy used by the average inhabitant of India.

Industrial Degradation

Industrialization and factory labor now characterize many societies in Latin America, Africa, the Pacific, and Asia. One effect of the spread of industrialization has been the destruction of indigenous economies, ecologies, and populations.

Two centuries ago, as industrialization was developing, 50 million people still lived beyond the periphery in politically independent bands, tribes, and chiefdoms. Occupying vast areas, those non-state societies, although not totally isolated, were only marginally affected by nation-states and the world capitalist economy. In 1800 bands, tribes, and chiefdoms controlled half the globe and 20 percent of its population (Bodley, ed. 1988). Industrialization tipped the balance in favor of states.

Map Atlas

Map 16 shows the annual consumption of commercial energy per capita by country.

See the Interactive Exercise for a quiz on the world system in the past

mhhe.com/kottak

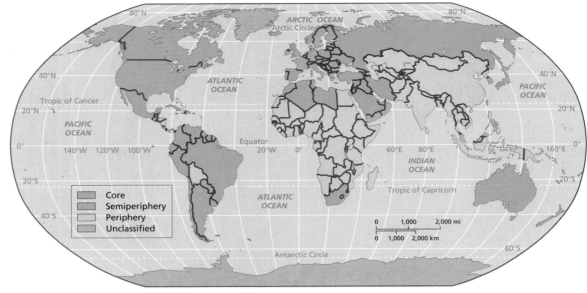

FIGURE 14.4 The World System in 2000.

| Core |
| Semiperiphery |
| Periphery |
| Unclassified |

TABLE 14.2   Energy Consumption in Various Contexts

Type of Society	Daily Kilocalories per Person
Bands and tribes	4,000–12,000
Preindustrial states	26,000 (maximum)
Early industrial states	70,000
Americans in 1970	230,000
Americans in 1990	275,000

SOURCE: John H. Bodley, *Anthropology and Contemporary Human Problems* (Mountain View, CA: Mayfield, 1985).

TABLE 14.3   Energy Consumption in Selected Countries, 2002

	Total	Per capita
World	411.2*	66**
United States	97.6	342
China	43.2	33
Russia	27.5	191
Germany	14.3	173
India	14.0	13
Canada	13.1	418
France	11.0	184
United Kingdom	9.6	162

*411.2 quadrillion (411,200,000,000,000,000) Btu.

**66 million Btu.

SOURCE: Based on data in *Statistical Abstract of the United States, 2004–2005* (Table 1367), and *Statistical Abstract of the United States, 2003* (Table 1365).

■ *Copsa Mica, Romania, may well be the world's most polluted city. A factory belches out smoke that leaves its mark on these boys' faces, food, and lungs. What's the term for such environmental devastation?*

As industrial states have conquered, annexed, and "developed" nonstates, there has been genocide on a grand scale. *Genocide* refers to a deliberate policy of exterminating a group through warfare or murder. Examples include the Holocaust, Rwanda in 1994, and Bosnia, as discussed in the chapter "Ethnicity and Race." Bodley (1988) estimates that an average of 250,000 indigenous people perished annually between 1800 and 1950. Besides warfare, the causes included foreign diseases (to which natives lacked resistance), slavery, land grabbing, and other forms of dispossession and impoverishment.

Many native groups have been incorporated within nation-states, in which they have become ethnic minorities. Some of these groups have been able to recoup their population. Many indigenous peoples survive and maintain their ethnic identity despite having lost their ancestral cultures to varying degrees (partial ethnocide). And many descendants of tribespeople live on as culturally distinct and self-conscious colonized peoples, many of whom aspire to autonomy. As the original inhabitants of their territories, they are called **indigenous peoples** (see Maybury-Lewis 2002).

Around the world many contemporary nations are repeating—at an accelerated rate—the process of resource depletion that started in Europe and the United States during the Industrial Revolution. Fortunately, however, today's world has some environmental watchdogs that did not exist during the first centuries of the Industrial Revolution. Given national and international cooperation and sanctions, the modern world may benefit from the lessons of the past.

See your OLC Internet Exercises for more on indigenous peoples

mhhe.com/kottak

SUMMARY

1. Local societies increasingly participate in wider systems—regional, national, and global. Columbus's voyages opened the way for a major and continuing exchange between the Old and New Worlds. Seventeenth-century plantation economies in the Caribbean and Brazil were based on sugar. In the 18th century, plantation economies based on cotton arose in the southeastern United States.

2. The capitalist world economy is based on production for sale, with the goal of maximizing profits. World capitalism has political and economic specialization based on three positions. Core, semiperiphery, and periphery have existed since the 16th century, although the particular countries filling these niches have changed.

3. The Industrial Revolution began around 1750. Transoceanic trade and commerce supplied capital for industrial investment. Industrialism began in England rather than in France because French industry could grow through expansion of the domestic system. England, with fewer people, had to industrialize.

4. Industrialization hastened the separation of workers from the means of production. Marx saw stratification as a sharp division between the bourgeoisie (capitalists) and the proletariat (propertyless workers). Class consciousness was a key part of Marx's view of class. Weber believed that social solidarity based on ethnicity, religion, race, or nationality could take priority over class.

Today's capitalist world system maintains the contrast between those who own the means of production and those who don't, but the division is now worldwide. Modern stratification systems also include a middle class of skilled and professional workers.

5. Nationalism has prevented global class solidarity. There is a substantial contrast between capitalists and workers in the core nations and workers on the periphery. The extent to which inequalities persist across the generations is a measure of the openness of the class system, the ease of social mobility it permits. Under world capitalism, stratification has taken many forms, including caste, slavery, and class systems.

6. The major forces influencing cultural interaction during the past 500 years have been commercial expansion and industrial capitalism. In the 19th century, industrialization spread to Belgium, France, Germany, and the United States. After 1870, businesses began a concerted search for more secure markets. This process led to European imperialism in Africa, Asia, and Oceania.

7. By 1900 the United States had become a core nation. Mass production gave rise to a culture that valued acquisitiveness and conspicuous consumption. One effect of industrialization has been the destruction of indigenous economies, ecologies, and populations. Two centuries ago, 50 million people lived in independent bands, tribes, and chiefdoms. Industrialization tipped the balance in favor of states.

bourgeoisie One of Marx's opposed classes; owners of the means of production (factories, mines, large farms, and other sources of subsistence).

capital Wealth or resources invested in business, with the intent of producing a profit.

capitalist world economy The single world system, which emerged in the 16th century, committed to production for sale, with the object of maximizing profits rather than supplying domestic needs.

caste system Closed, hereditary system of stratification, often dictated by religion; hierarchical social status is ascribed at birth, so that people are locked into their parents' social position.

core Dominant structural position in the world system; consists of the strongest and most powerful states with advanced systems of production.

imperialism A policy of extending the rule of a nation or empire over foreign nations or of taking and holding foreign colonies.

KEY TERMS

See the flash cards

mhhe.com/kottak

income   Earnings from wages and salaries.

indigenous peoples   The original inhabitants of particular territories; often descendants of tribespeople who live on as culturally distinct colonized peoples, many of whom aspire to autonomy.

Industrial Revolution   The historic transformation (in Europe, after 1750) of "traditional" into "modern" societies through industrialization of the economy.

open class system   Stratification system that facilitates social mobility, with individual achievement and personal merit determining social rank.

periphery   Weakest structural position in the world system.

semiperiphery   Structural position in the world system intermediate between core and periphery.

slavery   The most extreme, coercive, abusive, and inhumane form of legalized inequality; people are treated as property.

vertical mobility   Upward or downward change in a person's social status.

working class   Or proletariat; those who must sell their labor to survive; the antithesis of the bourgeoisie in Marx's class analysis.

CRITICAL THINKING QUESTIONS

For more self-testing, see the self-quizzes

mhhe.com/kottak

1. According to world-system theory, societies are subsystems of bigger systems, with the world system as the largest. What are the various systems, at different levels, in which you participate?

2. Give two examples each of core, semiperiphery, and periphery nations. Does any nation seem poised to move from one slot to another, such as semiperiphery to core, or vice versa? What's the last nation to make such a move?

3. How has social stratification in industrial societies changed over time? Think of comparing London of the 1850s (the era of Dickens and Marx) and today.

4. How did the views of Marx and Weber on stratification differ? Which approach makes the most sense to you? Why?

5. How open is the class system of your society? Describe what's open and what's closed about it.

SUGGESTED ADDITIONAL READINGS

Abu-Lughod, J. L.
  1989   *Before European Hegemony: The World System A. D. 1250–1350.* New York: Oxford University Press. Regional economies and politics before the age of European exploration and the capitalist world economy.

Arrighi, G.
  1994   *The Long Twentieth Century: Money, Power, and the Origins of Our Times.* New York: Verso. How core nations control finance and power in the modern world system.

Braudel, F.
  1973   *Capitalism and Material Life: 1400–1800.* London: Fontana. The role of the masses in the history of capitalism.
  1992   *Civilization and Capitalism, 15th–18th Century.* Volume III: The Perspective of the World. Berkeley: University of California Press. On the emergence of the world capitalist economy; case histories of European countries and various areas of the rest of the world.

Crosby, A. W., Jr.
  2003   *The Columbian Exchange: Biological and Cultural Consequences of 1492.* Westport, CT: Praeger. Describes how Columbus's voyages opened the way for a major exchange of people, resources, and ideas as the Old and New Worlds were forever joined together.

Diamond, J. M.
  1997   *Guns, Germs, and Steel: The Fates of Human Societies.* New York: W. W. Norton. An ecological approach to expansion and conquest in world history.

Fagan, B. M.
  1998   *Clash of Cultures,* 2nd ed. Walnut Creek, CA: AltaMira. Culture conflicts during European territorial expansion.

Kardulias, P. N.
  1999   *World-Systems Theory in Practice: Leadership, Production, and Exchange.* Lanham, MD: Rowman and Littlefield. Social systems, social change, and economic history in the context of world-system theory.

Kearney, M.
  2004   *Changing Fields of Anthropology: From Local to Global.* Lanham, MD: Rowman and Littlefield. Globalization from a Mexican perspective.

Mintz, S. W.
  1985   *Sweetness and Power: The Place of Sugar in Modern History.* New York: Viking Penguin. The place of sugar in the formation of the modern world system.

Shannon, T. R.
  1996   *An Introduction to the World-System Perspective,* 2nd ed. Boulder, CO: Westview Press. Useful review of world-system theory and developments.

Wallerstein, I. M.
  2004a   *The Decline of American Power: The U.S. in a Chaotic World.* New York: New Press. The reasons behind what Wallerstein sees as a coming U.S. decline within the world system of the 21st century.
  2004b   *World-Systems Analysis: An Introduction.* Durham, NC: Duke University Press. Basics of world-system theory from the master of that approach.

Wolf, E. R.

1982 *Europe and the People without History.* Berkeley: University of California Press. An anthropologist examines the effects of European expansion on tribal peoples and sets forth a world-system approach to anthropology.

Wolf, E. R., with S. Silverman

2001 *Pathways of Power: Building an Anthropology of the Modern World.* Berkeley: University of California Press. Political anthropology for the modern world, a comparative approach.

1. Read the page titled "Life of the Industrial Workers in Nineteenth-Century Britain" by Laura Del Col (**http://www.victorianweb.org/history/workers2.html**). The page contains excerpts from a report generated by a parliamentary panel charged with investigating conditions in British factories.
   a. What were conditions like for workers? What were their lives like? Their work? What were their expectations?
   b. What were the conditions like for children?
   c. In what way are these life stories different from those which might have been told 100 or 200 years earlier in preindustrial Britain?
   d. How are these conditions different from today's Britain? Are there areas of the world where workers might identify with these accounts?
2. Go to the United Nation's Human Development Report (HDR) website: **http://hdr.undp.org/statistics/data/**. At this site you have access to all sorts of data on the countries of the world, which you can retrieve by country, by indicator, or by data tables in the order they were published in the printed version of the HDR. Click on "Data by indicator." Click on "GDP per capita, in US$."

   a. View the countries in terms of their per capita GDP (gross domestic product) in 2002 (right-hand column). Which country has the highest GDP per capita? How do the Arab States compare with the least-developed countries in terms of GDP per capita (see bottom of table)? How about with the United States?
   b. Go back to the home site and click on the "Human Development and Income Growth" animation. Click on "next" at the bottom and view the three dimensions on which the Human Development Index (HDI) is based. What are they?
   c. Go back to the home site and click on "Data by country." Click on "Malaysia, data." How does Malaysia rank on the human poverty index (HPI)? Has Malaysia's Human Development Index been rising or falling since 1975?
   d. Go back to the home site and view data on three countries and indicators of your choice. Compare the three countries in terms of three key indicators.

See Chapter 14 at your McGraw-Hill Online Learning Center for additional review and interactive exercises.

Kottak, *Assault on Paradise*, 4th ed.

When Conrad Kottak revisited Arembepe in 1980, major and dramatic transformations were evident. Three economic changes had enmeshed Arembepe much more strongly in the Brazilian nation and the world capitalist economy: (1) changes in the fishing industry, from wind power to motors, (2) the opening of a paved highway and the rise of tourism, attracting people from all over the world, (3) the construction of a nearby factory and the resulting chemical pollution of Arembepe's waters. Read Chapter 8 and describe how these changes influenced Arembepe's economy and its pattern of socioeconomic stratification.

Peters-Golden, *Culture Sketches*, 4th ed.

This text chapter has discussed consequences of the spread of the industrial world system. Many foraging societies find their ways of life threatened. Two or three decades ago, the Ju/'hoansi maintained much more traditional lifestyles. They now find themselves fully drawn into a market economy, affected not only by institutions like schools and hospitals, but also by militarization, civil war, sedentism, resettlement, and governmental control. In *Culture Sketches* read Chapter 6, "Ju/'hoansi: Reciprocity and Sharing." Which effects of the modern world system are demonstrated in contemporary Ju/'hoansi life? The Ju/'hoansi tradition is one of egalitarianism and reciprocity. It is reported that the Dobe Ju/'hoansi still hold those values above all else. Do you think they can integrate their belief that no one should be denied the necessities of life with the demands of their modern situation? Why or why not?

Knauft, *The Gebusi*, 1st ed.

Read Chapter 7 and the conclusion. Based on Chapter 7, what influences of the modern world system had impacted Gebusi by 1998? How have these changes influenced Gebusi material aspirations? How have they influenced patterns of dominance between outsiders and Gebusi? Based on the conclusion, do you think the Gebusi's history of interaction with the modern world system has been fortunate or not compared with most other non-Western peoples? Why or why not?

15

Colonialism and Development

COLONIALISM

In the last chapter, we saw that after 1870, Europe began a concerted search for markets in Asia and Africa. That process led to European imperialism in Africa, Asia, and Oceania. Imperialism refers to a policy of extending the rule of a nation or empire, such as the British empire, over foreign nations and of taking and holding foreign colonies. **Colonialism** refers to the political, social, economic, and cultural domination of a territory and its people by a foreign power for an extended period of time. The influence of colonialism doesn't disappear just because formal independence has been granted.

OVERVIEW

Imperialism is the policy of extending the rule of a nation or empire over other nations. Colonialism is the long-term domination of a territory and its people by a foreign power. European colonialism had two broad phases. The first spanned the period from 1492 to 1825. The second, more imperialistic, phase ran from 1850 to just after the end of World War II. The British and French colonial empires reached their height around 1914.

Like colonialism, economic development has an intervention philosophy—an ideological justification for outsiders to lead—usually based on the assumption that particular social or economic models are beneficial and universally applicable. Development anthropology focuses on social issues in, and the cultural dimension of, economic development. Culturally compatible and successful development projects try to change just enough, not too much. Motives to change come from people's traditional culture and the small concerns of everyday life. The most productive strategy for change is to base the social design for innovation on traditional social forms in each affected area.

Imperialism

Imperialism goes back to early states, including Egypt in the Old World and the Incas in the New. A Greek empire was forged by Alexander the Great, and Julius Caesar and his successors spread the Roman empire. The term also has been used for more recent examples, including the British, French, and Soviet empires (Scheinman 1980).

If imperialism is almost as old as the state itself, colonialism can be traced back to the ancient Phoenicians, who established colonies along the eastern Mediterranean by 3,000 years

ago. The ancient Greeks and Romans were avid colonizers, as well as empire builders. Modern colonialism began with the European "Age of Discovery"—of the Americas and of a sea route to the Far East. After 1492, European states started founding colonies abroad. In South America, Portugal gained rule over Brazil. The Spanish, the original conquerors of the Aztecs and the Incas, explored the New World widely. They looked to the Caribbean, Mexico, and the southern portions of what was to become the United States, as well as colonizing in Central and South America. In what is now Latin America, especially in areas that had indigenous chiefdoms (e.g., Colombia and Venezuela) and states (e.g., Mexico, Guatemala, Peru, and Bolivia), native populations were large and dense. Today's Latin American population still reflects the intermingling of peoples and cultures during the first phase of colonialism. North of Mexico, indigenous populations were smaller and sparser. Such intermingling is less marked in the United States and Canada than in Latin America.

Rebellions and wars aimed at independence for American nations ended the first phase of European colonialism by the early 19th century. Brazil's independence from Portugal was declared in 1822. By 1825, most of Spain's colonies were politically independent. Spain held on to Cuba and the Philippines until 1898, but otherwise withdrew from the colonial field.

British Colonialism

At its peak about 1914, the British empire covered a fifth of the world's land surface and ruled a fourth of its population (see Figure 15.1). Like several other European nations, Britain had two

For a quiz on colonies throughout history, see the Interactive Exercise
mhhe.com/kottak

See your OLC Internet Exercises for more on the British colonization of the Americas
mhhe.com/kottak

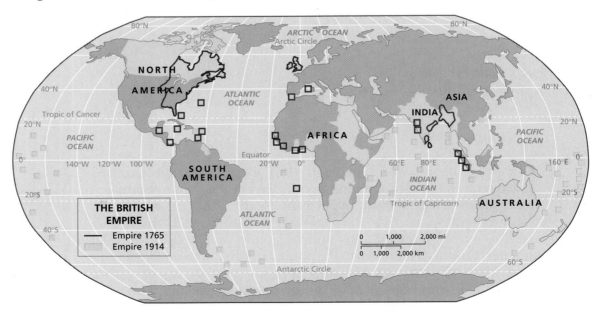

FIGURE 15.1 Map of the British Empire in 1765 and 1914. SOURCE: *Academic American Encyclopedia*, Vol. 3 (Danbury, CT: Grolier, 1998), p. 496.

Prediction Tool Puts Development in Hands of Locals

NATIONAL GEOGRAPHIC NEWS BRIEF

by John Roach
March 24, 2004

For Indonesia's poorest province, Papua, on the island of New Guinea, conservationists have introduced an innovative software program designed to assist local people in guiding their homeland toward sustainable development. The program allows local people to make informed judgments, based on anticipation and discussion of the likely effects of their decisions on their communities. Development anthropologists assume that motives to change come from people's traditional culture and the small concerns of everyday life. The software discussed here inputs cultural, social, and environmental, as well as economic, data in modeling potential development. This approach is unlike traditional economic development, which, like colonialism, has typically tried to impose an outsider's vision or blueprint, based on a particular intervention philosophy, on local people.

Indonesia's poorest province, Papua, is a natural-resource trove that is both awaiting exploitation and begging for protection. Conservationists hope an innovative software program will help residents guide the province to sustainable development. The program essentially allows local people to predict the effects of their civic decisions . . . on their communities.

"Papua significantly contributes to Indonesia's status as one of the biologically richest countries in the world," said Dessy Anggraeni, a resource economist in Indonesia with the Washington, D.C.-based environmental organization Conservation International (CI). "But its people are also among the poorest in Indonesia." . . .

To many people, Papua's lush forests of old-growth timber, latent precious metals, and untapped reserves of oil and natural gas are the answer to the province's poverty woes. But environmentalists have long argued against large-scale resource extraction, saying it benefits big, multinational corporations and leaves locals impoverished.

To determine if there is a way to alleviate the poverty of Papuans without irreparably harming the environment, CI has brought a planning tool, called Threshold 21, to Papua. The tool is a computerized development model that helps stakeholders and decision makers create and analyze strategies for the future.

"It won't predict the future, but it's the best way of getting a consistent idea of where things will lead," said John Shilling, a senior advisor with the Millennium Institute in Arlington, Virginia. With his colleagues, Shilling has worked over the past 20 years to develop the model.

Already customized for more than 15 different countries and regions around the world, CI recently asked the Millennium Institute to develop a version of Threshold 21 for Papua. Ultimately, CI hopes that Papuans will take control of the model and use it to chart their own course . . .

A deciding factor in CI's choice of Threshold 21 was the model's embrace of environmental and social factors in addition to economic factors as it analyzes any given strategy for the future.

The result of this integrated, three-pillar approach creates what the Millennium Institute says is a more "comprehensive" picture of what happens when one path is chosen over another. And that picture comes with all the details of how it was put together, a concept referred to as transparency.

For example, a local group in Bangladesh wanted to limit education to only men. So, using Threshold 21, they theoretically took women out of the schools and ran the computer program to find out what would happen. Shilling said that some things, like a reduction in gross domestic product and higher fertility rates, were predictable outcomes. But the local group was surprised to learn that by taking women out of the schools, male life expectancy went down. Since the model is transparent, they tracked back to find out why.

■ *Of various development scenarios, an urban development plan did the most to reduce poverty while also protecting the environment. These Papuan women are returning from a market town.*

"It turns out that women are significant health care providers," Shilling said. "If they are not educated, the health of the whole family declines." . . .

In the case of the model being developed for Papua, CI has a vision of poverty reduction and economic development for the local people. At the same time, they want to protect the environment, a goal the organization says is consistent with the challenges faced by the province's decentralized government . . .

The modelers solicit information from as many local everyday people and decision-makers as possible—specific data on the economy, the social structure, and the environment. With the data, the modelers prep the computer program to model the impact of strategies for future development.

"It is using the best information available," Shilling said. "It lays out a range of plausible scenarios and their implications so decision-makers have the best estimates on which to make their decisions. And it is transparent about the assumptions and the positive and negative outcomes." . . .

CI chose four widely discussed development strategies for Papua to run through the model as a means to demonstrate the model's effectiveness: keeping the status quo, a major roadbuilding and logging initiative, a major dambuilding and mining initiative, and a locally focused urban development initiative.

According to CI's analysis of the outcomes, the urban development initiative proved the best at providing poverty alleviation as well as protecting the environment, whereas the other scenarios led to greater environmental degradation with most of the money from resource extraction going to foreign investors and foreign workers.

Anggraeni said the goal of running the scenarios was not meant to dictate specific development paths. The goal was to impart this approach and method to local planners and other residents. Then they could use the approach to analyze the effects of several widely discussed scenarios and come up with their own agreed strategy. Feedback from the two workshops held so far suggests CI's plan is working.

"Indeed, most of the participants are really enthusiastic to discuss the results of the model and the model itself," Anggraeni said.

SOURCE: John Roach, "Prediction Tool Puts Development in Hands of Locals," *National Geographic News*, March 24, 2004. National Geographic Society. http://news.nationalgeographic.com/news/2004/03/0324_040324_indonesia.html.

Bringing It All Together

See the "Bringing It All Together" essay that immediately follows the chapter "Language and Communication" for information on Canada's Anglo-French heritage.

stages of colonialism. The first began with the Elizabethan voyages of the 16th century. During the seventeenth century, Britain acquired most of the eastern coast of North America, Canada's St. Lawrence basin, islands in the Caribbean, slave stations in Africa, and interests in India.

The British shared the exploration of the New World with the Spanish, Portuguese, French, and Dutch. The British by and large left Mexico, along with Central and South America, to the Spanish and the Portuguese. The end of the Seven Years' War in 1763 forced a French retreat from most of Canada and India, where France had previously competed with Britain (Cody 1998; Farr 1980).

The American revolution ended the first stage of British colonialism. A second colonial empire, on which the "sun never set," rose from the ashes of the first. Beginning in 1788, but intensifying after 1815, the British settled Australia. Britain had acquired Dutch South Africa by 1815. The establishment of Singapore in 1819 provided a base for a British trade network that extended to much of South Asia and along the coast of China. By this time, the empires of Britain's traditional rivals, particularly Spain, had been severely diminished in scope. Britain's position as imperial power and the world's leading industrial nation was unchallenged (Cody 1998; Farr 1980).

During the Victorian era (1837–1901), as Britain's acquisition of territory and of further trading concessions continued, Prime Minister Benjamin Disraeli implemented a foreign policy justified by a view of imperialism as shouldering "the white man's burden"—a phrase coined by the poet Rudyard Kipling. People in the empire were seen as unable to govern themselves, so that British guidance was needed to civilize and Christianize them. This paternalistic and racist doctrine served to legitimize Britain's acquisition and control of parts of central Africa and Asia (Cody 1998).

After World War II, the British empire began to fall apart, with nationalist movements for independence. India became independent in 1947, as did Ireland in 1949. Decolonization in Africa and Asia accelerated during the late 1950s. Today, the ties that remain between Britain and its former colonies are mainly linguistic or cultural rather than political (Cody 1998).

French Colonialism

French colonialism also had two phases. The first began in the early 1600s. The second came late in the 19th century. This was the French manifestation of a more general European imperialism that followed the spread of industrialization and the search for new markets, raw materials, and cheap labor. However, compared with Great Britain, where the drive for profit led expansion, French colonialism was spurred more by the state, church, and armed forces than by business interests. Prior to the French Revolution, in 1789, missionaries, explorers, and traders had led French expansion. They carved niches for France in Canada, the Louisiana territory, and several Caribbean islands, along with parts of India, which were lost, along with Canada (New France), to Great Britain in 1763. By 1815, only West Indian sugar islands and scattered African and Asian posts remained under French control (Harvey 1980).

The foundations of the second French empire were established between 1830 and 1870. France acquired Algeria and part of what eventually became Indochina. Like Britain, France rode a post-1870 wave of new imperialism. By 1914, the French empire covered 4 million square miles and included some 60 million people (see Figure 15.2). By 1893, French rule had been fully established in Indochina, and Tunisia and Morocco became French protectorates (Harvey 1980).

To be sure, the French, like the British, had substantial business interests in their colonies. But they also sought, again like the British, international glory and prestige. The French intervention philosophy was that of a *mission civilisatrice,* their equivalent of Britain's "white man's burden." The goal was to implant French culture, language, and religion—in the form of Roman Catholicism—throughout the colonies (Harvey 1980).

The French used two forms of colonial rule. They used *indirect rule,* governing through native leaders and established political structures, in

areas with long histories of state organization, such as Morocco and Tunisia. They brought *direct rule* by French officials to many areas of Africa. Here, the French imposed new government structures to control diverse tribes and cultures, many of them previously stateless. Like the British empire, the French empire began to disintegrate after World War II. France fought long—and ultimately futile—wars to keep its empire intact in Indochina and Algeria (Harvey 1980).

Colonialism and Identity

Many geopolitical labels in the news today had no equivalent meaning before colonialism. Whole countries, along with social groups and divisions

On January 1, 1900 a British officer in India receives a pedicure from a servant. What does this photo say to you about colonialism? Who gives pedicures in your society?

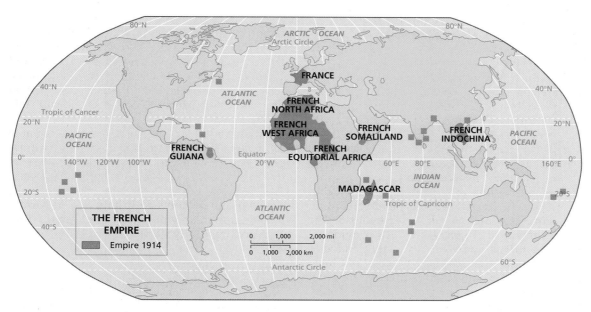

FIGURE 15.2 Map of the French Empire at Its Height around 1914. SOURCE: *Academic American Encyclopedia,* Vol. 8 (Danbury, CT: Grolier, 1998), p. 309.

within them, were colonial inventions. In West Africa, for example, by geographic logic, several adjacent countries could be one (Togo, Ghana, Côte d'Ivoire, Guinea, Guinea-Bissau, Sierra Leone, Liberia) (Figure 15.3). Instead, they are separated by linguistic, political, and economic contrasts promoted under colonialism.

Hundreds of ethnic groups and "tribes" are colonial constructions (see Ranger 1996). The Sukuma of Tanzania, for instance, were first registered as a single tribe by the colonial administration. Then missionaries standardized a series of dialects into a single Sukuma language as they translated the Bible and other religious texts. Thereafter, those texts were taught in missionary schools, and to European foreigners and other non-Sukuma speakers. Over time, this standardized the Sukuma language and ethnicity (Finnstrom 1997).

As in much of East Africa, in Rwanda and Burundi, farmers and herders live in the same areas and speak the same language. Historically, they have shared the same social world, although their social organization is "extremely hierarchical," almost "castelike" (Malkki 1995, p. 24). There has been a tendency to see the pastoral Tutsis as superior to the agricultural Hutus. Tutsis have been presented as nobles, Hutus as commoners. Yet when distributing identity cards in Rwanda, the Belgian colonizers simply identified all people with more than 10 head of cattle as Tutsi. Owners of fewer cattle were registered as Hutus (Bjuremalm 1997). Years later, these arbitrary colonial registers were used systematically for "ethnic" identification during the mass killings (genocide) that took place in Rwanda in 1994.

Postcolonial Studies

In anthropology, history, and literature, the field of postcolonial studies has gained prominence since the 1970s (see Ashcroft, Griffiths, and Tiffin 1989; Cooper and Stoler, eds. 1997). **Postcolonial** refers to the study of the interactions between European nations and the societies they colonized (mainly after 1800). In 1914, European empires, which broke up after World War II, ruled more than 85 percent of the world (Petraglia-Bahri 1996). The term *postcolonial* also has been used to describe the second half of the 20th century in general, the period succeeding colonialism. Even more generically, "postcolonial" may be used to signify a position against imperialism and Eurocentrism (Petraglia-Bahri 1996).

The former colonies (*postcolonies*) can be divided into settler, nonsettler, and mixed (Petraglia-Bahri 1996). The settler countries, with large numbers of European colonists and sparser native populations, include Australia and Canada. Examples of nonsettler countries include India, Pakistan, Bangladash, Sri Lanka, Malaysia, Indonesia, Nigeria, Senegal, Madagascar, and Jamaica. All these had substantial native populations and relatively few European settlers. Mixed countries include South Africa, Zimbabwe, Kenya (photo on page 555), and Algeria. Such countries had significant European settlement despite having sizable native populations.

FIGURE 15.3 Small West African Nations Created by Colonialism.

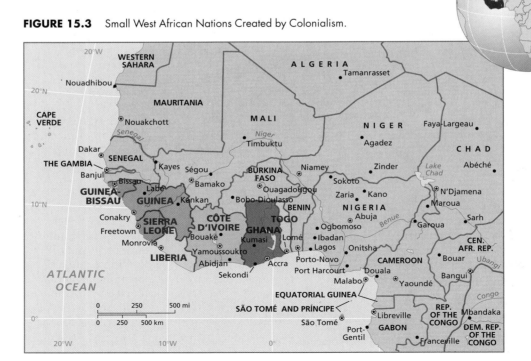

Given the varied experiences of such countries, "postcolonial" has to be a loose term. The United States, for instance, was colonized by Europeans and fought a war for independence from Britain. Is the United States a postcolony? It isn't usually perceived as such, given its current world power position, its treatment of native Americans (sometimes called internal colonization), and its annexation of other parts of the world (Petraglia-Bahri 1996). Research in postcolonial studies is growing, permitting a wide-ranging investigation of power relations in varied contexts. Broad topics in the field include the formation of an empire, the impact of colonization, and the state of the postcolony today (Petraglia-Bahri 1996).

Here are some common questions addressed in postcolonial studies: How did colonization affect colonized people—and their colonizers? How did colonial powers manage to subjugate so much of the world? How did people in the colonies resist colonial control? How have cultures and identities been affected by colonization? How do gender, race, and class function in colonial and postcolonial settings? How have colonial education systems influenced the postcolonies? With regard to literature, should postcolonial writers use a colonial language, like English or French, to reach a wider audience? Or should they write in their native language, to reach others in the postcolony? Finally, are new forms of imperialism, such as development and globalization, replacing old ones? (Petraglia-Bahri 1996).

DEVELOPMENT

During the Industrial Revolution, a strong current of thought viewed industrialization as a beneficial process of organic development and progress. Many economists still assume that industrialization increases production and income. They seek to create in Third World ("developing") countries a process—*economic development*—like the one that first occurred spontaneously in 18th-century Great Britain. Economic development generally aims at getting people to convert from subsistence to cash economies and thus to increase local participation in the world capitalist economy.

We just saw that Great Britain used the "white man's burden" to justify its imperialist expansion. Similarly, France claimed to be involved in a *mission civilisatrice*, a civilizing mission, in its colonies. Both of these ideas illustrate an **intervention philosophy,** an ideological justification for outsiders to guide in specific directions. Economic development plans also have intervention philosophies. John Bodley (1988) argues that the basic belief behind interventions—whether by colonialists, missionaries, governments, or development planners—has been the same for more

■ What traces of colonialism do you detect in this photo, taken recently at the Jockey Club in Nairobi, Kenya? What story is the photo telling you?

than 100 years. This belief is that industrialization, modernization, westernization, and individualism are desirable evolutionary advances and that development schemes that promote them will bring long-term benefits to local people. In a more extreme form, intervention philosophy may pit the assumed wisdom of enlightened colonial or other First World planners against the purported conservatism, ignorance, or "obsolescence" of "inferior" local people.

Neoliberalism

A recent and dominant intervention philosophy is neoliberalism. The term encompasses a set of assumptions and economic policies that have become widespread during the last 25 to 30 years and that are being implemented in capitalist and developing nations, including postsocialist societies. Neoliberalism is a new form of the old economic liberalism laid out in Adam Smith's famous capitalist manifesto, *The Wealth of Nations,* published in 1776, soon after the Industrial Revolution. Smith advocated laissez-faire economics as the basis of capitalism: The government should stay out of its nation's economic affairs. Free trade, Smith thought, was the best way for a nation's economy to develop. There should be no restrictions on manufacturing, no barriers to commerce, and no tariffs. Such ideas were "liberal" in the sense of advocating no controls. Economic liberalism encouraged "free" enterprise and competition, with the goal of generating profits. (Note the difference between this meaning of *liberal* and the one that has been popularized on American talk radio, in which "liberal" is used—usually as a derogatory term—as the opposite of "conservative." Ironically, Adam Smith's liberalism is today's capitalist "conservatism.")

For more on development efforts, see the Virtual Exploration
mhhe.com/kottak

Economic liberalism prevailed in the United States until President Franklin Roosevelt's New Deal during the 1930s. The Great Depression produced a turn to Keynesian economics, which challenged liberalism. John Maynard Keynes (1927, 1936) insisted that full employment was necessary for capitalism to grow, that governments and central banks should intervene to increase employment, and that government should promote the common good.

Especially since the fall of Communism (1989–1991), there has been a revival of economic liberalism, now known as neoliberalism, which has been spreading globally. Around the world, neoliberal policies have been imposed by powerful financial institutions such as the International Monetary Fund (IMF), the World Bank, and the Inter-American Development Bank (see Edelman and Haugerud 2004). In many developing countries, corruption in state-controlled industries has been an overwhelming problem, and free markets have been seen as a way out.

Neoliberalism differs little from Adam Smith's original idea that governments should not regulate private enterprise and market forces. Neoliberalism entails open (tariff and barrier free) international trade and investment. Profits are sought through lowering of costs, whether through improved productivity, laying off workers, or seeking workers who accept lower wages. To obtain loans, the governments of postsocialist and developing nations have been required to accept the neoliberal premise that deregulation leads to economic growth, which eventually will benefit everyone through a process sometimes called "trickle down." Accompanying the belief in free markets and the idea of cutting costs is a tendency to impose austerity measures that cut government expenses. This means reduced public spending on education, health care, and other social services (Martinez and Garcia 2000). Throughout the world, neoliberal policies have promoted deregulation and privatization—the sale to private investors of state-owned enterprises, such as banks, key industries, railroads, toll highways, utilities, schools, hospitals, and even fresh water. With its characteristic capitalist focus on individualism, neoliberalism places more emphasis on "individual responsibility" than on "the common good." The effects of neoliberal policies vary among countries. In some nations, social programs are negligible to begin with, and health care benefits go mainly to the elites.

THE SECOND WORLD

Remember from the chapter "Ethnicity and Race" that the labels "First World," "Second World," and "Third World" represent a com-mon, although ethnocentric, way of categorizing nations. *First World* refers to the "democratic West"—traditionally conceived as being in opposition to a "Second World" ruled by "communism." *Second World* refers to the Warsaw Pact nations, including the former Soviet Union and the socialist and once-socialist countries of Eastern Europe and Asia. Proceeding with this classification, the "less-developed countries" or "developing nations" make up the *Third World*, to which we turn after a discussion of Communism and its fall.

Communism

The two meanings of communism involve how it is written, whether with a lowercase (small) or a capital (large) *c*. Small-*c* **communism** describes a social system in which property is owned by the community and in which people work for the common good. Large-*C* **Communism** was a political movement and doctrine seeking to overthrow capitalism and establish a form of communism such as that which prevailed in the Soviet Union (USSR) from 1917 to 1991. The heyday of Communism was a 40-year period from 1949 to 1989 when more Communist regimes existed than at any time before or after. By the year 2000, there were only five Communist states left, including China, Cuba, Laos, North Korea, and Vietnam, compared with 23 in 1985. For Communists the term *Communism* has meant both an international movement dedicated to the overthrow of capitalism and a classless future society. What Americans called Communist systems were called socialist by the Communists themselves, as in the Union of Soviet Socialist Republics. (*Socialism* is a political-economic theory advocating that land, natural resources, and major industries should be owned by society as a whole. Social democratic parties in many nations have sought to achieve this goal through democratic elections.)

Communism, which originated with Russia's Bolshevik Revolution in 1917, and took its inspiration from Karl Marx and Friedrich Engels, was not uniform over time or among countries. All Communist systems were authoritarian (promoting obedience to authority rather than individual freedom). Many were totalitarian (banning rival parties and demanding total submission of the individual to the state.) Several features distinguished Communist societies from other authoritarian regimes (e.g., Spain under Franco) and from socialism of a social democratic type. First, the Communist party monopolized power in every Communist state. Second, relations within the party were highly centralized and strictly disciplined. Third, Communist nations had state ownership, rather than private ownership, of the means of production. Finally, all Communist regimes, with the goal of advancing communism,

Before and after communism. Above: on May Day (May 1, 1975), large photos of Politburo members (Communist party leaders) adorn buildings in Moscow. Below: on January 31, 2006 in a Moscow electronics store, a potential customer considers a display of TV sets, broadcasting live the annual press conference of Russian President Vladimir Putin.

cultivated a sense of belonging to an international movement (Brown 2001).

Social scientists have tended to refer to such societies as socialist rather than Communist. Today there is a great deal of research by anthropologists and others on postsocialist societies—those that once emphasized bureaucratic redistribution of wealth according to a central plan (Verdery 2001). In the postsocialist period, states that once had planned economies have been following the neoliberal agenda by divesting themselves of state-owned resources in favor of privatization. These societies in transition are undergoing democratization and marketization. Some common problems of the transition have included (1) the rise of nationalism, in the form of ethnic-religious minorities, (2) corruption, (3) unemployment and poverty, and (4) difficulties in establishing new values, social relations, and groups. Some of these societies have moved toward formal liberal democracy, with political parties, elections, and a balance of powers (Grekova 2001).

Postsocialist Transitions

Neoliberal economists assumed that dismantling the Soviet Union's planned economy would raise GDP (gross domestic product) and living standards. The goal was to enhance production by substituting a decentralized market system and providing incentives through privatization. In October 1991, Boris Yeltsin, who had been elected president of Russia that June, announced a program of radical market-oriented reform, pursuing a changeover to capitalism. Yeltsin's program of "shock therapy" cut subsidies to farms and industries and ended price controls. Since then, postsocialist Russia has faced many problems. The anticipated gains in productivity did not materialize. After the fall of the Soviet Union, Russia's GDP fell by half. Poverty increased, with a quarter of the population now living below the poverty line. Life expectancy and the birth rate also declined. Let's look more closely at two problems mentioned above as common to postsocialist transitions: ethnic/religious nationalism and corruption.

Ethnic/Religious Nationalism

In the chapter "Ethnicity and Race" we saw how Russians dominated the former Soviet Union. Ethnic minorities had only limited self-rule in republics and regions controlled by Moscow. To cement Soviet rule Russian colonists were sent to many areas, such as Tajikistan (see Figure 15.4), to diminish the cohesion and clout of the local people. Tajikistan is a small, poor state (and former Soviet republic) in central Asia, bordering Afghanistan. In Tajikistan, as in central Asia generally, most people are Muslims. Since the fall of the Soviet empire, Islam, as an alternative way of ordering spiritual and social life, has been replacing socialist ideology. This follows more than 70 years of official atheism and suppression of religion. Although the Soviets destroyed mosques and discouraged religious practice, Islam survived in homes, around the kitchen table, and so it has been called "kitchen Islam." When the Russians left Tajikistan, the force of Russian culture and language receded. Islamic influence has grown, with more and more people speaking and praying in Tajik, a language related to Persian (which is spoken in Iran) (Erlanger 1992).

Compared with Tajikistan, the postsocialist transition was much more violent in Yugoslavia, whose breakup was examined in the chapter "Ethnicity and Race." The Socialist Federal Republic of Yugoslavia was a nonaligned country outside the USSR. Yugoslavia's disintegration took place in the wake of the dramatic collapse of Communism throughout Eastern Europe in fall 1989. The spirit of change spread rapidly in Yugoslavia, offering the prospect of democracy and freedom. In Bosnia, one of Yugoslavia's republics, the fall of Communism seemed to herald the free expression of religion without the fear of accusations of Muslim nationalism or "fundamentalism." Under Communism it had been difficult for Bosnian Muslims to combine their duties as workers in a factory or shop with those of devout Muslims. Having a job and working for the state kept Muslims from performing their ritual obligations. There were no officially recognized times or places for prayer and rituals (Bringa 1995).

In 1989 few Yugoslavs foresaw that the end of Communism would also mean the end of their country. Well into 1990, Yugoslavia's federal government continued to enjoy widespread support. After Yugoslavia's Communist party disbanded in January 1990, the opening toward political pluralism proceeded rapidly. During the first months of 1990, dozens of new political parties were formed. The scheduling of elections for April and May in the republics of Slovenia and Croatia provided less than four months to select the first post-Communist governments. By the end of 1990, nationalist parties had won elections in the republics. A series of secessions began, and the federal government lost its electoral base. Just two years separated the end of 1989, with its expectation of democratic change, and the end of 1991, when the European Community decided to recognize the seceded republics as independent states. An ethnic war that began in Croatia shortly thereafter then engulfed Bosnia (Bower 2000).

This first war in Europe in almost 50 years generated tremendous interest in the region. Media coverage took two approaches. The first assumed the various ethnic groups in Bosnia had always hated each other. Whatever tolerance and coexistence had existed there previously had been imposed by the Communist regime. The second was an idealized view that Bosnia previously had been a harmonious multicultural society. Its problems originated mainly with the fall of Communism and the collapse of the federal government, due in part to the imposition of neoliberal austerity measures (Bringa 1995).

Corruption

Corruption has been mentioned as a second common problem in postsocialist nations. Since 1996, the World Bank and other international organiza-

FIGURE 15.4 Former Soviet Socialist Republics of Central Asia, Including Tajikistan.

tions have launched anticorruption programs worldwide. *Corruption* is defined as the abuse of public office for private gain. The World Bank's approach to corruption assumes, erroneously, that the state (public)–private dichotomy is universal and takes a similar form in all societies. (This illustrates the fallacy of underdifferentiation, as discussed later in this chapter.)

According to Janine Wedel (2002), postsocialist states, which now, guided by neoliberalism, are divesting themselves of state-owned resources, provide rich contexts in which to explore diversity and flux in state–private relationships. The societies feature competition for influence at the intersection of the public and private spheres. For example, in Poland there are informal circles of people (dubbed "institutional nomads") whose primary loyalty is to their circle rather than to the formal positions they occupy (in government, business, or wherever). The Russian "clan," as Olga Kryshtanovskaya (1997) describes it, is a similar informal group of elites whose members promote their mutual interests. These informal groups place their members in formal positions in order to advantage their "clan." They maximize their influence by bridging and blending the spheres of public and private.

The anthropologist Alexei Yurchak (2002) describes two spheres within the contemporary Russian state. We'll call them the official-public and the personal-public. They refer to different systems that coexist and sometimes overlap. State officials may respect the law (official-public), while also working with informal or even criminal groups (personal-public). Officials switch from official-public to personal-public behavior all the time, in order to accomplish specific tasks.

Consider an illustrative case from Poland. A man selling an apartment he had inherited was to pay a huge sum in taxes. He visited the state tax office, where a bureaucrat informed him of how much he was being assessed (official-public). She also told him how to avoid paying it (personal-public). He followed her advice and saved a lot of money. The man did not know the bureaucrat personally. She didn't expect anything in return, and he didn't offer anything. She said she routinely offers such help.

What is legal (official-public) and what is considered morally correct don't necessarily correspond. The bureaucrat just described seemed still to be operating under the old communist notion that state property (tax dollars in this case) belongs both to everyone and to no one. For a further illustration of this view of state property, imagine two people working in the same state-owned construction enterprise. To take home for private use materials belonging to the enterprise (that is, to everyone and no one) is morally acceptable. No one will fault you for it, because "everyone does it." However, if a fellow worker comes along and takes materials someone else had planned to take home, that is considered stealing, and morally wrong (Wedel 2002). In evaluating charges of corruption, anthropologists such as Janine Wedel (2002) are well aware that property notions and spheres of official action in postsocialist societies are in transition.

In postsocialist and developing nations, as well as in contemporary North America, the neoliberal agenda has included the promotion of **civil society.** This concept refers to voluntary collective action around shared interests, goals, and values. Civil society encompasses such organizations as NGOs (nongovernmental organizations), registered charities, community groups, women's organizations, faith-based and professional groups, trade unions, self-help groups, social movements, business associations, coalitions, and advocacy groups. In theory, civil society is distinct from the state, family, and market. In practice, those boundaries are often complex, blurred, and negotiated, as we just saw in the discussion of institutional nomads and Russian "clans" in postsocialist societies (London School of Economics 2004).

DEVELOPMENT ANTHROPOLOGY

Applied anthropology, already examined in Chapter 2, refers to the application of anthropological perspectives, theory, methods, and data to identify, assess, and solve social problems. **Development anthropology** is the branch of applied anthropology that focuses on social issues in, and the cultural dimension of, economic development. Development anthropologists do not just carry out development policies planned by others; they also plan and guide policy. (For more detailed discussions of issues in development anthropology, see Escobar [1995], Ferguson [1994], and Robertson [1995].)

However, ethical dilemmas often confront development anthropologists (Escobar 1991, 1995). Our respect for cultural diversity is often offended because efforts to extend industry and technology may entail profound cultural changes. Foreign aid doesn't usually go where need and suffering are greatest. It is spent on political, economic, and strategic priorities as international donors, political leaders, and powerful interest groups perceive them. Planners' interests don't always coincide with the best interests of the local people.

Although the aim of most development projects is to enhance the quality of life, living standards often decline in the target area (Bodley, ed. 1988).

Studying people at the local level, enthnographers have a unique view of the impact of national and international development planning on intended "beneficiaries." Local-level research often reveals inadequacies in the measures that economists use to assess development and a nation's economic health. For example, per capita income and gross national product don't measure the distribution of wealth. Because the first is an average and the second is a total, they may rise as the rich get richer and the poor get poorer.

Today, many government agencies, international groups, NGOs, and private foundations encourage attention to local-level social factors and the cultural dimension of economic development, as we saw in the "News Brief" at the beginning of this chapter. Anthropological expertise in economic development planning is important because social problems can doom even potentially beneficial projects to failure. A study of 50 economic development projects (Lance and McKenna 1975) judged only 21 to be successes. Social and cultural incompatabilities had doomed most of the failed projects.

For example, a 1981 anthropological study of a multimillion-dollar development project in Madagascar uncovered several reasons for its failure. The project had been planned and funded by the World Bank in the late 1960s. The planners (no anthropologists among them) anticipated none of the problems that emerged. The project was aimed at draining and irrigating a large plain to increase rice production. Its goal was to raise production through machinery and double cropping—growing two crops annually on the same plot. However, the planners disregarded several things, including the unavailability of spare parts and fuel for the machines. The designers also ignored the fact, well known to anthropologists, that cross-culturally, intensive cultivation is associated with dense populations. If there are no machines to do the work, there have to be people around to do it. However, population densities in the project area were much too low to support intensive cultivation without modern machinery.

The planners should have known that labor and machinery for the project were unavailable. Furthermore, many local people were understandably hostile toward the project because it gave their ancestral land away to outsiders. (Unfortunately, this is a common occurrence in development projects.) Many land-grant recipients were members of regional and national elites. They used their influence to get fields that were intended for poor farmers. The project also suffered from technical problems. The foreign firm hired to dig the irrigation canals dug them lower than the land they had to irrigate. The water couldn't flow up into the fields.

Millions of development dollars could have been spent more wisely if anthropologists, consulting with local farmers, had helped plan, implement, and monitor the project. It stands to reason that experts, such as anthropologists, who are familiar with the language and customs of a country can better evaluate prospects of project success than can those who are not. Accordingly, anthropologists increasingly work in organizations that promote, manage, and assess programs that influence human life in the United States and abroad.

The Greening of Java

Anthropologist Richard Franke (1977) conducted a classic study of discrepancies between goals and results in a scheme to promote social and economic change in Java, Indonesia (Figure 15.5). Experts and planners in the 1960s and 1970s assumed that as small-scale farmers got modern technology and more productive crop varieties,

FIGURE 15.5 Location of Java (yellow) in Indonesia (orange).

An anthropological study of an irrigated rice project in Madagascar found several reasons why it failed. If there are no machines to do the work, there have to be people around to do it—like these Betsileo women who are transplanting rice in the traditional manner.

their lives would improve. The media publicized new, high-yielding varieties of wheat, maize, and rice. These new crops, along with chemical fertilizers, pesticides, and new cultivation techniques, were hailed as the basis of a **green revolution.** This "revolution" was expected to increase the world's food supply and thus improve the diets and living conditions of victims of poverty, particularly in land-scarce, overcrowded regions.

The green revolution was an economic success. It did increase the global food supply. New strains of wheat and rice doubled or tripled farm supplies in many Third World countries. Thanks to the green revolution, world food prices declined by more than 20 percent during the 1980s (Stevens 1992). But its social effects were not what its advocates had intended, as we learn from Javanese experience.

Java received a genetic cross between rice strains from Taiwan and Indonesia—a high-yielding "miracle" rice known as IR-8. This hybrid could raise the productivity of a given plot by at least half. Governments throughout southern Asia, including Indonesia, encouraged the cultivation of IR-8, along with the use of chemical fertilizers and pesticides.

The Indonesian island of Java, one of the most densely populated places in the world (over 2,000 people per square mile), was a prime target for the green revolution. Java's total crop was insufficient to supply its people with minimal daily requirements of calories (2,150) and protein (55 grams). In 1960, Javanese agriculture supplied 1,950 calories and 38 grams of protein per capita. By 1967, these already inadequate figures had fallen to 1,750 calories and 33 grams. Could miracle rice, by increasing crop yields 50 percent, reverse the trend?

■ *Many Asian governments have promoted the cultivation of new rice varieties, along with the use of chemical fertilizers and pesticides. What costs and benefits may accompany such changes? Shown here is Vietnam's Can Tho Rice Research Institute.*

Java shares with many other underdeveloped nations a history of socioeconomic stratification and colonialism. Indigenous contrasts in wealth and power were intensified by Dutch colonialism. Although Indonesia gained political independence from the Netherlands in 1949, internal stratification continued. Today, contrasts between the wealthy (government employees, businesspeople, large landowners) and the poor (small-scale peasants) exist even in small farming communities. Stratification led to problems during Java's green revolution.

In 1963, the University of Indonesia's College of Agriculture launched a program in which students went to live in villages. They worked with peasants in the fields and shared their knowledge of new agricultural techniques while learning from the peasants. The program was a success. Yields in the affected villages increased by half. The program, directed by the Department of Agriculture, was expanded in 1964; nine universities and 400 students joined. These intervention programs succeeded where others had failed because the outside agents recognized that economic development rests not only on technological change but on political change as well. Students could observe firsthand how interest groups resisted attempts by peasants to improve their lot. Once, when local officials stole fertilizer destined for peasant fields, students got it back

by threatening in a letter to turn evidence of the crime over to higher-level officials.

The combination of new work patterns and political action was achieving promising results when, in 1965–1966, there was an insurrection against the government. In the eventual military takeover, Indonesia's President Sukarno was ousted and replaced by President Suharto, who ruled Indonesia until 1998. Efforts to increase agricultural production resumed soon after Suharto took control. However, the new government assigned the task to multinational corporations based in Japan, West Germany, and Switzerland rather than to students and peasants. These industrial firms were to supply miracle rice and other high-yielding seeds, fertilizers, and pesticides. Peasants adopting the whole green revolution kit were eligible for loans that would allow them to buy food and other essentials in the lean period just before harvesting.

Java's green revolution soon encountered problems. One pesticide, which had never been tested in Java, killed the fish in the irrigation canals and thus destroyed an important protein resource. Java's green revolution also encountered problems at the village level because of entrenched interests. Traditionally, peasants had fed their families by taking temporary jobs, or borrowing, from wealthier villagers before the harvest. However, having accepted loans, the peasants were obliged to work for wages lower than those paid on the open market. Low-interest loans would have made peasants less dependent on wealthy villagers, thus depriving local patrons of cheap labor.

Local officials were put in charge of spreading information about how the program worked. Instead, they limited peasant participation by withholding information. Wealthy villagers also discouraged peasant participation more subtly: They raised doubts about the effectiveness of the new techniques and about the wisdom of taking government loans when familiar patrons were nearby. Faced with the thought that starvation might follow if innovation failed, peasants were reluctant to take risks—an understandable reaction.

Production increased, but wealthy villagers rather than small-scale farmers reaped the benefits of the green revolution. Just 20 percent of one village's 151 households participated in the program. However, because they were the wealthiest households, headed by people who owned the most land, 40 percent of the land was being cultivated by means of the new system. Some large-scale landowners used their green revolution profits at the peasants' expense. They bought up peasants' small plots and purchased labor-saving machinery, including rice-milling machines and tractors. As a result, the poorest peasants lost both their means of subsistence—land—and local work opportunities. Their only recourse was to move to cities, where a growing pool of unskilled laborers depressed already low wages.

In a complementary view of the green revolution's social effects, Ann Stoler (1977) focused on gender and stratification. She took issue with Esther Boserup's (1970) contention that colonialism and development inevitably hurt Third World women more than men by favoring commercial agriculture and excluding women from farming. Stoler found that the green revolution had permitted some women to gain power over other women and men. Javanese women were not a homogeneous group but varied by class. Stoler found that whether the green revolution helped or harmed Javanese women depended on their position in the class structure. The status of landholding women rose as they gained control over more land and the labor of more poor women. The new economy offered wealthier women higher profits, which they used in trading. However, poor women suffered along with poor men as traditional economic opportunities declined. Nevertheless, the poor women fared better than did the poor men, who had no access at all to off-farm work.

These studies of the local effects of the green revolution reveal results different from those foreseen by policy makers, planners, and the media. We see the unintended and undesirable effects of development programs that ignore traditional social, political, and economic divisions. New technology, no matter how promising, does not inevitably help the intended beneficiaries. It may very well hurt them if vested interests interfere. The Javanese student–peasant projects of the 1960s worked because peasants need not just technology but also political clout. This ambitious development program in Java, although designed to alleviate poverty, actually increased it. Peasants stopped relying on their own subsistence production and started depending on a more volatile pursuit— cash sale of labor. Agricultural production became profit-oriented, machine-based, and chemical-dependent. Local autonomy diminished as linkages with the world system increased. Production rose, as the rich got richer and poverty increased.

Equity

A commonly stated goal of recent development policy is to promote equity. **Increased equity** means reduced poverty and a more even distribution of wealth. However, if projects are to increase equity, they must have the support of reform-minded governments. Wealthy and powerful people typically resist projects that threaten their vested interests.

Some types of development projects, particularly irrigation schemes, are more likely than others to widen wealth disparities, that is, to have a negative equity impact. An initial uneven distribu-

tion of resources (particularly land) often becomes the basis for greater skewing after the project. The social impact of new technology tends to be more severe, contributing negatively to quality of life and to equity, when inputs are channeled to or through the rich, as in Java's green revolution.

Many fisheries projects also have had negative equity results. In Bahia, Brazil (Kottak 2006), sailboat owners (but not nonowners) got loans to buy motors for their boats. To repay the loans, the owners increased the percentage of the catch they took from the men who fished in their boats. Over the years, they used their rising profits to buy larger and more expensive boats. The result was stratification—the creation of a group of wealthy people within a formerly egalitarian community. These events hampered individual initiative and interfered with further development of the fishing industry. With new boats so expensive, ambitious young men who once would have sought careers in fishing no longer had any way to obtain their own boats. They sought wage labor on land instead. To avoid such results, credit-granting agencies must seek out enterprising young fishers rather than giving loans only to owners and established businesspeople.

STRATEGIES FOR INNOVATION

Development anthropologists, who are concerned with social issues in, and the cultural dimension of, economic development, must work closely with local people to assess and help realize their own wishes and needs for change. Too many true local needs cry out for a solution to waste money funding development projects that are inappropriate in area A but needed in area B, or unnecessary anywhere. Development anthropology can

A mix of boats harbored at Dai-Lanh fishing village in Vietnam. A boat owner gets a loan to buy a motor. To repay it, he increases the share of the catch he takes from his crew. Later, he uses his rising profits to buy a more expensive boat, and takes even more from his crew. Can a more equitable solution be found?

Bringing Development to the Quichua
Track 15

This long and interesting clip describes the development process as a series of changes among Quichua Indians living near a national park created at Guagua Sumaco in Ecuador's Amazonian rain forest. It describes the supportive role of a German development agency (GTZ) in assisting (rather than imposing) development projects. Local people are interviewed about their development goals and the pluses and minuses of change. One of the main changes has been the arrival of electricity, from which the community derives part of its income. The clip describes how development has shifted the Quichua way of life from foraging to farming and work for cash. Yet aspects of their social organization—such as the clan system—remain and have been incorporated in the development process. Which changes would you regard as positive, and which as negative? The clip offers a good definition of sustainable development. What is it? After viewing the entire clip, do you agree with the narrator that development among the Quichua is sustainable?

help sort out the A's and B's and fit projects accordingly. Projects that put people first by consulting with them, and responding to their expressed needs, must be identified (Cernea 1991). Thereafter, development anthropologists can work to ensure socially compatible ways of implementing the project.

In a comparative study of 68 rural development projects from all around the world, I found the *culturally compatible* economic development projects to be twice as successful financially as the incompatible ones (Kottak 1990*b*, 1991). This finding shows that using applied anthropological expertise in planning, to ensure cultural compatibility, is cost-effective. To maximize social and economic benefits, projects must (1) be culturally compatible, (2) respond to locally perceived needs, (3) involve men and women in planning and carrying out the changes that affect them, (4) harness traditional organizations, and (5) be flexible.

Overinnovation

In my comparative study, the compatible and successful projects avoided the fallacy of **overinnovation** (too much change). We would expect people to resist development projects that require major changes in their daily lives, especially ones that interfere with subsistence pursuits. People usually want to change just enough to keep what they have. Motives for modifying behavior come from the traditional culture and the small concerns of ordinary life. Peasants' values are not such abstract ones as "learning a better way," "progressing," "increasing technical know-how,"

Change, we think, is good. Leaders are expected to offer "visions" of change. Few politicians get elected by promising, "I'm going to keep things just as they are." The assumption usually is that change is better—but what kind of change? From this discussion of the fallacy of overinnovation there are lessons to be learned and applied in our own lives.

Like most people, contemporary North Americans generally seek changes that will enable them to maintain or improve their lifestyles—not to revise them radically. Imagine someone chosen to lead an organization, someone from outside who is unfamiliar with the culture of that organization. He or she should follow the anthropologist's example and study the local culture before trying to change it. The leader should try to determine what works and what doesn't and what the natives (i.e., the men and women within the organization) want and really need. After local perceptions and needs have been assessed, if change seems in order, the leader must determine how to plan and implement change in the least disruptive way. Again, he or she should follow the applied anthropologist's strategy of consulting with and enlisting the help and support of local people throughout the process of change. To be an effective "change agent" requires listening and trying to tailor innovation to fit the local culture.

This process of study and collaboration illustrates participatory change—change from the "bottom up." By contrast, top-down change is often problematic. A top-down leader typically draws on an organizational blueprint—perhaps one he or she has brought from another organization. Unmodified blueprints usually don't work. Just as the linguistic blueprint in our brain is modified to fit a particular language, an organizational blueprint must be flexible enough to be modified to fit a specific organization. If it is not, that blueprint should be discarded. The fallacies of blueprint planning and overinnovation aren't just obscure lessons from failed development projects. They are vital considerations for any leader who wishes to run, or change, an organization.

"improving efficiency," or "adopting modern techniques." (Those phrases exemplify intervention philosophy.) Instead, their objectives are down-to-earth and specific ones. People want to improve yields in a rice field, amass resources for a ceremony, get a child through school, or have enough cash to pay the tax bill on time. The goals and values of subsistence producers differ from those of people who produce for cash, just as they differ from the intervention philosophies of development planners. Different value systems must be considered during planning.

In the comparative study, the projects that failed were usually both economically and culturally incompatible. For example, one South Asian project promoted the cultivation of onions and peppers, expecting this practice to fit into a preexisting labor-intensive system of rice growing. Cultivation of these cash crops wasn't traditional in the area. It conflicted with existing crop priorities and other interests of farmers. Also, the labor peaks for pepper and onion production coincided with those for rice, to which the farmers naturally gave priority.

Throughout the world, project problems have arisen from inadequate attention to, and consequent lack of fit with, local culture. Another naive and incompatible project was an overinnovative scheme in Ethiopia. Its major fallacy was to try to convert nomadic herders into sedentary cultivators. It ignored traditional land rights. Outsiders—commercial farmers—were to get much of the herders' territory. The pastoralists were expected to settle down and start farming. This project helped wealthy outsiders instead of the natives. The planners naively expected free-ranging herders to give up a generations-old way of life to work three times harder growing rice and picking cotton.

Underdifferentiation

The fallacy of **underdifferentiation** is the tendency to view "the less-developed countries" as more alike than they are. Development agencies often have ignored cultural diversity (e.g., between Brazil and Burundi) and adopted a uniform approach to deal with very different sets of people. Neglecting cultural diversity, many projects also have tried to impose incompatible property notions and social units. Most often, the faulty social design assumes either (1) individualistic productive units that are privately owned by an individual or couple and worked by a nuclear family or (2) cooperatives that are at least partially based on models from the former Eastern bloc and socialist countries.

Often, development aims at generating *individual* cash wealth through exports. This goal contrasts with the tendency of bands and tribes to share resources and to depend on local ecosystems and renewable resources (Bodley, ed. 1988). Development planners commonly emphasize benefits that will accrue to individuals. More concern with the effects on communities is needed (Bodley, ed. 1988).

One example of faulty Euro-American models (the individual and the nuclear family) was a West

■ *In Bangladesh, women count money at a weekly meeting where loans from the female-run Grameen Credit Bank are repaid. Groups promoting development can be particularly effective when they are based on traditional social organization or on a socioeconomic similarity among members.*

African project designed for an area where the extended family was the basic social unit. The project succeeded despite its faulty social design because the participants used their traditional extended family networks to attract additional settlers. Eventually, twice as many people as planned benefited as extended family members flocked to the project area. Here, settlers modified the project design that had been imposed on them by following the principles of their traditional society.

The second dubious foreign social model that is common in development strategy is the cooperative. In the comparative study of rural development projects, new cooperatives fared badly. Cooperatives succeeded only when they harnessed preexisting local-level communal institutions. This is a corollary of a more general rule: Participants' groups are most effective when they are based on traditional social organization or on a socioeconomic similarity among members.

Neither foreign social model—the nuclear family farm nor the cooperative—has an unblemished record in development. An alternative is needed: greater use of Third World social models for Third World development. These are traditional social units, such as the clans, lineages, and other extended kinship groups of Africa, Oceania, and many other areas, with their communally held estates and resources. The most humane and productive strategy for change is to base the social design for innovation on traditional social forms in each target area.

Third World Models

Many governments are not genuinely, or realistically, committed to improving the lives of their citizens. Interference by major powers also has kept governments from enacting needed reforms. In highly stratified societies, the class structure is very rigid. Movement of individuals into the

■ An effective social design for innovation may incorporate existing groups and institutions, such as descent groups in Africa and Oceania. Here, in Bali, Indonesia, a traditional system of planning and management by Hindu temples and priests has been harnessed for culturally appropriate agricultural development (see Lansing 1991).

Malagasy communities, where residence is based on descent, are more cohesive and homogeneous than are communities in Java or Latin America. Madagascar gained political independence from France in 1960. Although it was still economically dependent on France when I first did research there in 1966–1967, the new government was committed to a form of economic development designed to increase the ability of the Malagasy to feed themselves. Government policy emphasized increased production of rice, a subsistence crop, rather than cash crops. Furthermore, local communities, with their traditional cooperative patterns and solidarity based on kinship and descent, were treated as partners in, not obstacles to, the development process.

In a sense, the descent group is preadapted to equitable national development. In Madagascar, members of local descent groups have customarily pooled their resources to educate their ambitious members. Once educated, these men and women gain economically secure positions in the nation. They then share the advantages of their new positions with their kin. For example, they give room and board to rural cousins attending school and help them find jobs.

Malagasy administrations appear generally to have shared a commitment to democratic economic development. Perhaps this is because government officials are of the peasantry or have strong personal ties to it. By contrast, in Latin American countries, the elites and the lower class typically have different origins and no strong connections through kinship, descent, or marriage.

Furthermore, societies with descent-group organization contradict an assumption that many social scientists and economists seem to make. It is not inevitable that as nations become more tied to the world capitalist economy, native forms of social organization will break down into nuclear family organization, impersonality, and alienation. Descent groups, with their traditional communalism and corporate solidarity, have important roles to play in economic development.

middle class is difficult. It is equally hard to raise the living standards of the lower class as a whole. Many nations have a long history of government control by antidemocratic leaders and powerful interest groups, which tend to oppose reform.

In some nations, however, the government acts more as an agent of the people. Madagascar provides an example. As in many areas of Africa, precolonial states had developed in Madagascar before its conquest by the French in 1895. The people of Madagascar, the Malagasy, had been organized into descent groups before the origin of the state. The Merina, creators of the major precolonial state of Madagascar, wove descent groups into its structure, making members of important groups advisers to the king and thus giving them authority in government. The Merina state made provisions for the people it ruled. It collected taxes and organized labor for public works projects. In return, it redistributed resources to peasants in need. It also granted them some protection against war and slave raids and allowed them to cultivate their rice fields in peace. The government maintained the water works for rice cultivation. It opened to ambitious peasant boys the chance of becoming, through hard work and study, state bureaucrats.

Throughout the history of the Merina state—and continuing in modern Madagascar—there have been strong relationships between the individual, the descent group, and the state. Local

Realistic development promotes change but not overinnovation. Many changes are possible if the aim is to preserve local systems while making them work better. Successful economic development projects respect, or at least don't attack, local cultural patterns. Effective development draws on indigenous cultural practices and social structures.

1. Imperialism is the policy of extending the rule of a nation or empire over other nations and of taking and holding foreign colonies. Colonialism is the domination of a territory and its people by a foreign power for an extended time. European colonialism has had two main phases. The first started in 1492 and lasted through 1825. For Britain this phase ended with the American Revolution. For France it ended when Britain won the Seven Years' War, forcing the French to abandon Canada and India. For Spain, it ended with Latin American independence. The second phase of European colonialism extended approximately from 1850 to 1950. The British and French empires were at their height around 1914, when European empires controlled 85 percent of the world. Britain and France had colonies in Africa, Asia, Oceania, and the New World.

2. Political, ethnic, and tribal labels and identities were created under colonialism. Postcolonial studies is a growing academic field. It studies the interactions between European nations and the societies they colonized (mainly after 1800). Its topics include the impact of colonization and the state of postcolonies today.

3. Like colonialism, economic development has an intervention philosophy. This provides a justification for outsiders to guide native peoples toward particular goals. Development is usually justified by the idea that industrialization and modernization are desirable evolutionary advances. Yet many problems faced by Third World peoples have been caused by their incorporation in the world cash economy. Roads, mining, hydroelectric projects, ranching, lumbering, and agribusiness threaten indigenous peoples and their ecosystems. Neoliberalism revives and extends classic economic liberalism: the idea that governments should not regulate private enterprise and that free market forces should rule. This intervention philosophy currently dominates aid agreements with postsocialist and developing nations.

4. Spelled with a lowercase c, communism describes a social system in which property is owned by the community and in which people work for the common good. Spelled with a capital C, Communism indicates a political movement and doctrine seeking to overthrow capitalism and to establish a form of communism such as that which prevailed in the Soviet Union from 1917 to 1991. The heyday of Communism was between 1949 and 1989. The fall of Communism can be traced to 1989–1990 in eastern Europe and 1991 in the Soviet Union. Postsocialist states have followed the neoliberal agenda, through privatization, deregulation, and democratization. Common problems of the postsocialist transition include the rise of nationalism, in the form of ethnic-religious minorities, and corruption. Civil society encompasses NGOs, charities, community groups, women's organizations, faith-based and professional groups, unions, self-help groups, social movements, business associations, coalitions, and advocacy groups.

5. Development anthropology focuses on social issues in, and the cultural dimension of, economic development. Development projects typically promote cash employment and new technology at the expense of subsistence economies. Research in Java found that the green revolution was failing. The reason: It promoted only new technology, rather than a combination of technology and peasant political organization.

6. Not all governments seek to increase equality and end poverty. Resistance by elites to reform is typical—and hard to combat. Local people rarely cooperate with projects requiring major changes in their daily lives, especially ones that interfere with customary subsistence pursuits. Many projects seek to impose inappropriate property notions and incompatible social units on their intended beneficiaries. The best strategy for change is to base the social design for innovation on traditional social forms in each target area.

civil society Voluntary collective action around shared interests, goals, and values. Encompasses such organizations as NGOs, registered charities, community groups, women's organizations, faith-based and professional groups, trade unions, self-help groups, social movements, business associations, coalitions, and advocacy groups.

colonialism The political, social, economic, and cultural domination of a territory and its people by a foreign power for an extended time.

communism Spelled with a lowercase c, describes a social system in which property is owned by the community and in which people work for the common good.

Communism Spelled with a capital C, a political movement and doctrine seeking to overthrow capitalism and to establish a form of communism such as that which prevailed in the Soviet Union from 1917 to 1991.

development anthropology The branch of applied anthropology that focuses on social issues in, and the cultural dimension of, economic development.

equity, increased A reduction in absolute poverty and a fairer (more even) distribution of wealth.

green revolution Agricultural development based on chemical fertilizers, pesticides, 20th-century cultivation techniques, and new crop varieties such as IR-8 ("miracle rice").

intervention philosophy Guiding principle of colonialism, conquest, missionization, or development; an ideological justification for outsiders to guide native peoples in specific directions.

neoliberalism Revival of Adam Smith's classic economic liberalism, the idea that governments should not regulate private enterprise and that free market forces should rule; a currently dominant intervention philosophy.

overinnovation Characteristic of projects that require major changes in natives' daily lives, especially ones that interfere with customary subsistence pursuits.

postcolonial Referring to interactions between European nations and the societies they colonized (mainly after 1800); more generally, "postcolonial" may be used to signify a position against imperialism and Eurocentrism.

underdifferentiation Planning fallacy of viewing less-developed countries as an undifferentiated group; ignoring cultural diversity and adopting a uniform approach (often ethnocentric) for very different types of project beneficiaries.

CRITICAL THINKING QUESTIONS

For more self-testing, see the self-quizzes

mhhe.com/kottak

1. How is the diversity you see in your classroom related to the colonies and empires discussed in this chapter?

2. Think of a recent case in which a core nation, such as the United States, has intervened in the affairs of another nation. What was the intervention philosophy used to justify the action?

3. Devise a plan to equalize the distribution of computers in your public school system. What kind of opposition would you expect? Who would your supporters be?

4. Thinking of your own society and recent history, give an example of a proposal or policy that failed because it was overinnovative.

5. Think of a change you'd like to see happen. What groups would you enlist to make it happen? What would their roles be, from start to finish?

SUGGESTED ADDITIONAL READINGS

Arce, A., and N. Long, eds.
2000 *Anthropology, Development, and Modernities: Exploring Discourses, Counter-Tendencies, and Violence.* New York: Routledge. Applied anthropology, rural development, social change, violence, and social and economic policy in developing countries.

Bodley, J. H.
2001 *Anthropology and Contemporary Human Problems,* 4th ed. Boston: McGraw-Hill. Overview of major problems of today's industrial world: overconsumption, the environment, resource depletion, hunger, overpopulation, violence, and war.
2003 *The Power of Scale: A Global History Approach.* Armonk, NY: M. E. Sharpe. Capitalism and geopolitics in world history.

Bodley, J. H., ed.
1988 *Tribal Peoples and Development Issues: A Global Overview.* Mountain View, CA: Mayfield. An overview of case studies, policies, assessments, and recommendations concerning tribal peoples and development.

Bremen, J. V., and A. Shimizu, eds.
1999 *Anthropology and Colonialism in Asia and Oceania.* London: Curzon. One in a series on the anthropology of Asia.

Cernea, M. M., ed.
1991 *Putting People First: Sociological Variables in Rural Development,* 2nd ed. New York: Oxford University Press (published for the World Bank). First collection of articles by social scientists based on World Bank files and project experiences. Examines development successes and failures and the social and cultural reasons for them.

Cooper, F., and A. L. Stoler, eds.
1997 *Tensions of Empire: Colonial Cultures in a Bourgeois World.* Berkeley: University of California Press. The social complexity of colonial encounters is explored in several articles.

Edelman, M., and A. Haugerud
2004 *The Anthropology of Development and Globalization: From Classical Political Economy to Contemporary Neoliberalism.* Malden, MA: Blackwell. Surveys theories and approaches to development and the global.

Escobar, A.
1995 *Encountering Development: The Making and Unmaking of the Third World.* Princeton, NJ: Princeton University Press. A critique of economic development and development anthropology.

Lansing, J. S.
1991 *Priests and Programmers: Technologies of Power in the Engineered Landscape of Bali.* Princeton, NJ: Princeton University Press. The role of a traditional priesthood in managing irrigation and culturally appropriate economic development in Bali, Indonesia.

Nolan, R. W.

    2002 *Development Anthropology: Encounters in the Real World.* Boulder, CO: Westview Press. Cases in development anthropology.

    2003 *Anthropology in Practice.* Boulder, CO: Lynne Reiner. Putting anthropology to work for change.

Nussbaum, M. C.

    2000 *Women and Human Development: The Capabilities Approach.* New York: Cambridge University Press. The untapped power of women in developing countries.

INTERNET EXERCISES

1. Colonialism in California: Go to the Original Voices website, **http://originalvoices.org/Homepage.htm**, and read the chapters on Precontact Culture and Economy, Human Price of Gold Rush, and U.S. Government Roles.

    a. What cultures lived in Northern California before the gold rush? What were their lifestyles like?

    b. What were the gold miners' attitudes toward the indigenous people? What actions did they take that reflected those attitudes? Would you characterize these actions as ethnocide or genocide?

    c. What role did the U.S. government play in the gold rush? Did it just tolerate the actions of the miners or did it encourage them?

    d. Some names of professional sports teams have been in the news recently because some Native Americans consider them offensive (e.g., Washington Redskins, Atlanta Braves, Cleveland Indians). After reading this page, what do you think native groups from Northern California might feel about the name of the San Francisco 49ers (named after the gold rushers of 1849)?

2. Human Rights: Read the preamble and skim the articles of the United Nations Universal Declaration of Human Rights, **http://www.un.org/Overview/rights.html**.

    a. What are the central points of the declaration?

    b. Do you agree with them? Do you find them all reasonable? Is anything missing?

    c. How do colonial strategies and development projects threaten human rights as spelled out in this declaration?

    d. How would you suggest the U.N. enforce these rights?

See Chapter 15 at your McGraw-Hill Online Learning Center for additional review and interactive exercises.

LINKAGES

Kottak, *Assault on Paradise*, 4th ed.

Read Chapters 4 and 8 and describe the main changes affecting Arembepe's fishing industry during the period of study. How does Arembepe's experience illustrate this text chapter's point (in the section "Equity") about appropriate strategies for developing a local fishing industry?

Peters-Golden, *Culture Sketches*, 4th ed.

This text chapter has discussed the far-reaching and long-lasting results of colonialism. In *Culture Sketches*, read Chapter 4, "Haiti: A Nation in Turmoil." How do you think Haiti's colonial past has contributed to its contemporary situation? What sorts of problems does Haiti face owing to development, or lack thereof? How does Haiti compare to some other examples mentioned in the text chapter?

Knauft, *The Gebusi*, 1st ed.

Read Chapters 7, 9, and the conclusion. Based on Chapter 7 and the conclusion, how benign or brutal do you think the Gebusi's experience with colonialism has been? What evidence would you use to support your opinion? Based on Chapter 9, why do you think economic development is so relatively undeveloped among Gebusi—despite their strong desire for it? In an attempt to gain access to money, what kinds of economic activity are pursued by Gebusi women, and how successful are these activities?

16

Cultural Exchange and Survival

ACCULTURATION

Since at least the 1920s anthropologists have investigated the changes—on both sides—that arise from contact between industrial and nonindustrial societies. Studies of "social change" and "acculturation" are abundant. British and American ethnographers, respectively, have used these terms to describe the same process. *Acculturation* refers to changes that result when groups come into continuous firsthand contact—changes in the cultural patterns of either or both groups (Redfield, Linton, and Herskovits 1936, p. 149).

Acculturation differs from diffusion, or cultural borrowing, which can occur without firsthand contact. For example, most North Americans who eat hot dogs ("frankfurters") have never been to Frankfurt, Germany, nor have most North American Toyota owners or sushi

CONTACT AND DOMINATION

Different degrees of destruction, domination, resistance, survival, adaptation, and modification of native cultures may follow interethnic contact. In the most destructive encounters, native and subordinate cultures face obliteration. In cases where contact between the indigenous societies and more powerful outsiders leads to destruction—a situation that is particularly characteristic of colonialist and expansionist eras—a "shock phase" often follows the initial encounter (Bodley, ed. 1988). Outsiders may attack or exploit the native people. Such exploitation may increase mortality, disrupt subsistence, fragment kin groups, damage social support systems, and inspire new religious movements, such as the cargo cults examined in the chapter "Religion" (Bodley, ed. 1988). During the shock phase, there may be civil repression backed by military force. Such factors may lead to the group's cultural collapse (*ethnocide*) or physical extinction (*genocide*).

Outsiders often attempt to remake native landscapes and cultures in their own image. Political and economic colonialists have tried to redesign conquered and dependent lands, peoples, and cultures, imposing their cultural standards on others. The aim of many agricultural development projects, for example, seems to have been to make the world as much like Iowa as possible, complete with mechanized farming and nuclear family ownership—despite the fact that these models may be inappropriate for settings outside the North American heartland.

Development and Environmentalism

Today it is often multinational corporations, usually based in core nations, rather than the governments of those nations, that are changing the nature of Third World economies. However, nations do tend to support the predatory enterprises that seek cheap labor and raw materials in countries outside the core, such as Brazil, where economic development has contributed to ecological devastation.

Simultaneously, environmentalists from core nations increasingly state their case, promoting conservation, to the rest of the world. The ecological devastation of the Amazon has become a focus of international environmentalist attention. Yet many Brazilians complain that northerners talk about global needs and saving the Amazon after having destroyed their own forests for First World economic growth. Akbar Ahmed (1992, 2004) concludes that non-Westerners tend to be cynical about Western ecological morality, seeing it as yet another imperialist message. "The Chinese have cause to snigger at the Western suggestion that they forgo the convenience of the fridge to save the ozone layer" (Ahmed 1992, p. 120).

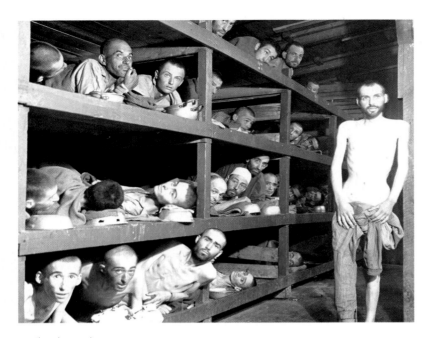

■ *This photo, taken on April 16, 1945, shows Holocaust survivors at the Buchenwald (Germany) Concentration Camp, which had just been liberated by U.S. troops. Genocidal policies, such as the Nazis' campaign against the Jews, aim at the physical extinction of a people.*

eaters ever visited Japan. Although *acculturation* can be applied to any case of cultural contact and change, the term most often has described **westernization**—the influence of Western expansion on indigenous peoples and their cultures. Thus, local people who wear store-bought clothes, learn Indo-European languages, and otherwise adopt Western customs are called acculturated. Acculturation may be voluntary or forced, and there may be considerable resistance to the process.

OVERVIEW

In our world in flux, new identities emerge, while others disappear. In worse cases, a culture may collapse or be absorbed (ethnocide). Its people may die off or be exterminated (genocide). Cultural imperialism refers to one culture's spread at the expense of others. A text, such as a media-born image, is interpreted by each person exposed to it. People may accept, resist, or oppose a text's established meaning. When outside forces enter new settings, they typically are indigenized—modified to fit the local culture. Mass media can diffuse the culture of a country within its borders, thus enhancing national identity. The mass media also play a role in preserving ethnic identities among people who lead transnational lives. Today's global culture is driven by flows of people, technology, finance, and information. Business and the media have stoked a global culture of consumption. Governments and international organizations have adopted policies, including constitutional reforms, designed to recognize and benefit indigenous peoples. Identity is a fluid, dynamic process, and there are multiple ways of being indigenous. No social movement exists apart from the nation and world that includes it.

Cultural Diversity Highest in Resource-Rich Areas, Study Says

NATIONAL GEOGRAPHIC NEWS BRIEF

by Stefan Lovgren
March 17, 2004

This chapter focuses on challenges to cultural diversity and cultural survival, and the resilience of people and cultures in the face of those challenges. This news story reports on a recent study of the origins and survival of cultural diversity. The point is made that people tend to move for economic reasons and that if resources are ample at home, people tend to stay put and continue doing what they have always done. This reinforces the point made in the last chapter that motives for modifying behavior come from the traditional culture and the small concerns of ordinary life.

An intriguing argument in this study is that patterns of cultural and biological diversity are similar, with diversity greatest in equatorial regions and least near the poles. Abundant resources in the tropics have allowed diverse societies to survive. When resources are less concentrated and abundant, people have to range widely to meet their daily needs. This movement works to homogenize cultures, as people constantly come into contact with others. This study also draws attention to a tendency for cultures to maintain themselves, even in the face of migration to new areas, such as North American cities, so that ethnic and other cultural distinctions remain important in a globalizing world.

We may rightfully beat our drums and toot our horns: No species come close to the wealth of culture that humans boast. We have different religions, marriage systems, languages, and dances.

"Humans are a very young species with very little genetic diversity, yet we've got enormous cultural diversity that other species really don't have," said Mark Pagel, a professor of evolutionary biology . . . at the University of Reading in England. But what explains our extreme cultural diversity?

In an article in this week's issue of the science journal *Nature,* Pagel and Ruth Mace, an anthropologist at the University College London, argue that our cultural evolution is driven in large part by a desire to control resources.

"Humans have a proclivity for drawing a ring around themselves and say[ing], 'This is my territory and I'm going to exclude others from occupying it,'" Pagel said. "That leads to different cultures arising through the usual processes of diversification and drifting apart when they're isolated from each other."

It may seem strange to talk about our great cultural diversity at a time when many of us fear that a cultural homogenization is sweeping the world . . .

Pagel doesn't deny that a cultural erosion is taking place. But, he says, it's happened far less than it appears. In fact, unless they're tempted financially to move and assimilate into a new culture, most people prefer to stay where they are and continue doing what they have always done. "What's remarkable is how little movement we have seen in people, given the ability we have to move

people," he said. "It's the natural tendency for cultures to be quite cohesive and exclusive that we want to draw attention to."

The study found that human cultures distribute themselves around the world in patterns similar to animal species. In animals, a trend known as Rapaport's rule holds that the density of species is highest in the equatorial regions and declines steadily toward the poles. Different languages—the standard by which the study differentiates cultures—are spoken every few square miles in some equatorial areas, while less climatologically hospitable regions have few languages.

Some 700 to 1,000 different languages, about 15 percent of the total on Earth, are spoken in Papua New Guinea. By comparison, only 90 languages are spoken in China.

"When resources are abundant, it is possible for a small group of humans to survive, while in areas where resources are not very abundant people have to range over large areas to meet their daily needs, and that seems to homogenize cultures, because they're constantly coming into contact with other people," Pagel said.

But how come humans don't form one large and homogenous cultural group in ecologically rich areas like Papua New Guinea?

Pagel says that's because humans display forms of social behavior that favor living in small groups, such as rewarding cooperation, punishing those who deviate from the norms, and being wary of outsiders. "In trying to control resources and excluding others from using them, we have developed [sophisticated group behaviors such as] hunting and warfare," he said. "These things require

Linguistic and cultural diversity characterizes Papua New Guinea, where this man lives. Body decoration is one way of marking cultural differences.

enormous amounts of cooperation, coherence, and communication among individuals."

It may also be a matter of choice. While our genes are transmitted vertically and can't be chosen, cultural traits can be accepted or rejected. However, most people still get their traits from their ancestors rather than other cultures.

"People tend to speak the same language as their parents, and have the same political and religious beliefs," Pagel said.

Although our cultural diversity is still strong, it is perhaps only a fraction of what it was, say, 10,000 years ago, when agriculturists moved out of Mesopotamia and replaced hunter-gatherer cultures in Europe and elsewhere, wiping out languages in the process.

"There are only about 50 languages spoken in Europe today," Pagel said. "If it hadn't been for the advance of the agriculturists, we would probably have greater linguistic diversity in Europe, and probably greater cultural diversity too."

We may be in another state of transition now. While some experts suggest that mass migrations of people moving from poor regions to rich areas will dent our cultural diversity, Pagel is not so sure. "Whether things will change in the next hundred years and we'll have one big homogenous world, we can't really say," he said . . .

After all, Pagel says, you can walk down a street in Manhattan and find three generations of Italian speakers. Walk a few blocks more, and people are speaking Chinese. "The cultural differences in Manhattan still remain," he said.

SOURCE: Stefan Lovgren, "Cultural Diversity Highest in Resource-Rich Areas, Study Says," *National Geographic News*, March 17, 2004. National Geographic Society. http://news.nationalgeographic.com/news/2004/03/0317_040317_cultures.html.

■ At a mall in Poodong district, China, consumers can shop in one of Asia's biggest supermarkets. What would be the environmental effects if China had a level of consumption paralleling that of the United States?

In the last chapter, we saw that development projects usually fail if they try to replace native forms with culturally alien property concepts and productive units. A strategy that incorporates the native forms is more effective than the fallacies of overinnovation and underdifferentiation. The same caveats would seem to apply to an intervention philosophy that seeks to impose global ecological morality without due attention to cultural variation and autonomy. Countries and cultures may resist interventionist philosophies aimed at either development or globally justified environmentalism.

A clash of cultures related to environmental change may occur when *development threatens indigenous peoples and their environments.* Hundreds of native groups throughout the world, including the Kayapó Indians of Brazil (Turner 1993) and the Kaluli of Papua New Guinea (see "Interesting Issues" on pp. 372–373), have been threatened by plans and forces, such as dam construction or commercially driven deforestation, that would destroy their homelands.

A second clash of cultures related to environmental change occurs when *external regulation threatens indigenous peoples.* Native groups may actually be threatened by environmental plans that seek to *save* their homelands. Sometimes outsiders expect local people to give up many of their customary economic and cultural activities without clear substitutes, alternatives, or incentives in order to conserve endangered species. The traditional approach to conservation has been to restrict access to protected areas, hire guards, and punish violators.

Problems often arise when external regulation replaces the native system. Like development projects, conservation schemes may ask people to change the way they have been doing things for generations to satisfy planners' goals rather than local goals. Ironically, well-meaning conservation efforts can be as insensitive as development schemes that promote radical changes without involving local people in planning and carrying out the policies that affect them. When people are asked to give up the basis of their livelihood, they usually resist.

Consider the case of a Tanosy man who lives on the edge of the Andohahela forest reserve of southeastern Madagascar. For years he has relied on rice fields and grazing land inside that reserve. Now external agencies are trying to get him to abandon this land for the sake of conservation. This man is a wealthy *ombiasa* (traditional sorcerer-healer). With four wives, a dozen children, and 20 head of cattle, he is an ambitious, hardworking, and productive peasant. With money, social support, and supernatural authority, he is mounting effective resistance against the park ranger who has been trying to get him to abandon his fields. The *ombiasa* claims he has already relinquished some of his land, but he is waiting for compensatory fields. His most effective resistance has been supernatural. The death of the ranger's son was attributed to the *ombiasa's* magical power. Since then, the ranger has been less vigilant in his enforcement efforts.

Given the threat that deforestation poses to global biodiversity, it is vitally important to devise conservation strategies that will work. Laws and enforcement may help stem the tide of commercially driven deforestation, which takes the form of burning and clear-cutting. However, local people also use and abuse forested lands. A challenge for the environmentally oriented applied anthropologist is to make forest preservation attractive to people like the Tanosy of Madagascar. Like development plans, effective conservation strategies must pay attention to the customs, needs, and incentives of the people living in the affected area. Conservation depends on local cooperation. In the Tanosy case, the guardians of the reserve must do more to satisfy the *ombiasa* and other affected people, through boundary adjustments, negotiation, and compensation. For effective conservation (as for development), the task is to devise culturally appropriate strategies. Neither development agencies nor NGOs (nongovernmental organizations) will succeed if they try to impose their goals without considering the practices, customs, rules, laws, beliefs, and values of the people to be affected (see Johansen 2003; Reed 1997).

Religious Change

Religious proselytizing can promote ethnocide, as native beliefs and practices are replaced by Western ones. Sometimes a religion and associated customs are replaced by ideology and behavior more compatible with Western culture. One example is the Handsome Lake religion (as described in the chapter on religion), which led the Iroquois to copy European farming techniques, stressing male rather than female labor. The Iroquois also gave up their communal longhouses and matrilineal descent groups for nuclear family households. The teachings of

Handsome Lake led to a new church and religion. This revitalization movement helped the Iroquois survive in a drastically modified environment, but much ethnocide was involved.

Handsome Lake was a native who created a new religion, drawing on Western models. More commonly, missionaries and proselytizers representing the major world religions, especially Christianity and Islam, are the proponents of religious change. Protestant and Catholic missionization continues even in remote corners of the world. Evangelical Protestantism, for example, is advancing in Peru, Brazil, and other parts of Latin America. It challenges an often jaded Catholicism that has too few priests and that is sometimes seen mainly as women's religion.

Sometimes the political ideology of a nation-state is pitted against traditional religion. Officials of the former Soviet empire discouraged Catholicism, Judaism, and Islam. In Central Asia, Soviet dominators destroyed Muslim mosques and discouraged religious practice. On the other hand, governments often use their power to advance a religion, such as Islam in Iran or Sudan (see Figure 16.1).

A military government seized power in Sudan in 1989. It immediately launched a campaign to change that country of more than 35 million people, where one-quarter were not Muslims, into an Islamic nation. Sudan adopted a policy of religious, linguistic, and cultural imperialism. The government sought to extend Islam and the Arabic language to the non-Muslim south. This was

For information on Sarawak cultural survival, see your OLC Internet Exercises

mhhe.com/kottak

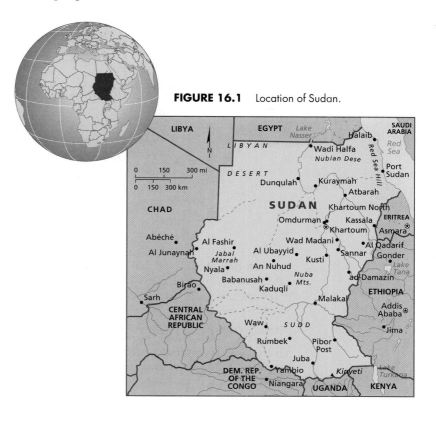

FIGURE 16.1 Location of Sudan.

Voices of the Rainforest

The government of Papua New Guinea has approved oil exploration by American, British, Australian, and Japanese companies in the rainforest habitat of the Kaluli (Figure 16.2) and other indigenous peoples. The forest degradation that usually accompanies logging, ranching, road building, and drilling endangers plants, animals, peoples, and cultures. Lost along with trees are songs, myths, words, ideas, artifacts, and techniques—the cultural knowledge and practices of rainforest people like the Kaluli, whom the anthropologist and ethnomusicologist Steven Feld has been studying for more than 20 years.

Feld teamed up with Mickey Hart of the Grateful Dead in a project designed to promote the cultural survival of the Kaluli through their music. For years, Hart has worked to preserve musical diversity through educational funding, concert promotion, and recording, including a successful series called "The World" on the Rykodisc label. *Voices of the Rainforest* was the first CD completely devoted to indigenous music from Papua New Guinea. In 1 hour, it encapsulates 24 hours of a day in Kaluli life in Bosavi village. The recording permits a form of cultural survival and diffusion in a high-quality commercial product. Bosavi is presented as a "soundscape" of blended music and natural environmental sounds. Kaluli weave the natural sounds of birds, frogs, rivers, and streams into their texts, melodies, and rhythms. They sing and whistle with birds and waterfalls. They compose instrumental duets with birds and cicadas.

FIGURE 16.2   Location of the Kaluli in Papua New Guinea.

The Kaluli project was launched on Earth Day 1991 at *Star Wars* creator George Lucas's Skywalker Ranch. There, Randy Hayes, the executive director of the Rainforest Action Network, and musician Mickey Hart spoke about the linked issues of rainforest destruction and musical survival.

an area of Christianity and tribal religions that had resisted the central government for a decade (Hedges 1992*a*). Resistance continues.

Cultural Imperialism

Cultural imperialism refers to the spread or advance of one culture at the expense of others, or its imposition on other cultures, which it modifies, replaces, or destroys—usually because of dif-ferential economic or political influence. Thus, children in the French colonial empire learned French history, language, and culture from standard textbooks also used in France. Tahitians, Malagasy, Vietnamese, and Senegalese learned the French language by reciting from books about "our ancestors the Gauls."

To what extent is modern technology, especially the mass media, an agent of cultural imperialism? Some commentators see modern technology as

Next came a San Francisco benefit dinner for the Bosavi People's Fund. This is the trust established to receive royalties from the Kaluli recording—a financial prong in Steven Feld's strategy to foster Kaluli cultural survival.

Voices of the Rainforest has been marketed as "world music." This term is intended to point up musical diversity, the fact that musics originate from all world regions and all cultures. "Tribal" music joins Western music as a form of artistic expression worth performing, hearing, and preserving. Hart's series offers musics of non-Western origin as well as those of ethnically dominated groups of the Western world.

Hart's record series aims at preserving "endangered music" against the artistic loss suffered by indigenous peoples. Its intent is to give a "world voice" to people who are being silenced by the dominant world system. In 1993, Hart launched a new

series, the Library of Congress Endangered Music Project, which includes digitally remastered field recordings collected by the American Folklife Center. The first of this series, *The Spirit Cries*, concentrated on music from a broad range of cultures in South and Central America and the Caribbean. Proceeds from this project were used to support the performers and their cultural traditions.

In *Voices of the Rainforest*, Feld and Hart excised all "modern" and "dominant" sounds from their recording. Gone are the world-system sounds that Kaluli villagers now hear every day. The recording temporarily silences the "machine voices": the tractor that cuts the grass on the local airstrip, the gas generator, the sawmill, the helicopters, and light planes buzzing to and from the oil-drilling areas. Gone, too, are the village church bells, Bible readings, evangelical prayers and hymns, and

the voices of teachers and students at an English-only school.

Initially, Feld anticipated criticism for attempting to create an idealized Kaluli "soundscape" insulated from invasive forces and sounds. Among the Kaluli, he expected varied opinions about the value of his project:

> It is a soundscape world that some Kaluli care little about, a world that other Kaluli momentarily choose to forget, a world that some Kaluli are increasingly nostalgic and uneasy about, a world that other Kaluli are still living and creating and listening to. It is a sound world that increasingly fewer Kaluli will actively know about and value, but one that increasingly more Kaluli will only hear on cassette and sentimentally wonder about. (Feld 1991, p. 137)

Despite these concerns, Feld was met with an overwhelmingly positive response when he returned to Papua New Guinea in 1992 armed with a boombox and the recording. The people of Bosavi reacted very favorably. Not only did they appreciate the recording, they also have been able to build a much-needed community school with the *Voices of the Rainforest* royalties that have been donated to the Bosavi People's Fund.

SOURCE: Based on Steven Feld, "Voices of the Rainforest," *Public Culture* 4(1): 131–140 (1991).

erasing cultural differences, as homogeneous products reach more people worldwide. But others see a role for modern technology in allowing social groups (local cultures) to express themselves and to survive (Marcus and Fischer 1999) (see "Interesting Issues" on p. 376). Modern radio and TV, for example, constantly bring local happenings (for example, a "chicken festival" in Iowa) to the attention of a larger public. The North American media play a role in stimulating local activities of

many sorts. Similarly, in Brazil, local practices, celebrations, and performances are changing in the context of outside forces, including the mass media and tourism.

In the town of Arembepe Brazil (Kottak 1999*a*), TV coverage has stimulated participation in a traditional annual performance, the *Chegança*. This is a fishermen's danceplay that reenacts the Portuguese discovery of Brazil. Arembepeiros have traveled to the state capital to perform the

Chegança before television cameras, for a TV program featuring traditional performances from many rural communities.

One national Brazilian Sunday-night variety program (*Fantástico*) is especially popular in rural areas because it shows such local events. In several towns along the Amazon River, annual folk ceremonies are now staged more lavishly for TV cameras. In the Amazon town of Parantíns, for example, boatloads of tourists arriving any time of year are shown a videotape of the town's annual Bumba Meu Boi festival. This is a costumed performance mimicking bullfighting, parts of which have been shown on *Fantástico*. This pattern, in which local communities preserve, revive, and intensify the scale of traditional ceremonies to perform for TV and tourists, is expanding.

Brazilian television also has played a "top-down" role, by spreading the popularity of holidays like Carnaval and Christmas (Kottak 1990a). TV has aided the national spread of Carnaval beyond its traditional urban centers. Still, local reactions to the nationwide broadcasting of Carnaval and its trappings (elaborate parades, costumes, and frenzied dancing) are not simple or uniform responses to external stimuli.

Rather than direct adoption of Carnaval, local Brazilians respond in various ways. Often they don't take up Carnaval itself but modify their local festivities to fit Carnaval images. Others actively spurn Carnaval. One example is Arembepe, where Carnaval has never been important, probably because of its calendrical closeness to the main local festival, which is held in February to honor Saint Francis of Assisi. In the past, villagers couldn't afford to celebrate both occasions. Now, not only do the people of Arembepe reject Carnaval, they are also increasingly hostile to their own main festival. Arembepeiros resent the

For more on strategies of cultural survival, see your OLC Internet Exercises

mhhe.com/kottak

fact that Saint Francis has become "an outsiders' event," because it draws thousands of tourists to Arembepe each February. The villagers think that commercial interests and outsiders have appropriated Saint Francis.

In opposition to these trends, many Arembepeiros now say they like and participate more in the traditional June festivals honoring Saint John, Saint Peter, and Saint Anthony. In the past, these were observed on a much smaller scale than was the festival honoring Saint Francis. Arembepeiros celebrate them now with a new vigor and enthusiasm, as they react to outsiders and their celebrations, real and televised.

MAKING AND REMAKING CULTURE

Any media-borne image, such as that of Carnaval, can be analyzed in terms of its nature and effects. It also can be analyzed as a **text.** We usually think of a text as a textbook, like this one. But the term has a more general meaning. Anthropologists use text to refer to anything that may be "read," interpreted, and assigned meaning by anyone exposed to it. In this sense, a text doesn't have to be written. The term may refer to a film, an image, or an event, such as Carnaval. As Brazilians participate in Carnaval, they "read" it as a text. These "readers" derive their own meanings and feelings from Carnaval events, images, and activities. Such meanings may be very different from what the creators of the text, such as official sponsors, imagined. (The "reading" or meaning that the creators intended—or the one that the elites consider to be the intended or correct meaning—can be called the *hegemonic reading.*)

"Readers" of media messages constantly produce their own meanings. They may resist or oppose the hegemonic meanings of a text, or they may seize on the antihegemonic aspects of a text. Previously, we saw this process when American slaves preferred the biblical story of Moses and deliverance to the hegemonic lessons of acceptance and obedience that their masters taught.

Popular Culture

In his book *Understanding Popular Culture* (1989), John Fiske views each individual's use of popular culture as a creative act (an original "reading" of a text). (For example, Madonna, the Rolling Stones, and *The Lord of the Rings* mean something different to each of their fans.) As Fiske puts it, "the meanings I make from a text are pleasurable when I feel that they are *my* meanings and that they relate to *my* everyday life in a practical, direct way" (1989, p. 57). All of us can creatively "read" magazines, books, music, television, films, celebrities, and other popular culture products (see Fiske and Hartley 2003).

Individuals also draw on popular culture to express resistance. Through their use of popular culture, people can symbolically resist the unequal power relations they face each day—in the family, at work, and in the classroom. Popular culture (from hip-hop music to comedy) can be used to express discontent and resistance by groups that are or feel powerless or oppressed.

Indigenizing Popular Culture

To understand culture change, it is important to recognize that meaning may be locally manufactured. People assign their own meanings and value to the texts, messages, and products they receive. Those meanings reflect their cultural backgrounds and experiences. When forces from world centers enter new societies, they are **indigenized**—modified to fit the local culture. This is true of cultural forces as different as fast food, music, housing styles, science, terrorism, celebrations, and political ideas and institutions (Appadurai 1990).

Consider the reception of the movie *Rambo* in Australia as an example of how popular culture may be indigenized. Michaels (1986) found *Rambo* to be very popular among aborigines in the deserts of central Australia, who had manufactured their own meanings from the film. Their "reading" was very different from the one imagined by the movie's creators, and by most North Americans. The Native Australians saw Rambo as a representative of the Third World who was engaged in a battle with the white officer class. This reading expressed their negative feelings about white paternalism and about existing race relations. The Native Australians also imagined that there were tribal ties and kin links between Rambo and the prisoners he was rescuing. All this made sense, based on their experience. Native Australians are disproportionately represented in Australian jails. Their most likely liberator would be someone with a personal link to them. These readings of *Rambo* were relevant meanings produced *from* the text, not *by* it (Fiske 1989).

A World System of Images

All cultures express imagination—in dreams, fantasies, songs, myths, and stories. Today, however, more people in many more places imagine "a wider set of 'possible' lives than they ever did before. One important source of this change is the mass media, which present a rich, ever-changing store of possible lives" (Appadurai 1991, p. 197). The United States as a media center has been joined by Canada, Japan, Western Europe, Brazil, Mexico, Nigeria, Egypt, India, and Hong Kong.

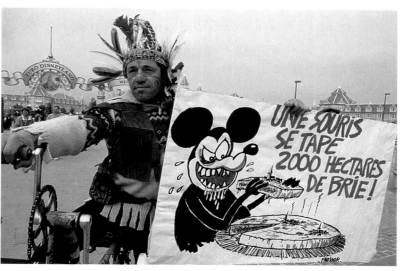

As print has done for centuries (Anderson 1991), the electronic mass media also can spread, even help create, national and ethnic identities. Like print, television and radio can diffuse the cultures of different countries within their own boundaries, thus enhancing national cultural identity. For example, millions of Brazilians who were formerly cut off (by geographic isolation or illiteracy) from urban and national events and information now participate in a national communication system, through TV networks (Kottak 1990a).

Cross-cultural studies of television contradict a belief Americans ethnocentrically hold about televiewing in other countries. This misconception is that American programs inevitably triumph over local products. This doesn't happen when there is appealing local competition. In Brazil, for example, the most popular network (TV Globo) relies heavily on native productions. TV Globo's most popular programs are *telenovelas,* locally made serials that are similar to American soap operas. Globo plays each night to the world's largest and most devoted audience (60 to 80 million viewers throughout the nation). The programs that attract this horde are made by Brazilians, for Brazilians. Thus, it is not North American culture but a new pan-Brazilian national culture that Brazilian TV is propagating. Brazilian productions also compete internationally. They are exported to over 100 countries, spanning Latin America, Europe, Asia, and Africa.

We may generalize that programming that is culturally alien won't do very well anywhere when a quality local choice is available. Confirmation comes from many countries. National productions are highly popular in Japan, Mexico, India, Egypt, and Nigeria. In a survey during the mid-1980s, 75 percent of Nigerian viewers preferred local productions. Only 10 percent favored

▪ *Native children throughout the French colonial empire learned the French language by reciting from books about "our ancestors the Gauls." More recently, French citizens have criticized or resisted what they see as American "cultural imperialism"—one prominent symbol of which has been Euro Disneyland. Has there also been resistance to the expansion of Disney enterprises in the United States?*

Using Modern Technology to Preserve Linguistic and Cultural Diversity

Although some see modern technology as a threat to cultural diversity, others see a role for this technology in allowing social groups to express themselves. The anthropologist H. Russell Bernard has been a pioneer in teaching speakers of endangered languages how to write their language using a computer. Bernard's work permits the preservation of languages and cultural memories. Native peoples from Mexico to Cameroon are using their mother tongue to express themselves as individuals and to provide insiders' accounts of different cultures.

Jesús Salinas Pedraza, a rural schoolteacher in the Mexican state of Hidalgo, sat down to a word processor a few years back and produced a monumental book, a 250,000-word description of his own Indian culture written in the Nähñu language. Nothing seems to be left out: folktales and traditional religious beliefs, the practical uses of plants and minerals and the daily flow of life in field and village . . .

Mr. Salinas is neither a professional anthropologist nor a literary stylist. He is, though, the first person to write a book in Nähñu (NYAW-hnyu), the native tongue of several hundred thousand Indians but a previously unwritten language.

Such a use of microcomputers and desktop publishing for languages with no literary tradition is now being encouraged by anthropologists for recording ethnographies from an insider's perspective. They see this as a means of preserving cultural diversity and a wealth of human knowledge.

With even greater urgency, linguists are promoting the techniques as a way of saving some of the world's languages from imminent extinction.

Half of the world's 6,000 languages are considered by linguists to be endangered. These are the languages spoken by small societies that are dwindling with the encroachment of larger, more dynamic cultures. Young people feel economic pressure to learn only the language of the dominant culture, and as the older people die, the non-written language vanishes, unlike languages with a history of writing, like Latin.

Dr. H. Russell Bernard, the anthropologist at the University of Florida at Gainesville who taught Mr. Salinas to read and write his native language, said: "Languages have always come and gone . . . But languages seem to be disappearing faster than ever before." . . .

Dr. Michael E. Krauss, the director of the Alaska Native Language Center at the University of Alaska in Fairbanks, estimates that 300 of the 900 indigenous languages in the Americas are moribund. That is, they are no longer being spoken by children, and so could disappear in a generation or two. Only two of the 20 native languages in Alaska are still being learned by children . . .

In an effort to preserve language diversity in Mexico, Dr. Bernard and Mr. Salinas decided in 1987 on a plan to teach the Indian people to read and write their own language using microcomputers. They established a native literacy center in Oaxaca, Mexico,

where others could follow in the footsteps of Mr. Salinas and write books in other Indian languages.

The Oaxaca center goes beyond most bilingual education programs, which concentrate on teaching people to speak and read their native languages. Instead, it operates on the premise that, as Dr. Bernard decided, what most native languages lack is native authors who write books in their own languages . . .

The Oaxaca project's influence is spreading. Impressed by the work of Mr. Salinas and others, Dr. Norman Whitten, an anthropologist at the University of Illinois, arranged for schoolteachers from Ecuador to visit Oaxaca and learn the techniques.

Now Ecuadorian Indians have begun writing about their cultures in the Quechua and Shwara languages. Others from Bolivia and Peru are learning to use the computers to write their languages, including Quechua, the tongue of the ancient Incas, still spoken by about 12 million Andean Indians . . .

Dr. Bernard emphasized that these native literacy programs are not intended to discourage people from learning the dominant language of their country as well. "I see nothing useful or charming about remaining monolingual in any Indian language if that results in being shut out of the national economy," he said.

SOURCE: Excerpted from John Noble Wilford, "In a Publishing Coup, Books in 'Unwritten' Languages," *New York Times*, December 31, 1991, pp. B5, B6.

imports, and the remaining 15 percent liked the two options equally. Local productions are successful in Nigeria because "they are filled with everyday moments that audiences can identify with. These shows are locally produced by Nigerians" (Gray 1986). Thirty million people watched one of the most popular series, *The Village Headmaster,* each week. That program brought rural values to the screens of urbanites who had lost touch with their rural roots (Gray 1986).

The mass media also can play a role in maintaining ethnic and national identities among people who lead transnational lives. Arabic-speaking Muslims, including migrants, in several countries follow the TV network Al Jazeera, based in Qatar, which helps reinforce ethnic and religious identities. As groups move, they can stay linked to each other and to their homeland through the media. Diasporas (people who have spread out from an original, ancestral homeland) have enlarged the markets for media, communication, and travel services targeted at specific ethnic, national, or religious audiences. For a fee, a PBS station in Fairfax, Virginia, offers more than 30 hours a week to immigrant groups in the D.C. area, to make programs in their own languages.

A Transnational Culture of Consumption

Besides the electronic media, another key transnational force is finance. Multinational corporations and other business interests look beyond national boundaries for places to invest and draw profits. As Arjun Appadurai (1991, p. 194) puts it, "money, commodities, and persons unendingly chase each other around the world." Residents of many Latin American communities now depend on outside cash, remitted from international labor migration. Also, the economy of the United States is increasingly influenced by foreign investment, especially from Britain, Canada, Germany, the Netherlands, and Japan (Rouse 1991). The American economy also has increased its dependence on foreign labor—through both the immigration of laborers and the export of jobs.

Contemporary global culture is driven by flows of people, technology, finance, information, images, and ideology (Appadurai 1990, 2001). Business, technology, and the media have increased the craving for commodities and images throughout the world (Gottdiener 2000). This has forced nation-states to open to a global culture of consumption. Almost everyone today participates in this culture. Few people have never seen a T-shirt advertising a Western product. American and English rock stars' recordings blast through the streets of Rio de Janeiro, while taxi drivers from Toronto to Madagascar play Brazilian music tapes. Peasants and tribal people participate in the modern world system not only because they have been hooked on cash, but also because their products and images are appropriated by world capitalism (Root 1996). They are commercialized by others (like the San in the movie *The Gods Must Be Crazy*). Furthermore, indigenous peoples also market their own images and products, through outlets like Cultural Survival (see Mathews 2000).

PEOPLE IN MOTION

The linkages in the modern world system have both enlarged and erased old boundaries and distinctions. Arjun Appadurai (1990, p. 1) characterizes today's world as a "translocal" "interactive system" that is "strikingly new." Whether as refugees, migrants, tourists, pilgrims, proselytizers, laborers, businesspeople, development workers, employees of nongovernmental organizations, politicians, terrorists, soldiers, sports figures, or media-borne images, people appear to travel more than ever.

In previous chapters, we saw that foragers and herders are typically seminomadic or nomadic. Today, however, the scale of human movement has expanded dramatically. So important is transnational migration that many Mexican villagers find "their most important kin and friends are as likely to be living hundreds or thousands of miles away as immediately around them" (Rouse 1991). Most migrants maintain their ties with their native land (phoning, e-mailing, visiting, sending money, watching "ethnic TV"). In a sense, they live multilocally—in different places at once. Dominicans in New York City, for example, have been characterized as living "between two islands": Manhattan and the Dominican Republic (Grasmuck and Pessar 1991). Many Dominicans—like migrants from other countries—migrate to the United States temporarily, seeking cash to transform their lifestyles when they return to the Caribbean.

With so many people "in motion," the unit of anthropological study expands from the local community to the **diaspora**—the offspring of an area who have spread to many lands. Anthropologists increasingly follow descendants of the villages we have studied as they move from rural to urban areas and across national boundaries. For the 1991 annual meeting of the American Anthropological Association in Chicago, the anthropologist Robert Kemper organized a session of presentations about long-term ethnographic field work. Kemper's own longtime research focus has been the Mexican village of Tzintzuntzan, which,

■ *When products and images enter new settings, they are typically indigenized—modified to fit the local culture. Jeans Street, in Bandung, Indonesia, is a strip of stores, vendors, and restaurants catering to young people interested in Western pop culture. How is the poster of Batman and Robin indigenized?*

and breakdown of established canons (rules or standards), categories, distinctions, and boundaries. The word is taken from **postmodernism**—a style and movement in architecture that succeeded modernism, beginning in the 1970s. Postmodern architecture rejected the rules, geometric order, and austerity of modernism. Modernist buildings were expected to have a clear and functional design. Postmodern design is "messier" and more playful. It draws on a diversity of styles from different times and places—including popular, ethnic, and non-Western cultures. Postmodernism extends "value" well beyond classic, elite, and Western cultural forms. *Postmodern* is now used to describe comparable developments in music, literature, and visual art. From this origin, *postmodernity* describes a world in which traditional standards, contrasts, groups, boundaries, and identities are opening up, reaching out, and breaking down.

Globalization promotes intercultural communication, including travel and migration, which bring people from different societies into direct contact. The world is more integrated than ever. Yet *dis*integration also surrounds us. Nations dissolve (Yugoslavia, the Soviet Union), as do political blocs (the Warsaw Pact nations) and ideologies ("Communism"). The notion of a "Free World" collapses because it existed mainly in opposition to a group of "Captive Nations"—a label once applied by the United States and its allies to the former Soviet empire that has lost much of its meaning today.

Simultaneously, new kinds of political and ethnic units are emerging. In some cases, cultures and ethnic groups have banded together in larger associations. There is a growing pan-Indian identity (Nagel 1996) and an international pantribal movement as well. Thus, in June 1992, the World Conference of Indigenous Peoples met in Rio de Janeiro concurrently with UNCED (the United Nations Conference on the Environment and Development). Along with diplomats, journalists, and environmentalists came 300 representatives of the tribal diversity that survives in the modern world—from Lapland to Mali (Brooke 1992; see also Maybury-Lewis 2002).

with his mentor George Foster, he has studied for decades. However, their database now includes not just Tzintzuntzan, but its descendants all over the world. Given the Tzintzuntzan diaspora, Kemper was even able to use some of his time in Chicago to visit people from Tzintzuntzan who had established a colony there. In today's world, as people move, they take their traditions and their anthropologists along with them.

Postmodernity describes our time and situation: today's world in flux, these people on the move who have learned to manage multiple identities depending on place and context. In its most general sense, **postmodern** refers to the blurring

INDIGENOUS PEOPLES

The term and concept *indigenous people* gained legitimacy within international law with the creation in 1982 of the United Nations Working Group on Indigenous Populations (WGIP). This group, which meets annually, has representation from all six continents. The draft of the Declaration of Indigenous Rights, produced by the WGIP in 1989, was accepted by the U.N. for discussion in 1993. Convention 169, an ILO (International Labor Organization) document that supports cul-

There's a difference between being a member of a diaspora and having a diasporic identity, such as a pan-Indian or pan-African identity. Diasporic identities, which have been abetted by the media and by various political and cultural organizations devoted to spreading or reinforcing such identities, are increasingly important in today's world. As for being a member of some diaspora, all humans are. All Americans, including Native Americans, originated somewhere else. Several groups, including English, French, Spanish, Portuguese, Dutch, Italians, Poles, Jews, Muslims, Lebanese, Africans, and Chinese, have migrated widely and settled in many countries. But there were older migrations, such as the one the led to the settling of the Polynesian islands—the Polynesian diaspora—starting around 3,000 years ago. Diasporas of ancestral Native Americans spread throughout North and South America. Australia was first settled, probably from Indonesia, between 50,000 and 60,000 years ago, and was "resettled" much later as part of the British colonial diaspora.

Once hunting was incorporated into the human adaptive strategy, *Homo erectus* extended the human range out of Africa and into Eurasia and beyond. Migrating bands of *Homo erectus* were part of a highly significant diaspora, but they certainly lacked a diasporic identity. There would be later diasporas out of Africa, including the migration that took ancient anatomically modern humans to Europe, Asia, and eventually the Americas. The forced migration out of Africa that occurred under slavery was responsible for a more recent African diaspora, contributing to the settlement of the United States, the Caribbean, Brazil, and many other countries in the Western Hemisphere. Although many of us lack any conscious diasporic identity, exposure to anthropology should certainly convince us that we all have the right to such an identity. Few, if any, of us can claim to belong to a lineage that has lived eternally in its homeland.

tural diversity and indigenous empowerment, was approved in 1989. Such declarations and documents, along with the work of the WGIP, have influenced governments, NGOs, and international agencies, including the World Bank, to express greater concern for, and to adopt policies designed to benefit, indigenous peoples. Social movements worldwide have adopted the term

■ *With so many people on the move, the unit of anthropological study has expanded from the local community to the diaspora. This refers to the offspring of an area (e.g., Africa) who have spread to many lands, such as these Afro-Caribbean pub owners in West Broomwich, England. Do you belong to a diaspora?*

"indigenous people" as a self-identifying and political label based on past oppression but now legitimizing a search for social, cultural, and political rights (de la Peña 2005).

In Spanish-speaking Latin America, social scientists and politicians favor the term *indígena* (indigenous person) over *indio* (Indian)—the colonial term that the Spanish and Portuguese conquerors used to refer to the native inhabitants of the Americas. With the national independence movements that ended Latin American colonialism, the situation of indigenous peoples did not necessarily improve. For the white and *mestizo* (mixed) elites of the new nations, *indios* and their lifestyle were perceived as alien to (European) civilization. But Indians also were seen as redeemable by intellectuals, who argued for social policies to improve their welfare (de la Peña 2005).

Until the mid- to late 1980s, Latin American public discourse and state policies emphasized assimilation and discouraged indigenous identification and mobilization. Indians were associated with a romanticized past, but marginalized in the present, except for museums, tourism, and folkloric events. Argentina's Indians were all but invisible. Indigenous Bolivians and Peruvians were encouraged to self-identify as *campesinos* (peasants). The past 30 years have seen a dramatic shift. The emphasis has shifted from biological and cultural assimilation—*mestizaje*—to identities that value difference, especially Indianness. In Ecuador groups seen previously as Quichua-speaking peasants are classified now as indigenous communities with assigned territories. Other Andean "peasants" have experienced reindigenization as well. Brazil has recognized 30

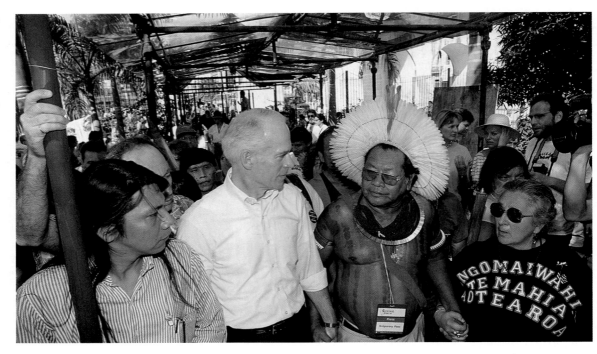

new indigenous communities in the northeast, a region previously seen as having lost its indigenous population (see "Beyond the Classroom"). In Guatemala, Nicaragua, Brazil, Colombia, Mexico, Paraguay, Ecuador, Argentina, Bolivia, Peru, and Venezuela, constitutional reforms have recognized those nations as multicultural (Jackson and Warren 2005). Several national constitutions now recognize the rights of indigenous peoples to cultural distinctiveness, sustainable development, political representation, and limited self-government. In Colombia, for example, indigenous communities have been confirmed as rightful owners of large territories. Their leaders and councils have the same benefits as any local government. Two seats in the Colombian senate are reserved for Indian representatives (de la Peña 2005).

In Latin America, the drive by indigenous peoples for self-determination has emphasized (1) their cultural distinctiveness; (2) political reforms involving a restructuring of the state; (3) territorial rights and access to natural resources, including control over economic development; and (4) reforms of military and police powers over indigenous peoples (Jackson and Warren 2005).

The indigenous rights movement, and government responses to it, take place in the context of globalization, including transnational social movements focusing on such issues as human rights, women's rights, and environmentalism. Transnational organizations have helped indigenous peoples influence national legislative agendas. NGOs specializing in development and human rights have come to see indigenous peoples as clients. Many Latin American countries

have signed international human rights treaties and covenants.

Although Latin America has experienced a general shift from authoritarian to democratic rule since the 1980s, ethnic and racial discrimination and inequality haven't disappeared. We should recognize as well that indigenous organizing has a high toll, including assassinations of indigenous leaders and their supporters. Especially in Guatemala, Peru, and Colombia there has been severe political repression, along with thousands of indigenous deaths, indigenous refugees, and internally displaced persons (Jackson and Warren 2005).

Ceuppens and Geschiere (2005) explore a recent upsurge of the notion of *autochthony* (being native to, or formed in, the place where found)—with an implicit call for excluding strangers—in different parts of the world. The terms *autochthony* and *indigenous* both go back to classical Greek history, with similar implications. *Autochthony* refers to self and soil. *Indigenous* literally means born inside, with the connotation in classical Greek of being born "inside the house." Both notions stress the need to safeguard ancestral lands (patrimony) from strangers, along with the rights of first-comers to special rights and protection versus later immigrants—legal or illegal (Ceuppens and Geschiere 2005).

During the 1990s, autochthony became an issue in many parts of Africa, inspiring violent efforts to exclude "strangers"—especially in Francophone (French-speaking) areas, but spilling over into Anglophone (English-speaking) countries as well. Simultaneously, autochthony became

BEYOND THE CLASSROOM

Urban Indigenous Identity in Salvador, Bahia, Brazil

BACKGROUND INFORMATION

STUDENT:
Jessica F. Nelson

SUPERVISING PROFESSOR:
Conrad P. Kottak

SCHOOL:
University of Michigan

YEAR IN SCHOOL/MAJOR:
Senior/Cultural Anthropology

FUTURE PLANS:
Graduate School
in Cultural Anthropology

PROJECT TITLE:
Urban Indigenous Identity
in Salvador, Bahia, Brazil

As an exchange student in Brazil, I recall walking along *Baixa dos Sapateiros,* the street known as "Shoemakers' Hollow," as it curved its way through the hills of the historic district of Salvador, the capital city of Bahia state. I had heard that this street was once a river, the boundary between Portuguese and Indian territories, and the scene of the first of their battles. I wondered about the stories such places held. This inspired me to design an independent study through which I planned to discover the stories of the indigenous people of Salvador.

My intent was to identify the concepts of identity held by indigenous people and their descendants living in Salvador, as well as the general public. I hoped also to learn how those who claim to be indigenous construct such an identity. Though aware of entering a cultural context in which indigenous identity might be considered irrelevant, I was unprepared to be confronted with statements that indigenous people do not exist in Salvador. Many residents of that city, Brazil's third largest, warned me that I would "be disappointed." Yet nearly every neighborhood had at least one person whose nickname was *índio,* or "Indian." "Why?" I asked. "Oh, because he or she *is* Indian," would be the response.

This contradiction gave new purpose to my research. Why, despite so many signs of indigenous people living in Salvador, do people believe they have disappeared? How could concepts of both identity and disappearance exist simultaneously?

For six months, I compiled information through participant observation, literary research, and taped interviews with indigenous people and their descendants, representing three generations. During these interviews, which were informal, I gathered quantifiable information, such as the names, ages, and birthplaces of family members. I also asked open-ended questions designed to lead into stories of personal experiences and perspectives. I worked with a list of questions, so as to facilitate later comparisons of information, although our conversations often drifted from those topics. Unforeseen information surfaced as we talked, joked, and spent time together. Interviewing allowed me to get to know people I otherwise never would have met, some of whom became good friends. At times intensely personal, their stories were candid testimonies of struggle and inner strength. No less moving perhaps were stories I could not collect: those of people who might have claimed, but who chose to deny, indigenous identity. I learned of such people through my own observation, and at times from their own family members who did claim indigenous identity.

Through the interviews, I discovered that many people construct their indigenous identity by using elements and symbols of popular culture, such as stereotypical clothing, ornaments, and body decorations associated with Indians in the media—though with sharply contrasting intent and message. After decades of virtual silence, when it was physically and socially dangerous to be *índio,* many ethnic groups have "emerged," or officially reclaimed their existence within the eyes of the law. Others, who have had this recognition, though often left unnoticed on the margins of society, are becoming increasingly vocal about their rights. Many people in Salvador now are claiming indigenous identity on a personal level. This is happening within a cultural context that has assumed indigenous people to have been assimilated; either entirely, or by occupying a *caboclo,* or mixed racial and cultural, status. Like many others in Latin America, indigenous people and their descendants in Salvador are challenging their "disappearance," and redefining what it means to be Indian.

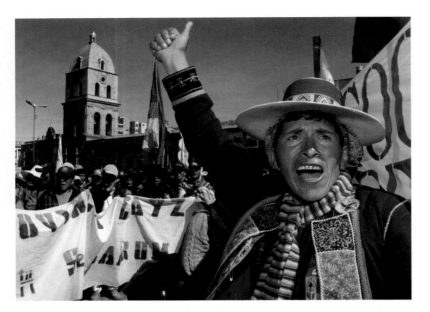

■ La Paz, Bolivia, May 23, 2005: Bolivians claiming an Indian (indigenous) identity rally for indigenous rights and the nationalization of that country's gas resources. In December 2005, Bolivians elected as their president Evo Morales, the candidate of the Indigenous Movement toward Socialism party. The party made further gains in 2006 parliamentary elections.

be managed in the context of, other identity components, including religion, race, and gender. Identities always must be seen as (1) potentially plural, (2) emerging through a specific process, and (3) ways of being someone or something in particular times and places (Jackson and Warren 2005).

Indigenous Peoples and Ethnography

How have indigenous movements, political mobilization, and identity politics affected ethnography? Pauline Turner Strong (2005) answers this question through an extensive review of recent ethnographic research among Native Americans in North America. The hallmark of traditional ethnographic research has been intensive, long-term participant observation in a local community. Such research continues among North American Indians today, but often it takes place in institutional settings such as tribal schools, museums, cultural centers, casinos, and tourist complexes. This shift in part reflects indigenous preferences: These institutions mediate between indigenous communities and the outside world. At such sites anthropologists can contribute to community-based research without intruding on private life. Also, these settings are ideal for the study of self-representation, self-determination, repatriation, and economic development. Museum studies, for example, have generated new ethnographies on tribal cultural centers (Strong 2005). One of these is a collaborative ethnography on the Cultural and Research Center of the Makah, whose whale hunt was described in the "News Brief" for the chapter "Culture" (Erickson, Ward, and Wachendorf 2002).

Increasingly as well, ethnographic research with Native Americans is situated in governmental institutions, including tribal offices, courts, and social service agencies. Such research may rely as much on formal interviews and archival research as it does on participant observation. Topics of such studies include (1) the articulation of tribal politics with the regional, national, and global political economy; (2) political divisions within, and alliances between, indigenous communities; (3) racial politics within indigenous communities and between them and surrounding non-Indian communities; and (4) governing and judicial bodies in tribal communities (Strong 2005). Sovereignty and the politics of identity have emerged as central themes, and anthropologists have worked as researchers for tribes in their efforts aimed at recognition, acknowledgment, and repatriation.

Compared with research in North America and Latin America since the 1990s, anthropological studies of social movements and identity politics have been less characteristic of Australia, whose

a key notion in debates about immigration and multiculturalism in Europe. Unlike "indigenous peoples," the label *autochthon* has been claimed by majority groups in Europe. This term highlights the prominence that the exclusion of strangers has assumed in day-to-day politics worldwide (Ceuppens and Geschiere 2005). One familiar example is the United States, as represented in the congressional debate that broke out, beginning in spring 2006, over illegal immigration.

Identity in Indigenous Politics

Essentialism describes the process of viewing an identity as established, real, and frozen, to hide the historical processes and politics within which that identity developed. One example would be the ethnic labels "Hutu" and "Tutsi" in Rwanda, as discussed in the chapter "Colonialism and Development." Those labels actually had nothing to do with ethnicity when they were created. Nation-states have used essentializing strategies (e.g., the Tutsi–Hutu distinction) to perpetuate hierarchies and to justify violence against categories seen as less than fully human.

Identities, emphatically, are not fixed. We saw in the chapter "Ethnicity and Race" that identities are fluid and multiple. People seize on particular, sometimes competing, self-labels and identities. Some Peruvian groups, for instance, self-identify as *mestizos* but still see themselves as indigenous. Identity is a fluid, dynamic process, and there are multiple ways of being indigenous. Neither speaking an indigenous language nor wearing "native" clothing is required. Identities are asserted at particular times and places by particular individuals and groups, and after various kinds of negotiations. Indigenous identity co-exists with, and must indigenous peoples comprise about 2 percent of the national population. In Australia, the 1990s were a decade of reconciliation, with the aim of creating a new relationship between settler Australia and its indigenous peoples. The Council for Aboriginal Reconciliation (CAR) situated itself within a people's movement. On May 28, 2000, in the People's Walk for Reconciliation, a quarter of a million people crossed Sydney's Harbor Bridge on foot, following a major public event called Corroboree 2000. CAR produced its final report in December 2002. Although Aboriginal and other Australians have been working together to recognize and help heal the wounds of the past, the federal government has not yet officially recognized the 2002 CAR report (Merlan 2005).

Francesca Merlan (2005) writes that until fairly recently, views of Australian indigenous peoples and their cultures tended to overlook their responses to colonization and settlement by Europeans. Indigenous societies were seen either as having been crushed by colonial impact (in areas of major European settlement), or, in more remote areas, as unchanging. Anthropologists valued Australia's indigenous cultures to the extent that they could be viewed as traditional and distinct from the dominant society. With the focus on the "traditional" life and institutions, interactions of indigenous peoples and outsiders were neglected.

One exception was Ronald Berndt (1969), who described what he saw as a gradual and late emergence of indigenous protest in Australia. Berndt found outside agents to be behind most of the protests. He saw activist Aborigines as "for all practical purposes Australian-Europeans," seeking common identity in the Aboriginal past, this trend itself a "kind of social movement" (p. 41). He concluded that once people "see themselves in relation to others, once they are in a position to compare, the way becomes wide open for . . . protest" (p. 42). In other words, although the protests reflected marginalization and oppression, the ideas and styles of activism that have guided Native Australian protest have arisen in interaction with Australian national culture (Merlan 2005). This is not unusual. No social movement exists apart from the nation that includes it. Nor is any contemporary nation isolated from the world system, globalization, and transnational organization.

THE CONTINUANCE OF DIVERSITY

Anthropology has a crucial role to play in promoting a more humanistic vision of social change, one that respects the value of human biological and cultural diversity. The existence of anthropology is itself a tribute to the continuing need to understand similarities and differences among human beings throughout the world. Anthropology teaches us that the adaptive responses of humans can be more flexible than can those of other species because our main adaptive means are sociocultural. However, the cultural forms, institutions, values, and customs of the past always influence subsequent adaptation, producing continued diversity and giving a certain uniqueness to the actions and reactions of different groups. With our knowledge and our awareness of our professional responsibilities, let us work to keep anthropology, the study of humankind, the most humanistic of all the sciences.

SUMMARY

1. Different degrees of destruction, domination, resistance, survival, and modification of native cultures may follow interethnic contact. This may lead to a tribe's cultural collapse (ethnocide) or its physical extinction (genocide). Multinational corporations have fueled economic development and ecological devastation. Either development or external regulation may pose a threat to indigenous peoples, their cultures, or their environments. The most effective conservation strategies pay attention to the needs, incentives, and customs of people living in the affected area.

2. *Cultural imperialism* refers to the spread of one culture and its imposition on other cultures, which it modifies, replaces, or destroys—usually because of differential economic or political influence. Some worry that modern technology, including the mass media, is destroying traditional cultures. But others see an important role for new technology in allowing local cultures to express themselves.

3. The term *text* is used here to describe anything that can be creatively "read," interpreted, and assigned meaning by someone who receives it. People may resist the hegemonic meaning of a text. Or they may seize on its antihegemonic aspects. When forces from world centers enter new societies, they are *indigenized.* Like print, the electronic mass media can help diffuse a national culture within its own boundaries. The media also play a role in preserving ethnic and national identities among people who lead transnational lives. Business, technology, and the media have increased the craving for commodities and images throughout the world, creating a global culture of consumption.

4. People travel more than ever. But migrants also maintain ties with home, so they live multi-locally. With so many people "in motion," the unit of anthropological study expands from the local community to the diaspora. *Postmodernity* describes this world in flux, such people on the move who manage multiple social identities depending on place and context. New kinds of political and ethnic units are emerging as others break down or disappear.

5. The term and concept *indigenous people* has gained legitimacy within international law. Governments, NGOs, and international agencies have adopted policies designed to recognize and benefit indigenous peoples. Social movements worldwide have adopted this term as a self-identifying and political label based on past oppression but now signaling a search for social, cultural, and political rights. In Latin America, emphasis has shifted from biological and cultural assimilation to identities that value difference. Several national constitutions now recognize the rights of indige-nous peoples. Transnational organizations have helped indigenous peoples influence national legislative agendas. Recent use of the notion of *autochthony* (being native to, or formed in, the place where found) includes a call to exclude strangers, such as recent and illegal immigrants. Identity is a fluid, dynamic process, and there are multiple ways of being indigenous.

6. Indigenous movements and identity politics have affected anthropology. Ethnographic research among North American Indians today often takes place in institutional and government settings. Topics of such studies include the articulation of tribal politics with the regional, national, and global political economy and political divisions within, and alliances between, indigenous communities. In Australia, where native resistance has been downplayed by anthropologists, the ideas and styles of activism that have guided indigenous protest have arisen in interaction with Australian national culture. No social movement exists apart from the nation and world that includes it.

KEY TERMS

See the flash cards
mhhe.com/kottak

cultural imperialism The rapid spread or advance of one culture at the expense of others, or its imposition on other cultures, which it modifies, replaces, or destroys—usually because of differential economic or political influence.

diaspora The offspring of an area who have spread to many lands.

essentialism The process of viewing an identity as established, real, and frozen, to hide the historical processes and politics within which that identity developed.

indigenized Modified to fit the local culture.

postmodern In its most general sense, describes the blurring and breakdown of established canons (rules, standards), categories, distinctions, and boundaries.

postmodernism A style and movement in architecture that succeeded modernism. Compared with modernism, postmodernism is less geometric, less functional, less austere, more playful, and more willing to include elements from diverse times and cultures; postmodern now describes comparable developments in music, literature, visual art, and anthropology.

postmodernity Condition of a world in flux, with people on the move, in which established groups, boundaries, identities, contrasts, and standards are reaching out and breaking down.

text Something that is creatively "read," interpreted, and assigned meaning by each person who receives it; includes any media-borne image, such as Carnaval.

westernization The acculturative influence of Western expansion on native cultures.

CRITICAL THINKING QUESTIONS

For more self-testing,
see the self-quizzes
mhhe.com/kottak

1. Are you a conservationist? What do you see as the pros and cons of forcing people, businesses, or communities to conserve when such conservation conflicts with cultural patterns or economic interests? Revisit the "News Brief" in the chapter "Culture" on Makah whale hunting. What's your opinion about cultural rights in the context of conservationist initiatives?

2. Consider majority and minority rights in the context of contemporary events involving religion, politics, and law. Should religion be an ascribed or an achieved status? Should someone in a Muslim nation be allowed to convert to a different religion? In your country, how much influence should majority and minority religions be allowed to have on politics and the law?

3. How do you participate in a world system of images? Are the images to which you relate mainly national, or foreign/international as well?

4. How do you use the media? Is there a program or group that has special meaning for you? Are you personally irritated when someone questions your meaning?

5. Do you now live, or have you ever lived, multi-locally? How so?

Ahmed, A. S.
2004 *Postmodernism and Islam: Predicament and Promise,* rev. ed. New York: Routledge. Clear presentation of postmodernism in relation to the media and to images of Islam.

Appadurai, A. , ed.
2001 *Globalization.* Durham, NC: Duke University Press. The flows that create today's world system.

Bodley, J. H.
1999 *Victims of Progress,* 4th ed. Mountain View, CA: Mayfield. Social change, acculturation, and culture conflict involving indigenous peoples.

Cultural Survival Inc.
1992 *At the Threshold.* Cambridge, MA: Author. Originally published as the Spring 1992 issue of *Cultural Survival Quarterly.* Manual for the promotion of the rights of indigenous peoples. Highlights activist successes, gives instructions for affecting policy, working in schools and communities, directly helping native societies, and using the media as a human rights ally.

Feld, S.
1990 *Sound and Sentiment: Birds, Weeping, Poetics, and Song in Kaluli Expression,* 2nd ed. Philadelphia: University of Pennsylvania Press. Ethnographic study of sound as a cultural system among the Kaluli people of Papua New Guinea.

Fiske, J., and J. Hartley
2003 *Reading Television,* 2nd ed. New York: Routledge. Interpreting television and its content as a text.

Gottdiener, M., ed.
2000 *New Forms of Consumption: Consumers, Culture, and Commodification.* Lanham, MD: Rowman and Littlefield. Cultural consumption, diversity, and market segmentation in today's global economy.

Johansen, B. E.
2003 *Indigenous Peoples and Environmental Issues: An Encyclopedia.* Westport, CT: Greenwood. A compendium of knowledge about environmental issues as they affect and reflect local communities.

Laird, S. A.
2002 *Biodiversity and Traditional Knowledge: Equitable Partnerships in Practice.* Sterling, VA: Earthscan. What local people and scientists have to offer each other in regard to biodiversity.

Lutz, C., and J. L. Collins
1993 *Reading National Geographic.* Chicago: University of Chicago Press. How the cultural narratives of the magazine are received and interpreted; the relation between images of other peoples, cultures, and lifestyles and middle-class North American values.

Marcus, G. E., and M. M. J. Fischer
1999 *Anthropology as Cultural Critique: An Experimental Moment in the Human Sciences,* 2nd ed. Chicago: University of Chicago Press. New edition of an influential book on modern and postmodern anthropology.

Maybury-Lewis, D.
2002 *Indigenous Peoples, Ethnic Groups, and the State,* 2nd ed. Boston: Allyn & Bacon. Indigenous peoples and ethnicity in the contemporary world.

Nagel, J.
1996 *American Indian Ethnic Renewal: Red Power and the Resurgence of Identity and Culture.* New York: Oxford University Press. The meaning of activism for Native American individual ethnic identification; the role of federal, tribal, and personal politics in the growth of American Indian identity.

Reed, R.
1997 *Forest Dwellers, Forest Protectors: Indigenous Models for International Development.* Boston: Allyn & Bacon. Applying indigenous knowledge and practices to economic development.

Robbins, R.
2005 *Global Problems and the Culture of Capitalism,* 3rd ed. Boston: Pearson/Allyn & Bacon. Examines issues of domination, resistance, and social and economic problems in today's world.

Root, D.
1996 *Cannibal Culture: Art, Appropriation, and the Commodification of Difference.* Boulder, CO: Westview Press. How Western art and commerce classify, co-opt, and commodify "native" experiences, creations, and products.

Scott, J. C.
1990 *Domination and the Arts of Resistance.* New Haven, CT: Yale University Press. A study of institutionalized forms of domination, such as colonialism, slavery, serfdom, racism, caste, concentration camps, prisons, and old-age homes— and the forms of resistance that oppose them.

1. Peacemaking among the Nuer and Dinka: Read the *Washington Post* article about the recent history of these groups, **http://www.washingtonpost.com/wp-srv/inatl/daily/july99/sudan7.htm**.
   a. Anthropologists in the middle of the 20th century recorded conflict between the Nuer and the Dinka. In this article, they became allies against what opponent? How did conflict reemerge between the Nuer and the Dinka?
   b. What were the traditional views of warfare and death among the Nuer and the Dinka? How did these change with the introduction of modern machine guns?
   c. What impact did these new views have on the recent Nuer–Dinka conflicts?
   d. Despite the cultural changes brought about by the pressures of modern nations and the introduction of machine guns, the Nuer and the Dinka used traditional cultural symbols to help bring about peace. What are some examples?
   e. Do you think this peace will be short-lived? What needs to take place in order to maintain peace?

2. Ishi and Cultural Survival: Visit the website **http://www.mohicanpress.com/mo08019.html** and read about Ishi.
   a. Who was Ishi? To what tribe did he belong, and what happened to it?
   b. In what way was Ishi successful in preserving native culture and educating people about it? Who was Alfred Kroeber, and what role did he play in Ishi's life?
   c. How did Ishi's family perish? Where did he live after he was rescued?
   d. The website draws parallels between Ishi and James Fennimore Cooper's *The Last of the Mohicans*. Do you think those parallels are apt?

See Chapter 16 at your McGraw-Hill Online Learning Center for additional review and interactive exercises.

LINKAGES

Kottak, *Assault on Paradise*, 4th ed.

Read the section of Chapter 6 titled "The Magic of Success and the Growth of Religion." How was the increase in *candomblé* activity related to new economic opportunities in Arembepe? Both the textbook and *Assault on Paradise* (Chapter 12) have discussed how Arembepeiros resisted outsiders' appropriation of their traditional February festival. Having finished *AOP*, provide three other examples of resistance by Arembepeiros to the ideas or actions of outsiders, such as people claiming higher status, hippies, or fish buyers.

Peters-Golden, *Culture Sketches*, 4th ed.

This text chapter discusses the potentially grave consequences of economic development and environmental degradation. Outside exploitation poses a threat to indigenous peoples. In *Culture Sketches*, read Chapter 15, "The Yanomamo: Challenges in the Rainforest." What are some challenges faced by the Yanomamo (aka Yanomami)? What is the anthropologist's role in conflicts between indigenous peoples and the governments of the countries in which they live? Should an anthropologist be an objective observer, an advocate, or neither of these things? What are some difficulties involved in choosing a position?

Knauft, *The Gebusi*, 1st ed.

Read Chapter 11 and the conclusion. Based on Chapter 11, what features of Gebusi culture are preserved, transformed, or made fun of at Independence Day celebrations? What extra-local images, activities, and social relations are evident in the celebrations? In what ways is Gebusi culture becoming blurred with regional or national culture? Based on the conclusion, do you think Gebusi culture has changed more than it has stayed the same? What evidence can be used to support your opinion? In what ways have Gebusi become modern in a unique cultural fashion?

The Biology and Culture of Overconsumption

In the chapter "The Modern World System," we learned that Americans are the world's foremost consumers. Using some 275,000 calories of energy per day, the average American is 35 times more expensive than the average forager or tribesperson, who uses just 8,000 calories. Since 1900, the United States has increased its total energy consumption 30-fold. And in the last two decades, Americans have increased their *food* consumption by an average of 200 calories per day. American agribusiness now produces 500 food calories more per person per day than it did 30 years ago, which is about 1,000 more calories per day than most people need (Pollan 2003). This provides a dramatic contrast with the food scarcity that accompanies poverty in the less-developed countries. In the chapter "Colonialism and Development," for example, we saw that in Java, daily food calories available per capita had dropped from 1,950 to 1,750, less than half the current American figure of 3,800 (Pollan 2003).

In his book *Fat Land: Supersizing America* (2003), Greg Critser examines how Americans rapidly are becoming the fattest people on earth. Sixty percent of all Americans, and 25 percent of American children, are now overweight. Since 1970, the percentage of American children who are overweight has doubled. Food companies have fueled this epidemic of obesity as they have attempted to maintain their profitability—by getting people to eat more—at a time when the American food supply has been growing much faster than the American population has. A key ingredient in the fattening of America has been the rise and spread of "supersizing."

Critser (2003) traces how David Wallerstein—an executive at McDonald's—invented supersizing. In the 1960s, Wallerstein, then working for a movie theater chain, was looking for ways to expand sales of soda pop and popcorn. He discovered that although the typical moviegoer was reluctant to buy more than one drink or bag of popcorn, people would consume more drink and popcorn if they came in a single large serving. Such supersizing is an effective business strategy because the raw materials for soda, popcorn, fries, and burgers make up only a small fraction of their price—compared with the costs of labor, packaging, and advertising. Expanding the size of portions allowed businesses to raise prices and increase sales without adding much to costs.

Ray Kroc, the founder of McDonald's, adopted Wallerstein's strategy of supersizing. In McDonald's advertising, Big Macs and large fries replaced "regular" (i.e., small) hamburgers and fries. Dave Thomas offered "biggie" fries and drinks at Wendy's. All the fast-food chains started hawking combos (for breakfast, lunch, or later). This greatly enhanced the American (and worldwide) consumption of that old Peruvian domesticate, the "Irish" potato, in the form of "French" fries. (Talk about a world system!)

When people are offered larger portions, studies show they will eat up to 30 percent more than they otherwise would. (Think about our holiday feasts.) For human hunger to be elastic like this makes evolutionary sense. By feasting whenever they had the chance, our hunter-gatherer ancestors could store fat to use later when they were confronted with food scarcity or famine. We've seen that in Papua New Guinea and Melanesia, "big men" and their followers work hard to organize feasts at which pigs are killed and cooked and pork is widely distributed and eaten. In those societies it's a rare and welcome treat to "pig out." In the contemporary United States it's easy to "pig out" any day of the year. If a "thrifty

■ *Fast food leaves its imprint on the body. The 4-year-old Russian boy on the right weighs 123 pounds. The Georgian boy on the left has just turned 5 and weighs 112 pounds. After a wrestling match in which they tied, they went off to enjoy a meal in Tbilisi, Georgia, on July 9, 2003.*

See your OLC Bringing
It All Together links
mhhe.com/kottak

Whether in North America or in Denmark, as shown here on May 13, 2002, McDonald's presents itself as a place where families can eat comfortably.

only the United States but also the consuming (middle and upper) classes of nations around the world.

The sun, it was said, never set on the British empire. We could make the same observation about the global presence of McDonald's in the 21st century. The number of McDonald's outlets today far surpasses the total number of fast-food restaurants in the United States in 1945. McDonald's has grown from a single hamburger stand in San Bernardino, California, into today's international web of thousands of outlets.

The success of McDonald's is founded on modern technology, particularly automobiles, television, work away from home, and the short lunch break (see Brown and Krick 2001). Several years ago, I began to notice certain ritual-like aspects of Americans' behavior at fast-food restaurants, especially at McDonald's. Tell your fellow Americans that going to a fast-food restaurant is similar in some ways to going to church and their bias as natives will reveal itself in laughter, denial, or questions about your sanity. McDonald's, for natives, is just a place to eat. However, an analysis of what natives do there will reveal a very high degree of formal, uniform behavior by staff members and customers alike. It is particularly interesting that this invariance in word and deed has developed without any theological doctrine. It is striking that a commercial organization should be so successful in producing behavioral invariance. Factors other than low cost, fast service, and the taste of the food—all of which are approximated by other chains—have contributed to our acceptance of McDonald's and adherence to its rules.

Remarkably, when Americans travel abroad, even in countries noted for good food, many go to the local McDonald's outlet. The same factors that lead us to visit McDonald's at home are responsible. Because Americans are thoroughly familiar with how to eat and more or less what they will pay at McDonald's, in its outlets overseas they have a home away from home. In Paris, whose people aren't known for making tourists, particularly Americans, feel at home, McDonald's offers sanctuary (along with relatively clean, free rest rooms). It is, after all, an originally American institution where natives, programmed by years of prior experience, can feel completely at home.

This devotion to McDonald's rests in part on uniformities associated with its outlets: food, setting, architecture, ambience, acts, and utterances. The McDonald's symbol, the golden arches, is an almost universal symbol, as familiar to Americans as Mickey Mouse, Oprah, and the flag. A McDonald's (now closed) near my university was a brick structure whose stained-glass windows had golden arches as their central theme. Sunlight flooded in through a skylight that was like the clerestory of a church.

gene" facilitating fat storage was adaptive for our hunter-gatherer ancestors, it has become maladaptive today given the food surplus just described (see Brown and Bentley-Condit 1996; Farb and Armelagos 1980).

The American epidemic of obesity is a consequence of cheap and abundant food. As applied anthropologists know, changes take place as part of systems: One change leads to other changes, which are related and compensatory. Thus, as Critser (2003) notes, to accommodate fatter customers, restaurants have increased the size of their seats. American government agencies have relaxed their weight, fitness, and dietary guidelines. Named diets and fitness centers have proliferated, and clothing sizes have been recalibrated to make fatter people feel thinner. "It runs large" and "it runs small" are common phrases in the linguistic strategies of garment salespeople.

Overeating has clear health consequences. The new American diet has ushered in an epidemic of Type 2 diabetes, formerly known as "adult-onset diabetes," which, however, now afflicts millions of children. The cost of overconsumption to the American health system runs to billions of dollars annually. According to Pollan (2003), the fattening of America may be emerging as a political issue. A grassroots parents' movement seeks to remove fast food and vending machines from schools. Obese customers have filed lawsuits against fast-food chains, seeking to hold those companies liable for health problems, as tobacco companies have been held liable through legal action. Questions have been raised about the ethics of marketing unhealthy products to children.

We've seen how the business strategy of supersizing fueled the expansion of fast food and overeating. An anthropological perspective can reveal more subtle cultural factors within the culture of overconsumption, which characterizes not

Americans enter a McDonald's restaurant for an ordinary, secular act—eating. However, the surroundings tell us we are somehow apart from the variability of the world outside. We know what we are going to see, what we are going to say, and what will be said to us. We know what we will eat, how it will taste, and how much it will cost. Behind the counter, agents wear similar attire. Permissible utterances by customer and worker are written above the counter. Throughout the United States, with only minor variations, the menu is in the same place, contains the same items, and has the same prices. The food, again with only minor variation, is prepared according to plan and varies little in taste. Obviously, customers are limited in what they can choose. Less obviously, they are limited linguistically—in terms of what they can say. Each item has its appropriate designation: "large fry," "quarter pounder with cheese." The novice who innocently asks, "What kind of hamburgers do you have?" or "What's a Big Mac?" is out of place.

A linguistic anthropologist would notice that other ritual phrases are uttered by the person behind the counter. After the customer has completed an order, if no potatoes are requested, the agent ritually asks, "You want the combo?" Once food is presented and picked up, the agent conventionally says, "Have a nice day." (McDonald's has surely played a strong role in the diffusion of this linguistic cliché into every corner of contemporary American life.)

Understandably, as the world's number one fast-food chain, McDonald's evokes hostility. The Ann Arbor campus McDonald's once was the scene of a ritual rebellion—desecration by the Radical Vegetarian League, which held a "puke-in." Standing on the second-story balcony just below the clerestory, a dozen vegetarians gorged themselves on mustard and water and vomited down on the customer waiting area. McDonald's, defiled, lost many customers that day. Worldwide, McDonald's has become one of the most potent symbols of globalization and perceived American cultural and economic imperialism. McDonald's has felt the brunt of cultural, including religious, opposition to its meals, meats, and mission.

Eating at McDonald's and religious feasts are in complementary distribution in American life. That is, when one occurs, the other doesn't. Most Americans would consider it inappropriate to eat at a fast-food restaurant on Christmas, Thanksgiving, Easter, or Passover. Our culture regards these as family days, occasions when relatives and close friends get together. However, although Americans neglect McDonald's on holidays, television reminds us that McDonald's still endures, that it will welcome us back once our holiday is over. The television presence of McDonald's is particularly evident on such occasions—whether through a float in the Macy's Thanksgiving Day

On April 18, 2002, students hold a sit-in at a McDonald's outlet in Beirut, Lebanon, as part of a campaign to boycott American products. McDonald's international success has made it a target of protests against perceived American cultural imperialism.

parade or through sponsorship of special programs, particularly "family entertainment."

Although Burger King, Wendy's, and Arby's compete with McDonald's for the fast-food business, none has equaled the success of McDonald's. The explanation may lie in the particularly skillful ways in which McDonald's advertising plays up the features just discussed. On Saturday morning television, with its steady stream of cartoons, McDonald's has been a ubiquitous sponsor. Breakfast at McDonald's has been promoted by a fresh-faced, sincere, happy, clean-cut young woman. Actors gambol on ski slopes or in mountain pastures. The single theme that for years has run through the commercials is personalism. McDonald's, the commercials drone on, is something other than a fast-food restaurant. It's a warm, friendly place where you are graciously welcomed and feel at home, where your children won't get into trouble. McDonald's commercials tell you that you aren't simply an anonymous face in an amorphous crowd. You find respite from a hectic and impersonal society, the break you deserve. Your individuality and dignity are respected at McDonald's. And "I'm lovin it."

McDonald's advertising tries to deemphasize the fact that the chain is a commercial organization. One jingle proclaimed, "You, you're the one; we're fixin' breakfast for ya"—not "We're making millions off ya." "Family" television entertainment often is "brought to you by McDonald's."

McDonald's commercials regularly tell us that it supports and works to maintain the values of American family life.

I am not arguing here that McDonald's has become a religion. I merely am suggesting that specific ways in which Americans participate in McDonald's bear analogies to religious systems involving myth, symbol, and ritual. Just as in rituals, participation in McDonald's requires temporary subordination of individual differences in a social and cultural collectivity. In a land of ethnic, social, economic, and religious diversity, we demonstrate that we share something with millions of others. Furthermore, as in rituals, participation in McDonald's is linked to a cultural system that transcends the chain itself. By eating there, we say something about ourselves as Americans, about our acceptance of certain collective values, customs, and ways of living.

Such widespread learned behavior patterns, fueled in this case by a savvy business model, also have biological—weight and health—consequences, as we saw at the beginning of this essay. Consider finally the explosion of paper, plastic, and Styrofoam associated with the fast-food industry. Such material remains, along with distinctive arches and architecture, offer evidence that contemporary garbologists, or future archaeologists, might use to reconstruct the culture of consumption in the early 21st century.

Appendix 1
A History of Theories in Anthropology

Anthropology has various fathers and mothers. The fathers include Lewis Henry Morgan, Sir Edward Burnett Tylor, Franz Boas, and Bronislaw Malinowski. The mothers include Ruth Benedict and especially Margaret Mead. Some of the fathers might be classified better as grandfathers, since one, Franz Boas, was the intellectual father of Mead and Benedict, and since what is known now as Boasian anthropology arose mainly in opposition to the 19th-century evolutionism of Morgan and Tylor.

My goal here is to survey the major theoretical perspectives that have characterized anthropology since its emergence in the second half of the 19th century. Evolutionary perspectives, especially those associated with Morgan and Tylor, dominated early anthropology. The early 20th century witnessed various reactions to 19th-century evolutionism. In Great Britain, functionalists such as Malinowski and Alfred Reginald Radcliffe-Brown abandoned the speculative historicism of the evolutionists in favor of studies of present-day living societies. In the United States, Boas and his followers rejected the search for evolutionary stages in favor of a historical approach that traced borrowing between cultures and the spread of culture traits across geographic areas. Functionalists and Boasians alike saw cultures as integrated and patterned. The functionalists especially viewed societies as systems in which various parts worked together to maintain the whole.

By the mid-20th century, following World War II and the collapse of colonialism, there was a revived interest in change, including new evolutionary approaches. Other anthropologists concentrated on the symbolic basis and nature of culture, using symbolic and interpretive approaches to uncover patterned symbols and meanings. By the 1980s anthropologists had grown more interested in the relation between culture and the individual, and the role of human action (agency) in transforming culture. There was also a resurgence of historical approaches, including those that viewed local cultures in relation to colonialism and the world system. Contemporary anthropology is marked by increasing specialization, based on special topics and identities. Reflecting this specialization, some universities have moved away from the holistic, biocultural view of anthropology that is reflected in this book. However, the Boasian view of anthropology as a four-subfield discipline—including biological, archaeological, cultural, and linguistic anthropology—continues to thrive at many universities as well.

EVOLUTIONISM

Both Tylor and Morgan wrote classic books during the 19th century. Tylor (1871/1958) offered a classic definition of culture and proposed it as a topic that could be studied scientifically. Morgan's influential books included *Ancient Society* (1877/1963), *The League of the Ho-dé-no-sau-nee or Iroquois* (1851/1966), and *Systems of Consanguinity and Affinity of the Human Family* (1870/1997). The first was a key work in cultural evolution. The second was an early ethnography. The third was the first systematic compendium of cross-cultural data on systems of kinship terminology.

Ancient Society is a key example of 19th-century evolutionism applied to society. Morgan assumed that human society had evolved through a series of stages, which he called savagery, barbarism, and civilization. He subdivided savagery and barbarism into three substages each: lower, middle, and upper savagery and lower, middle, and upper barbarism. In Morgan's scheme, the earliest humans lived in lower savagery, with a subsistence based on fruits and nuts. In middle savagery people started fishing and gained control over fire. The invention of the bow and arrow ushered in upper savagery. Lower barbarism began when humans started making pottery. Middle barbarism in the Old World depended on the domestication of plants and animals, and in the Americas on irrigated agriculture. Iron smelting and the use of iron tools ushered in upper barbarism. Civilization, finally, came about with the invention of writing.

Morgan's brand of evolutionism is known as *unilinear evolutionism,* because he assumed there was one line or path through which all societies had to evolve. Any society in upper barbarism, for example, had to include in its history, in order, periods of lower, middle, and upper savagery, and then lower and middle barbarism. Stages could not be skipped. Furthermore, Morgan believed that the societies of his time could be placed in the various stages. Some had not advanced beyond upper savagery. Others had made it to middle barbarism, while others had attained civilization.

Critics of Morgan disputed various elements of his scheme, particularly the criteria he used for progress. Thus, because Polynesians never developed pottery, they were frozen, in Morgan's scheme, in upper savagery. In fact, in sociopolitical terms, Polynesia was an advanced region, with many chiefdoms and at least one state— ancient Hawaii. We know now, too, that Morgan was wrong in assuming that societies pursued only one evolutionary path. Societies (e.g., Maya versus Mesopotamia) followed different paths to civilization, based on very different economies.

In his book *Primitive Culture* (1871/1958), Tylor developed his own evolutionary approach to the anthropology of religion, as was discussed in the chapter "Religion." Like Morgan, Tylor proposed a unilinear path—from animism to polytheism, then monotheism, and finally science. Religion would end, Tylor thought, when it lost its primary function—to explain the unexplainable. In Tylor's view, religion would retreat as science provided better and better explanations. Both Tylor and Morgan were interested in *survivals,* practices that survived in contemporary society form earlier evolutionary stages. The belief in ghosts today, for example, would represent a survival from the stage of animism—the belief in spiritual beings. Survivals were taken as evidence that a particular society had passed through earlier evolutionary stages.

Morgan is well known also for *The League of the Iroquois,* anthropology's earliest ethnography. It was based on occasional rather than protracted fieldwork. Morgan, although one of anthropology's founders, was not himself a professionally trained anthropologist. He was a lawyer in upper New York state, who was fond of visiting a nearby Seneca reservation and learning about their history and customs. The Seneca were one of six Iroquois tribes. Through his fieldwork, and his friendship with Ely Parker (see Chapter 1), an educated Iroquois man, Morgan was able to describe the social, political, religious, and economic principles of Iroquois life, including the history of their confederation. He laid out the structural principles on which Iroquois society was based. Morgan also used his skills as a lawyer to help the Iroquois in their fight with the Ogden Land Company, which was attempting to seize their lands.

Although Morgan was a strong advocate for the Iroquois, his work contains some assumptions that would be considered racist today. There are statements in *The League* and elsewhere suggesting, erroneously, that cultural traits, such as hunting and a type of kinship terminology, have a biological basis. Morgan assumed that the desire to hunt was intrinsic to being Indian, transmitted "in the blood" rather than through enculturation. It was up to Franz Boas, writing decades later, to show that cultural traits are transmitted culturally rather than genetically, and to show the malleability of human biology and its openness to variable enculturation.

THE BOASIANS

Four-Field Anthropology

Indisputably, Boas is the father of four-field American anthropology. His book *Race, Language, and Culture* (1940/1966) is a collection of essays on those key topics. Boas contributed to cultural, biological, and linguistic anthropology. His biological studies of European immigrants to the United States revealed and measured phenotypical plasticity. The children of immigrants differed physically from their parents not because of genetic change but because they had grown up in a different environment. Boas showed that human biology was plastic. It could be changed by the environment, including cultural forces. Boas and his students worked hard to demonstrate that biology (including race) did not determine culture. In an important book, Ruth Benedict (1940) stressed the idea that people of many races have contributed to major historical advances and that civilization is the achievement of no single race.

As was mentioned in Chapter 1, the four subfields of anthropology initially formed around interests in Native Americans—their cultures, histories, languages, and physical characteristics. Boas himself studied language and culture among Native Americans, most notably the Kwakiutl of the North Pacific coast of the United States and Canada.

Historical Particularism

Boas and his many influential followers, who studied with him at Columbia University in New York City, took issue with Morgan on many counts. They disputed the criteria he used to define his stages. They disputed the idea of one evolutionary path. They argued that the same cultural result, for example, totemism, could not have a single explanation, because there were many paths to totemism. Their position was one of *historical particularism.* Because the particular histories of totemism in societies A, B, and C had all been different, those forms of totemism had different causes, which made them incomparable. They might seem to be the same, but they were really different because they had different histories. Any cultural form, from totemism to clans, could develop, they believed, for all sorts of reasons. Boasian historical particularism rejected what those scholars called the *comparative method,* which was associated not only with Morgan and Tylor, but with any anthropologist interested in cross-cultural comparison. The evolutionists had compared societies in attempting to reconstruct the evolutionary history of *Homo sapiens.* Later anthropologists, such as Émile Durkheim and Claude Lévi-Strauss (see below), also compared societies in attempting to explain cultural phenomena such as totemism. As we have seen throughout this text, cross-cultural comparison is alive and well in contemporary anthropology.

Independent Invention versus Diffusion

Remember from the chapter "Culture" that *cultural generalities* are shared by some but not all societies. To explain cultural generalities, such as totemism and the clan, the evolutionists had stressed independent invention: Eventually people in many areas (as they evolved along a preordained evolutionary path) had come up with the same cultural solution to a common problem. Agriculture, for example, was invented several times. The Boasians, while not denying independent invention, stressed the importance of diffusion, or borrowing, from other cultures. The analytic units they used to study diffusion were the culture trait, the trait complex, and the culture area. A culture trait was something like a bow and arrow. A trait complex was the hunting pattern that went along with it. A culture area was based on the diffusion of traits and trait complexes across a particular geographic area, such as the Plains, the Southwest, or the North Pacific coast of North America. Such areas usually had environmental boundaries that could limit the spread of culture traits outside that area. For the Boasians historical particularism and diffusion were complementary. As culture traits diffused, they developed their particular histories as they entered and moved through particular societies. Boasians such as Alfred Kroeber, Clark Wissler, and Melville Herskovits studied the distribution of traits and developed culture area classifications for Native North America (Wissler and Kroeber) and Africa (Herskovits).

Historical particularism was based on the idea that each element of culture, such as the culture trait or trait complex, had its own distinctive history, and that social forms (such as totemism in different societies) that might look similar were far from identical because of their different histories. Historical particularism rejected comparison and generalization in favor of an individuating historical approach. In this rejection, historical particularism stands in contrast to most of the approaches that have followed it.

FUNCTIONALISM

Another challenge to evolutionism (and to historical particularism) came from Great Britain. *Functionalism* postponed the search for origins (through evolution or diffusion) and instead focused on the role of culture traits and practices in contemporary society. The two main strands of functionalism are associated with Alfred Reginald Radcliffe-Brown and Bronislaw Malinowski, a Polish anthropologist who taught mainly in Great Britain.

Malinowski

Both Malinowski and Radcliffe-Brown focused on the present rather than on historical reconstruction. Malinowski did pioneering field work among living people. Usually considered the father of ethnography by virtue of his years of field work in the Trobriand Islands, Malinowski was a functionalist in two senses. In the first, rooted in his ethnography, he believed that all customs and institutions in society were integrated and interrelated, so that if one changed, others would change as well. Each, then, was a function of the others. A corollary of this belief was that the ethnography could begin anywhere and eventually get at the rest of the culture. Thus, a study of Trobriand fishing eventually would lead the ethnographer to study the entire economic system, the role of magic and religion, myth, trade, and kinship. The second strand of Malinowski's functionalism is known as *needs functionalism.* Malinowski (1944) believed that humans had a set of universal biological needs, and that customs developed to fulfill those needs. The function of any practice was the role it played in satisfying those universal biological needs, such as the need for food, sex, shelter, and so on.

Conjectural History

According to Radcliffe-Brown (1962/1965), although history is important, social anthropology could never hope to discover the histories of people without writing. (*Social anthropology* is what cultural anthropology is called in Great Britain.) He trusted neither evolutionary nor diffusionist reconstructions. Since all history was conjectural, Radcliffe-Brown urged social anthropologists to focus on the role that particular practices play in the life of societies today. In a famous essay Radcliffe-Brown (1962/1965) examined the prominent role of the mother's brother among the Ba Thonga of Mozambique. An evolutionist priest working in Mozambique previously had explained the special role of the mother's brother in this patrilineal society as a survival from a time when the descent rule had been matrilineal. (The unilinear evolutionists believed all human societies had passed through a matrilineal stage.) Since Radcliffe-Brown believed that the history of Ba Thonga society could only be conjectural, he explained the special role of the mother's brother with reference to the institutions of present rather than past Ba Thonga society. Radcliffe-Brown advocated that social anthropology be a *synchronic* rather than a *diachronic* science, that is, that it study societies as they exist today (synchronic, at one time) rather than across time (diachronic).

Structural Functionalism

The term *structural functionalism* is associated with Radcliffe-Brown and Edward Evan Evans-Pritchard, another prominent British social anthropologist. The latter is famous for many books, including *The Nuer* (1940), an ethnographic classic that laid out very clearly the structural principles that organized Nuer society in Sudan. According to functionalism and structural functionalism, customs (social practices) function to preserve the social structure. In Radcliffe-Brown's view, the *function* of any practice is what it does to maintain the system of which it is a part. That system has a structure whose parts work or function to maintain the whole. Radcliffe-Brown saw social systems as comparable to anatomical and physiological systems. The function of organs and physiological processes is their role in keeping the body running smoothly. So, too, he thought, did customs, practices, social roles, and behavior function to keep the social system running smoothly.

Dr. Pangloss versus Conflict

Given this suggestion of harmony, some functionalist models have been criticized as Panglossian, after Dr. Pangloss, a character in Voltaire's *Candide* who was fond of proclaiming this "the best of all possible worlds." Panglossian functionalism means a tendency to see things as functioning not just to maintain the system but to do so in the most optimal way possible, so that any deviation from the norm would only damage the system. A group of British social anthropologists working at the University of Manchester, dubbed the Manchester school, are well known for their research in African societies and their departure from a Panglossian view of social harmony. Manchester anthropologists Max Gluckman and Victor Turner made conflict an important part of their analysis, such as when Gluckman wrote about rituals of rebellion. However, the Manchester school did not abandon functionalism totally. Its members examined how rebellion and conflict were regulated and dissipated, thus maintaining the system.

Functionalism Persists

A form of functionalism persists in the widely accepted view that there are social and cultural systems and that their elements, or constituent parts, are functionally related (are functions of each other) so that they covary: when one part changes, others also change. Also enduring is the idea that some elements—often the economic ones—are more important than others are. Few would deny, for example, that significant economic changes, such as the increasing cash employment of women, have led to changes in family and household organization, and in related variables such as age at marriage and frequency of divorce. Changes in work and family arrangements then affect other variables, such as frequency of church attendance, which has declined in the United States and Canada.

CONFIGURATIONALISM

Two of Boas's students, Benedict and Mead, developed an approach to culture that has been called *configurationalism*. This is related to functionalism in the sense that culture is seen as integrated. We've seen that the Boasians traced the geographic distribution of culture traits. But Boas recognized that diffusion wasn't automatic. Traits might not spread if they met environmental barriers, or if they were not accepted by a particular culture. There had to be a fit between the culture and the trait diffusing in, and borrowed traits would be reworked to fit the culture adopting them. This process recalls the discussion, in the chapter "Cultural Exchange and Survival," of how borrowed traits are indigenized—modified to fit the existing culture. Although traits may diffuse in from various directions, Benedict stressed that culture traits—indeed, whole cultures—are uniquely patterned or integrated. Her best-selling book *Patterns of Culture* (1934/1959) described such culture patterns.

Mead also found patterns in the cultures she studied, including Samoa, Bali, and Papua New Guinea. Mead was particularly interested in how cultures varied in their patterns of enculturation. Stressing the plasticity of human nature, she saw culture as a powerful force that created almost endless possibilities. Even among neighboring societies, different enculturation patterns could produce very different personality types and cultural configurations. Mead's best-known—albeit controversial—book is *Coming of Age in Samoa* (1928/1961). Mead traveled to Samoa to study female adolescence there in order to compare it with the same period of life in the United States. Suspicious of biologically determined universals, she assumed that Samoan adolescence would differ from the same period in the United States and that this would affect adult personality. Using her Samoan ethnographic findings, Mead contrasted the apparent sexual freedom and experimentation there with the repression of adolescent sexuality in the United States. Her findings supported the Boasian view that culture, not biology or race, determines variation in human behavior and personality. Mead's later field work among the Arapesh, Mundugumor, and Tchambuli of New Guinea resulted in *Sex and Temperament in Three Primitive Societies* (1935/1950). That book documented variation in male and female personality traits and behavior across cultures. She offered it as further support for cultural determinism. Like Benedict, Mead was more interested in describing how cultures were uniquely patterned or configured than in explaining how they got to be that way.

NEOEVOLUTIONISM

Around 1950, with the end of World War II and a growing anticolonial movement, anthropologists renewed their interest in culture change and even evolution. The American anthropologists Leslie White and Julian Steward complained that the Boasians had thrown the baby (evolution) out with the bath water (the particular flaws of 19th-century evolutionary schemes). There was a need, the neoevolutionists contended, to reintroduce within the study of culture a powerful concept—evolution itself. This concept, after all, remains basic to biology. Why should it not apply to culture as well?

In his book *The Evolution of Culture* (1959), White claimed to be returning to the same concept of cultural evolution used by Tylor and Morgan, but now informed by a century of archaeological

discoveries and a much larger ethnographic record. White's approach has been called *general evolution,* the idea that over time and through the archaeological, historical, and ethnographic records, we can see the evolution of culture as a whole. For example, human economies have evolved from Paleolithic foraging, through early farming and herding, to intensive forms of agriculture, and to industrialism. Sociopolitically, too, there has been evolution, from bands and tribes to chiefdoms and states. There can be no doubt, White argued, that culture has evolved. But unlike the unilinear evolutionists of the 19th century, White realized that particular cultures might not evolve in the same direction.

Julian Steward, in his influential book *Theory of Culture Change* (1955), proposed a different evolutionary model, which he called *multilinear evolution.* He showed how cultures had evolved along several different lines. For example, he recognized different paths to statehood (e.g., those followed by irrigated versus nonirrigated societies). Steward was also a pioneer in a field of anthropology he called *cultural ecology,* today generally known as *ecological anthropology,* which considers the relationships between cultures and environmental variables.

Unlike Mead and Benedict, who were not interested in causes, White and Steward were. For White, energy capture was the main measure and cause of cultural advance: Cultures advanced in proportion to the amount of energy harnessed per capita per year. In this view, the United States is one of the world's most advanced societies because of all the energy it harnesses and uses. White's formulation is ironic in viewing societies that deplete nature's bounty as being more advanced than those that conserve it.

Steward was equally interested in causality, and he looked to technology and the environment as the main causes of culture change. The environment and the technology available to exploit it were seen as part of what he called the *culture core*—the combination of subsistence and economic activities that determined the social order and the configuration of that culture in general.

CULTURAL MATERIALISM

In proposing *cultural materialism* as a theoretical paradigm, Marvin Harris adapted multilayered models of determinism associated with White and Steward. For Harris (1979/2001) all societies had an *infrastructure,* corresponding to Steward's culture core, consisting of technology, economics, and demography—the systems of production and reproduction without which societies could not survive. Growing out of infrastructure was *structure*—social relations, forms of kinship and descent, patterns of distribution and consumption. The third layer was *superstructure:* religion, ideology, play—aspects of culture furthest away from the meat and bones that enable cultures to survive. Harris's key belief, shared with White, Steward, and Karl Marx, was that in the final analysis infrastructure determines structure and superstructure.

Harris therefore took issue with theorists (he called them "idealists") such as Max Weber who argued for a prominent role of religion (the Protestant ethic, as discussed in the chapter "Religion") in changing society. Weber didn't argue that Protestantism had caused capitalism. He merely contended that the individualism and other traits associated with early Protestantism were especially compatible with capitalism and therefore aided its spread. One could infer from Weber's argument that without Protestantism, the rise and spread of capitalism would have been much slower. Harris probably would counter that given the change in economy, some new religion compatible with the new economy would appear and spread with that economy, since infrastructure (what Karl Marx called the base) always determines in the final analysis.

SCIENCE AND DETERMINISM

Harris's influential books include *The Rise of Anthropological Theory* (1968/2001) and *Cultural Materialism: The Struggle for a Science of Culture* (1979/2001). Like most of the anthropologists discussed so far, Harris insisted that anthropology is a *science;* that science is based on explanation, which uncovers relations of cause and effect; and that the role of science is to discover causes, to find determinants. One of White's two influential books was *The Science of Culture* (1949). Malinowski set forth his theory of needs functionalism in a book titled *A Scientific Theory of Culture, and Other Essays* (1944). Mead viewed anthropology as a humanistic science of unique value in understanding and improving the human condition.

Like Harris, White, and Steward, all of whom looked to infrastructural factors as determinants, Mead was a determinist, but of a very different sort. Mead's cultural determinism viewed human nature as more or less a blank slate on which culture could write almost any lesson. Culture was so powerful that it could change drastically the expression of adolescence in Samoa and the United States. Mead stressed the role of culture rather than economy, environment, or material factors in this difference.

CULTURE AND THE INDIVIDUAL

Culturology

Interestingly, Leslie White, the avowed evolutionist and champion of energy as a measure of cultural progress, was, like Mead, a strong advocate of the importance of culture. White saw cultural anthropology as a science, and he named that science *culturology.* Cultural forces, which rested on the unique human capacity for symbolic thought, were so powerful, White believed, that individuals made little difference. White disputed what was then called the "great man theory of history," the idea that particular individuals were responsible for great discoveries and epochal changes. White looked instead to the constellation of cultural forces that produced great individuals. During certain historical periods, such as the Renaissance, conditions were right for the expression of creativity and greatness, and individual genius blossomed. At other times and places, there may have been just as many great minds, but the culture did not encourage their expression. As proof of this theory, White pointed to the simultaneity of discovery. Several times in human history, when culture was ready, people working independently in different places have come up with the same revolutionary idea or achievement. Examples include the formulation of the theory of evolution through natural selection by Charles Darwin and Alfred Russel Wallace, the independent rediscovery of Mendelian genetics by three separate scientists in 1917, and the independent invention of flight by the Wright brothers in the United States and Santos Dumont in Brazil.

The Superorganic

Much of the history of anthropology has been about the roles and relative prominence of culture and the individual. Like White, the prolific Boasian anthropologist Alfred Kroeber stressed the power of culture. Kroeber (1952/1987) called the cultural realm, whose origin converted an ape into an early hominid, the *superorganic.* The superorganic opened up a new domain of analysis separable from, but comparable in importance to, the organic (life—without which there could be no superorganic) and the inorganic (chemistry and physics—the basis of the organic). Like White (and long before him Tylor, who first proposed a science of culture), Kroeber saw culture as the basis of a new science, which became cultural anthropology. Kroeber (1923) laid out the basis of this science in anthropology's first textbook. He attempted to demonstrate the power of culture over the individual by focusing on particular styles and fashions, such as those involving women's hem lengths. According to Kroeber (1944), hordes of individuals were carried along helplessly by the alternating trends of various times, swept up in the undulation of styles. Unlike White, Steward, and Harris, Kroeber did not attempt to explain such shifts; he simply used them to show the power of culture over the individual. Like Mead, he was a cultural determinist.

Durkheim

In France, Émile Durkheim had taken a similar approach, calling for a new social science to be based in what he called, in French, the *conscience collectif.* The usual translation of this as "collective consciousness" does not convey adequately the similarity of this notion to Kroeber's superorganic and White's culturology. This new science, Durkheim proposed, would be based on the study of *social facts,* analytically distinct from the individuals from whose behavior those facts were inferred. Many anthropologists agree with the central promise that the role of the anthropologist is to study something larger than the individual. Psychologists study individuals; anthropologists study individuals as representative of something more. It is those larger systems, which consist of social positions—statuses and roles—and which are perpetuated across the generations through enculturation, that anthropologists should study.

Of course sociologists also study such social systems, and Durkheim, as was discussed in the chapter "Culture," is a common father of anthropology and sociology. Durkheim wrote of religion in Native Australia as readily as of suicide rates in modern societies. As analyzed by Durkheim, suicide rates (1897/1951) and religion (1912/2001) are collective phenomena. Individuals commit suicide for all sorts of reasons, but the variation in rates (which apply only to collectivities) can and should be linked to social phenomena, such as a sense of anomie, malaise, or alienation at particular times and in particular places.

SYMBOLIC AND INTERPRETIVE ANTHROPOLOGY

Victor Turner was a colleague of Max Gluckman in the Department of Social Anthropology at the University of Manchester, and thus a member of the Manchester school, previously described, before moving to the United States, where he taught at the University of Chicago and the University of Virginia. Turner wrote several important books and essays on ritual and symbols. His monograph *Schism and Continuity in an African Society* (1957/1996) illustrates the interest in conflict and its resolution previously mentioned as characteristic of the Manchester school. *The Forest of Symbols* (1967) is a collection of essays about symbols and rituals among the Nbembu of Zambia, where Turner did his major field work. In *The Forest of Symbols* Turner examines how symbols and rituals are used to redress, regulate, anticipate, and avoid conflict. He also examines a hierarchy of meanings of symbols, from their social meanings and functions to their internalization within individuals.

Turner recognized links between *symbolic anthropology* (the study of symbols in their social and cultural context), a school he pioneered, and such other fields as social psychology, psychology, and psychoanalysis. The study of symbols is all important in psychoanalysis, whose founder, Sigmund Freud, also recognized a hierarchy of symbols, from potentially universal ones to those that had meaning for particular individuals and emerged during the analysis and interpretation of their dreams. Turner's symbolic anthropology flourished at the University of Chicago, where another major advocate, David Schneider (1968), developed a symbolic approach to American culture in his book *American Kinship: A Cultural Account* (1968).

Related to symbolic anthropology, and also associated with the University of Chicago (and later with Princeton University), is *interpretive anthropology,* whose main advocate is Clifford Geertz. As mentioned in the chapter "Culture," Geertz defines culture as ideas based on cultural learning and symbols. During enculturation, individuals internalize a previously established system of meanings and symbols. They use this cultural system to define their world, express their feelings, and make their judgments.

Interpretive anthropology (Geertz 1973, 1983) approaches cultures as texts whose forms and, especially, meanings must be deciphered in particular cultural and historical contexts. Geertz's approach recalls Malinowski's belief that the ethnographer's primary task is "to grasp the native's point of view, his relation to life, to realize *his* vision of *his* world" (1922/1961, p. 25—Malinowski's italics). Since the 1970s, interpretive anthropology has considered the task of describing and interpreting that which is meaningful to natives. Cultures are texts that natives constantly "read" and ethnographers must decipher. According to Geertz (1973), anthropologists may choose anything in a culture that interests or engages them (such as a Balinese cockfight he interprets in a famous essay), fill in details, and elaborate to inform their readers about meanings in that culture. Meanings are carried by public symbolic forms, including words, rituals, and customs.

STRUCTURALISM

In anthropology structuralism mainly is associated with Claude Lévi-Strauss, a prolific and long-lived French anthropologist. Lévi-Strauss's structuralism evolved over time, from his early interest in the structures of kinship and marriage systems to his later interest in the structure of the human mind. In this latter sense, Lévi-Straussian structuralism (1967) aims not at explaining relations, themes, and connections among aspects of culture but at discovering them.

Structuralism rests on Lévi-Strauss's belief that human minds have certain universal characteristics which originate in common features of the *Homo sapiens* brain. These common mental structures lead people everywhere to think similarly regardless of their society or cultural background. Among these universal mental characteristics are the need to classify: to impose order on aspects of nature, on people's relation to nature, and on relations between people.

According to Lévi-Strauss, a universal aspect of classification is opposition, or contrast. Although many phenomena are continuous rather than discrete, the mind, because of its need to impose order, treats them as being more different than they are. One of the most common means of classifying is by using binary opposition. Good and evil, white and black, old and young, high and low are oppositions that, according to Lévi-Strauss, reflect the universal human need to convert differences of degree into differences of kind.

Lévi-Strauss applied his assumptions about classification and binary opposition to myths and folk tales. He showed that these narratives have simple building blocks—elementary structures or "mythemes." Examining the myths of different cultures, Lévi-Strauss shows that one tale can be converted into another through a series of simple operations, for example, by doing the following:

1. Converting the positive element of a myth into its negative

2. Reversing the order of the elements

3. Replacing a male hero with a female hero

4. Preserving or repeating certain key elements

Through such operations, two apparently dissimilar myths can be shown to be variations on a common structure, that is, to be transformations of each other. One example is Lévi-Strauss's (1967) analysis of "Cinderella," a widespread tale whose elements vary between neighboring cultures. Through reversals, oppositions, and negations, as the tale is told, retold, diffused, and incorporated within the traditions of successive societies, "Cinderella" becomes "Ash Boy," along with a series of other oppositions (e.g., stepfather versus stepmother) related to the change in gender from female to male.

PROCESSUAL APPROACHES: PRACTICE THEORY

Agency

Structuralism has been faulted for being overly formal and for ignoring social process. We saw in the chapter "Culture" that culture conventionally has been seen as social glue transmitted across the generations, binding people through their common past. More recently, anthropologists have come to see culture as something continually created and reworked in the present. The tendency to view culture as an entity rather than a process is changing. Contemporary anthropologists now emphasize how day-to-day action, practice, or resistance can make and remake culture (Gupta and Ferguson, eds. 1997b). *Agency* refers to the actions that individuals take, both alone and in groups, in forming and transforming cultural identities.

Practice Theory

The approach to culture known as *practice theory* (Ortner 1984) recognizes that individuals within a society or culture have diverse motives and intentions and different degrees of power and influence. Such contrasts may be associated with gender, age, ethnicity, class, and other social variables. Practice theory focuses on how such varied individuals—through their actions and practices—influence and transform the world they live in. Practice theory appropriately recognizes a reciprocal relation between culture and the individual. Culture shapes how individuals experience and respond to external events, but individuals also play an active role in how society functions and changes. Practice theory recognizes both constraints on individuals and the flexibility and changeability of cultures and social systems. Well-known practice theorists include Sherry Ortner, an American anthropologist, and Pierre Bourdieu and Anthony Giddens, French and British social theorists, respectively.

Leach

Some of the germs of practice theory, sometimes also called action theory (Vincent 1990), can be traced to the British anthropologist Edmund Leach, who wrote the influential book *Political Systems of Highland Burma* (1954/1970). Influenced by the Italian social theorist Vilfredo Pareto, Leach focused on how individuals work to achieve power and how their actions can transform society. In the Kachin Hills of Burma, now Myanmar, Leach described three forms of sociopolitical organization, which he called *gumlao, gumsa,* and Shan. Greatly oversimplifying, these three forms in that order suggest tribal, chiefdom, and state organization as discussed in previous chapters. But Leach made a tremendously important point by taking a regional rather than a local perspective. The Kachins participated in a regional system that included all three forms of organization. Traditional typologies suggest that tribes, chiefdoms, and states are separate units. Leach showed how they coexist and interact, as forms and possibilities known to everyone, in the same region. He also showed how Kachins creatively use power struggles, for example, to convert *gumlao* into *gumsa* organization, and how they negotiate their own identities within the regional system. Leach brought process to the formal models of structural functionalism. By focusing on power and how individuals get and use it, he showed the creative role of the individual in transforming culture.

WORLD-SYSTEM THEORY AND POLITICAL ECONOMY

Leach's regional perspective was not all that different from another development at the same time. Julian Steward, discussed previously as a neoevolutionist, joined the faculty of Columbia University in 1946, where he worked with several graduate students, including Eric Wolf and Sidney Mintz. Steward, Mintz, Wolf, and others planned and conducted a team research project in Puerto Rico, described in Steward's volume *The People of Puerto Rico* (1956). This project exemplified a post–World War II turn of anthropology away from "primitive" and nonindustrial societies, assumed to be somewhat isolated and autonomous, to contemporary societies recognized as forged by colonialism and participating fully in the modern world system. The team studied communities in different parts of Puerto Rico. The field sites were chosen to sample major events and adaptations, such as the sugar plantation, in the island's history. The approach emphasized economics, politics, and history.

Wolf and Mintz retained their interest in history throughout their careers. Wolf wrote the modern classic *Europe and the People without History* (1982), which viewed local people, such as Native Americans, in the context of world system events, such as the fur trade in North America. Wolf focused on how such "people without history"—that is, nonliterate people, those who lacked written histories of their own—participated in and were transformed by the world system and the spread of capitalism. Mintz's *Sweetness and Power* (1985) is another example of historical anthropology focusing on *political economy* (the web of interrelated economic and power relations). Mintz traces the domestication and spread of sugar, its transformative role in England, and its impact on the New World, where it became the basis for slave-based plantation economies in the Caribbean and Brazil. Such works in political economy illustrate a movement of anthropology toward interdisciplinarity, drawing on other academic fields, such as history and sociology. Any world-system approach in anthropology would have to pay attention to sociologist Immanuel Wallerstein's writing on world-system theory, including his model of core, periphery, and semiperiphery, as discussed in the chapter "The Modern World System." World-system approaches in anthropology have been criticized for overstressing the influence of outsiders, and for paying insufficient attention to the transformative actions of "the people without history" themselves.

CULTURE, HISTORY, POWER

More recent approaches in historical anthropology, while sharing an interest in power with the world-system theorists, have focused more on local agency, the transformative actions of individuals and groups within colonized societies. Archival work has been prominent in recent historical anthropology, particularly on areas, such as Indonesia, for which colonial and postcolonial archives contain valuable information on relations between colonizers and colonized and the actions of various actors in the colonial context. Studies of culture, history, and power have drawn heavily on the work of European social theorists such as Antonio Gramsci and Michel Foucault.

As we saw in the chapter "Political Systems," Gramsci (1971) developed the concept of *hegemony* for a stratified social order in which subordinates comply with domination by internalizing their rulers' values and accepting domination as "natural." Both Pierre Bourdieu (1977) and Foucault (1979) contend that it is easier to dominate people in their minds than to try to control their bodies. Contemporary societies have devised various forms of social control in addition to physical violence. These include techniques of persuading, coercing, and managing people and of monitoring and recording their beliefs, behavior, movements, and contacts. Anthropologists interested in culture, history and power, such as Ann Stoler (1995, 2002), have examined systems of power, domination, accommodation, and resistance in various contexts, including colonies, postcolonies, and other stratified contexts.

ANTHROPOLOGY TODAY

Early American anthropologists, such as Morgan, Boas, and Kroeber, were interested in, and made contributions to, more than a single subfield. If there has been a single dominant trend in anthropology since the 1960s, it has been one of increasing specialization. During the 1960s, when this author attended graduate school at Columbia University, I had to study and take qualifying exams in all four subfields. This has changed. There are still strong four-field anthropology departments, but many excellent departments lack one or more of the subfields. Four-field departments such as the University of Michigan's still require courses and teaching expertise across the subfields, but graduate students must choose to specialize in a particular subfield, and take qualifying exams only in that subfield. In Boasian anthropology, all four subfields shared a single theoretical assumption about human plasticity. Today, following specialization, the theories that guide the subfields differ. Evolutionary paradigms of various sorts still dominate biological anthropology and remain strong in archaeology as well. Within cultural anthropology, it has been decades since evolutionary approaches thrived.

Ethnography, too, has grown more specialized. Cultural anthropologists now head for the field with a specific problem in mind, rather than with the goal of producing a holistic ethnography—a complete account of a given culture—as Morgan and Malinowski intended when they studied, respectively, the Iroquois and the people of the Trobriand Islands. We've seen, too, in previous chapters that "the field" has become more amorphous over time. Boas, Malinowski, and Mead went somewhere and stayed there for a while, studying the local culture. Today the field has expanded to include regional and national systems and the movement of people, such as immigrants and diasporas, across national boundaries. Many anthropologists now follow the flows of people, information, finance, and media to multiple sites. Such movement has been made possible by advances in transportation and communication. However, with so much time in motion and with the need to adjust to various field sites and contexts, the richness of traditional ethnography may diminish.

Anthropology also has witnessed a crisis in representation—questions about the role of the ethnographer and the nature of ethnographic authority. What right do ethnographers have to represent a people or culture to which they don't belong? Some argue that insiders' accounts are more valuable and appropriate than are studies by outsiders, because native anthropologists not only know the culture better, they also should be in charge of representing their culture to the public. Reflecting the trends just described, the AAA (American Anthropological Association) now has all sorts of subgroups. In its beginning, there were just anthropologists within the AAA. Now there are groups representing biological anthropology, archaeology, and linguistic, cultural, and applied anthropology, as well as dozens of groups formed around particular interests and identities. These groups represent psychological anthropology, urban anthropology, culture and agriculture, anthropologists in small colleges, midwestern anthropologists, senior anthropologists, lesbian and gay anthropologists, Latino/a anthropologists, and so on. Many of the identity-based groups accept the premise that group members are better qualified to study issues and topics involving that group than outsiders are.

The chapter "Cultural Exchange and Survival" described *postmodernity*—our world in flux, where mobile people manage multiple identities depending on place and context. The term *postmodern* refers to the blurring and breakdown of established canons, categories, distinctions, and boundaries. Postmodernity has influenced anthropology in many ways. It has changed our units of analysis. Postmodernism is like anthropology itself in extending value beyond high culture to the culture of ordinary people from all over the world. Yet postmodern approaches in anthropology also question established assumptions, such as the outside ethnographer's right to represent. Science itself is challenged. Doubters argue that science can't be trusted because it is carried out by scientists. All scientists, the doubters contend, come from particular individual or cultural backgrounds that prevent objectivity, leading to artificial and biased accounts that have no more value than do those of insiders who are nonscientists.

What are we to do if we, as I do, continue to share Mead's view of anthropology as a humanistic science of unique value in understanding and improving the human condition? We must try to stay aware of our biases and our inability totally to escape them. The best scientific choice would seem to be to combine the perpetual goal of objectivity with skepticism about achieving it. Kluckhohn's statement (1944, p. 9) of the need for anthropology's scientific objectivity still stands: "Anthropology provides a scientific basis for dealing with the crucial dilemma of the world today: how can peoples of different appearance, mutually unintelligible languages, and dissimilar ways of life get along peaceably together?" In this world of failed states, terrorism, and preemptive war, most anthropologists never would have chosen their profession had they doubted that anthropology could play a significant role in answering such questions.

Appendix 2
Ethics and Anthropology

As the main organization representing the breadth of anthropology (all four subfields, academic and applied dimensions), the American Anthropological Association believes that generating and appropriately using knowledge of the peoples of the world, past and present, is a worthy goal. The production of anthropological knowledge is a dynamic process involving different and ever-evolving approaches. The mission of the AAA is to advance anthropological research and encourage the spread of anthropological knowledge through publications, teaching, public education, and application. Part of that mission is to help educate AAA members about ethical obligations and challenges (http://www.aaanet.org).

As anthropologists conduct research and engage in other professional activities, ethical issues inevitably arise. Anthropologists have typically worked abroad, outside their own society. In the context of international contacts and cultural diversity, different value systems will meet, and often compete. To guide its members in making decisions involving ethics and values, the AAA offers a Code of Ethics. The most recent Code was approved in June 1998 and updated on March 31, 1999. The Code's preamble states that anthropologists have obligations to their scholarly field, to the wider society and culture, and to the human species, other species, and the environment. This Code's aim is to offer guidelines and to promote discussion and education. Although the AAA has investigated allegations of misconduct by anthropologists, it does not adjudicate such claims. The AAA also recognizes that anthropologists belong to multiple groups—including, perhaps, a family, a community, a religion, and other organizations—each of which may have its own ethical and moral rules. Because anthropologists can find themselves in complex situations and subject to more than one ethical code, the AAA Code provides a framework, not an ironclad formula, for making decisions.

The AAA wants its members to be attentive to ethical issues, and it urges anthropology departments to include ethical training in their curricula. The AAA Code addresses several contexts in which anthropologists work. Its main points about the ethical dimensions of research may be summarized.

> Anthropologists should be open and honest about all dimensions of their research projects with funding agencies, colleagues, and all parties affected by the research. These parties should be informed about the purpose(s), potential impacts, and source(s) of support for the research. Anthropologists should disseminate the results of their research in an appropriate and timely way.
>
> Researchers should not compromise anthropological ethics in order to conduct research. They should also pay attention to proper relations between themselves as guests and the host nations and communities where they work. The AAA does not advise anthropologists to avoid taking stands on issues. Indeed, the Code states that leadership in seeking to shape actions and policies may be as ethically justifiable as inaction.

Here are some of the headings and subheadings of the Code:

A. RESPONSIBILITY TO PEOPLE AND ANIMALS

1. The primary ethical obligation of the anthropologist is to the people, species, and materials they study. This obligation takes precedence over the goal of seeking new knowledge. It can also lead to the decision not to undertake, or to discontinue, research when ethical conflicts arise. This primary

ethical obligation—anthropology's "prime directive"—entails:

Avoiding harm or wrong.

Understanding that the production of knowledge can have positive or negative effects on the people or animals worked with or studied.

Respecting the well-being of humans and non-human primates.

Working for the long-term conservation of the archaeological, fossil, and historical records.

Consulting actively with the affected individuals or group(s), with the goal of establishing a working relationship that will benefit all parties.

2. Researchers must do all they can to preserve the safety, dignity, and privacy of the people with whom they work. Anthropologists working with animals should not endanger their safety, psychological well-being, or survival.

3. Anthropologists should determine whether their hosts wish to remain anonymous or to receive recognition, and should try to comply with those wishes. Researchers should make clear to research participants that, despite the best efforts of the anthropologist, anonymity may be compromised or recognition fail to materialize.

4. Researchers must obtain the *informed consent* of affected parties. That is, prior to their agreement to participate, people should be told about the purpose, nature, and procedures of the research and its potential impact on them. Informed consent (agreement to take part in the research) should be obtained from anyone providing information, owning materials being studied, or otherwise having an interest that might be impacted by the research. Informed consent does not necessarily imply or require a written or signed form.

5. Researchers who develop ongoing relationships with individuals providing information or with hosts must continue to respect the obligations of openness and informed consent.

6. Anthropologists may gain personally from their work, but they should not exploit individuals, groups, animals, or cultural or biological materials. They should recognize their debt to the communities and societies in which they work and to the people with whom they work. They should reciprocate in appropriate ways.

B. RESPONSIBILITY TO SCHOLARSHIP AND SCIENCE

1. Anthropologists should attempt to identify potential ethical conflicts and dilemmas when preparing proposals, and as projects proceed.

2. Anthropologists are responsible for the integrity and reputation of their field, of scholarship, and of science. They are subject to the general moral rules of scientific and scholarly conflict. They should not deceive or knowingly misrepresent (i.e., fabricate evidence, falsify, plagiarize). They should not attempt to prevent reporting of misconduct, or obstruct the scholarly research of others.

3. Anthropologists should do all they can to preserve opportunities for future researchers to follow them to the field.

4. To the extent possible, anthropologists should disseminate their findings to the scientific and scholarly community.

5. Anthropologists should consider all reasonable requests for access to their data and materials for purposes of research. They should preserve their data for use by posterity.

C. RESPONSIBILITY TO THE PUBLIC

1. Anthropologists should strive to ensure that their findings are contextualized properly and used responsibly. Anthropologists should also consider the social and political implications of their conclusions. They should be honest about their qualifications and philosophical and political biases. They must be alert to possible harm their information might cause people with whom they work, or colleagues.

2. Anthropologists may move beyond disseminating research results to a position of advocacy. This is an individual decision, but not an ethical responsibility.

D. ETHICS PERTAINING TO APPLIED ANTHROPOLOGY

1. The same ethical guidelines apply to all anthropological work—academic and applied. Applied anthropologists should use their results appropriately (i.e., publi-

cation, teaching, program and policy development) within a reasonable time. Applied anthropologists should be honest about their skills and intentions. They should monitor the effects of their work on everyone affected.

2. In dealings with employers, applied anthropologists should be honest about their qualifications, abilities, and goals. The applied anthropologist should review the aims and interests of the prospective employer, taking into consideration the employer's past activities and future goals. Applied anthropologists should not accept conditions contrary to professional ethics.

The full Code of Ethics, which is abbreviated and paraphrased here, is available at the AAA website (http://www.aaanet.org).

Appendix 3
American Popular Culture

Culture is shared. But all cultures have divisive as well as unifying forces. Tribes are divided by residence in different villages and membership in different descent groups. Nations, though united by government, are divided by class, region, ethnicity, religion, and political party. Unifying forces in tribal cultures include marriage, trade, and a belief in common descent. In any society, of course, a common cultural tradition also may provide a basis for uniformity.

Whatever unity contemporary American culture has doesn't rest on a particularly strong central government. Nor is national unity based on a belief in common descent or marital exchange networks. In fact, many of the commonalities of experience, belief, behavior, and activity that enable us to speak of "contemporary American culture" are relatively new. Like the globalizing forces discussed in the chapter "Cultural Exchange and Survival," they are founded on and perpetuated by recent developments, particularly in business, transportation, and the mass media.

ANTHROPOLOGISTS AND AMERICAN CULTURE

When anthropologists study urban ethnic groups or relationships between class and household organization, they focus on variation, a very important topic. When we look at the creative use that each individual makes of popular culture, as we did in the chapter "Cultural Exchange and Survival," we are also considering variation. However, anthropology traditionally has been concerned as much with uniformity as with variation. "National character" studies of the 1940s and 1950s foreshadowed anthropology's interest in unifying themes in modern nations. Unfortunately, those studies, of such countries as Japan and Russia, focused too much on the psychological characteristics of individuals.

Contemporary anthropologists interested in national culture realize that culture is an attribute of groups. Despite increasing ethnic diversity, we can still talk about an "American national culture." Through common experiences in their enculturation, especially through the media, most Americans do come to share certain knowledge, beliefs, values, and ways of thinking and acting (as was discussed in the chapter "Culture"). The shared aspects of national culture override differences among individuals, genders, regions, or ethnic groups.

The chapter "Cultural Exchange and Survival" examined the creative use that individuals and cultures make of introduced cultural forces, including media images. That chapter discussed how, through different "readings" of the same media "text," individuals and cultures constantly make and remake popular culture. Here we take a different approach. We focus on a few texts that have diffused most successfully in a given national (i.e., American) culture. Other such texts examined in previous chapters include *Star Wars* and *The Wizard of Oz*. These texts have spread because they are culturally appropriate. For various reasons, they are able to carry some sort of meaning to millions of people. Previous chapters focused on variation and diversity, but this appendix stresses unifying factors: common experiences, actions, and beliefs in American culture.

Anthropologists *should* study American society and culture. Anthropology, after all, deals with universals, generalities, and uniqueness. A national culture is a particular cultural variant, as interesting as any other. Although survey research traditionally is used to study modern nations, techniques developed to interpret and analyze smaller-scale societies, where sociocultural uniformity is more marked, also can contribute to an understanding of American life.

Native anthropologists are those who study their own cultures, for example, American anthropologists working in the United States, Canadian anthropologists working in Canada, or Nigerians working in Nigeria. Anthropological training and fieldwork abroad provide an anthropologist with a certain degree of detachment and objectivity that most natives lack. However, life experience as a native gives an advantage to anthropologists who wish to study their own cultures. Nevertheless, more than when working abroad, the native anthropologist is both participant and observer, often emotionally and intellectually involved in the events and beliefs being studied. Native anthropologists must be particularly careful to resist their own biases and prejudices as natives. They must strive to be as objective in describing their own cultures as they are in analyzing others.

Natives often see and explain their behavior very differently than anthropologists do. For example, most Americans have probably never considered the possibility that apparently secular, commercial, and recreational institutions such as sports, movies, and fast-food restaurants have things in common with myths, religious beliefs, symbols, and behavior. However, these similarities do exist. A key theme of this book has been that *anthropology helps us understand ourselves*. By studying other cultures, we learn both to appreciate and to question aspects of our own culture. Furthermore, the same techniques that anthropologists use in describing and analyzing other cultures can be applied to American culture.

American readers may not find the analyses that follow convincing. In part, this is because you are natives, who know much more about your own culture than you do about any other. Also, as we saw in the chapter "Cultural Exchange and Survival," people in a culture may "read" that culture differently. Furthermore, American culture assigns a high value to differences in individual opinion—and to the belief that one opinion is as good as another. Here I am trying to extract *culture* (widely shared aspects of behavior) from diverse *individual* opinions, actions, and experiences.

The following analyses depart from areas that can be easily quantified, such as demography and economics. We are entering a more impressionistic domain, where cultural analysis sometimes seems much more like literary analysis than like science. You will be right in questioning some of the conclusions that follow. Some are surely debatable; some may be plain wrong. However, if they illustrate how anthropology can be used to shed light on aspects of your own life and experience and to revise and broaden your understanding of your own culture, they will have served a worthwhile function.

A reminder (from the chapter "Culture") about culture, ethnocentrism, and native anthropologists is needed here. For anthropologists, *culture* means much more than refinement, cultivation, education, and appreciation of "classics" and "fine arts"—its popular usage. Curiously, however, when some anthropologists confront their own culture, they seem to forget this. Like other academics and intellectuals, they may regard American "pop" culture as trivial and unworthy of serious study. In doing so, they demonstrate ethnocentrism and reveal a bias that comes with being members of an academic-intellectual subculture.

In examining American culture, native anthropologists must be careful to overcome the bias associated with the academic subculture. Although some academics discourage their children from watching television, the fact that TVs outnumber toilets in American households is a significant cultural datum that anthropologists can't afford to ignore. My own research on Michigan college students may be generalizable to other young Americans. They visit fast-food restaurants more often than they visit houses of worship. I found that almost all had seen a Walt Disney movie and had attended rock concerts or football games. Such shared experiences are major features of American enculturation patterns. As we saw in the last "Bringing It All Together" essay, they affect our bodies as well as our minds. Certainly, any extraterrestrial anthropologist doing field work in the United States would stress such aspects of mass culture. Within the United States, the mass media and the culture of consumption have created major themes in contemporary national culture. These themes merit study.

From the popular domains of sports, TV, and movies I have chosen certain very popular texts to discuss here. (Other features of popular culture, such as fast food, have been discussed previously.) I could have used other texts (for example, blue jeans, baseball, or pizza) to make the same points: that there are powerful shared aspects of contemporary American national culture and that anthropological techniques can be used to interpret them.

FOOTBALL

Football, we say, is only a game, yet it has become a popular spectator sport. On fall Saturdays, millions of people travel to and from college football games. Smaller congregations meet in high school stadiums. Millions of Americans watch televised football. Indeed, nearly half the adult population of the United States watches the Super Bowl. Because football is of general interest to Americans, it is a unifying cultural institution that merits attention. Our most popular sports manage to attract fans of diverse ethnic backgrounds, regions, religions, political parties, jobs, social statuses, levels of wealth, and even genders.

The popularity of football, particularly professional football, depends directly on the mass media, especially television. Is football, with its territorial incursion, hard hitting, and violence—occasionally resulting in injury—popular because Americans are violent people? Are football spectators vicariously realizing their own hostile and aggressive tendencies? The anthropologist W. Arens (1981) discounts this interpretation. He points out that football is a peculiarly American pastime. Although a similar game is played in Canada, it is less popular there. Baseball has become a popular sport in the Caribbean, parts of Latin America, and Japan. Basketball and volleyball also are spreading. However, throughout most of the world, soccer is the most popular sport. Arens argues that if football were a particularly effective channel for expressing aggression, it would have spread (like soccer and baseball) to many other countries, where people have as many aggressive tendencies and hostile feelings as Americans do. Furthermore, he suggests that if a sport's popularity rested simply on a bloodthirsty temperament, boxing, a far bloodier sport, would be America's national pastime. Arens concludes that the explanation for the sport's popularity lies elsewhere, and I agree.

He contends that football is popular because it symbolizes certain key features of American life. In particular, it is characterized by teamwork based on specialization and division of labor, which are pervasive features of modern life. Susan Montague and Robert Morais (1981) take the analysis a step further. They argue that Americans appreciate football because it presents a miniaturized and simplified version of modern organizations. People have trouble understanding organizational bureaucracies, whether in business, universities, or government. Football, the anthropologists argue, helps us understand how decisions are made and rewards are allocated in organizations.

Montague and Morais link football's values, particularly teamwork, to those associated with business. Like corporate workers, the ideal players are diligent and dedicated to the team. Within corporations, however, decision making is complicated, and workers aren't always rewarded for their dedication and good job performance. Decisions are simpler and rewards are more consistent in football, these anthropologists contend, and this helps explain its popularity. Even if we can't figure out how General Motors and Microsoft run, any fan can become an expert on football's rules, teams, scores, statistics, and patterns of play. Even more important, football suggests that the values stressed by business really do pay off. Teams whose members work the hardest, show the most spirit, and best develop and coordinate their talents can be expected to win more often than other teams do.

STAR TREK*

Star Trek, a familiar, powerful, and enduring force in American popular culture, can be used to illustrate the idea that popular media content often is derived from prominent values expressed in many other domains of culture. Americans first encountered the Starship *Enterprise* on NBC in 1966. *Star Trek* was shown in prime time for just three seasons. However, the series not only survives but thrives today in syndication, reruns, books, websites, cassettes, and theatrical films. Revived as a regular weekly series with an entirely new cast in 1987, *Star Trek: The Next Generation* became the third most popular syndicated program in the United States (after *Wheel of Fortune* and *Jeopardy*). *Deep Space Nine, Voyager,* and *Enterprise* have been somewhat less popular successors in the *Star Trek* family.

What does the enduring mass appeal of *Star Trek* tell us about American culture? I believe the answer to be this: *Star Trek* is a transformation of a fundamental American origin myth. The same myth shows up in the image and celebration of Thanksgiving, a distinctively American holiday. Thanksgiving sets the myth in the past, and *Star Trek* sets it in the future.

The myths of contemporary America are drawn from a variety of sources, including such popular-culture fantasies as *Star Wars, The Wizard of Oz* (see the chapter on the arts), and *Star Trek.*

*This section is adapted from Conrad Phillip Kottak, *Prime-Time Society: An Anthropological Analysis of Television and Culture* (Belmont, CA: Wadsworth, 1990).

Our myths also include real people, particularly national ancestors, whose lives have been reinterpreted and endowed with special meaning over the generations. The media, schools, churches, communities, and parents teach the national origin myths to American children. The story of Thanksgiving, for example, continues to be important. It recounts the origin of a national holiday celebrated by Protestants, Catholics, and Jews. All those denominations share a belief in the Old Testament God, and they find it appropriate to thank God for their blessings.

Again and again, Americans have heard idealized retellings of that epochal early harvest. We have learned how Indians taught the Pilgrims to farm in the New World. Grateful Pilgrims then invited the Indians to share their first Thanksgiving. Native American and European labor, techniques, and customs thus blended in that initial biethnic celebration. Annually reenacting the origin myth, the American public schools commemorate "the first Thanksgiving" as children dress up as Pilgrims, Indians, and pumpkins.

More rapidly and pervasively as the mass media grow, each generation of Americans writes its own revisionist history. Our culture constantly reinterprets the origin, nature, and meaning of national holidays. The collective consciousness of contemporary Americans includes TV-saturated memories of "the first Thanksgiving" and "the first Christmas." Our mass culture has instilled the widely shared images of a *Peanuts*-peopled Pilgrim-and-Indian "love-in."

We also conjure up a fictionalized Nativity with Mary, Joseph, Jesus, manger animals, shepherds, three eastern kings, a little drummer boy, and, in some versions, Rudolph the Red-Nosed Reindeer. Note that the interpretation of the Nativity that American culture perpetuates is yet another variation on the same dominant myth. We remember the Nativity as a Thanksgiving involving interethnic contacts (e.g., the three kings) and gift giving. It is set in Bethlehem rather than Massachusetts.

We impose our present on the past as we reinterpret quasi-historic and actual events. For the future, we do it in our science-fiction and fantasy creations. *Star Trek* places in the future what the Thanksgiving story locates in the past: *the myth of the assimilationist, incorporating, melting-pot society.* The myth says that America is distinctive not just because it is assimilationist but because it is *founded* on unity in diversity. (Our *origin* is unity in diversity. After all, we call ourselves "the United States.") Thanksgiving and *Star Trek* illustrate the credo that unity through diversity is essential for survival (whether of a harsh winter or of the perils of outer space). Americans survive by sharing the fruits of specialization.

Star Trek proclaims that the sacred principles that validate American society, because they lie at its foundation, will endure across the generations and even the centuries. The Starship *Enterprise* crew is a melting pot. Captain James Tiberius Kirk is symbolic of real history. His clearest historic prototype is Captain James Cook, whose ship, the *Endeavor,* also sought out new life and civilizations. Kirk's infrequently mentioned middle name, from the Roman general and eventual emperor, links the captain to the earth's imperial history. Kirk is also symbolic of the original Anglo American. He runs the *Enterprise* (America is founded on free enterprise), just as laws, values, and institutions derived from England continue to guide the United States.

McCoy's Irish (or at least Gaelic) name represents the next wave, the established immigrant. Sulu is the successfully assimilated Asian American. The African American female character Uhura, "whose name means freedom," indicates that blacks will become full partners with all other Americans. However, Uhura was the only major female character in the original crew. Female extradomestic employment was less characteristic of American society in 1966 than it is now.

One of *Star Trek*'s constant messages is that strangers, even enemies, can become friends. Less obviously, this message is about cultural imperialism, the assumed irresistibility of American culture and institutions. Russian nationals (Chekhov) could be seduced and captured by an expansive American culture. Spock, although from Vulcan, is half human, with human qualities. We learn, therefore, that our assimilationist values eventually will not just rule the earth but extend to other planets as well. By "the next generation," Klingons, even more alien than Vulcans, and personified by Bridge Officer Worf, had joined the melting pot.

Even God was harnessed to serve American culture, in the person of Scotty. His role was that of the ancient Greek *deus ex machina.* He was a stage controller who "beamed" people up and down, back and forth, from earth to the heavens. Scotty, who kept society going, was also a servant-employee who did his engineering for management—illustrating loyalty and technical skill.

The Next Generation contained many analogues of the original characters. Several "partial people" were single-character personifications of particular human qualities represented in more complex form by the original *Star Trek* crew members. Kirk, Spock, and McCoy were split into multiple characters. Captain Jean-Luc Picard possessed the intellectual and managerial attributes of James T. Kirk. With his English accent and

French name, Picard, like Kirk, drew his legitimacy from symbolic association with historic Western European empires. First Officer Riker replaced Kirk as a romantic man of action.

Spock, an alien (strange ears) who represented science, reason, and intellect, was split in two. One half was Worf, a Klingon bridge officer whose cranial protuberances were analogous to Spock's ears. The other was Data, an android whose brain contained the sum of human knowledge. Two female characters, an empath and the ship's doctor, replaced Dr. McCoy as the repository of healing, emotion, and feeling.

Mirroring contemporaneous American culture, *The Next Generation* featured prominent black, female, and physically challenged characters. An African American actor played the Klingon Mr. Worf. Another, LeVar Burton, appeared as Geordi La Forge. Although blind, Geordi managed, through a vision-enhancing visor, to see things that other people could not. His mechanical vision expressed the characteristic and enduring American faith in technology. So did the android, Data.

During its first year, *The Next Generation* had three prominent female characters. One was the ship's doctor, a working professional with a teenage son. Another was an empath, the ultimate "helping professional." The third was the ship's security officer.

America had become more specialized, differentiated, and professional than it was in the 1960s. The greater role specificity and diversity of *Next Generation* characters reflected this. Nevertheless, both series convey the central *Star Trek* message, one that dominates the culture that created them: Americans are diverse. Individual qualities, talents, and specialties divide us. However, we make our livings and survive as members of cohesive, efficient groups. We explore and advance as members of a crew, a team, an enterprise, or, most generally, a society. Our nation is founded on and endures through assimilation—effective subordination of individual differences within a smoothly functioning multiethnic team. The team is American culture. It worked in the past. It works today.

It will go on working across the generations. Orderly and progressive democracy based on mutual respect is best. Inevitably, American culture will triumph over all others—by convincing and assimilating rather than conquering them. Unity in diversity guarantees human survival.

ANTHROPOLOGY AND "POP" CULTURE

The examples of mass or popular culture considered in this appendix and elsewhere in this book are shared cultural forms that have appeared and spread rapidly because of major changes in the material conditions of American life—particularly work organization, communication, and transportation. Most contemporary Americans deem at least one automobile a necessity. Televisions outnumber toilets in our households. Through the mass media, institutions such as sports, movies, TV shows, amusement parks, and fast-food restaurants have become powerful elements of national culture. They provide a framework of common expectations, experiences, and behavior overriding differences in region, class, formal religious affiliation, political sentiments, gender, ethnic group, and place of residence. Although some of us may not like these changes, it's difficult to deny their significance.

The rise of these institutions is linked not just to the mass media but also to decreasing American participation in traditional religion and the weakening of ties based on kinship, marriage, and community within industrial society. Neither a single church, a strong central government, nor a belief in common descent unites most Americans.

These dimensions of contemporary culture are dismissed as passing, trivial, or "pop" by some. However, because millions of people share them, they deserve and are receiving scholarly attention. Such studies help fulfill the promise that by studying anthropology, we can better understand ourselves.

Appendix 4
Methods in Cultural Anthropology

This appendix begins with a brief discussion of some of the ethical considerations that anthropologists face as they plan and conduct their fieldwork. See also Appendix 2, which summarizes the Code of Ethics of the American Anthropological Association (AAA). That code offers guidelines for anthropologists as they plan and conduct research, and as they deal with colleagues at home and abroad. The discussion of methods here focuses on cultural anthropology, especially on ethnography.

ETHICAL CONSIDERATIONS: NETWORKING AND RECIPROCATION

Ethnographers (fieldworkers in cultural anthropology) typically have done fieldwork outside their nations of origin. In the host country, the ethnographer seeks permissions, cooperation, and knowledge from government officials, scholars, and many others, most importantly the people of the community being studied. Cultural sensitivity is paramount when the research subjects are living people into whose lives the anthropologist intrudes. Anthropologists need to establish and maintain appropriate, collaborative, and nonexploitative relationships with colleagues and communities in the host country.

To work in a host country and community, researchers must inform officials and colleagues there about the purpose and funding, and the anticipated results and impacts, of the research. Researchers have to gain the informed consent of all affected parties—from the authorities who control access to the field site to the members of the community to be studied. Before the research begins, people should be informed about the purpose, nature, and procedures of the research and its potential costs and benefits to them. *Informed consent* (agreement to take part in the research) should be obtained from anyone who provides information or who might be affected by the research.

A process of culturally appropriate networking, which will vary from country to country, is necessary before fieldwork can begin. As one illustration, consider how I prepared for my first fieldwork in Madagascar, which began in 1966. Before arriving in Madagascar I obtained a visa to do research there from Madagascar's embassy in France, where I spent six months on language preparation. I needed to learn Malagasy, the language of Madagascar, a former colony of France. Once I reached Antananarivo, Madagascar's capital, I visited university anthropologists there to draw on their expertise and get their advice about my plans. Later, when I arrived in the territory of the ethnic group (Betsileo) I planned to study, I met with the province chief. Eventually I met with the heads of all the lower-level administrative units where I would be working. Next, I became friendly with knowledgeable people in the small town where I first settled. Townfolk have social networks that extend to rural areas—where I would be doing the bulk of my ethnographic fieldwork. Through personal contacts, I created a network that eventually enabled me to work in several rural villages, one of which was my primary field site. Throughout my stay in Madagascar, I tried to stay in touch with the scholars and officials who had helped me at the outset. When I later applied for grants to return to Madagascar, I included two of those scholars as funded participants in the research. Such networking is an important part of any field research project in cultural or linguistic anthropology.

Anthropologists have a debt to the people they work with in the field, and they should reciprocate in appropriate ways. For example, it is highly appropriate for North American anthropologists working in another country to (1) include host country colleagues in their research plans and funding requests, (2) establish collaborative relationships with those colleagues and their institutions, and (3) include host country colleagues in publication of the research results.

METHODS—ETHNOGRAPHY

Cultural anthropology started to separate from sociology around the turn of the 20th century. Early students of society, such as the French scholar Émile Durkheim, were among the founders of both sociology and anthropology. Theorizing about the organization of simple and complex societies, Durkheim drew on written accounts of the religions of Native Australia (Durkheim 1912/2001) as well as considering mass phenomena (such as suicide rates) in modern nations (Durkheim 1897/1951). Eventually anthropology would specialize in the former, sociology in the latter. (See Appendix 1 for more on Durkheim and early anthropology.)

Anthropology developed into a separate field as early scholars, such as Franz Boas (1940/1966), worked on Indian (Native American) reservations and traveled to distant lands to study small groups of foragers and cultivators. This type of firsthand personal study of local settings is called ethnography. Traditionally, the process of becoming a cultural anthropologist has required field experience in another society. Early ethnographers lived in small-scale, relatively isolated societies with simple technologies and economies.

Ethnography thus emerged as a research strategy in societies with greater cultural uniformity and less social differentiation than are found in large, modern industrial nations. In such nonindustrial settings, ethnographers have needed to consider fewer paths of enculturation (the process by which one acquires cultural knowledge) to understand social life. Traditionally, ethnographers have tried to understand the whole of a particular culture (or, more realistically, as much as they can, given limitations of time and perception). To pursue this goal, ethnographers adopt a free-ranging strategy for gathering information. In a given society or community, the ethnographer moves from setting to setting, place to place, and subject to subject to discover the totality and interconnectedness of social life.

By expanding our knowledge of the range of human diversity, ethnography provides a foundation for generalizations about human behavior and social life. Chapter 1 pointed out that ethnography involves fieldwork in a particular society, whereas *ethnology* is the comparative aspect of cultural anthropology. The goals of ethnology are to identify, compare, and explain cultural differences and similarities, and to build theory about how social and cultural systems work. You might want to review the section of Chapter 1 titled "Science, Explanation, and Hypothesis Testing." That section discusses how ethnographic data, gathered through the techniques discussed here, can be used to compare and contrast, and to make generalizations about, societies and cultures.

In this appendix we focus on ethnographic field techniques. Ethnographers draw on a variety of techniques to piece together a picture of otherwise alien lifestyles. Anthropologists usually employ several (but rarely all) of the techniques discussed here (see also Bernard 2006; O'Reilly 2004).

ETHNOGRAPHIC TECHNIQUES

The characteristic *field techniques* of the ethnographer include the following:

1. Direct, firsthand observation of daily behavior, including *participant observation.*

2. Conversation with varying degrees of formality, from the daily chitchat that helps maintain rapport and provides knowledge about what is going on to prolonged *interviews,* which can be unstructured or structured. Formal, printed *interview schedules* or questionnaires may be used to ensure that complete, comparable information is available for everyone of interest to the study.

3. The *genealogical method.*

4. Detailed work with *key consultants* about particular areas of community life.

5. In-depth interviewing, often leading to the collection of *life histories* of particular people (narrators).

6. Discovery of local beliefs and perceptions, which may be compared with the ethnographer's own observations and conclusions.

7. Problem-oriented research of many sorts.

8. Longitudinal research—the continuous long-term study of an area or site.

9. Team research—coordinated research by multiple ethnographers.

10. Large-scale approaches that recognize the complexity of modern life.

Observation and Participant Observation

Ethnographers get to know their hosts and usually take an interest in the totality of their lives. Ethnographers must pay attention to hundreds of details of daily life, seasonal events, and unusual happenings. They must observe individual and collective behavior in varied settings. They should record what they see as they see it. Things will never seem quite as strange as they do during the first few days and weeks in the field. The ethnographer eventually gets used to, and accepts as normal, cultural patterns that were initially alien. Ethnographers typically spend more than a year in the field. This permits them to observe the entire annual cycle. Staying a bit more than a year allows the ethnographer to repeat the season of his or her arrival, when certain events and processes may have been missed because of initial unfamiliarity and culture shock.

Many ethnographers record their impressions in a personal *diary,* which is kept separate from more formal *field notes.* Later, this record of early impressions will help point out some of the most basic aspects of cultural diversity. Such aspects include distinctive smells, noises people make, how they cover their mouths when they eat, and how they gaze at others. These patterns, which are so basic as to seem almost trivial, are part of what Bronislaw Malinowski called "the imponderabilia of native life and of typical behavior" (Malinowski 1922/1961, p. 20). These features of culture are so fundamental that local people take them for granted. They are too basic even to talk about, but the unaccustomed eye of the fledgling anthropologist picks them up. Thereafter, becoming familiar, they fade to the edge of consciousness. Initial impressions are valuable and should be recorded. First and foremost, ethnographers should try to be accurate observers, recorders, and reporters of what they see in the field.

Ethnographers don't study animals in laboratory cages. The experiments that psychologists do with pigeons, chickens, guinea pigs, and rats are very different from ethnographic procedure. Anthropologists don't systematically control subjects' rewards and punishments or their exposure to certain stimuli. Our subjects are not speechless animals but human beings. It is not part of ethnographic procedure to manipulate them, control their environments, or experimentally induce certain behaviors.

Ethnographers strive to establish *rapport*—a good, friendly working relationship based on personal contact—with our hosts. One of ethnography's most characteristic procedures is *participant observation,* which means that we take part in community life as we study it. As human beings living among others, we cannot be totally impartial and detached observers. We also must take part in many of the events and processes we are observing and trying to comprehend. By participating, we may learn how and why natives find such events meaningful, as well as see how they are organized and conducted.

To exemplify participant observation, let me describe aspects of my own ethnographic fieldwork in Madagascar, a large island off the southeastern coast of Africa, and in Brazil. During the 14 months I lived in Madagascar in 1966–1967, I observed and participated on many occasions in Betsileo life. I helped out at harvest time, joining other people who climbed atop—in order to stomp down on and compact—accumulating stacks of rice stalks. One September, for a reburial ceremony, I bought a silk shroud for a village ancestor. I entered the village tomb and watched people rewrap the bones and decaying flesh of their ancestors. I accompanied Betsileo peasants to town and to market. I observed their dealings with outsiders and sometimes offered help when problems arose.

In Arembepe, Brazil, I learned about fishing by sailing on the Atlantic in simple boats with local fishermen. I gave Jeep rides into the capital to malnourished babies, to pregnant mothers, and once to a teenage girl possessed by a spirit. All those people needed to consult specialists outside the village. I danced on Arembepe's festive occasions, drank libations commemorating new births, and became a godfather to a village girl. Most anthropologists have similar field experiences. The common humanity of the student and the studied, the ethnographer and the research community, makes participant observation inevitable.

Conversation, Interviewing, and Interview Schedules

Participating in local life means that ethnographers constantly talk to people and ask questions. As their knowledge of the local language and culture increases, they understand more. There are several stages in learning a field language. First is the naming phase—asking name after name of the objects around us. Later we are able to pose more complex questions and understand the replies. We begin to understand simple conversations between two villagers. If our language expertise proceeds far enough, we eventually become able to comprehend rapid-fire public discussions and group conversations.

One data-gathering technique I have used in both Arembepe and Madagascar involves an ethnographic survey that includes an interview schedule. In 1964, my fellow fieldworkers and I attempted to complete an interview schedule in each of Arembepe's 160 households. We entered almost every household (fewer than 5 percent refused to participate) to ask a set of questions on a printed form.

Our results provided us with a census and basic information about the village. We wrote down the name, age, and sex of each household member. We gathered data on family type, political party, religion, present and previous jobs, income, expenditures, diet, possessions, and many other items on our eight-page form.

Although we were doing a survey, our approach differed from the survey research design routinely used by sociologists and other social scientists working in large, industrial nations. That survey research, discussed below, involves *sampling* (choosing a small, manageable study group from a larger population) and impersonal data collection. We did not select a partial sample from the total population. Instead, we tried to interview all households in the community we were studying (that is, to have a total sample). We used an interview schedule rather than a questionnaire. With the **interview schedule,** the ethnographer talks face to face with people, asks the questions, and writes down the answers. **Questionnaire** procedures tend to be more indirect and impersonal; the respondent often fills in the form.

Our goal of getting a total sample allowed us to meet almost everyone in the village and helped us establish rapport. Decades later, Arembepeiros still talk warmly about how we were interested enough in them to visit their homes and ask them questions. We stood in sharp contrast to the other outsiders the villagers had known, who considered them too poor and backward to be taken seriously.

Like other survey research, however, our interview-schedule survey did gather comparable quantifiable information. It gave us a basis for assessing patterns and exceptions in village life. Our schedules included a core set of questions that were posed to everyone. However, some interesting side issues often came up during the interview, which we would pursue then or later.

We followed such leads into many dimensions of village life. One woman, for instance, a midwife, became the key cultural consultant we sought out later when we wanted detailed information about local childbirth. Another woman had done an internship in an Afro-Brazilian cult (*candomblé*) in the city. She still went there regularly to study, dance, and get possessed. She became our *candomblé* expert.

Thus, our interview-schedule survey provided a structure that *directed but did not confine* us as researchers. It enabled our ethnography to be both quantitative and qualitative. The quantitative part consisted of the basic information we gathered and later analyzed statistically. The qualitative dimension came from our follow-up questions, open-ended discussions, pauses for gossip, and work with key consultants.

The Genealogical Method

As ordinary people, many of us learn about our own ancestry and relatives by tracing our genealogies. Nowadays various computer programs allow us to trace our "family trees" and degrees of relationship. The **genealogical method** is a well-established ethnographic technique. Early ethnographers developed notation and symbols (see the chapter on "Families, Kinship, and Descent") to deal with kinship, descent, and marriage. Genealogy is a prominent building block in the social organization of nonindustrial societies, where people live and work each day with their close kin. Anthropologists need to collect genealogical data to understand current social relations and to reconstruct history. In many nonindustrial societies, kin links are basic to social life. Anthropologists even call such cultures "kin-based societies." Everyone is related to each other and spends most of his or her time with relatives. Rules of behavior attached to particular kin relations are basic to everyday life (see Carsten 2004). Marriage is also crucial in organizing nonindustrial societies because strategic marriages between villages, tribes, and clans create political alliances.

Key Cultural Consultants

Every community has people who by accident, experience, talent, or training can provide the most complete or useful information about particular aspects of life. These people are **key cultural consultants,** also called *key informants*. In Ivato, the Betsileo village where I spent most of my time, a man named Rakoto was particularly knowledgeable about village history. However, when I asked him to work with me on a genealogy of the 50 to 60 people buried in the village tomb, he called in his cousin Tuesdaysfather, who knew more about this subject. Tuesdaysfather had survived an epidemic of influenza that ravaged Madagascar, along with much of the world, around 1919. Immune to the disease himself, Tuesdaysfather had the grim job of burying his kin as they died. He kept track of everyone buried in the tomb. Tuesdaysfather helped me with the tomb genealogy. Rakoto joined him in telling me personal details about the deceased villagers.

Life Histories

In nonindustrial societies as in our own, individual personalities, interests, and abilities vary. Some villagers prove to be more interested in the ethnographer's work and are more helpful, interesting, and pleasant than others. Anthropologists develop likes and dislikes in the field as we do at home. Often, when we find someone unusually interesting, we collect his or her **life history.** This recollection of a lifetime of experiences provides a more intimate and personal cultural portrait than would be possible otherwise. Life histories, which may be recorded or videotaped for later review and analysis, reveal how specific people perceive, react to, and contribute to changes that affect their lives. Such accounts can illustrate diversity, which exists within any community, since the focus is on how different people interpret and deal with some of the same problems. Many ethnographers include the collection of life histories as an important part of their research strategy.

Local Beliefs and Perceptions, and the Ethnographer's

One goal of ethnography is to discover local views, beliefs, and perceptions, which may be compared with the ethnographer's own observations and conclusions. In the field, ethnographers typically combine two research strategies: the emic (local-oriented) and the etic (scientist-oriented). These terms, derived from linguistics, have been applied to ethnography by various anthropologists. Marvin Harris (1968) has popularized the following meanings of the terms. An **emic** approach investigates how local people think. How do they perceive and categorize the world? What are their rules for behavior? What has meaning for them? How do they imagine and explain things? Operating emically, the ethnographer seeks the "local viewpoint," relying on local people to explain things and to say whether something is significant or not. The term **cultural consultant** or *informant* refers to individuals the ethnographer gets to know in the field, the people who teach him or her about their culture, who provide the emic perspective.

The **etic** (scientist-oriented) approach shifts the focus from local categories, expressions, explanations, and interpretations to those of the anthropologist. The etic approach realizes that members of a culture are often too involved in what they are doing to interpret their cultures impartially. Operating etically, the ethnographer emphasizes what he or she (the observer) notices and considers important. As a trained scientist, the ethnographer should try to bring an objective and comprehensive viewpoint to the study of other cultures. Of course, the ethnographer, like any other scientist, is also a human being with cultural blinders that prevent complete objectivity. As in other sciences, proper training can reduce, but not totally eliminate, the observer's bias. But anthropologists do have special training to compare behavior between different societies.

Ethnographers typically combine emic and etic strategies in their fieldwork. Local statements, perceptions, categories, and opinions help ethnographers understand how cultures work. Local beliefs are also interesting and valuable in themselves. However, local people often don't admit, or even recognize, certain causes and consequences of their behavior. This is as true of North Americans as it is of people in other soci-eties. To describe and interpret culture, ethnographers should recognize biases that come from their own culture as well as those of the people being studied.

The Evolution of Ethnography

The Polish anthropologist Bronislaw Malinowski (1884–1942), who spent most of his professional life in England, is generally considered the father of ethnography. Like most anthropologists of his time, Malinowski did *salvage ethnography,* in the belief that the ethnographer's job is to study and record cultural diversity threatened by westernization (see also Boas 1940/1966). Early ethnographic accounts (*ethnographies*), such as Malinowski's classic *Argonauts of the Western Pacific* (1922/1961), were similar to earlier traveler and explorer accounts in describing the writer's discovery of unknown people and places. However, the *scientific* aims of ethnographies set them apart from books by explorers and amateurs.

More recently, the style that dominated "classic" ethnographies has been characterized as *ethnographic realism.* The writer's goal was to present an accurate, objective, scientific account of a different way of life, written by someone who knew it firsthand. This knowledge came from immersion in an alien language and culture. Ethnographers derived their authority—both as scientists and as voices of "the native" or "the other"—from this personal research experience.

Malinowski's ethnographies were guided by the assumption that aspects of culture are linked and intertwined. Beginning by describing a Trobriand sailing expedition, the ethnographer then follows the links between that entry point and other areas of the culture, such as magic, religion, myths, kinship, and trade. Compared with Malinowski, today's ethnographies tend to be less inclusive and holistic, focusing on particular topics, such as kinship or religion.

According to Malinowski, a primary task of the ethnographer is "to grasp the native's point of view, his relation to life, to realize *his* vision of *his* world" (1922/1961, p. 25—Malinowski's italics). This is a good statement of the need for the emic perspective, as was discussed earlier. Since the 1970s, *interpretive anthropology* has considered the task of describing and interpreting that which is meaningful to natives. Interpretivists such as Clifford Geertz (1973) view cultures as meaningful texts that natives constantly "read" and ethnographers must decipher. According to Geertz, anthropologists may choose anything in a culture that interests them, fill in details, and elaborate to inform their readers about meanings in that culture. Meanings are carried by public symbolic forms, including words, rituals, and customs. (For more on Malinowski and Geertz, see Appendix 1.)

One trend in ethnographic writing since the 1980s has been to question traditional goals, methods, and styles, including ethnographic realism and salvage ethnography (Clifford 1982, 1988; Marcus and Cushman 1982). Marcus and Fischer argue that experimentation in ethnographic writing is necessary because all peoples and cultures have already been "discovered" and must now be "*re*discovered . . . in changing historical circumstances" (1986, p. 24).

In general, experimental anthropologists see ethnographies as works of art as well as works of science. Ethnographic texts may be viewed as literary creations in which the ethnographer, as mediator, communicates information from the "natives" to readers. Some experimental ethnographies are "dialogic," presenting ethnography as a dialogue between the anthropologist and one or more native informants (e.g., Behar 1993; Dwyer 1982). These works draw attention to ways in which ethnographers, and by extension their readers, communicate with other cultures. However, some such ethnographies have been criticized for spending too much time talking about the anthropologist and too little time describing the natives and their culture.

The dialogic ethnography is one genre within a larger experimental category—that is, *reflexive ethnography* (Davies 1999). Here the ethnographer-writer puts his or her personal feelings and reactions to the field situation right in the text. Experimental writing strategies are prominent in reflexive accounts. The ethnographer may adopt some of the conventions of the novel, including first-person narration, conversations, dialogues, and humor. Experimental ethnographies, using new ways of showing what it means to be a Samoan or a Brazilian, may convey to the reader a richer and more complex understanding of human experience.

Linked to salvage ethnography was the idea of the *ethnographic present*—the period before Westernization, when the "true" native culture flourished. This notion often gives classic ethnographies an unrealistic timeless quality. Providing the only jarring note in this idealized picture are occasional comments by the author about traders or missionaries, suggesting that in actuality the natives were already part of the world system. Anthropologists now recognize that the ethnographic present is a rather unrealistic construct. Cultures have been in contact—and have been changing—throughout history (Boas 1940/1966). Most native cultures had at least one major foreign encounter before any anthropologist ever came their way. Most of them had already been incorporated in some fashion into nation–states or colonial systems.

Contemporary ethnographies usually recognize that cultures constantly change and that an ethnographic account applies to a particular moment. A current trend in ethnography is to focus on the ways in which cultural ideas serve political and economic interests. Another trend is to describe how various particular "natives" participate in broader historical, political, and economic processes (Shostak 1981).

Problem-Oriented Ethnography

We see, then, a tendency to move away from holistic accounts toward more problem-focused ethnographies. Although anthropologists are interested in the whole context of human behavior, it is impossible to study everything, and field research usually addresses specific questions. Most ethnographers now enter the field with a specific problem to investigate, and they collect data about variables deemed relevant to that problem. And local people's answers to questions are not the only data source. Anthropologists also gather information on factors such as population density, environmental quality, climate, physical geography, diet, and land use. Sometimes this involves direct measurement—of rainfall, temperature, fields, yields, dietary quantities, or time allocation (Bailey 1990; Johnson 1978). Often it means that we consult government records or archives.

The information of interest to ethnographers is not limited to what local people can and do tell us. In an increasingly interconnected and complicated world, local people lack knowledge about many factors that affect their lives. Our local consultants may be as mystified as we are by the exercise of power from regional, national, and international centers.

Longitudinal Research

Geography limits anthropologists less now than in the past, when it could take months to reach a field site and return visits were rare. New systems of transportation allow anthropologists to widen the area of their research and to return repeatedly. Ethnographic reports now routinely include data from two or more field stays. **Longitudinal research** is the long-term study of a community, region, society, culture, or other unit, usually based on repeated visits. One example of such research is the longitudinal study of Gwembe District, Zambia. This study, planned in 1956 as a longitudinal project by Elizabeth Colson and Thayer Scudder, continues with Colson, Scudder, and their associates of various nationalities. Thus, as is often the case with longitudinal research, the Gwembe study also illustrates team research—coordinated research by multiple ethnographers. The Gwembe research project is both longitudinal (multitime) and *multisited* (considering several field sites) (Colson and Scudder 1975; Scudder and Colson 1980). Four villages, in different areas, have been followed for five decades. Periodic village censuses provide basic data on population, economy, kinship, and religious behavior. Censused people who have moved are traced and interviewed to see how their lives compare with those of people who have stayed in the villages.

A series of different research questions have emerged, while basic data on communities and individuals continue to be collected. The first focus of study was the impact of a large hydroelectric dam, which subjected the Gwembe people to forced resettlement. The dam also spurred road building and other activities that brought the people of Gwembe more closely in touch with the rest of Zambia (Colson 1971; Scudder 1982; Scudder and Habarad 1991).

Later on, education became the research focus. Scudder and Colson (1980) examined how education provided access to new opportunities as it also widened a social gap between people with different educational levels. A third major study then examined a change in brewing and drinking patterns, including a rise in alcoholism, in relation to changing markets, transportation, and exposure to town values (Colson and Scudder 1988).

Team Research

As mentioned, longitudinal research is often team research. My own field site of Arembepe, Brazil, for example, first entered the world of anthropology as a field-team village in the 1960s. It was one of four sites for the now-defunct Columbia–Cornell–Harvard–Illinois Summer Field Studies Program in Anthropology. For at least three years, that program sent a total of about 20 undergraduates annually, the author included, to do brief summer research abroad. We were stationed in rural communities in four countries: Brazil, Ecuador, Mexico, and Peru. Since my wife, Isabel Wagley Kottak, and I began studying it in 1962, Arembepe has become a longitudinal field site. There generations of researchers have monitored various aspects of change and development. The community has changed from a village into a town. Its economy, religion, and social life have been transformed.

Brazilian and American researchers worked with us on team research projects during the 1980s (on television's impact) and the 1990s (on ecological awareness and environmental risk perception). Graduate students from the University of Michigan have drawn on our baseline information from the 1960s as they have studied various topics in Arembepe. In 1990, Doug Jones, a Michigan student doing biocultural research, used Arembepe as a field site to investigate standards of physical attractiveness. In 1996–1997, Janet Dunn studied family planning and changing female reproductive strategies (Dunn 2000). Chris O'Leary, who first visited Arembepe in summer 1997, has investigated a striking aspect of religious change in Arembepe—

the arrival of Protestantism. Later he did a study of changing food preferences (O'Leary 2002).

Arembepe is thus a site where various fieldworkers have worked as members of a longitudinal team. The more recent researchers have built on prior contacts and findings to increase knowledge about how local people meet and manage new circumstances. I think that scholarship should be a community enterprise. The information we gathered in the past is there for new generations to use. To monitor changing attitudes and to understand the relation between television and family planning, Janet Dunn reinterviewed many of the women we had interviewed in the 1980s. Similarly, Chris O'Leary, who compared food habits and nutritional status in Arembepe and another Brazilian town, had access to dietary information from our 1964 interviews.

Contemporary forces of change are too pervasive and complex to be understood fully by a "lone ethnographer"—a researcher who starts from scratch and works alone, for a limited period of time, and who views his or her field site as relatively discrete and isolated. No longer can any ethnographer imagine that his or her field site represents some sort of pristine or autonomous entity. Nor should the ethnographer assume that he or she has exclusive (owner's) rights to the site, or even to the data gathered there. That information, after all, has been produced in friendship, cooperation, and consultation with local people. More and more anthropological field sites, including Malinowski's Trobriand Islands, have been restudied. Ideally, later ethnographers collaborate with and build on the work of their predecessors. Compared with the lone ethnographer model, team work across time (as in Arembepe) and space (as in our comparative studies in various Brazilian towns) produces better understanding of cultural change and social complexity.

Culture, Space, and Scale

The previous sections on longitudinal and team research illustrate an important shift in cultural anthropology. Traditional ethnographic research focused on a single community or "culture," which was treated as more or less isolated and unique in time and space. The shift has been toward recognition of ongoing and inescapable flows of people, technology, images, and information. The study of such flows and linkages is now part of the anthropological analysis. And, reflecting today's world—in which people, images, and information move about as never before—fieldwork must be more flexible and on a larger scale. Ethnography is increasingly multitimed and multisited. Malinowski could focus on Trobriand culture and spend most of his field time in a particular community. Nowadays we cannot afford to ignore, as Malinowski did, the "outsiders" who increasingly impinge on the places we study (e.g., migrants, refugees, terrorists, warriors, tourists, developers). Integral to our analyses now are the external organizations and forces (e.g., governments, businesses, nongovernmental organizations) laying claim to land, people, and resources throughout the world. Also important is increased recognition of power differentials and how they affect cultures, and of the importance of diversity within culture and societies.

In two volumes of essays edited by Akhil Gupta and James Ferguson (1997a and 1997b), several anthropologists describe problems in trying to locate cultures in bounded spaces. John Durham Peters (1997), for example, notes that, particularly because of the mass media, contemporary people simultaneously experience the local and the global. He describes those people as culturally "bifocal"—both "near-sighted" (seeing local events) and "far-sighted" (seeing images from far away). Given their "bifocality," their interpretations of the local are always influenced by information from outside. Thus, their attitude about a clear blue sky at home is tinged by their knowledge, through weather reports, that a hurricane may be approaching. The national news may not at all fit opinions voiced in local conversations, but national opinions find their way into local discourse.

The mass media, which anthropologists increasingly study, are oddities in terms of culture and space. Whose image and opinions are these? What culture or community do they represent? They certainly aren't local. Media images and messages flow electronically. TV brings them right to you. The Internet lets you discover new cultural possibilities at the click of a mouse. The Internet takes us to virtual places, but in truth, the electronic mass media are placeless phenomena, which are transnational in scope and play a role in forming and maintaining cultural identities.

Anthropologists increasingly study people in motion. Examples include people living on or near national borders, nomads, seasonal migrants, homeless and displaced people, immigrants, and refugees. Anthropological research today may take us traveling along with the people we study, as they move from village to city, cross the border, or travel internationally on business. As we saw in the chapter on "Cultural Exchange and Survival," ethnographers increasingly follow the people and images they study. As fieldwork changes, with less and less of a spatially set field, what can we take from traditional ethnography? Gupta and Ferguson correctly cite the "characteristically anthropological emphasis on daily routine and lived experience" (1997a, p. 5). The treatment of communities as discrete entities may be a thing of the past. However, "anthropology's traditional attention to the close observation of particular lives in particular places" (Gupta and Ferguson

1997b, p. 25) has an enduring importance. The method of close observation helps distinguish cultural anthropology from sociology and survey research, to which we now turn.

SURVEY RESEARCH

As anthropologists work increasingly in large-scale societies, they have developed innovative ways of blending ethnography and survey research (Fricke 1994). Before considering such combinations of field methods, I must describe survey research and the main differences between survey research and ethnography as traditionally practiced. Working mainly in large, populous nations, sociologists, political scientists, and economists have developed and refined the **survey research** design, which involves sampling, impersonal data collection, and statistical analysis. Survey research usually draws a **sample** (a manageable study group) from a much larger population. By studying a properly selected and representative sample, social scientists can make accurate inferences about the larger population.

In smaller-scale societies, ethnographers get to know most of the people, but given the greater size and complexity of nations, survey research cannot help being more impersonal. Survey researchers call the people they study *respondents*. These are people who respond to questions during a survey. Sometimes survey researchers personally interview them. Sometimes, after an initial meeting, they ask respondents to fill out a questionnaire. In other cases, researchers mail printed questionnaires to randomly selected sample members or have graduate students interview or telephone them. (In a **random sample,** all members of the population have an equal statistical chance of being chosen for inclusion. A random sample is selected by randomizing procedures, such as tables of random numbers, which are found in many statistics textbooks.)

Anyone who has grown up recently in the United States or Canada has heard of sampling. Probably the most familiar example is the polling used to predict political races. The media hire agencies to estimate outcomes and do exit polls to find out what kinds of people voted for which candidates. During sampling, researchers gather information about age, gender, religion, occupation, income, and political party preference. These characteristics (**variables**—attributes that vary among members of a sample or population) are known to influence political decisions.

The number of variables influencing social identity and behavior increases with, and can be considered a measure of, social complexity. Many more variables affect social identities, experiences, and activities in a modern nation than is the case in the small communities where ethnography grew up. In contemporary North America, hundreds of factors influence our social behavior and attitudes. These social predictors include our religion; the region of the country in which we grew up; whether we come from a town, suburb, or city; and our parents' professions, ethnic origins, and income levels. Because survey research deals with large and diverse groups and with samples and probability, its results must be analyzed statistically.

Ethnography can be used to supplement and fine-tune survey research. Anthropologists can transfer the personal, firsthand techniques of ethnography to virtually any setting that includes human beings. A combination of survey research and ethnography can provide new perspectives on life in **complex societies** (large and populous societies with social stratification and central governments). Preliminary ethnography also can help develop relevant and culturally appropriate questions for inclusion in surveys.

In my own courses in Ann Arbor, Michigan, undergraduates have done ethnographic research on sororities, fraternities, teams, campus organizations, and the local homeless population. Other students have systematically observed behavior in public places. These include racquetball courts, restaurants, bars, football stadiums, markets, malls, and classrooms. Other "modern anthropology" projects use anthropological techniques to interpret and analyze mass media. Anthropologists have been studying their own cultures for decades, and anthropological research in the United States and Canada is booming today. Wherever there is patterned human behavior, there is grist for the anthropological mill.

In any complex society, many predictor variables (*social indicators*) influence behavior and opinions. Because we must be able to detect, measure, and compare the influence of social indicators, many contemporary anthropological studies have a statistical foundation. Even in rural fieldwork, more anthropologists now draw samples, gather quantitative data, and use statistics to interpret them (see Bernard 2006). Quantifiable information may permit a more precise assessment of similarities and differences between communities. Statistical analysis can support and round out an ethnographic account of local social life.

However, in the best studies, the hallmark of ethnography remains: Anthropologists enter the community and get to know the people. They participate in local activities, networks, and associations, in the city or in the countryside. They observe and experience social conditions and problems. They watch the effects of national policies and programs on local life. I believe that the ethnographic method and the emphasis on personal relationships in social research are valuable gifts that cultural anthropology brings to the study of a complex society.

Bibliography

Abelmann, N., and J. Lie
    1995   *Blue Dreams: Korean Americans and the Los Angeles Riots.* Cambridge, MA: Harvard University Press.

Abiodun, R.
    1996   Foreword. In *Art and Religion in Africa,* by R. I. J. Hackett, pp. viii–ix. London: Cassell.

Abu-Lughod, J. L.
    1989   *Before European Hegemony: The World System a.d. 1250–1350.* New York: Oxford University Press.

Adams, R. M.
    1981   *Heartland of Cities.* Chicago: Aldine.

Adepegba, C. O.
    1991   The Yoruba Concept of Art and Its Significance in the Holistic View of Art as Applied to African Art. *African Notes* 15: 1–6.

Adherents.com
    2002   Major Religions of the World Ranked by Number of Adherents. http://www.adherents.com/Religions_By_Adherents.html.

Agar, M. H.
    1980   *The Professional Stranger: An Informal Introduction to Ethnography.* New York: Academic Press.

Ahmed, A. S.
    1992   *Postmodernism and Islam: Predicament and Promise.* New York: Routledge.
    2004   *Postmodernism and Islam: Predicament and Promise,* rev. ed. New York: Routledge.

Albert, B.
    1989   Yanomami "Violence": Inclusive Fitness or Ethnographer's Representation? *Current Anthropology* 30: 637–640.

Altman, D.
    2001   *Global Sex.* Chicago: University of Chicago Press.

Amadiume, I.
    1987   *Male Daughters, Female Husbands.* Atlantic Highlands, NJ: Zed.
    1997   *Reinventing Africa: Matriarchy, Religion, and Culture.* New York: Zed.

American Almanac 1994–1995
    1994   *Statistical Abstract of the United States,* 114th ed. Austin, TX: Reference Press.

American Almanac 1996–1997
    1996   *Statistical Abstract of the United States,* 116th ed. Austin, TX: Reference Press.

American Anthropological Association
    AAA Guide: A Guide to Departments, a Directory of Members. (Formerly *Guide to Departments of Anthropology.*) Published annually by the American Anthropological Association, Washington, DC.
    Anthropology Newsletter. Published nine times annually by the American Anthropological Association, Washington, DC.
    General Anthropology: Bulletin of the Council for General Anthropology.

Amick III, B., S. Levine, A. R. Tarlov, and D. C. Walsh, eds.
    1995   *Society and Health.* New York: Oxford University Press.

Anderson, B.
    1991   *Imagined Communities: Reflections on the Origin and Spread of Nationalism,* rev. ed. London: Verso.
    1998   *The Spectre of Comparisons: Nationalism, Southeast Asia, and the World.* New York: Verso.

Anderson, R.
    1989   *Art in Small Scale Societies.* Upper Saddle River, NJ: Prentice Hall.
    2000   *American Muse: Anthropological Excursions into Art and Aesthetics.* Upper Saddle River, NJ: Prentice Hall.

2004 *Calliope's Sisters: A Comparative Study of Philosophy of Art,* 2nd ed. Upper Saddle River, NJ: Prentice Hall.

Anderson, R., and K. Field, eds.
1993 *Art in Small-Scale Societies: Contemporary Readings.* Upper Saddle River, NJ: Prentice Hall.
1996 *Magic, Science, and Health: The Aims and Achievements of Medical Anthropology.* Fort Worth: Harcourt Brace.

Angrosino, M. V., ed..
Doing Cultural Anthropology: Projects for Ethnographic Data Collection. Prospect Heights, IL: Waveland.

Antoun, R. T.
2001 *Understanding Fundamentalism: Christian, Islamic, and Jewish Movements.* Walnut Creek, CA: AltaMira.

Aoki, M. Y., and M. B. Dardess, eds.
1981 *As the Japanese See It: Past and Present.* Honolulu: University Press of Hawaii.

Aoyagi, K., P. J. M. Nas, and J. Traphagan, eds.
1998 *Toward Sustainable Cities: Readings in the Anthropology of Urban Environments.* Leiden, Netherlands: Leiden Development Studies, Institute of Cultural and Social Studies, University of Leiden.

Apostolopoulos, Y., S. Sönmez, and D. J. Timothy
2001 *Women as Producers and Consumers of Tourism in Developing Regions.* Westport, CT: Praeger.

Appadurai, A.
1990 Disjuncture and Difference in the Global Cultural Economy. *Public Culture* 2(2): 1–24.
1991 Global Ethnoscapes: Notes and Queries for a Transnational Anthropology. In *Recapturing Anthropology: Working in the Present,* ed. R. G. Fox, pp. 191–210. Santa Fe: School of American Research Advanced Seminar Series.

Appadurai, A., ed.
2001 *Globalization.* Durham, NC: Duke University Press.

Appel, R., and P. Muysken
1987 *Language Contact and Bilingualism.* London: Edward Arnold.

Appell, G. N.
1978 *Ethical Dilemmas in Anthropological Inquiry: A Case Book.* Waltham, MA: Crossroads Press.

Appiah, K. A.
1990 Racisms. In *Anatomy of Racism,* ed. David Theo Goldberg, pp. 3–17. Minneapolis: University of Minnesota Press.

Applebome, P.
1996 English Unique to Blacks Is Officially Recognized. *New York Times,* December 20. http://www.nytimes.com.

1997 Dispute over Ebonics Reflects a Volatile Mix. *New York Times,* March 1. http://www.nytimes.com.

Arce, A., and N. Long, eds.
2000 *Anthropology, Development, and Modernities: Exploring Discourses, Counter-Tendencies, and Violence.* New York: Routledge.

Archer, M. S.
1996 *Culture and Agency: The Place of Culture in Social Theory,* rev ed. Cambridge, UK: Cambridge University Press.

Arens, W.
1981 Professional Football: An American Symbol and Ritual. In *The American Dimension: Cultural Myths and Social Realities,* 2nd ed., ed. W. Arens and S. P. Montague, pp. 1–10. Sherman Oaks, CA: Alfred.

Arens, W., and S. P. Montague
1981 *The American Dimension: Cultural Myths and Social Realities,* 2nd ed. Sherman Oaks, CA: Alfred.

Arensberg, C.
1987 Theoretical Contributions of Industrial and Development Studies. In *Applied Anthropology in America,* ed. E. M. Eddy and W. L. Partridge. New York: Columbia University Press.

Arrighi, G.
1994 *The Long Twentieth Century: Money, Power, and the Origins of Our Times.* New York: Verso.

Ashcroft, B., G. Griffiths, and H. Tiffin
1989 *The Empire Writes Back: Theory and Practice in Post-Colonial Literatures.* New York: Routledge.

Ashmore, W., and R. Sharer
2000 *Discovering Our Past: A Brief Introduction to Archaeology,* 3rd ed. Boston: McGraw-Hill.

Askew, K. M.
2001 *Performing the Nation: Swahili Music and Cultural Politics in Tanzania.* Chicago: University of Chicago Press.

Baer, H. A., M. Singer, and I. Susser
2003 *Medical Anthropology and the World System.* Westport, CT: Praeger.

Bailey, E. J.
2000 *Medical Anthropology and African American Health.* Westport, CT: Bergin and Garvey.

Bailey, R. C.
1990 *The Behavioral Ecology of Efe Pygmy Men in the Ituri Forest, Zaire.* Ann Arbor: Anthropological Papers, Museum of Anthropology, University of Michigan, no. 86.

Bailey, R. C., G. Head, M. Jenike, B. Owen, R. Rechtman, and E. Zechenter
1989 Hunting and Gathering in Tropical Rain Forests: Is It Possible? *American Anthropologist* 91: 59–82.

Bakhtin, M.
1984   *Rabelais and His World.* Translated by Helen Iswolksy. Bloomington: Indiana University Press.

Balick, M. J., and P. A. Cox
1996   *Plants, People, and Culture: The Science of Ethnobotany.* New York: Scientific American Library.

Balick, M. J., E. Elisabetsky, and S. A. Laird
1995   *Medicinal Resources of the Tropical Forest: Biodiversity and Its Importance to Human Health.* New York: Columbia University Press.

Banton, M.
1957   *West African City: A Study in Tribal Life in Freetown.* London: Oxford University Press.

Barber, B. R.
1992   Jihad vs. McWorld. *Atlantic Monthly* 269(3): 53–65, March 1992.
1995   *Jihad vs. McWorld.* New York: Times Books.

Barlett, P. F., ed.
1980   *Agricultural Decision Making: Anthropological Contribution to Rural Development.* New York: Academic Press.

Barnaby, F., ed.
1984   *Future War: Armed Conflict in the Next Decade.* London: M. Joseph.

Barnard, A.
1979   Kalahari Settlement Patterns. In *Social and Ecological Systems*, ed. P. Burnham and R. Ellen, pp. 131–144. New York: Academic Press.

Barnouw, V.
1985   *Culture and Personality*, 4th ed. Belmont, CA: Wadsworth.

Baron, D.
1986   *Grammar and Gender.* New Haven, CT: Yale University Press.

Barringer, F.
1989   32 Million Lived in Poverty in '88, a Figure Unchanged. *New York Times,* October 19, p. 18.
1992   New Census Data Show More Children Living in Poverty. *New York Times,* May 29, pp. A1, A12, A13.

Barry, H., M. K. Bacon, and I. L. Child
1959   Relation of Child Training to Subsistence Economy. *American Anthropologist* 61: 51–63.

Barth, F.
1964   *Nomads of South Persia: The Basseri Tribe of the Khamseh Confederacy.* London: Allen and Unwin.
1968   (orig. 1958). Ecologic Relations of Ethnic Groups in Swat, North Pakistan. In *Man in Adaptation: The Cultural Present*, ed. Yehudi Cohen, pp. 324–331. Chicago: Aldine.

1969   *Ethnic Groups and Boundaries: The Social Organization of Cultural Difference.* London: Allen and Unwin.

Batalla, G. B.
1966   Conservative Thought in Applied Anthropology: A Critique. *Human Organization* 25: 89–92.

Bates, D. G.
2005   *Human Adaptive Strategies: Ecology, Culture, and Politics,* 3rd ed. Boston: Allyn & Bacon.

Bateson, M. C.
1984   *With a Daughter's Eye: A Memoir of Margaret Mead and Gregory Bateson.* New York: William Morrow.

Beckerman, S., and P. Valentine
2002   *Cultures of Multiple Fathers: The Theory and Practice of Partible Paternity in Lowland South America.* Gainesville: University of Florida Press.

Beeman, W.
1986   *Language, Status, and Power in Iran.* Bloomington: Indiana University Press.

Behar, R.
1993   *Translated Woman: Crossing the Border with Esperanza's Story.* Boston: Beacon Press.

Behar, R., and D. A. Gordon, eds.
1995   *Women Writing Culture.* Berkeley: University of California Press.

Bell, W.
1981   Neocolonialism. In *Encyclopedia of Sociology*, p. 193. Guilford, CT: DPG Publishing.

Bellah, R. N.
1978   Religious Evolution. In *Reader in Comparative Religion: An Anthropological Approach*, 4th ed., ed. W. A. Lessa and E. Z. Vogt, pp. 36–50. New York: Harper & Row.

Benedict, B.
1970   Pluralism and Stratification. In *Essays in Comparative Social Stratification*, ed. L. Plotnicov and A. Tuden, pp. 29–41. Pittsburgh: University of Pittsburgh Press.

Benedict, R.
1940   *Race, Science and Politics.* New York: Modern Age Books.
1946   *The Chrysanthemum and the Sword.* Boston: Houghton Mifflin.
1959   (orig. 1934). *Patterns of Culture.* New York: New American Library.

Bennett, J. W.
1969   *Northern Plainsmen: Adaptive Strategy and Agrarian Life.* Chicago: Aldine.

Bennett, J. W., and J. R. Bowen, eds.
1988   *Production and Autonomy: Anthropological Studies and Critiques of Development.* Monographs in Economic Anthropology, no. 5, Society for Economic Anthropology. New York: University Press of America.

Berg, B. L.
  2004   *Qualitative Research Methods for the Social Sciences,* 5th ed. Boston: Pearson.

Berlin, B. D., E. Breedlove, and P. H. Raven
  1974   *Principles of Tzeltal Plant Classification: An Introduction to the Botanical Ethnography of a Mayan-Speaking People of Highland Chiapas.* New York: Academic Press.

Berlin, B. D., and P. Kay
  1969   *Basic Color Terms: Their Universality and Evolution.* Berkeley: University of California Press.
  1991   *Basic Color Terms: Their Universality and Evolution,* 2nd ed. Berkeley: University of California Press.
  1999   *Basic Color Terms: Their Universality and Evolution.* Stanford, CA: Center for the Study of Language and Information.

Bernard, H. R.
  1994   *Research Methods in Cultural Anthropology,* 2nd ed. Thousand Oaks, CA: Sage.
  2006   *Research Methods in Anthropology: Qualitative and Quantitative Methods,* 4th ed. Walnut Creek, CA: AltaMira.

Bernard, H. R., ed.
  1998   *Handbook of Methods in Cultural Anthropology.* Walnut Creek, CA: AltaMira.

Berndt, R. M.
  1969   The Concept of Protest within an Australian Aboriginal Context. In *A Question of Choice: An Australian Aboriginal Dilemma,* ed. R. M. Berndt, pp. 25–43. Nedlands: University of West Australia Press.

Berreman, G. D.
  1962   Pahari Polyandry: A Comparison. *American Anthropologist* 64: 60–75.
  1975   Himalayan Polyandry and the Domestic Cycle. *American Ethnologist* 2: 127–138.

Besteman, C. L., and H. Gusterson
  2005   *Why America's Top Pundits Are Wrong: Anthropologists Talk Back.* Berkeley: University of California Press.

Bettelheim, B.
  1975   *The Uses of Enchantment: The Meaning and Importance of Fairy Tales.* New York: Vintage.

Bicker, A., P. Sillitoe, and J. Pottier, eds.
  2004   *Investigating Local Knowledge: New Directions, New Approaches.* Burlington, VT: Ashgate.

Biology-Online.org
  2005   Natural selection in action: Industrial melanism. http://www.biology-online.org/2/11_natural_selection.htm.

Bird-David, N.
  1992   Beyond "The Original Affluent Society": A Culturalist Reformulation. *Current Anthropology* 33(1): 25–47.

Bjuremalm, H.
  1997   Rättvisa kan skipas i Rwanda: Folkmordet 1994 går att förklara och analysera på samma sätt som förintelsen av judarna. *Dagens Nyheter* [06-03-1997, p. B3].

Blackwood, E.
  2000   *Webs of Power: Women, Kin, and Community in a Sumatran Village.* Lanham, MD: Rowman and Littlefield.

Blackwood, E., and S. Wieringa, eds.
  1999   *Female Desires: Same-Sex Relations and Transgender Practices across Cultures.* New York: Columbia University Press.

Bloch, M., ed.
  1975   *Political Language and Oratory in Traditional Societies.* London: Academic.

Blum, H. F.
  1961   Does the Melanin Pigment of Human Skin Have Adaptive Value? *Quarterly Review of Biology* 36: 50–63.

Boas, F.
  1966   (orig. 1940). *Race, Language, and Culture.* New York: Free Press.

Bock, P. K.
  1980   *Continuities in Psychological Anthropology.* San Francisco: W. H. Freeman.

Bodley, J. H.
  1985   *Anthropology and Contemporary Human Problems,* 2nd ed. Mountain View, CA: Mayfield.
  1995   *Anthropology and Contemporary Human Problems,* 3rd ed. Mountain View, CA: Mayfield.
  1999   *Victims of Progress,* 4th ed. Mountain View, CA: Mayfield.
  2001   *Anthropology and Contemporary Human Problems,* 4th ed. Boston: McGraw-Hill.
  2003   *The Power of Scale: A Global History Approach.* Armonk, NY: M. E. Sharpe.

Bodley, J. H., ed.
  1988   *Tribal Peoples and Development Issues: A Global Overview.* Mountain View, CA: Mayfield.

Bogoras, W.
  1904   The Chukchee. In *The Jesup North Pacific Expedition,* ed. F. Boas. New York: Memoir of the American Museum of Natural History.

Bohannan, P.
  1955   Some Principles of Exchange and Investment among the Tiv. *American Anthropologist* 57: 60–70.
  1971   Artist and Critic in an African Society. In *Anthropology and Art: Readings in Cross-Cultural Aesthetics,* ed. C. Otten, pp. 172–181. Austin: University of Texas Press.
  1995   *How Culture Works.* New York: Free Press.

Bohannan, P., and J. Middleton, eds.
1968 *Marriage, Family, and Residence.* Garden City, NY: Natural History Press.

Bolton, R.
1981 Susto, Hostility, and Hypoglycemia. *Ethnology* 20(4): 227–258.

Bond, G. C., J. Kreniske, I. Susser, and J. Vincent, eds.
1996 *AIDS in Africa and the Caribbean.* Boulder, CO: Westview Press.

Bonvillain, N.
2001 *Women and Men: Cultural Constructions of Gender,* 3rd ed. Upper Saddle River, NJ: Prentice Hall.
2003 *Language, Culture, and Communication: The Meaning of Messages,* 4th ed. Upper Saddle River, NJ: Prentice Hall.

Borneman, J.
1998 *Subversions of International Order: Studies in the Political Anthropology of Culture.* Albany: State University of New York Press.

Boserup, E.
1965 *The Conditions of Agricultural Growth.* Chicago: Aldine.
1970 *Women's Role in Economic Development.* London: Allen and Unwin.

Bourdieu, P.
1977 *Outline of a Theory of Practice.* Translated by Richard Nice. Cambridge, UK: Cambridge University Press.
1982 *Ce Que Parler Veut Dire.* Paris: Fayard.
1984 *Distinction: A Social Critique of the Judgment of Taste.* Translated by R. Nice. Cambridge, MA: Harvard University Press.

Bourguignon, E.
1979 *Psychological Anthropology: An Introduction to Human Nature and Cultural Differences.* New York: Harcourt Brace Jovanovich.

Bourque, S. C., and K. B. Warren
1981 *Women of the Andes: Patriarchy and Social Change in Two Peruvian Villages.* Ann Arbor: University of Michigan Press.
1987 Technology, Gender and Development. *Daedalus* 116(4): 173–197.

Bower, B.
2000 Inside Violent Worlds—Social Scientists Study Social Consequences of Violent Conflicts. *Science News Online,* August 5. http://www.sciencenews.org/articles/20000805/bob8ref.asp.

Bowie, F.
2006 *The Anthropology of Religion: An Introduction.* Malden, MA: Blackwell.

Bradley, C., C. Moore, M. Burton, and D. White
1990 A Cross-Cultural Historical Analysis of Subsistence Change. *American Anthropologist* 92(2): 447–457.

Brady, I., ed.
1983 Special Section: Speaking in the Name of the Real: Freeman and Mead on Samoa. *American Anthropologist* 85: 908–947.

Braudel, F.
1973 *Capitalism and Material Life: 1400–1800.* Translated by M. Kochan. London: Weidenfeld and Nicolson.
1981 *Civilization and Capitalism, 15th–18th Century.* Volume I: *The Structure of Everyday Life: The Limits.* Translated by S. Reynolds. New York: Harper & Row.
1982 *Civilization and Capitalism, 15th–18th Century.* Volume II: *The Wheels of Commerce.* New York: HarperCollins.
1984 *Civilization and Capitalism, 15th–18th Century.* Volume III: *The Perspective of the World.* New York: HarperCollins.
1992 *Civilization and Capitalism, 15th–18th Century.* Volume III: *The Perspective of the World.* Berkeley: University of California Press.

Bremen, J. V., and A. Shimizu, eds.
1999 *Anthropology and Colonialism in Asia and Oceania.* London: Curzon.

Brenneis, D.
1988 Language and Disputing. *Annual Review of Anthropology* 17: 221–237.

Brettell, C. B., and C. F. Sargent, eds.
2005 *Gender in Cross-Cultural Perspective.* Upper Saddle River, NJ: Pearson/Prentice Hall.

Brim, J. A., and D. H. Spain
1974 *Research Design in Anthropology.* New York: Harcourt Brace Jovanovich.

Bringa, T.
1995 *Being Muslim the Bosnian Way: Identity and Community in a Central Bosnian Village.* Princeton, NJ: Princeton University Press.

Brogger, J.
1992 *Nazaré: Women and Men in a Prebureaucratic Portuguese Fishing Village.* Fort Worth: Harcourt Brace.

Bronfenbrenner, U.
1975 Nature with Nurture: A Reinterpretation of the Evidence. In *Race and IQ,* ed. A. Montagu, pp. 114–144. New York: Oxford University Press.

Brooke, J.
1992 Rio's New Day in Sun Leaves Laplander Limp. *New York Times,* June 1, p. A7.
2000 A Commercial Makes Canadian Self-Esteem Bubble to the Surface. *New York Times,* May 29, late edition, final, section A, p. 6, column 1.

Brown, A.
2001 Communism. *International Encyclopedia of the Social & Behavioral Sciences,* pp. 2323–2326. New York: Elsevier.

Brown, D.
1991   *Human Universals.* New York: McGraw-Hill.

Brown, J. K.
1975   Iroquois Women: An Ethnohistoric Note. In *Toward an Anthropology of Women,* ed. R. Reiter, pp. 235–251. New York: Monthly Review Press.

Brown, K. M.
2001   *Mama Lola: A Vodou Priestess in Brooklyn,* rev. ed. Berkeley: University of California Press.

Brown, P. J.
1998   *Understanding and Applying Medical Anthropology.* Boston: McGraw-Hill.

Brown, P. J., and V. Bentley-Condit
1996   Culture, Evolution, and Obesity. In *Obesity: Its Causes and Management,* eds. A. J. Stunkard and T. Wadden. New York: Raven Press.

Brown, P. J., and S. V. Krick
2001   Culture and Economy in the Etiology of Obesity: Diet, Television and the Illusions of Personal Choice. Atlanta, GA: Emory University MARIAL Center, Working Paper 003-01.

Brown, R. W.
1958   *Words and Things.* Glencoe, IL: Free Press.

Bryant, B., and P. Mohai
1991   Race, Class, and Environmental Quality in the Detroit Area. In *Environmental Racism: Issues and Dilemmas,* ed. B. P. Bryant and Mohai. Ann Arbor: University of Michigan Office of Minority Affairs.

Bryson, K.
1996   Household and Family Characteristics: March 1995, P20-488, November 26, 1996. United States Department of Commerce, Bureau of Census, Public Information Office, CB96-195.

Buchler, I. R., and H. A. Selby
1968   *Kinship and Social Organization: An Introduction to Theory and Method.* New York: Macmillan.

Burke, P., and R. Porter
1987   *The Social History of Language.* Cambridge, UK: Cambridge University Press.

Burling, R.
1970   *Man's Many Voices: Language in Its Cultural Context.* New York: Harcourt Brace Jovanovich.

Burns, J. F.
1992a   Bosnian Strife Cuts Old Bridges of Trust. *New York Times,* May 22, pp. A1, A6.
1992b   A Serb, Fighting Serbs, Defends Sarajevo. *New York Times,* July 12, section 4, p. E3.
1997   A Year of Harsh Islamic Rule Weighs Heavily for Afghans. *New York Times,* September 24, late edition, final, section A, p. 6, column 1.

Buvinic, M.
1995   The Feminization of Poverty? Research and Policy Needs. In *Reducing Poverty through Labour Market Policies.* Geneva: International Institute for Labour Studies.

Caldeira, T. P. R.
1996   Fortified Enclaves: The New Urban Segregation. *Public Culture* 8(2): 303–328.

Calhoun, C., D. Light, and S. Keller
1997   *Sociology,* 7th ed. New York: McGraw-Hill.

Carlson, T. J. S., and L. Maffi
2004   *Ethnobotany and Conservation of Biocultural Diversity.* Bronx: New York Botanical Garden Press.

Carneiro, R. L.
1956   Slash-and-Burn Agriculture: A Closer Look at Its Implications for Settlement Patterns. In *Men and Cultures,* Selected Papers of the Fifth International Congress of Anthropological and Ethnological Sciences, pp. 229–234. Philadelphia: University of Pennsylvania Press.
1968   (orig. 1961). Slash-and-Burn Cultivation among the Kuikuru and Its Implications for Cultural Development in the Amazon Basin. In *Man in Adaptation: The Cultural Present,* ed. Y. A. Cohen, pp. 131–145. Chicago: Aldine.
1970   A Theory of the Origin of the State. *Science* 69: 733–738.
1990   Chiefdom-Level Warfare as Exemplified in Fiji and the Cauca Valley. In *The Anthropology of War,* ed. J. Haas, pp. 190–211. Cambridge, UK: Cambridge University Press.
1991   The Nature of the Chiefdom as Revealed by Evidence from the Cauca Valley of Colombia. In *Profiles in Cultural Evolution,* ed. A. T. Rambo and K. Gillogly, *Anthropological Papers* 85, pp. 167–190. Ann Arbor: University of Michigan Museum of Anthropology.

Carrier, J.
1995   *De Los Otros: Intimacy and Homosexuality among Mexican Men: Hidden in the Blood.* New York: Columbia University Press.

Carsten, J.
2004   *After Kinship.* New York: Cambridge University Press.

Carver, T.
1996   *Gender Is Not a Synonym for Women.* Boulder, CO: Lynne Rienner.

Casper, L., and K. Bryson
1998   Growth in Single Fathers Outpaces Growth in Single Mothers, Census Bureau Reports. http://www.census.gov/Press-Release/cb98-228.html.

Casson, R.
1983   Schemata in Cognitive Anthropology. *Annual Review of Anthropology* 12: 429–462.

Centers for Disease Control and Prevention (CDC)
  2006 *National Vital Statistics Report,* v. 54,
    no. 12, March 3, 2006. http://www.cdc.gov/
    nchs/products/pubs/pubd/nvsr/54/
    54-pre.htm.

Cernea, M. M., ed.
  1991 *Putting People First: Sociological Variables
    in Rural Development,* 2nd ed. New York:
    Oxford University Press (published for the
    World Bank).

Cernea, M. M., and C. McDowell, eds.
  2000 *Risks and Reconstruction: Experiences
    of Resettlers and Refugees.* Washington, DC:
    World Bank.

Chagnon, N. A.
  1967 *Yanomamo Warfare: Social Organization
    and Marriage Alliances.* Ann Arbor, MI:
    University Microfilms.
  1968 *Yanomamo: The Fierce People.* New York:
    Holt, Rinehart and Winston.
  1997 *Yanomamö,* 5th ed. Fort Worth: Harcourt
    Brace.

Chagnon, N. A., and W. Irons, eds.
  1979 *Evolutionary Biology and Human Social
    Behavior: An Anthropological Perspective.* North
    Scituate, MA: Duxbury.

Chambers, E.
  1985 *Applied Anthropology: A Practical Guide.*
    Englewood Cliffs, NJ: Prentice Hall.
  1987 Applied Anthropology in the Post-
    Vietnam Era: Anticipations and Ironies.
    Annual Review of Anthropology 16: 309–337.
  2000 *Native Tours: The Anthropology of Travel
    and Tourism.* Prospect Heights, IL: Waveland.

Chambers, E., ed.
  1997 *Tourism and Culture: An Applied Perspec-
    tive.* Albany: State University of New York
    Press.

Chatty, D.
  1996 *Mobile Pastoralists: Development
    Planning and Social Change in Oman.* New
    York: Columbia University Press.

Cheater, A. P., ed.
  1999 *The Anthropology of Power: Empowerment
    and Disempowerment in Changing Structures.*
    New York: Routledge.

Cheney, D. L., and R. M. Seyfarth
  1990 In the Minds of Monkeys: What Do
    They Know and How Do They Know It? *Nat-
    ural History,* September, pp. 38–46.

Cherlin, A. J.
  1992 *Marriage, Divorce, Remarriage.*
    Cambridge, MA: Harvard University Press.

Child, A. B., and I. L. Child
  1993 *Religion and Magic in the Life of
    Traditional Peoples.* Englewood Cliffs, NJ:
    Prentice Hall.

Chiseri-Strater, E., and B. S. Sunstein
  2002 *Fieldworking: Reading and Writing
    Research,* 2nd ed. Upper Saddle River, NJ:
    Prentice Hall.

Chomsky, N.
  1955 *Syntactic Structures.* The Hague:
    Mouton.

Cigno, A.
  1994 *Economics of the Family.* New York:
    Oxford University Press.

Clammer, J., ed.
  1976 *The New Economic Anthropology.* New
    York: St. Martin's Press.

Clarke, S. C.
  1995 Advance Report of Final Divorce Statis-
    tics, 1989 and 1990. *Monthly Vital Statistics
    Report,* v. 43, nos. 8, 9. Hyattsville, MD:
    National Center for Health Statistics.

Clifford, J.
  1982 *Person and Myth: Maurice Leenhardt in
    the Melanesian World.* Berkeley: University of
    California Press.
  1988 *The Predicament of Culture: Twentieth-
    Century Ethnography, Literature, and Art.* Cam-
    bridge, MA: Harvard University Press.

Clifton, J. A., ed.
  1970 *Applied Anthropology: Readings in the
    Uses of the Science of Man.* Boston: Houghton
    Mifflin.

Coates, J.
  1986 *Women, Men, and Language.* London:
    Longman.

Cody, D.
  1998 British Empire. http://www.
    victorianweb.org/.

Cohen, M.
  1998 *Culture of Intolerance: Chauvinism, Class,
    and Racism.* New Haven, CT: Yale University
    Press.

Cohen, Roger
  1995 Serbs Shift Opens a Chance for Peace, a
    U.S. Envoy Says. *New York Times,* September
    1, pp. A1, A6.

Cohen, Ronald
  1967 *The Kanuri of Bornu.* New York:
    Harcourt Brace Jovanovich.

Cohen, Ronald, and E. R. Service, eds.
  1978 *Origins of the State: The Anthropology of
    Political Evolution.* Philadelphia: Institute for
    the Study of Human Issues.

Cohen, Y. A.
  1974a *Man in Adaptation: The Cultural Present,*
    2nd ed. Chicago: Aldine.
  1974b Culture as Adaptation. In *Man in
    Adaptation: The Cultural Present,* 2nd ed., ed.
    Y. A. Cohen, pp. 45–68. Chicago: Aldine.

Collier, J. F.
 1997 *From Duty to Desire: Remaking Families in a Spanish Village.* Princeton, NJ: Princeton University Press.

Collier, J. F., ed.
 1988 *Marriage and Inequality in Classless Societies.* Stanford, CA: Stanford University Press.

Collier, J. F., and S. J. Yanagisako, eds.
 1987 *Gender and Kinship: Essays toward a Unified Analysis.* Stanford, CA: Stanford University Press.

Collins, T. W.
 1989 Rural Economic Development in Two Tennessee Counties: A Racial Dimension. Paper presented at the annual meetings of the American Anthropological Association, Washington, DC.

Colson, E.
 1971 *The Social Consequences of Resettlement: The Impact of the Kariba Resettlement on the Gwembe Tonga.* Manchester, UK: Manchester University Press.

Colson, E., and T. Scudder
 1975 New Economic Relationships between the Gwembe Valley and the Line of Rail. In *Town and Country in Central and Eastern Africa,* ed. David Parkin, pp. 190–210. London: Oxford University Press.
 1988 *For Prayer and Profit: The Ritual, Economic, and Social Importance of Beer in Gwembe District, Zambia, 1950–1982.* Stanford, CA: Stanford University Press.

Comaroff, J.
 1982 Dialectical Systems, History and Anthropology: Units of Study and Questions of Theory. *Journal of Southern African Studies* 8: 143–172.

Combs-Schilling, E.
 1989 *Sacred Performances: Islam, Sexuality, and Sacrifice.* New York: Columbia University Press.

Conklin, H. C.
 1954 *The Relation of Hanunóo Culture to the Plant World.* Unpublished Ph.D. dissertation, Yale University.

Connell, R. W.
 1995 *Masculinities.* Berkeley: University of California Press.
 2002 *Gender.* Malden, MA: Blackwell.

Connor, W.
 1972 Nation-Building or Nation Destroying. *World Politics* 24(3): 319–355.

Cook-Gumperz, J.
 1986 *The Social Construction of Literacy.* Cambridge, UK: Cambridge University Press.

Cooper, F., and A. L. Stoler
 1989 Introduction, Tensions of Empire: Colonial Control and Visions of Rule. *American Ethnologist* 16: 609–621.

Cooper, F., and A. L. Stoler, eds.
 1997 *Tensions of Empire: Colonial Cultures in a Bourgeois World.* Berkeley: University of California Press.

Coote, J., and A. Shelton, eds.
 1992 *Anthropology, Art, and Aesthetics.* New York: Oxford University Press.

Crane, J. G., and M. V. Angrosino
 1992 *Field Projects in Anthropology: A Student Handbook,* 3rd ed. Prospect Heights, IL: Waveland.

Crapo, R. H.
 2006 *Anthropology of Religion: The Unity and Diversity of Religions.* Boston: McGraw-Hill.

Cresswell, T.
 2006 *On the Move: Mobility in the Modern West.* New York: Routledge.

Critser, G.
 2003 *Fat Land: How Americans Became the Fattest People in the World.* Boston: Houghton Mifflin.

Crosby, A. W.
 2003 *The Columbian Exchange: Biological and Cultural Consequences of 1492.* Westport, CT: Praeger.

Cueppens, B., and P. Geschiere
 2005 Autocthony: Local or Global? New Modes in the Struggle over Citizenship and Belonging in Africa and Europe. *Annual Review of Anthropology* 34: 385–407.

Cultural Survival Inc.
 1992 *At the Threshold.* Cambridge, MA: Cultural Survival. Originally published as the Spring 1992 issue of *Cultural Survival Quarterly.*

Cultural Survival Quarterly
 Quarterly journal. Cambridge, MA: Cultural Survival.

Cunningham, G.
 1999 *Religion and Magic: Approaches and Theories.* New York: New York University Press.

Dahlberg, F., ed.
 1981 *Woman the Gatherer.* New Haven, CT: Yale University Press.

Dalton, G., ed.
 1967 *Tribal and Peasant Economies.* Garden City, NY: Natural History Press.

DaMatta, R.
 1991 *Carnivals, Rogues, and Heroes: An Interpretation of the Brazilian Dilemma.* Translated from the Portuguese by John Drury. Notre Dame, IN: University of Notre Dame Press.

D'Andrade, R.
1984 Cultural Meaning Systems. In *Culture Theory: Essays on Mind, Self, and Emotion*, ed. R. A. Shweder and R. A. Levine, pp. 88–119. Cambridge, UK: Cambridge University Press.
1995 *The Development of Cognitive Anthropology.* New York: Cambridge University Press.

Das, V.
1995 *Critical Events: An Anthropological Perspective on Contemporary India.* New York: Oxford University Press.

Davies, C. A.
1999 *Reflexive Ethnography: Guide to Researching Selves and Others.* New York: Routledge.

Davis, D. L., and R. G. Whitten
1987 The Cross-Cultural Study of Human Sexuality. *Annual Review of Anthropology* 16: 69–98.

Degler, C.
1970 *Neither Black nor White: Slavery and Race Relations in Brazil and the United States.* New York: Macmillan.

Delamont, S.
1995 *Appetites and Identities: An Introduction to the Social Anthropology of Western Europe.* London: Routledge.

de la Peña, G.
2005 Social and Cultural Policies toward Indigenous Peoples: Perspectives from Latin America. *Annual Review of Anthropology* 34: 717–739.

Dentan, R. K.
1979 *The Semai: A Nonviolent People of Malaya*, fieldwork edition. New York: Harcourt Brace.

Desjarlais, R., L. Eisenberg, B. Good, and A. Kleinman, eds.
1995 *World Mental Health: Problems and Priorities in Low-Income Countries.* New York: Oxford University Press.

DeVita, P. R.
1992 *The Naked Anthropologist: Tales from around the World.* Belmont, CA: Wadsworth.

DeVita, P. R., and J. D. Armstrong, eds.
2002 *Distant Mirrors: America as a Foreign Culture*, 3rd ed. Belmont, CA: Wadsworth.

De Vos, G. A.
1971 *Japan's Outcastes: The Problem of the Burakumin.* London: Minority Rights Group.

De Vos, G. A., and H. Wagatsuma
1966 *Japan's Invisible Race: Caste in Culture and Personality.* Berkeley: University of California Press.

De Vos, G. A., W. O. Wetherall, and K. Stearman
1983 *Japan's Minorities: Burakumin, Koreans, Ainu and Okinawans.* Report no. 3. London: Minority Rights Group.

Di Leonardo, M., ed.
1991 *Gender at the Crossroads of Knowledge: Feminist Anthropology in the Postmodern Era.* Berkeley: University of California Press.

Divale, W. T., and M. Harris
1976 Population, Warfare, and the Male Supremacist Complex. *American Anthropologist* 78: 521–538.

Douglass, W. A.
1969 *Death in Murelaga: Funerary Ritual in a Spanish Basque Village.* Seattle: University of Washington Press.
1975 *Echalar and Murelaga: Opportunity and Rural Exodus in Two Spanish Basque Villages.* London: C. Hurst
1992 Basques. *Encyclopedia of World Cultures*, ed. L. Bennett, vol. 4. Boston: GK Hall. http://ets.umdl.umich.edu/cgi/e/ehraf/ehraf-idx?c=ehrafe&view=owc&owc=EX08.

Downes, W.
1998 *Language and Society*, 2nd ed. New York: Cambridge University Press.

Draper, P.
1975 !Kung Women: Contrasts in Sexual Egalitarianism in Foraging and Sedentary Contexts. In *Toward an Anthropology of Women*, ed. R. Reiter, pp. 77–109. New York: Monthly Review Press.

Dublin, M.
2001 *Native America Collected: The Culture of an Art World.* Albuquerque: University of New Mexico Press.

Dunn, J. S.
2000 *The Impact of Media on Reproductive Behavior in Northeastern Brazil.* Ph.D. dissertation, Department of Anthropology, University of Michigan, Ann Arbor.

Durkheim, E.
1951 (orig. 1897). *Suicide: A Study in Sociology.* Glencoe, IL: Free Press.
2001 (orig. 1912). *The Elementary Forms of the Religious Life.* Translated by Carol Cosman. Abridged with an introduction and notes by Mark S. Cladis. New York: Oxford University Press.

Dwyer, K.
1982 *Moroccan Dialogues: Anthropology in Question.* Baltimore: Johns Hopkins University Press.

Eagleton, T.
1983 *Literary Theory: An Introduction.* Minneapolis: University of Minnesota Press.

Earle, T. K.
1987 Chiefdoms in Archaeological and Ethnohistorical Perspective. *Annual Review of Anthropology* 16: 279–308.
1991 *Chiefdoms: Power, Economy, and Ideology.* New York: Cambridge University Press.

1997 *How Chiefs Come to Power: The Political Economy in Prehistory.* Stanford, CA: Stanford University Press.

Eastman, C. M.
1975 *Aspects of Language and Culture.* San Francisco: Chandler and Sharp.

Echeverria, J.
1999 *Home away from Home: A History of Basque Boardinghouses.* Reno: University of Nevada Press.

Eckert, P.
1989 *Jocks and Burnouts: Social Categories and Identity in the High School.* New York: Teachers College Press, Columbia University.
2000 *Linguistic Variation as Social Practice: The Linguistic Construction of Identity in Belten High.* Malden, MA: Blackwell.

Eckert, P., and S. McConnell-Ginet
2003 *Language and Gender.* New York: Cambridge University Press.

Eckert, P., and J. R. Rickford, eds.
2001 *Style and Sociolinguistic Variation.* New York: Cambridge University Press.

Eddy, E. M., and W. L. Partridge, eds.
1987 *Applied Anthropology in America,* 2nd ed. New York: Columbia University Press.

Edelman, M., and A. Haugerud
2004 *The Anthropology of Development and Globalization: From Classical Political Economy to Contemporary Neoliberalism.* Malden, MA: Blackwell.

Eder, J.
1987 *On the Road to Tribal Extinction: Depopulation, Deculturation, and Adaptive Well-Being among the Batak of the Philippines.* Berkeley: University of California Press.

Edgerton, R.
1965 "Cultural" versus "Ecological" Factors in the Expression of Values, Attitudes and Personality Characteristics. *American Anthropologist* 67: 442–447.

Eggert, K.
1988 Malafaly as Misnomer. In *Madagascar: Society and History,* ed. C. P. Kottak, J. A. Rakotoarisoa, A. Southall, and P. Verin, pp. 321–336. Durham, NC: Carolina Academic Press.

Ellen, R., P. Parkes, and A. Bicker, eds.
2000 *Indigenous Environmental Knowledge and its Transformations.* Amsterdam: Harwood Academic.

Ember, C., and Ember, M.
2001 *Cross-Cultural Research Methods.* Walnut Creek, CA: AltaMira.

Ember, M., and C. R. Ember
1997 Science in Anthropology. In *The Teaching of Anthropology: Problems, Issues, and Decisions,* ed. C. P. Kottak, J. J. White, R. H. Furlow, and

P. C. Rice, pp. 29–33. Mountain View, CA: Mayfield.

Erickson P., H. Ward, and K. Wachendorf
2002 *Voices of a Thousand People: The Makah Cultural and Research Center.* Lincoln/London: University of Nebraska Press.

Erlanger, S.
1992 An Islamic Awakening in Central Asian Lands. *New York Times,* June 9, pp. A1, A7.

Errington, F., and D. Gewertz
1987 *Cultural Alternatives and a Feminist Anthropology: An Analysis of Culturally Constructed Gender Interests in Papua New Guinea.* New York: Cambridge University Press.

Ervin, A. M.
2005 *Applied Anthropology: Tools and Perspectives for Contemporary Practice.* 2nd ed. Boston: Pearson/Allyn & Bacon.

Escobar, A.
1991 Anthropology and the Development Encounter: The Making and Marketing of Development Anthropology. *American Ethnologist* 18: 658–682.
1994 Welcome to Cyberia: Notes on the Anthropology of Cyberculture. *Current Anthropology* 35(3): 211–231.
1995 *Encountering Development: The Making and Unmaking of the Third World.* Princeton, NJ: Princeton University Press.

Eskridge, W. N., Jr.
1996 *The Case for Same-Sex Marriage: From Sexual Liberty to Civilized Commitment.* New York: Free Press.

Evans-Pritchard, E. E.
1940 *The Nuer: A Description of the Modes of Livelihood and Political Institutions of a Nilotic People.* Oxford: Clarendon Press.
1970 Sexual Inversion among the Azande. *American Anthropologist* 72: 1428–1433.

Ezra, K.
1986 *A Human Ideal in African Art: Bamana Figurative Sculpture.* Washington, DC: Smithsonian Institution Press for the National Museum of African Art.

Farb, P., and G. Armelagos.
1980 *Consuming Passions: The Anthropology of Eating.* Boston: Literary Guild.

Farner, R. F., ed.
2004 *Nationalism, Ethnicity, and Identity: Cross-National and Comparative Perspectives.* New Brunswick, NJ: Transaction.

Farnsworth, C. H.
1992 Canada to Divide Its Northern Land. *New York Times,* May 6, p. A7.

Farooq, M.
1966 Importance of Determining Transmission Sites in Planning Bilharziasis Control: Field

Observations from the Egypt-49 Project Area. *American Journal of Epidemiology* 83: 603–612.

Farr, D. M. L.
1980   British Empire. *Academic American Encyclopedia*, vol. 3, pp. 495–496. Princeton, NJ: Arete.

Fasold, R. W.
1990   *The Sociolinguistics of Language.* Oxford: Blackwell.

Feld, S.
1990   *Sound and Sentiment: Birds, Weeping, Poetics, and Song in Kaluli Expression*, 2nd ed. Philadelphia: University of Pennsylvania Press.
1991   Voices of the Rainforest. *Public Culture* 4(1): 131–140.

Ferguson, J.
1994   *The Anti-Politics Machine: "Development," Depoliticization, and Bureaucratic Power in Lesotho.* Minneapolis: University of Minnesota Press.

Ferguson, R. B.
1995   *Yanomami Warfare: A Political History.* Santa Fe, NM: School of American Research.
2002   *The State, Identity, and Violence: Political Disintegration in the Post–Cold War Era.* New York: Routledge.

Ferguson, R. B., and N. L. Whitehead
1991   *War in the Tribal Zone: Expanding States and Indigenous Warfare.* Santa Fe, NM: School of American Research Press.

Ferraro, G. P.
2006   *The Cultural Dimension of International Business*, 5th ed. Upper Saddle River, NJ: Prentice Hall.

Fields, J. M., and L. M. Casper
2001   America's Families and Living Arrangements: Population Characteristics, 2000. U.S. Census Bureau. *Current Population Reports*, P20-537, June 2001. http://www.census.gov/prod/2001pubs/p20-537.pdf.

Finke, R., and R. Stark
2005   *The Churching of America, 1776–2005: Winners and Losers in Our Religious Economy.* New Brunswick, NJ: Rutgers University Press.

Finkler, K.
1985   *Spiritualist Healers in Mexico: Successes and Failures of Alternative Therapeutics.* South Hadley, MA: Bergin and Garvey.
2000   *Experiencing the New Genetics: Family and Kinship on the Medical Frontier.* Philadelphia: University of Pennsylvania Press.

Finnstrom, S.
1997   Postcoloniality and the Postcolony: Theories of the Global and the Local. http://www.postcolonialweb.org/.

Fiske, J.
1989   *Understanding Popular Culture.* Boston: Unwin Hyman.

Fiske, J., and J. Hartley
2003   *Reading Television,* 2nd ed. New York: Routledge.

Fleisher, M. L.
1998   Cattle Raiding and Its Correlates: The Cultural-Ecological Consequences of Market-Oriented Cattle Raiding among the Kuria of Tanzania. *Human Ecology* 26(4): 547–572.
2000   *Kuria Cattle Raiders: Violence and Vigilantism on the Tanzania/Kenya Frontier.* Ann Arbor: University of Michigan Press.

Foley, W. A.
1997   *Anthropological Linguistics: An Introduction.* Cambridge, MA: Blackwell.

Ford, C. S., and F. A. Beach
1951   *Patterns of Sexual Behavior.* New York: Harper Torchbooks.

Forman, S., ed.
1994   *Diagnosing America: Anthropology and Public Engagement.* Ann Arbor: University of Michigan Press.

Fortes, M.
1950   Kinship and Marriage among the Ashanti. In *African Systems of Kinship and Marriage*, ed. A. R. Radcliffe-Brown and D. Forde, pp. 252–284. London: Oxford University Press.

Foster, G. M.
1965   Peasant Society and the Image of Limited Good. *American Anthropologist* 67: 293–315.

Foster, G. M., and B. G. Anderson
1978   *Medical Anthropology.* New York: McGraw-Hill.

Foucault, M.
1979   *Discipline and Punish: The Birth of the Prison.* Translated by Alan Sheridan. New York: Vintage Books, University Press.

Fouts, R.
1997   *Next of Kin: What Chimpanzees Have Taught Me about Who We Are.* New York: William Morrow.

Fouts, R. S., D. H. Fouts, and T. E. Van Cantfort
1989   The Infant Loulis Learns Signs from Cross-Fostered Chimpanzees. In *Teaching Sign Language to Chimpanzees*, ed. R. A. Gardner, B. T. Gardner, and T. E. Van Cantfort, pp. 280–292. Albany: State University of New York Press.

Fox, Richard. G., ed.
1990   Nationalist Ideologies and the Production of National Cultures. American Ethnological Society Monograph Series, no. 2. Washington, DC: American Anthropological Association.

Fox, Robin
1985   *Kinship and Marriage.* New York: Viking Penguin.

Frake, C. O.
  1961   The Diagnosis of Disease among the
         Subanun of Mindanao. *American Anthropolo-
         gist* 63: 113–132.

Franke, R.
  1977   Miracle Seeds and Shattered Dreams in
         Java. In *Readings in Anthropology,* pp. 197–201.
         Guilford, CT: Dushkin.

Free Dictionary
  2004   Honorific. http://encyclopedia.
         thefreedictionary.com/Honorific.

Freeman, D.
  1983   *Margaret Mead and Samoa: The Making
         and Unmaking of an Anthropological Myth.*
         Cambridge, MA: Harvard University Press.

Freilich, M., D. Raybeck, and J. Savishinsky
  1991   *Deviance: Anthropological Perspectives.*
         Westport, CT: Bergin and Garvey.

French, H. W.
  1992   Unending Exodus from the Caribbean,
         with the U.S. a Constant Magnet. *New York
         Times,* May 6, pp. A1, A8.
  2002   Whistling Past the Global Graveyard.
         New York Times, July 14. http://www.
         nytimes.com/2002/07/14/weekinreview/
         14FREN.html.

Freud, S.
  1950   (orig. 1918). *Totem and Taboo.* Translated
         by J. Strachey. New York: W. W. Norton.

Fricke, T.
  1994   *Himalayan Households: Tamang Demogra-
         phy and Domestic Processes,* 2nd ed. New York:
         Columbia University Press.

Fried, M. H.
  1960   On the Evolution of Social Stratification
         and the State. In *Culture in History,* ed. S. Dia-
         mond, pp. 713–731. New York: Columbia
         University Press.
  1967   *The Evolution of Political Society: An
         Essay in Political Anthropology.* New York:
         McGraw-Hill.

Friedan, B.
  1963   *The Feminine Mystique.* New York:
         W. W. Norton.

Friedl, E.
  1975   *Women and Men: An Anthropologist's
         View.* New York: Harcourt Brace Jovanovich.

Friedman, J.
  1994   *Cultural Identity and Global Process.*
         Thousand Oaks, CA: Sage.

Friedman, J., ed.
  2003   *Globalization, the State, and Violence.*
         Walnut Creek, CA: AltaMira.

Friedman, J., and M. J. Rowlands, eds.
  1978   *The Evolution of Social Systems.*
         Pittsburgh: University of Pittsburgh Press.

Fry, D. P.
  2006   *The Human Potential for Peace: An
         Anthropological Challenge to Assumptions
         about War and Violence.* New York: Oxford
         University Press.

Fry, D. P., and K. Bjorkqvist, eds.
  1997   *Cultural Variation in Conflict Resolution:
         Alternatives to Violence.* Mahwah, NJ:
         Erlbaum.

Gal, S.
  1989   Language and Political Economy.
         Annual Review of Anthropology 18: 345–367.

Garbarino, M. S., and R. F. Sasso
  1994   *Native American Heritage,* 3rd ed.
         Prospect Heights, IL: Waveland.

Gardner, R. A., B. T. Gardner, and T. E. Van
Cantfort, eds.
  1989   *Teaching Sign Language to Chimpanzees.*
         Albany: State University of New York Press.

Gargan, E. A.
  1992   A Single-Minded Man Battles to Free
         Slaves. *New York Times,* June 4, p. A7.

Geertz, C.
  1973   *The Interpretation of Cultures.* New York:
         Basic Books.
  1980   Blurred Genres: The Refiguration of
         Social Thought. *American Scholar* 29(2):
         165–179.
  1983   *Local Knowledge.* New York: Basic Books.
  1995   *After the Fact: Two Countries, Four
         Decades, One Anthropologist.* Cambridge, MA:
         Harvard University Press.

Geis, M. L.
  1987   *The Language of Politics.* New York:
         Springer-Verlag.

Gellner, E.
  1983   *Nations and Nationalism.* Ithaca, NY:
         Cornell University Press.
  1997   *Nationalism.* New York: New York
         University Press.

*General Anthropology: Bulletin of the Council
for General Anthropology*

Gibbons, A.
  2001   The Peopling of the Pacific. *Science* 291:
         1735. http://www.familytreedna.com/pdf/
         Gibbons_Science2001.pdf.

Gibbs, N.
  1989   How America Has Run Out of Time.
         Time, April 24, pp. 59–67.

Giddens, A.
  1973   *The Class Structure of the Advanced Soci-
         eties.* New York: Cambridge University Press.

Gilmore, D.
  1987   *Aggression and Community: Paradoxes of
         Andalusian Culture.* New Haven, CT: Yale
         University Press.

2001   *Misogyny: The Male Malady.* Philadelphia: University of Pennsylvania Press.

Gledhill, J.
2000   *Power and Its Disguises: Anthropological Perspectives on Politics.* Sterling, VA: Pluto Press.

Glick-Schiller, N., and G. Fouron
1990   "Everywhere We Go, We Are in Danger": Ti Manno and the Emergence of Haitian Transnational Identity. *American Ethnologist* 17(2): 327–347.

Gmelch, G.
1978   Baseball Magic. *Human Nature* 1(8): 32–40.
2001   *Inside Pitch: Life in Professional Baseball.* Washington, DC: Smithsonian Institution Press.

Gmelch, G., and W. Zenner
2002   *Urban Life: Readings in the Anthropology of the City.* Prospect Heights, IL: Waveland.

Goldberg, D. T.
1997   *Racial Subjects: Writing on Race in America.* New York: Routledge.

Goldberg, D. T., ed.
1990   *Anatomy of Racism.* Minneapolis: University of Minnesota Press.

Goldberg, P., V. T. Holliday, and C. R. Ferring
2000   *Earth Sciences and Archaeology.* New York: Kluwer Academic/Plenum Press.

Golden, T.
1997   Oakland Revamps Plan to Teach Black English. *New York Times,* January 14. http://www.nytimes.com.

Goldschmidt, W.
1965   Theory and Strategy in the Study of Cultural Adaptability. *American Anthropologist* 67: 402–407.

Goodale, J., and J. D. Koss
1971   The Cultural Context of Creativity among Tiwi. In *Anthropology and Art: Readings in Cross-Cultural Aesthetics,* ed. C. Otten, pp. 182–203. Austin: University of Texas Press.

Goodenough, W. H.
1953   *Native Astronomy in the Central Carolines.* Philadelphia: University of Pennsylvania Press.

Goodman, J., P. E. Lovejoy, and A. Sherratt
1995   *Consuming Habits: Drugs in History and Anthropology.* London: Routledge.

Goody, J.
1977   *Production and Reproduction: A Comparative Study of the Domestic Domain.* New York: Cambridge University Press.

Goody, J., and S. T. Tambiah
1973   *Bridewealth and Dowry.* Cambridge, UK: Cambridge University Press.

Gordon, A. A.
1996   *Transforming Capitalism and Patriarchy: Gender and Development in Africa.* Boulder, CO: Lynne Rienner.

Gorer, G.
1943   Themes in Japanese Culture. *Transactions of the New York Academy of Sciences* (Series II) 5: 106–124.

Gottdiener, M., ed.
2000   *New Forms of Consumption: Consumers, Culture, and Commodification.* Lanham, MD: Rowman and Littlefield.

Gough, E. K.
1959   The Nayars and the Definition of Marriage. *Journal of Royal Anthropological Institute* 89: 23–34.

Graburn, N.
1976   *Ethnic and Tourist Arts: Cultural Expressions from the Fourth World.* Berkeley: University of California Press.

Graburn, N., ed.
1971   *Readings in Kinship and Social Structure.* New York: Harper & Row.

Gramsci, A.
1971   *Selections from the Prison Notebooks.* Edited and translated by Quenten Hoare and Geoffrey Nowell Smith. London: Wishart.

Grasmuck, S., and P. Pessar
1991   *Between Two Islands: Dominican International Migration.* Berkeley: University of California Press.

Grassmuck, K.
1985   Local Educators Join Push for "A Computer in Every Classroom." *Ann Arbor News,* February 10, p. A11. (Quotes testimony of Linda Tarr-Whelan of the National Education Association to the House Committee on Science, Research and Technology.)

Gray, J.
1986   With a Few Exceptions, Television in Africa Fails to Educate and Enlighten. *Ann Arbor News,* December 8.

Greaves, T. C.
1995   Problems Facing Anthropologists: Cultural Rights and Ethnography. *General Anthropology* 1(2): 1, 3–6.

Green, E. C.
1992   (orig. 1987). The Integration of Modern and Traditional Health Sectors in Swaziland. In *Applying Anthropology,* ed. A. Podolefsky and P. J. Brown, pp. 246–251. Mountain View, CA: Mayfield.

Greenwood, D. J.
1976   *Unrewarding Wealth: The Commercialization and Collapse of Agriculture in a Spanish Basque Town.* Cambridge, UK: Cambridge University Press.

Greiner, T. M.
　2003　What Is the Difference between Hominin and Hominid When Classifying Humans? MadSci Network: Evolution. http://www.madsci.org/posts/archives/Apr2003/1050350684.Ev.r.html.

Grekova, M.
　2001　Postsocialist Societies. *International Encyclopedia of the Social and Behavioral Sciences*, pp. 11877–11881. New York: Elsevier.

Griffin, P. B., and A. Estioko-Griffin, eds.
　1985　*The Agta of Northeastern Luzon: Recent Studies*. Cebu City, Philippines: University of San Carlos.

Gross, D.
　1971　The Great Sisal Scheme. *Natural History*, March, pp. 49–55.

Gross, D., and B. Underwood
　1971　Technological Change and Caloric Costs: Sisal Agriculture in Northeastern Brazil. *American Anthropologist* 73: 725–740.

Gudeman, S.
　2001　*The Anthropology of Economy: Community, Market, and Culture*. Malden, MA: Blackwell.

Gudeman, S., ed.
　1998　*Economic Anthropology*. Northhampton, MA: E. Elgar.

Gugliotta, G.
　2005　Tools Found in Britain Show Much Earlier Human Existence. *Washington Post*, December 15, p. A-24.

Gulliver, P. H.
　1974　(orig. 1965). The Jie of Uganda. In *Man in Adaptation: The Cultural Present*, 2nd ed., ed. Y. A. Cohen, pp. 323–345. Chicago: Aldine.

Gumperz, J. J.
　1982　*Language and Social Identity*. Cambridge, UK: Cambridge University Press.

Gumperz, J. J., and S. C. Levinson, eds.
　1996　*Rethinking Linguistic Relativity*. New York: Cambridge University Press.

Gunther, E.
　1971　Northwest Coast Indian Art. In *Anthropology and Art: Readings in Cross-Cultural Aesthetics*, ed. C. Otten, pp. 318–340. Austin: University of Texas Press.

Gupta, A., and J. Ferguson
　1997a　Culture, Power, Place: Ethnography at the End of an Era. In *Culture, Power, Place: Explorations in Critical Anthropology*, ed. A. Gupta and J. Ferguson, pp. 1–29. Durham, NC: Duke University Press.
　1997b　Beyond "Culture": Space, Identity, and the Politics of Difference. In *Culture, Power, Place: Explorations in Critical Anthropology*, ed. A. Gupta and J. Ferguson, pp. 33–51. Durham, NC: Duke University Press.

Gupta, A., and J. Ferguson, eds.
　1997a　*Anthropological Locations: Boundaries and Grounds of a Field Science*. Berkeley: University of California Press.
　1997b　*Culture, Power, Place: Explorations in Critical Anthropology*. Durham, NC: Duke University Press.

Guthrie, S.
　1995　*Faces in the Clouds: A New Theory of Religion*. New York: Oxford University Press.

Gwynne, M. A.
　2003　*Applied Anthropology: A Career-Oriented Approach*. Boston: Allyn & Bacon.

Haapala, A.
　1998　Literature: Invention of the Self. *Canadian Aesthetics Journal* 2. http://www.uqtr.ca/AE/vol_2/haapala.html.

Hackett, R. I. J.
　1996　*Art and Religion in Africa*. London: Cassell.

Hall, E. T.
　1990　*Understanding Cultural Differences*. Yarmouth, ME: Intercultural Press.
　1992　*An Anthropology of Everyday Life: An Autobiography*. New York: Doubleday.

Hall, T. D., ed.
　1999　*A World-System Reader: New Perspectives on Gender, Urbanism, Cultures, Indigenous Peoples, and Ecology*. Lanham, MD: Rowman and Littlefield.

Hallowell, A. I.
　1955　*Culture and Experience*. Philadelphia: University of Pennsylvania Press.

Hamilton, M. B.
　1995　*The Sociology of Religion: Theoretical and Comparative Perspectives*. London: Routledge.

Hanks, W. F.
　1995　*Language and Communicative Practices*. Boulder, CO: Westview Press.

Hansen, K. V.
　2004　*Not-So-Nuclear Families: Class, Gender, and Networks of Care*. New Brunswick, NJ: Rutgers University Press.

Hansen, K. V., and A. I. Garey, eds.
　1998　*Families in the U.S.: Kinship and Domestic Politics*. Philadelphia: Temple University Press.

Harding, S.
　1975　Women and Words in a Spanish Village. In *Toward an Anthropology of Women*, ed. R. Reiter, pp. 283–308. New York: Monthly Review Press.

Hargrove, E. C.
　1986　*Religion and Environmental Crisis*. Athens: University of Georgia Press.

Harris, M.
1970   Referential Ambiguity in the Calculus of Brazilian Racial Identity. *Southwestern Journal of Anthropology* 26(1): 1–14.
1974   *Cows, Pigs, Wars, and Witches: The Riddles of Culture.* New York: Random House.
1978   *Cannibals and Kings.* New York: Vintage.
1989   *Our Kind: Who We Are, Where We Came from, Where We Are Going.* New York: Harper & Row.
2001   (orig. 1979). *Cultural Materialism: The Struggle for a Science of Culture.* Walnut Creek, CA: AltaMira.
2001   (orig. 1968). *The Rise of Anthropological Theory.* Walnut Creek, CA: AltaMira.

Harris, M., and C. P. Kottak
1963   The Structural Significance of Brazilian Racial Categories. *Sociologia* 25: 203–209.

Harrison, G. G., W. L. Rathje, and W. W. Hughes
1994   Food Waste Behavior in an Urban Population. In *Applying Anthropology: An Introductory Reader,* 3rd ed., ed. A. Podolefsky and P. J. Brown, pp. 107–112. Mountain View, CA: Mayfield.

Hart, C. W. M., A. R. Pilling, and J. C. Goodale
1988   *The Tiwi of North Australia,* 3rd ed. Fort Worth: Harcourt Brace.

Harvey, D. J.
1980   French Empire. *Academic American Encyclopedia,* vol. 8, pp. 309–310. Princeton, NJ: Arete.

Harvey, K.
1996   Online for the Ancestors: The Importance of Anthropological Sensibility in Information Superhighway Design. *Social Science Computing Review* 14(1): 65–68.

Hastings, A.
1997   *The Construction of Nationhood: Ethnicity, Religion, and Nationalism.* New York: Cambridge University Press.

Hatcher, E. P.
1999   *Art as Culture: An Introduction to the Anthropology of Art,* 2nd ed. Westport, CT: Bergin & Garvey.

Hatfield, E., and R. L. Rapson
1996   *Love and Sex: Cross-Cultural Perspectives.* Needham Heights, MA: Allyn & Bacon.

Hausfater, G., and S. Hrdy, eds.
1984   *Infanticide: Comparative and Evolutionary Perspectives.* Hawthorne, NY: Aldine.

Hawkes, K., J. O'Connell, and K. Hill
1982   Why Hunters Gather: Optimal Foraging and the Aché of Eastern Paraguay. *American Ethnologist* 9: 379–398.

Hawley, J. S,. ed.
1994   *Sati, the Blessing and the Curse: The Burning of Wives in India.* New York: Oxford University Press.

Hayden, B.
1981   Subsistence and Ecological Adaptations of Modern Hunter/Gatherers. In *Omnivorous Primates: Gathering and Hunting in Human Evolution,* ed. R. S. Harding and G. Teleki, pp. 344–421. New York: Columbia University Press.

Headland, T. N., ed.
1992   *The Tasaday Controversy: Assessing the Evidence.* Washington, DC: American Anthropological Association.

Headland, T. N., and L. A. Reid
1989   Hunter-Gatherers and Their Neighbors from Prehistory to the Present. *Current Anthropology* 30: 43–66.

Heath, D. B., ed.
1995   *International Handbook on Alcohol and Culture.* Westport, CT: Greenwood Press.

Hedges, C.
1992*a*   Sudan Presses Its Campaign to Impose Islamic Law on Non-Muslims. *New York Times,* June 1, p. A7.
1992*b*   Sudan Gives Its Refugees a Desert to Contemplate. *New York Times,* June 3, p. A4.

Heider, K. G.
1988   The Rashomon Effect: When Ethnographers Disagree. *American Anthropologist* 90: 73–81.
1997   *Grand Valley Dani: Peaceful Warriors,* 3rd ed. Fort Worth: Harcourt Brace.

Heller, M.
1988   *Codeswitching: Anthropological and Sociolinguistic Perspectives.* Berlin: Mouton de Gruyter.

Helman, C.
2001   *Culture, Health, and Illness: An Introduction for Health Professionals,* 4th ed. Boston: Butterworth-Heinemann.

Henry, D. O.
1989   *From Foraging to Agriculture: The Levant at the End of the Ice Age.* Philadelphia: University of Pennsylvania Press.
1995   *Prehistoric Cultural Ecology and Evolution: Insights from Southern Jordan.* New York: Plenum Press.

Henry, J.
1955   Docility, or Giving Teacher What She Wants. *Journal of Social Issues* 2: 33–41.

Herdt, G.
1981   *Guardians of the Flutes.* New York: McGraw-Hill.
1986   *The Sambia: Ritual and Gender in New Guinea.* Fort Worth: Harcourt Brace.

Herdt, G. H., ed.
1984   *Ritualized Homosexuality in Melanesia.* Berkeley: University of California Press.

Herrnstein, R. J.
1971 I.Q. *Atlantic* 228(3): 43–64.

Herrnstein, R. J., and C. Murray
1994 *The Bell Curve: Intelligence and Class Structure in American Life.* New York: Free Press.

Herskovits, M.
1937 *Life in a Haitian Valley.* New York: Knopf.

Hess, D. J.
1995 A Democratic Research Agenda in the Social Studies of the National Information Infrastructure. Paper prepared for the National Science Foundation Workshop on Culture, Society, and Advanced Information Technology. Washington, DC: May 31–June 1, 1995.

Hess, D. J., and R. A. DaMatta, eds.
1995 *The Brazilian Puzzle: Culture on the Borderlands of the Western World.* New York: Columbia University Press.

Hewitt, R.
1986 *White Talk, Black Talk.* Cambridge, UK: Cambridge University Press.

Heyneman, D.
1984 Development and Disease: A Dual Dilemma. *Journal of Parasitology* 70: 3–17.

Hicks, D., ed.
2001 *Ritual and Belief: Readings in the Anthropology of Religion,* 2nd ed. Boston: McGraw-Hill.

Hill, C. E., ed.
1986 Current Health Policy Issues and Alternatives: An Applied Social Science Perspective. *Southern Anthropological Society Proceedings.* Athens: University of Georgia Press.

Hill, J. H.
1978 Apes and Language. *Annual Review of Anthropology* 7: 89–112.

Hill, K., H. Kaplan, K. Hawkes, and A. Hurtado
1987 Foraging Decisions among Aché Hunter-Gatherers: New Data and Implications for Optimal Foraging Models. *Ethology and Sociobiology* 8: 1–36.

Hill-Burnett, J.
1978 Developing Anthropological Knowledge through Application. In *Applied Anthropology in America,* ed. E. M. Eddy and W. L. Partridge, pp. 112–128. New York: Columbia University Press.

Hobhouse, L. T.
1915 *Morals in Evolution,* rev. ed. New York: Holt.

Hobsbawm, E. J.
1992 *Nations and Nationalism since 1780: Programme, Myth, Reality,* 2nd ed. New York: Cambridge University Press.

Hoebel, E. A.
1954 *The Law of Primitive Man.* Cambridge, MA: Harvard University Press.

1968 (orig. 1954). The Eskimo: Rudimentary Law in a Primitive Anarchy. In *Studies in Social and Cultural Anthropology,* ed. J. Middleton, pp. 93–127. New York: Crowell.

Holden, A.
2005 *Tourism Studies and the Social Sciences.* New York: Routledge.

Holland, D., and N. Quinn, eds.
1987 *Cultural Models in Language and Thought.* Cambridge, UK: Cambridge University Press.

Holmes, L. D.
1987 *Quest for the Real Samoa: The Mead/ Freeman Controversy and Beyond.* South Hadley, MA: Bergin and Garvey.

Holtzman, J.
2000 *Nuer Journeys, Nuer Lives.* Boston: Allyn & Bacon.

Hopkins, T., and I. Wallerstein
1982 Patterns of Development of the Modern World System. In *World System Analysis: Theory and Methodology,* by T. Hopkins, I. Wallerstein, R. Bach, C. Chase-Dunn, and R. Mukherjee, pp. 121–141. Thousand Oaks, CA: Sage.

Hopkins, T. K.
1996 *The Age of Transition: Trajectory of the World-System 1945–2025.* Atlantic Highlands, NJ: Zed.

Horton, R.
1963 The Kalabari Ekine Society: A Borderland of Religion and Art. *Africa* 33: 94–113.
1993 *Patterns of Thought in Africa and the West: Essays on Magic, Religion, and Science.* New York: Cambridge University Press.

Hostetler, J., and G. E. Huntington
1992 *Amish Children: Education in the Family,* 2nd ed. Fort Worth: Harcourt Brace.
1996 *The Hutterites in North America,* 3rd ed. Fort Worth: Harcourt Brace.

Hughes, R., Jr.
1996 Demographics of Divorce. http://missourifamilies.org/features/divorcearticles/divorcefeature17.htm.

Human Organization
Quarterly journal. Oklahoma City: Society for Applied Anthropology.

Hunter, M. L.
2005 *Race, Gender, and the Politics of Skin Tone.* New York: Routledge.

Hutchinson, S. E.
1996 *Nuer Dilemmas: Coping with Money, War, and the State.* Berkeley: University of California Press.

Ingold, T., D. Riches, and J. Woodburn
1991 *Hunters and Gatherers.* New York: Berg (St. Martin's Press).

Ingraham, C.
1999 *White Weddings: Romancing Heterosexuality in Popular Culture.* New York: Routledge.

Inhorn, M. C., and P. J. Brown
1990   The Anthropology of Infectious Disease. *Annual Review of Anthropology* 19: 89–117.

Irving, W. N.
1985   Context and Chronology of Early Man in the Americas. *Annual Review of Anthropology* 14: 529–555.

Ives, E. D.
1995   *The Tape-Recorded Interview: A Manual for Fieldworkers in Folklore and Oral History,* 2nd ed. Knoxville: University of Tennessee Press.

Jackson, B.
1987   *Fieldwork.* Champaign–Urbana: University of Illinois Press.

Jackson, J., and K. B. Warren
2005   Indigenous Movements in Latin America, 1992–2004: Controversies, Ironies, New Directions. *Annual Review of Anthropology* 34: 549–573.

Jacoby, R., and N. Glauberman, eds.
1995   *The Bell Curve Debate: History, Documents, Opinions.* New York: Free Press. New York: Random House/Times Books.

Jameson, F.
1984   Postmodernism, or the Cultural Logic of Late Capitalism. *New Left Review* 146: 53–93.
1988   *The Ideologies of Theory: Essays 1971–1986.* Minneapolis: University of Minnesota Press.

Jankowiak, W. R., and E. F. Fischer
1992   A Cross-Cultural Perspective on Romantic Love. *Ethnology* 31(2): 149–156.

Jenks, C.
2004   *Culture,* 2nd ed. New York: Routledge.

Jensen, A.
1969   How Much Can We Boost I.Q. and Scholastic Achievement? *Harvard Educational Review* 29: 1–123.

Jodelet, D.
1991   *Madness and Social Representations: Living with the Mad in One French Community.* Translated from the French by Gerard Duveen. Berkeley: University of California Press.

Johansen, B. E.
2003   *Indigenous Peoples and Environmental Issues: An Encyclopedia.* Westport, CT: Greenwood Press.

Johnson, A. W.
1978   *Quantification in Cultural Anthropology: An Introduction to Research Design.* Stanford, CA: Stanford University Press.

Johnson, A. W., and T. Earle, eds.
1987   *The Evolution of Human Societies: From Foraging Group to Agrarian State.* Stanford, CA: Stanford University Press.

2000   *The Evolution of Human Societies: From Foraging Group to Agrarian State,* 2nd ed. Stanford, CA: Stanford University Press.

Johnson, T. J., and C. F. Sargent, eds.
1990   *Medical Anthropology: A Handbook of Theory and Method.* New York: Greenwood Press.

Johnston, F. E., and S. Low
1994   *Children of the Urban Poor: The Sociocultural Environment of Growth, Development, and Malnutrition in Guatemala City.* Boulder, CO: Westview Press.

Jones, D.
1999   Hot Asset in Corporate: Anthropology Degrees. *USA Today,* February 18, p. B1.

Joralemon, D.
1999   *Exploring Medical Anthropology.* Boston: Allyn & Bacon.

Jordan, A.
2003   *Business Anthropology.* Prospect Heights, IL: Waveland.

Kan, S.
1986   The 19th-Century Tlingit Potlatch: A New Perspective. *American Ethnologist* 13: 191–212.
1989   *Symbolic Immortality: The Tlingit Potlatch of the Nineteenth Century.* Washington, DC: Smithsonian Institution Press.

Kantor, P.
1996   Domestic Violence against Women: A Global Issue. http://www.ucis.unc.edu/resources/pubs/carolina/Abuse/Abuse.html.

Kaplan, R. D.
1994   The Coming Anarchy: How Scarcity, Crime, Overpopulation, and Disease Are Rapidly Destroying the Social Fabric of Our Planet. *Atlantic Monthly,* February, pp. 44–76.

Kardiner, A., ed.
1939   *The Individual and His Society.* New York: Columbia University Press.

Kardulias, P. N.
1999   *World-Systems Theory in Practice: Leadership, Production, and Exchange.* Lanham, MD: Rowman and Littlefield.

Kearney, M.
1996   *Reconceptualizing the Peasantry: Anthropology in Global Perspective.* Boulder, CO: Westview Press.
2004   *Changing Fields of Anthropology: From Local to Global.* Lanham, MD: Rowman and Littlefield.

Kehoe, A. B.
1989   *The Ghost Dance Religion: Ethnohistory and Revitalization.* Fort Worth: Harcourt Brace.

Keiser, L.
1991   *Friend by Day, Enemy by Night: Organized Vengeance in a Kohistani Community.* Fort Worth: Harcourt Brace.

Kelly, R. C.

1976 Witchcraft and Sexual Relations: An Exploration in the Social and Semantic Implications of the Structure of Belief. In *Man and Woman in the New Guinea Highlands*, ed. P. Brown and G. Buchbinder, pp. 36–53. Special Publication, no. 8. Washington, DC: American Anthropological Association.

1985 *The Nuer Conquest: The Structure and Development of an Expansionist System.* Ann Arbor: University of Michigan Press.

2000 *Warless Societies and the Origin of War.* Ann Arbor: University of Michigan Press.

Kelly, R. L.

1995 *The Foraging Spectrum: Diversity in Hunter-Gatherer Lifeways.* Washington, DC: Smithsonian Institution Press.

Kent, S.

1992 The Current Forager Controversy: Real versus Ideal Views of Hunter-Gatherers. *Man* 27: 45–70.

1996 *Cultural Diversity among Twentieth-Century Foragers: An African Perspective.* New York: Cambridge University Press.

1998 *Gender in African Prehistory.* Walnut Creek, CA: AltaMira.

Kent, S., and H. Vierich

1989 The Myth of Ecological Determinism: Anticipated Mobility and Site Organization of Space. In *Farmers as Hunters: The Implications of Sedentism*, ed. S. Kent, pp. 96–130. New York: Cambridge University Press.

Keynes, J. M.

1927 *The End of Laissez-Faire.* London: L. and Virginia Woolf.

1936 *General Theory of Employment, Interest, and Money.* New York: Harcourt Brace.

Kimmel, M. S.

2004 *The Gendered Society,* 2nd ed. New York: Oxford University Press.

Kimmel, M. S., J. Hearn, and R. W. Connell

2005 *Handbook of Studies on Men and Masculinities.* Thousand Oaks, CA: Sage.

Kimmel, M. S., and M. A. Messner, eds.

2007 *Men's Lives,* 7th ed. Boston: Allyn & Bacon.

Kimmel, M. S., and R. Plante

2004 *Sexualities: Identities, Behaviors, and Society.* New York: Oxford University Press.

King, B. J., ed.

1994 *The Information Continuum: Evolution of Social Information Transfer in Monkeys, Apes, and Hominids.* Santa Fe: School of American Research Press.

Kinsey, A. C., W. B. Pomeroy, and C. E. Martin

1948 *Sexual Behavior in the Human Male.* Philadelphia: W. B. Saunders.

Kirch, P. V.

1984 *The Evolution of the Polynesian Chiefdoms.* Cambridge, UK: Cambridge University Press.

2000 *On the Road of the Winds: An Archaeological History of the Pacific Islands before European Contact.* Berkeley: University of California Press.

Kirman, P.

1997 An Introduction to Ethnomusicology. http://www.insideworldmusic.com/library/weekly/aa101797.htm.

Klass, M.

1995 *Ordered Universes: Approaches to the Anthropology of Religion.* Boulder, CO: Westview Press.

2003 *Mind over Mind: The Anthropology and Psychology of Spirit Possession.* Lanham, MA: Rowman and Littlefield.

Klass, M., and M. Weisgrau, eds.

1999 *Across the Boundaries of Belief: Contemporary Issues in the Anthropology of Religion.* Boulder, CO: Westview Press.

Kleinfeld, J.

1975 Positive Stereotyping: The Cultural Relativist in the Classroom. *Human Organization* 34: 269–274.

Kleymeyer, C. D., ed.

1994 *Cultural Expression and Grassroots Development: Cases from Latin America and the Caribbean.* Boulder, CO: Lynne Rienner.

Klineberg, O.

1951 Race and Psychology. In *The Race Question in Modern Science.* Paris: UNESCO.

Kling, R.

1996 Synergies and Competition between Life in Cyberspace and Face-to-Face Communities. *Social Science Computing Review* 14(1): 50–54.

Kluckhohn, C.

1944 *Mirror for Man: A Survey of Human Behavior and Social Attitudes.* Greenwich, CT: Fawcett.

Korten, D. C.

1980 Community Organization and Rural Development: A Learning Process Approach. *Public Administration Review,* September–October, pp. 480–512.

Kosty, P.

2002 Indonesia's Matriarchal Minangkabau Offer an Alternative Social System, EurekAlert.org May 9. http://www.eurekalert.org/pub_releases/2002-05/uop-imm050902.php.

Kottak, C. P.

1980 *The Past in the Present: History, Ecology, and Social Organization in Highland Madagascar.* Ann Arbor: University of Michigan Press.

1990a *Prime-Time Society: An Anthropological Analysis of Television and Culture.* Belmont, CA: Wadsworth.

1990b Culture and Economic Development. *American Anthropologist* 92(3): 723–731.

1991 When People Don't Come First: Some Lessons from Completed Projects. In *Putting People First: Sociological Variables in Rural Development,* 2nd ed., ed. M. Cernea, pp. 429–464. New York: Oxford University Press.

1999a *Assault on Paradise: Social Change in a Brazilian Village,* 3rd ed. New York: McGraw-Hill.

1999b The New Ecological Anthropology. *American Anthropologist* 101(1): 23–35.

2004 An Anthropological Take on Sustainable Development: A Comparative Study of Change. *Human Organization* 63(4): 501–510.

2006 *Assault on Paradise: The Globalization of a Little Community in Brazil,* 4th ed. New York: McGraw-Hill.

Kottak, C. P., ed.
1982 *Researching American Culture: A Guide for Student Anthropologists.* Ann Arbor: University of Michigan Press.

Kottak, C. P., and A. C. G. Costa
1993 Ecological Awareness, Environmentalist Action, and International Conservation Strategy. *Human Organization* 52(4): 335–343.

Kottak, C. P., L. L. Gezon, and G. Green
1994 Deforestation and Biodiversity Preservation in Madagascar: The View from Above and Below. CIESIN Human Dimensions Kiosk. http://www.ciesin.com.

Kottak, C. P., and K. A. Kozaitis
2003 *On Being Different: Diversity and Multiculturalism in the North American Mainstream,* 2nd ed. Boston: McGraw-Hill.

Kottak, N. C.
2002 *Stealing the Neighbor's Chicken: Social Control in Northern Mozambique.* Ph.D. dissertation. Department of Anthropology, Emory University, Atlanta, GA.

Kramarae, R., M. Shulz, and M. O'Barr, eds.
1984 *Language and Power.* Thousand Oaks, CA: Sage.

Kreider, R. M., and J. M. Fields
2002 Number, Timing and Duration of Marriages and Divorces: 1996. U.S. Census Bureau. *Current Population Reports,* P70–80, February, 2002. http://www.census.gov/prod/2002pubs/p70-80.pdf.

Kristof, N. D.
1995 Japan's Feminine Falsetto Falls Right out of Favor. *New York Times,* December 13, pp. A1, A4.

Kroeber, A. L.
1923 *Anthropology.* New York: Harcourt, Brace.

1944 *Configurations of Cultural Growth.* Berkeley: University of California Press.

1987 (orig. 1952). *The Nature of Culture.* Chicago: University of Chicago Press.

Kroeber, A. L., and C. Kluckhohn
1963 *Culture: A Critical Review of Concepts and Definitions.* New York: Vintage.

Kryshtanovskaya, O.
1997 Illegal Structures in Russia. *Trends in Organized Crime* 3(1): 14–17.

Kulick, D.
1998 *Travesti: Sex, Gender, and Culture among Brazilian Transgendered Prostitutes.* Chicago: University of Chicago Press.

Kunitz, S. J.
1994 *Disease and Social Diversity: The European Impact on the Health of Non-Europeans.* New York: Oxford University Press.

Kuper, L.
2006 *Race, Class, and Power: Ideology and Revolutionary Change in Plural Societies.* New Brunswick, NJ: Transaction.

Kurtz, D. V.
2001 *Political Anthropology: Power and Paradigms.* Boulder, CO: Westview Press.

Kutsche, P.
1998 *Field Ethnography: A Manual for Doing Cultural Anthropology.* Upper Saddle River, NJ: Prentice Hall.

LaBarre, W.
1945 Some Observations of Character Structure in the Orient: The Japanese. *Psychiatry* 8: 326–342.

Labov, W.
1972a *Language in the Inner City: Studies in the Black English Vernacular.* Philadelphia: University of Pennsylvania Press.

1972b *Sociolinguistic Patterns.* Philadelphia: University of Pennsylvania Press.

La Fraugh, R. J.
n.d. Euskara: The History, a True Mystery. The La Fraugh Name History. http://planetrjl.tripod.com/LaFraughName/id5.html.

Laguerre, M. S.
1984 *American Odyssey: Haitians in New York.* Ithaca, NY: Cornell University Press.

1998 *Diasporic Citizenship: Haitian Americans in Transnational America.* New York: St. Martin's Press.

1999 *The Global Ethnopolis: Chinatown, Japantown, and Manilatown in American Society.* New York: St. Martin's Press.

2001   *Urban Multiculturalism and Globalization in New York City.* New York: Palgrave Macmillan.

Laird, S. A.
2002   *Biodiversity and Traditional Knowledge: Equitable Partnerships in Practice.* Sterling, VA: Earthscan.

Lakoff, R. T.
2000   *Language War.* Berkeley: University of California Press.
2004   *Language and Woman's Place.* New York: Harper & Row.

Lamphere, L., H. Ragone, and P. Zavella, eds.
1997   *Situated Lives: Gender and Culture in Everyday Life.* New York: Routledge.

Lancaster, R. N., and M. Di Leonardo, eds.
1997   *The Gender/Sexuality Reader: Culture, History, Political Economy.* New York: Routledge.

Lance, L. M., and E. E. McKenna
1975   Analysis of Cases Pertaining to the Impact of Western Technology on the Non-Western World. *Human Organization* 34: 87–94.

Lansing, J. S.
1991   *Priests and Programmers: Technologies of Power in the Engineered Landscape of Bali.* Princeton, NJ: Princeton University Press.

Larson, A.
1989   Social Context of Human Immunodeficiency Virus Transmission in Africa: Historical and Cultural Bases of East and Central African Sexual Relations. *Review of Infectious Diseases* 11: 716–731.

Lassiter, L. E.
1998   *The Power of Kiowa Song: A Collaborative Ethnography.* Tucson: University of Arizona Press.

Layton, R.
1991   *The Anthropology of Art,* 2nd ed. New York: Cambridge University Press.

Leach, E. R.
1955   Polyandry, Inheritance and the Definition of Marriage. *Man* 55: 182–186.
1961   *Rethinking Anthropology.* London: Athlone Press.
1970   (orig. 1954). *Political Systems of Highland Burma: A Study of Kachin Social Structure.* London: Athlone Press.
1985   *Social Anthropology.* New York: Oxford University Press.

LeClair, E. E., and H. K. Schneider, eds.
1968   (orig. 1961). *Economic Anthropology: Readings in Theory and Analysis.* New York: Holt, Rinehart and Winston.

Lee, R. B.
1974   (orig. 1968). What Hunters Do for a Living, or, How to Make Out on Scarce Resources. In *Man in Adaptation: The Cultural Present,* 2nd ed., ed. Y. A. Cohen, pp. 87–100. Chicago: Aldine.
1979   *The !Kung San: Men, Women, and Work in a Foraging Society.* New York: Cambridge University Press.
1984   *The Dobe !Kung.* New York: Holt, Rinehart and Winston.
2003   *The Dobe Ju/'hoansi,* 3rd ed. Belmont, CA: Wadsworth.

Lee, R. B., and R. H. Daly
1999   *The Cambridge Encyclopedia of Hunters and Gatherers.* New York: Cambridge University Press.

Lee, R. B., and I. DeVore, eds.
1977   *Kalahari Hunter-Gatherers: Studies of the !Kung San and Their Neighbors.* Cambridge, MA: Harvard University Press.

Lehmann, A. C., J. E. Meyers, and P. A. Moro, eds.
2005   *Magic, Witchcraft, and Religion: An Anthropological Study of the Supernatural,* 6th ed. Mountain View, CA: Mayfield.

Leman, J.
2001   *The Dynamics of Emerging Ethnicities: Immigrant and Indigenous Ethnogenesis in Confrontation.* New York: Peter Lang.

Lenski, G.
1966   *Power and Privilege: A Theory of Social Stratification.* New York: McGraw-Hill.

Lessa, W. A., and E. Z. Vogt, eds.
1979   *Reader in Comparative Religion: An Anthropological Approach,* 4th ed. New York: Harper & Row.

Lévi-Strauss, C.
1963   *Totemism.* Translated by R. Needham. Boston: Beacon Press.
1967   *Structural Anthropology.* New York: Doubleday.
1969   (orig. 1949). *The Elementary Structures of Kinship.* Boston: Beacon Press.

Levine, N. E.
1988   *The Dynamics of Polyandry: Kinship, Domesticity, and Population on the Tibetan Border.* Chicago: University of Chicago Press.

Levine, R. A.
1982   *Culture, Behavior, and Personality: An Introduction to the Comparative Study of Psychosocial Adaptation,* 2nd ed. Chicago: Aldine.

Levine, R. A., ed.
1974   *Culture and Personality: Contemporary Readings.* Chicago: Aldine.

Levy, J. E., with B. Pepper
1992   *Orayvi Revisited: Social Stratification in an "Egalitarian" Society.* Santa Fe, NM: School of American Research Press, and Seattle: University of Washington Press.

Lewis, H. S.
1989   *After the Eagles Landed: The Yemenites of Israel.* Boulder, CO: Westview Press.

Lewis, O.
1959   *Five Families*. New York: Basic Books.

Lewis, P.
1992   U.N. Sees a Crisis in Overpopulation. *New York Times,* April 30, p. A6.

Lewontin, R.
2000   *It Ain't Necessarily So: The Dream of the Human Genome and Other Illusions.* New York: New York Review of Books.

Lie, J.
2001   *Multiethnic Japan.* Cambridge, MA: Harvard University Press.

Lieban, R. W.
1977   The Field of Medical Anthropology. In *Culture, Disease, and Healing: Studies in Medical Anthropology,* ed. D. Landy, pp. 13–31. New York: Macmillan.

Light, D., S. Keller, and C. Calhoun
1994   *Sociology,* 6th ed. New York: McGraw-Hill.

Linden, E.
1986   *Silent Partners: The Legacy of the Ape Language Experiments.* New York: Times Books.

Lindenbaum, S.
1972   Sorcerers, Ghosts, and Polluting Women: An Analysis of Religious Belief and Population Control. *Ethnology* 11: 241–253.

Lindholm, C.
2001   *Culture and Identity: The History, Theory, and Practice of Psychological Anthropology.* Boston: McGraw-Hill.

Linton, R.
1927   Report on Work of Field Museum Expedition in Madagascar. *American Anthropologist* 29: 292–307.
1943   Nativistic Movements. *American Anthropologist* 45: 230–240.

Lipke, D. J.
2000   Dead End Ahead? Income May Be the Real Barrier to the Internet On-Ramp. *American Demographics,* August. http://www.demographics.com/publications/ad/00_ad/ad000805c.htm.

Little, K.
1965   *West African Urbanization: A Study of Voluntary Associations in Social Change.* Cambridge, UK: Cambridge University Press.
1971   *Some Aspects of African Urbanization South of the Sahara. McCaleb Modules in Anthropology.* Reading, MA: Addison-Wesley.

Lizot, J.
1985   *Tales of the Yanomami: Daily Life in the Venezuelan Forest.* New York: Cambridge University Press.

Lockwood, W. G.
1975   *European Moslems: Economy and Ethnicity in Western Bosnia.* New York: Academic Press.

Lockwood, Y. R.
1983   *Text and Context: Folksong in a Bosnian Muslim Village.* Columbus, OH: Slavica.

Lohr, S.
2005   Cutting Here, but Hiring Over There. *New York Times,* June 24. http://www.nytimes.com/2005/06/24/technology/24blue.html?pagewanted=print.

Loomis, W. F.
1967   Skin-Pigmented Regulation of Vitamin-D Biosynthesis in Man. *Science* 157: 501–506.

London School of Economics
2004   Definition of Civil Society. LSE Centre for Civil Society, March 22. http://www.lse.ac.uk/collections/CCS/introduction.htm.

Loveday, L.
1986   Japanese Sociolinguistics: An Introductory Survey. *Journal of Pragmatics* 10: 287–326.
2001   *Explorations in Japanese Sociolinguistics.* Philadelphia: J. Benjamins.

Lowie, R. H.
1935   *The Crow Indians.* New York: Farrar and Rinehart.
1961   (orig. 1920). *Primitive Society.* New York: Harper & Brothers.

Lugaila, T.
1998a   Numbers of Divorced and Never-Married Adults Increasing, Says Census Bureau Report. http://www.census.gov/Press-Release/cb98-56.html.
1998b   Marital Status and Living Arrangements, March 1998 (Update). http://www.census.gov/prod/99pubs/p20-514.pdf.
1999   Married Adults Still in the Majority, Census Bureau Reports. http://www.census.gov/Press-Release/www/1999/cb99-03.html.

Lutz, C., and J. L. Collins
1993   *Reading National Geographic.* Chicago: University of Chicago Press.

Lyell, C.
1969   (orig. 1830–37). *Principles of Geology.* New York: Johnson.

Lyotard, J. F.
1993   *The Postmodern Explained.* Translated by J. Pefanis, M. Thomas, and D. Barry. Minneapolis: University of Minnesota Press.

Madra, Y. M.
2004   Karl Polanyi: Freedom in a Complex Society. *Econ-Atrocity Bulletin: In the History of Thought.* http://www.fguide.org/Bulletin/polanyi.htm.

Maher, J. C., and G. MacDonald, eds.
1995   *Diversity and Language in Japanese Culture.* New York: Columbia University Press.

Mair, L.
  1969   *Witchcraft.* New York: McGraw-Hill.

Malinowski, B.
  1926   *Crime and Custom in Savage Society.*
     London: Routledge and Kegan Paul.
  1927   *Sex and Repression in Savage Society.*
     London and New York: International Library
     of Psychology, Philosophy and Scientific
     Method.
  1929a   Practical Anthropology. *Africa* 2: 23–38.
  1929b   *The Sexual Life of Savages in North-
     Western Melanesia.* New York: Harcourt,
     Brace, and World.
  1944   *A Scientific Theory of Culture, and Other
     Essays.* Chapel Hill: University of North
     Carolina Press.
  1961   (orig. 1922). *Argonauts of the Western
     Pacific.* New York: Dutton.
  1978   (orig. 1931). The Role of Magic and
     Religion. In *Reader in Comparative Religion: An
     Anthropological Approach,* 4th ed., ed. W. A.
     Lessa and E. Z. Vogt, pp. 37–46. New York:
     Harper & Row.
  2001   (orig. 1927). *Sex and Repression in Savage
     Society.* Chicago: University of Chicago Press.

Malkki, L. H.
  1995   *Purity and Exile: Violence, Memory, and
     National Cosmology among Hutu Refugees in
     Tanzania.* Chicago: University of Chicago
     Press.

Manners, R.
  1973   (orig. 1956). Functionalism, Realpolitik
     and Anthropology in Underdeveloped Areas.
     America Indigena 16. Also in *To See Ourselves:
     Anthropology and Modern Social Issues,* gen. ed.
     T. Weaver, pp. 113–126. Glenview, IL: Scott,
     Foresman.

Maquet, J.
  1964   Objectivity in Anthropology. *Current
     Anthropology* 5: 47–55 (also in Clifton, ed.,
     1970).
  1986   *The Aesthetic Experience: An Anthropolo-
     gist Looks at the Visual Arts.* New Haven, CT:
     Yale University Press.

Mar, M. E.
  1997   Secondary Colors: The Multiracial
     Option. *Harvard Magazine,* May–June 1997,
     pp. 19–20.

Marcus, G. E., and D. Cushman
  1982   Ethnographies as Texts. *Annual Review
     of Anthropology* 11: 25–69.

Marcus, G. E., and M. M. J. Fischer
  1986   *Anthropology as Cultural Critique: An
     Experimental Moment in the Human Sciences.*
     Chicago: University of Chicago Press.
  1999   *Anthropology as Cultural Critique: An
     Experimental Moment in the Human Sciences,*
     2nd ed. Chicago: University of Chicago Press.

Marcus, G. E., and F. R. Myers, eds.
  1995   *The Traffic in Culture: Refiguring Art
     and Anthropology.* Berkeley: University of
     California Press.

Margolis, M.
  1984   *Mothers and Such: American Views of
     Women and How They Changed.* Berkeley:
     University of California Press.
  1994   *Little Brazil: An Ethnography of Brazilian
     Immigrants in New York City.* Princeton, NJ:
     Princeton University Press.
  2000   *True to Her Nature: Changing Advice
     to American Women.* Prospect Heights, IL:
     Waveland.

Marks, J. M.
  1995   *Human Biodiversity: Genes, Race, and
     History.* New York: Aldine.

Marshack, A.
  1972   *Roots of Civilization.* New York:
     McGraw-Hill.

Martin, E.
  1987   *The Woman in the Body: A Cultural
     Analysis of Reproduction.* Boston: Beacon
     Press.

Martin, J.
  1992   *Cultures in Organizations: Three Perspec-
     tives.* New York: Oxford University Press.

Martin, K., and B. Voorhies
  1975   *Female of the Species.* New York: Colum-
     bia University Press.

Martin, P., and E. Midgley
  1994   Immigration to the United States: Jour-
     ney to an Uncertain Destination. *Population
     Bulletin* 49(3): 1–47.

Martinez, E., and A. Garcia
  2000   What Is Neo-Liberalism: A Brief Defini-
     tion. Updated February 26, 2000. http://
     www.globalexchange.org/campaigns/
     econ101/neoliberalDefined.html.

Marx, K., and F. Engels
  1976   (orig. 1848). *Communist Manifesto.* New
     York: Pantheon.

Mascia-Lees, F., and N. J. Black
  2000   *Gender and Anthropology.* Prospect
     Heights, IL: Waveland.

Mathews, G.
  2000   *Global Culture/Individual Identity: Search-
     ing for Home in the Cultural Supermarket.* New
     York: Routledge.

Maybury-Lewis, D.
  2002   *Indigenous Peoples, Ethnic Groups, and the
     State,* 2nd ed. Boston: Allyn & Bacon.

McAllester, D. P.
  1954   *Enemy Way Music: A Study of Social and
     Esthetic Values as Seen in Navaho Music.* Cam-
     bridge, MA: Peabody Museum of American
     Archaeology and Ethnology, Papers 41(3).

McDonald, G.
　　1984　*Carioca Fletch.* New York: Warner Books.

McDonald, J. H., ed.
　　2002　*The Applied Anthropology Reader.* Boston: Allyn & Bacon.

McElroy, A., and P. K. Townsend
　　1996　*Medical Anthropology in Ecological Perspective,* 3rd ed. Boulder, CO: Westview Press.

McGraw, T. K., ed.
　　1986　*America versus Japan.* Boston: Harvard Business School Press.

McKinley, J.
　　1996　Board's Decision on Black English Stirs Debate. *New York Times,* December 21. http://www.nytimes.com.

Mead, M.
　　1930　*Growing Up in New Guinea.* New York: Blue Ribbon.
　　1937　*Cooperation and Competition among Primitive Peoples.* New York: McGraw-Hill.
　　1950　(orig. 1935). *Sex and Temperament in Three Primitive Societies.* New York: New American Library.
　　1961　(orig. 1928). *Coming of Age in Samoa.* New York: Morrow Quill.
　　1972　*Blackberry Winter: My Earlier Years.* New York: Simon & Schuster.

Meigs, A., and K. Barlow
　　2002　Beyond the Taboo: Imagining Incest. *American Anthropologist* 104(1): 38–49.

Merlan, F.
　　2005　Indigenous Movements in Australia. *Annual Review of Anthropology* 34: 473–494.

Merriam, A.
　　1971　The Arts and Anthropology. In *Anthropology and Art: Readings in Cross-Cultural Aesthetics,* ed. C. Otten, pp. 93–105. Austin: University of Texas Press.

Michaels, E.
　　1986　Aboriginal Content. Paper presented at the meeting of the Australian Screen Studies Association, December, Sydney.

Michaelson, K.
　　1996　Information, Community, and Access. *Social Science Computing Review* 14(1): 57–59.

Michrina, B. P., and C. Richards
　　1996　*Person to Person: Fieldwork, Dialogue, and the Hermeneutic Method.* Albany: State University of New York Press.

Middleton, J.
　　1967　Introduction. In *Myth and Cosmos: Readings in Mythology and Symbolism,* ed. John Middleton, pp. ix–xi. Garden City, NY: Natural History Press.
　　1993　*The Lugbara of Uganda,* 2nd ed. Fort Worth: Harcourt Brace.

Middleton, J., ed.
　　1967　*Gods and Rituals.* Garden City, NY: Natural History Press.

Miles, H. L.
　　1983　Apes and Language: The Search for Communicative Competence. In *Language in Primates,* ed. J. de Luce and H. T. Wilder, pp. 43–62. New York: Springer-Verlag.

Miller, B. D.
　　1997　*The Endangered Sex: Neglect of Female Children in Rural North India.* New York: Oxford University Press.

Miller, B. D., ed.
　　1993　*Sex and Gender Hierarchies.* New York: Cambridge University Press.

Miller, J.
　　n.d.　Alaskan Tlingit and Tsimtsian. Seattle: University of Washington Libraries, Digital Collections. http://content.lib.washington.edu/aipnw/miller1.html.

Miller, L.
　　2004　The Ancient Bristlecone Pine, Dendrochronology. http://www.sonic.net/bristlecone/dendro.html.

Miller, N., and R. C. Rockwell, eds.
　　1988　*AIDS in Africa: The Social and Policy Impact.* Lewiston, ME: Edwin Mellen.

Mills, G.
　　1971　Art: An Introduction to Qualitative Anthropology. In *Anthropology and Art: Readings in Cross-Cultural Aesthetics,* ed. C. Otten, pp. 66–92. Austin: University of Texas Press.

Mintz, S. W.
　　1985　*Sweetness and Power: The Place of Sugar in Modern History.* New York: Viking Penguin.

Mirzoeff, N.
　　1999　*An Introduction to Visual Culture.* New York: Routledge.

Mishler, E. G.
　　1991　*Research Interviewing: Context and Narrative.* Cambridge, MA: Harvard University Press.

Mitchell, J. C.
　　1966　Theoretical Orientations in African Urban Studies. In *The Social Anthropology of Complex Societies,* ed. M. Banton, pp. 37–68. London: Tavistock.

Moerman, M.
　　1965　Ethnic Identification in a Complex Civilization: Who Are the Lue? *American Anthropologist* 67(5 Part I): 1215–1230.

Moisala, P., and B. Diamond, eds.
　　2000　*Music and Gender.* Champaign–Urbana: University of Illinois Press.

Molnar, S.
　　2005　*Human Variation: Races, Types, and Ethnic Groups,* 6th ed. Upper Saddle River, NJ: Prentice Hall.

Moncure, S.
  1998 Anthropologist Assists in Police Investigations. *University of Delaware Update* 17, no. 39, August 20. http://www.udel.edu/PR/UpDate/98/39/anthrop.html.

Montagu, A.
  1975 *The Nature of Human Aggression.* New York: Oxford University Press.
  1981 *Statement on Race: An Annotated Elaboration and Exposition of the Four Statements on Race Issued by the United Nations Educational, Scientific, and Cultural Organization.* Westport, CT: Greenwood Press.

Montagu, A., ed.
  1996 *Race and IQ,* expanded ed. New York: Oxford University Press.
  1997 *Man's Most Dangerous Myth: The Fallacy of Race,* 6th ed. Walnut Creek, CA: AltaMira.
  1999 *Race and IQ,* expanded ed. New York: Oxford University Press.

Montague, S., and R. Morais
  1981 Football Games and Rock Concerts: The Ritual Enactment. In *The American Dimension: Cultural Myths and Social Realities,* 2nd ed., ed. W. Arens and S. B. Montague, pp. 33–52. Sherman Oaks, CA: Alfred.

Moore, S. F.
  1986 *Social Facts and Fabrications.* Cambridge, UK: Cambridge University Press.

Moran, E. F.
  1982 *Human Adaptability: An Introduction to Ecological Anthropology.* Boulder, CO: Westview Press.

Moran, L.
  1993 Evolution Is a Fact and a Theory. The Talk Origins Archive. http://www.talkorigins.org/faqs/evolution-fact.html.

Morgan, L. H.
  1963 (orig. 1877). *Ancient Society.* Cleveland: World Publishing.
  1966 (orig. 1851). *League of the Ho-dé-no-sau-nee or Iroquois.* New York: B. Franklin.
  1997 (orig. 1870). *Systems of Consanguinity and Affinity of the Human Family.* Lincoln: University of Nebraska Press.

Morgen, S., ed.
  1989 *Gender and Anthropology: Critical Reviews for Research and Teaching.* Washington, DC: American Anthropological Association.

Morris, B.
  1987 *Anthropological Studies of Religion: An Introductory Text.* New York: Cambridge University Press.

Mount Holyoke College
  1999 Dung-Covered Madonna Sparks Controversy; Art Professor Michael Davis Takes a Look. *College Street Journal* 13(6), October 8. http://www.mtholyoke.edu/offices/comm/csj/991008/madonna.html.

Muhlhausler, P.
  1986 *Pidgin and Creole Linguistics.* London: Blackwell.

Mukhopadhyay, C., and P. Higgins
  1988 Anthropological Studies of Women's Status Revisited: 1977–1987. *Annual Review of Anthropology* 17: 461–495.

Mullings, L., ed.
  1987 *Cities of the United States: Studies in Urban Anthropology.* New York: Columbia University Press.

Murdock, G. P.
  1934 *Our Primitive Contemporaries.* New York: Macmillan.
  1957 World Ethnographic Sample. *American Anthropologist* 59: 664–687.

Murdock, G. P., and C. Provost
  1973 Factors in the Division of Labor by Sex: A Cross-Cultural Analysis. *Ethnology* XII(2): 203–225.

Murphy, R. F.
  1990 *The Body Silent.* New York: W. W. Norton.

Murphy, R. F., and L. Kasdan
  1959 The Structure of Parallel Cousin Marriage. *American Anthropologist* 61: 17–29.

Murray, S. O., and W. Roscoe, eds.
  1998 *Boy-Wives and Female Husbands: Studies in African Homosexualities.* New York: St. Martin's Press.

Mydans, S.
  1992a Criticism Grows over Aliens Seized during Riots. *New York Times,* May 29, p. A8.
  1992b Judge Dismisses Case in Shooting by Officer. *New York Times,* June 4, p. A8.

Myers, F. R.
  2002 *Painting Culture: The Making of an Aboriginal High Art.* Durham, NC: Duke University Press.

Nagel, J.
  1996 *American Indian Ethnic Renewal: Red Power and the Resurgence of Identity and Culture.* New York: Oxford University Press.

Nanda, S.
  2000 *Gender Diversity: Crosscultural Variations.* Prospect Heights, IL: Waveland.

Napier, A. D.
  1992 *Foreign Bodies: Performance, Art, and Symbolic Anthropology.* Berkeley: University of California Press.

Narayan, U.
  1997 *Dislocating Cultures: Identities, Traditions, and Third World Feminisms.* New York: Routledge.

Nash, D.
  1999 *A Little Anthropology,* 3rd ed. Upper Saddle River, NJ: Prentice Hall.

Nash, J., and H. Safa, eds.
  1986   *Women and Change in Latin America.*
          South Hadley, MA: Bergin and Garvey.
National Association for the Practice
of Anthropology
  1991   *NAPA Directory of Practicing Anthropologists.* Washington, DC: American Anthropological Association.
National Vital Statistics Reports
  2000   Births, Marriages, Divorces, and Deaths: Provisional Data for November 1999. October 31, 2000. Hyattsville, MD: U.S. Department of Health and Human Services, Center for Disease Control and Prevention, National Center for Health Statistics.
  2001   *National Vital Statistics Reports,* vol. 46, no. 6. http://www.cdc.gov/nchs/data/nvsr/nvsr49/nvsr49_06.pdf.
Naylor, L. L.
  1996   *Culture and Change: An Introduction.* Westport, CT: Bergin and Garvey.
Nelson, S. N., and M. Rosen-Ayalon, eds.
  2002   *In Pursuit of Gender: Worldwide Archaeological Approaches.* Walnut Creek, CA: AltaMira.
Netting, R. M. C., R. R. Wilk, and E. J. Arnould, eds.
  1984   *Households: Comparative and Historical Studies of the Domestic Group.* Berkeley: University of California Press.
New York Times
  1990   Tropical Diseases on March, Hitting 1 in 10. March 28, p. A3.
  1992a   Alexandria Journal: TV Program for Somalis Is a Rare Unifying Force. December 18.
  1992b   Married with Children: The Waning Icon. August 23, p. E2.
  2005   Intelligent Design Derailed. Editorial Desk, December 22. http://www.nytimes.com/2005/12/22/opinion/22thur1.html?ex=1292907600&en=af56b21719a9dd8f&ei=5090&partner=rssuserland&emc=rss.
Newman, M.
  1992   Riots Bring Attention to Growing Hispanic Presence in South-Central Area. *New York Times,* May 11, p. A10.
Nielsson, G. P.
  1985   States and Nation-Groups: A Global Taxonomy. In *New Nationalisms of the Developed World,* ed. E. A. Tiryakian and R. Rogowski, pp. 27–56. Boston: Allen and Unwin.
Nolan, R. W.
  2002   *Development Anthropology: Encounters in the Real World.* Boulder, CO: Westview Press.
  2003   *Anthropology in Practice.* Boulder, CO: Lynne Rienner.

Nussbaum, M. C.
  2000   *Women and Human Development: The Capabilities Approach.* New York: Cambridge University Press.
Nussbaum, M., and J. Glover, eds.
  1995   *Women, Culture, and Development: A Study of Human Capabilities.* New York: Oxford University Press.
O'Dougherty, M.
  2002   *Consumption Intensified: The Politics of Middle-Class Daily Life in Brazil.* Durham, NC: Duke University Press.
Okpewho, I.
  1977   Principles of Traditional African Art. *Journal of Aesthetics and Art Criticism* 35(3): 301–314.
O'Leary, C. M.
  2002   *Class Formation, Diet and Economic Transformation in Two Brazilian Fishing Communities.* Ph.D. Dissertation, Department of Anthropology, University of Michigan, Ann Arbor.
Omohundro, J. T.
  2001   *Careers in Anthropology,* 2nd ed. Boston: McGraw-Hill.
Ong, A.
  1987   *Spirits of Resistance and Capitalist Discipline: Factory Women in Malaysia.* Albany: State University of New York Press.
  1989   Center, Periphery, and Hierarchy: Gender in Southeast Asia. In *Gender and Anthropology: Critical Reviews for Research and Teaching,* ed. S. Morgen, pp. 294–312. Washington, DC: American Anthropological Association.
  2006   *Neoliberalism as Exception: Mutations in Citizenship and Sovereignty.* Durham, NC: Duke University Press.
Ong, A., and S. J. Collier, eds.
  2005   *Global Assemblages: Technology, Politics, and Ethics as Anthropological Problems.* Malden, MA: Blackwell.
Ontario Consultants on Religious Tolerance
  1996   Religious Access Dispute Resolved. Internet Mailing List, April 12.
  1997   Swiss Cult Promotes Cloning.
  2001   Religions of the World: Number of Adherents; Rates of growth. http://www.religioustolerance.org/worldrel.htm.
O'Reilly, K.
  2004   *Ethnographic Methods.* New York: Routledge.
Ortner, S. B.
  1984   Theory of Anthropology Since the Sixties. *Comparative Studies in Society and History* 126(1): 126–166.
Ott, S.
  1981   *The Circle of Mountains: A Basque Shepherding Community.* Oxford, UK: Clarendon Press.

Otten, C. M., ed.
1971 *Anthropology and Art; Readings in Cross-Cultural Aesthetics.* Garden City, NY: American Museum of Natural History.

Ottenheimer, M.
1996 *Forbidden Relatives: The American Myth of Cousin Marriage.* Champaign–Urbana: University of Illinois Press.

Otterbein, K. F.
1968 (orig. 1963). Marquesan Polyandry. In *Marriage, Family and Residence,* ed. P. Bohannan and J. Middleton, pp. 287–296. Garden City, NY: Natural History Press.
2004 *How War Began.* College Station: Texas A&M University Press.

Palmer, S.
2001 The Rael Deal. *Religion in the News* 4:2. Hartford, CT: Trinity College, The Leonard E. Greenberg Center for the Study of Religion in Public Life. http://www.trincoll.edu/depts/csrpl/RINVol4No2/Rael.htm.

Parker, S., and R. Kleiner
1970 The Culture of Poverty: An Adjustive Dimension. *American Anthropologist* 72: 516–527.

Parkin, R.
1997 *Kinship: An Introduction to Basic Concepts.* Cambridge, MA: Blackwell.

Parkin, R., and L. Stone, eds.
2004 *Kinship and Family: An Anthropological Reader.* Malden, MA: Blackwell.

Pasternak, B., C. R. Ember, and M. Ember
1997 *Sex, Gender, and Kinship: A Cross-Cultural Perspective.* Upper Saddle River, NJ: Prentice Hall.

Patterson, F.
1978 Conversations with a Gorilla. *National Geographic,* October, pp. 438–465.

Paul, R.
1989 Psychoanalytic Anthropology. *Annual Review of Anthropology* 18: 177–202.

Pear, R.
1992 Ranks of U.S. Poor Reach 35.7 Million, the Most Since '64. *New York Times,* September 3, pp. A1, A12.

Peletz, M.
1988 *A Share of the Harvest: Kinship, Property, and Social History among the Malays of Rembau.* Berkeley: University of California Press.

Pelto, P.
1973 *The Snowmobile Revolution: Technology and Social Change in the Arctic.* Menlo Park, CA: Cummings.

Pelto, P. J., and G. H. Pelto
1978 *Anthropological Research: The Structure of Inquiry,* 2nd ed. New York: Cambridge University Press.

Peplau, L. A., ed.
1999 *Gender, Culture, and Ethnicity: Current Research about Women and Men.* Mountain View, CA: Mayfield.

Peters, J. D.
1997 Seeing Bifocally: Media, Place, Culture. In *Culture, Power, Place: Explorations in Critical Anthropology,* ed. A. Gupta and J. Ferguson, pp. 75–92. Durham, NC: Duke University Press.

Peters-Golden, H.
2006 *Culture Sketches,* 4th ed. Boston: McGraw-Hill.

Petraglia-Bahri, D.
1996 Introduction to Postcolonial Studies. http://www.emory.edu/ENGLISH/Bahri/.

Piddington, R.
1970 Action Anthropology. In *Applied Anthropology: Readings in the Uses of the Science of Man,* ed. James Clifton, pp. 127–143. Boston: Houghton Mifflin.

Piddocke, S.
1969 The Potlatch System of the Southern Kwakiutl: A New Perspective. In *Environment and Cultural Behavior,* ed. A. P. Vayda, pp. 130–156. Garden City, NY: Natural History Press.

Plattner, S., ed.
1989 *Economic Anthropology.* Stanford, CA: Stanford University Press.

Podolefsky, A.
1992 *Simbu Law: Conflict Management in the New Guinea Highlands.* Fort Worth: Harcourt Brace.

Podolefsky, A., and P. J. Brown, eds.
1992 *Applying Anthropology: An Introductory Reader,* 2nd ed. Mountain View, CA: Mayfield.
2007 *Applying Anthropology: An Introductory Reader,* 8th ed. Boston: McGraw-Hill.

Polanyi, K.
1968 *Primitive, Archaic and Modern Economies: Essays of Karl Polanyi.* Edited by G. Dalton. Garden City, NY: Anchor Books.

Pollan, M.
2003 You Want Fries with That? *New York Times Book Review,* January 12, p. 6.

Pollard, T. M., and S. B. Hyatt
1999 *Sex, Gender, and Health.* New York: Cambridge University Press.

Pospisil, L.
1963 *The Kapauku Papuans of West New Guinea.* New York: Harcourt Brace Jovanovich.

Potash, B., ed.
1986 *Widows in African Societies: Choices and Constraints.* Stanford, CA: Stanford University Press.

Price, R., ed.
  1973 *Maroon Societies.* New York: Anchor Press, Doubleday.

Public Culture
  Journal published by the University of Chicago.

Punch, M.
  1985 *The Politics and Ethics of Fieldwork.* Beverly Hills, CA: Sage.

Quinn, N., and C. Strauss
  1989 A Cognitive Cultural Anthropology. Paper presented at the Invited Session "Assessing Developments in Anthropology," American Anthropological Association 88th Annual Meeting, November 15–19, 1989, Washington, DC.
  1994 A Cognitive Cultural Anthropology. *In Assessing Cultural Anthropology,* ed. R. Borofsky. New York: McGraw-Hill.

Radcliffe-Brown, A. R.
  1965 (orig. 1962). *Structure and Function in Primitive Society.* New York: Free Press.

Radcliffe-Brown, A. R., and D. Forde, eds.
  1994 *African Systems of Kinship and Marriage.* New York: Columbia University Press.

Ramirez, R. R., and G. P. de la Cruz
  2003 The Hispanic Population in the United States. *Current Population Reports,* P20-545. U.S. Census Bureau.

Random House College Dictionary
  1982 Revised ed. New York: Random House.

Ranger, T. O.
  1996 Postscript. In *Postcolonial Identities,* ed. R. Werbner and T. O. Ranger. London: Zed.

Rappaport, R. A.
  1974 Obvious Aspects of Ritual. *Cambridge Anthropology* 2: 2–60.
  1979 *Ecology, Meaning, and Religion.* Richmond, CA: North Atlantic Books.
  1999 *Holiness and Humanity: Ritual in the Making of Religious Life.* New York: Cambridge University Press.

Rathje, W. L.
  2001 *Rubbish!: The Archaeology of Garbage.* Tucson: University of Arizona Press.

Rathus, S. A., J. S. Nevid, and J. Fichner-Rathus
  1997 *Human Sexuality in a World of Diversity,* 3rd ed. Boston: Allyn & Bacon.
  2005 *Human Sexuality in a World of Diversity,* 6th ed. Boston: Allyn & Bacon.

Redfield, R.
  1941 *The Folk Culture of Yucatan.* Chicago: University of Chicago Press.

Redfield, R., R. Linton, and M. Herskovits
  1936 Memorandum on the Study of Acculturation. *American Anthropologist* 38: 149–152.

Reed, R.
  1997 *Forest Dwellers, Forest Protectors: Indigenous Models for International Development.* Boston: Allyn & Bacon.

Reese, W. L.
  1999 *Dictionary of Philosophy and Religion: Eastern and Western Thought.* Amherst, NY: Humanities Books.

Reiter, R.
  1975 Men and Women in the South of France: Public and Private Domains. In *Toward an Anthropology of Women,* ed. R. Reiter, pp. 252–282. New York: Monthly Review Press.

Reiter, R., ed.
  1975 *Toward an Anthropology of Women.* New York: Monthly Review Press.

Richards, D.
  1994 *Masks of Difference: Cultural Representations in Literature, Anthropology, and Art.* New York: Cambridge University Press.

Richards, P.
  1973 The Tropical Rain Forest. *Scientific American* 229(6): 58–67.

Rickford, J. R.
  1997 Suite for Ebony and Phonics. http://www.stanford.edu/~rickford/papers/SuiteForEbonyandPhonics.html (also published in *Discover,* December 1997).
  1999 *African American Vernacular English: Features, Evolution, Educational Implications.* Malden, MA: Blackwell.

Rickford, J. R., and Rickford, R. J.
  2000 *Spoken Soul: The Story of Black English.* New York: Wiley.

Ricoeur, P.
  1971 The Model of the Text: Meaningful Action Considered as a Text. *Social Research* 38: 529–562.

Robbins, R.
  2005 *Global Problems and the Culture of Capitalism,* 3rd ed. Boston: Pearson/Allyn & Bacon.

Roberts, S.
  1979 *Order and Dispute: An Introduction to Legal Anthropology.* New York: Penguin.

Robertson, A. F.
  1995 *The Big Catch: A Practical Introduction to Development.* Boulder, CO: Westview Press.

Robertson, J.
  1992 Koreans in Japan. Paper presented at the University of Michigan Department of Anthropology, Martin Luther King Jr. Day Panel, January 1992. Ann Arbor: University of Michigan Department of Anthropology (unpublished).

Rogers, C.
    2005   A Conversation with Carel van Schaik; Revealing Behavior in 'Orangutan Heaven and Human Hell.' *New York Times,* November 15, late edition, final, p. F2.

Romaine, S.
    1994   *Language in Society: An Introduction to Sociolinguistics.* New York: Oxford University Press.
    1999   *Communicating Gender.* Mahwah, NJ: Erlbaum.

Root, D.
    1996   *Cannibal Culture: Art, Appropriation, and the Commodification of Difference.* Boulder, CO: Westview Press.

Rosaldo, M. Z.
    1980a   *Knowledge and Passion: Notions of Self and Social Life.* Stanford, CA: Stanford University Press.
    1980b   The Use and Abuse of Anthropology: Reflections on Feminism and Cross-Cultural Understanding. *Signs* 5(3): 389–417.

Rosaldo, M. Z., and L. Lamphere, eds.
    1974   *Woman, Culture, and Society.* Stanford, CA: Stanford University Press.

Roseberry, W.
    1988   Political Economy. *Annual Review of Anthropology* 17: 161–185.

Rouse, R.
    1991   Mexican Migration and the Social Space of Postmodernism. *Diaspora* 1(1): 8–23.

Royal Anthropological Institute
    1951   *Notes and Queries on Anthropology,* 6th ed. London: Routledge and Kegan Paul.

Rushing, W. A.
    1995   *The AIDS Epidemic: Social Dimension of an Infectious Disease.* Boulder, CO: Westview Press.

Rushing, W. Jackson, ed.
    1999   *Native American Art in the Twentieth Century.* New York: Routledge.

Russell, D.
    1986   *The Secret Trauma: Incest in the Lives of Girls and Women.* New York: Basic Books.

Ryan, S.
    1990   *Ethnic Conflict and International Relations.* Brookfield, MA: Dartmouth.
    1995   *Ethnic Conflict and International Relations,* 2nd ed. Brookfield, MA: Dartmouth.

Sachs, C. E.
    1996   *Gendered Fields: Rural Women, Agriculture, and Environment.* Boulder, CO: Westview Press.

Sahlins, M. D.
    1961   The Segmentary Lineage: An Organization of Predatory Expansion. *American Anthropologist* 63: 322–345.
    1968   *Tribesmen.* Englewood Cliffs, NJ: Prentice Hall.
    1981   *Historical Metaphors and Mythical Realities: Structure in the Early History of the Sandwich Islands Kingdom.* Ann Arbor: University of Michigan Press.
    2004 (orig. 1974).   *Stone Age Economics.* New York: Routledge.

Saitoti, T. O.
    1988   *The Worlds of a Maasai Warrior: An Autobiography.* Berkeley: University of California Press.

Saluter, A.
    1995   Household and Family Characteristics: March 1994, P20-483, Press release, October 16, CB95-186, Single-Parent Growth Rate Stabilized; 2-parent Family Growth Renewed, Census Bureau Reports. United States Department of Commerce, Bureau of Census, Public Information Office.
    1996   Marital Status and Living Arrangements: March 1994, P20-484, U.S. Census Bureau, Press release, March 13, 1996, CB96-33. United States Department of Commerce, Bureau of Census, Public Information Office, http://www.census.gov/prod/www/titles.html#popspec.

Salzman, P. C.
    1974   Political Organization among Nomadic Peoples. In *Man in Adaptation: The Cultural Present,* 2nd ed., ed. Y. A. Cohen, pp. 267–284. Chicago: Aldine.
    2004   *Pastoralists: Equality, Hierarchy, and the State.* Boulder, CO: Westview Press.

Salzman, P. C., and J. G. Galaty, eds.
    1990   *Nomads in a Changing World.* Naples: Istituto Universitario Orientale.

Salzmann, Z.
    2004   *Language, Culture, and Society: An Introduction to Linguistic Anthropology,* 3rd ed. Boulder, CO: Westview Press.

Sanday, P. R.
    1974   Female Status in the Public Domain. In *Woman, Culture, and Society,* ed. M. Z. Rosaldo and L. Lamphere, pp. 189–206. Stanford, CA: Stanford University Press.
    2002   *Women at the Center: Life in a Modern Matriarchy.* Ithaca, NY: Cornell University Press.

Sankoff, G.
    1980   *The Social Life of Language.* Philadelphia: University of Pennsylvania Press.

Santino, J.
    1983   Night of the Wandering Souls. *Natural History* 92(10): 42.

Sapir, E.
    1931   Conceptual Categories in Primitive Languages. *Science* 74: 578–584.

Sargent, C. F., and C. B. Brettell
    1996   *Gender and Health: An International Perspective.* Upper Saddle River, NJ: Prentice Hall.

Sargent, C. F., and T. J. Johnson, eds.
1996   *Medical Anthropology: A Handbook of Theory and Method,* rev. ed. Westport, CT: Praeger.

Schaefer, R.
1989   *Sociology,* 3rd ed. New York: McGraw-Hill.

Schaik, C. V.
2004   *Among Orangutans: Red Apes and the Rise of Human Culture.* Tucson: University of Arizona Press.

Scheffler, H. W.
2001   *Filiation and Affiliation.* Boulder, CO: Westview Press.

Scheidel, W.
1997   Brother-Sister Marriage in Roman Egypt. *Journal of Biosocial Science* 29(3): 361–371.

Scheinman, M.
1980   Imperialism. *Academic American Encyclopedia,* vol. 11, pp. 61–62. Princeton, NJ: Arete.

Scheper-Hughes, N.
1987   Culture, Scarcity, and Maternal Thinking: Mother Love and Child Death in Northeast Brazil. In *Child Survival,* ed. N. Scheper-Hughes, pp. 187–208. Boston: D. Reidel.
1992   *Death without Weeping: The Violence of Everyday Life in Brazil.* Berkeley: University of California Press.

Schieffelin, E.
1976   *The Sorrow of the Lonely and the Burning of the Dancers.* New York: St. Martin's Press.

Schildkrout, E., and C. A. Keim
1990   *African Reflections: Art from Northeastern Zaire.* Seattle: University of Washington Press.

Schlee, G., ed.
2002   *Imagined Differences: Hatred and the Construction of Identity.* New York: Palgrave.

Schneider, D. M.
1968   *American Kinship: A Cultural Account.* Englewood Cliffs, NJ: Prentice Hall.

Schneider, D. M., and K. Gough, eds.
1961   *Matrilineal Kinship.* Berkeley: University of California Press.

Scholte, J. A.
2000   *Globalization: A Critical Introduction.* New York: St. Martin's Press.

Scott, J.
2002   Prehistoric Human Footpaths Lure Archaeologists Back to Costa Rica. University of Colorado Press Release, May 20. http://www.eurekalert.org/pub_releases/2002-05/uoca-phf052002.php.

Scott, J. C.
1985   *Weapons of the Weak.* New Haven, CT: Yale University Press.

1990   *Domination and the Arts of Resistance.* New Haven, CT: Yale University Press.
1998   *Seeing Like a State: How Certain Schemes to Improve the Human Condition Have Failed.* New Haven, CT: Yale University Press.

Scudder, T.
1982   The Impact of Big Dam-building on the Zambezi River Basin. In *The Careless Technology: Ecology and International Development,* ed. M. T. Farvar and J. P. Milton, pp. 206–235. New York: Natural History Press.

Scudder, T., and E. Colson
1980   *Secondary Education and the Formation of an Elite: The Impact of Education on Gwembe District, Zambia.* London: Academic Press.

Scudder, T., and J. Habarad
1991   Local Responses to Involuntary Relocation and Development in the Zambian Portion of the Middle Zambezi Valley. In *Migrants in Agricultural Development,* ed. J. A. Mollett, pp. 178–205. New York: New York University Press.

Scupin, R.
2003   *Race and Ethnicity: An Anthropological Focus on the United States and the World.* Upper Saddle River, NJ: Prentice Hall.

Seligson, M. A.
1984   *The Gap between Rich and Poor: Contending Perspectives on the Political Economy of Development.* Boulder, CO: Westview Press.

Sered, S. S.
1996   *Priestess, Mother, Sacred Sister: Religions Dominated by Women.* New York: Oxford University Press.

Service, E. R.
1962   *Primitive Social Organization: An Evolutionary Perspective.* New York: McGraw-Hill.
1966   *The Hunters.* Englewood Cliffs, NJ: Prentice Hall.
1975   *Origins of the State and Civilization: The Process of Cultural Evolution.* New York: W. W. Norton.

Shabecoff, P.
1989a   Ivory Imports Banned to Aid Elephant. *New York Times,* June 7, p. 15.
1989b   New Lobby Is Helping Wildlife of Africa. *New York Times,* June 9, p. 14.

Shanklin, E.
1994   *Anthropology and Race.* Belmont, CA: Wadsworth.

Shannon, T. R.
1989   *An Introduction to the World-System Perspective.* Boulder, CO: Westview Press.
1996   *An Introduction to the World-System Perspective,* 2nd ed. Boulder, CO: Westview Press.

Shepher, J.
1983   *Incest, a Biosocial View.* New York: Academic Press.

Shigeru, K.

1994   *Our Land Was a Forest: An Ainu Memoir.* Boulder, CO: Westview Press.

Shivaram, C.

1996   Where Women Wore the Crown: Kerala's Dissolving Matriarchies Leave a Rich Legacy of Compassionate Family Culture. *Hinduism Today* 96(02). http://www.hinduism-today.com/archives/1996/2/1996-2-03.shtml.

Shore, B.

1996   *Culture in Mind: Meaning, Construction, and Cultural Cognition.* New York: Oxford University Press.

Shostak, M.

1981   *Nisa, the Life and Words of a !Kung Woman.* New York: Vintage Books.

2000   *Return to Nisa.* Cambridge, MA: Harvard University Press.

Shweder, R., and H. Levine, eds.

1984   *Culture Theory: Essays on Mind, Self, and Emotion.* Cambridge, UK: Cambridge University Press.

Signo, A.

1994   *Economics of the Family.* New York: Oxford University Press.

Silberbauer, G.

1981   *Hunter and Habitat in the Central Kalahari Desert.* New York: Cambridge University Press.

Simons, A.

1995   *Networks of Dissolution: Somalia Undone.* Boulder, CO: Westview Press.

Simpson, B.

1998   *Changing Families: An Ethnographic Approach to Divorce and Separation.* New York: Berg.

Sinnott, M. J.

2004   *Toms and Dees: Transgender Identity and Female Same-Sex Relationships in Thailand.* Honolulu: University of Hawaii Press.

Slade, M. F.

1984   Displaying Affection in Public. *New York Times,* December 17, p. B14.

Smith, C. A.

1990   The Militarization of Civil Society in Guatemala: Economic Reorganization as a Continuation of War. *Latin American Perspectives* 17: 8–41.

Smith, M. G.

1965   *The Plural Society in the British West Indies.* Berkeley: University of California Press.

Smitherman, G.

1986   *Talkin and Testifyin: The Language of Black America.* Detroit: Wayne State University Press.

Solway, J., and R. Lee

1990   Foragers, Genuine and Spurious: Situating the Kalahari San in History (with CA treatment). *Current Anthropology* 31(2): 109–146.

Spickard, P., ed.

2004   *Race and Nation: Ethnic Systems in the Modern World.* New York: Routledge.

Spindler, G. D., ed.

1978   *The Making of Psychological Anthropology.* Berkeley: University of California Press.

1982   *Doing the Ethnography of Schooling: Educational Anthropology in Action.* New York: Holt, Rinehart and Winston.

2000   *Fifty Years of Anthropology and Education, 1950–2000: A Spindler Anthology.* Mahwah, NJ: Erlbaum.

2005   *New Horizons in the Anthropology of Education.* Mahwah, NJ: Erlbaum.

Spiro, M. E.

1993   *Oedipus in the Trobriands.* New Brunswick, NJ: Transaction.

Sponsel, L. E., and T. Gregor, eds.

1994   *The Anthropology of Peace and Nonviolence.* Boulder, CO: Lynne Rienner.

Spradley, J. P.

1979   *The Ethnographic Interview.* New York: Harcourt Brace Jovanovich.

Srivastava, J., N. J. H. Smith, and D. A. Forno

1999   *Integrating Biodiversity in Agricultural Intensification: Toward Sound Practices.* Washington, DC: World Bank.

Stacey, J.

1996   *In the Name of the Family: Rethinking Family Values in the Postmodern Age.* Boston: Beacon Press.

1998   *Brave New Families: Stories of Domestic Upheaval in Late Twentieth Century America.* Berkeley: University of California Press.

Stack, C. B.

1975   *All Our Kin: Strategies for Survival in a Black Community.* New York: Harper Torchbooks.

Statistical Abstract of the United States

1991   111th ed. Washington, DC: U.S. Bureau of the Census, U.S. Government Printing Office.

1996   116th ed. Washington, DC: U.S. Bureau of the Census, U.S. Government Printing Office.

2003   *Statistical Abstract of the United States, 2003.* http://www.census.gov/statab/www/.

Statistics Canada

1998   1996 Census: Ethnic Origin, Visible Minorities. *The Daily,* February 17. http://www.statcan.ca/Daily/English/980217/d980217.htm.

2001a   1996 Census. Nation Tables. http://www.statcan.ca/english/census96/nation.htm.

2001b Selected Religions, Provinces and Territories. http://www40.statcan.ca/101/cst01/demo30a.htm.

Staub, S.
1989 *Yemenis in New York City: The Folklore of Ethnicity.* Philadelphia: Balch Institute Press.

Stein, R. L., and P. L. Stein
2005 *The Anthropology of Religion, Magic, and Witchcraft.* Boston: Pearson/Allyn & Bacon.

Stephens, S., ed.
1996 *Children and the Politics of Culture.* Princeton, NJ: Princeton University Press.

Stephens, W. R.
2002 *Careers in Anthropology: What an Anthropology Degree Can Do for You.* Boston: Allyn & Bacon.

Stevens, W. K.
1992 Humanity Confronts Its Handiwork: An Altered Planet. *New York Times,* May 5, pp. B5–B7.

Stevenson, D.
2003 *Cities and Urban Cultures.* Philadelphia: Open University Press.

Stevenson, R. F.
1968 *Population and Political Systems in Tropical Africa.* New York: Columbia University Press.

Steward, J. H.
1955 *Theory of Culture Change.* Urbana: University of Illinois Press.
1956 *The People of Puerto Rico: A Study in Social Anthropology.* Urbana: University of Illinois Press.

Stocking, G. W., ed.
1986 *Malinowski, Rivers, Benedict and Others: Essays on Culture and Personality.* Madison: University of Wisconsin Press.

Stoler, A.
1977 Class Structure and Female Autonomy in Rural Java. *Signs* 3: 74–89.

Stoler, A. L.
1995 *Race and the Education of Desire: Foucault's History of Sexuality and the Colonial Order of Things.* Durham, NC: Duke University Press.
2002 *Carnal Knowledge and Imperial Power: Race and the Intimate in Colonial Rule.* Berkeley: University of California Press.

Stone, L.
2000 *Kinship and Gender: An Introduction,* 2nd ed. Boulder, CO: Westview Press.
2001 *New Directions in Anthropological Kinship.* Lanham, MD: Rowman and Littlefield.

Strathern, A., and P. J. Stewart
1999 *Curing and Healing: Medical Anthropology in Global Perspective.* Durham, NC: Carolina Academic Press.

Strathern, M.
1988 *The Gender of the Gift: Problems with Women and Problems with Society in Melanesia.* Berkeley: University of California Press.

Strong, P. T.
2005 Recent Ethnographic Research on North American Indigenous Peoples. *Annual Review of Anthropology* 34: 253–268.

Suarez-Orozco, M. M., G. Spindler, and L. Spindler, eds.
1994 *The Making of Psychological Anthropology II.* Fort Worth: Harcourt Brace.

Susser, I., and T. C. Patterson, eds.
2000 *Cultural Diversity in the United States: A Critical Reader.* Malden, MA: Blackwell.

Suttles, W.
1960 Affinal Ties, Subsistence, and Prestige among the Coast Salish. *American Anthropologist* 62: 296–395.

Swift, M.
1963 Men and Women in Malay Society. In *Women in the New Asia,* ed. B. Ward, pp. 268–286. Paris: UNESCO.

Tanaka, J.
1980 *The San Hunter-Gatherers of the Kalahari.* Tokyo: University of Tokyo Press.

Tannen, D.
1990 *You Just Don't Understand: Women and Men in Conversation.* New York: Ballantine.

Tannen, D., ed.
1993 *Gender and Conversational Interaction.* New York: Oxford University Press.

Tanner, N.
1974 Matrifocality in Indonesia and Africa and among Black Americans. In *Women, Culture, and Society,* ed. M. Z. Rosaldo and L. Lamphere, pp. 127–156. Stanford, CA: Stanford University Press.

Taylor, A.
1993 *Women Drug Users: An Ethnography of a Female Injecting Community.* New York: Oxford University Press.

Taylor, C.
1987 Anthropologist-in-Residence. In *Applied Anthropology in America,* 2nd ed., ed. E. M. Eddy and W. L. Partridge. New York: Columbia University Press.
1996 *The Black Churches of Brooklyn.* New York: Columbia University Press.

Thomas, L., and S. Wareing, eds.
2004 *Language, Society and Power.* New York: Routledge.

Thomason, S. G., and T. Kaufman
1988 *Language Contact, Creolization and Genetic Linguistics.* Berkeley: University of California Press.

Thompson, W.
 1983 Introduction: World System with and without the Hyphen. In *Contending Approaches to World System Analysis,* ed. W. Thompson, pp. 7–26. Thousand Oaks, CA: Sage.

Tice, K.
 1997 Reflections on Teaching Anthropology for Use in the Public and Private Sector. In *The Teaching of Anthropology: Problems, Issues, and Decisions,* ed. C. P. Kottak, J. J. White, R. H. Furlow, and P. C. Rice, pp. 273–284. Mountain View, CA: Mayfield.

Titiev, M.
 1992 *Old Oraibi: A Study of the Hopi Indians of Third Mesa.* Albuquerque: University of New Mexico Press.

Toner, R.
 1992 Los Angeles Riots Are a Warning, Americans Fear. *New York Times,* May 11, pp. A1, A11.

Trask, L.
 1996 FAQs about Basque and the Basques. http://www.cogs.susx.ac.uk/users/larryt/basque.faqs.html.

Trehub, S. E.
 2001 Musical Predispositions in Infancy. *Annals of the New York Academy of Sciences* 930(1): 1–16.

Trudgill, P.
 1983 *Sociolinguistics: An Introduction to Language and Society,* rev. ed. Baltimore: Penguin.
 2000 *Sociolinguistics: An Introduction to Language and Society,* 4th ed. New York: Penguin.

Turnbull, C.
 1965 *Wayward Servants: The Two Worlds of the African Pygmies.* Garden City, NY: Natural History Press.

Turner, B. S.
 1998 *Readings in the Anthropology and Sociology of Family and Kinship.* London: Routledge/Thoemmes.

Turner, T.
 1993 The Role of Indigenous Peoples in the Environmental Crisis: The Example of the Kayapo of the Brazilian Amazon. *Perspectives in Biology and Medicine* 36: 526–545.

Turner, V. W.
 1967 *The Forest of Symbols: Aspects of Ndembu Ritual.* Ithaca, NY: Cornell University Press.
 1995 (orig. 1969). *The Ritual Process.* Hawthorne, NY: Aldine.
 1996 (orig. 1957). *Schism and Continuity in an African Society: A Study of Ndembu Village Life.* Washington, DC: Berg.

Tylor, E. B.
 1889 On a Method of Investigating the Development of Institutions: Applied to Laws of Marriage and Descent. *Journal of the Royal Anthropological Institute* 18: 245–269.
 1958 (orig. 1871). *Primitive Culture.* New York: Harper Torchbooks.

Urban, Greg
 2001 *Metaculture: How Culture Moves through the World.* Minneapolis: University of Minnesota Press.

U.S. Census Bureau
 1998 Unpublished Tables—Marital Status and Living Arrangements, March 1998 (Update). http://www.census.gov/prod/99pubs/p20-514u.pdf.
 1999 *Statisical Abstract of the United States.* http://www.census.gov/prod/99pubs/99statab/sec01.pdf and http://www.census.gov/prod/99pubs/99statab/sec02.pdf.
 2004 *Statistical Abstract of the United States, 2003.* Table 688, p. 459. http://www.census.gov/prod/2004pubs/03statab/income.pdf.
 2005 *Statistical Abstract of the United States, 2004.* http://www.census.gov/prod/2004pubs/04statab/labor.pdf.
 2006 *Statistical Abstract of the United States, 2006.* http://www.census.gov/prod/www/statistical-abstract.html.

University of Virginia
 n.d. American Studies Program, Armory Show of 1913. http://xroads.virginia.edu/~MUSEUM/Armory/ofili.html.

Valentine, C.
 1968 *Culture and Poverty.* Chicago: University of Chicago Press.

Van Cantfort, T. E., and J. B. Rimpau
 1982 Sign Language Studies with Children and Chimpanzees. *Sign Language Studies* 34: 15–72.

Van der Elst, D., and P. Bohannan
 2003 *Culture as Given, Culture as Choice.* 2nd ed. Prospect Heights, IL: Waveland.

Van Willingen, J.
 1987 *Becoming a Practicing Anthropologist: A Guide to Careers and Training Programs in Applied Anthropology.* NAPA Bulletin 3. Washington, DC: American Anthropological Association/National Association for the Practice of Anthropology.
 2002 *Applied Anthropology: An Introduction,* 3rd ed. Westport CT: Bergin and Garvey.

Vayda, A. P.
 1968 (orig. 1961). Economic Systems in Ecological Perspective: The Case of the Northwest Coast. In *Readings in Anthropology,* 2nd ed., vol. 2, ed. M. H. Fried, pp. 172–178. New York: Crowell.

Veblen, T.
 1934 *The Theory of the Leisure Class: An Economic Study of Institutions.* New York: The Modern Library.

Verdery, K.
2001 Socialist Societies: Anthropological Aspects. *International Encyclopedia of the Social & Behavioral Sciences*, pp. 14496–14500. New York: Elsevier.

Verlinden, C.
1980 Colonialism. *Academic American Encyclopedia*, vol. 5, pp. 111–112. Princeton, NJ: Arete.

Vidal, J.
2003 Every Third Person Will be a Slum Dweller within 30 Years, UN Agency Warns: Biggest Study of World's Cities Finds 940 Million Already Living in Squalor. *The Guardian*, October 4. http://www.guardian.co./uk/international/story/0,3604,1055785,00.html.

Vietnam Labor Watch
1997 Nike Labor Practices in Vietnam, March 20. http://www.saigon.com/~nike/reports/report1.html.

Vincent, J.
1990 *Anthropology and Politics: Visions, Traditions, and Trends.* Tucson: University of Arizona Press.

Vincent, J., ed.
2002 *The Anthropology of Politics: A Reader in Ethnography, Theory, and Critique.* Malden, MA: Blackwell.

Wade, N.
2001 Gene Study Shows Ties Long Veiled in Europe. *New York Times*, April 10. http://www.angelfire.com/nt/dragon9/BASQUES2.html.

Wade, P.
2002 *Race, Nature, and Culture: An Anthropological Perspective.* Sterling, VA: Pluto Press.

Wagley, C. W.
1968 (orig. 1959). The Concept of Social Race in the Americas. In *The Latin American Tradition*, ed. C. Wagley, pp. 155–174. New York: Columbia University Press.

Wagner, R.
1981 *The Invention of Culture*, rev. ed. Chicago: University of Chicago Press.

Wallace, A. F. C.
1956 Revitalization Movements. *American Anthropologist* 58: 264–281.
1966 *Religion: An Anthropological View.* New York: McGraw-Hill.
1970 *The Death and Rebirth of the Seneca.* New York: Knopf.

Wallerstein, I. M.
1974 *The Modern World-System: Capitalist Agriculture and the Origins of the European World-Economy in the Sixteenth Century.* New York: Academic Press.
1980 *The Modern World System II: Mercantilism and the Consolidation of the Euro-pean World-Economy, 1600–1750.* New York: Academic Press.
1982 The Rise and Future Demise of the World Capitalist System: Concepts for Comparative Analysis. In *Introduction to the Sociology of "Developing Societies,"* ed. H. Alavi and T. Shanin, pp. 29–53. New York: Monthly Review Press.
2000 *The Essential Wallerstein.* New York: New Press, W. W. Norton.
2004a *The Decline of American Power: The U.S. in a Chaotic World.* New York: New Press.
2004b *World-Systems Analysis: An Introduction.* Durham, NC: Duke University Press.

Wallman, S., ed.
1977 *Perceptions of Development.* New York: Cambridge University Press.

Ward, C.
2003 The Evolution of Human Origins. *American Anthropologist* 105(1): 77–88.

Ward, M. C., and M. Edelstein
2006 *A World Full of Women*, 4th ed. Needham Heights, MA: Allyn & Bacon.

Warren, K. B.
1998 *Indigenous Movements and Their Critics: Pan-Maya Activism in Guatemala.* Princeton, NJ: Princeton University Press.

Watson, P.
1972 *Can Racial Discrimination Affect IQ? In Race and Intelligence; The Fallacies behind the Race-IQ Controversy*, ed. K. Richardson and D. Spears, pp. 56–67. Baltimore: Penguin.

Weaver, T., gen. ed.
1973 *To See Ourselves: Anthropology and Modern Social Issues.* Glenview, IL: Scott, Foresman.

Weber, M.
1958 (orig. 1904). *The Protestant Ethic and the Spirit of Capitalism.* New York: Scribner.
1968 (orig. 1922). *Economy and Society.* Translated by E. Fischoff et al. New York: Bedminster Press.

Webster's New World Encyclopedia
1993 College Edition. Englewood Cliffs, NJ: Prentice Hall.

Wedel, J.
2002 Blurring the Boundaries of the State-Private Divide: Implications for Corruption. Paper presented at the European Association of Social Anthropologists (EASA) Conference in Copenhagen, August 14–17. http://www.anthrobase.com/Txt/W/Wedel_J_01.htm.

Weiner, A.
1988 *The Trobrianders of Papua New Guinea.* New York: Holt, Rinehart and Winston.

Weise, E.
1999 Anthropologists Adapt Technology to World's Cultures. *USA Today*, May 26. http://eclectic.ss.uci.edu/~drwhite/center/news/USAToday5-25-99.htm.

Werner, O., and G. M. Shoepfle
  1987   *Systematic Fieldwork.* Newbury Park, CA: Sage.

Westermarck, E.
  1894   *The History of Human Marriage.* London: Macmillan.

Weston, K.
  1991   *Families We Choose: Lesbians, Gays, Kinship.* New York: Columbia University Press.

White, L. A.
  1949   *The Science of Culture: A Study of Man and Civilization.* New York: Farrar, Strauss.
  1959   *The Evolution of Culture: The Development of Civilization to the Fall of Rome.* New York: McGraw-Hill.

Whiting, B. E., ed.
  1963   *Six Cultures: Studies of Child Rearing.* New York: Wiley.

Whiting, J. M.
  1964   Effects of Climate on Certain Cultural Practices. In *Explorations in Cultural Anthropology: Essays in Honor of George Peter Murdock,* ed. W. H. Goodenough, pp. 511–544. New York: McGraw-Hill.

Whorf, B. L.
  1956   A Linguistic Consideration of Thinking in Primitive Communities. In *Language, Thought, and Reality: Selected Writings of Benjamin Lee Whorf,* ed. J. B. Carroll, pp. 65–86. Cambridge, MA: MIT Press.

Whyte, M. F.
  1978   Cross-Cultural Codes Dealing with the Relative Status of Women. *Ethnology* 17(2): 211–239.

Wikipedia
  2004   Fundamentalism, in *Wikipedia, the Free Encyclopedia.* http://en.wikipedia.org/wiki/Fundamentalism.

Wilford, J. N.
  2005   For Neandertals and *Homo Sapiens,* Was It De-Lovely? *New York Times,* February 15. http://www.nytimes.com/2005/02/15/science/15nean.html?ex=1147492800&en=7d5fadb91364f1d5&ei=5070.

Wilk, R. R.
  1996   *Economies and Cultures: An Introduction to Economic Anthropology.* Boulder, CO: Westview Press.

Williams, B.
  1989   A Class Act: Anthropology and the Race to Nation across Ethnic Terrain. *Annual Review of Anthropology* 18: 401–444.

Williams, L. M., and D. Finkelhor
  1995   Paternal Caregiving and Incest: Test of a Biosocial Model. *American Journal of Orthopsychiatry* 65(1): 101–113.

Willie, C. V.
  2003   *A New Look at Black Families.* Walnut Creek, CA: AltaMira.

Wilmsen, E. N.
  1989   *Land Filled with Flies: A Political Economy of the Kalahari.* Chicago: University of Chicago Press.

Wilmsen, E. N., and P. McAllister, eds.
  1996   *The Politics of Difference: Ethnic Premises in a World of Power.* Chicago: University of Chicago Press.

Wilson, C.
  1995   *Hidden in the Blood: A Personal Investigation of AIDS in the Yucatan.* New York: Columbia University Press.

Wilson, R., ed.
  1996   *Human Rights: Culture and Context: Anthropological Perspectives.* Chicago: Pluto Press.

Winter, R.
  2001   Religions of the World: Number of Adherents; Names of Houses of Worship; Names of Leaders; Rates of Growth. http://www.religioustolerance.org/worldrel.htm.

Winzeler, R. L.
  1995   *Latah in Southeast Asia: The Ethnography and History of a Culture-Bound Syndrome.* New York: Cambridge University Press.

Wittfogel, K. A.
  1957   *Oriental Despotism: A Comparative Study of Total Power.* New Haven, CT: Yale University Press.

Wolf, E. R.
  1966   *Peasants.* Englewood Cliffs, NJ: Prentice Hall.
  1982   *Europe and the People without History.* Berkeley: University of California Press.
  1999   *Envisioning Power: Ideologies of Dominance and Crisis.* Berkeley: University of California Press.

Wolf, E. R., with S. Silverman
  2001   *Pathways of Power: Building an Anthropology of the Modern World.* Berkeley: University of California Press.

Wolpoff, M., B. Senut, M. Pickford, and J. Hawks
  2002   Sahelanthropus or "Sahelpithecus"? *Nature* 419: 581–582.

Woolard, K. A.
  1989   *Double Talk: Bilingualism and the Politics of Ethnicity in Catalonia.* Stanford, CA: Stanford University Press.

World Almanac & Book of Facts
  Published annually. New York: Newspaper Enterprise Association.

World Health Organization
  1997   *World Health Report.* Geneva: World Health Organization.

Worsley, P.

    1984   *The Three Worlds: Culture and World Development.* Chicago: University of Chicago Press.

    1985   (orig. 1959). Cargo Cults. In *Readings in Anthropology 85/86.* Guilford, CT: Dushkin.

Wright, S., ed.

    1994   *Anthropology of Organizations.* London: Routledge.

Wulff, R. M., and S. J. Fiske, eds.

    1987   *Anthropological Praxis: Translating Knowledge into Action.* Boulder, CO: Westview Press.

Yanagisako, S. J.

    2002   *Producing Culture and Capital: Family Firms in Italy.* Princeton, NJ: Princeton University Press.

Yetman, N., ed.

    1991   *Majority and Minority: The Dynamics of Race and Ethnicity in American Life,* 5th ed. Boston: Allyn & Bacon.

    1999   *Majority and Minority: The Dynamics of Race and Ethnicity in American Life,* 6th ed. Boston: Allyn & Bacon.

Young, W. C.

    1996   *The Rashaayada Bedouin: Arab Pastoralists of Eastern Sudan.* Fort Worth: Harcourt Brace.

Yurchak, A.

    2002   Entrepreneurial Governmentality in Postsocialist Russia. In *The New Entrepreneurs of Europe and Asia,* ed. V. Bonnell and T. Gold, p. 301. Armonk, NY: M.E. Sharpe.

    2005   *Everything Was Forever Until It Was No More: The Last Soviet Generation.* Princeton, NJ: Princeton University Press.

Zou, Y., and E. T. Trueba

    2002   *Ethnography and Schools: Qualitative Approaches to the Study of Education.* Lanham, MD: Rowman and Littlefield.

Zulaika, J.

    1988   *Basque Violence: Metaphor and Sacrament.* Reno: University of Nevada Press.

Glossary

Audible pronunciations for many of the following terms are provided in the electronic Glossary at the Online Learning Center for this book.

A. afarensis   Early form of *Australopithecus,* known from Hadar in Ethiopia ("Lucy") and Laetoli in Tanzania; the Hadar remains date to 3.3–3.0 m.y.a.; the Laetoli remains are older, dating to 3.8–3.6 m.y.a.; despite its many apelike features, *A. afarensis* was an upright biped.

acculturation   The exchange of cultural features that results when groups come into continuous firsthand contact; the cultural patterns of either or both groups may be changed, but the groups remain distinct.

achieved status   Social status that comes through talents, choices, actions, and accomplishments, rather than ascription.

aesthetics   Appreciation of the qualities perceived in works of art; the mind and emotions in relation to a sense of beauty.

affinals   Relatives by marriage, whether of lineals (e.g., son's wife) or collaterals (e.g., sister's husband).

age set   Group uniting all men or women born during a certain time span; this group controls property and often has political and military functions.

agriculture   Nonindustrial systems of plant cultivation characterized by continuous and intensive use of land and labor.

ambilineal   Principle of descent that does not automatically exclude the children of either sons or daughters.

anatomically modern humans (AMHs)   Including the Cro-Magnons of Europe (31,000 B.P.) and the older fossils from Skhūl (100,000), Qafzeh (92,000), Herto, and other sites; continue through the present.

animism   Belief in souls or doubles.

anthropology   The study of the human species and its immediate ancestors.

anthropology and education   Anthropological research in classrooms, homes, and neighborhoods, viewing students as total cultural creatures whose enculturation and attitudes toward education belong to a larger context that includes family, peers, and society.

antimodernism   The rejection of the modern in favor of what is perceived as an earlier, purer, and better way of life.

applied anthropology   The application of anthropological data, perspectives, theory, and methods to identify, assess, and solve contemporary social problems.

archaeological anthropology   The study of human behavior and cultural patterns and processes through the culture's material remains.

archaic *H. sapiens*   Early *H. sapiens,* consisting of the Neandertals of Europe and the Middle East, the Neandertal-like hominins of Africa and Asia, and the immediate ancestors of all these hominins; lived from about 300,000 to 28,000 B.P.

art   An object or event that evokes an aesthetic reaction—a sense of beauty, appreciation, harmony, and/or pleasure; the quality, production, expression, or realm of what is beautiful or of more than ordinary significance; the class of objects subject to aesthetic criteria.

arts   The arts include the visual arts, literature (written and oral), music, and theater arts.

ascribed status   Social status (e.g., race or gender) that people have little or no choice about occupying.

assimilation The process of change that a minority group may experience when it moves to a country where another culture dominates; the minority is incorporated into the dominant culture to the point that it no longer exists as a separate cultural unit.

australopithecines Varied group of early hominins. The term is derived from their former classification as members of a distinct subfamily, the Australopithecinae; now they are distinguished from *Homo* only at the genus level, as *Australopithecus (A.).*

balanced reciprocity See *generalized reciprocity.*

band Basic unit of social organization among foragers. A band includes fewer than 100 people; it often splits up seasonally.

bifurcate collateral kinship terminology Kinship terminology employing separate terms for M, F, MB, MZ, FB, and FZ.

bifurcate merging kinship terminology Kinship terminology in which M and MZ are called by the same term, F and FB are called by the same term, and MB and FZ are called by different terms.

big man Regional figure found among tribal horticulturalists and pastoralists. The big man occupies no office but creates his reputation through entrepreneurship and generosity to others. Neither his wealth nor his position passes to his heirs.

bilateral kinship calculation A system in which kinship ties are calculated equally through both sexes: mother and father, sister and brother, daughter and son, and so on.

biocultural Referring to the inclusion and combination (to solve a common problem) of both biological and cultural approaches—one of anthropology's hallmarks.

biological anthropology The study of human biological variation in time and space; includes evolution, genetics, growth and development, and primatology.

bipedalism Upright two-legged locomotion, the key feature differentiating early hominins from the apes.

Black English Vernacular (BEV) A rule-governed dialect of American English with roots in southern English. BEV is spoken by African-American youth and by many adults in their casual, intimate speech.

bourgeoisie One of Marx's opposed classes; owners of the means of production (factories, mines, large farms, and other sources of subsistence).

bridewealth See *progeny price.*

call systems Systems of communication among nonhuman primates, composed of a limited number of sounds that vary in intensity and duration. Tied to environmental stimuli.

capital Wealth or resources invested in business, with the intent of producing a profit.

capitalist world economy The single world system, which emerged in the 16th century, committed to production for sale, with the object of maximizing profits rather than supplying domestic needs.

cargo cults Postcolonial, acculturative religious movements, common in Melanesia, that attempt to explain European domination and wealth and to achieve similar success magically by mimicking European behavior.

caste system Closed, hereditary system of stratification, often dictated by religion; hierarchical social status is ascribed at birth, so that people are locked into their parents' social position.

catharsis Intense emotional release.

chiefdom Form of sociopolitical organization intermediate between the tribe and the state; kin-based with differential access to resources and a permanent political structure.

civil society Voluntary collective action around shared interests, goals, and values. Encompasses such organizations as NGOs, registered charities, community groups, women's organizations, faith-based and professional groups, trade unions, self-help groups, social movements, business associations, coalitions, and advocacy groups.

clan Unilineal descent group based on stipulated descent.

collateral relative A genealogical relative who is not in ego's direct line, such as B, Z, FB, or MZ.

colonialism The political, social, economic, and cultural domination of a territory and its people by a foreign power for an extended time.

communal religions In Wallace's typology, these religions have, in addition to shamanic cults, communal cults in which people organize community rituals such as harvest ceremonies and rites of passage.

Communism Spelled with a capital C, a political movement and doctrine seeking to overthrow capitalism and to establish a form of communism such as that which prevailed in the Soviet Union from 1917 to 1991.

communism Spelled with a lowercase *c*, describes a social system in which property is owned by the community and in which people work for the common good.

communitas Intense community spirit, a feeling of great social solidarity, equality, and togetherness; characteristic of people experiencing liminality together.

complex societies Nations; large and populous, with social stratification and central governments.

core Dominant structural position in the world system; consists of the strongest and most powerful states with advanced systems of production.

core values Key, basic, or central values that integrate a culture and help distinguish it from others.

correlation An association between two or more variables such that when one changes (varies), the other(s) also change(s) (covaries); for example, temperature and sweating.

cross cousins Children of a brother and a sister.

cultivation continuum A continuum based on the comparative study of nonindustrial cultivating societies in which labor intensity increases and fallowing decreases.

cultural anthropology The study of human society and culture; describes, analyzes, interprets, and explains social and cultural similarities and differences.

cultural consultants Subjects in ethnographic research; people the ethnographer gets to know in the field, who teach him or her about their culture.

cultural imperialism The rapid spread or advance of one culture at the expense of others, or its imposition on other cultures, which it modifies, replaces, or destroys—usually because of differential economic or political influence.

cultural relativism The position that the values and standards of cultures differ and deserve respect. Anthropology is characterized by methodological rather than moral relativism: In order to understand another culture fully, anthropologists try to understand its members' beliefs and motivations. Methodological relativism does not preclude making moral judgments or taking action.

cultural resource management (CRM) The branch of applied archaeology aimed at preserving sites threatened by dams, highways, and other projects.

cultural rights Doctrine that certain rights are vested in identifiable groups, such as religious and ethnic minorities and indigenous societies. Cultural rights include a group's ability to preserve its culture, to raise its children in the ways of its forebears, to continue its language, and not to be deprived of its economic base by the nation-state in which it is located.

cultural transmission A basic feature of language; transmission through learning.

culture Distinctly human; transmitted through learning; traditions and customs that govern behavior and beliefs.

curer Specialized role acquired through a culturally appropriate process of selection, training, certification, and acquisition of a professional image; the curer is consulted by patients, who believe in his or her special powers, and receives some form of special consideration; a cultural universal.

daughter languages Languages developing out of the same parent language; for example, French and Spanish are daughter languages of Latin.

descent Rule assigning social identity on the basis of some aspect of one's ancestry.

descent group A permanent social unit whose members claim common ancestry; fundamental to tribal society.

development anthropology The branch of applied anthropology that focuses on social issues in, and the cultural dimension of, economic development.

diaspora The offspring of an area who have spread to many lands.

differential access Unequal access to resources; basic attribute of chiefdoms and states. Superordinates have favored access to such resources, while the access of subordinates is limited by superordinates.

diffusion Borrowing of cultural traits between societies, either directly or through intermediaries.

diglossia The existence of "high" (formal) and "low" (informal, familial) dialects of a single language, such as German.

discrimination Policies and practices that harm a group and its members.

disease A scientifically identified health threat caused by a bacterium, virus, fungus, parasite, or other pathogen.

displacement A basic feature of language; the ability to speak of things and events that are not present.

domestic–public dichotomy Contrast between women's role in the home and men's role in public life, with a corresponding social devaluation of women's work and worth.

dowry A marital exchange in which the wife's group provides substantial gifts to the husband's family.

economizing The rational allocation of scarce means (or resources) to alternative ends (or uses); often considered the subject matter of economics.

economy A population's system of production, distribution, and consumption of resources.

ego Latin for *I*. In kinship charts, the point from which one views an egocentric genealogy.

emic The research strategy that focuses on local explanations and criteria of significance.

enculturation The social process by which culture is learned and transmitted across the generations.

endogamy Rule or practice of marriage between people of the same social group.

equity, increased A reduction in absolute poverty and a fairer (more even) distribution of wealth.

ethnic group Group distinguished by cultural similarities (shared among members of that group) and differences (between that group and others); ethnic-group members share beliefs, customs, and norms, and, often, a common language, religion, history, geography, and kinship.

ethnicity Identification with, and feeling part of, an ethnic group, and exclusion from certain other groups because of this affiliation.

ethnocentrism The tendency to view one's own culture as best and to judge the behavior and beliefs of culturally different people by one's own standards.

ethnography Field work in a particular culture.

ethnology Cross-cultural comparison; the comparative study of ethnographic data, society, and culture.

ethnomusicology The comparative study of the musics of the world and of music as an aspect of culture and society.

ethnosemantics The study of lexical (vocabulary) contrasts and classifications in various languages.

etic The research strategy that emphasizes the ethnographer's rather than the locals' explanations, categories, and criteria of significance.

evolution Belief that species arose from others through a long and gradual process of transformation, or descent with modification.

exogamy Rule requiring people to marry outside their own group.

expressive culture The arts; people express themselves creatively in dance, music, song, painting, sculpture, pottery, cloth, storytelling, verse, prose, drama, and comedy.

extended family household Expanded household including three or more generations.

extradomestic Outside the home; within or pertaining to the public domain.

family of orientation Nuclear family in which one is born and grows up.

family of procreation Nuclear family established when one marries and has children.

fiscal Pertaining to finances and taxation.

focal vocabulary A set of words and distinctions that are particularly important to certain groups (those with particular foci of experience or activity), such as types of snow to Eskimos or skiers.

folk Of the people; originally coined for European peasants; refers to the art, music, and lore of ordinary people, as contrasted with the "high" art or "classic" art of the European elites.

food production Cultivation of plants and domestication (stockbreeding) of animals; first developed 10,000 to 12,000 years ago.

functional explanation Explanation that establishes a correlation or interrelationship between social customs. When customs are functionally interrelated, if one changes, the others also change.

fundamentalism Describes antimodernist movements in various religions. Fundamentalists assert an identity separate from the larger religious group from which they arose; they advocate strict fidelity to the "true" religious principles on which the larger religion was founded.

gender roles The tasks and activities that a culture assigns to each sex.

gender stereotypes Oversimplified but strongly held ideas about the characteristics of males and females.

gender stratification Unequal distribution of rewards (socially valued resources, power, prestige, and personal freedom) between men and women, reflecting their different positions in a social hierarchy.

genealogical method Procedures by which ethnographers discover and record connections of kinship, descent, and marriage, using diagrams and symbols.

general anthropology The field of anthropology as a whole, consisting of cultural, archaeological, biological, and linguistic anthropology.

generality Culture pattern or trait that exists in some but not all societies.

generalized reciprocity Principle that characterizes exchanges between closely related individuals. As social distance increases, reciprocity becomes balanced and finally negative.

generational kinship terminology Kinship terminology with only two terms for the parental generation, one designating M, MZ, and FZ and the other designating F, FB, and MB.

genitor Biological father of a child.

globalization The accelerating interdependence of nations in a world system linked economically and through mass media and modern transportation systems.

gracile Opposite of *robust; gracile* indicates that members of *A. africanus* were a bit smaller and slighter, less robust, than were members of *A. robustus.*

green revolution Agricultural development based on chemical fertilizers, pesticides, 20th-century cultivation techniques, and new crop varieties such as IR-8 ("miracle rice").

head, village A local leader in a tribal society who has limited authority, leads by example and persuasion, and must be generous.

health-care systems Beliefs, customs, and specialists concerned with ensuring health and preventing and curing illness; a cultural universal.

hegemony As used by Antonio Gramsci, a stratified social order in which subordinates comply with domination by internalizing its values and accepting its "naturalness."

hidden transcript As used by James Scott, the critique of power by the oppressed that goes on offstage—in private—where the power holders can't see it.

historical linguistics Subdivision of linguistics that studies languages over time.

holistic Interested in the whole of the human condition: past, present, and future; biology, society, language, and culture.

hominid A member of the taxonomic family that includes humans and the African apes and their immediate ancestors.

hominin A member of the human lineage after its split from ancestral chimps; the term *hominin* is used to describe all the human species that ever have existed, including the extinct ones, and excluding chimps and gorillas.

Homo habilis Term coined by L. S. B. and Mary Leakey; immediate ancestor of *H. erectus;* lived from about 2.0 to 1.7 m.y.a.

honorific A term, such as "Mr." or "Lord," used with people, often by being added to their names, to "honor" them.

horticulture Nonindustrial system of plant cultivation in which plots lie fallow for varying lengths of time.

human rights Doctrine that invokes a realm of justice and morality beyond and superior to particular countries, cultures, and religions. Human rights, usually seen as vested in individuals, would include the right to speak freely, to hold religious beliefs without persecution, and not to be murdered, injured, enslaved, or imprisoned without charge.

hypodescent Rule that automatically places the children of a union or mating between members of different socioeconomic groups in the less-privileged group.

illness A condition of poor health perceived or felt by an individual.

imperialism A policy of extending the rule of a nation or empire over foreign nations or of taking and holding foreign colonies.

incest Forbidden sexual relations with a close relative.

income Earnings from wages and salaries.

independent invention Development of the same cultural trait or pattern in separate cultures as a result of comparable needs, circumstances, and solutions.

indigenized Modified to fit the local culture.

indigenous peoples The original inhabitants of particular territories; often descendants of tribespeople who live on as culturally distinct colonized peoples, many of whom aspire to autonomy.

Industrial Revolution The historic transformation (in Europe, after 1750) of "traditional" into "modern" societies through industrialization of the economy.

international culture Cultural traditions that extend beyond national boundaries.

intervention philosophy Guiding principle of colonialism, conquest, missionization, or development; an ideological justification for outsiders to guide native peoples in specific directions.

interview schedule Ethnographic tool for structuring a formal interview. A prepared form (usually printed or mimeographed) that guides interviews with households or individuals being compared systematically. Contrasts with a *questionnaire* because the researcher has personal contact with the local people and records their answers.

IPR Intellectual property rights, consisting of each society's cultural base—its core beliefs and principles. IPR are claimed as a group right—a cultural right—allowing indigenous groups to control who may know and use their collective knowledge and its applications.

key cultural consultant Person who is an expert on a particular aspect of local life.

kinesics The study of communication through body movements, stances, gestures, and facial expressions.

kinship calculation The system by which people in a particular society reckon kin relationships.

language Human beings' primary means of communication; may be spoken or written; features productivity and displacement and is culturally transmitted.

law A legal code, including trial and enforcement; characteristic of state-organized societies.

leveling mechanism A custom or social action that operates to reduce differences in wealth and thus to bring standouts in line with community norms.

levirate Custom by which a widow marries the brother of her deceased husband.

lexicon Vocabulary; a dictionary containing all the morphemes in a language and their meanings.

life history Of a key consultant or narrator; provides a personal cultural portrait of existence or change in a culture.

liminality The critically important marginal or in-between phase of a rite of passage.

lineage Unilineal descent group based on demonstrated descent.

lineal kinship terminology Parental generation kin terminology with four terms: one for M, one for F, one for FB and MB, and one for MZ and FZ.

lineal relative Any of ego's ancestors or descendants (e.g., parents, grandparents, children, grandchildren) on the direct line of descent that leads to and from ego.

linguistic anthropology The descriptive, comparative, and historical study of language and of linguistic similarities and differences in time, space, and society.

longitudinal research Long-term study of a community, region, society, culture, or other unit, usually based on repeated visits.

magic Use of supernatural techniques to accomplish specific aims.

mana Sacred impersonal force in Melanesian and Polynesian religions.

market principle Profit-oriented principle of exchange that dominates in states, particularly industrial states. Goods and services are bought and sold, and values are determined by supply and demand.

mater Socially recognized mother of a child.

matrifocal Mother-centered; often refers to a household with no resident husband-father.

matrilineal descent Unilineal descent rule in which people join the mother's group automatically at birth and stay members throughout life.

matrilocality Customary residence with the wife's relatives after marriage, so that children grow up in their mother's community.

means (or factors) of production Land, labor, technology, and capital—major productive resources.

medical anthropology Unites biological and cultural anthropologists in the study of disease, health problems, health-care systems, and theories about illness in different cultures and ethnic groups.

m.y.a. Million years ago.

mode of production Way of organizing production—a set of social relations through which labor is deployed to wrest energy from nature by means of tools, skills, and knowledge.

monotheism Worship of an eternal, omniscient, omnipotent, and omnipresent supreme being.

morphology The study of form; used in linguistics (the study of morphemes and word construction) and for form in general—for example, biomorphology relates to physical form.

multiculturalism The view of cultural diversity in a country as something good and desirable; a multicultural society socializes individuals not only into the dominant (national) culture but also into an ethnic culture.

mutation Change in the DNA molecules of which genes and chromosomes are built.

nation Once a synonym for "ethnic group," designating a single culture sharing a language, religion, history, territory, ancestry, and kinship; now usually a synonym for state or *nation-state*.

national culture Cultural experiences, beliefs, learned behavior patterns, and values shared by citizens of the same nation.

nationalities Ethnic groups that once had, or wish to have or regain, autonomous political status (their own country).

nation-state An autonomous political entity; a country like the United States or Canada.

natural selection The process by which the forms most fit to survive and reproduce in a given environment do so in greater numbers than others in the same population; more than survival of the fittest, natural selection is differential reproductive success.

Neandertals Members of an archaic *H. sapiens* group that lived in Europe and the Middle East between 130,000 and 28,000 B.P.

negative reciprocity See *generalized reciprocity*.

neoliberalism Revival of Adam Smith's classic economic liberalism, the idea that governments should not regulate private enterprise and that free market forces should rule; a currently dominant intervention philosophy.

neolocality Postmarital residence pattern in which a couple establishes a new place of residence rather than living with or near either set of parents.

nomadism, pastoral Movement throughout the year by the whole pastoral group (men, women, and children) with their animals; more generally, such constant movement in pursuit of strategic resources.

office Permanent political position.

Oldowan Earliest (2.5 to 2.0 m.y.a.) stone tools; first discovered in 1931 by L. S. B. and Mary Leakey at Olduvai Gorge.

Olympian religions In Wallace's typology, develop with state organization; have full-time religious specialists—professional priesthoods.

open class system Stratification system that facilitates social mobility, with individual achievement and personal merit determining social rank.

overinnovation Characteristic of projects that require major changes in natives' daily lives, especially ones that interfere with customary subsistence pursuits.

Paleolithic Old Stone Age (from Greek roots meaning "old" and "stone"); divided into Lower (early), Middle, and Upper (late).

parallel cousins Children of two brothers or two sisters.

particularity Distinctive or unique culture trait, pattern, or integration.

pastoralists People who use a food-producing strategy of adaptation based on care of herds of domesticated animals.

pater Socially recognized father of a child; not necessarily the genitor.

patriarchy Political system ruled by men in which women have inferior social and political status, including basic human rights.

patrilineal descent Unilineal descent rule in which people join the father's group automatically at birth and stay members throughout life.

patrilineal-patrilocal complex An interrelated constellation of patrilineality, patrilocality, warfare, and male supremacy.

patrilocality Customary residence with the husband's relatives after marriage, so that children grow up in their father's community.

peasant Small-scale agriculturalist living in a state with rent fund obligations.

periphery Weakest structural position in the world system.

phenotype An organism's evident traits, its "manifest biology"—anatomy and physiology.

phoneme Significant sound contrast in a language that serves to distinguish meaning, as in minimal pairs.

phonemics The study of the sound contrasts (phonemes) of a particular language.

phonetics The study of speech sounds in general; what people actually say in various languages.

phonology The study of sounds used in speech.

physical anthropology See *biological anthropology*.

plural marriage Any marriage with more than two spouses, aka polygamy.

plural society A society that combines ethnic contrasts and economic interdependence of the ethnic groups.

polyandry Variety of plural marriage in which a woman has more than one husband.

polygyny Variety of plural marriage in which a man has more than one wife.

polytheism Belief in several deities who control aspects of nature.

postcolonial Referring to interactions between European nations and the societies they colonized (mainly after 1800); more generally, "postcolonial" may be used to signify a position against imperialism and Eurocentrism.

postmodern In its most general sense, describes the blurring and breakdown of established canons (rules, standards), categories, distinctions, and boundaries.

postmodernism A style and movement in architecture that succeeded modernism. Compared with modernism, postmodernism is less geometric, less functional, less austere, more playful, and more willing to include elements from diverse times and cultures; postmodern now describes comparable developments in music, literature, visual art, and anthropology.

postmodernity Condition of a world in flux, with people on the move, in which established groups, boundaries, identities, contrasts, and standards are reaching out and breaking down.

potlatch Competitive feast among Indians on the North Pacific Coast of North America.

power The ability to exercise one's will over others—to do what one wants; the basis of political status.

practicing anthropologists Used as a synonym for applied anthropology; anthropologists who practice their profession outside of academia.

prejudice Devaluing (looking down on) a group because of its assumed behavior, values, capabilities, attitudes, or other attributes.

prestige Esteem, respect, or approval for acts, deeds, or qualities considered exemplary.

productivity A basic feature of language; the ability to use the rules of one's language to create new expressions comprehensible to other speakers.

progeny price A gift from the husband and his kin to the wife and her kin before, at, or after marriage; legitimizes children born to the woman as members of the husband's descent group.

protolanguage Language ancestral to several daughter languages.

public transcript As used by James Scott, the open, public interactions between dominators and oppressed—the outer shell of power relations.

questionnaire Form (usually printed) used by sociologists to obtain comparable information from respondents. Often mailed to and filled in by research subjects rather than by the researcher.

race An ethnic group assumed to have a biological basis.

racism Discrimination against an ethnic group assumed to have a biological basis.

random sample A sample in which all members of the population have an equal statistical chance of being included.

reciprocity One of the three principles of exchange; governs exchange between social equals; major exchange mode in band and tribal societies.

redistribution Major exchange mode of chiefdoms, many archaic states, and some states with managed economies.

refugees People who have been forced (involuntary refugees) or who have chosen (voluntary refugees) to flee a country, to escape persecution or war.

religion Belief and ritual concerned with supernatural beings, powers, and forces.

revitalization movements Movements that occur in times of change, in which religious leaders emerge and undertake to alter or revitalize a society.

rites of passage Culturally defined activities associated with the transition from one place or stage of life to another.

ritual Behavior that is formal, stylized, repetitive, and stereotyped, performed earnestly as a social act; rituals are held at set times and places and have liturgical orders.

robust Large, strong, sturdy; said of skull, skeleton, muscle, and teeth; opposite of *gracile.*

sample A smaller study group chosen to represent a larger population.

Sapir-Whorf hypothesis Theory that different languages produce different ways of thinking.

science A systematic field of study or body of knowledge that aims, through experiment, observation, and deduction, to produce reliable explanations of phenomena, with reference to the material and physical world.

scientific medicine As distinguished from Western medicine, a health-care system based on scientific knowledge and procedures, encompassing such fields as pathology, microbiology, biochemistry, surgery, diagnostic technology, and applications.

semantics A language's meaning system.

semiperiphery Structural position in the world system intermediate between core and periphery.

sexual dimorphism Marked differences in male and female biology besides the contrasts in breasts and genitals.

sexual orientation A person's habitual sexual attraction to, and activities with, persons of the opposite sex, heterosexuality; the same sex, homosexuality; or both sexes, bisexuality.

shaman A part-time religious practitioner who mediates between ordinary people and supernatural beings and forces.

slavery The most extreme, coercive, abusive, and inhumane form of legalized inequality; people are treated as property.

social control Those fields of the social system (beliefs, practices, and institutions) that are most actively involved in the maintenance of norms and the regulation of conflict.

social race A group assumed to have a biological basis but actually perceived and defined in a social context, by a particular culture rather than by scientific criteria.

sociolinguistics Study of relationships between social and linguistic variation; study of language (performance) in its social context.

sodality, pantribal A non-kin-based group that exists throughout a tribe, spanning several villages.

sororate Custom by which a widower marries the sister of his deceased wife.

state (nation-state) Complex sociopolitical system that administers a territory and populace with substantial contrasts in occupation, wealth, prestige, and power. An independent, centrally organized political unit; a government. A form of social and political organization with a formal, central government and a division of society into classes.

status Any position that determines where someone fits in society; may be ascribed or achieved.

stratification Characteristic of a system with socioeconomic strata—groups that contrast in regard to social status and access to strategic resources. Each stratum includes people of both sexes and all ages.

stratified Class-structured; stratified societies have marked differences in wealth, prestige, and power between social classes.

style shifts Variations in speech in different contexts.

subcultures Different cultural traditions associated with subgroups in the same complex society.

subgroups Languages within a taxonomy of related languages that are most closely related.

subordinate The lower, or underprivileged, group in a stratified system.

superordinate The upper, or privileged, group in a stratified system.

survey research Characteristic research procedure among social scientists other than anthropologists. Studies society through sampling, statistical analysis, and impersonal data collection.

symbol Something, verbal or nonverbal, that arbitrarily and by convention stands for something else, with which it has no necessary or natural connection.

syncretisms Cultural mixes, including religious blends, that emerge from acculturation—the exchange of cultural features when cultures come into continuous firsthand contact.

syntax The arrangement and order of words in phrases and sentences.

taboo Set apart as sacred and off-limits to ordinary people; prohibition backed by supernatural sanctions.

taxonomy Classification scheme; assignment to categories (*taxa*; singular, *taxon*).

text Something that is creatively "read," interpreted, and assigned meaning by each person who receives it; includes any media-borne image, such as Carnaval.

theory A set of ideas formulated (by reasoning from known facts) to explain something. The main value of a theory is to promote new understanding. A theory suggests patterns, connections, and relationships that may be confirmed by new research.

transhumance One of two variants of pastoralism; part of the population moves seasonally with the herds while the other part remains in home villages.

tribe Form of sociopolitical organization usually based on horticulture or pastoralism. Socioeconomic stratification and centralized rule are absent in tribes, and there is no means of enforcing political decisions.

underdifferentiation Planning fallacy of viewing less developed countries as an undifferentiated group; ignoring cultural diversity and adopting a uniform approach (often ethnocentric) for very different types of project beneficiaries.

uniformitarianism Belief that explanations for past events should be sought in ordinary forces that continue to work today.

unilineal descent Matrilineal or patrilineal descent.

universal Something that exists in every culture.

Upper Paleolithic Blade-tool-making traditions associated with early *H. sapiens sapiens*; named from their location in upper, or more recent, layers of sedimentary deposits.

variables Attributes (e.g., sex, age, height, weight) that differ from one person or case to the next.

vertical mobility Upward or downward change in a person's social status.

wealth All a person's material assets, including income, land, and other types of property; the basis of economic status.

westernization The acculturative influence of Western expansion on native cultures.

working class Or proletariat; those who must sell their labor to survive; the antithesis of the bourgeoisie in Marx's class analysis.

Credits

Photo Credits

CHAPTER 1

2: © Jean-Leo Dugast /Peter Arnold; **5:** © Francesco Broli/The New York Times; **8:** © Smithsonian Institution; **9:** © Lauren Greenfield/VII; **11:** © Randy Olson/Aurora Photos; **14:** Courtesy Alicia Wilbur; **17:** © Bruce Avera Hunter/National Geographic Image Collection; **18:** © William Campbell/Homefire Productions/Corbis Images

CHAPTER 2

22: © Mark Edwards/Peter Arnold; **25:** © Ozier Muhammad/The New York Times; **27:** © Mike Yamashita/Woodfin Camp & Associates; **28:** © Will & Deni McIntyre/Corbis Images; **30:** © Paul Conklin/Photo Edit, Inc.; **31:** © Charles Harbutt/Actuality, Inc.; **32:** © Hahn/Laif/Aurora Photos; **33:** © Ron Giling/Peter Arnold; **34:** © Erich Lessing/Magnum Photos; **35:** © UNEP/Peter Arnold; **36:** Courtesy, Ann L. Bretnall; **37:** Professor Marietta Baba, Michigan State University

CHAPTER 3

42: Courtesy, Kenneth Garrett; **45:** © Bolante Anthony/Corbis Images; **47:** © Jed Jacobsohn/Getty Images; **49** (*left*): © Jason Homa/Getty Images; **49** (*right*): © Ted Spiegel/Corbis Images; **50** (*left*): © William Gottlieb/Corbis; **45** (*right*): © Jamie Rose/Aurora; **51:** © Sean Sprague/Image Works; **53:** © Joao Silva/PIcturenet Africa; **55** (*top*): © Hideo Haga/Image Works; **55** (*bottom*): © Carl D. Walsh/Aurora Photos; **56:** © Barry Iverson; **57:** Courtesy, Mark Dennis

CHAPTER 4

62: AAAC/Topham/The Image Works; **65:** Reprinted by permission of the publisher from *Among Orangutans: Red Apes and the Rise of Human Culture* by Carel van Schaik, Cambridge, Mass.: The Belknap Press of Harvard University Press, Copyright © 2004 by the President and Fellows of Harvard College; **67:** English Heritage/Topham-HIP/The Image Works; **69:** Kenneth Garrett/ National Geographic Society; **71:** Sandra Dawes/The Image Works; **72:** Mike K. Nichols/Magnum Photos; **73:** C. Novellino/Peter Arnold, Inc.; **77:** John Reader/Science Photo Library/Photo Researchers, Inc.; **79:** Luba Dmytryk/National Geographic Society; **80:** Peter Bostrom; **81:** Kenneth Garrett/

National Geographic Society; **83:** Luba Dmytryk/National Geographic Society; **86:** Courtesy Kelsey Foster; **88:** French Ministry of Culture and Communication, Regional Direction for Cultural Affairs, Rhône-Alpes region, Regional department of archaeology; **89:** Kenneth Garrett/National Geographic Society

CHAPTER 5

54: © Sidali Djenidi/Gamma Presse; **98:** © Werner Forman/Corbis; **100:** © T. Arruza/Image Works; **101:** © Ronald Martinez/Getty Images; **103:** Gretchen M. Haupt; **105:** © PJ. Griffiths/Magnum Photos; **107** (*all*): Conrad P. Kottak; **108:** © Mary Ann Chatain/AP/Wide World Photos; **111:** ICTY, Via APTN (Television)/AP Photo; **112:** © Mark Edwards/Peter Arnold; **113:** © Alain Buu/Gamma Presse; **114:** © Michael Ainsworth/Dallas Morning News/Corbis; **115:** © Thomas Grabka/Laif/Redux; **116** (*left*): © Bradley Mayhew/Lonely Planet Images; **116** (*right*): © Yuri Kochetkov/Epa/Corbis

CHAPTER 6

122: © Stuart Franklin/Magnum Photos; **124:** © Michael Nichols/Magnum Photos; **125:** © Hector Amezcua/The Sacramento Bee/ZUMA Press; **127:** © Michael Nichols/National Geographic Society; **128:** © David William Hamilton; **129:** © Lonny Shavelson; **133:** © Ira Block/National Geographic Image Collection; **134:** © Vincent Laforet/New York Times Pictures; **136:** © PhotoFest; **137:** © Jim Goldberg/Magnum Photos; **139:** Gary Hershorn/Reuters/Corbis; **141:** Courtesy, Jason A. DeCaro; **142:** © Photos 12/Polaris; **146:** © Rod Macivor/AP/Wide World Photos; **147:** © Reuters/Corbis; **148:** © Andre Forget/AP/Wide World Photos

CHAPTER 7

150: © Max Galli/laif/Redux; **153:** © B.C. Alexander/Photo Researchers; **156:** Courtesy, Jennifer A. Kelly; **157:** © Georg Gerster/Photo Researchers; **158:** © D. Halleux/BIOS/Peter Arnold; **160:** © Paul Chesley/Getty Images; **161** (*top*): © Bruno Barbey/Magnum Photos; **161** (*center*): © H. Schwarzbach/Argus Fotoarchiv/Peter Arnold; **163:** © David Austen/Woodfin Camp & Associates; **165:** © Darcy Padilla/Redux; **167:** © Carl D. Walsh/Aurora; **169:** © John Eastcott/Yva Momatiuk/Woodfin Camp & Associates; **172** (*top*): © American Museum of Natural History,

Neg# 336116; **172** (*center*): © Lawrence Migdale/Stock Boston

CHAPTER 8

176: © Christain Hartmann/Epa/Corbis; **178:** © Sarah Leen/National Geographic Image Collection; **179:** © Abbas/Magnum Photos; **181:** © Joy Tessman/National Geographic Society; **185:** © Burt Glinn/Magnum Photos; **187:** © Library of Congress (LC-USZC2-3231); **188:** © Douglas Kirkland; **189:** © Michael Schneps; **190:** Courtesy, Abrigail Dreibelbis; **191:** © John A. Novak/Animals Animals; **192:** © James Davis/Eye Ubiquitous/Corbis Images; **193:** © Greg Ruffing/Getty Images; **195:** © Catherine Karnow/Woodfin Camp & Associates; **196:** © Renzo Gostoli/AP/Wide World Photos; **198:** © Nicholas C. Kottak

CHAPTER 9

204: © Julio Donoso/Woodfin Camp & Associates; **206:** © Eastcott-Momatiuk/The Image Works; **207:** © Stephen Beckerman/Pennsylvania State University; **208:** © Reuters/Str Old; **209:** © Caleb Kenna/IPN Stock; **210:** © Najlah Feanny/Stock Boston; **215** (*top*): © Ognen Teofilovski/Reuters; **215** (*bottom*): © D.H. Hessell/Stock Boston; **218:** © Larry Williams/Corbis Images

CHAPTER 10

226: © Danny Zhan/AP/WideWorld Photos; **229:** © AFP/Getty Images; **231:** © Mark Edwards/Still Photos/Peter Arnold; **232:** Kenneth Garrett; **233:** © DPA/Image Works; **235:** © Pablo Bartholomew/Getty Images; **236:** © National Pictures/Topham/The Image Works; **237:** © James Marshall/Image Works; **238:** Courtesy, Kim Shah; **239:** © Cary Wolinsky/Stock Boston; **244:** © Earl & Nazima Kowall/Corbis Images

CHAPTER 11

250: © Jodi Cobb/National Geographic Image Collection; **252:** Ziva Santop; **253:** © Lindsay Hebberd/Corbis Images; **256:** © Amit Dave/Reuters/Corbis; **258:** © Bryan & Cherry Alexander/Arctic Photo; **259** (*top*): © Wendy Stone; **259** (*bottom*): © Stuart Franklin/Magnum Photos; **261** (*top*): © David Allan Harvey/Magnum Photos; **261** (*bottom*): © George Holton/Photo Researchers; **263:** © Martha Cooper/Peter Arnold; **265:** © National Archives; **268:** "Memories of Rio de Janeiro"; **274:** John Bigelow Taylor/Art Resource and ARS, NY; **276** (*top*): © David Alan Harvey/Magnum Photos; **276** (*bottom*): © Mountain Light Photography/Odyssey/Chicago; **277:** © Stephen Saks/Lonely Planet

CHAPTER 12

278: © R. Giling/Peter Arnold; **281:** © M. and E. Bernheim/Woodfin Camp & Associates; **282:** © Erich Lessing/Art Resource; **283:** © Rick Silva/AP/Wide World Photos; **284:** © Peter Essick/Aurora Photos; **286** (*top*): © Thierry Secretan/COSMOS/Woodfin Camp & Associates; **286** (*bottom*): © Joe McNally/IPNstock.com; **287:** © Michele Burgess; **289:** Courtesy, Charlie Graham; **290:** © Sara Terry/Polaris; **292:** © National Anthropological Archives. Neg.#85-8666; **296:** © Kal Muller/Woodfin Camp & Associates; **297:** © Robert Nickelsberg/Getty Images

CHAPTER 13

302: © Robert Fried Photography; **304:** © Gilles Peress/Magnum Photos; **305:** © The Kobal Collection/ABC-TV/Getty Images; **307:** © David Berkwitz/Polaris; **310:** © John Moss/Photo Researchers; **312:** © James P. Blair/National Geographic Image Collection; **313:** © Robert Frerck; **315** (*top*): © Stephanie Maze/Woodfin Camp & Associates; **315** (*bottom*): © Yva Momatiuk & John Eastcott/Woodfin Camp & Associates; **318:** © James P. Blair/National Geographic Image Collection; **319:** © Inge Yspeert/Corbis Images; **320:** © Joan Marcus

CHAPTER 14

324: © Chris Stowers/Panos; **326:** © Hu Sheng/epa/Corbis; **327:** © Archives Charmet/Bridgeman Art Library; **329** (*top*): © Bruce Dale/National Geographic Image Collection; **329** (*bottom*): © David Reed; **331:** © ARPL/Topham/Image Works; **332** (*top*): © Michael Nichols/National Geographic Image Collection; **332** (*bottom*): © Culver Pictures; **335:** MinBuZa/Peter Arnold; **336:** © The New York Public Library/Art Resource, NY; **339:** Robin Nelson/PhotoEdit, Inc.; **340:** © V. Leloup/Gamma Press

CHAPTER 15

344: © Mark Edwards/Still Pictures/Peter Arnold; **347:** © Rob Huibers/Panos Pictures; **349:** © Hulton Archive/Getty Images; **351:** © Stuart Franklin/Magnum Photos; **353** (*top*): © Bettmann/Corbis Images; **353** (*bottom*): © Denis Sinyakov/AFP/Getty Images; **357:** © Alexander Low/Woodfin Camp & Associates; **358:** © Jorgen Schytte/Still Pictures/Peter Arnold; **359:** © J.L. Dugast/Lineair/Peter Arnold; **361:** © Noorani/Still Pictures/Peter Arnold; **362:** © Dr. Steven Lansing

CHAPTER 16

366: © S. Nagendra/Photo Researchers; **368:** United States Holocaust Memorial Museum, Courtesy of National Archives; **369:** © Jodi Cobbs/National Geographic Image Collection; **370:** © Gueorgui Pinkhassov/Magnum Photos; **373:** © Steven Feld; **374:** © Buu Deville Turpin/Gamma Presse; **377:** © Andres Hernandez/Getty Images; **378** (*top*): © Julio Etchart/Peter Arnold; **378** (*bottom*): © Christopher Morris; **379:** © Peter Marlow/Magnum Photos; **380:** © Ricardo Funari; **381:** Jessica Nelson; **382:**© Jose Luis Quintana/Reuters/Corbis; **387:**AP/Wide World Photos; **388:** Francis Dean/Image Works; **389:** Mohamed Azakir/Reuters/Landov

Text and Illustration Credits

FRONT MATTER

xxxvi-xxxvii: From *Student Atlas of World Geography*, Third Edition, by John L. Allen. Copyright © 2003 by The McGraw-Hill Companies, Inc. Reprinted by permission of McGraw-Hill/Dushkin, a division of The McGraw-Hill Companies, Guilford, CT 06437.

CHAPTER 1

5-6: Excerpts from Marc Lacey, "Remote and Poked, Anthropology's Dream Tribe," *New York Times*, December 18, 2005, section 1, p. 1. Copyright © 2005 by The New York Times Co. Reprinted with permission.

CHAPTER 2

25-26: Excerpts from John Schwartz, "Archaeologist in New Orleans Finds a Way to Help the Living," *New York*

CHAPTER 3

CHAPTER 4

CHAPTER 5

CHAPTER 6

CHAPTER 7

CHAPTER 8

CHAPTER 9

CHAPTER 10

CHAPTER 11

CHAPTER 12

CHAPTER 13

CHAPTER 14

CHAPTER 15

CHAPTER 16

Wilford, "In a Publishing Coup, Books in 'Unwritten' Languages," *New York Times*, December 31, 1991, pp. B5, B6. Copyright © 1991 by The New York Times Co. Reprinted with permission.

APPENDIX 2

A11-A13: AAA Code of Ethics. Adapted from http://www.aaanet.org/committees/ethics/ethcode.htm. With permission of the American Anthropological Association.

APPENDIX 3

A16-A18: Adapted from *Prime-Time Society: An Anthropological Analysis of Television and Culture*, 1st edition, by Conrad Phillip Kottak. © 1990. Reprinted with permission of Wadsworth, a division of Thomson Learning: www.thomsonrights.com. Fax 800 730-2215.

Name Index

Subject Index

creative thought and, 85–88
culture and, 309–315, 318–320
definition of, 303, 304, 321
ethnomusicology, 310–312
folk art, 310–311
Greek theater, 319
impressionism, 309
individuality and, 308–309, 314
ornamentation and, 88–89
overview of, 303–304
placement of, 307
politics and, 313–314
religion and, 304, 306–307, 312
tradition and, 312
Arts, definition of, 303, 321
Ascribed status, 99, 118
Asexuality, 267
Asian people, 96
Assault on Paradise (Kottak), 216
Assimilation, 111–112, 115, 118
Attractiveness standards, 8
Australia, 8, 154, 307, 318, 325–326, 382
Australopithecines, 75, 78, 79, 91
Authority, definition of, 177
Autochthony, 380–381
Awls, 85, 88
Azande people, 269
Aztecs, 346

B
Baha'i, 294, 295
Balance reciprocity, definition of, 169, 173
Bali, 315, 318
Bamana people, 303
Bands
    definition of, 155, 173, 178
    energy consumption and, 340
    foraging and, 155, 181, 194
    industrialization and, 339
    kinship and, 180, 181
    land and, 164
    manufacturing and, 164
    marriage and, 181
    overview of, 180
Bangladesh, 281, 347
Barí people, 207
Bart, 215
Baseball, 283, 284
Basongye people, 311
Basques, 115, 274–277
Basseri people, 162, 188
"BBC English," 135
Beagle, 66
Bedouins, 5, 179–180
Behavioral modernity, 85–89
Beijing man, 81
Bell Curve (Murray), 107
Beloit College, 38
Berdaches, 236, 269, 292
Beringia, 89
Betsileo people
    burial ceremonies, 55
    child fosterage, 220
    descent and, 213
    division of labor and, 262
    plural marriage and, 244–245
    rice cultivation, 163
    scarcity and, 166–167
    witchcraft and, 290–291
BEV. *See* Black English Vernacular (BEV)
Bias, 18
Bible, 64

Bifurcate collateral kinship terminology, 221, 222
Bifurcate merging kinship terminology, 219–221, 222
"Big men," 182, 184–185, 201, 296, 387
Bilateral kinship calculation, 217, 222
Biocultural, definition of, 8, 19
Biological adaptation, 4, 6–7
Biological anthropology
    applications of, 27
    culture and, 4, 8–9
    definition of, 19
    overview of, 11–13
    primatology and, 13
Biomedicine, 34
Bipedalism, 74–75, 77, 91
Birth control, 18
Birthing process, 215
Bisexuality, 267
Bison, 186
Black English Vernacular (BEV), 30–31, 132, 138–139, 143
Blade tools, 84–85
Blindness, 70
Blombos Cave, 84, 88, 309–310
Blood feuds, 182
Bolivia, 379, 380
Bone tools, 88, 310
Book of Kells, 142
Bosavi People's Fund, 373
Bosnia, 115, 311, 340, 354
Bosnia-Herzegovina, 110–111, 115
Boston University, 6
Botswana, 334–335
Bourgeoisie, definition of, 331, 341
Brachaition, 70, 77
Brain, 69–70, 75, 78–80, 81, 83, 88, *See also* Skull
Brazil
    anthropological studies in, 12
    assimilation in, 112
    capoeira and, 319
    Chegança performance and, 373
    development and, 368, 370
    division of labor in, 256
    environmentalism and, 368
    faith healers in, 288
    family and, 212
    female body perspectives, 8, 9
    foraging and, 154
    indigenous population, 380, 381–382
    kinship in, 216
    marriage in, 228
    nonverbal communication in, 129
    Portugal and, 346, 373–374
    race and, 106
    as semiperiphery nation, 328
    slavery and, 336, 379
    television in, 55
    touching and, 49
    transvestitism in, 268
Bridewealth, 229, 237, 239–242, 246
Brooklyn Museum of Art, 313
Buddhism, 293, 294, 295, 304
Buganda, 193, 245
Bulgaria, 110
Burakumin, 105–106
Burger King, 389
Burial practices, 25, 55, 318
Burma, 132

C
Caboclo, 381
Call systems, 124, 126–128, 143

Camels, 161
Campesinos, 379
Canada
    American settlement and, 90
    Basques and, 275
    Canadian Immigration Act, 147
    childcare and, 256–257
    diversity in culture and language in, 146–148
    domestic violence and, 263
    Employment Equity Act, 104, 148
    energy consumption in, 340
    family and, 211, 217
    female swimmers and, 8
    foraging and, 154
    French colonization of, 349
    pantribal societies in, 186
    race and, 104
    same-sex marriage and, 236
    subcultures and, 51–52
Candomblé, 295
Cannibals, 166
Cao Dai, 294
Capital, 138
    definition of, 326, 341
Capitalism, 162, 164–167, 168, 293, 354
Capitalist world economy, definition of, 326, 341
Capoeira, 319
Cargo cults, 295–297, 299
Carnaval, 268, 374
Cash crops, 326
Cash economies, 164–167
Cassava, 152, 160
Caste systems, 335–336, 341
Castration, 286
Catastrophism, 64
Catharsis, definition of, 313, 321
Cathedrals, 306
Cattle
    as bridewealth, 239–240
    cattle rustling, 167, 170, 187
    food production and, 159, 161, 163
    as sacred, 287
Cave art, 85, 87, 88, 309–310
Celebrity, 306
Center for Ethnographic Research, 38
Ceremonial funds, 167
Chad, 74
Chat rooms, 179–180
Chauvet cave paintings, 85, 87, 88
Chegança performance, 373
Cherokee, 168–169
Chicano, 100
Chiefdoms
    definition of, 178, 180, 201
    development of, 189
    economic systems in, 191, 194
    industrialization and, 339
    political systems in, 191
    redistribution and, 191
    social ranking, 191–193
Chiefly redistribution, 191
Childhood dependency, 75, *See also* Parental investment
Chile, 90
Chimpanzees
    humans and, 70
    hunting and, 72–73
    incest and, 232
    sociality of, 65
    termiting and, 72
    tool use and, 71–72

China
  Asian factory women, 333
  energy consumption in, 338–340
  Homo erectus and, 81
  Islam and, 281
  languages spoken in, 369
  states and, 189
Chinese traditional religion, 293, 294
Chisels, 85
Choppers, 79
Christianity, 171, 291–295, 297, 371
Chukchee people, 292
CI. *See* Conservation International (CI)
Circumcision, 52, 187
Citicorp, 38
Civil rights, 97
Civil society, 356, 363
civilization and Capitalism, 15th–18th Centure (Braudel), 326
Clans, 213–214, 222, 355, 356
Class consciousness, definition of, 331
Clitoridectomy, 52
Closed class systems, 335–336
Clothing, 83, 85
Clovis tradition, 90
Cold War, 56
Cold-adapted Neandertals, 82–83
Collateral households, 209
Collateral relatives, definition of, 219, 222
Collective liminality, 285–286
College of William & Mary, 26
Colombia, 380
Colonial anthropology, 28
Colonialism
  British colonialism, 346, 348
  cultural colonialism, 117
  definition of, 115, 118, 337, 345, 363
  French colonialism, 348–349
  identity and, 349–350
  imperialism and, 337, 345–346
  Indonesia and, 358
  overview of, 346
  postcolonial, 350–351
Color vision, 68
Columbia University, 12
Communal religions, 291, 292, 299
Communication and language, *See also* Sociolinguistics
  accents and, 132
  art and, 312–313
  Basque language, 275
  Creole languages, 56, 131, 138
  cultural diversity and, 369
  cybercommunication, 141
  daughter languages, 140, 143
  diglossia and, 135, 143
  displacement and, 127, 143
  education and, 29–31
  focal vocabulary, 133, 143
  global communications, 7
  historical linguistics, 124, 140–142, 143
  Hopi language, 132
  kinesics, 129, 143
  language defined, 143
  language subgroups, 140, 143
  linguistic anthropology, 13, 15
  meaning and, 133–134
  missionaries and, 350
  mutation and, 88
  nationalities and, 109
  nonhuman primate communication, 124, 126–128

nonverbal communication, 124, 128–130, 135
origin of language, 128
ornamentation and, 89
overview of, 123–124
pidgin languages, 56, 131
preservations of languages, 376
primates and, 13
productivity and, 127, 143
protolanguages, 140
Sapir-Whorf hypothesis, 131–133, 143
sign language, 126–128
social stratification and, 379
sociolinguistics, 134–139, 143
speech sounds, 130
status position and, 136–138
structure of language, 130–131
symbols and, 47
thought and culture and, 131–134
universal grammar, 131
Communism, 352, 352–354, 363
Communitas, 285–286, 300
Confessional rituals, 215
Confucianism, 293
Congo, 84, 311
Conservation International (CI), 347
Consumption activities, 10
Contagious magic, 283
Cooperation and sharing, 73
Cooperatives, 361
Copula deletion, 139
Core nations, 328, 333, 337, 341, 368
Core tools, 79
Core values, definition of, 50, 58
Correlation, 155, 157–158, 173
Corruption, 354–356
Cotton, 326, 329
Cousins, 228, 230
Covenant on Civil and Political Rights (UN), 53
Covenant on Economic, Social and Cultural Rights (UN), 53
Creationism, 64
Creativity, 85–89, *See also* Art
Creole languages, 56, 131, 138
Crime, 239
Cro-Magnon, 83, 88, 89
Croatia, 110, 354
Cross cousins, 228, 233, 246
Crow Indians, 218, 292
Cuba, 346, 352
Cult houses, 308
Cultivation, 158–161, 173
Cultivation continuum, 159–160, 173
Cults, 286, 295–297, 308
Cultural anthropology
  applications of, 27
  definition of, 7, 19
  educational research and, 29–30
  overview of, 9–10
  sociology and, 15–16
  studies focus of, 7–8
Cultural colonialism, 117
Cultural exchange
  acculturation and, 367–368
  contact and domination and, 368, 370–374
  indigenous peoples and, 378–383
  popular culture and, 374–375
  religious change and, 371–372
  remaking culture, 374–377
  text and, 374, 384
Cultural imperialism, 372–374, 384
Cultural relativism, 52, 58

Cultural resource management (CRM), 28, 39
Cultural rights, definition of, 53, 58
Cultural transmission, 127, 143
Culture
  acculturation, 56, 58
  adaptation and, 4, 7, 50, 64
  as all-encompassing, 48
  art and, 309–315, 318–320
  attractiveness standards and, 8
  biology and, 4, 8–9
  body effected by, 8
  concept of, 43–44, 46–47, 50
  consumption activities, 10
  cultural change mechanisms, 56
  cultural relativism, 52, 58
  cultural transmission, 127, 143
  culture clashes, 45–46
  definition of, 4, 19
  diffusion, 51, 54, 55, 56, 58
  enculturation, 43, 44, 46, 58
  ethnocentrism and, 27, 49, 52, 58
  expressive culture, 303, 321
  folklore and, 57
  generality and, 54–55, 58
  globalization and, 56–58
  independent invention and, 56, 58
  individuality and, 48, 50–51
  as integrated, 48, 50
  international culture, 51, 59
  as learned, 44
  levels of, 51–52
  as maladaptive, 50
  national culture, 51, 59
  nature and, 47–48
  overview of, 44
  particularity and, 55, 59
  personal space and, 44, 49
  popular culture, 305–306, 374–375, 381
  propriety and, 8
  race and, 7
  as shared, 44, 46
  subcultures, 51–52, 59, 146
  symbols and, 44, 46–47, 51, 59
  text and, 374, 384
  universal traits and, 54, 59
Cultures of Multiple Fathers: The Theory and Practice of Partible Paternity in Lowland South America (Beckerman and Valentine), 207
Curers, 34–35, 39
Cybercommunication, 141
Cyrillic alphabet, 110

D
Dance, 312, 318, 319
Daughter languages, 140, 143
Deafness, 70
Deforestation, 160, 371
Demonstrated descent, 213
Dentition, 75–77, 83
Depth perception, 68
Descent
  ambilineal descent, 214, 222
  clans and, 213–214
  definition of, 118
  demonstrated descent, 213
  descent groups, 182, 212–213, 222
  ego and, 215, 217, 218, 222, 230
  family versus, 213–214
  lineages and, 213–214
  local descent groups, 213
  matrilineal descent, 198, 212–213, 222
  moiety and, 228, 230

patrilineal descent, 213, 223
race and, 101
stipulated descent, 213
unilineal descent, 213, 223, 230
Descent groups, 182, 212–213, 222
Descriptive linguistics, 130
Development
civil society and, 356
communism and, 352–354
corruption and, 354–356
descent-groups and, 362
developmental anthropology and, 356–359, 363
environmentalism and, 357–359, 368, 370–371
equity and, 359, 363
greening of Java, 357–359
innovation strategies, 359–362
intervention philosophy and, 351, 364
neoliberalism and, 351–352, 364
overinnovation, 360–361, 364
overview of, 351
privatization, 353
Second World and, 352–356
Third World models, 361–362
underdifferentiation, 361, 364
Developmental anthropology, 356–359, 363
Diaspora
African diaspora, 97, 109, 379
Basque diaspora, 274
definition of, 377, 384
media and, 377
slavery and, 97
Didgeridoo, 320
Diet and nutrition, *See also* Disease; Health
Ariaal and, 5
body effected by, 8
dentition and, 76–77
education about, 36
of foragers, 160
health and, 216
poverty and, 9
sexual behavior and, 17–18
tool advances and, 84–85
Differential access, definition of, 192, 201
Diffusion, 51, 54, 55, 56, 58, 367, 368
Diglossia, 135, 143
Direct diffusion, 56
Direct rule, 349
Disaster Mortuary Operational Response Teams (Dmort), 25
Discourse, definition of, 197
Discovery Channel, 312
Discrimination, 105–106, 114, 118
Disease, *See also* Diet and nutrition; Health
AIDS/HIV, 33–34, 313
curers and, 34–35, 39
definition of, 32–33, 39
disease-theory systems, 34
health-care systems and, 34–35, 39
illness differentiated from, 33
schistosomiasis (liver flukes), 33
sexually transmitted diseases, 33–34
taboos and, 17–18
Displacement, 127, 143
Diversity, 51, 125–126, 135, 146–148, 369–370
"Divje babe flute," 310
Divorce, 50, 206, 210, 242–243
Diwaniya, 179

Dmanisi site, 80
DNA (deoxyribonucleic acid), 14, 84
Domestic-public dichotomy, 258, 271
Dowries, 229, 237, 239–241, 246, 263

E
Early hominins, 75–79
East African Standard, 229
Ecology, definition of, 10–11
Economic capital, 138
Economics, *See also* Adaptive strategies; Trade
adaptive strategies and, 151–152
cash economies, 164–167
chiefdoms and, 191
definition of, 162, 173
disease and, 33
economizing and, 165–168, 173
global economy, 7
industrial economies, 162, 164–165
laissez-faire economics, 351
maximization and, 165–168
plantation economies, 326
potlatching, 170–172, 174
profit motives, 166
sociopolitical types and, 194
Economizing, 165–168, 173
Economy, definition of, 162
Ecosystems, 10
Ecuador, 379, 380
Education
anthropology and education, 29–31, 39
business careers and, 38
diet and nutrition education, 36
enculturation and, 29–30
ethnographic studies and, 27
linguistic anthropology and, 27
Efe people, 152
Egalitarian societies, 157–158, 182
Ego, 215, 217, 218, 222, 230
Egypt
food production and, 7
imperialism of, 346
incest and, 232
pyramids, 11
royal endogamy and, 235
schistosomiasis (liver flukes) and, 33, 34
television and, 375–376
Emic approach, definition of, 26
Emotionalistic disease theories, 34
Employment. *See* Labor
Enculturation
art and, 314–315, 318
definition of, 4, 43, 58
education and, 29–30
language and, 123–124
process of, 44
symbols and, 46
Endeavor Alternative School, 125–126
Endogamy, 234–235
Energy consumption, 338–340
Enforcement, 194–195
English language
"BBC English," 135
Black English Vernacular (BEV) and, 30–31, 132, 138–139, 143
Standard English (SE), 30, 130, 132, 135
Environment
adaptability and, 4, 6–7
development and, 357–359, 368, 370–371
intensive agriculture and, 160

Equity, 359, 363
Eritrea, 81
Eskimos, 86, 133, 154, 218
Essentialism, 381–382, 384
Estrus, 73
Ethics, applied anthropologists and, 28
Ethiopia, 74, 76, 81, 84
Ethnic expulsion, 115
Ethnic group, definition of, 96, 118
Ethnicity
assimilation and, 111–112
definition of, 96, 118
discrimination and, 114
ethnic conflict, 114–117
marriage and, 234
multiculturalism, 112–114
nationalities and, 109–110
overview of, 95–96, 99
plural societies, 112
prejudice and, 114
state and, 109
Ethnocentrism, 27, 49, 52, 58
Ethnocide, 115, 368, 371
Ethnography
applied anthropology and, 29
definition of, 9, 12, 16, 19
development and, 356
emic approach, 26
foraging and, 73
indigenous peoples and, 382–383
market research and, 37
Ethnology, 9, 10, 16–17, 19
Ethnology, 240
Ethnomedicine, 53
Ethnomusicology, 15, 310–312, 321
Ethnosamantics, 133–134, 143
Etoro people, 267
EU (European Union), 56
European Union (EU), 56
"Eve," 84
Evolution
American settlement and, 89–90
anatomically modern humans (AMHs) and, 78, 80, 83–85
australopithines and early homo, 79
behavioral modernity, 85–89
definition of, 91
early hominins and, 75–79
fossil evidence and, 74–75
Homo erectus, 80–81
Homo sapiens, 81–82
human and nonhuman primate comparisons and, 67–73
Neandertals, 82–85
overview of, 64, 66
theory of, 64, 66, 82
Ewe people, 288–289
Exogamy
bands and, 157
definition of, 54, 246
descent groups and, 212–213
human and nonhuman primate comparison and, 73
incest and, 228, 230–231
Expressive culture, definition of, 303, 321
Extended family households, 206, 208–209, 222
Extradomestic, 262, 271

F
Faith healers, 288
Falsification, 18

Lebanon, 88

Les Miserables, 314

Leveling mechanisms, definition of, 291, 300

Levirate, 242, 246

Lexicon, definition of, 130, 143

Library of Congress Endangered Music Project, 373

Liminality, definition of, 285, 300

Lincoln University, 97

Lineages, 213–214, 222

Lineal kinship terminology, 219, 221, 222

Lineal relatives, 219, 222

Linguistic anthropology
definition of, 19
education and, 27
McDonald's ritual phrases and, 389
overview of, 13, 15, 124

Linguistic relativity, 135

Linnaean Society of London, 66

Literacy, 110, 315

Liver flukes, 33

Llamas, 161

Llongot, 254

Local descent groups, 213

Long-term physiological adaptation, 6–7

Louisiania territory, 349

Love, 240–241

Lovedu, 237

Lower Paleolithic, 80

Lower Pleistocene, 81

Lucy skeleton, 76–77, 79

M

McDonald's Corporation, 387–390

McGill University, 6

"McTeague" (Norris), 305

McWorld, 297

Madagascar
burial ceremonies in, 55
descent and, 213, 362
development and, 356
foraging and, 154
nonverbal communication in, 129
plural marriage and, 244–245
rice cultivation, 163
witchcraft and, 290–291

Magic, 283–284, 300

Magico-religious specialists, 34–35

Makah Indians, 45–46, 197–198, 215, 382

Malaysia, 35, 154, 165, 169

Male sexual jealousy, 207–208

Male-female avoidance, 261–262, 270

Mali, 303

Mana, 283, 300

Manifest function, definition of, 235

Manioc, 152, 159

Manon Lescaut, 26

Marine Mammal Protection Act, 46

Market principle, 168, 173

Marriage, *See also* Family; Kinship
adultery, 52, 182, 257
age at first marriage, 48, 50, 210, 264
Ariaal people and, 5
bands and, 181
bridewealth and, 229, 237, 239–241, 242, 246
"common law" marriage, 228
cousins and, 228, 230, 233
culture and, 48, 50
divorce and, 50, 242–243

dowries and, 229, 237, 239–241, 246

endogamy and, 234–235

exogamy and, 54, 73, 157, 212–213, 228, 230–231, 246

female husbands, 261

fertility and, 240, 241

as group alliance, 237, 239–242

human and nonhuman primate comparison and, 73–74

incest taboo and, 54, 228, 230–235

levirate, 242, 246

love and, 240–241

matrimonial advertisements, 238

moiety and, 228, 230

music and, 311–312

overview of, 227–228

plural marriage, 228, 229–230, 240–241, 243–246

post-marital resident rules, 208, 213–214, 223, 259–260

race and, 105

rights and obligations and, 216, 235–237

same-sex marriage, 228, 235–237, 261

sororate, 241–242, 246

wife stealing, 182

Marrow Utility Index, 86

Masai, 5, 187, 188

Matai system, 32

Maters, 236, 246

Mating. *See* Sexual behavior

Matriarchy, 253–254

Matrifocal societies, 260–261, 271

Matrilineal descent, 198, 212–213, 222

Matrilineal families, 209, 215

Matrilineal kinship, 16

Matrilocality, 215, 223, 259–260

Maximization, 165–168

Mbuti people, 152, 157, 170, 255

Meaning in language, 133–134

Means of production, 163–164, 173

Meat Utility Index, 86

Medical anthropology, 32–35, 40

Melanasia, 186, 283, 295–296, 387

Mende, 188

Men's Health, 6

Mesoamerica, state formation in, 189

Mestizos, 379, 382

Mexico
cheap labor and, 329
colonialism and, 346
endangered languages and, 376
foraging and, 155
pyramids, 11
television and, 375–376
transnational migration and, 377
urban versus rural societies and, 31

Michigan State University, 37

Microenculturation, definition of, 35

Middle East, 152, *See also* specific countries

Middle Paleolithic, 80

Middle Pleistocene, 81

Millennium Institute, 347

Minangkabau, 253–254

Minority groups, 100

Mission Civilsatrice, 349, 351

Missionaries, 184, 241, 269, 349, 350

Mitochondrial DNA (mtDNA), 84

Mladec site, 83

Modern world system. *See* World system

Modes of production, 162–165, 173

Moiety, 228, 230

Molson Canadian beer, 146–147

Monkeys, 13, 67–68, 70–71

Monocrop production, 326

Monotheistic religion, 291, 292, 300

Morocco, 81, 349

Morphology, definition of, 130, 143

Motivation, 165–166

Motorola, 38

Mozambique, 197–198, 215

MtDNA. *See* Mitochondrial DNA (mtDNA)

Multiculturalism, 112–114, 118

Museum of Modern Art in New York, 307

Music, 304, 306, 307, 310, 310–315, 320

Mutations, 67, 87–88, 91

M.y.a. (million years ago), 74, 91

N

NAACP. *See* National Association for the Advancement of Colored People (NAACP)

NAFTA (North American Free Trade Agreement), 56

Nähñu language, 376

Namibia, 334–335

NAPA. *See* National Association for the Practice of Anthropology (NAPA).

Nariokotome boy, 79, 81

Nation, definition of, 109, 118

Nation-states, definition of, 109, 118

National Association for the Advancement of Colored People (NAACP), 102

National Association for the Practice of Anthropology (NAPA), 27

National Council of La Raza, 102, 125–126

National culture, 51, 59

National Endowment for the Arts, 314

National Geographic, 5

National Oceanic and Atmospheric Administration, 46

National Organization of Women (NOW), 264, 266

Nationalities, definition of, 109–110, 118

Native Americans, *See also* specific tribes
anthropological studies of, 7, 14
berdaches and, 236, 269, 292
biological anthropology and, 14
division of labor and, 255
family and, 212
foraging and, 154
intelligence and, 107
livestock and, 161
"noble savage myth," 327–328
religion and, 285, 288–291
rites of passage and, 285, 311–312

Nativist movements, 294

Natural selection, 66–67, 75, 82, 91

Naturalistic disease theories, 34

Navajo Indians, 161, 314, 318, 320

Nayars, 54, 208–209

Nazis, 115

Ndembu, 285

Neandertals, 81–85, 89, 91

Negative reciprocity, 169–170, 173

Négritude, 110

Neo-Paganism, 294

Proletarianization, definition of, 331
Promiscuity, 215
Propriety, 8
Protestant Ethic and the Spirit of Capitalism (Weber), 293
Protolanguages, 140
"Psychic unity of man," 44
Psychology, 16
Public policy, 27–28
Public transcript, 196, 201
Pygmies, 141, 152

Q

Qashqai, 162, 188
Quichua language, 379

R

Race
  census and, 102, 104
  culture and, 7
  definition of, 100, 118
  discrimination and, 105–106
  hypodescent, 101–102
  intelligence and, 106–109
  overview of, 100–101
  perceptions of, 103
  social construction of, 101–102, 104–106
Racism
  Apartheid, 107, 114, 134–135, 282, 334–336
  definition of, 100, 105, 118
  "white man's burden" and, 348, 351
Radical Vegetarian League, 389
Raelian Movement, 298
Rainforest, 372
Rainforest Action Network, 372–373
Rambo, 375
Rapaport's rule, 369
Rastafarianism, 294
Real culture, definition of, 51
Reciprocity, 169–170, 174
Redistribution, 168–169, 174, 191
Refugees, 115, 118
Reindeer, 84–86, 153–154
Religion
  of American slaves, 197
  animism, 280, 282, 299
  anxiety control and, 283–284
  art and, 304, 306–307, 312
  capitalism and, 293
  cargo cults, 295–297, 299
  change and, 294–298
  creation and, 64
  cults, 286, 295–297
  cultural ecology and, 287
  cultural exchange and, 371–372
  definition of, 279–280, 300
  disease spread and, 33
  functions of, 280–287
  fundamentalism, 294, 297–298, 300
  kinds of, 291–292
  McDonald's and religious ritual, 388–390
  magic and, 283, 283–284, 300
  mana and, 283, 300
  marriage and, 234
  new age and, 298
  as ordering mechanism, 354
  origins of, 280–287
  plural marriage and, 243
  potlatching and, 171
  religious artifacts, 25
  rites of passage and, 284–286
  secular rituals and, 298–299

shamans and, 34, 291–292, 300
  social control and, 288–291
  states and, 292–293
  syncretisms, 295–297, 300
  taboo and, 283, 300
  totemism, 286–287
  world religions, 293–294
Rendille, 6
Rent funds, 167
Replacement funds, 167
Reputation, 197–198
Resources, 163–164, 368–370
Revitalization movements, 294–295, 300, 371
Rice, 159, 160, 356, 357
Rising Sun Hotel, 26
Rites of passage, 285, 300, 311–312
Ritual, 215, 283–287, 298–300, 388–390
Robust, 78, 92
Roman alphabet, 110
Roman Catholic Church, 47, 293, 294, 349
Royal endogamy, 235
Rubinstein-Taybi Syndrome, 14
Russia, 8, 110, 340, 354, 355
Rutgers University, 238, 327
Rwanda, 340, 350

S

Sahelanthropus tchadensis, 74
Salish, 170, 171
Samburu, 6
Same-sex marriage, 228, 235–237, 261
Samis, 153–154, 161
Samoans, 32
San ("Bushmen")
  division of labor and, 157
  foraging and, 152, 154, 155
  Ju/'hoansi people, 152, 154, 164, 169, 181, 258–259
  means of production and, 164
  media representation of, 377
  reciprocity and, 169
Santeria, 295
Sapir-Whorf hypothesis, 131–133, 143
Sati, 239
SATs. *See* Scholastic Achievement Tests (SATs)
Saudi Arabia, 290
Schistosomiasis (liver flukes), 33
Scholastic Achievement Tests (SATs), 108
Science
  anthropology and, 16–17
  bias and, 18
  definition of, 15, 19
  hypotheses and, 17
  theories and, 17
"Science in Anthropology" (Ember and Ember), 17
Scientific medicine, 34–35, 40
Scientology, 294, 298
SE. *See* Standard English (SE)
Second World, 116, 352–356
Secret societies, 188
Sectorial fallowing, 160
Semai, 169
Semantics, definition of, 143
Semiperiphery nations, 328, 333, 337, 342
Serbian Orthodox Church, 110–111
Serial monogamy, 243
Sexual behavior
  adultery and, 52, 182, 257
  birth control and, 18

diet and, 17–18
  female genital mutilation and, 52
  human and nonhuman primate comparison, 73–74
  male-female avoidance, 261–262, 270
  polygamy and, 6
  sexual orientation and, 267–270, 271
  transvestism, 268, 269, 292
  universal traits and, 54
Sexual dimorphism, definition of, 251–252, 271
Sexual orientation, 267–270, 271
Sexually transmitted diseases, 33–34
SfAA. *See* Society for Applied Anthropology (SfAA)
Shamans, 34, 291–292, 300, 328
Shame, 197–199, 291
Sharing and cooperation and, 73
Sheep, 161, 276–277
Shifting cultivation, 158
Shinto, 294, 295
Short-term adaptation, 6–7
Shoshoni Indians, 212
Sierra Leone, 188
Sight, 68–70
Sign language, 126–128
Sikhism, 294
Single-parent families, 210–211
Situational negotiation of identity, 99, 100
Skull, *See also* Brain
  evolution of, 75, 77, 83–84
  Homo erectus and, 80
  Kabwe skull, 82
  language and, 13
  Toumai skull, 74
Slash-and-burn techniques, 158
Slavery
  definition of, 342
  Ghana and, 97–98
  hypodescent rule and, 106
  language development and, 138
  overview of, 336
  resistance to, 196–197
  sugar demand and, 326
Slovenia, 110, 354
Smell sense, 68–70
Smell to sight adaptation, 68–69
Smith College, 5
Smithsonian Institution, 3, 6
Social adaptation, 7
Social capital, 138
Social control, 195–200, 201, 288–291
Social funds, 167
Social races, 101, 118
Socialism, definition of, 352
Society, definition of, 4
Society for Applied Anthropology (SfAA), 27
Socioeconomic status (SES), 234
Sociolinguistics, *See also* Communication and language
  definition of, 15, 19, 124, 143
  educational research and, 29–30
  gender speech contrasts, 135–136
  linguistic diversity, 135
  overview of, 134–139
Sociology, 15–16
Sodality, pantribal, 185–188, 201
Sorcery, 197–198, 199, 371
Sororate, 241–242, 246
Sororities, 190
South Africa, 78, 84, 88, 107, 237, 282, 309–310, 334–335, 354–355

MAP ATLAS

CONTENTS

MAP 1

Annual Percent of World Forest Loss, 1990–2000

Deforestation is a major environmental problem. In the tropics, large corporations clear forests seeking hardwoods for the global market in furniture and fine woods. As well, the agriculturally driven clearing of the great rain forests of the Amazon Basin, west and central Africa, Middle America, and Southeast Asia has drawn public attention. Reduced forest cover means the world's vegetation system will absorb less carbon dioxide, resulting in global warming. Of concern, too, is the loss of biodiversity (large numbers of plants and animals), the destruction of soil systems, and disruptions in water supply that accompany clearing.

QUESTIONS

Look at Map 1, "Annual Percent of World Forest Loss, 1990–2000."

1. On what continents do you find stable or increased forest cover?

2. Are there areas of Africa with stable or increased forest cover? Where are they? What might the reasons be for this lack of deforestation?

3. How does deforestation in India compare with the area to its east, which includes mainland and insular Southeast Asia?

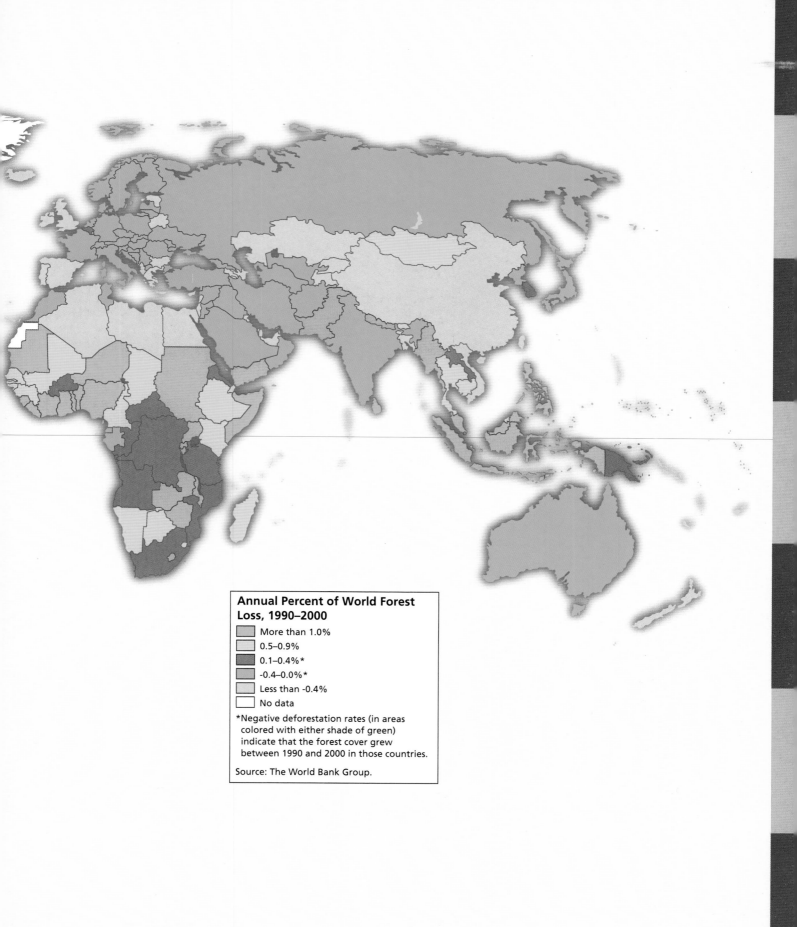

Annual Percent of World Forest Loss, 1990–2000

More than 1.0%
0.5–0.9%
0.1–0.4%*
-0.4–0.0%*
Less than -0.4%
No data

*Negative deforestation rates (in areas colored with either shade of green) indicate that the forest cover grew between 1990 and 2000 in those countries.

Source: The World Bank Group.

MAP 2

Major Primate Groups

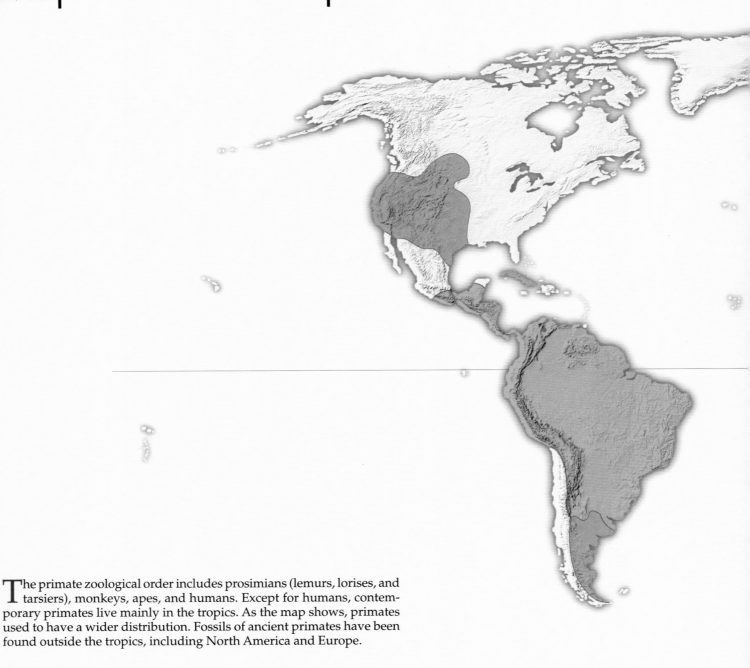

The primate zoological order includes prosimians (lemurs, lorises, and tarsiers), monkeys, apes, and humans. Except for humans, contemporary primates live mainly in the tropics. As the map shows, primates used to have a wider distribution. Fossils of ancient primates have been found outside the tropics, including North America and Europe.

QUESTIONS

Look at Map 2, "Major Primate Groups."

1. On what continents are there nonhuman primates today? How does this differ from the past? What primate thrives today in North America?

2. What nonhuman primates live on the island of Madagascar? Are they monkeys or what? Where do other members of their suborder live?

3. On what continents can you find apes in the wild today? What continent that used to have apes lacks them today (except, of course, in zoos).

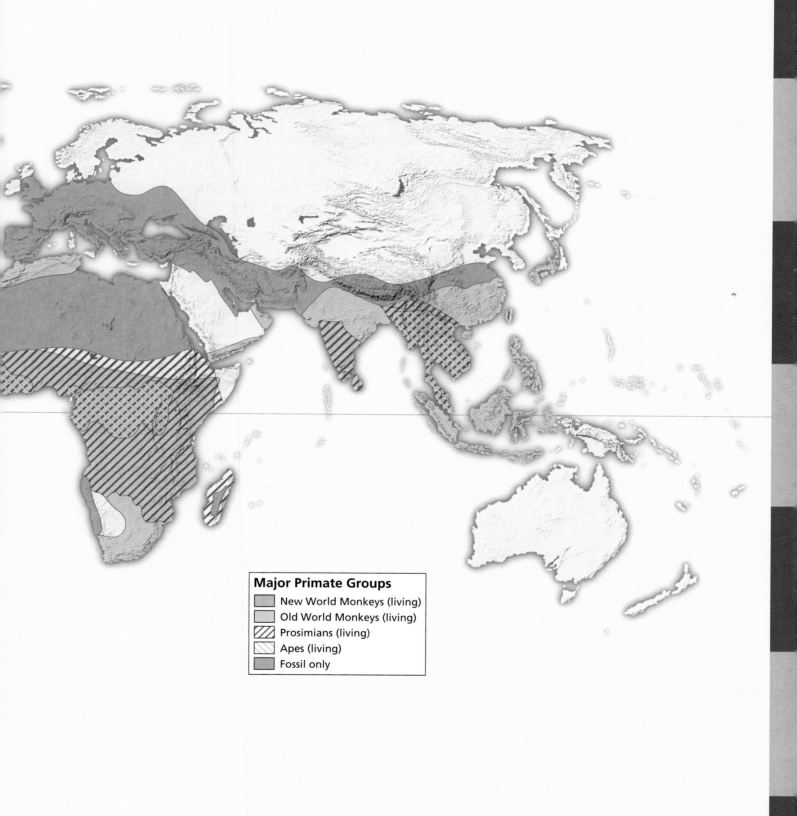

Major Primate Groups

- New World Monkeys (living)
- Old World Monkeys (living)
- Prosimians (living)
- Apes (living)
- Fossil only

MAP 3
Evolution of the Primates

Scientists trace modern primates, including humans, back to ancestral forms. Prosimians evolved earliest, perhaps by 60 million years ago. Their fossils have been found in North America, Europe, Asia, and Africa. Fossil sites with the ancestors of New World monkeys date back between 37 and 23 million years (to the Oligocene epoch). Old World monkeys and apes evolved at about the same time, but Old World monkeys spread into many parts of the Old World only in the last 5 million years. Apes lived in Africa, Europe, and Asia during the Miocene (23–5 million years ago).

QUESTIONS

Look at Map 3, "Evolution of the Primates."

1. What continent(s) had the first primates? What kinds of primates were those?

2. On what continent has the evolution of primates been most continuous? Does this have implications for human evolution?

3. Which continent with several of the earliest primates has the fewest nonhuman primates today?

Evolution of the Primates

- Eocene: 57–37 million years ago
- Oligocene: 37–23 million years ago
- Miocene: 23–5 million years ago

OM Old World monkeys
NM New World monkeys
P Prosimians
A Apes

See Inset

0   100   200 Miles
0   100   200 Kilometers

ETHIOPIA

Lake Turkana

UGANDA

Lake Baringo

Lake Victoria

KENYA

TANZANIA

MAP 4

Early Hominids:
Origins and Diffusion

The earliest hominids, which included the ancestors of modern humans, evolved in Africa around 6 million years ago. There are many sites dating to the late Miocene (8-5 million years ago) when the lines leading to modern humans, chimps, and gorillas may have separated. Some sites dating to the end of the Pliocene epoch (5-1.8 million years ago) contain fossil remains of human ancestors, *Homo*. During the Pleistocene Era (1.8 million–11,000 years ago), humans spread all over the world.

QUESTIONS

Look at Map 4, "Early Hominids: Origins and Diffusion."

1. How many African countries have hominid sites? How many have sites from the Miocene? From the Pliocene? And from the Pleistocene?

2. Compare the African distribution of nonhuman primate fossils in Map 3 with the distribution of early hominids in Map 4. Which fossil record is better—the one for nonhuman primates or the one for hominids?

3. Compare the distribution of contemporary African apes, as shown in Map 2, with the distribution of early hominid sites in Map 4. Also look at the distribution of extinct African apes in Map 3. What patterns do you notice? Where did early hominids overlap with the African apes (extinct and contemporary)? Where were there apes but no known early hominids, and vice versa?

Early Hominids: Origins and Diffusion

▫ Late Miocene localities
◼ Pliocene localities
△ Early and Middle Pleistocene localities

Pierolapithecus catalaunicus

Bahr el Ghazal

Toumai

CHAD

• N'Djamena

Middle Awash

Hadar

ETHIOPIA

W. Turkana

Omo

Lothagam

Fejej

Koobi Fora

Kanapoi

Tugen Hills

Chesawanja

Lukeino

Chemeron

Kanam

Peninj

KENYA

TANZANIA

ATLANTIC OCEAN

INDIAN OCEAN

Gladysvale

Sterkfontein

Makapansgat

Swartkrans

• Pretoria

Kromdraai

• Johannesburg

Taung

Drimolen

• Kimberley

SOUTH AFRICA

40°N

30°N

20°N

10°N

0°

10°S

20°S

30°S

10°W

0°

10°E

20°E

30°E

40°E

MAP 5
The Emergence of Modern Humans

Early forms of *Homo (H.) erectus,* sometimes called *H. ergaster,* have been found in East Africa and the former Soviet Georgia. By 1.7 million years ago, *H. erectus* had spread from Africa into Asia, including Indonesia, and eventually Europe. The *H. erectus* period may have lasted until 300,000 years ago. Other archaic forms of *Homo,* including fossils sometimes called *H. antecessor* and *H. heidelbergensis,* have been found in various parts of the Old World.

QUESTIONS

Look at Map 5, "The Emergence of Modern Humans."

1. Locate the site of Dmanisi (Georgia). Locate the site of Nariokotome (East Turkana, Kenya). These are sites where similarly dated early remains of *Homo erectus* (or *Homo ergaster*) have been found. Find two additional sites where hominins with similar dates (1.8–1.6 m.y.a.) have been found.

2. Considering Africa and Asia, name five sites (other than Dmanisi and Nariokotome) where *Homo erectus* fossils have been found.

3. Locate Heidelberg and Ceprano. What kinds of hominin fossils have been found there?

Dmanisi (1.7–1.8 m.y.a.)

CAUCASUS MTS.

Black Sea

Teshik Tash

Caspian Sea

Shanidar

Kebara

n Sea

Skhul   Amud

Tabun   Zuttiyen

Qafzeh

Hominid migration

ASIA

Zhoukoudian, "Peking man" (450,000 years ago)

Lantian

Langtandong

Yunxian

Red Sea

Nazlet Khatir

Yuanmou (Earliest evidence of hominids in East Asia, 1.7 million years ago)

Maba

Tham Khuyen

Buia

AFRICA

Herto

Hadar

Bouri

Konso-Gardula

Omo

Nariokotome   Koobi Fora

Lake Turkana, "Nariokotome boy" (1.6 m.y.a.)

Olduvai Gorge

INDIAN OCEAN

Sangiran, Java (1.6–1.8 m.y.a)   Kedungbrubus

Trinil, "Java man" (700,000 years ago)

ARCHAEOLOGICAL SITE
- *Homo habilis*
- *Homo erectus*
- Archaic *Homo sapiens*
- Neandertals
- *Homo sapiens*

Cave of Hearths

Sterkfontein (2 m.y.a.)

Border Cave

Swartkrans (1.5 m.y.a.)

AUSTRALIA

es River Mouth
 of some of the earliest
 vn anatomically modern
ans, c. 100,000 years ago)

MAP 6
Origins and Distribution of Modern Humans

Homo sapiens sapiens, aka anatomically modern humans (AMHs), appeared earliest in Africa (at Herto) and spread into the rest of the Old World after 130,000 years ago. Whether these early modern humans interbred with archaic humans, such as Neandertals, outside of Africa is still debated. Sometime between 25,000 and 9,000 years ago, humans colonized the New World.

QUESTIONS

Look at Map 6, "Origins and Distribution of Modern Humans."

1. When and from where was Australia first settled?

2. When and from where was North America first settled? How many migrations are shown as figuring in the settlement of North America? How were these migrations related to the glacial ice cover? Did they all follow the same route?

3. Locate three sites providing early evidence of AMHs in Africa. How do their dates compare with those of AMHs in Europe?

Corridor
opened
from
11,300 B.P.

BERINGIA
(c. 80,000 to 7,000 B.P.)

LAURENTIDE ICE SHEET
St. Lawrence R.
Great Lakes

**NORTH
AMERICA**

ROCKY MTS.

GREAT PLAINS

APPALACHIAN MTS.

Meadowcroft

Clovis

Rio Grande

Mississippi
R.

West Indies

*ATLANTIC
OCEAN*

A

ukoudian

JAPAN

First settled
c. 40,000 B.P.

East Asia:
Earliest evidence of
hominid colonization
dates to c. 1.7 million B.P.

PACIFIC OCEAN

*Philippine
Islands*

*New
Guinea*

*Solomon
Islands*

sis
00 B.P.)

USTRALIA

Lake Mungo

Keilor

Tasmania

New Zealand

inoco R.

ANDES

GUIANA
HIGHLANDS

*AMAZON
BASIN*

Pedra
Furada

Monte
Verde

PATAGONIA

**Origins and Distribution
of Modern Humans**

➤ Possible settlement direction

▲ Archaic *Homo sapiens* (c. 650,000–28,000 B.P.)

△ Neandertals (c. 130,000–28,000? B.P.)

■ Modern *Homo sapiens* (c. 130,000 B.P.–present)

☐ Areas covered by ice in late
Pleistocene era (18,000 B.P.)

▨ Beringia

MAP 7

The Distribution of Human Skin Color (Before A.D. 1400)

Human skin color varies. The pigmentation is caused by the presence of melanin in the skin, which protects the skin from damage due to ultraviolet radiation. In areas with much UV radiation, people biologically adapted to their environments by increased melanin production.

QUESTIONS

Look at Map 7, "The Distribution of Human Skin Color (Before A.D. 1400)."

1. Where are the Native Americans with the darkest skin color located? What factors help explain this distribution?

2. In both western and eastern hemispheres, is the lightest skin color found in the north or the south? Outside Asia, where do you find skin color closest to northern Asian skin color? Is this surprising given what you have read about migrations and settlement history?

3. Where are skin colors darkest? How might you explain this distribution?

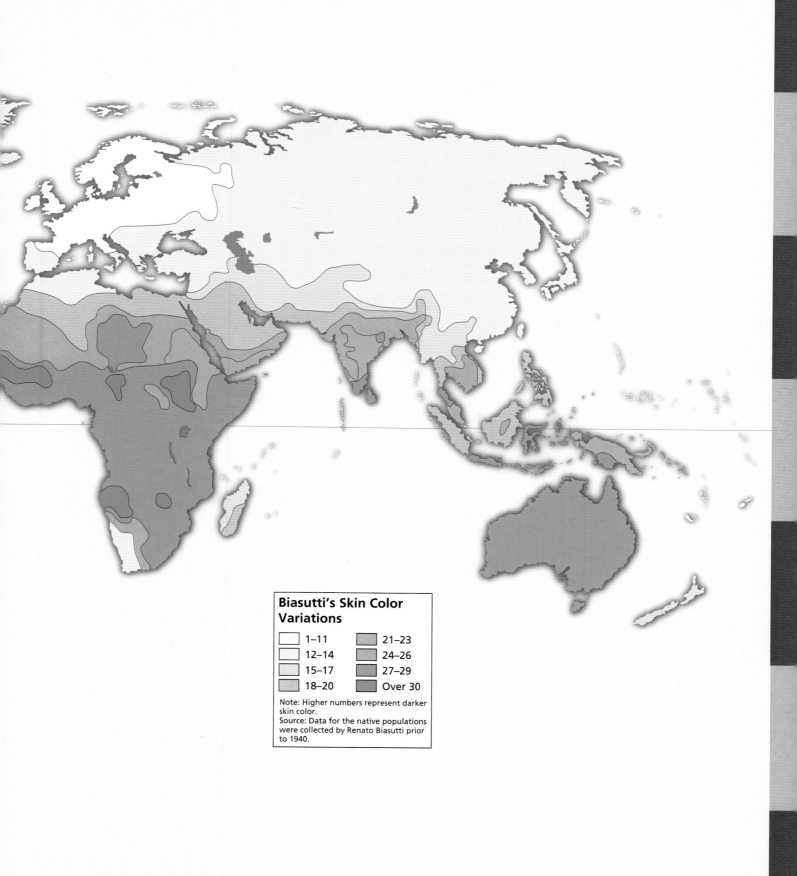

Biasutti's Skin Color Variations

☐ 1–11	☐ 21–23
☐ 12–14	☐ 24–26
☐ 15–17	☐ 27–29
☐ 18–20	☐ Over 30

Note: Higher numbers represent darker skin color.
Source: Data for the native populations were collected by Renato Biasutti prior to 1940.

MAP 8
The Origin and Spread of Food Production

The Neolithic, or New Stone Age, refers to the period of early farming settlements when people who had been foragers shifted to food production. This pattern of subsistence was based on the domestication of plants and animals. Through domestication, people transformed plants and animals from their wild state to a form more useful to humans. The Neolithic began in the fertile crescent area of the Middle East over 10,000 years ago. It spread to the Levant and Mediterranean, finally reaching Britain and Scandinavia around 5,000 years ago.

QUESTIONS

Look at Map 8, "The Origin and Spread of Food Production."

1. Considering the map and the timeline, name three regions where cattle were domesticated. Based on the timeline, what animals were domesticated in North America?

2. Did Ireland receive Middle Eastern domesticates? What is the origin of the "Irish potato," or white potato (see the timeline), which became, much later, the caloric basis of Irish subsistence?

3. Besides cattle, what animals were domesticated more than once? Where were those areas of domestication?

Early Neolithic Sites of the Middle East and Europe

- Settlement region and date
- Settlement sites
- Possible migration routes
- Areas of domestication

Lake Ladoga

Lake Peipus

Baltic Sea

Aral Sea

Elbe R.

Goose

Bug R.

Oder R.

Rhine R.

Vistula R.

Dniester R.

Dnieper R.

Horse

Danube R.

Volga R.

Ural R.

Caspian Sea

Po R.

Sava R.   7,500

Adriatic Sea   7,700

7,700   Danube R.   7,800

Black Sea

8,000   7,800   9,000

Cattle   8,400

9,000   8,900

Mediterranean Sea

Cattle

10,300   Sheep

Pig

9,800   Goat

9,600

9,400?

Tigris R.   Goat

Euphrates R.

Persian Gulf

10,300

Dromedary

Sea of Azov

Ass
Honey Bee
Cat

Mediterranean Domestication

Barley	Dates	Grapes
Cattle	Garlic	Lentils
Celery	Goat	Lettuce
		Olives

Southwest Asia Domestication

Barley	Duck	Melons
Beans	Fruits (seed	Oats
Beets	and stone)	Oil seeds
Camel (Bactrian)	Goat	Onions
Carrots	Grapes	Rye
Cattle	Hemp	Sheep
Dog	Horse	Wheat

Yam, oil palm

Cat (Egypt)

Chickens (south-central Asia)

4000	3000	2000	1000 Years Ago
Marsh elder	Lamb's quarters	Maize	
Sunflower			
Squash	North America		

White potato

MAP 9
Ancient Civilizations of the Old World

A rchaic states developed in many parts of the Old World at different periods. The earliest civilizations, such as Mesopotamia, Egypt, and the Indus Valley, are generally placed at about 5500 B.P. States developed later in Asia, Africa, and the Americas (see Map 13).

QUESTIONS

Look at Map 9, "Ancient Civilizations of the Old World."

1. What contemporary nations would you have to visit if you wanted to see all the places where ancient civilizations developed in the Old World? Would some countries be off limits for political reasons? How do you think such limitations have affected the archaeological record?

2. Of the ancient states shown on Map 9, which developed latest? Why do you think the first states developed when and where they did?

3. In which of the ancient states shown on Map 9 were Middle Eastern domesticates basic to the economy? In which states shown on Map 9 were other domesticates basic to the economy?

Minoan-Mycenaean
4100–3050 B.P.

Yellow River (Shang)
4000 B.P.–3027 B.P.

Lake Baikal

Caspian Sea

**Tigris-Euphrates
(Mesopotamia and
Babylonia)**
5500 B.P.–4000 B.P.

an Sea

**Nile
(Ancient Egypt)**
4920 B.P.–3100 B.P..

Red Sea

**Indus-Ganges
(Harappan and Vedic Civilizations)**
5000 B.P.–2150 B.P.

*Arabian
Sea*

Bay of Bengal

*Sea
of
Japan*

*East
China
Sea*

Khmer
A.D. 802–1218

Funan
A.D. 100–546

*South
China
Sea*

Chenla
A.D. 611–802

*PACIFIC
OCEAN*

Meroe (Nubia)
2591 B.P.–
1675 B.P. (A.D. 325)

Aksum/Axum
?2200 B.P.–1300 B.P. (A.D. 700)

INDIAN OCEAN

Zimbabwe
A.D. 1000–1450

**Ancient Civilizations of
the Old World**

5500–3000 B.P.
4100–3000 B.P.
After 2600 B.P.

Years (B.P.)				
Funan				
Meroe (Nubia)				
Aksum/Axum				
Chenia				
Jenne-jeno				
Ghana				
Khmer				
Rome				
Zimbabwe				
Mali				
Songhay/Songhai				

2500   2000   1500
                (500 A.D)   1000
                             (1000 A.D)   500
                                           (1500 A.D)

Years (B.P.)

MAP 10
Ethnographic Study Sites Prior to 1950

The development of anthropology as a scientific discipline can be traced to the middle to late part of the 19th century (see Appendix 1). In cultural anthropology, ethnographic field work became usual and common during the early 20th century. American ethnographers turned to the study of Native Americans, while European anthropologists often studied people living in world areas, such as Africa, which had been conquered and/or colonized by the anthropologist's nation of origin.

QUESTIONS

Look at Map 10, "Ethnographic Study Sites Prior to 1950."

1. Anthropology originated as the scientific study of nonwestern peoples and cultures. Yet Map 10 shows that many anthropological studies conducted prior to 1950 were done in North America. What societies were being studied in North America? Were they considered western or nonwestern? What does this tell us about the concept of "western"?

2. How would you describe the range of ethnographic sites prior to 1950? Were some world areas being neglected, such as the Middle East or mainland Asia? What might be the reasons for such omissions?

3. Think about how changes in transportation and communication have affected the way anthropologists do their research. How might a list of contemporary ethnographic sites contrast with the distribution shown in Map 10. How has longitudinal research been affected by changes in transportation and communication?

Ethnographic Study Sites Prior to 1950

North America
1. Eastern Eskimo
2. Central Eskimo
3. Naskapi
4. Iroquois
5. Delaware
6. Natchez
7. Shawnee
8. Kickapoo
9. Sioux
10. Crow
11. Nez Percé
12. Shoshone
13. Paviotso
14. Kwakiutl
15. Tsimshian
16. Haida
17. Tlingit
18. Navajo
19. Hopi
20. Zuñi
21. Aztec
22. Tzintzuntzan and Cuanajo
23. Maya
24. Cherokee
25. San Pedro

South America
Ecuador
 26. Jívaro
Peru
 27. Inca
 28. Machiguenga
 29. Achuara
 30. Campa
Bolivia
 31. Aymara
Chile
 32. Yahgan
Venezuela
 33. Yanomamö
Brazil
 34. Tapirapé
 35. Mundurucu
 36. Mehinacu
 37. Kuikuru
 38. Caingang

Africa
Ghana
 39. Ashanti
Nigeria
 40. Kadar

Sudan
 41. Fur
 42. Dinka
 43. Nuer
 44. Azaṅde
Uganda
 45. Bunyoro
 46. Ganda
Dem. Rep. of Congo
 47. Mbuti
Rwanda
 48. Watusi
Kenya
 49. Masai
Tanzania
 50. Nyakyusa
 51. Lovedu
Zambia
 52. Ndembu
 53. Barotse
Mozambique
 54. Bathonga
South Africa
 55. !Kung Bushmen
 56. Zulu

Asia
Sri Lanka
 57. Vedda
 58. Sinhalese
India
 59. Andaman
 60. Nayar
 61. Tamil
 62. Rajput
Siberia
 63. Tungus
Japan
 64. Ainu
China
 65. Luts'un village
Taiwan
 66.Taiwan Chinese
Vietnam
 67. Mnong-Gar
Malaya
 68. Semai

Pacific
Philippines
 69. Tasaday
Indonesia Area
 70. Dyaks
 71. Alorese
 72. Tetum
Australia
 73. Tiwi
 74. Arunta
 75. Murngin
 76. Saibai Islanders
New Guinea
 77. Arapesh
 78. Dani
 79. Gururumba
 80. Kai
 81. Kapauku
 82. Mae Enga
 83. Kuma
 84. Mundugumor
 85. Tchambuli
 86. Tsembaga Maring
 87. Tavade
 88. Foré
 89. Etoro

Melanesian Islands
90. Manus Islanders
91. New Hanover Islanders
92. Trobriand Islanders
93. Dobuans
94. Rossel Islanders
95. Kaoka
96. Malaita Islanders
97. Espiritu Santo Islanders
98. Tana Islanders
99. Tikopia
100. Sivai
Polynesian Islands
101. Maori
102. Tongans
103. Samoans
104. Mangians
105. Tahitians
106. Hawaiians
Micronesian Islands
107. Truk

MAP 11
Major Families of World Languages

Language, like religion, is an important identifying and distinguishing characteristic of culture. Knowing the distribution of the major world languages and language families helps us understand some of the reasons behind important current events. In areas that have emerged from recent colonial rule, for example, the participants in conflicts over territory and power are often defined in terms of linguistic groups. Language distributions also help us understand our past by providing clues that enable us to chart the course of human migrations, as is suggested by the distribution of Indo-European, Austronesian, and Hamito-Semitic languages.

QUESTIONS

Look at Map 11, "Major Families of World Languages."

1. Name three language families or subfamilies that are spoken on more than one continent. How do you explain this distribution?

2. Where are the Austronesian languages spoken? How might one explain this distribution?

3. What language families are spoken on the African continent? Locate the Niger-Congo language family, of which the Bantu languages comprise a subfamily.

Major Families of World Languages

Indo-European

1	Germanic	6	Indo-Aryan
2	Romance	7	Celtic
3	Slavic	8	Greek
4	Baltic	9	Armenian
5	Iranian		

- Eskimo-Aleut
- Native American
- Hamito-Semitic
- Niger-Congo
- Nilo-Saharan
- Austronesian
- Australian
- Samoyed
- Finno-Ugric
- Basque
- Khosian
- Ural-Altaic
- Caucasian
- Sino-Tibetan
- Paleo-Siberian
- Korean
- Japanese
- Burushaski
- Austro-Asiatic
- Vietnamese
- Thai-Kadai
- Papuan
- Dravidian
- Unpopulated Regions

MAP 12
World Land Use, A.D. 1500

In the late 1400s there were a variety of self-sustaining economies in the world. Foragers hunted and gathered wild forms of animals and plants. Horticulturalists practiced a simple form of cultivation, using hoes or digging sticks as their basic tools. They sometimes cleared their land by burning, and then planted crops. Pastoralists herded animals as their basic subsistence pattern. Some state-level societies, such as the Mongols, had pastoralism as their economic base. Intensive agriculturalists based their subsistence economies on complicated irrigation systems and/or the plow and draft animals. Wheat and rice were two kinds of crops that supported large populations

QUESTIONS

Look at Map 12, "World Land Use, A.D. 1500."

1. Name three continents with significant herding economies. On which continents was pastoralism absent?

2. How do the various types of agriculture vary among the continents? Which continent had the largest area under intensive cultivation? Which continent or continents had the least amount of intensive cultivation?

3. What were the main uses of land in Europe when the European age of discovery and conquest began?

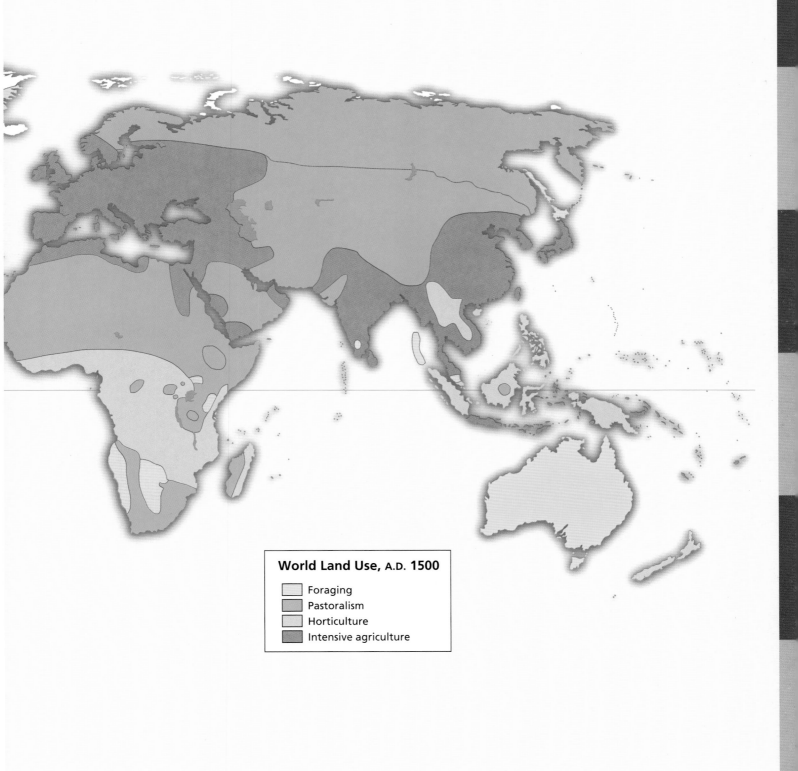

World Land Use, A.D. 1500

- Foraging
- Pastoralism
- Horticulture
- Intensive agriculture

MAP 13
Organized States and Chiefdoms, A.D. 1500

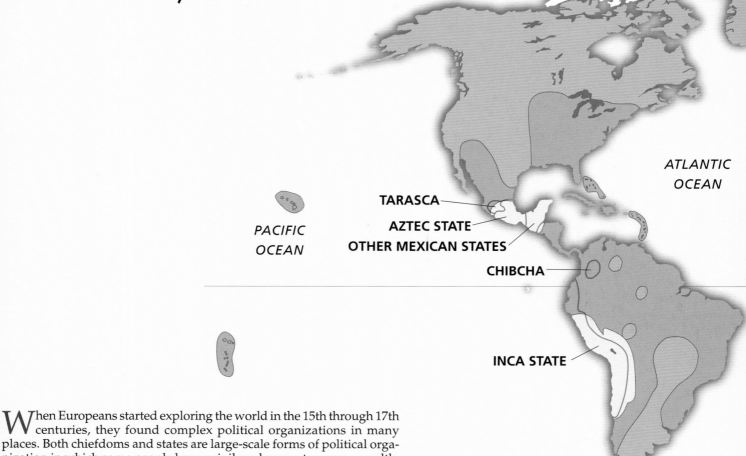

ATLANTIC OCEAN

PACIFIC OCEAN

TARASCA
AZTEC STATE
OTHER MEXICAN STATES
CHIBCHA
INCA STATE

When Europeans started exploring the world in the 15th through 17th centuries, they found complex political organizations in many places. Both chiefdoms and states are large-scale forms of political organization in which some people have privileged access to power, wealth, and prestige. Chiefdoms are kin-based societies in which redistribution is the major economic pattern. States are organized in terms of socio-economic classes, headed by a centralized government that is led by an elite. States include a full-time bureaucracy and specialized subsystems for such activities as military action, taxation, and social control.

QUESTIONS

Look at Map 13, "Organized States and Chiefdoms, A.D. 1500."

1. Locate and name the states that existed in the Western Hemisphere in A.D. 1500. Compare Map 12, "World Land Use: A.D. 1500," with Map 13. Looking at the Western Hemisphere, can you detect a correlation between land use (and economy) and the existence of states? What's the nature of that correlation? Does that correlation also characterize other parts of the world?

2. Locate three regions of the world where chiefdoms existed in A.D. 1500. Compare Map 12, "World Land Use: A.D. 1500," with Map 13. Can you detect a correlation between land use (and economy) and the existence of chiefdoms? What's the nature of that correlation?

3. Some parts of the world lacked either chiefdoms or states in A.D. 1500. What are some of those areas? What kinds of political systems did they probably have?

EUROPEAN
STATES

SEMI NOMADIC
STATES

JAPAN

ISLAMIC STATES

CHINA

PACIFIC
OCEAN

SONGHAI

KANEM-
BORNU

INDIAN
STATES

PHILIPPINES

HINDU/
MUSLIM
STATES

ETHIOPIA

Ceylon

Malaya

Strait
of Malacca

Moluccas

NEW
GUINEA

OYO
BENIN

Zanzibar

Sumatra

KONGO

• Kilwa

Java

LUBA

THE
EAST INDIES

INDIAN
OCEAN

• Sofala

AUSTRALIA

MONOMATAPA

**Organized States and
Chiefdoms, A.D. 1500**

　No chiefdoms or states

　Chiefdoms

◯　States

MAP 14

Female/Male Inequality in Education and Employment

Women in developed countries have made significant advances in socioeconomic status in recent years. In most of the world, however, females suffer from significant inequality when compared with their male counterparts. Although women can vote in most countries, in over 90 percent of those countries that right was granted only during the last 50 years. In most regions, literacy rates for women still fall far short of those for men. In Africa and Asia, for example, only about half as many women are as literate as men. Inequalities in education and employment are perhaps the most telling indicators of the unequal status of women in most of the world. Even where women are employed in positions similar to those held by men, they tend to receive less compensation. The gap between rich and poor involves not only a clear geographic differentiation, but a clear gender differentiation as well.

QUESTIONS

Look at Map 14 "Female/Male Inequality in Education and Employment."

1. Locate and name three Third World countries with the same degree of gender-based inequality as the United States and Canada.

2. Two of the world's largest developing nations are coded as having "less inequality." What are they?

3. Most European countries are coded as having "least inequality." Which western European countries are exceptions?

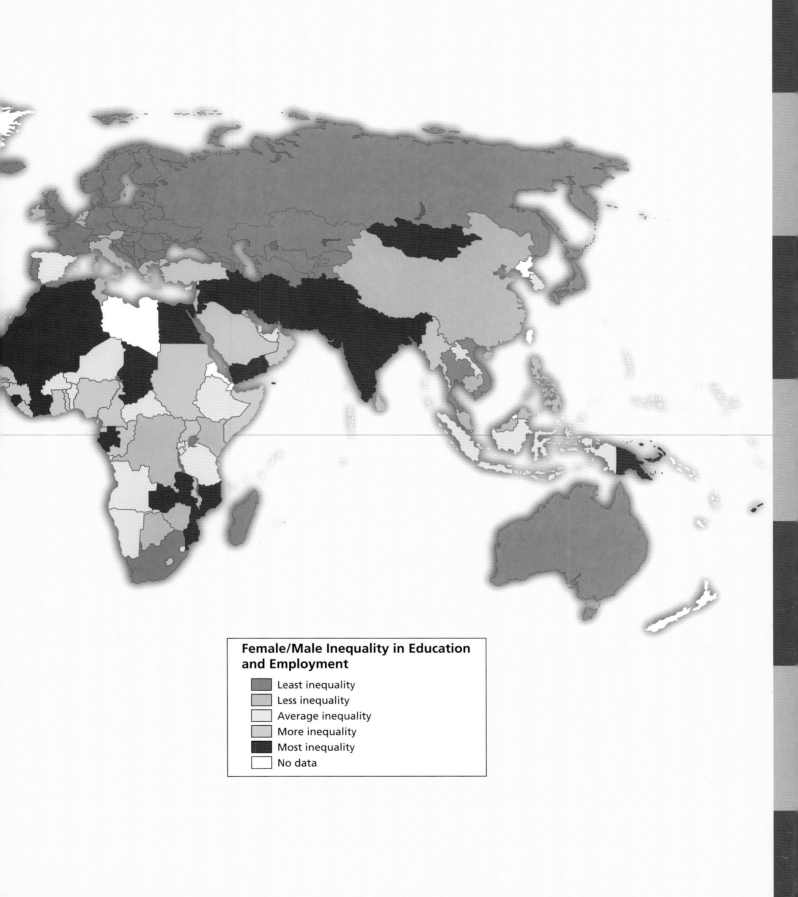

Female/Male Inequality in Education and Employment

- Least inequality
- Less inequality
- Average inequality
- More inequality
- Most inequality
- No data

MAP 15
World Religions

Because religion is a fundamental characteristic of human culture, a depiction of the spatial distribution of religions comes close to a map of cultural patterns. More than just a set of behavior patterns having to do with worship and ceremony, religion influences the ways in which people deal with one another, with their institutions, and with their environments. An examination of this map in the context of conflict within and among nations also shows that the tension between countries and the internal stability of states are also functions of the spatial distribution of religion.

QUESTIONS

Look at Map 15, "World Religions."

1. Which continent has the most diversity with respect to the major religions?

2. Which continent is most Protestant? Why do you think that is the case?

3. Where in the world are "tribal" religions still practiced?

Predominant Religions

Christianity (C)*
Roman Catholic
Protestant
Mormon (LDS)
Eastern Churches
Mixed

Islam (M)
Sunni
Shi'a

Buddhism (B)
Hinayanistic
Lamaistic

Hinduism (H)

Judaism (J)

Sikhism

Animism (Tribal)

Chinese Complex
(Confucianism, Taoism, and
Buddhism)

Korean Complex
(Buddhism, Confucianism,
Christianity, and Chondogyo)

Japanese Complex
(Shinto and Buddhism)

Vietnamese Complex
(Buddhism, Taoism,
Confucianism, and Cao Dai)

Unpopulated Regions

*Capital letters indicate the presence of
locally important minority adherents of
nonpredominant faiths.

MAP 16

Annual Energy Consumption per Capita

All of the countries defined by the World Bank as having high incomes consume at least 100 gigajoules of commercial energy (the equivalent of more than 10 metric tons of coal) per person per year. With the exception of the oil-rich Persian Gulf states, where consumption figures include the costly "burning off" of excess energy in the form of natural gas flares at wellheads, most of the highest-consuming countries are concentrated in North America and Western Europe. At the other end of the scale are low-income countries, whose consumption rates are often less than 1 percent of those of the United States and other high consumers. These figures don't include the consumption of noncommercial energy—the traditional fuels of firewood, animal dung, and other organic matter—widely used in the less developed parts of the world.

QUESTIONS

Look at Map 16, "Annual Energy Consumption Per Capita."

1. Compare energy consumption in Europe and North America. Do all European countries consume energy at the same rate as the United States and Canada?

2. What are some exceptions to the generalization that the highest rates of energy consumption are in core countries, with the lowest rates on the periphery.

3. How is energy consumption related to measures of the quality of life, as shown in Map 17?

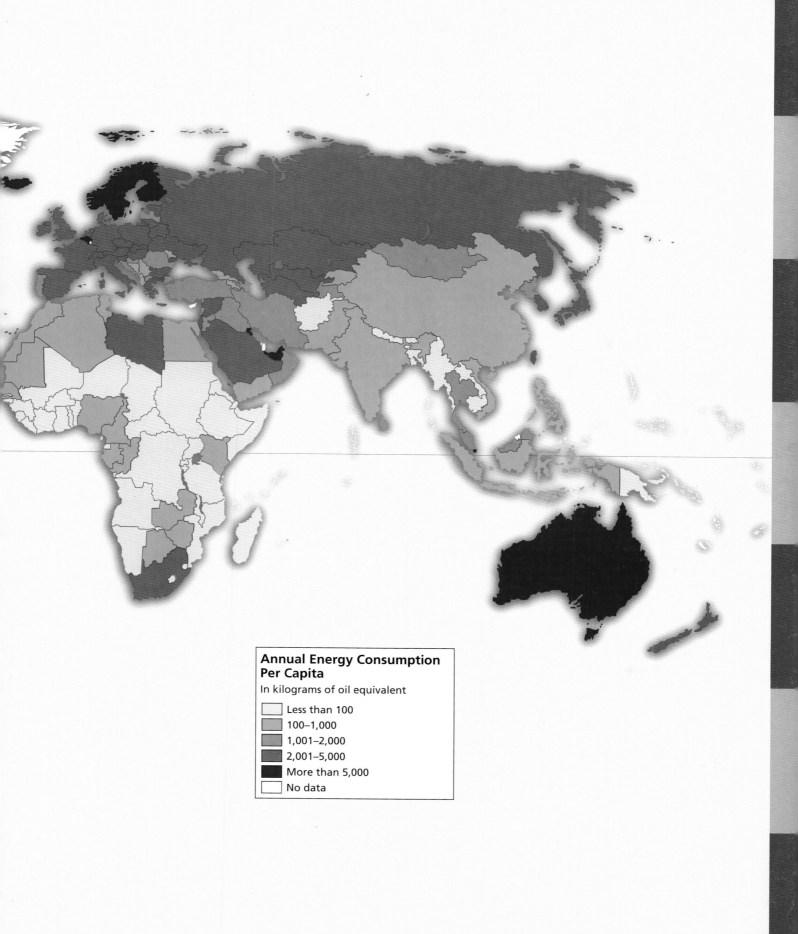

Annual Energy Consumption Per Capita

In kilograms of oil equivalent

- Less than 100
- 100–1,000
- 1,001–2,000
- 2,001–5,000
- More than 5,000
- No data

MAP 17

The Quality of Life: The Index of Human Development

The development index upon which this map is based takes into account a wide variety of demographic, health, and educational data, including population growth, per capita gross domestic income, longevity, literacy, and years of schooling. The map reveals significant improvement in the quality of life in Middle and South America. It is questionable whether the gains made in those regions can be maintained given the dramatic population increases expected over the next 30 years. This map illustrates a near desperate situation in Africa and South Asia, where population growth threatens to overwhelm all efforts to improve the quality of life. Africa and South Asia face the challenge of providing basic access to health care, education, and jobs for a rapidly increasing population. The map also illustrates the striking difference in quality of life between those who inhabit the world's equatorial and tropical regions and those fortunate enough to live in the temperate zones, where the quality of life is significantly higher.

QUESTIONS

Look at Map 17, "The Quality of Life: The Index of Human Development."

1. What countries in central and South America have Human Development Index (HDI) scores comparable to those of some European nations? Does this surprise you?

2. Given that Brazil has one of the world's top 10 economies, does its HDI score surprise you? How do Brazil, Mexico, and Venezuela compare in terms of the HDI?

3. Do you notice a correlation between deforestation (Map 1) and quality of life? Does India fit this correlation?